M000316460

PARASITES AND DISEASES
OF WILD MAMMALS IN FLORIDA

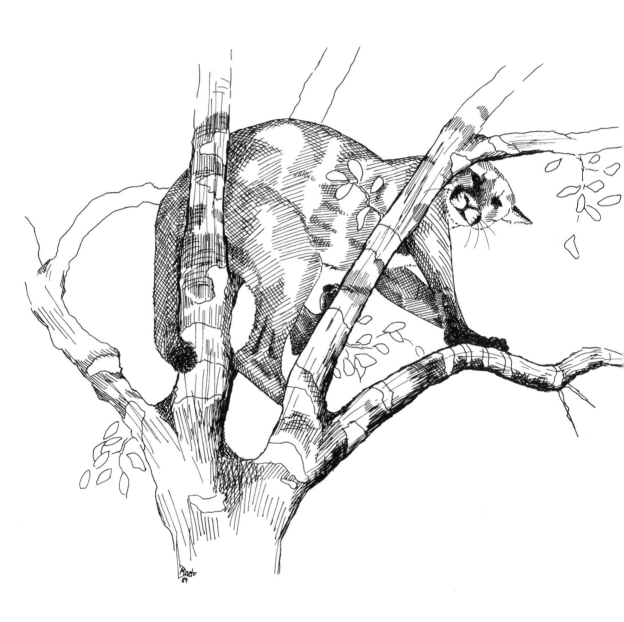

Parasites and Diseases of Wild Mammals in Florida

Donald J. Forrester

Wildlife Drawings by David S. Maehr

To: Rebecca
With my best regards,
Don Forrester
6/24/97

UNIVERSITY PRESS OF FLORIDA

Gainesville Tallahassee Tampa Boca Raton Pensacola Orlando Miami Jacksonville

Copyright © 1992 by the Board of Regents of the State of Florida
All rights reserved
Printed in the U.S.A. on acid-free paper ∞

Library of Congress Cataloging-in-Publication Data

Forrester, Donald J., 1937–
    Parasites and diseases of wild mammals in Florida / Donald J.
Forrester.
        p. cm.
    Includes bibliographical references and index.
    ISBN 0–8130–1072–1
    1. Wildlife diseases—Florida. 2. Mammals—Diseases—Florida.
3. Mammals—Parasites—Florida. I. Title.
    [DNLM: 1. Animal Diseases. 2. Mammals—parasitology.
3. Parasitic Diseases—epidemiology—Florida. 4. Parasitic
Diseases—veterinary. SF 997 F731p]
SF996.4.F65   1991   91–536
639.9′6′09759—dc20   CIP
DNLM/DLC
for Library of Congress

The University Press of Florida is the scholarly publishing agency of the State University System of Florida, comprised of Florida A & M University, Florida Atlantic University, Florida International University, Florida State University, University of Central Florida, University of Florida, University of North Florida, University of South Florida, and University of West Florida.

University Press of Florida, 15 Northwest 15th Street, Gainesville, FL 32611

Published in cooperation with the Florida Game and Fresh Water Fish Commission Division of Wildlife.

Partially funded by the Federal Aid in Wildlife Restoration Program (Pittman–Robertson Act)

I dedicate this book to my mother and father,

A. Emily Forrester (1906–1989)

and

J. Ronald Forrester (1904–1976)

who understood and fostered my early interest in wildlife during
my youth in New England. I will always remember
their love and encouragement.

Contents

Figures

Foreword

Stressed wildlife populations naturally serve as hosts to many pathogens and vectors of diseases that may affect not only their individual health, but the health of wildlife populations, domestic animals, and humans as well. Factors that may traumatize wildlife, such as poor nutrition, social stress, loss of habitat, harassment, and environmental changes, typically reduce the individual animal's ability to combat infectious agents, ultimately resulting in reduced thriftiness, disease, mortality, and/ or population decline.

Both parasites and diseases may in some cases affect wildlife as independent agents, but in most cases are clinically manifested in response to declining health of the stressed animal or population. Because many wildlife disease events are density-dependent, any management treatments, heretofore, typically have been designed to artificially reduce animal numbers to accelerate improved health of the population. Although such an approach represents a treatment of symptoms rather than causes, it has served the need well in cases where populations are not already compromised by low numbers. Florida wildlife and their habitats are currently being affected by pressures of unprecedented human growth, however, and more in-depth understanding of the role of diseases and parasites in wildlife biology is now essential. This reality is particularly true in the recovery of such endangered mammals as the Florida panther and the Florida manatee. This book seeks to partially fulfill that need.

Parasites and Diseases of Wild Mammals in Florida is a product of more than 20 years of scientific work that Dr. Donald J. Forrester has performed under contract for the Florida Game and Fresh Water Fish Commission to further our understanding of wild animal health in Florida. While unquestionably valuable to wildlife managers in Florida, this volume should also serve as a technical contribution to the wildlife literature.

Tom H. Logan
Bureau of Wildlife Research
Florida Game and Fresh Water Fish Commission

Preface

*Then God commanded, "Let the earth produce all kinds of animal life:
domestic and wild, large and small"—and it was done.*
Genesis 1:24 (TEV)

Because of its exceptional combination of climate and geography, Florida has a rich and diverse mammalian fauna. Of the 96 species found in the state or its waters, 85 are native and 11 have been introduced or recently have expanded their range into Florida. Among Florida's mammals are a number of unique species or subspecies, such as round-tailed muskrats, panthers, manatees, and Key deer, as well as important game animals, for example, rabbits, squirrels, white-tailed deer, and wild hogs. Others are of interest because of their esthetic value or their role in the transmission of diseases to man or domesticated animals.

An understanding of the health and diseases of these mammals is necessary in order to properly manage and preserve this valuable natural resource. The purpose of this book is to provide a reference to the available information on various parasites, diseases, and other factors that cause morbidity (sickness) and mortality (death) in Florida wild mammals, with emphasis on distribution, prevalence, and significance. Information is included on 61 native and 8 non-native species. Much of this information was found scattered throughout the published literature, in the "gray literature," and in the personal files, notes, and reports of numerous individuals and organizations. A large amount of unpublished data has been included through the cooperation and generosity of many people. Much of this information has come from my own research and that of my graduate students and postdoctoral associates over the past 21 years as well as numerous colleagues at the University of Florida and other universities and agencies.

For some mammals (i.e., white-tailed deer, wild hogs, raccoons, and manatees) the coverage is fairly extensive, whereas for others (i.e., moles, shrews, armadillos, pocket gophers) it is more limited. This was not by choice, but because many mammals in Florida have not been well studied and little is known about their parasites and diseases. It is hoped that this book will help wildlife biologists, mammalogists, conservationists, resource administrators, educators, students, veterinarians, and others in the health professions to understand what is known and to thereby stimulate further research, especially on those mammals that have been poorly studied or neglected.

Acknowledgments

Funding for much of the original research reported in this book and for its publication was provided by the Florida Game and Fresh Water Fish Commission and the federal Pittman–Robertson Wildlife Restoration Program. Tom H. Logan was particularly supportive, as were Lovett E. Williams, Jr., Fred W. Stanberry, James A. Powell, James R. Brady, and Tommy C. Hines.

A number of organizations and people generously contributed information, much of it unpublished. I am especially indebted to the personnel of the Southeastern Cooperative Wildlife Disease Study (SCWDS) at the University of Georgia for their cooperation and help in providing considerable data on Florida mammals. Data were obtained also from the Florida State Collection of Arthropods, Gainesville, Florida, and from the U.S. National Parasite Collection, Beltsville, Maryland. Personnel from these organizations and many others who contributed include C.A. Beck, H.N. Becker, W.J. Bigler, R.K. Bonde, E.A. Bowerman, J.R. Brady, C.D. Buergelt, M.J. Burridge, M.B. Calderwood-Mays, D.K. Caldwell, W.R. Davidson, G.L. Doster, E.P.J. Gibbs, B. Goodson, N. Gourlie, E.C. Greiner, G.L. Hoff, H. Hoogstraal, S.R. Humphrey, J.M. Kinsella, J.N. Layne, R.G. McLean, D.S. Maehr, L. Matthews, J.C. Mead, E.G. Milstrey, V.F. Nettles, P.L. Nicoletti, D.K. Odell, T.J. O'Shea, J.A. Popp, M.E. Roelke, C.E. Roessler, H.L. Rubin, S.W. Russell, J.J. Sacks, G.C. Steers, E.R. Stetzer, F.I. Townsend, H.Y. Wassef, J.O. Whitaker, F.H. White, N.A. Wilson, M.M. Wong, J.C. Woodard, J.B. Wooding, and S.D. Wright.

The following people reviewed various chapters and provided helpful suggestions: C.A. Beck, H.N. Becker, R.C. Belden, W.J. Bigler, R.R. Bonde, J.R. Brady, C.D. Buergelt, D.K. Caldwell, J.A. Conti, W.R. Davidson, E.P.J. Gibbs, E.C. Greiner, T.C. Hines, G.L. Hoff, S.R. Humphrey, J.M. Kinsella, T.H. Logan, R.G. McLean, D.S. Maehr, V.F. Nettles, D.K. Odell, T.J. O'Shea, M.E. Roelke, M.G. Spalding, J.E. Thul, M.T. Walsh, F.H. White, J.C. Woodard, S.D. Wright, and M.D. Young. J.N. Layne read the entire manuscript and provided a number of very useful suggestions, especially related to mammalogy.

Those who donated or assisted with the preparation of photographs and figures included J.R. Brady, C.D. Buergelt, J. Cooley, W.R. Davidson, G.W. Foster, R.T. Goldston, E.C. Greiner, G.L. Hoff, J.N. Layne, M.D. Little, D.B. Pence, W.L. Shoop, M.G. Spalding, F.I. Townsend, J.B. Wooding, and S.D. Wright. Most of the distribution maps were made by S.A. Ross and M.G. Spalding. The wildlife line drawings were done by D.S. Maehr, to whom I am especially grateful. Others who helped in various ways are L.M. Bielsa, J.H. Bogue, G.L. Cornish, D.K. Couch, N.R. Hall, P.K. Humphlett, P.P. Humphrey, J.R. Litchenfels, G. Migaki, S.E. Ross, D.E. Wood, and M.D. Young.

Special thanks go to Sandy Bolton, Sherri Clark, Kandi Crosier, Rita Day, Tammy Gault, Phillip Liston, Jan Machnik, Marianne Rarick, Barbara Rowe, Joan Swofford, and Lisa Weppner for patiently providing the word processing of many revisions of the manuscript and for their suggestions on improving the format.

Finally I wish to thank my family, especially my wife, Gabriele, for understanding and encouragement during the long process of writing this book.

I am grateful to the following publishers and authors for permission to use figures from their publications:

Journal of Parasitology for Figures 2-1, 2-2, and 2-3
Laboratory Animals for Figure 5-1
J. Perran Ross for Figure 8-1
Zoologica for Figure 10-3
Bulletin of the Wildlife Disease Association for Figure 10-4
Florida Department of Health and Rehabilitative Services for Figures 4-2 and 12-2
Journal of Wildlife Diseases for Figures 12-4 and 23-9
Southeastern Association of Fish and Wildlife Agencies for Figures 14-1 and 14-2
American Journal of Tropical Medicine and Hygiene for Figure 17-4
Whalewatcher for Figure 19-2
Florida Wildlife for Figure 23-2
Journal of the American Veterinary Medical Association for Figure 23-4
Melody E. Roelke for Figures 15-1 and 15-2

How to Use This Book

Parasites and Diseases of Wild Mammals in Florida is not a diagnostic manual, although it may prove to be of some value in that regard since a knowledge of the diseases and parasites that occur in a given mammal may aid in a differential diagnosis. For help in the recognition of the common diseases and parasites of many of the mammals in Florida, the reader is referred to the recent publication by Davidson and Nettles (1988). This excellent manual contains a number of color plates along with descriptions of clinical signs and lesions for many diseases of mammals in the southeastern United States, and should be utilized as a companion volume to the present book. The reader is cautioned, however, that the diagnostic process can be a complicated one and, as stated by Davidson and Nettles, "highly trained disease specialists with access to sophisticated diagnostic tests often have difficulty in confirming a diagnosis" (p. 1). They state further that where "there is any doubt about the identity of any disease or parasite, specimens should be sent to a professional diagnostician for examination" (p. 1). Davidson and Nettles' manual also contains a section on field investigations and outlines the procedures to be followed for such studies of disease outbreaks and gives general guidelines for the collection and handling of samples for diagnostic purposes.

This book is intended to be a reference in

which data on the distribution, prevalence, and significance of parasites and diseases are assembled. The material is presented on a host basis, that is, the chapters are organized by species of mammal rather than by disease agents as is so often done in books on diseases. This should facilitate the use of this book by wildlife biologists and others who most often are host-oriented and may wish to know the health/disease status of a certain mammal. Because many diseases and parasites occur in more than one host, information on them appears in more than one chapter. To avoid repetition of details on etiology, transmission, pathology, and so on, such general information is presented only in the chapter concerning the host in which this disease or parasite is of most significance in Florida. Rabies, for example, is discussed most thoroughly in the chapter on raccoons, whereas additional data on prevalence and distribution of rabies will be found in a number of other chapters. To assist the reader in locating the chapters containing this type of general information, the page numbers of such are indicated in boldface type in the index.

Each chapter is preceded by an introduction in which the population and survival status of the mammal or group of mammals in question are discussed. In addition, pertinent reviews or bibliographies are mentioned in this section along with references dealing with hematology, serum chemistry, nutrition, urinalysis, and various physiological topics. If the species is hunted or trapped, information on the numbers of animals harvested is also provided. After the introduction there are sections on various morbidity/mortality factors, disease agents, and conditions in which the distribution, prevalence, and, in some cases, intensity of each is given. This is followed by statements of the significance of these diseases to natural populations as well as considerations of public health aspects. Each chapter ends with a summary and conclusion followed by a list of references cited. At the end of the book there is a glossary to assist the reader in understanding the technical terms used.

Literature cited

Davidson, W. R., and V. F. Nettles. 1988. Field manual of wildlife diseases in the southeastern United States. Southeastern Cooperative Wildlife Disease Study, Univ. of Georgia, Athens. 309 pp.

CHAPTER ONE

Introduction

*The role of disease in wildlife conservation
has probably been radically underestimated.*
Aldo Leopold (1933)

The term *disease* has been defined in many different ways. For the purposes of this book a broad definition is employed as presented by Wobeser (1981, p. 1): disease is "any impairment that interferes with or modifies the performance of normal functions." This definition would include diseases caused by infectious agents (viruses, rickettsia, bacteria, fungi) and parasites (protozoans, trematodes, cestodes, nematodes, acanthocephalans, pentastomes, ticks, mites, fleas, lice, biting flies) as well as other factors such as environmental contaminants, trauma, inclement weather, neoplasia, anomalies, and nutritional deficiencies. The causes of morbidity and mortal-

ity can be grouped into 12 categories (Table 1-1), which include the items listed above and others.

A clear distinction must be made between the terms *infection* and *disease*. They are not the same. An animal can have an infection, that is, it can be a host to bacteria, viruses, or parasites and experience little or no effects, or it can have a disease in which case the infectious agent may overpower the resistance of the animal and cause considerable harm, possibly resulting in death. Often the suffix *-iasis* is added to a word to indicate an infection, while *-osis* is used for disease. For example, small numbers of the abomasal nematode

Table 1-1
The 12 fundamental categories of morbidity and mortality in wild mammals

Category	Comments
1. Anomalies	Usually are rare; confined to an occasional mammal.
2. Stress	Varies depending on the nature of the stress or stressors. Usually reflects other conditions such as chronic malnutrition or extreme parasitism.
3. Trauma	Includes predation, road-kills, and intraspecific conflicts.
4. Suffocation	Can be caused by drowning or verminous pneumonia.
5. Neoplasms	Includes both benign and malignant tumors; most cause only occasional mortality.
6. Toxicoses	May cause considerable mortality in a localized area. Most are caused by environmental contaminants and are due to man's activities.
7. Nutritional diseases	Malnutrition due to deficient intake of energy and protein. Often is associated with infectious diseases and is most severe in the young and the very old.
8. Viral and rickettsial diseases	Can cause widespread and rapid mortality.
9. Bacterial diseases	Can result in considerable mortality especially in dense populations, but also can be of an insidious nature.
10. Mycotic diseases	Usually are secondary invaders along with or following other diseases.
11. Parasitic diseases	Most are insidious and cause morbidity and mortality over a long period of time. Commonly are associated with overpopulation and malnutrition.
12. Senility	Not usually an important mortality factor in wild mammals.

Source: Adapted from Hayes and Prestwood (1969); Kellogg (1981).

Haemonchus contortus infecting white-tailed deer result in haemonchiasis, but if large numbers of the nematode are involved and disease is a consequence, the condition is called haemonchosis. These two concepts should be kept in mind when reading this book, where both conditions are presented sometimes without clear distinction. A given mammal may have a long list of infectious agents, parasites, and other conditions, but not all may cause disease, or, if they do, the effects may not be serious. Wild mammals often serve as reservoir hosts or carrier hosts, in which case they maintain infections with little or no apparent harm to themselves but serve as a source of infection for other wild mammals, domestic mammals, or man. In many cases the mechanisms whereby infections become diseases are poorly understood or not known at all.

Another concept that must be emphasized is that disease agents and conditions often in-

teract within a host and result in synergistic effects. This interaction can mean that separately various infectious and parasitic agents may cause little harm to an animal, but concurrent infections can be more harmful than would be expected from a mere additive effect. In addition, various factors, such as nutrition, environmental contaminants, stress due to overcrowding, or inclement weather, may interact with infectious and parasitic agents and result in serious disease. This complex phenomenon is only partially understood for most wildlife diseases.

Basic to an understanding of wildlife diseases is information on distribution, prevalence, and intensity. The distribution of diseases in time and space is of great relevance. Some diseases are widespread geographically, occur at all times of the year, and infect many different species of mammals. Others are more restricted in distribution and occur only at certain times of the year. Still others are found only in one host or in a few closely related species. In addition, the prevalence of diseases or disease agents is of great interest. The term *prevalence* refers to the number or percentage of animals in a sample or population that are infected with a given disease or parasite. It is helpful to understand prevalence in terms of the time span during which the data were collected. *Intensity* is also of value in assessing the significance of infections and relates to the number of disease agents (i.e., worms, protozoans, arthropods) per infected mammal. Uninfected animals are not taken into consideration by the concept of intensity. It is not always possible to determine the intensity of infections, but where it can be done the information is of great value.

Diseases that cause large-scale mortality (epizootics) often receive considerable attention because the results are dramatic. The effects of more subtle or chronic problems, however, can be important as well. An attempt is made in each chapter to assess the importance of the various diseases to the host in question and to relate it to three aspects: effects on the populations of wild mammals; effects on and interactions with domesticated animals; and public health implications. Much of the information on these topics is incomplete, sketchy, or lacking entirely. An attempt is made in the summary (Chapter 24) to bring the available information for Florida's mammals into focus, but the reader should understand that the discipline of wildlife disease investigation is still in its infancy compared to human and veterinary medicine. There is much to be done, but the first steps are to assemble and examine what is known about the various diseases and their distribution and prevalence among native populations. This information should form the basis for future research as well as provide a foundation for management and conservation plans for the valuable and unique mammalian fauna of Florida.

Literature cited

Hayes, F.A., and A.K. Prestwood. 1969. Some considerations for diseases and parasites of white-tailed deer in the southeastern United States. Proc. White-tailed Deer in the Southern Forest Habitat Symp., USDA, Forest Service, Southern For. Exp. Sta., Nacogdoches, Tex. pp. 32–36.

Kellogg, F.E. 1981. Field considerations. In: Diseases and parasites of white-tailed deer. W.R. Davidson et al. (eds.). Misc. Pub. No. 7, Tall Timbers Research Station, Tallahassee, Fla. pp. 1–5.

Leopold, A. 1933. Game management. Charles Scribner's Sons, New York. 481 pp.

Wobeser, G.A. 1981. Diseases of wild waterfowl. Plenum Press, New York. 300 pp.

Opossums

I. Introduction

The Virginia opossum (*Didelphis virginiana* Kerr) is abundant and distributed widely throughout the state of Florida (Brown 1987). Interest in the opossum is considerable due to its value as a research animal and its significance as a reservoir of zoonotic diseases. The biology of this marsupial has been reviewed recently by Gardner (1982), and a brief summary of mortality factors, including predation, trauma, diseases, and parasites, was included. More detailed accounts have been given by Barr (1963) and Potkay (1970, 1977). The 1977 review by Potkay is especially helpful, and includes data on viruses, rickettsiae, bacteria, fungi, parasites, and a

compilation of a number of specific anatomical lesions and conditions.

II. Trauma

Gardner (1982) discussed the published accounts of trauma in Virginia opossums and pointed out that this animal often seems to have excessive numbers of cuts, scratches, ripped ears, lost toes, broken teeth, and broken bones. There is little published information on trauma in opossums from Florida, but a few such observations have been made. The most important predators appear to be dogs and great horned owls (Gardner 1982). The skull of an opossum was found in the nest of a bald eagle in Highlands County (Rand and Host 1942). Road-killed opossums are common in Florida, and trauma of this type will be of increasing importance as Florida's human population grows.

III. Environmental contaminants

Very little information is available on environmental contaminants in opossums in Florida. In one study, residues of mirex (a chlorinated hydrocarbon) were determined in three opossums from the Dee Dot Ranch in Duval County (Wheeler et al. 1977). One animal was killed and examined at 1 month, 6 months, and 18 months after the area was treated for fire ant control. Concentrations of mirex in brain, fat, liver, muscle, and stomach contents were less than 1 ppm except for the fat samples at 1 month and 6 months, which measured 1.72 and 3.35 ppm, respectively. The significance of these findings is unknown.

In another study (Jenkins and Fendley 1968) 14 opossums were examined for gamma ray-emitting radioisotopes. The most important isotope was cesium-137. The exact locality for these opossums was not given, but they were from the lower coastal plain in Florida. Mean concentrations of cesium-137 were 19,372 pCi/kg, and ranged from 11,474 to 29,057 pCi/kg. The authors felt that these concentrations would not constitute a serious public health hazard should these animals be consumed. The significance to opossum populations is unknown.

IV. Rabies

Rabies is uncommon in opossums (Burridge et al. 1986). Only two cases have been reported in Florida, one from Duval County (1970) and one from Escambia County (1981). The clinical signs of rabies in opossums are those of "dumb rabies" rather than "furious rabies," and this would make it unlikely that rabid wild opossums would transmit the disease to other animals by biting (Barr 1963). Experimental studies have shown that the opossum is extremely resistant to rabies. More than 16,000 times the amount of virus that causes foxes to die of rabies is needed to cause fatal infections in opossums (Barr 1961; Beamer et al. 1960). These data indicate that rabies is not an important disease to opossums and that the opossum does not have an important role in the epidemiology of this disease in Florida.

V. Arboviruses

Five arboviruses have been reported from opossums in Florida (Table 2-1). These include eastern equine encephalomyelitis (EEE), St. Louis encephalitis, Everglades, Keystone, and Sawgrass viruses. There is no indication that any of these viruses have an adverse effect on opossums. Experimental infections with EEE virus have shown that opossums exhibit no clinical evidence of disease—even when massive doses of virus are given (Syverton and Berry 1940). Opossums may serve some role as reservoir hosts for these viruses, particularly Everglades virus, in southern Florida.

VI. Miscellaneous viruses

The possible role of opossums in the epidemiology of encephalomyocarditis (EMC) virus was studied during an outbreak of EMC in domestic swine near Winter Haven, Florida, in 1966 (Gainer and Bigler 1967; Gainer et al.

Table 2-1
Arboviruses reported from opossums in Florida

Arbovirus[a]	Date	No. opossums		Locality (county)	Data source
		Exam.	Pos.		
EEE	1963–70	194	2	Hillsborough	Wellings et al. (1972)
	1965–74	199	1	Statewide	Bigler et al. (1975)
SLE	1962	3	1	Hillsborough	Jennings et al. (1969)
	1965–74	199	2	Statewide	Bigler et al. (1975)
	1968	NG[b]	2	Dade	" " " "
Highlands J	1965–74	159	0	Statewide	" " " "
Everglades	1965–74	184	1	Statewide	" " " "
	1965–66	66	0	Collier	Lord et al. (1973)
	1965–66	52	20	Monroe	" " " "
	1969–70	93	1[c]	Statewide	Bigler (1971)
	1966–68	23	0	"South Florida"	Bigler (1969)
Keystone	1964–67	113	1	Hillsborough	Jennings et al. (1968), Taylor et al. (1971)
Sawgrass	1964	4	4[d]	Hillsborough	Sather et al. (1970)

Note: All data (except as noted otherwise) are from serologic studies.
[a] EEE = eastern equine encephalomyelitis, SLE = St. Louis encephalitis.
[b] NG = not given by authors.
[c] The positive animal was from Collier County, where 4 opossums were examined.
[d] Sawgrass virus was isolated from ticks (Dermacentor variabilis) taken from 4 opossums.

1968). As part of a general survey of wildlife, three opossums from a farm where EMC had occurred were examined for serologic evidence of infection, and attempts were made to isolate EMC virus. All results were negative.

Antibodies to canine distemper (CD) virus were found in 4 of 61 (7%) opossums in Manatee County and in 1 of 14 (7%) in Sarasota County in 1968–69 (McLean 1988). The importance of this virus to opossums is unknown. For more information on CD virus in carnivores in Florida, see Chapters 12 (Raccoons) and 16 (Foxes and Coyotes).

Serological tests for antibodies to infectious canine hepatitis virus were conducted also on the same animals listed above (McLean 1988). All were negative.

There are no data available on pseudorabies in opossums in Florida. Since this animal has been shown to be susceptible to pseudorabies (Trainer and Karstad 1963), it would be helpful to know what role opossums play

in the epidemiology of this virus in Florida, where it is common in feral hog populations (see Chapter 23).

VII. Bacterial diseases

Three surveys have been conducted to detect infections of leptospires in various wild mammals in southern Georgia and Florida. All of these included examinations of opossums. In the investigation during 1954–1956 by McKeever et al. (1958a), cultures were made of kidneys from opossums from three areas near the Florida border (site nos. 10, 11, 12). Leptospires were cultured from 5 of 81 opossums, and *Leptospira ballum* was identified in 3 of these isolates. In another study (Shotts et al. 1975) 17 opossums from the Florida panhandle and southwestern Georgia were examined serologically and via culture techniques. *Leptospira ballum* was identified se-

Table 2-2
Helminths reported from opossums in Florida

Helminth	No. opossums Exam.	Inf.	(%)	Locality (county)	Data source
Trematoda					
Brachylaeme virginianum	NG[a]	+[b]	(—)	Highlands	Kinsella (1987)
Mesostephanus appendiculatoides	c	c	(—)	—	Hutton (1964)
Phagicola longa	c	c	(—)	—	" "
Rhopalias baculifer	NG	+	(—)	Leon	Loftin (1961)
Rhopalias coronatus	NG	+	(—)	Leon	" "
Rhopalias macracanthus	NG	+	(—)	Highlands	Kinsella (1987)
Stictodora cursitans	1	1	(100)	Levy	Kinsella & Heard (1974)
Nematoda					
Anatrichosoma buccalis	64	23	(36)	Highlands	Kinsella & Winegarner (1975)
Capillaria hepatica	6	0	(0)	Several[d]	Layne (1968)
Cruzia americana	NG	+	(—)	Highlands	Kinsella (1987)
	1	1	(100)	Alachua	Forrester (1990)
Dipetalonema didelphis[e]	NG	+	(—)	"Florida"	Esslinger & Smith (1979)
	26	0	(0)	Indian R.	Sauerman & Nayar (1985)
Gnathostoma didelphis	NG	+	(—)	Levy	Penner (1987)
Longistriata didelphis	NG	+	(—)	Highlands	Kinsella (1987)
Physaloptera ackerti	NG	+	(—)	"Florida"	Penner (1987)
Physaloptera turgida	NG	+	(—)	NG	Morgan (1941)
	NG	+	(—)	"Florida"	Walton (1927)
	NG	+	(—)	"Florida"	Penner (1987)
Trichinella spiralis	65	3	(5)	Marion	Scholtens & Norman (1971)
Viannaia viannai	NG	+	(—)	Highlands	Kinsella (1987)
Acanthocephala					
Hamanniella tortuosa	NG	+	(—)	Levy	Penner (1987)

[a] NG = not given by author.
[b] + = presence of the parasite reported by author, but no data given on prevalence.
[c] Hutton (1964) included these two species in his checklist and added a notation that these were "experimental" infections. It is not known if these trematodes infect opossums naturally in Florida.
[d] Alachua, Highlands, and Levy counties.
[e] This filariid was described by Esslinger and Smith (1979) from specimens collected from an opossum in Florida. The specific locality was not given.

rologically in five animals and was cultured from seven. Unfortunately Shotts et al. combined their data from Florida and Georgia, so it is not possible to determine how many of these positive opossums were from Florida. McLean (1988) found seropositive animals (serovar not determined) in Manatee County (6 of 69 opossums) and Sarasota County (1 of 16) in 1968–1969. The importance of these leptospiral infections to opossums is un-known, but this marsupial is considered to be an important reservoir of leptospirosis for other wildlife and for humans (Gardner 1982).

Antibodies to *Francisella tularensis,* the etiologic agent of tularemia, were identified in 6 of 24 opossums from Leon County during 1955–57 (McKeever et al. 1958b). *Francisella tularensis* was isolated from the spleen of one of these seropositive opossums. Hoff

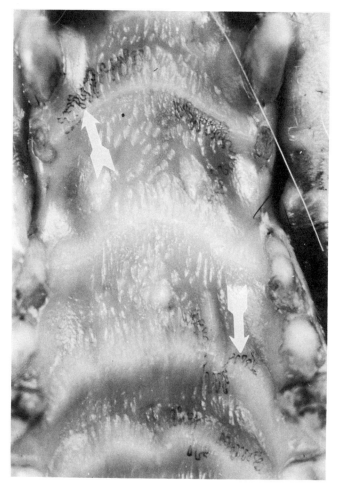

FIGURE 2-1. View of hard palate of a Virginia opossum showing tunnels (arrows) filled with eggs of *Anatrichosoma buccalis* in the mucosal epithelium (× 3). (After Pence and Little 1972.)

et al. (1975) reported that 5 of 451 opossums from Florida (specific localities not given) were seropositive for *F. tularensis*. These animals were sampled between 1965 and 1973. Opossums may have a significant role in the spread of this zoonotic disease.

In September 1975 White (1988) cultured five opossums from Dade County; three were positive for *Salmonella*. Two animals were infected with *S. newport* and *S. bareilly* and one animal was positive for *S. saint-paul*.

These cultures were made from intestinal contents and not from tissues, so these findings probably represent the carrier state rather than disease situations.

Hoff et al. (1974) examined sera from 169 opossums from Florida (specific localities not given) for agglutinins to *Brucella canis*. All samples were negative. McLean (1988) examined 61 opossums from Manatee County and 14 from Sarasota County in 1968–69; all were seronegative for *B. canis*.

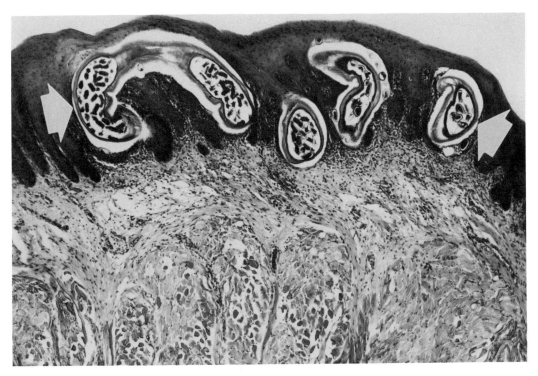

FIGURE 2-2. Section of tongue of a Virginia opossum showing transverse sections of female *Anatricho-soma buccalis* (arrows) (× 43). (After Pence and Little 1972.)

VIII. Mycotic infections

During 1954–1956, 436 opossums from southwestern Georgia and northwestern Florida were examined for ringworm fungi (McKeever et al. 1958d). Seventeen (3.9%) of these were infected. Eleven of the 17 animals were positive for a *Microsporum* (red variety), and six were positive for *Trichophyton mentagrophytes*. The significance of these findings is questionable since none of the opossums showed any sign of fungal infection. The authors concluded that the origin of the fungi was from contaminated fur rather than a true ringworm infection. *Microsporum* has been recovered from soil and attempts to infect experimental animals have not been successful. *Trichophyton mentagrophytes* causes ringworm in cattle and horses, and these animals rather than opossums may

have been the source of this fungus in the area.

IX. Protozoan parasites

Two protozoan parasites have been reported from opossums in Florida; both are of zoonotic concern. McKeever et al. (1958c) found 93 of 552 (17%) opossums from southwestern Georgia and northwestern Florida infected by a *Trypanosoma cruzi*–like organism. Further studies on this organism by Norman et al. (1959) showed that this trypanosome was indistinguishable from *T. cruzi*. Irons (1971) examined 201 opossums from 23 counties in Florida; all were seronegative for *T. cruzi*.

Antibodies to *Toxoplasma gondii* were found in 37 of 349 (11%) opossums from

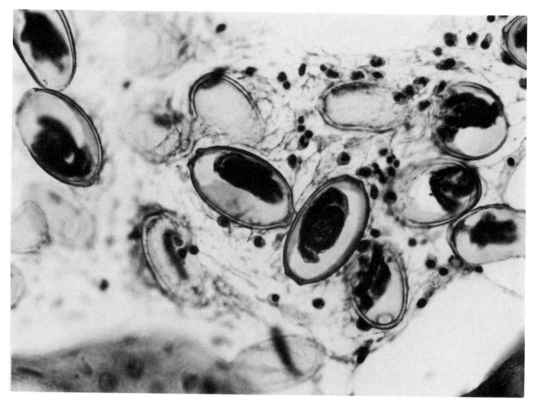

FIGURE 2-3. Section of hard palate of a Virginia opossum showing eggs of *Anatrichosoma buccalis* in a tunnel. Note that the eggs are thick-walled, bipolar, and contain developing larvae (× 360). (After Pence and Little 1972.)

throughout Florida (Burridge et al. 1979). The prevalence of infection was significantly higher in adult animals (15%) than in non-adults (1%). There were no differences in prevalence according to sex or geographic location within the state. In another study, McLean (1988) found 1 of 62 and none of 14 opossums seropositive in Manatee and Sarasota counties, respectively, in 1968.

There is no information available concerning the effects of these two protozoans on opossums.

X. Helminths

The helminths of the Virginia opossum have been well studied in several parts of its range,

but not in Florida. Gardner (1982) lists 70 species of helminths, including 30 nematodes, 26 trematodes, 7 cestodes, and 7 acanthocephalans. These are composite data and a given population will have a much smaller number of species. For example, two studies in North Carolina resulted in the finding of 13 (Miller and Harkema 1970) and 17 species (Feldman et al. 1972). Stewart and Dean (1971) gave data on nine species of helminths from four opossums in southern Georgia.

Five species of trematodes, nine species of nematodes, and one acanthocephalan are known from opossums in Florida (Table 2-2). Only one of these (*Trichinella spiralis*) is of zoonotic concern.

For most of these parasites there are no data on pathology or other biological as-

Table 2-3

Ticks reported from opossums in Florida

Species of tick	Location (county)	Data source
Dermacentor variabilis	"Northern Florida"	Rogers (1953)
	Hillsborough	Sather et al. (1970), Worth (1950b), Taylor (1951)
	Osceola, Orange, Collier	Travis (1941)
	Brevard, Indian R.	FSCA,[a] Wilson & Kale (1972)
	Alachua, Gilchrist, Sumter	Taylor (1951)
	Alachua	Boardman (1929)
	Palm Beach	Carpenter et al. (1946)
	"Statewide"	Hoff et al. (1975)
Ixodes scapularis	"Northern Florida"	Rogers (1953)
	Hillsborough	Worth (1950b), Taylor (1951)
	Monroe	Worth (1950a)
	Alachua, Dade, Sumter	Taylor (1951)
	Alachua	Boardman (1929)
	Orange, Osceola, Collier	Travis (1941)
	Indian R., Brevard	FSCA
	Palm Beach	Carpenter et al. (1946)
Amblyomma americanum (nymphs)	"Florida"	Bishopp & Trembley (1945)

[a] FSCA = records from the Florida State Collection of Arthropods, Division of Plant Industry, Florida Department of Agriculture, Gainesville, Fla.

Table 2-4

Mites reported from opossums in Florida

Species of mite	Location (county)	Data source
Haemogamasus harperi	"Florida"	Keegan (1951)
Ornithonyssus bacoti	Hillsborough	Worth (1950a, 1950b)
Walchia americana	Alachua	Rohani & Cromroy (1979)
Eutrombicula splendens	Levy	" " " "
	Collier	Ewing (1943)
Eutrombicula sp.	Hillsborough	Worth (1950b)

pects. The one exception is *Anatrichosoma buccalis*. Kinsella and Winegarner (1975) provided data on the prevalence of *A. buccalis* in opossums of various ages in Highlands County. The youngest animals with infections were five months of age. By six months 50% of the opossums were infected and by seven months 63% were infected. This parasite is found in tunnels in the superficial layers of the mucosa of the hard palate, gums, and tongue (Figure 2-1). Female worms (Figure 2-2) deposit eggs (Figure 2-3) in these tunnels, which eventually are liberated into the mouth due to sloughing of the surface epithelium. The eggs pass out of the opossum by way of the digestive tract (Pence and Little 1972). Kinsella and Winegarner (1975) observed that lesions caused by this egg-laying activity in the tunnels disappeared in as little as three days. Infections of high intensity were

Table 2-5
Fleas reported from opossums in Florida

Species of flea	Location (county)	Data source
Xenopsylla cheopis	Hillsborough	Worth (1950b)
Pulex simulans	Hillsborough	" "
	Alachua, Highlands	Layne (1971)
Ctenocephalides felis	Hillsborough	Worth (1950b)
	Alachua, Highlands	Layne (1971), FSCA[a]
	Levy, Marion	FSCA
Echidnophaga gallinacea	Hillsborough	Worth (1950b)
	Alachua, Highlands	Layne (1971), FSCA
Polygenis gwyni	Hillsborough	Worth (1950b)
	Collier	FSCA
	Dade	Worth (1950a)
	Osceola	Fox (1940)
	Alachua, Highlands, Levy	Layne (1971)
Orchopeas howardii	Indian River	" "

[a] FSCA = records from the Florida State Collection of Arthropods, Division of Plant Industry, Florida Department of Agriculture, Gainesville, Fla.

rare and would indicate that this nematode is of minor consequence to opossums.

A comprehensive study of the helminths of opossums in Florida should be conducted in order to evaluate the significance of these parasites to populations of this marsupial.

XI. Arthropods

Fifteen species of parasitic arthropods are known from opossums in Florida. These include three species of ticks (Table 2-3), five species of mites (Table 2-4), six species of fleas (Table 2-5), and one blowfly (Diptera).

The three species of ticks (*Dermacentor variabilis, Ixodes scapularis,* and *Amblyomma americanum*) have been found on many other mammals in Florida, including white-tailed deer, feral hogs, fox squirrels, black bears, gray foxes, bobcats, and Florida panthers. These ticks are common also on various mammals in Georgia, including opossums (Wilson and Baker 1972). All of the ticks can cause tick paralysis, although no

records of this in opossums in Florida were found. *Dermacentor variabilis* also is a vector of the etiologic agent of Rocky Mountain spotted fever (Strickland et al. 1976).

Chiggers such as *Walchia americana* and *Eutrombicula* spp. can produce itching and may lead to secondary bacterial infections (Rohani and Cromroy 1979). Two of the mites (*O. bacoti* and *E. splendens*) are primarily parasites of cotton rats and rice rats in Florida (Worth 1950a). In addition, one of these (*O. bacoti*) is a biological vector of filarial worms (*Litomosoides carinii* and *L. scotti*) of cotton rats and rice rats in Florida (Forrester and Kinsella 1973). It is not known if these filariids infect opossums.

The sticktight flea (*Echidnophaga gallinacea*) is primarily a parasite of domestic fowl, and opossums probably acquire infestations from their association with poultry houses (Layne 1971). The most ubiquitous flea of small mammals in Florida is *Polygenis gwyni,* and this probably accounts for its being reported from opossums in seven counties in Florida. Layne (1971) reported that this flea was more prevalent during the cooler times of year in Florida and more abundant in the spring. The primary host in Florida is the cotton rat (Layne 1971). Some of the fleas and ticks reported from opossums might serve as vectors for *Francisella tularensis,* the etiologic agent of tularemia (Jellison 1974).

In April 1969 an opossum was found in Lake County with a blowfly infection, probably secondary to trauma of some kind (records from the Florida State Collection of Arthropods). Twenty-three larvae of *Lucilia illustris* were collected and identified by W.P. Henderson, who wrote: "These were found on an opossum wandering around with his eyes and nose completely eaten away down to the bone. A gruesome sight to say the least. I don't know what kept him alive." This species of blowfly normally breeds in meat or carrion, but can function as a parasite and result in facultative traumatic myiasis as seen in the opossum described above (Harwood and James 1979).

XII. Summary and conclusions

Forty-eight different parasites, disease agents, and environmental contaminants have been identified from opossums in Florida. These include one pesticide, one radionuclide, seven viruses, five bacteria, two fungi, two protozoans, five trematodes, nine nematodes, one acanthocephalan, three ticks, five mites, six fleas, and one blowfly. There is no evidence that any of these are of significance to populations of opossums in Florida. A number of these disease agents are of public health importance, including the agents of rabies, encephalitis, leptospirosis, tularemia, Chagas' disease, toxoplasmosis, and trichinellosis. Several of the ticks, mites, and fleas may infest man, at least temporarily.

XIII. Literature cited

Barr, T.R.B. 1961. Experimental rabies in the opossum (*Didelphis marsupialis virginiana* Kerr). Ph.D. diss., Univ. of Illinois, Urbana. 83 pp.

———. 1963. Infectious diseases in the opossum: A review. J. Wildl. Manage. 27:53–71.

Beamer, P.D., C.O. Mohr, and T.R.B. Barr. 1960. Resistance of the opossum to rabies virus. Am. J. Vet. Res. 21:507–510.

Bigler, W.J. 1969. Venezuelan encephalitis antibody studies in certain Florida wildlife. Bull. Wildl. Dis. Assoc. 5:267–270.

———. 1971. Serologic evidence of Venezuelan equine encephalitis virus infections in raccoons of south central Florida. J. Wildl. Dis. 7:166–170.

Bigler, W.J., E. Lassing, E. Buff, A.L. Lewis, and G.L. Hoff. 1975. Arbovirus surveillance in Florida: Wild vertebrate studies 1965–1974. J. Wildl. Dis. 11:348–356.

Bishopp, F.C., and H.L. Trembley. 1945. Distribution and hosts of certain North American ticks. J. Parasitol. 31:1–54.

Boardman, E.T. 1929. Ticks of the Gainesville area. M.S. thesis, Univ. of Florida, Gainesville. 57 pp.

Brown, L.N. 1987. A checklist of Florida's mammals. Florida Game and Fresh Water Fish Commission, Tallahassee. 6 pp.

Burridge, M.J., L.A. Sawyer, and W.J. Bigler. 1986. Rabies in Florida. Department of Health and Rehabilitative Services, Tallahassee, Fla. 147 pp.

Burridge, M.J., W.J. Bigler, D.J. Forrester, and J.M. Hennemann. 1979. Serologic survey for *Toxoplasma gondii* in wild animals in Florida. J. Am. Vet. Med. Assoc. 175:964–967.

Carpenter, S.J., R.W. Chamberlain, and L. Peeples. 1946. Tick collections at army installations in the Fourth Service Command. Entomol. News 57:71–76.

Esslinger, J.H., and J.L. Smith. 1979. *Dipetalonema* (*Acanthocheilonema*) *didelphis* sp.n. (Nematoda: Filarioidea) from opossums, with a redescription of *D.* (*A.*) *pricei* (Vaz and Pereira 1934). J. Parasitol. 65:928–933.

Ewing, H.E. 1943. The American chiggers (larvae of the Trombiculinae) of the genus *Acariscus*, new genus. Proc. Entomol. Soc. Wash. 45:57–66.

Feldman, D.B., J.A. Moore, M.W. Harris, and J.L. Self. 1972. Characteristics of common helminths of the Virginia opossum (*Didelphis virginiana*) from North Carolina. Lab. Anim. Sci. 22:183–189.

Forrester, D.J. 1990. Unpublished data. Univ. of Florida, Gainesville.

Forrester, D.J., and J.M. Kinsella. 1973. Comparative morphology and ecology of two species of *Litomosoides* (Nematoda: Filarioidea) of rodents in Florida, with a key to the species of *Litomosoides* Chandler, 1931. Int. J. Parasitol. 3:255–263.

Fox, I. 1940. Fleas of eastern United States. Iowa State Coll. Press, Ames. 191 pp.

Gainer, J.H., and W.J. Bigler. 1967. Encephalomyocarditis (EMC) virus recovered from two cotton rats and a raccoon. Bull. Wildl. Dis. Assoc. 3:47–49.

Gainer, J.H., J.R. Sandefur, and W.J. Bigler. 1968. High mortality in a Florida swine herd infected with the encephalomyocarditis virus. An accompanying epizootiologic survey. Cornell Vet. 58:31–47.

Gardner, A.L. 1982. Virginia opossum. In: Wild mammals of North America. J.A. Chapman and G.A. Feldhamer (eds.). Johns Hopkins Univ. Press, Baltimore. pp. 3–36.

Harwood, R.F., and M.T. James. 1979. Entomology in human and animal health. 7th ed. Macmillan, New York. 548 pp.

Hoff, G.L., W.J. Bigler, and E.C. Prather. 1975. One-half century of tularemia in Florida. J. Fla. Med. Assoc. 62:35–37.

Hoff, G.L., W.J. Bigler, D.O. Trainer, J.G. Debbie, G.M. Brown, W.G. Winkler, S.H. Richards, and M. Reardon. 1974. Survey of selected carnivore and opossum serums for agglutinins to *Brucella canis*. J. Am. Vet. Med. Assoc. 165:830–831.

Hutton, R.F. 1964. A second list of parasites from marine and coastal animals of Florida. Trans. Am. Micros. Soc. 83:439–447.

Irons, E.M. 1971. A survey of the state of Florida for the incidence of American trypanosomiasis in insect vectors and reservoir animals. M.S. thesis, Univ. of Florida, Gainesville. 71 pp.

Jellison, W.L. 1974. Tularemia in North America. Univ. of Montana Foundation, Missoula. 276 pp.

Jenkins, J.H., and T.T. Fendley. 1968. The extent of contamination, detection, and health significance of high accumulations of radioactivity in southern game populations. Proc. Ann. Conf. S.E. Assoc. Game Fish Comm. 22:89–95.

Jennings, W.L., A.L. Lewis, G.E. Sather, W.M. Hammon, and J.O. Bond. 1968. California-encephalitis-group viruses in Florida rabbits: Report of experimental and sentinel studies. Am. J. Trop. Med. Hyg. 17:781–787.

Jennings, W.L., W.G. Winkler, D.D. Stamm, P.H. Coleman, and A.L. Lewis. 1969. Serologic studies of possible avian or mammalian reservoirs of St. Louis encephalitis virus in Florida. Fla. State Board of Health Monogr. Series, no. 12, pp. 118–125.

Keegan, H.L. 1951. The mites of the subfamily Haemogamasinae (Acari: Laelaptidae). Proc. U.S. Nat. Mus. 101:203–268.

Kinsella, J.M. 1987. Unpublished data. Archbold Biological Station, Lake Placid, Fla.

Kinsella, J.M., and R.W. Heard. 1974. Morphology and life cycle of *Stictodora cursitans* n. comb. (Trematoda: Heterophyidae) from mammals in Florida salt marshes. Trans. Am. Micros. Soc. 93:408–412.

Kinsella, J.M., and C.E. Winegarner. 1975. A field study of *Anatrichosoma* infections in the opossum, *Didelphis virginiana*. J. Parasitol. 61:779–781.

Layne, J.N. 1968. Host and ecological relationships of the parasitic helminth *Capillaria hepatica* in Florida mammals. Zoologica 53:107–122.

———. 1971. Fleas (Siphonaptera) of Florida. Fla. Entomol. 54:35–51.

Loftin, H. 1961. An annotated check-list of trematodes and cestodes and their vertebrate hosts from northwest Florida. Quart. J. Fla. Acad. Sci. 23:302–314.

Lord, R.D., C.H. Calisher, W.D. Sudia, and T.H. Work. 1973. Ecological investigations of vertebrate hosts of Venezuelan equine encephalomyelitis virus in south Florida. Am. J. Trop. Med. Hyg. 22:116–123.

McKeever, S., G.W. Gorman, J.D. Chapman, M.M. Galton, and D.K. Powers. 1958a. Incidence of leptospirosis in wild mammals from southwestern Georgia, with a report of new hosts for six serotypes of leptospires. Am. J. Trop. Med. Hyg. 7:646–655.

McKeever, S., J.H. Schubert, M.D. Moody, G.W. Gorman, and J.F. Chapman. 1958b. Natural occurrence of tularemia in marsupials, carnivores, lagomorphs, and large rodents in southwestern Georgia and northwestern Florida. J. Inf. Dis. 103:120–126.

McKeever, S., G.W. Gorman, and L. Norman. 1958c. Occurrence of a *Trypanosoma cruzi*–like organism in some mammals from southwestern Georgia and northwestern Florida. J. Parasitol. 44:583–587.

McKeever, S., W. Kaplan, and L. Ajello. 1958d. Ringworm fungi of large wild mammals in southwestern Georgia and northwestern Florida. Am. J. Vet. Res. 19:973–975.

McLean, R.G. 1988. Unpublished data. CDC, Fort Collins, Colo.

Miller, G.C., and R. Harkema. 1970. Helminths of the opossum (*Didelphis virginiana*) in North Carolina. Proc. Helminthol. Soc. Wash. 37:36–39.

Morgan, B.B. 1941. A summary of the Physalopterinae (Nematoda) of North America. Proc. Helminthol. Soc. Wash. 8:28–30.

Norman, L., M.M. Brooke, D.S. Allain, and G.W. Gorman. 1959. Morphology and virulence of *Trypanosoma cruzi*–like hemoflagellates isolated from wild mammals in Georgia and Florida. J. Parasitol. 45:457–463.

Pence, D.P., and M.D. Little. 1972. *Anatrichosoma buccalis* sp.n. (Nematoda: Trichosomoididae) from the buccal mucosa of the common opossum, *Didelphis marsupialis* L. J. Parasitol. 58: 767–773.

Penner, L.R. 1987. Unpublished data. Archbold Biological Station, Lake Placid, Fla.

Potkay, S. 1970. Diseases of the opossum (*Didelphis marsupialis*): A review. Lab. Anim. Care 20:502–511.

———. 1977. Diseases of marsupials. In: The biology of marsupials. D. Hunsaker (ed.). Academic, New York. pp. 415–506.

Rand, A.L., and P. Host. 1942. Results of the Archbold Expeditions No. 45. Mammal notes from Highlands County, Florida. Bull. Am. Mus. Nat. Hist. 80:1–21.

Rogers, A.J. 1953. A study of the ixodid ticks of northern Florida, including the biology and life history of *Ixodes scapularis* Say (Ixodidae: Acarina). Ph.D. diss., Univ. of Maryland, College Park. 191 pp.

Rohani, I.B., and H.L. Cromroy. 1979. Taxonomy and distribution of chiggers (Acarina: Trombiculidae) in northcentral Florida. Fla. Entomol. 62:363–376.

Sather, G.E., A.L. Lewis, W. Jennings, J.O. Bond, and W.M. Hammon. 1970. Sawgrass virus: A newly described arbovirus in Florida. Am. J. Trop. Med. Hyg. 19:319–326.

Sauerman, D.M., Jr., and J.K. Nayar. 1985. Prevalence of presumed *Dirofilaria tenuis* microfilariae in raccoons near Vero Beach, Florida. J. Parasitol. 71:130–132.

Scholtens, R.G., and L. Norman. 1971. *Trichinella spiralis* in Florida wildlife. J. Parasitol. 57:1103.

Shotts, E.B., C.L. Andrews, and T.W. Harvey. 1975. Leptospirosis in selected wild mammals of the Florida panhandle and southwestern Georgia. J. Am. Vet. Med. Assoc. 167:587–589.

Stewart, T.B., and D. Dean. 1971. *Didelphonema longispiculata* (Hill, 1939) Wolfgang, 1953 (Nematoda: Spiruroidea) and other helminths from the opossum (*Didelphis marsupialis virginiana*) in Georgia. J. Parasitol. 57:687–688.

Strickland, R.K., R.R. Gerrish, J.L. Hourigan, and G.O. Schubert. 1976. Ticks of veterinary importance. APHIS-USDA Agr. Handbook No. 485. Washington, D.C. 122 pp.

Syverton, J.T., and G.P. Berry. 1940. Host range of equine encephalomyelitis: Susceptibility of the North American cottontail rabbit, jack rabbit, field vole, woodchuck and opossum to experimental infection. Am. J. Hyg. 32:19–23.

Taylor, D.J. 1951. The distribution of ticks in Florida. M.S. thesis, Univ. of Florida, Gainesville. 124 pp.

Taylor, D.J., A.L. Lewis, J.D. Edman, and W.L. Jennings. 1971. California group arboviruses in Florida. Am. J. Trop. Med. Hyg. 20:139–145.

Trainer, D.O., and L.H. Karstad. 1963. Experimental pseudorabies in some North American mammals. Zoon. Res. 2: 135–151.

Travis, B.V. 1941. Examinations of wild animals for the cattle tick *Boophilus annulatus microplus* (Can.) in Florida. J. Parasitol. 27:465–467.

Walton, A.C. 1927. A revision of the nematodes of the Leidy collections. Proc. Acad. Nat. Sci. Phila. 79:49–163.

Wellings, F.M., A.L. Lewis, and L.V. Pierce. 1972. Agents encountered during arboviral ecological studies: Tampa Bay area, Florida, 1963 to 1970. Am. J. Trop. Med. Hyg. 21:201–213.

Wheeler, W.B., D.P. Jouvenaz, D.P. Wojcik, W.A. Banks, C.H. VanMiddelem, C.S. Lofgren, S. Nesbitt, L. Williams, and R. Brown. 1977. Mirex residues in nontarget organisms after application of 10-5 bait for fire ant control, northeast Florida, 1972–74. Pest. Monit. J. 11:146–156.

White, F.H. 1988. Unpublished data. Univ. of Florida, Gainesville.

Wilson, N., and W.W. Baker. 1972. Ticks of Georgia (Acarina: Metastigmata). Bull. Tall Timbers Res. Sta. 10:1–29.

Wilson, N., and H.W. Kale. 1972. Ticks collected from Indian River County, Florida (Acari: Metastigmata: Ixodidae). Fla. Entomol. 55:53–57.

Worth, C.B. 1950a. Observations on ectoparasites of some small mammals in Everglades National Park and Hillsborough County, Florida. J. Parasitol. 36:326–335.

———. 1950b. A preliminary host-ectoparasite register for some small mammals of Florida. J. Parasitol. 36:497–498.

Moles and Shrews

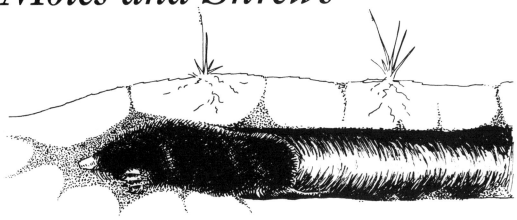

I. Introduction

Four species of insectivores are found in Florida, including three shrews and one mole (Table 3-1). One of these, the southeastern shrew, is Florida's smallest mammal (Brown 1978). Subspecies of two of the shrews are listed as species of special concern by the Florida Game and Fresh Water Fish Commission (Wood 1990). These are the Homosassa shrew (*S. l. eionis*), found only in the vicinity of Homosassa Springs in Citrus County (Brown 1978), and Sherman's short-tailed shrew (*B. c. shermani*), which occurs only in Lee County about two miles north of Fort Myers (Layne 1978). The survival status of the Anastasia Island mole (*Scalopus aquaticus anastasae*) is under review by the U.S. Fish and Wildlife Service, but according to Humphrey et al. (1987) it is secure. The Englewood mole (*S. a. bassi*) is under study by the U.S. Fish and Wildlife Service (Wood 1990) and may be endangered.

Lowery (1974) gave some information on the parasites of these four insectivores. In his discussion of the parasites of the Eastern mole, he stated that moles "have few external parasites," but a recent summary of parasites of moles in North America (Yates and Pedersen 1982, p. 91) listed 5 species of fleas, 1 sucking louse, and 10 mites from the Eastern mole.

Table 3-1
Species of insectivores that occur in Florida

Common and scientific names	Range in Florida	Status
Family Soricidae		
(Shrews)		
Southeastern shrew		
(*Sorex longirostris* Bachman)	No. 2/3	Rare
Southern short-tailed shrew		
(*Blarina carolinensis* [Bachman])	Statewide[a]	Common
Least shrew		
(*Cryptotis parva* [Say])	Statewide[a]	Common
Family Talpidae		
(Moles)		
Eastern mole		
(*Scalopus aquaticus* [L.])	Statewide[a]	Abundant

Source: Brown (1987).
[a]Absent from the Florida Keys.

II. Environmental contaminants

The only information available on environmental contaminants in insectivores in Florida relates to residues of mirex in a controlled study conducted on the Dee Dot Ranch in Duval and St. Johns counties during 1972–74. In that study, one least shrew was examined six months after aerial application of mirex for control of fire ants and had 1.29 ppm of mirex residue. This concentration was considered moderately high, reflected the insectivorous feeding habits of the shrew, and was comparable to residues in other insectivorous species such as armadillos and certain passeriforms (Wheeler et al. 1977). The significance of this finding to shrew populations in Florida is not known.

III. Rabies

From 1975 to 1983, 56 moles and 2 shrews (species not given) were examined for rabies virus in Florida (Burridge et al. 1986). All were negative. As is the case for rodents, in-

sectivores are probably of little or no importance in the epidemiology of rabies.

IV. Bacteria

Only one study has been conducted in which insectivores in Florida were cultured for bacteria. Shotts et al. (1975) recovered a strain of *Leptospira* from one least shrew (locality not given). The serovar was not identified and the significance of this finding is unknown.

V. Helminths

There is little information on helminths of insectivores in Florida. Layne (1968) examined 10 least shrews from Alachua County, 5 southern short-tailed shrews from Alachua County and 1 from Highlands County, and 4 Eastern moles from Alachua County and 1 from Lake County for infections by *Capillaria hepatica*. All were negative. Kinsella (1987) identified two species of trematodes (*Ectosiphonus rhomboideus* and *Panopistus*

Table 3-2
Arthropod parasites recorded from insectivores in Florida

Host Arthropod	County	Data source
Least shrews		
Ticks		
Ixodes scapularis[a]	Indian River	Wilson & Kale (1972)
Mites		
Haemolaelaps glasgowi[b]	Hillsborough	Worth (1950)
Fleas		
Ctenocephalides felis	Sumter	Layne (1971)
Xenopsylla cheopis[b]	Hillsborough	Worth (1950)
Corrodopsylla hamiltoni	Alachua	Layne (1971)
Eastern moles		
Mites		
Haemogamasus harperi	Putnam	Keegan (1951)
	Alachua	FSCA[c]

[a]All specimens were larvae.

[b]Recorded as being from a short-tailed shrew by Worth (1950), but he gave the scientific name of the shrew as *Cryptotis parva*. It is assumed that the scientific name is correct and that this is a least shrew, not a short-tailed shrew.

[c]FSCA = records from the Florida State Collection of Arthropods, Division of Plant Industry, Florida Department of Agriculture, Gainesville, Fla. This specimen is labeled as from *Scapanus latimanus*, the broad-footed mole, which is found in the western United States. It is assumed that this was actually from the Eastern mole, which is the only mole occurring in Florida.

pricei) from a southern short-tailed shrew in Highlands County.

An immature male Eastern mole from Alachua County (1973) was examined for helminths. One specimen of a species of *Strongyloides* was in its stomach (Forrester 1987). No other helminths were found.

VI. Arthropods

Six species of arthropod parasites have been reported from insectivores in Florida, and include one tick, two mites, and three fleas (Table 3-2). The data on these arthropods are too meager to determine their importance to insectivore populations or their zoonotic significance, although the flea *Xenopsylla cheopis* is of concern since it is a vector of the agents of plague and typhus.

VII. Summary and conclusions

Very little information is available on the parasites and diseases of insectivores in Florida, and what is known is limited to records of one environmental contaminant, one bacterium, three helminths, one tick, two mites, and three fleas. Of these, the bacterium (*Leptospira*) and one of the fleas (*Xenopsylla cheopis*) may be of public health significance.

VIII. Literature cited

Brown, L.N. 1978. Southeastern shrew and Homosassa shrew. In: Rare and endangered biota of Florida. Vol. 1. Mammals. J.N. Layne (ed.). Univ. Presses of Florida, Gainesville. pp. 30–31.

———. 1987. A checklist of Florida's mammals. Florida Game and Fresh Water Fish Commission, Tallahassee. 8 pp.

Burridge, M.J., L.A. Sawyer, and W.J. Bigler. 1986. Rabies in Florida. Department of Health and Rehabilitative Services, Tallahassee, Fla. 147 pp.

Forrester, D.J. 1987. Unpublished data. Univ. of Florida, Gainesville.

Humphrey, S.R., W.H. Kern, Jr., and M.S. Ludlow. 1987. Status survey of seven Florida mammals. Fla. Coop. Fish & Wildl. Res. Unit Tech. Rep. No. 25. 39 pp.

Keegan, H.L. 1951. The mites of the subfamily Haemogamasinae (Acari: Laelaptidae). Proc. U.S. Nat. Mus. 101:203–268.

Kinsella, J.M. 1987. Unpublished data. Archbold Biological Station, Lake Placid, Fla.

Layne, J.N. 1968. Host and ecological relationships of the parasitic helminth *Capillaria hepatica* in Florida mammals. Zoologica. 53:107–122.

———. 1971. Fleas (Siphonaptera) of Florida. Fla. Entomol. 54:35–51.

———. 1978. Sherman's short-tailed shrew. In: Rare and endangered biota of Florida. Vol. 1. Mammals. J.N. Layne (ed.). Univ. Presses of Florida, Gainesville. pp. 42–43.

Lowery, G.H., Jr. 1974. The mammals of Louisiana and its adjacent waters. Louisiana State Univ. Press, Baton Rouge. 565 pp.

Shotts, E.B., C.L. Andrews, and T.W. Harvey. 1975. Leptospirosis in selected wild mammals of the Florida panhandle and southwestern Georgia. J. Am. Vet. Med. Assoc. 167:587–589.

Wheeler, W.B., D.P. Jouvenaz, D.P. Wojcik, W.A. Banks, C.H. VanMiddelem, C.S. Lofgren, S. Nesbitt, L. Williams, and R. Brown. 1977. Mirex residues in nontarget organisms after application of 10-5 bait for fire ant control, northeast Florida, 1972–1974. Pest. Monit. J. 11:146–156.

Wilson, N., and H.W. Kale. 1972. Ticks collected from Indian River County, Florida (Acari: Metastigmata: Ixodidae). Fla. Entomol. 55:53–57.

Wood, D.A. 1990. Official lists of endangered and potentially endangered fauna and flora in Florida. Florida Game and Fresh Water Fish Commission, Tallahassee. 19 pp.

Worth, C.B. 1950. A preliminary host-ectoparasite register for some small mammals of Florida. J. Parasitol. 36:497–498.

Yates, T.L., and R.J. Pedersen. 1982. Moles (Talpidae). In: Wild mammals of North America. Biology, management, and economics. J.A. Chapman and G.A. Feldhamer (eds.). Johns Hopkins Univ. Press, Baltimore. pp. 37–51.

Bats

I. Introduction

Bats are "among the most abundant mammals on earth today" (Gillette and Kimbrough 1970, p. 262). Currently there are more than 940 species in the world (Nowak and Paradiso 1983), of which 16 occur in Florida (Brown 1987). Stevenson (1976) listed the Jamaican fruit-eating bat, *Artibeus jamaicensis* Leach, from Key West, but Humphrey and Brown (1986) determined that this record was not valid. Of the 16 species, 14 are vespertilionid bats (Family Vespertilionidae) and 2 are free-tailed bats (Family Molossidae). Several species are listed as rare or endangered (Table 4-1).

The literature on parasites and diseases of bats of North America has been reviewed by Ubelaker (1970) and Humphrey (1982). Several other authors have written on the public health aspects of bats and diseases (Constantine 1970; Sulkin and Allen 1970; Tuttle and Kern 1981; Constantine 1985). The review by Constantine (1970) is especially well done and thorough.

II. Trauma

The importance of predation and accidents as mortality factors for bats was discussed by Gillette and Kimbrough (1970). They listed

Table 4-1
Species of bats that occur in Florida

Common and scientific names	Range in Florida	Status
Family Vespertilionidae		
(Vespertilionid bats)		
1. Little brown bat		
Myotis lucifugus (Le Conte)	No. border	Uncommon
2. Gray bat		
Myotis grisescens A.H. Howell	No. panhandle	Uncommon[a]
3. Keen's bat		
Myotis keenii (Merriam)	No. panhandle	Uncommon[b]
4. Southeastern brown bat		
Myotis austroriparius (Rhoads)	No. 2/3	Abundant
5. Indiana bat		
Myotis sodalis Miller and G.M. Allen	No. panhandle	Uncommon[a]
6. Silver-haired bat		
Lasionycteris noctivagans (Le Conte)	Panhandle	Uncommon
7. Eastern pipistrelle		
Pipistrellus subflavus (F. Cuvier)	Statewide[c]	Common
8. Rafinesque's big-eared bat		
Plecotus rafinesquii Lesson	No. 2/3	Uncommon[b]
9. Big brown bat		
Eptesicus fuscus (Palisot de Beauvois)	Statewide[c]	Uncommon[b]
10. Hoary bat		
Lasiurus cinereus (Palisot de Beauvois)	No. 1/3	Common[b]
11. Red bat		
Lasiurus borealis (Muller)	No. 2/3	Common
12. Seminole bat		
Lasiurus seminolus (Rhoads)	Statewide[c]	Common
13. Yellow bat		
Lasiurus intermedius H. Allen	Statewide[c]	Abundant
14. Evening bat		
Nycticeius humeralis Rafinesque	Statewide[c]	Common
Family Molossidae		
(Free-tailed bats)		
15. Brazilian free-tailed bat		
Tadarida brasiliensis (I. Geoffroy)	Statewide[c]	Common
16. Wagner's mastiff bat		
Eumops glaucinus (Wagner)	So. 1/4[c]	Uncommon

Source: Brown (1987).
[a] Listed as "endangered" by the Florida Game and Fresh Water Fish Commission and the U.S. Fish and Wildlife Service (Wood 1990).
[b] Classified as "rare" by the Florida Committee on Rare and Endangered Plants and Animals (Layne 1978).
[c] Absent from the Florida Keys.

the known cases of predation by mammals, birds, reptiles, amphibians, fish, and invertebrates, and also documented a number of deaths due to adverse weather, flooding of caves, fires, entanglement in plants or on fences, and the like.

There is little specific information on such mortality among bats in Florida. Rice (1957) stated that predation by rat snakes (*Elaphe obsoleta*), corn snakes (*Elaphe guttata*), and opossums (*Didelphis virginiana*) was a significant factor in populations of southeastern brown bats in Florida. He also reported that very young bats frequently were preyed upon by cockroaches (*Periplaneta americana* and *P. australasiae*) after falling to the floors of caves. He felt that these roaches were important predators and ranked next only to rat snakes in significance.

III. Environmental contaminants

Bats are known to be affected adversely by PCBs and a number of pesticides, including DDT, dieldrin, endrin, and chlordane (Luckens and Davis 1964, 1965; Kunz et al. 1977; Clark and Lamont 1976; Clark 1988). Because of their sensitivity to chlorinated hydrocarbons, such compounds often have been used to kill bats in areas where they are unwanted (Constantine 1970). Clark et al. (1986) examined guano samples from three bat caves in Jackson County, Florida, for residues of p,p'-DDE, p,p'-DDD, p,p'-DDT, dieldrin, heptachlor epoxide, oxychlordane, cis-chlordane, trans-nonachlor, cis-nonachlor, endrin, toxaphene, and PCBs. This was done since it has been determined that analysis of a single sample of guano from beneath a colony of bats will provide an accurate measure of the pesticide contamination of those bats (Clark et al. 1982). The samples contained only small amounts (< 1 ppm) of

DDT, dieldrin, and PCBs (quantified as Aroclor 1260) that were far below concentrations associated with harmful effects in bats (Clark 1978; Clark et al. 1982). All three caves contained predominantly southeastern brown bats and a smaller number (approximately 10%) of gray bats. In July 1984, 30 red and Seminole bats from Bay, Escambia, and Santa Rosa counties were examined for residues of organochlorines. Trace amounts (< 1 ppm) of DDE, dieldrin, and heptachlor epoxide were detected in samples of liver and gastrointestinal contents (SCWDS records).

The same guano samples mentioned above were analyzed for concentrations of lead, chromium, zinc, and cadmium. In addition, livers and kidneys from 20 southeastern brown bats (10 from Judges Cave in Jackson County and 10 from beneath a highway bridge in Gainesville, Alachua County) were analyzed for the same four metals. Judges Cave is the most important gray bat cave in Florida and is located on the Chipola River 11.3 km upstream from a part of the river that is contaminated by metals originating from a battery salvage plant (Clark et al. 1986). Concentrations of chromium, zinc, and cadmium were elevated in guano samples from two of the caves (Judges and Sneads caves) and cadmium was higher also at Geromes Cave. Concentrations of lead (considered slightly elevated) were found in guano from one of the caves (Geromes Cave). Details are presented in Table 4-2. Concentrations of cadmium were elevated in livers and kidneys of bats from Judges Cave compared to bats from Gainesville (Table 4-3). The authors concluded that these concentrations were below those associated with pathologic effects in other mammals and that this amount of metal pollution was not harmful to the bats (Clark et al. 1986).

Wheeler et al. (1977) conducted a monitoring study in which two red bats and two

Table 4-2

Concentrations (ppm dry wt) of metals in single samples of bat guano from 3 caves in Jackson County, Florida in 1981

Cave	Lead	Chromium	Zinc	Cadmium
Judges	3.4	2.7	640	2.2
Geromes	6.1	0.83	390	1.9
Sneads	3.9	5.0	530	2.3

Source: Clark et al. (1986).

Table 4-3

Mean concentrations (ppm wet wt) of metals in livers and kidneys of 20 southeastern brown bats from Jackson and Alachua counties, 1983

Area	N	Liver Zinc	Liver Cadmium	Kidney Cadmium
Judges Cave	10	31.0	0.612	0.998
Gainesville	10	28.5	0.256	0.266

Source: Clark et al. (1986).

evening bats were collected before mirex (an organochlorine insecticide formerly used for control of fire ants, *Solenopsis invicta*) was applied aerially to the Dee Dot Ranch in Duval and St. Johns counties. No residues (at > 0.01 ppm concentration) were detected in the four bats. One evening bat was collected one year after application, and two were collected two years after application. At one year no residues were detected, but at two years after application residues of 0.09 ppm were found in the two evening bats. The authors did not draw any conclusions concerning these findings in bats, but stated that mammals in general had higher concentrations of mirex in fat tissues than did other vertebrates and invertebrates. The significance of these observations to bat populations is unknown.

IV. Rabies

Constantine (1970) published a very detailed review of rabies in bats, and since that time several other shorter summaries have appeared (Beran 1981; Humphrey 1982). The situation in Florida bats has been reviewed by Bigler et al. (1975) and Burridge et al. (1986).

The first record of rabies in a bat in Florida was in 1953 (Venters et al. 1954). In that instance a rabid yellow bat attacked a boy and bit him in the upper chest. Since that first report 9 of the 16 species of Florida bats have been found to be infected with rabies virus (Burridge et al. 1986). These are summarized in Table 4-4. Rabid bats have been found throughout Florida except in the extreme southern end of the state (Burridge et al. 1986) (Figure 4-1).

Up until 1983 most of the cases were in yellow bats. In that year, however, the picture changed somewhat in that the number of cases of bat rabies increased statewide and actually outnumbered the number of cases reported from raccoons (69 vs. 56). This was largely due to outbreaks that occurred in Duval (n = 18 bats) and Escambia (n = 19 bats)

Table 4-4

Species of bats found rabid in Florida, 1953–73

Species	No. rabid	% of all rabid bats
Colonial		
Gray bat	1	0.4
Evening bat	3	1.2
Southeastern brown bat	4	1.6
Eastern pipistrelle	6	2.4
Brazilian free-tailed bat	13	5.2
Noncolonial		
Hoary bat	1	0.4
Red bat	7	2.8
Seminole bat	25	10.1
Yellow bat	188	75.8

Source: Burridge et al. (1986).

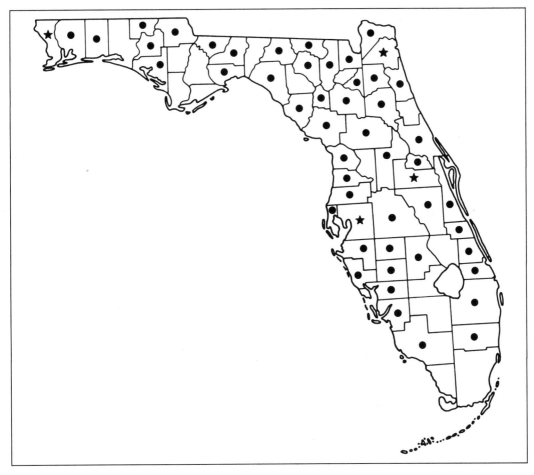

FIGURE 4-1. Counties in Florida in which rabid bats were found from 1953 to 1987. Solid circles identify counties in which rabid bats were found. Stars indicate counties in which epizootics have occurred. (After Burridge et al. 1986; Bigler 1988.)

counties. Most of the bats involved were red and Seminole bats (Department of Health and Rehabilitative Services, 1983). During the next four years the numbers of rabid bats from Duval County declined, but in 1986 another outbreak (n = 14 bats) occurred in Escambia County (Bigler 1988). Yellow, red, and Seminole bats are noncolonial. In other parts of the United States rabies is more common in colonial species of bats (Baer and Adams 1970).

There is a seasonal trend in the occurrence of rabies in bats in Florida (Figure 4-2); most infections occur during the month of August. This has been seen throughout the United States (Baer and Adams 1970; Burridge et al. 1986) and has been attributed to patterns of bat migration and hibernation (Baer 1975).

The usual method of transmission of rabies virus from bats to other animals is by biting, but there are reports of airborne transmission of the virus in caves in Texas that have large colonies of bats (Constantine 1962). It is unknown if airborne transmission occurs in caves in Florida. Recently Smith et al. (1990) determined that bats were not

MONTHLY DISTRIBUTION OF BAT RABIES IN FLORIDA

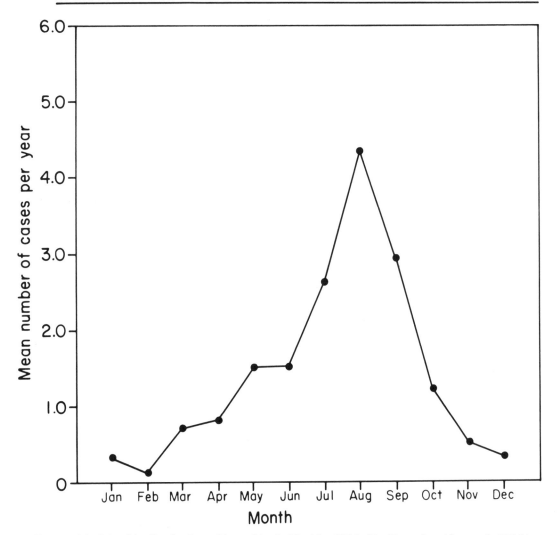

FIGURE 4-2. Monthly distribution of bat rabies in Florida, 1955–83. (From Burridge et al. 1986.)

important in the transmission of rabies virus to terrestrial animals in Florida, at least in 1987 and 1988. Through a monoclonal antibody study they were able to show that raccoons, but not bats, were the source of terrestrial animal rabies in Florida.

The effect of rabies on bats is variable and depends on the species of bat involved and the strain of rabies virus (Sulkin and Allen 1975). Mass mortality due to rabies has been known to occur (Constantine 1967), but

there is evidence that bats can recover from rabies (Sulkin and Allen 1975). It is also known that rabies virus can persist for extended periods of time in bats that show no overt signs of disease (Sulkin and Allen 1970). Nothing is known about the effects of rabies on populations of bats in Florida.

The reader is referred to Burridge et al. (1986) for further information on bat rabies and suggestions for control of this disease in Florida.

V. Histoplasmosis

Histoplasmosis is a respiratory disease caused by the fungus *Histoplasma capsulatum*. Normally this organism is a soil saprophyte, but it proliferates to an increased extent when soil becomes enriched with animal feces. Infections of animals occur when airborne spores are inhaled (Hoff and Bigler 1981). The disease is known from a number of domestic and wild mammals (including opossums, bats, and rodents) and in man (Constantine 1970). The organism survives well in sites that are protected from extremes of climate (Constantine 1970), including old buildings, attics, and bat caves. In the United States the disease is endemic in the Mississippi and Missouri river valleys (Lottenberg et al. 1979). Histoplasmosis has been documented in humans in Florida on numerous occasions and since 1955 five incidents were associated with exposures traced to bat caves (Table 4-5; Figure 4-3).

Two surveys of *Histoplasma capsulatum* in caves in Florida have been published, the results of which establish Florida as an endemic area for histoplasmosis. Tesh and Schneidau (1967) examined 156 southeastern brown bats from three caves. In one of the caves (Grant's Cave in Alachua County, according to additional information provided by DiSalvo et al. 1970) 80 of 105 (76%) of the bats were positive for *H. capsulatum*.

Two other caves (names not given) had 23 of 50 (46%) and none of one bats infected. The survey by DiSalvo et al. (1970) was more extensive and included examinations of both bats and samples of soil/guano mixtures from bat caves. Ten of 148 soil/guano samples from nine caves were positive for *H. capsulatum* (Table 4-6). These positive samples were from caves in Alachua, Jackson, and Marion counties (Figure 4-3). *Histoplasma capsulatum* was isolated from 80 of 165 (48%) southeastern brown bats, but none of 101 eastern pipistrelles and 71 Brazilian free-tailed bats. Positive bats came from Alachua, Jackson, Marion, Citrus, and Hillsborough counties (Table 4-7; Figure 4-3).

Little is known about the effects of *H. capsulatum* on natural populations of bats. In one experimental study on free-tailed bats (Tesh and Schneidau 1966) 80% of the exposed animals died of disseminated disease. These bats, however, had been inoculated intraperitoneally. This route of infection may have resulted in more serious disease than if the animals had been exposed via the inhalation route. In several other experimental studies with neotropical bats, infections were established via the inhalation route, but resulted in no morbidity or mortality (McMurray and Greer 1979; McMurray et al. 1978). We have no specific information on the significance of histoplasmosis to Florida bats, but suspect that it could be important. None

Table 4-5
Human cases of histoplasmosis associated with bats in Florida, 1955–1982

Year	No. cases	Species of bats associated with the exposures	Location (county)	Pos. soil samples	Data source
1955	1	Not determined	NG[a]	Yes	Tegeris & Smith (1958)
1966	1	Southeastern brown bat	Alachua	Yes	Johnson et al. (1970)
1972	3	Southeastern brown bat	Citrus	Yes	Hoff & Bigler (1981)
1973	23	Southeastern brown bat and eatern pipistrelle	Suwannee	Yes	Lottenberg et al. (1979)
1982	6	NG	Citrus	NG	Sacks (1982)

[a] NG = not given by authors.

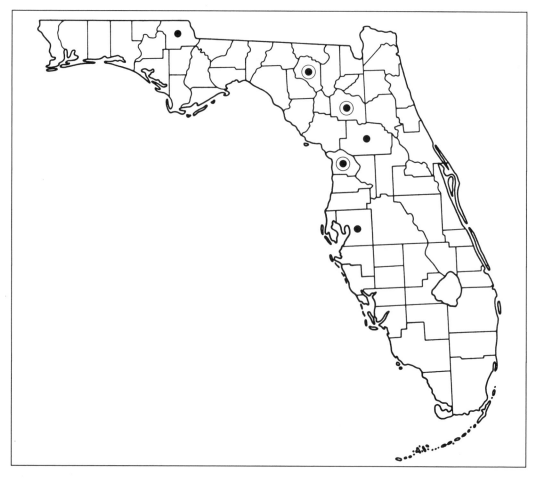

FIGURE 4-3. Distribution of *Histoplasma capsulatum* in Florida. Black dots indicate counties in which infected bats have been found. Circled black dots indicate counties where infected bats have been found and humans have become infected by entering bat caves.

of 80 southeastern brown bats that were infected naturally with *H. capsulatum* showed signs of illness at the time of capture (DiSalvo et al. 1970).

VI. Protozoan parasites

A number of protozoans have been reported from bats throughout the world, and include trypanosomes, hemosporidians, and coccidia (Constantine 1970; Ubelaker 1970).

There is only one record of a protozoan from a Florida bat. Foster (1979) reported *Polychromophilus deani* from 2 of 250 southeastern brown bats from three roosting sites in north-central Florida during 1976 and 1977. Two species of dipteran ectoparasites were found on the infected bats and included a nycteribiid (*Trichobius major*). One of these might be the vector for *P. deani*, but this has not been determined. The pathogenicity of this blood parasite is unknown.

Rice (1957) examined about 100 southeastern brown bats from northern Florida, but found no blood protozoans.

Table 4-6
Recovery of *Histoplasma capsulatum* from
samples of soil from bat caves in Florida, 1968

Location	No. samples exam.	No. samples pos.
Alachua County		
Grant's Cave	23	2
Jones Cave	25	0
Newberry Bat Cave	9	0
Savior Cave	34	0
Seven Sisters Cave	12	0
Citrus County		
No Name Cave	10	0
Jackson County		
Indian Cave	15	3
Small Picnic Area Cave	10	0
Marion County		
Turnley Cave	10	5
Total	148	10

Source: DiSalvo et al. (1970).

VII. Helminths

Bats are hosts for a large number and variety of helminths, including trematodes, cestodes, nematodes, and acanthocephalans (Ubelaker 1970). Two species of helminths have been reported from bats in Florida. Loftin (1961) recorded a trematode (*Lecithodendrium* sp.) from a yellow bat from St. Marks Wildlife Refuge (Wakulla County) and Kinsella (1987) found a trematode (*Dicrocoelium rileyi*) in an evening bat from Highlands County.

Further investigation will undoubtedly lead to the finding of a rich helminth fauna in bats in Florida. An extensive study of 18 species of bats in Cuba resulted in the identification of 12 species of trematodes, 9 cestodes, 27 nematodes, and 2 acanthocephalans (Rutkowska 1980; Zdzitowiecki and Rutkowska 1980a, 1980b). Similar results could be expected in Florida.

Table 4-7
Recovery of *Histoplasma capsulatum* from
colonial bats in Florida, 1968

Location	Species of bat[a]	No. bats exam.[b]	No. bats pos.
Alachua County			
Savior Cave	SBB	20	1
Jones Cave	SBB	3	2
Seven Sisters Cave	EP	12	0
Newberry Bat Cave	EP	3	0
	SBB	1	0
Jackson County			
Indian Cave	EP	1	0
	SBB	6	4
Small Picnic Area	EP	2	0
Cave	SBB	7	4
Marion County			
Turnley Cave	SBB	37	23
Citrus County			
No Name Cave	SBB	58	37
Hernando County			
Brooksville (attic)	BFB	71	0
Hillsborough County			
Tampa (sewer)	SBB	15	9

Source: DiSalvo et al. (1970).
[a] SBB = southeastern brown bat, EP = eastern pipistrelle, BFB = Brazilian free-tailed bat.
[b] DiSalvo et al. (1970) listed 29 additional bats that were examined for *H. capsulatum*. These were animals submitted for rabies testing and all (except for 2 yellow bats from Fort Lauderdale) came from areas north of Orlando. Among these were 5 southeastern brown bats, 14 yellow bats, 4 Seminole bats, and 6 evening bats. The only bat positive for *H. capsulatum* was one of the southeastern brown bats from Lake County.

VIII. Arthropods

Eleven species of parasitic arthropods are known from three species of bats in Florida, namely, the southeastern brown bat, the evening bat, and the Brazilian free-tailed bat. These include one tick, six mites, one flea, two flies, and one bug (Table 4-8).

Ticks are not found often on bats (Ubelaker 1970). The record of *Ornithodoros yumatensis* from a southeastern brown bat in Gainesville (Bain and Zinn 1982, p. 510) was

Table 4-8
Arthropod parasites reported from bats in Florida

| | Species of bat | | | | |
Arthropod	Southeastern brown bat	Evening bat	Brazilian free-tailed bat	Locality (county)	Data source
Ticks					
Ornithodoros yumatensis	L[a]			Alachua[b]	Bain (1981), Bain & Zinn (1982)
Mites					
Steatonyssus ceratognathus		+		Lee	FSCA[c]
Ichoronyssus quadridentatus	+[d]			Alachua	Rice (1957), Baker & Strandtmann (1959)
Chiroptonyssus robustipes			A	Hamilton	Radovsky (1967)
Radfordia floridensis			A	Leon	Ewing (1938)
Radfordia inaequalis			A	Leon	" "
Spirturnix sp.	+[d]			Alachua	Rice (1957), Baker & Strandtmann (1959)
Fleas					
Sternopsylla distincta	A[e]		A[f]	See footnotes e and f	See footnotes e and f
Flies					
Basilia boardmani	A			Alachua[g]	Bain (1981)
Trichobius major	A			Alachua[g]	" "
Bugs					
Cimex adjunctus		A		Alachua, Lee	Bain (1981), FSCA

[a] L = larvae, A = adults, + = stage not given.
[b] Wilson and Baker (1972) in their publication on the ticks of Georgia mentioned a record of larvae of O. _yumatensis_ in a colony of eastern pipistrelles in a cave in Grady County, southern Georgia. Free-flying bats of the same species were examined from a locality in Leon County, Florida, less than 30 miles south of the cave in Georgia, but all were free of ticks.
[c] FSCA = records from the Florida State Collection of Arthropods, Division of Plant Industry, Florida Department of Agriculture, Gainesville, Fla.
[d] Rice (1957) did not give specific localities in Florida, but did state that both species of mites were "abundant on the wing membranes of virtually every bat examined" (p. 30). Baker and Strandtmann (1959) examined adult mites submitted to them by Rice and reported that they were from Alachua County.
[e] Found in Alachua County (Fox 1940) and Columbia County (Layne 1971; FSCA). Rice (1957) also reported this flea from southeastern brown bats in Florida, but did not give a specific locality.
[f] Found in Alachua County (Fuller 1943), Collier County (Schwartz 1952), Columbia County (Layne 1971; FSCA), Hamilton County (FSCA), and Leon County (Fox 1940).
[g] Rice (1957) reported that these two species of Diptera were found commonly in the fur of southeastern brown bats in Florida, but gave no specific data on localities. Foster (1979) also reported these two species from southeastern brown bats, but gave no prevalence data or localities for the bats other than "north-central Florida."

a rare event. The authors stated that they had examined "thousands of these bats in north-central Florida in the past five years and found ticks on only one individual." There are a number of records of other species of _Ornithodoros_ infesting humans (Constantine 1970), but it is unknown if O. _yumatensis_ is of zoonotic concern.

One of the mites (_Chiroptonyssus robustipes_) is known to infest humans also and cause dermatitis (Constantine 1970). Other species of mites serve as vectors of trypanosomes and hemosporidians (Constantine 1970), but information on this topic is lacking for Florida.

The flea, _Sternopsylla distincta_, is a typical

parasite of free-tailed bats and in Florida occurs on the Brazilian free-tailed bat. It has been found on the southeastern brown bat only when free-tailed bats also are present in the same cave or refugia (Layne 1971).

Two species of bat flies (Diptera) are found commonly on southeastern brown bats in Florida. These are very host-specific and occur only on bats (Ubelaker 1970). One of these (*Trichobius major*) is known to bite humans (Constantine 1970). Their effects on bat populations are unknown.

Cimex adjunctus is a close relative of the bedbug of man and may be an occasional parasite of humans (Constantine 1970). Little is known about its biology (Ubelaker 1970) and its effects on bat populations are unknown.

IX. Summary and conclusions

Twenty-five different parasites, disease agents, and environmental contaminants have been identified in bats from Florida. These include 5 organochlorines, 4 metals, 1 virus, 1 fungus, 1 protozoan, 2 trematodes, and 11 arthropods. Of these the most important diseases appear to be rabies and histoplasmosis. These two diseases could have adverse effects on bat populations and are significant because of their zoonotic status. With the exception of arthropods, the parasites of bats in Florida have been neglected. Attention should be given to the helminths and protozoans in order to understand their role in the health and diseases of the bats of Florida.

X. Literature cited

Baer, G.M. 1975. Rabies in nonhematophagous bats. In: The natural history of rabies. Vol. 2. G.M. Baer (ed.). Academic Press, New York. pp. 79–97.

Baer, G.M., and D.B. Adams. 1970. Rabies in insectivorous bats in the United States, 1953–65. Pub. Health Rep. 85:637–645.

Bain, J.R. 1981. Roosting ecology of three Florida bats: *Nycticeius humeralis, Myotis austroriparius,* and *Tadarida brasiliensis.* M.S. thesis, Univ. of Florida, Gainesville. 131 pp.

Bain, J.R., and T.L. Zinn. 1982. *Ornithodoros yumatensis* from the southeastern brown bat (*Myotis austroriparius*) in Florida. J. Parasitol. 68:510–511.

Baker, E.W., and R.W. Strandtmann. 1959. Further notes on *Ichoronyssus quadridentatus* Strandtmann and Hunt, with a description of the female (Acarina, Dermanyassidae, Macronyssinae). Proc. Entomol. Soc. Wash. 61:225–228.

Beran, G.W. 1981. Rabies and infections by rabies-related viruses. In: CRC handbook series in zoonoses. J.H. Steele (ed.). CRC Press, Boca Raton, Fla. pp. 57–135.

Bigler, W.J. 1988. Unpublished data. HRS, Tallahassee, Fla.

Bigler, W.J., G.L. Hoff, and E.E. Buff. 1975. Chiropteran rabies in Florida: A twenty-year analysis, 1954 to 1973. Am. J. Trop. Med. Hyg. 24:347–352.

Brown, L.N. 1987. A checklist of Florida's mammals. Florida Game and Fresh Water Fish Commission, Tallahassee. 8 pp.

Burridge, M.J., L. Sawyer, and W.J. Bigler. 1986. Rabies in Florida. Department of Health and Rehabilitative Services, Tallahassee, Fla. 147 pp.

Clark, D.R. 1978. Uptake of dietary PCB by pregnant big brown bats (*Eptesicus fuscus*) and their fetuses. Bull. Environ. Contam. Toxicol. 19:707–714.

———. 1988. How sensitive are bats to insecticides? Wildl. Soc. Bull. 16:399–403.

Clark, D.R., and T.G. Lamont. 1976. Organochlorine residues and reproduction in the big brown bat. J. Wildl. Manage. 40:249–254.

Clark, D.R., R.K. LaVal, and M.D. Tuttle. 1982. Estimating pesticide burdens of bats from guano analyses. Bull. Environ. Contam. Toxicol. 29:214–220.

Clark, D.R., A.S. Wenner, and J.F. Moore. 1986. Metal residues in bat colonies, Jackson County, Florida, 1981–1983. Fla. Field Nat. 14:38–45.

Constantine, D.G. 1962. Rabies transmission by nonbite route. Pub. Health Rep. 77:287–289.

———. 1967. Activity patterns of the Mexican free-tailed bat. Univ. of New Mexico Pub. Biol. 7. 79 pp.

———. 1970. Bats in relation to the health, welfare, and economy of man. In: Biology of bats. W.A. Wimsath (ed). Academic Press, New York. pp. 319–449.

———. 1985. Disease exchange between bats and researchers: Problems and precautions. Aust. Mammal. 8:325–329.

Department of Health and Rehabilitative Services. 1983. Florida morbidity statistics, 1983. HRS, Tallahassee, Fla. 116 pp.

DiSalvo, A.F., W.J. Bigler, L. Ajello, J.E. Johnson, and J. Palmer. 1970. Bat and soil studies for sources of histoplasmosis in Florida. Pub. Health Rep. 85:1063–1069.

Ewing, H.E. 1938. North American mites of the subfamily Myobiinae, new subfamily (Arachnida). Proc. Entomol. Soc. Wash. 40:180–197.

Foster, G.W. 1979. *Polychromophilus* from southeastern brown bats (*Myotis austroriparius*) in north-central Florida. J. Parasitol. 65:465–466.

Fox, I. 1940. Fleas of eastern United States. Iowa State Coll. Press, Ames. 191 pp.

Fuller, H.S. 1943. Studies on Siphonaptera of eastern North America. Bull. Brooklyn Entomol. Soc. 38:18–23.

Gillette, D.D., and J.D. Kimbrough. 1970. Chiropteran mortality. In: About bats. B.H. Slaughter and D.W. Walton (eds.). Southern Methodist Univ. Press, Dallas. pp. 262–283.

Hoff, G.L., and W.J. Bigler. 1981. The role of bats in the propagation and spread of histoplasmosis: A review. J. Wildl. Dis. 17:191–196.

Humphrey, S.R. 1982. Bats. In: Wild mammals of North America. J.A. Chapman and G.A.

Feldhamer (eds). Johns Hopkins Univ. Press, Baltimore. pp. 52–70.

Humphrey, S.H., and L.N. Brown. 1986. Report of a new bat (Chiroptera: *Artibeus jamaicensis*) in the United States is erroneous. Fla. Sci. 49:262–263.

Johnson, J.E., G. Radimer, A.F. DiSalvo, L. Ajello, and W. Bigler. 1970. Histoplasmosis in Florida. I. Report of a case and epidemiologic studies. Am. Rev. Resp. Dis. 101:299–305.

Kinsella, J.M. 1987. Unpublished data. Archbold Biological Station, Lake Placid, Fla.

Kunz, T.H., E.L.P. Anthony, and W.T. Rumage. 1977. Mortality of little brown bats following multiple pesticide applications. J. Wildl. Manage. 41:476–483.

Layne, J.N. 1971. Fleas (Siphonaptera) of Florida. Fla. Entomol. 54:35–51.

———. (ed.). 1978. Rare and endangered biota of Florida. Vol. 1. Mammals. Univ. Presses of Florida, Gainesville. 52 pp.

Loftin, H. 1961. An annotated check-list of trematodes and cestodes and their vertebrate hosts from northwest Florida. Quart. J. Fla. Acad. Sci. 23:302–314.

Lottenberg, R., R.H. Waldman, L. Ajello, G.L. Hoff, W. Bigler, and S.R. Zellner. 1979. Pulmonary histoplasmosis associated with exploration of a bat cave. Am. J. Epidem. 110:156–161.

Luckens, M.M., and W.H. Davis. 1964. Bats: Sensitivity to DDT. Science 146:948.

———. 1965. Toxicity of dieldrin and endrin to bats. Nature 207:879–880.

McMurray, D.N., and D.L. Greer. 1979. Immune responses in bats following intranasal infection with *Histoplasma capsulatum*. Am. J. Trop. Med. Hyg. 28:1036–1039.

McMurray, D.N., M.E. Thomas, D.L. Greer, and N.L. Tolentino. 1978. Humoral and cell-mediated immunity to *Histoplasma capsulatum* during experimental infection in neotropical bats (*Artibeus lituratus*). Am. J. Trop. Med. Hyg. 27:815–821.

Nowak, R.M., and J.L. Paradiso. 1983. Walker's mammals of the world. 4th ed. Johns Hopkins Univ. Press, Baltimore. 1,362 pp.

Radovsky, F.J. 1967. The Macronyssidae and

Laelapidae (Acarina: Mesostigmata) parasitic on bats. Univ. Calif. Publ. Entomol. 46:1–288.

Rice, D.W. 1957. Life history and ecology of *Myotis austroriparius* in Florida. J. Mammal. 38:15–32.

Rutkowska, M.A. 1980. The helminthofauna of bats (Chiroptera) from Cuba. I. A review of nematodes and acanthocephalans. Acta Parasit. Pol. 26:153–186.

Sacks, J.J. 1982. Unpublished data. HRS, Tallahassee, Fla.

Schwartz, A. 1952. The land mammals of southern Florida and the upper Florida Keys. Ph.D. diss., Univ. of Michigan, Ann Arbor.

Smith, J.S., P.A. Yager, W.J. Bigler, and E.C. Hartwig, Jr. 1990. Surveillance and epidemiologic mapping of monoclonal antibody-defined rabies variants in Florida. J. Wildl. Dis. 26: 473–485.

Stevenson, H.M. 1976. Vertebrates of Florida. Identification and distribution. Univ. Presses of Florida, Gainesville. 607 pp.

Sulkin, S.E., and R. Allen. 1970. Bats: Carriers of human disease–producing agents. In: About bats. B.H. Slaughter and D.W. Walton (eds.). Southern Methodist Univ. Press, Dallas. pp. 284–302.

Sulkin, S.E., and R. Allen. 1975. Experimental rabies virus infection in bats. In: The natural history of rabies. Vol. 2. G.M. Baer (ed.). Academic Press, New York. pp. 99–114.

Tegeris, A.S., and D.T. Smith. 1958. Acute disseminated pulmonary histoplasmosis treated with cortisone and MRO-112. Ann. Int. Med. 48:1414–1420.

Tesh, R.B., and J.D. Schneidau. 1966. Experimental infection of North American insectivorous bats (*Tadarida brasiliensis*) with *Histoplasma capsulatum* from bats in the United States. Am. J. Trop. Med. Hyg. 15:544–550.

Tesh, R.B., and J.D. Schneidau. 1967. Naturally occurring histoplasmosis among bat colonies in the southeastern United States. Am. J. Epidem. 86:545–551.

Tuttle, M.D., and S.J. Kern. 1981. Bats and public health. Milwaukee Public Museum Contrib. in Biol. and Geol. 48:1–11.

Ubelaker, J.E. 1970. Some observations on ecto- and endoparasites of Chiroptera. In: About bats. B.H. Slaughter and D.W. Walton (eds.). Southern Methodist Univ. Press, Dallas. pp. 247–261.

Venters, H.D., W.R. Hoffert, J.E. Scatterday, and A.V. Hardy. 1954. Rabies in bats in Florida. Am. J. Public Health 44: 182–185.

Wheeler, W.B., D.P. Jouvenaz, D.P. Wojcik, W.A. Banks, C.H. Van Middelem, C.S. Lofgren, S. Nesbitt, L. Williams, and R. Brown. 1977. Mirex residues in nontarget organisms after application of 10-5 bait for fire ant control, Northeast Florida—1972–1974. Pest. Monit. J. 11:146–156.

Wilson, N., and W.W. Baker. 1972. Ticks of Georgia (Acarina: Metastigmata). Bull. Tall Timbers Res. Sta. 10:1–29.

Wood, D.A. 1990. Official lists of endangered and potentially endangered fauna and flora in Florida. Florida Game and Fresh Water Fish Commission, Tallahassee. 19 pp.

Zdzitowiecki, K., and M.A. Rutkowska. 1980a. The helminthofauna of bats (Chiroptera) from Cuba. II. A review of cestodes with description of four new species and a key to Hymenolepididae of American bats. Acta Parasit. Pol. 26:187–200.

Zdzitowiecki, K., and M.A. Rutkowska. 1980b. The helminthofauna of bats (Chiroptera) from Cuba. III. A review of trematodes. Acta Parasit. Pol. 26:201–214.

Armadillos

I. Introduction

At the beginning of this century the common long-nosed or nine-banded armadillo (*Dasypus novemcinctus* L.) was found in the United States only in the semiarid regions of Texas south of latitude 33°N (Galbreath 1982). Since then armadillos have moved to the north and east and into the Florida panhandle (Wolfe 1968; Humphrey 1974). Between 1920 and 1936 there were three introductions of armadillos into the Atlantic coast region of Florida (Talmage and Buchanan 1954). Since 1972 the western population and the introduced peninsular populations have expanded until they merged. Armadillos are now abundant throughout Florida except for the Keys and parts of the Everglades and

Big Cypress swamp (Galbreath 1982; Brown 1987). Humphrey (1974, p. 460) pointed out that the "92-year history of armadillo movement is one of a few well-documented cases of range expansion among mammals." He further indicated that drought and cold are important factors that affect the distribution of armadillos.

The common long-nosed armadillo has been the subject of considerable interest in recent years due to a number of unique features. It has a relatively low body temperature (32–34°C), a long delay in implantation of its blastocyst, and always gives birth to four young of the same sex and of identical genetic makeup (Szabuniewicz and McCrady

1969). In addition, it has been useful as a laboratory model for the study of leprosy and other human diseases (Storrs 1971; Kirchheimer and Storrs 1971; Storrs et al. 1974). Various aspects of embryology, morphology, physiology, blood chemistry, and nutrition have been reviewed by several authors (Talmage and Buchanan 1954; Szabuniewicz and McCrady 1969; Storrs 1971; Ramsey et al. 1981; Herbst et al. 1989).

The literature on parasites and diseases of armadillos has been discussed by a number of authors (Chandler 1954; Storrs 1971; Lowery 1974; Galbreath 1982). All have remarked that armadillos are remarkably free of parasites, especially when compared to other mammals such as opossums, raccoons, and skunks, with which they live sympatrically.

II. Trauma

Armadillos are among the most common animals killed by vehicles in the state of Florida (Galbreath 1982). Humphrey (1974) conducted a questionnaire-type survey of eight southeastern states (including Florida) and found that the numbers of armadillos killed by vehicles were particularly high. He pointed out that the armadillo's habit of jumping upwards when startled probably contributes to the high mortality caused by vehicles, which otherwise would pass over these animals without harming them. A similar statement was made by Lowery (1974) concerning armadillos in Louisiana. Second to road-kills by vehicles is predation by dogs as a mortality factor (Humphrey 1974; Lowery 1974; Galbreath 1982).

III. Climatic effects

In Florida, the armadillo, like the manatee (see Chapter 19), is at or near the northern limits of its distribution under present climatic conditions (Galbreath 1982). Humphrey (1974) determined that the distribution of armadillos in the southern United States was linked with annual rainfall and the number of freeze-days per year. His data indicated that the lower limit for annual rainfall was 380 mm and an upper limit for freeze-days was nine per year. Populations of armadillos in Texas (Kalmbach 1943) and Louisiana (Fitch et al. 1952) have been reduced significantly by cold spells. In January and February 1948, a local population of armadillos in western Louisiana was reduced by almost 80% due to severe cold weather (Fitch et al. 1952). Such declines have not been recorded in Florida, but Layne and Glover (1985) observed emaciated and weakened animals after prolonged cold spells in southern Florida. There are also records in the literature of local populations declining due to drought (Kalmbach 1943; Taber 1945; Clark 1951).

IV. Environmental contaminants

The armadillo should be a useful animal in which to monitor pesticide residues since it is at the top of the soil food chain in many areas of the South where such crops as cotton, sugarcane, rice, soybeans, and yams are produced in large quantities (Wheeler et al. 1975). This mammal is mostly a generalist that preys on invertebrates that live in soil, litter, and rotten wood (Galbreath 1982). Beetles are the single most important food item; in a study conducted in Florida they accounted for 78.5% of the diet by volume (Nesbitt et al. 1977). Hymenoptera, Diptera, and Orthoptera were also important. Similar findings were reported in another study in Florida conducted in 1959–1962 (Wirtz et al. 1985).

With the exception of a small amount of

information from a single study (Wheeler et al. 1977), there are no data on pesticides in armadillos in Florida. In that study one armadillo was tested before and seven were tested after the aerial application of mirex for the control of fire ants. The study was conducted on the Dee Dot Ranch in Duval and St. Johns counties in 1972–1974. Values for the residues ranged from undetectable to 1.68 ppm. The highest value was in adipose tissue of an armadillo obtained six months after the application of mirex. These values are low compared to those obtained from armadillos in Louisiana and Texas, where residues varied from undetectable to 25 ppm in adipose tissue (Wheeler et al. 1975). The significance of these findings to armadillo populations is not known.

V. Viruses

Rabies has never been diagnosed in armadillos in Florida. Between 1975 and 1983 eight armadillos were tested for rabies virus (Burridge et al. 1986). All were negative.

Bigler et al. (1975) tested sera of 11 armadillos for antibodies to SLE, Everglades, and EEE viruses, and six for Highlands J virus. One was positive for SLE and two for Everglades virus. Localities for positive animals were not given. The importance of these observations to armadillo populations is unknown.

VI. Leprosy

Leprosy or Hansen's disease in humans is caused by the bacterium *Mycobacterium leprae* and characteristically occurs as a chronic disease of the skin, nerves, and certain mucous membranes (Brubaker 1976). Over 10 million people in the world have leprosy, which is widespread in tropical and subtropi-

cal areas of Asia, central Africa, and South and Central America. It is endemic also in southern California, southeastern Texas, Louisiana, and Florida (especially Key West, Miami, and Tampa) (Brubaker 1976).

In 1971 it was shown that leprosy developed in a common long-nosed armadillo 17 months after *M. leprae* bacilli were inoculated from an infected human (Kirchheimer and Storrs 1971; Storrs 1971). Subsequently it has been demonstrated that the armadillo is an excellent experimental model for studying leprosy (Storrs et al. 1974).

Leprosy in wild armadillos was first reported in 1975 in Louisiana (Walsh et al. 1975). Since that time there have been additional reports of leprosy in armadillos in Texas, Mississippi, and Mexico, with prevalences varying from 0.5% to 10%. No infections have been found in more than 2,500 armadillos examined from 15 counties in Florida (Table 5-1).

The mode of transmission of leprosy in humans and armadillos is unknown (Storrs and Burchfield 1985). Filice et al. (1977) determined that there was no association between armadillo contact and leprosy in 18 infected humans in Louisiana. In the area studied leprosy had been endemic for 200 years, whereas armadillos have been in Louisiana only for the past 50 years (Filice et al. 1977). Further studies on the epidemiology of leprosy in humans and armadillos are needed before the full significance of this disease can be appreciated. At the present time it does not appear to be a problem in populations of armadillos in Florida.

VII. Other bacterial infections

Five types of bacterial infections have been reported from armadillos in Florida (Table 5-2). These included 10 serovars of *Leptospira*

Table 5-1
Prevalence of leprosy in common long-nosed armadillos from several areas of
the United States and Mexico

| Area | No. armadillos | | | Data source |
	Exam.	Pos.	(%)	
Louisiana	70	7	(10.0)	Walsh et al. (1975)
	691	47	(6.8)	" " " "
Texas	451	21	(4.7)	Smith et al. (1983)
Mexico	96	1	(1.0)	Amezcua et al. (1984)
Mississippi	179	1	(0.5)	Storrs & Burchfield (1985)
Florida				
Bay Co.	26	0	(0)	Howerth et al. (1990)
Brevard Co.	209	0	(0)	Storrs (1989)
Calhoun Co.	12	0	(0)	Howerth et al. (1990)
Escambia Co.	13	0	(0)	" " " "
Gadsden Co.	1	0	(0)	" " " "
Glades Co.	2,087	0	(0)	Storrs (1989)
Gulf Co.	23	0	(0)	Howerth et al. (1990)
Jackson Co.	3	0	(0)	" " " "
Okaloosa Co.	2	0	(0)	" " " "
Orange Co.	4	0	(0)	Storrs (1989)
Osceola Co.	121	0	(0)	" "
Santa Rosa Co.	2	0	(0)	Howerth et al. (1990)
Taylor Co.	1	0	(0)	" " " "
Walton Co.	1	0	(0)	" " " "
Washington Co.	9	0	(0)	" " " "

interrogans, the most common of which was *shermani.* Serovars *autumnalis, canicola,* and *pomona* have been identified also in armadillos in Louisiana (Roth et al. 1964; Stuart et al. 1977). The significance of this information is not clear. Stuart et al. (1977) studied renal lesions in a series of armadillos from Louisiana, but found no association between interstitial nephritis and serologic or cultural evidence of leptospires.

One of 68 armadillos from Florida examined by Hoff et al. (1975) was seropositive for agglutinins to *Francisella tularensis,* the etiologic agent of tularemia. The locality of the positive animal was not given. The pathologic significance of tularemia to armadillo populations is not known.

White (1987) isolated *Edwardsiella tarda* from two of five armadillos from Alachua County. The hemolytic activity of one of these isolates was studied and it was concluded that the production of a cell-associated hemolysin might explain the association of *E. tarda* with hemorrhagic enteritis in some species (Watson and White 1979). Five serovars of *Salmonella* were isolated from armadillos from Glades County. Both *E. tarda* and *Salmonella* were isolated from contents of the large intestines. Since they were not associated with lesions, they probably represented the carrier state.

Nocardia sp. was isolated from the lungs of 2 of 18 armadillos from Glades County in 1971 (White 1987). One of these armadillos was also positive for *Salmonella muenster.* The significance of these infections by *Nocardia* is not known, but in other animals, such as dogs and marine mammals, this fungus-

Table 5-2
Summary of findings on bacterial infections of armadillos in Florida

Bacteria	No. armadillos			Date	Location (county)	Basis of diagnosis	Data source
	Exam.	Inf.	(%)				
Leptospira interrogans	18	2[a]	(11)	1970–72	Glades	Culture of kidneys	White (1987)
	5	0	(0)	1970–72	Alachua	Culture of kidneys	" "
	286	32[b]	(11)	1980–83	Glades	Serology	Motie et al. (1986)
Francisella tularensis	68	1	(1.5)	1965–73	NG[c]	Serology	Hoff et al. (1975)
Edwardsiella tarda	18	0	(0)	1970–72	Glades	Culture of L.I. contents	White (1987)
	5	2	(40)	1970–72	Alachua	Culture of L.I. contents	" "
Salmonella spp.	18	5[d]	(28)	1970–72	Glades	Culture of L.I. contents	" "
	5	0	(0)	1970–72	Alachua	Culture of L.I. contents	" "
Nocardia sp.	18	2	(11)	1970–72	Glades	Culture of lungs	" "
	5	0	(0)	1970–72	Alachua	Culture of lungs	" "

[a] Serovar *autumnalis*.
[b] Serovars *shermani, canicola, tarasovi, pomona, javanica, australis, grippotyphosa, bataviae,* and *celledoni.*
[c] NG = not given by authors.
[d] Serovars *oranienburg, hartford, barta, havana,* and *muenster.*

like bacterium is known to cause respiratory disease (Pier 1979). One of the common sources of infection by *Nocardia* is through contaminated soil. These armadillos probably became infected via that method due to their burrowing habits.

All of the bacteria discussed above are of zoonotic concern, and the armadillo may serve as a reservoir host. Its role as such needs to be studied more carefully, however.

Skin infections by staphylococci and *Proteus* spp. are found as a common sequel to any form of trauma in captive armadillos (Wampler 1969; Baskerville and Francis 1981). Such problems are often the cause of death. There are no reports of this situation in free-ranging animals, although it probably occurs.

VIII. Protozoan parasites

Two protozoan parasites are known from armadillos in Florida: *Toxoplasma gondii* and *Trypanosoma cruzi*. Both represent potential disease hazards for man.

In a serologic survey, 12 of 63 (19%) armadillos in Florida were positive for antibodies to *Toxoplasma gondii* (Burridge et al. 1979). This was the highest prevalence of infection in 25 species of mammals examined. There were no significant differences in the prevalence of infection in male versus female armadillos or in adult versus younger animals. Infections were found throughout peninsular Florida. Armadillos become infected by ingestion of oocysts in feces of bobcats or domestic cats. The reader is referred to

Chapter 15 on Florida panthers and bobcats for more information on toxoplasmosis. Armadillos that are consumed should be cooked thoroughly to prevent infection of humans.

Irons (1971) examined 59 armadillos from seven counties in Florida (Alachua, Broward, Glades, Hardee, Highlands, Levy, and Orange) for serologic evidence of infection by *Trypanosoma cruzi*. One armadillo from Alachua County was seropositive. Armadillos are important reservoir hosts of *T. cruzi* in South America (Levine 1973), and Yeager (1982) found 25% of 60 armadillos from the New Orleans area infected. The effects on armadillos in Florida have not been studied. As pointed out in other chapters, *T. cruzi* causes Chagas' disease in humans and is a significant problem in Central and South America.

IX. Helminths

According to Chandler (1954) and Storrs (1971), the common long-nosed armadillo does not have much of a helminth fauna. The following numbers of species have been found: 3 trematodes, 2 cestodes, 20 nematodes (several of which are most certainly spurious infections), and 3 acanthocephalans. Herbst and Greiner (1990) found pinworms (*Aspidodera* sp.) in the large intestines of eight of nine armadillos from San Felasco Hammock (Alachua Co.) in 1988–1990. We have no other information on helminths of armadillos in Florida.

X. Arthropods

Compared to other animals such as raccoons, opossums, and skunks, the armadillo is infested with very few ectoparasites. Both Chandler (1954) and Storrs (1971) com-

mented on this and attributed the lack of parasitic arthropods to the armadillo's dorsal covering or carapace and sparse hair on its underbelly. They do list, however, four ticks, five fleas, one bot, and one pentastome from armadillos.

Baskerville and Francis (1981) reported mange problems in 8 of 20 adult armadillos from Florida (exact locality not given) that had been shipped to England within a few days after their capture. They described the lesions as dry, crumbling encrustations on the ventral surfaces of the neck, thorax, and abdomen. Mites (*Echimyopus dasypus*) were located in the epidermis (Figure 5-1) and in the deepest layers of keratin, but were absent from sweat glands and hair follicles. Moderate numbers of another species of mite (*Ornithonyssus* sp.) were also present on the carapace and ventral surface, but were not associated with the skin lesions. These captive animals were treated with a monosulfiram solution and recovery was complete. The significance of this mange problem to free-ranging armadillos is unknown. The authors were certain that the mites were acquired in the wild since the armadillos had been captured in Florida only a few days prior to examination. Herbst (1990) examined 130 armadillos from San Felasco Hammock (Alachua Co.) over a four-year period (1986–1990) and observed a mange-like condition on the ventral surfaces of two animals. This may have been caused by the same mite as described by Baskerville and Francis (1981), although mites were not seen in the latter two cases when skin scrapings were performed (Herbst 1990).

XI. Summary and conclusions

Twenty-seven parasites, disease agents, and environmental contaminants have been iden-

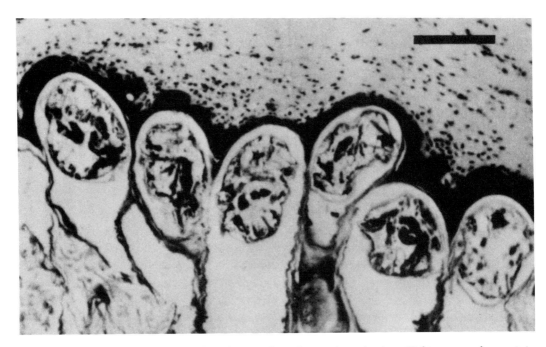

FIGURE 5-1. Section of armadillo skin showing hyperkeratosis and mites (*Echimyopus dasypus*) in lacunae in the epidermis. Line = 0.2 mm. (From Baskerville and Francis 1981.)

tified from armadillos in Florida. These include 1 chlorinated hydrocarbon, 2 arboviruses, 19 bacteria, 2 protozoans, 1 nematode, and 2 mites. With the possible exception of the chlorinated hydrocarbon, the nematode, and the mites, all these agents are of public health concern. None, however, has been associated with epizootics and they may not be of importance to armadillo populations, although this aspect has not been investigated properly.

XII. Literature cited

Amezcua, M.E., A. Escubar-Gutierrez, E.E. Storrs, A.M. Dhople, and H.P. Burchfield. 1984. Wild Mexican armadillo with leprosy-like infection. Int. J. Lepr. 52:254–255.

Baskerville, A., and L. Francis. 1981. Mange in newly-imported armadillos (*Dasypus novemcinctus*). Lab. Anim. 15:305–307.

Bigler, W.J., E. Lassing, E. Buff, A.L. Lewis, and G.L. Hoff. 1975. Arbovirus surveillance in Florida: Wild vertebrate studies 1965–1974. J. Wildl. Dis. 11:348–356.

Brown, L.N. 1987. A checklist of Florida's mammals. Florida Game and Fresh Water Fish Commission, Tallahassee. 8 pp.

Brubaker, M.L. 1976. Leprosy. In: Tropical medicine. 5th ed. G.W. Hunter, J.C. Swartzwelder, and D.F. Clyde (eds.). W.B. Saunders, Philadelphia. pp. 212–223.

Burridge, M.J., L.A. Sawyer, and W.J. Bigler. 1986. Rabies in Florida. Department of Health and Rehabilitative Services, Tallahassee, Fla. 147 pp.

Burridge, M.J., W.J. Bigler, D.J. Forrester, and J.M. Hennemann. 1979. Serologic survey for *Toxoplasma gondii* in wild animals in Florida. J. Am. Vet. Med. Assoc. 175:964–967.

Chandler, A.C. 1954. Parasites of armadillos. In: The armadillo (*Dasypus novemcinctus*): A review of its natural history, ecology, anatomy and reproductive physiology. Rice Inst. Pam. 41:43–66.

Clark, W.K. 1951. Ecological life history of the armadillo in the eastern Edwards Plateau Region. Am. Midl. Nat. 46:337–358.

Filice, G.A., R.N. Greenberg, and D.W. Fraser. 1977. Lack of observed association between armadillo contact and leprosy in humans. Am. J. Trop. Med. Hyg. 26:137–139.

Fitch, H.S., P. Goodrum, and C. Newman. 1952. The armadillo in the southeastern United States. J. Mammal. 33:21–37.

Galbreath, G.J. 1982. Armadillo. In: Wild mammals of North America. J.A. Chapman and G.A. Feldhamer (eds.). Johns Hopkins Univ. Press, Baltimore. pp. 71–79.

Herbst, L.H. 1990. Unpublished data. Univ. of Florida, Gainesville.

Herbst, L.H., and E.C. Greiner. 1990 Unpublished data. Univ. of Florida, Gainesville.

Herbst, L.H., A.I. Webb, R.M. Clemmons, M.R. Dorsey-Lee, and E.E. Storrs. 1989. Plasma and erythrocyte cholinesterase values for the common long-nosed armadillo, *Dasypus novemcinctus*. J. Wildl. Dis. 25:364–369.

Hoff, G.L., W.J. Bigler, and E.C. Prather. 1975. One-half century of tularemia in Florida. J. Fla. Med. Assoc. 62:35–37.

Howerth, E.W., D.E. Stallknecht, W.R. Davidson, and E.J. Wentworth. 1990. Survey for leprosy in nine-banded armadillos (*Dasypus novemcinctus*) from the southeastern United States. J. Wildl. Dis. 26:112–115.

Humphrey, S.R. 1974. Zoogeography of the nine-banded armadillo (*Dasypus novemcinctus*) in the United States. Bioscience 24:457–462.

Irons, E.M. 1971. A survey of the state of Florida for the incidence of American trypanosomiasis in insect vectors and reservoir animals. M.S. thesis, Univ. of Florida, Gainesville. 71 pp.

Kalmbach, E.R. 1943. The armadillo: Its relation to agriculture and game. Game, Fish, & Oyster Comm., Austin, Tex. 61 pp.

Kirchheimer, W.F., and E.E. Storrs. 1971. Attempts to establish the armadillo (*Dasypus novemcinctus* Linn.) as a model for the study of leprosy. I. Report of lepromatoid leprosy in an experimentally infected armadillo. Int. J. Lepr. 39:693–702.

Layne, J.N., and D. Glover. 1985. Activity patterns of the common long-nosed armadillo *Dasypus novemcinctus* in south-central Florida. In: The evolution and ecology of armadillos, sloths, and vermilinguas. G.G. Montgomery (ed.). Smithsonian Inst. Press, Washington, D.C. pp. 407–417.

Levine, N.P. 1973. Protozoan parasites of domestic animals and of man. Burgess Pub. Co., Minneapolis. 406 pp.

Lowery, G.W., Jr. 1974. The mammals of Louisiana and its adjacent waters. Louisiana State Univ. Press, Baton Rouge. 565 pp.

Motie, A., D.M. Myers, and E.E. Storrs. 1986. A serologic survey for leptospires in nine-banded armadillos (*Dasypus novemcinctus* L.) in Florida. J. Wildl. Dis. 22:423–424.

Nesbitt, S.A., W.M. Hetrick, L.E. Williams, Jr., and D.H. Austin. 1977. Foods of the nine-banded armadillo in Florida. Proc. Ann. Conf. S.E. Assoc. Game Fish Comm. 31:56–61.

Pier, A.C. 1979. Actinomycetes. In: CRC handbook series in zoonoses. Section A: Bacterial, rickettsial, and mycotic diseases. Vol. 1. J.H. Steele (ed.). CRC Press, Boca Raton, Fla. pp. 17–30.

Ramsey, P.R., D.F. Tyler, Jr., J.R. Waddill, and E.E. Storrs. 1981. Blood chemistry and nutritional balance of wild and captive armadillos (*Dasypus novemcinctus* L.). Comp. Biochem. Physiol. 69A:517–521.

Roth, E.E., B. Greer, M. Moore, K. Newman, G.E. Sanford, and W.V. Adams. 1964. Serological analysis of two new related leptospiral serotypes isolated in Louisiana. Zoon. Res. 3:31–38.

Smith, J.H., D.S. Folse, E.G. Long, J.D. Christie, D.T. Crouse, M.E. Tewes, A.M. Gatson, R.L. Ehrhardt, S.K. File, and M.T. Kelley. 1983. Leprosy in wild armadillos (*Dasypus novemcinctus*) of the Texas Gulf Coast: Epidemiology and mycobacteriology. J. Reticuloendoth. Soc. 34:75–88.

Storrs, E.E. 1971. The nine-banded armadillo: A model for leprosy and other biomedical research. Int. J. Lepr. 39:703–714.

———. 1989. Unpublished data. Florida Institute of Technology, Melbourne.

Storrs, E.E., and H.P. Burchfield. 1985. Leprosy in wild common long-nosed armadillos *Da-*

sypus novemcinctus. In: Evolution and ecology of armadillos, sloths, and vermilinguas. G.G. Montgomery (ed.). Smithsonian Inst. Press, Washington, D.C. pp. 265–268.

Storrs, E.E., G.P. Walsh, H.P. Burchfield, and C.H. Binford. 1974. Leprosy in the armadillo: New model for biomedical research. Science 183:851–852.

Stuart, B.P., W.A. Crowell, W.V. Adams, and J.C. Cartisle. 1977. Spontaneous renal disease in Louisiana armadillos (*Dasypus novemcinctus*). J. Wildl. Dis. 13:240–244.

Szabuniewicz, M., and J.D. McCrady. 1969. Some aspects of the anatomy and physiology of the armadillo. Lab. Anim. Care 19:843–848.

Taber, F.W. 1945. Contribution on the life history and ecology of the nine-banded armadillo. J. Mammal. 26:211–226.

Talmage, R.V., and G.D. Buchanan. 1954. The armadillo (*Dasypus novemcinctus*): A review of its natural history, ecology, anatomy and reproductive physiology. Rice Inst. Pam. 41:1–135.

Walsh, G.P., E.E. Storrs, W. Meyers, and C.H. Binford. 1977. Naturally acquired leprosy-like disease in the nine-banded armadillo (*Dasypus novemcinctus*): Recent epizootiologic findings. J. Reticuloendoth. Soc. 22:363–367.

Walsh, G.P., E.E. Storrs, H.P. Burchfield, E.H. Cottrell, M.F. Vidring, and C.H. Binford. 1975. Leprosy-like disease occurring naturally in armadillos. J. Reticuloendoth. Soc. 18:347–351.

Wampler, S.N. 1969. Husbandry and health problems of armadillos, *Dasypus novemcinctus.* Lab. Anim. Care 19:391–393.

Watson, J.J., and F.H. White. 1979. Hemolysins of *Edwardsiella tarda.* Can. J. Comp. Med. 43:78–83.

Wheeler, R.J., D.F. Friday, H.P. Burchfield, and E.E. Storrs. 1975. Use of the nine-banded armadillo for sampling soil insects for pesticide residue analysis. Environ. Qual. Safety 3 (Suppl.):129–134.

Wheeler, W.B., D.P. Jouvenaz, D.P. Wojcik, W.A. Banks, C.H. VanMiddelen, C.S. Lofgren, S. Nesbitt, L. Williams, and R. Brown. 1977. Mirex residues in nontarget organisms after application of 10-5 bait for fire ant control, Northeast Florida—1972–74. Pest. Monit. J. 11:146–156.

White, F.H. 1987. Unpublished data. Univ. of Florida, Gainesville.

Wirtz, W.O., D.H. Austin, and G.W. Deble. 1985. Food habits of the common long-nosed armadillo *Dasypus nomvemcinctus* in Florida, 1960–61. In: The evolution and ecology of armadillos, sloths, and vermilinguas. G.G. Montgomery (ed.). Smithsonian Inst. Press, Washington, D.C. pp. 439–451.

Wolfe, J.L. 1968. Armadillo distribution in Alabama and northwest Florida. Quart. J. Fla. Acad. Sci. 31:209–212.

Yeager, R.C. 1982. American trypanosomiasis. In: CRC handbook series in zoonoses. Section C: Parasitic zoonoses. Vol. 1. L. Jacobs and P. Arambulo (eds.). CRC Press, Boca Raton, Fla. pp. 105–119.

Rabbits

I. Introduction

Three species of rabbits occur in Florida. These include the Eastern cottontail, *Sylvilagus floridanus* (Allen), the marsh rabbit, *Sylvilagus palustris* (Bachman), and the black-tailed jackrabbit, *Lepus californicus* Gray (Stevenson 1976). The jackrabbit is rare and is found only in Broward, Dade, and Hillsborough counties, where it was introduced (Layne 1965, 1988). The other two species are abundant and distributed throughout Florida (Brown 1987). In 1986–1987 more than 41,000 rabbits were killed by hunters (Wright 1987). The Micco cottontail rabbit, *S. f. ammophilus,* is under review for survival status (Wood 1990), but its status may be secure according to Humphrey et al. (1987). The Lower

Keys rabbit, *S. p. hefneri,* is considered endangered according to the Florida Game and Fresh Water Fish Commission (Wood 1990).

The diseases and parasites of marsh rabbits and cottontails have been reviewed by Chapman et al. (1982). A similar review of the literature on cottontails was conducted by Andrews (1969). Dunn et al. (1982) reviewed the diseases and parasites of jackrabbits, although nothing is known about this host in Florida.

II. Environmental contaminants

Virtually nothing is known about pesticides and other contaminants in rabbit populations in Florida. Wheeler et al. (1977) examined one marsh rabbit from the Dee Dot Ranch (Duval and St. Johns counties). No residues of mirex were detected in brain, liver, and muscle samples from that animal.

III. Rabies

The records of the Florida Division of Health (Prather et al. 1975; Burridge et al. 1986) show that rabies has been diagnosed in 14 rabbits since 1905. The species involved were not given nor were domestic rabbits separated from wild rabbits, so the exact situation is not known for these incidents. Between 1957 and 1983, 2,342 rabbits (species not given) were examined for rabies in Florida. None was positive (Burridge et al. 1986). It has been concluded that lagomorphs are not involved to any significant degree in the epi-

zootiology of rabies in carnivores, even though they serve as important prey items and inflict wounds on carnivores when they are captured (Winkler 1972; Prather et al. 1975). The Florida Division of Health's recommendation for gray squirrels (see Chapter 7) also holds for rabbits, that is, rabies immunization is recommended only if a person is bitten by a rabbit that has exhibited unusual behavior or was obviously ill prior to the biting episode (Prather et al. 1975).

IV. Arboviruses

Three arboviruses (Tensaw, Sawgrass, and Keystone) are known to infect rabbits in Florida (Table 6-1). Sawgrass and Keystone viruses are not thought to be of public health significance, although Keystone virus has been documented sporadically in children in

Table 6-1
Arboviruses reported from rabbits in Florida

Arbovirus	Species of rabbit	No. rabbits Exam.	No. rabbits Pos.	Date	Location	Data source
Tensaw	Marsh rabbits	144	2	1963–70	Hillsborough	Wellings et al. (1972)[a]
		3	2	1965–74	NG	Bigler et al. (1975)
Sawgrass	Marsh rabbits	NG	2[b]	1964	Hillsborough	Sather et al. (1970)
Keystone	"Rabbits"	37	1[c]	1964–67	Hillsborough	Jennings et al. (1968), Taylor et al. (1971)
Everglades	Marsh rabbits	6	0	1968	"South Fla."	Bigler (1969)
		12	0	1965–69	Collier	Lord et al. (1973)
	Eastern cottontails	1	0	1968	Nassau	Bigler (1969)
		12	0	1965–69	Collier	Lord et al. (1973)
	"Rabbits"	43	0	1965–74	Statewide	Bigler et al. (1975)
SLE[d]	"Rabbits"	46	0	1965–74	Statewide	" " " "
EEE[e]	"Rabbits"	46	0	1965–74	Statewide	" " " "
Highlands J	"Rabbits"	46	0	1965–74	Statewide	" " " "

Note: All data (except as noted otherwise) are from serologic studies.
[a]Calisher et al. (1986) report what appears to be the same data. It is not clear if they were referring to Wellings et al. (1972), but they report the isolation of Tensaw virus from the blood of 2 swamp rabbits (*Sylvilagus aquaticus*). Since swamp rabbits do not occur in Florida, it is assumed that they were referring to Wellings' data on marsh rabbits.
[b]Sawgrass virus was isolated from 2 ticks (*Haemophysalis leporispalustris*) taken from a marsh rabbit.
[c]Keystone virus was isolated from a cottontail that had been raised in captivity and then used as a sentinel for 1 week.
[d]SLE = St. Louis encephalitis.
[e]EEE = eastern equine encephalomyelitis.

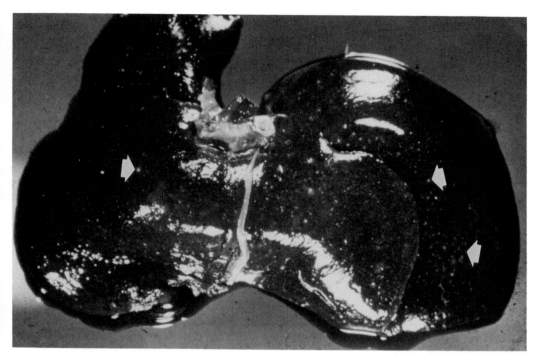

FIGURE 6-1. Liver of a rabbit showing whitish foci (arrows) typical of tularemia.

Florida (Gates et al. 1968). Tensaw virus is of public health concern (Seymour and Yuill 1981). Their importance to rabbit populations is not known.

V. Tularemia

Tularemia is an acute infectious disease caused by the bacterium *Francisella tularensis*. It is primarily a disease of wild lagomorphs and rodents and is also an important zoonotic disease (Bell and Reilly 1981). Transmission is by ectoparasites such as mites, ticks, flies, fleas, and lice, by direct contact with infected animals, or by environmental contamination (Bell and Reilly 1981). The disease is usually fatal for cottontails, and hence animals that survive the infection and produce antibodies rarely are found. McKeever et al. (1958b) examined 188 Eastern cottontails and 6 marsh rabbits in south-western Georgia and northwestern Florida and found only one seropositive animal, an Eastern cottontail. Hoff et al. (1975a) reported no positive sera from 4 cottontails and 47 marsh rabbits examined in Florida (localities not given). *Francisella tularensis* was isolated from skin scrapings of one of two men who contracted tularemia from killing, cleaning, and eating a marsh rabbit in Palm Beach County in November 1974 (Hoff et al. 1975b). Both men developed signs typical of tularemia (fever, chills, profuse perspiration, and bilateral axillary adenopathy) and significant antibody titers to *F. tularensis*. In response to these cases of tularemia, 34 mammals were collected in the vicinity where the marsh rabbit was obtained in Palm Beach County. These included two cottontails and five marsh rabbits, all of which were negative for the tularemia organisms via isolation techniques and serologic tests.

Tularemia, therefore, is present in Florida,

Table 6-2
Helminths recorded from Eastern cottontails in Florida

Helminth	Prevalence	Location (county)	Data source
Nematoda			
Capillaria hepatica	0/12[a]	Alachua, Brevard, Highlands, Lee	Layne (1968)
	1/17	Polk, Highlands	Layne (1970)
Trichostrongylus calcaratus	NG[b]	Highlands	Kinsella (1988)
Trichostrongylus affinis	NG	Highlands	" "
Longistriata noviberae	NG	Highlands	" "
Obeliscoides cuniculi	NG	Highlands	Kinsella (1988), Penner (1988)
Dirofilaria uniformis	NG	Highlands	Penner (1988)
Cestoda			
Taenia pisiformis	NG	Highlands	" "

[a]No. infected per no. examined.
[b]NG = not given by author.

but its impact on rabbit populations is unknown. Other mammals are known to be infected with *F. tularensis* in Florida (raccoons, opossums, armadillos, white-tailed deer, cotton rats, cotton mice, etc.) (Hoff et al. 1975a) and may be as important as rabbits in the transmission of tularemia to man. Since 247 cases of human tularemia were reported between 1924 and 1973 (Hoff et al. 1975a), hunters, wildlife biologists, and others who handle rabbits should be aware of tularemia and observe the necessary precautions. Rabbits with tularemia may not always display signs of the disease, but often they behave oddly, run slowly, and are captured easily. They do not raise their heads or carry their front feet well, and will rub their noses and forefeet into the ground. At necropsy typical gross lesions will include nodules or whitish foci on the liver (Figure 6-1), spleen, lungs, or lymph nodes (Bell and Reilly 1981). Rabbits with these conditions should not be further processed (or eaten) and should be discarded by burial or burning or, better still, submitted to a disease laboratory for definitive diagnosis.

For further information on tularemia, the reader is referred to Yeatter and Thompson (1952), Jellison (1974), and Bell and Reilly (1981). The latter two references provide excellent reviews of the disease in various species of wildlife, including rabbits.

VI. Leptospirosis

Shotts et al. (1975) isolated *Leptospira interrogans* serovar *grippotyphosa* from 1 of 25 cottontails examined in the Florida panhandle and southwestern Georgia. In another study in southern Georgia, 68 cottontails and 1 marsh rabbit from areas near the northern border of Florida were cultured for leptospiral organisms (McKeever et al. 1958c). All were negative. The significance of these findings is unknown, but it appears that rabbits are not important as reservoirs of the agent of leptospirosis.

VII. Mycotic diseases

During 1954 to 1956 McKeever et al. (1958d) examined 207 cottontails and 4

Table 6-3
Arthropod parasites reported from Eastern cottontails in Florida

Arthropod	Location (county)	Data source
Fleas		
Cediopsylla simplex	Alachua	Kohls (1940), Fuller (1943), Layne (1971)
Hoplopsyllus glacialis affinis	Dade	Kohls (1940)
	Highlands, Polk, Putnam	Layne (1971), FSCA[a]
	Orange	FSCA
Hoplopsyllus lynx	Osceola	"
Echidnophaga gallinacea	Alachua	Kohls (1940), Fuller (1943)
Pulex simulans	Alachua	Fuller (1943), Layne (1971), FSCA
Ctenocephalides felis	Alachua	Layne (1971)
Ticks[b]		
Haemaphysalis leporispalustris	"Throughout Fla."	Boardman (1929)
	Orange, Osceola, Collier	Travis (1941)
	Indian River	Worth (1950), Wilson & Kale (1972), FSCA
	Alachua, Gilchrist, Hillsborough, Marion	Taylor (1951)
	"Northern Fla."	Rogers (1953)
Ixodes scapularis	Alachua	Taylor (1951)
Dermacentor variabilis	"Northern Fla."	Rogers (1953)
Dermacentor sp.	Hillsborough	Taylor (1951)
Amblyomma americanum	Marion	" "
Amblyomma tuberculatum	Highlands	FSCA
	"Northern Fla."	Rogers (1953)
Mites		
Eutrombicula sp.	Hillsborough	Worth (1950)
Bots		
Cuterebra buccata	"Throughout Fla."	Sabrosky (1986)
Cuterebra cuniculi	St. Lucie	" "
	Polk	FSCA

[a]FSCA = records from the Florida State Collection of Arthropods, Division of Plant Industry, Florida Department of Agriculture, Gainesville, Fla.
[b]Boardman (1929) reported immature *Amblyomma tuberculatum* and adults of *A. maculatum* from "rabbits" in Florida, but did not say which species of rabbits. Likewise, Rogers (1953) reported nymphs of *Amblyomma americanum* from "rabbits" in northern Florida.

marsh rabbits in southwestern Georgia and northwestern Florida. Only one of the cottontails (and none of the marsh rabbits) was positive for fungi. A red variety of *Microsporum* was cultured from the fur of this rabbit. There were no signs of fungal disease and it was assumed by the authors that the animal had become contaminated by the organism from soil. This fungus is probably of limited consequence as a disease agent in rabbit populations.

VIII. Parasites

The parasites of Eastern cottontails have been well studied in several parts of North America, but not in Florida. Andrews (1969) listed 110 species of parasites from the host, including 20 protozoans, 5 flukes, 8 tapeworms, 23 nematodes, 5 dipterans, 23 fleas, 9 ticks, 16 mites, and 1 pentastome. Andrews et al. (1980) examined 260 Eastern cottontails from eight southeastern states (excluding

Table 6-4
Parasites recorded from marsh rabbits in Florida

Parasite	Occurrence or prevalence[a]	County	Data source
Protozoa			
Toxoplasma gondii	1/37	NG[b]	Burridge et al. (1979)
Nematoda			
Capillaria hepatica	0/4	Alachua, Levy, Pinellas	Layne (1968)
Fleas			
Cediopsylla simplex	+	Hillsborough	Worth (1950)
	+	Nassau, Putnam	Layne (1971)
Hoplopsyllus glacialis affinis	+	Lee	" "
Ticks[c]			
Haemaphysalis leporispalustris	+	Lee	FSCA[d]
	+	Hillsborough	Sather et al. (1970)
	+	Indian River	Wilson & Kale (1972), Worth (1950), FSCA
	+	"Throughout Fla."	Boardman (1929)
	+	"Northern Fla."	Rogers (1953)
Dermacentor variabilis	+	Hillsborough	Worth (1950), Taylor (1951), Sather et al. (1970)
	+	Levy	FSCA
	+	NG	Bishopp & Trembley (1945)
Ixodes scapularis	+	Hillsborough	Worth (1950), Taylor (1951)
Mites			
Ornithonyssus bacoti	+	Hillsborough	Worth (1950)
Chyletiella furmani[e]	+	Duval	Smiley (1970)
Bots			
Cuterebra cuniculi	+	"Throughout Fla."	Sabrosky (1986)
Cuterebra sp.	+	Hillsborough	Worth (1950)

[a]No. infected or infested per no. examined; + = parasite present, but no data available on prevalence.
[b]NG = not given by authors.
[c]Boardman (1929) reported immature *Amblyomma tuberculatum* and adults of *A. maculatum* from "rabbits" in Florida, but did not state which species of rabbits. Likewise, Rogers (1953) reported nymphs of *Amblyomma americanum* from "rabbits" in northern Florida.
[d]FSCA = records from the Florida State Collection of Arthropods, Division of Plant Industry, Florida Department of Agriculture, Gainesville, Fla.
[e]This species was described from specimens collected from a marsh rabbit by C. B. Worth in Jacksonville, Florida, on February 4, 1950 (Smiley 1970).

Florida), and reported 2 protozoans, 1 fluke, 3 tapeworms, 10 nematodes, and 1 pentastome species. Much less information is available on marsh rabbits and black-tailed jackrabbits, although Chapman et al. (1982) reported 2 species from marsh rabbits, and Dunn et al. (1982) reported 22 from black-tailed jackrabbits.

Twenty-two species of parasites have been reported from Eastern cottontails in Florida (Tables 6-2 and 6-3) and 10 species have been reported from marsh rabbits (Table 6-4).

There are no reports of parasites from black-tailed jackrabbits, although Layne (1971) postulated that the flea *Hoplopsyllus glacialis affinis* (a western North American species primarily) was introduced into Florida on black-tailed jackrabbits that were brought here in the 1930s for use in training racing greyhounds. This flea is now well established in Florida and, in addition to Eastern cottontails and marsh rabbits, has been found on deer mice, cotton rats, gray squirrels, and raccoons (Layne 1971). The typical host for the flea is the cottontail. The flea is most common in southern Florida, which may be related to the fact that the jackrabbit was introduced originally in the Miami area.

McKeever et al. (1958a) cultured 203 Eastern cottontails and 4 marsh rabbits from southwestern Georgia and northwestern Florida from 1954 to 1957. None was positive for trypanosomes. Burridge et al. (1979) found 1 of 37 marsh rabbits and none of 6 Eastern cottontails seropositive for *Toxoplasma gondii*.

Nothing is known about the effects of these parasites on rabbits in Florida. The ticks and fleas could be important as vectors of tularemia.

IX. Summary and conclusions

Little is known about the parasites and diseases of rabbits in Florida. Twenty-two species of parasites (6 nematodes, 1 cestode, and 15 arthropods), 2 bacterial diseases, and 1 fungal disease are known from Eastern cottontails. Ten parasites (1 protozoan and 9 arthropods), 2 viruses, and 1 bacterial disease are known from marsh rabbits. Nothing is known about parasites and diseases of the introduced black-tailed jackrabbit. Tensaw virus, tularemia, and toxoplasmosis are of public health importance. Tularemia may be

of significance to rabbit populations, although this has not been studied in Florida.

The paucity of information on the parasites and diseases of rabbits in Florida is presumably not due to their absence, but rather to the fact that rabbits have not been well studied in this area.

X. Literature cited

Andrews, C.L. 1969. Parasitism and other disease entities among selected populations of cottontail rabbits (*Sylvilagus floridanus*). Ph.D. diss., Univ. of Georgia, Athens. 185 pp.

Andrews, C.L., W.R. Davidson, and E.E. Provost. 1980. Endoparasites of selected populations of cottontail rabbits *Sylvilagus floridanus* in the southeastern United States. J. Wildl. Dis. 16:395–401.

Bell, J.F., and J.R. Reilly. 1981. Tularemia. In: Infectious diseases of wild mammals. 2d ed. J.W. Davis et al. (eds.). Iowa State Univ. Press, Ames. pp. 213–231.

Bigler, W.J. 1969. Venezuelan encephalitis antibody studies in certain Florida wildlife. Bull. Wildl. Dis. Assoc. 5:267–270.

Bigler, W.L., E. Lassing, E. Buff, A.L. Lewis, and G.L. Hoff. 1975. Arbovirus surveillance in Florida: Wild vertebrate studies 1965–1974. J. Wildl. Dis. 11:348–356.

Bishopp, F.C., and H.L. Trembley. 1945. Distribution and hosts of certain North American ticks. J. Parasitol. 31:1–54.

Boardman, E.T. 1929. Ticks of the Gainesville area. M.S. thesis, Univ. of Florida, Gainesville. 57 pp.

Brown, L.N. 1987. A checklist of Florida's mammals. Florida Game and Fresh Water Fish Commission, Tallahassee. 6 pp.

Burridge, M.J., L.A. Sawyer, and W.J. Bigler. 1986. Rabies in Florida. Department of Health and Rehabilitative Services, Tallahassee, Fla. 147 pp.

Burridge, M.J., W.J. Bigler, D.J. Forrester, and

J.M. Hennemann. 1979. Serologic survey for *Toxoplasma gondii* in wild animals in Florida. J. Am. Vet. Med. Assoc. 175:964–967.

Calisher, C.H., D.B. Francy, G.C. Smith, D.J. Muth, J.S. Lazuick, N. Karabatsos, W.L. Jakob, and R.G. McLean. 1986. Distribution of Bunyamwera serogroup viruses in North America, 1956–1984. Am. J. Trop. Med. Hyg. 35:429–443.

Chapman, J.A., J.G. Hockman, and W.R. Edwards. 1982. Cottontails. In: Wild mammals of North America. J.A. Chapman and G.A. Feldhamer (eds.). Johns Hopkins Univ. Press, Baltimore. pp. 83–123.

Dunn, J.P., J.A. Chapman, and R.E. Marsh. 1982. Jackrabbits. In: Wild mammals of North America. J.A. Chapman and G.A. Feldhamer (eds.). Johns Hopkins Univ. Press, Baltimore. pp. 124–145.

Fuller, H.S. 1943. Studies on Siphonaptera of eastern North America. Bull. Brooklyn Entomol. Soc. 38:18–23.

Gates, E.H., J.O. Bond, and A.L. Lewis. 1968. California group arbovirus encephalitis in Florida children. J. Fla. Med. Assoc. 55:37–40.

Hoff, G.L., W.J. Bigler, and E.C. Prather. 1975a. One-half century of tularemia in Florida. J. Fla. Med. Assoc. 62:35–37.

Hoff, G.L., W.J. Bigler, W. Hemmert, and D. Lawrence. 1975b. Tularemia in Florida: *Sylvilagus palustris* as a source of human infection. J. Wildl. Dis. 11:560–561.

Humphrey, S.R., W.H. Kern, Jr., and M.S. Ludlow. 1987. Status survey of seven Florida mammals. Fla. Coop. Fish & Wildl. Res. Unit Tech. Rep. No. 25. 39 pp.

Jellison, W.L. 1974. Tularemia in North America, 1930–1974. Univ. of Montana Foundation, Missoula. 276 pp.

Jennings, W.L., A.L. Lewis, G.E. Sather, W.M. Hammon, and J.O. Bond. 1968. California-encephalitis-group viruses in Florida rabbits: Report of experimental and sentinel studies. Am. J. Trop. Med. Hyg. 17:781–787.

Kinsella, J.M. 1988. Unpublished data. Archbold Biological Station, Lake Placid, Fla.

Kohls, G.M. 1940. Siphonaptera. A study of the species infesting wild hares and rabbits of North America north of Mexico. Nat. Inst. Health Bull. 175. 27 pp.

Layne, J.N. 1965. Occurrence of black-tailed jack rabbits in Florida. J. Mammal. 46:502.

———. 1968. Host and ecological relationships of the parasitic helminth *Capillaria hepatica* in Florida mammals. Zoologica 53:107–122.

———. 1970. New host records of *Capillaria hepatica* in Florida. Quart. J. Fla. Acad. Sci. 33:18–22.

———. 1971. Fleas (Siphonaptera) of Florida. Fla. Entomol. 54:35–51.

———. 1988. Unpublished data. Archbold Biological Station, Lake Placid, Fla.

Lord, R.D., C.H. Calisher, W.D. Sudia, and T.H. Work. 1973. Ecological investigations of vertebrate hosts of Venezuelan equine encephalomyelitis virus in south Florida. Am. J. Trop. Med. Hyg. 22:116–123.

McKeever, S., G.W. Gorman, and L. Norman. 1958a. Occurrence of a *Trypanosoma cruzi*–like organism in some mammals from southwestern Georgia and northwestern Florida. J. Parasitol. 44:583–587.

McKeever, S., J.H. Schubert, M.S. Moody, G.W. Gorman, and J.F. Chapman. 1958b. Natural occurrence of tularemia in marsupials, carnivores, lagomorphs, and large rodents in southwestern Georgia and northeastern Florida. J. Infect. Dis. 103:120–126.

McKeever, S., G.W. Gorman, J.F. Chapman, M.M. Galton, and D.K. Powers. 1958c. Incidence of leptospirosis in wild mammals from southwestern Georgia, with a report of new hosts for six serotypes of leptospires. Am. J. Trop. Med. Hyg. 7:646–655.

McKeever, S., W. Kaplan, and L. Ajello. 1958d. Ringworm fungi of large wild mammals in southwestern Georgia and northwestern Florida. Am. J. Vet. Res. 19:973–975.

Penner, L.R. 1988. Unpublished data. Archbold Biological Station, Lake Placid, Fla.

Prather, C.E., W.J. Bigler, G.L. Hoff, and J.A. Tomas. 1975. Rabies in Florida. History, status, trends. Fla. Div. of Health Monogr. Series, no. 14. Jacksonville. 122 pp.

Rogers, A.J. 1953. A study of the ixodid ticks of northern Florida, including the biology and life history of *Ixodes scapularis* Say (Ixodidae: Acarina). Ph.D. diss., Univ. of Maryland, College Park. 191 pp.

Sabrosky, C.W. 1986. North American species of *Cuterebra*, the rabbit and rodent bot flies (Diptera: Cuterebridae). Entomol. Soc. Am., College Park, Md. 240 pp.

Sather, G.E., A.L. Lewis, W. Jennings, J.O. Bond, and W.M. Hammon. 1970. Sawgrass virus: A newly described arbovirus in Florida. Am. J. Trop. Med. Hyg. 19:319–326.

Seymour, C., and T.M. Yuill. 1981. Arboviruses. In: Infectious diseases of wild mammals. 2d ed. J.W. Davis et al. (eds.). Iowa State Univ. Press, Ames. pp. 54–86.

Shotts, E.B., C.L. Andrews, and T.W. Harvey. 1975. Leptospirosis in selected wild mammals of the Florida panhandle and southwestern Georgia. J. Am. Vet. Med. Assoc. 167:387–389.

Smiley, R.L. 1970. A review of the family Cheyletiellidae (Acarina). Ann. Entomol. Soc. Am. 63:1056–1078.

Stevenson, H.M. 1976. Vertebrates of Florida. Identification and distribution. Univ. Presses of Florida, Gainesville. 607 pp.

Taylor, D.J. 1951. The distribution of ticks in Florida. M.S. thesis, Univ. of Florida, Gainesville. 121 pp.

Taylor, D.J., A.L. Lewis, J.D. Edman, and W.L. Jennings. 1971. California group arboviruses in Florida. Am. J. Trop. Med. Hyg. 20:139–145.

Travis, B.V. 1941. Examinations of wild animals for the cattle tick *Boophilus annulatus microplus* (Can.) in Florida. J. Parasitol. 27:465–467.

Wellings, F.M., A.L. Lewis, and L.V. Pierce. 1972. Agents encountered during arboviral ecological studies: Tampa Bay Area, Florida, 1963 to 1970. Am. J. Trop. Med. Hyg. 21:201–213.

Wheeler, W.B., D.P. Jouvenaz, D.P. Wojcik, W.A. Banks, C.H. VanMiddelen, C.S. Lofgren, S. Nesbitt, L. Williams, and R. Brown. 1977. Mirex residues in nontarget organisms after application of 10-5 bait for fire ant control, northeast Florida—1972–1974. Pest. Monit. J. 11:146–156.

Wilson, N., and H.W. Kale, II. 1972. Ticks collected from Indian River County, Florida (Acari: Metastigmata: Ixodidae). Fla. Entomol. 55:53–57.

Winkler, W.G. 1972. Rodent rabies in United States. J. Infect. Dis. 126:565–567.

Wood, D.A. 1990. Official lists of endangered fauna and flora in Florida. Florida Game and Fresh Water Fish Commission, Tallahassee. 19 pp.

Worth, C.B. 1950. A preliminary host-parasite register for some small mammals of Florida. J. Parasitol. 36:497–498.

Wright, T.J. 1987. Wildlife harvest and economic survey. Florida Game and Fresh Water Fish Commission, Tallahassee. P-R Report, W-33.

Yeatter, R.E., and D.H. Thompson. 1952. Tularemia, weather, and rabbit populations. Bull. Ill. Nat. Hist. Surv. 25:351–382.

Squirrels

I. Introduction

Five species of squirrels occur in Florida (Table 7-1). Two of these, the gray squirrel and the southern flying squirrel, are abundant and are found throughout the state. One, the Mexican red-bellied squirrel, is an introduced species and occurs only on Elliot Key. The Eastern chipmunk, although considered common in other parts of its range, occurs only in Oklaloosa County in Florida, where it is rare and considered a species of special concern (Wood 1990). The status of two subspecies of fox squirrels is also of concern. The Big Cypress fox squirrel, *Sciuris niger avicennia*, is considered threatened (Williams and Humphrey 1979; Wood 1990) and

Sherman's fox squirrel, *S. n. shermani*, is listed as a species of special concern (Wood 1990).

In 1986–1987 hunters in Florida killed an estimated 411,000 squirrels, most of which were gray squirrels (Wright 1987).

The parasites and diseases of gray and fox squirrels in North America were reviewed by Flyger and Gates (1982). The literature on parasites of gray squirrels is voluminous, although most of the publications deal with descriptions of new parasites and studies on local populations (Davidson 1975). A number of extensive reviews and bibliographies on the parasites of gray squirrels have been

Table 7-1
Species of squirrels that occur in Florida

Common and scientific names	Range in Florida	Status
1. Eastern chipmunk *Tamias striatus* (L.)	Okaloosa County	Rare[a]
2. Southern flying squirrel *Glaucomys volans* (L.)	Statewide[b]	Abundant
3. Gray squirrel *Sciurus carolinensis* Gmelin	Statewide	Abundant
4. Fox squirrel *Sciurus niger* L.	Statewide[b]	Common
5. Mexican red-bellied squirrel[c] *Sciurus aureogaster* Cuvier	Elliot Key	Common

Source: Brown (1987).
[a]Listed as "species of special concern" by the Florida Game and Fresh Water Fish Commission (Wood 1990).
[b]Absent from the Florida Keys.
[c]Introduced species.

published (Doran 1954a, 1954b, 1955a, 1955b; Katz 1939; Clark 1959; Parker 1971; Davidson 1975). Two extensive studies on endoparasites (Davidson 1975, 1976) and bacteria (Best 1977) have been conducted in the southeastern United States, but did not include Florida. Data from several collection sites in southern Georgia and Alabama, however, are of relevance to Florida squirrels. In Florida, two localized studies, one on gray squirrels in Duval County and one on fox squirrels in Putnam County, contributed the bulk of our knowledge of squirrel parasites and diseases in this state. No disease information is available on Eastern chipmunks and red-bellied squirrels in Florida.

Baseline values for serum proteins have been published for gray squirrels in Florida (Chan et al. 1976) as have various determinations on hematology, serum chemistry, and urinalysis (Hoff et al. 1976a, 1976b). The reader is referred to these publications for more details on these aspects of the health of gray squirrels.

II. Environmental contaminants

In 1974, samples of omental fat were obtained from 22 gray squirrels trapped in city parks and residential areas of the city of Jacksonville (Duval County) (Nalley et al. 1978). These were analyzed for pesticide residues. Low concentrations (less than 1 ppm) of the following compounds were detected: alpha-BHC, gamma-BHC, beta-BHC, aldrin, dieldrin, heptachlor, heptachlor epoxide, oxychlordane, nonachlor, o,p'-DDT, p,p'-DDT, o,p'-DDE, p,p'-DDE, o,p'-DDD, and p,p'-DDD. Up to 4 ppm of PCB was detected in 4 squirrels. The PCB compounds were not identified as to specific chlorine content. There was no relationship of residues with the age or sex of the squirrels.

Samples of hair from the tails of 66 gray squirrels from the Jacksonville area were analyzed for mercury concentrations (Jenkins et al. 1980). Values ranged from 0.07 to 9.2 ppm, with squirrels older than two years having significantly higher concentrations. The overall mean value (1.1 ppm) for these urban squirrels was significantly greater than concentrations (mean, 0.43 ppm) found in six gray squirrels from a rural area in Pasco County. The authors concluded that squirrels were good indicators of the presence of mercury in the environment, but not as good as raccoons. The source of mercury contamination in these squirrels was unknown.

In a related study, concentrations of lead, zinc, and cadmium were determined in 180 urban and 12 rural gray squirrels (Table 7-2). Concentrations of lead and zinc in the kidneys of the squirrels from Jacksonville were similar for all age groups, but concentrations of cadmium increased up to two years

Table 7-2

Mean concentrations of cadmium, zinc, and lead in kidneys of gray squirrels from 2 areas in northern Florida

Age (yr)	No. squirrels	Cadmium	Zinc	Lead
Jacksonville				
<1	75	4	28	1
1	69	9	30	1
2	20	15	31	1
3	10	16	23	1
4	6	16	23	1
Gulf Hammock				
1	5	2	14	1
2	7	5	19	1

Source: McKinnon et al. (1976).
Note: All values are in ppm wet wt.

of age. Values in the squirrels from Gulf Hammock Wildlife Management area (a rural area) were lower than those in squirrels from Jacksonville. One noteworthy facet of this study was the finding of the highest concentrations of lead in squirrels trapped from neighborhoods classified as low socioeconomic areas. The reasons for this were uncertain, but may have been related to automobile emissions (McKinnon et al. 1976).

Concentrations of cesium-137 ranged from 250 to 29,000 pCi/kg of muscle in 66 gray squirrels from Jacksonville (Jenkins et al. 1980). There were higher amounts of cesium in squirrels trapped near schools than in squirrels from other areas (low-income areas, parks, and cemeteries). Other studies have shown that squirrels from urban localities contain lower concentrations of cesium than squirrels from nearby rural areas (Jenkins and Fendley 1968). Jenkins et al. (1980) concluded that the concentrations in these squirrels were not of public health significance. They speculated also that cesium-137 was acquired by the squirrels from feeding on mushrooms, acorns, or palmetto berries, all

of which are known to accumulate cesium-137 (Johnson and Nayfield 1970; Stockbridge and Jenkins 1974). The original source was believed to be fallout from weapons testing before 1964. (See Chapter 20 for a discussion on radionuclide concentrations in white-tailed deer.)

The significance of the above findings on the health of gray squirrels in Florida is unknown. However, Bigler and Hoff (1976) concluded that gray squirrels were sensitive indicators of lead, cesium-137, and mercury, but not pesticides, and that they would serve as a "suitable animal for urban environmental monitoring" (p. 539). More information on toxicosis and environmental contamination is needed on gray squirrels in rural or "wild" situations in addition to similar types of data on the other three species of tree squirrels in Florida.

III. Neoplasia

An outbreak of squirrel fibromatosis was documented in February 1974 on Amelia Island, Nassau County (Forrester 1974). Several gray squirrels were observed in the wild with skin nodules. One animal was collected and submitted for necropsy. This animal was emaciated and had multiple skin tumors, especially on the head (Figure 7-1). The eyelids were involved to the degree that the squirrel was obviously blinded.

These tumors or fibromas are caused by a poxvirus (Yuill 1981), which is suspected of being transmitted from animal to animal by mosquitoes (Kilham 1955). Such infections are uncommon in the Southeast (Davidson and Nettles 1988) and the above outbreak is the only one known from Florida. Since this is not a prevalent disease, there is probably no significant effect at the population level,

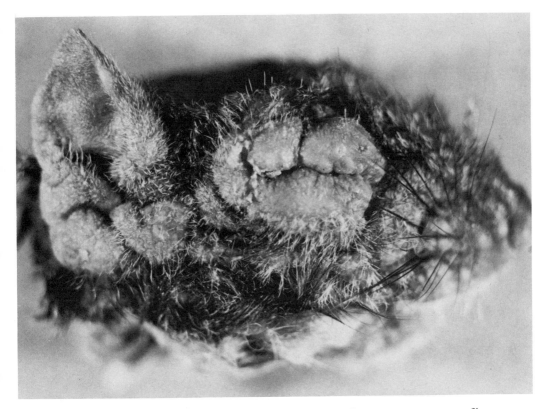

FIGURE 7-1. Head of a gray squirrel from Nassau County with numerous cutaneous fibromas.

although the effects on individuals can be fatal.

IV. Rabies

Gray squirrels in Florida have been shown to be susceptible to rabies virus (Winkler et al. 1972). Thirty gray squirrels were trapped near Orange Park, Florida, and were inoculated intramuscularly with rabies viruses, 15 with a virus obtained from a yellow bat from Tampa and 15 with a virus from a raccoon from Inverness. Twenty of the squirrels died, 7 that had received the bat virus and 13 that had received the raccoon virus. About half of the infected squirrels exhibited typical signs of the furious form of rabies, that is, aggressiveness and self-mutilation ("chewing tails and feet in some cases to the point of amputation"; Winkler et al. 1972, p. 101). The authors concluded that the squirrels were more susceptible to the rabies virus from raccoons than to the virus of bat origin.

In spite of the above findings, natural infections of squirrels by rabies virus are rare. In the United States 184 cases of rabies were diagnosed in various species of squirrels between 1953 and 1970 (Winkler 1972). Between 1957 and 1983, 9,304 squirrels (mostly gray squirrels) were tested for rabies in Florida. Only one squirrel (a flying squirrel from Putnam County) was positive (Venters and Jennings 1962). One other known case of rabies in squirrels in Florida was in a gray squirrel diagnosed in 1913 (Prather et al. 1975; Burridge et al. 1986).

Because rabies is so rarely seen in squirrels,

the U.S. Public Health Service states that bites by squirrels seldom, if ever, require rabies treatment (Winkler 1972). The Florida Division of Health recommends the use of rabies immunization after a person is bitten by a squirrel only if the animal exhibits bizarre behavior (unprovoked attack) or obvious illness prior to a bite (Prather et al. 1975).

V. Arboviruses

Two arboviruses (Keystone and SLE viruses) have been reported from gray squirrels in Florida (Table 7-3). SLE virus is of public health importance, whereas the significance of Keystone virus to human health is unknown (Karabatsos 1985). Both viruses are probably of little importance to squirrel populations in Florida.

VI. Other viruses

Encephalomyocarditis (EMC) virus has been isolated from brain tissue of two squirrels (species not given; probably gray squirrels) in Florida. The first squirrel was from Palm Beach County in 1954 (Kissling et al. 1956); the second squirrel was from Orange County in 1961 (Gainer 1961). In the latter instance the author attributed the cause of death to the viral infection, but gave no details on lesions and the like. EMC virus has been isolated also from cotton rats and raccoons in Florida (see Chapters 10 and 12).

Wildlife, therefore, may serve some role as reservoir hosts of EMC virus, which causes an important disease in domestic animals such as swine (Gainer 1967). This role may not be significant, however, since such infections in wild mammals are not common (Gainer and Bigler 1967).

Isolates of human echovirus 1/8 complex were obtained from feces of 5 of 180 squirrels from Duval County (Hoff et al. 1980). The significance of this finding to the health of gray squirrels or man is not known. Hoff et al. (1980) were unable to infect squirrels with the ECHO 1/8 complex virus *per os*. The source of virus was not determined, but it was suspected that the squirrels acquired it

Table 7-3
Arboviruses reported from gray squirrels in Florida

Arbovirus	No. squirrels		Date	Location (county)	Data source
	Exam.	Pos.			
Keystone	17	3	1964–67	Hillsborough	Jennings et al. (1968), Taylor et al. (1971)
	4	1	1965–74	Alachua	Bigler et al. (1975)
	180[a]	0[a]	1974	Duval	White et al. (1975)
SLE[b]	19	1	1962	Hillsborough	Jennings et al. (1969)
	180	0	1974	Duval	Bigler et al. (1975)
Everglades	180	0	1974	"	" " " "
EEE[c]	180	0	1974	"	" " " "

Note: All data are from serologic studies unless otherwise indicated.
[a]In addition to serologic studies on these animals, brain samples and blood clots were processed in an attempt to isolate arboviruses. None was found (White et al. 1975).
[b]SLE = St. Louis encephalitis virus.
[c]EEE = eastern equine encephalomyelitis virus.

from surface water contaminated with raw sewage.

VII. Rickettsial diseases

Epidemic typhus is a rickettsial disease of man caused by *Rickettsia prowazekii*. The disease is spread from man to man by the human body louse (*Pediculus humanus humanus*). Epidemic typhus resembles murine typhus (discussed in Chapter 9), but is usually more severe with mortality rates as high as 20% (Philip 1980). Flying squirrels were implicated as reservoir hosts of this disease when Bozeman et al. (1975) reported that in 1973–74, 104 of 215 flying squirrels from northern and central Florida were seropositive. *Rickettsia prowazekii* was isolated from six of these animals. Subsequent studies have shown that the rickettsial organism is transmitted from squirrel to squirrel by biting ectoparasites (primarily fleas, *Orchopeas howardii*, and sucking lice, *Neohaematopinus sciuropteri*), but that transmission to humans is due not to the bites of fleas and lice, but to the inhalation of ectoparasite feces that become aerosolized when squirrels groom themselves (McDade 1987). Although human cases of epidemic typhus associated with contacts with flying squirrels have been reported from a number of states (including Georgia, North Carolina, Tennessee, and Virginia), none has been recognized in Florida (McDade 1987). However, this potentially could occur since the rickettsia is present in flying squirrels in Florida and the proper species of fleas and sucking lice are known from Florida squirrels. Nothing is known about the effects of this rickettsia on flying squirrels.

White et al. (1975) found no serologic evidence of rickettsial infections in 180 gray squirrels examined from urban areas near Jacksonville.

VIII. Bacterial diseases

Shotts et al. (1975) examined 26 gray squirrels, 27 fox squirrels, and 1 flying squirrel for cultural or serologic evidence of leptospiral infection. These animals were collected at Tall Timbers Research Station in Leon County, Florida, and on three private plantations in southwestern Georgia. *Leptospira interrogans* serovar *grippotyphosa* was recovered from one fox squirrel and *L. interrogans* serovar *ballum* from one gray squirrel. The flying squirrel was negative. In another study of 180 gray squirrels from Jacksonville, no evidence of infections by leptospires was found (White et al. 1975). McKeever et al. (1958d) cultured 11 fox squirrels in southern Georgia (close to the Florida border) for leptospires. All were negative.

White et al. (1975) conducted other bacteriologic studies on the 180 gray squirrels and found no evidence of *Salmonella* or tularemia organisms. Cultures of the mouths of some of these squirrels were positive for alpha-hemolytic *Streptococcus* sp., *Staphylococcus epidermidis*, *Staphylococcus aureus*, *Enterobacter* sp., *Bacillus* sp., *Proteus vulgaris*, *Pseudomonas aeruginosa*, and *Esherichia coli*. Eight of 180 blood cultures were positive for bacteria. Three were positive for alpha-hemolytic *Streptococcus*, two for *Bacillus* sp., two for *Staphylococcus epidermidis*, and one for a gram-positive microaerophilic rod. The authors felt that these isolations of bacteria from a few blood cultures were probably due to contamination during collection.

McKeever et al. (1958b) tested six fox squirrels from Leon County for antibodies to *Francisella tularensis*, the etiologic agent of tularemia. All squirrels were negative, but one of nine fox squirrels in southern Thomas County, Georgia (just north of the Florida border), was seropositive. Hoff et al. (1975) reported three gray squirrels in Florida (locality not given) to be negative for antibodies to *F. tularensis*.

One case of pyogenic otitis media was found in a fox squirrel from Leon County in 1980 (SCWDS records), but the bacteria involved were not determined.

IX. Mycotic diseases

The study conducted on 180 gray squirrels from urban areas in Jacksonville resulted in 942 isolates of fungi representing 19 genera (Table 7-4). These were recovered from cul-

Table 7-4
Isolates of fungi from 180 gray squirrels in Jacksonville, Florida, 1974

	No. isolates	
Fungus	Hair-skin scrapings	Toe-nails
Alternaria sp.	82	45
Aspergillus glaucus[b]	3	5
Aspergillus niger[b]	29	20
Aspergillus sp.	60	28
Candida albicans[b]	0	2
Candida tropicalis	5	4
Cladosporium sp.	114	57
Curvularia sp.	2	0
Fusarium sp.	1	3
Helminthosporium sp.	13	3
Microsporum gypseum[b]	1	8
Mucor sp.[a,b]	50	53
Nigrospora sp.	1	1
Oospora sp.	5	3
Paecilomyces sp.	2	0
Penicillium sp.	133	97
Rhizopus sp.	1	0
Scopulariopsis brevicaulis[b]	7	52
Streptomyces sp.	4	0
Trichoderma sp.	4	4
Trichophyton mentagrophytes[a,b]	26	13
Trichothecium sp.	1	0
Totals	544	398

Source: Lewis et al. (1975).
[a]Potentially pathogenic for squirrels.
[b]Potentially pathogenic for humans.

tures of hair-skin scrapings and toenails (Lewis et al. 1975). Nine squirrels had minor skin lesions on the hindquarters and legs; *Trichophyton mentagrophytes* was isolated from six of these and *Mucor* sp. from one. These two fungi were isolated from 107 (59%) of these squirrels, although most of the animals exhibited no skin lesions. There were 114 squirrels carrying fungi of importance to humans. Four species of fungi were considered of significance: *Candida albicans*, *Microsporum gypseum*, *Scopulariopsis brevicaulis*, and *Trichophyton mentagrophytes*. These could pose a disease problem in hunters handling gray squirrels. One of the authors of the above-mentioned article contracted an infection by *T. mentagrophytes*. Similar infections were reported by DeLamater (1939) from handling gray squirrels.

McKeever et al. (1958c) examined 4 gray squirrels and 59 fox squirrels from southwestern Georgia and northwestern Florida and found no fungal infections.

X. Protozoan parasites

Davidson (1975) reviewed the literature on protozoan parasites of gray squirrels and listed 11 species from squirrels in various parts of the United States. Flyger and Gates (1982) gave information on gray and fox squirrels. An extensive survey of parasites of gray squirrels was conducted recently in the southeastern United States (Davidson 1976), but unfortunately no squirrels from Florida were included in the study. Several collection sites in southern Georgia and Alabama provided data of value to those interested in parasites of squirrels in Florida due to their proximity to the Florida border. In that study three species of coccidia were identified, one of which (*Eimeria confusa*) was found in squirrels collected in the southwestern tip of

Georgia (Decatur County). In addition, *Hepatozoon griseisciuri* and an unidentified species of *Sarcocystis* were found also in squirrels from southern Georgia and Alabama.

In 1974 fecal samples from 192 gray squirrels in the Jacksonville area were examined for coccidial oocysts (Forrester et al. 1977). Oocysts were found in 97% of the samples. These represented three species: *Eimeria lancasterensis*, *E. confusa*, and *E. ontarioensis* (Table 7-5). Squirrels were sampled each month throughout the year, but there was no variation in oocyst prevalence by season. *Eimeria lancasterensis* was recovered from a road-killed fox squirrel from Alachua County in 1977 (Forrester 1984). A new species of coccidia (*E. parasciurorum*) was described from fecal material collected from a flying squirrel in Gainesville (Bond and Bovee 1957).

Antibodies to *Toxoplasma gondii* were detected in 1 of 265 gray squirrels and none of 2 flying squirrels examined from Florida (Burridge et al. 1979). Blood films from four gray squirrels from Duval County were positive for *Hepatozoon griseisciuri* (Table 7-5).

McKeever et al. (1958a) cultured 3 gray squirrels and 48 fox squirrels in southwestern Georgia and northwestern Florida for trypanosomes. None was infected.

The pathologic significance of these protozoan parasites is uncertain. Davidson and Calpin (1976) concluded that infections by *H. griseisciuri* caused significant damage to the lungs and thereby could be related to gray squirrel mortality in late winter in the Southeast. Davidson (1976) did not find lesions associated with coccidial infections in gray squirrels and concluded that these protozoans were not harmful to squirrels unless infections were massive. Joseph (1972) felt that *Eimeria confusa* and *E. lancasterensis* were nonpathogenic.

XI. Helminths

Davidson (1975) listed 34 species of helminths from the gray squirrel throughout its range. These included 1 trematode, 1 acanthocephalan, 9 cestodes, and 23 nematodes.

In Florida our knowledge of the helminths of gray squirrels is based mainly on two stud-

Table 7-5
Protozoan parasites reported from gray squirrels in Florida

| | No. squirrels | | | | | Basis of | |
Protozoan	Exam.	Inf.	(%)	Date	County	diagnosis	Data source
Toxoplasma gondii	265	1	(<1)	NG[a]	NG	Serology[b]	Burridge et al. (1979)
Eimeria lancasterensis	192	184	(96)	1974	Duval	Fecal analysis	Forrester et al. (1977)
Eimeria confusa	192	30	(16)	1974	Duval	Fecal analysis	" " " "
Eimeria ontarioensis	192	5	(3)	1974	Duval	Fecal analysis	" " " "
Hepatozoon griseisciuri	180	4	(2)	1974	Duval	Blood smears	Forrester (1987)

[a]NG = not given by authors.
[b]Indirect fluorescent antibody test.

ies, one conducted in the Jacksonville area (Conti et al. 1984) and one in Marion County (Parker et al. 1972). Nine species of helminths (six nematodes, two cestodes, and one acanthocephalan) were found (Table 7-6).

The study on urban gray squirrels in the Jacksonville area resulted in several noteworthy findings. *Strongyloides robustus* was the most abundant species and made up 61% of the 4,098 worms collected from the 180 squirrels. The other species of helminths occurred infrequently and in low numbers. Of the 180 squirrels examined, 49 (27%) were

free of helminths. There were no differences in prevalence with respect to host sex or age, but male squirrels had significantly higher intensities of *S. robustus*. There were higher prevalences of *S. robustus* and *Heligmodendrium hassalli* during the winter months.

The helminth fauna of urban gray squirrels in Jacksonville was more sparse (nine species) compared to the number of species (24) reported by Davidson (1976) from gray squirrels from nonurban areas in the Southeast (excluding Florida). The prevalences of the helminths with indirect life cycles (the tape-

Table 7-6
Helminths of gray squirrels from Florida

Helminth	No. squirrels			Intensity		Date	County	Data source
	Exam.	Inf.	(%)	Mean	Range			
Nematoda								
Physaloptera sp. (larvae)	180	4	(2)	22	1–65	1974	Duval	Conti et al. (1984)
Strongyloides robustus	180	92	(51)	27	1–800	1974	Duval	" " " "
	4	1	(25)	25	—	1969	Marion	Parker et al. (1972)
	NG[a]	NG		NG	NG	NG	Highlands	Layne (1987)
Heligmodendrium hassalli	180	47	(26)	17	1–181	1974	Duval	Conti et al. (1984)
	4	3	(75)	53	1–115	1969	Marion	Parker et al. (1972)
	NG	NG		NG	NG	NG	Highlands	Layne (1987)
Trichostrongylus calcaratus	180	4	(2)	2	1–3	1974	Duval	Conti et al. (1984)
	4	1	(25)	1	—	1969	Marion	Parker et al. (1972)
Syphacia thompsoni	180	11	(6)	4	1–26	1974	Duval	Conti et al. (1984)
	4	2	(50)	1	1	1969	Marion	Parker et al. (1972)
Dipetalonema interstitium	180	5	(3)	1	1	1974	Duval	Conti et al. (1984)
Microfilariae (prob. of								
D. *interstitium*)	180	18	(10)	—	—	1974	Duval	" " " "
Capillaria hepatica	11	0	(0)	—	—	1957–64	Alachua, Highlands, Levy, Pinellas	Layne (1968)
Cestoda								
Raillietina bakeri	180	59	(33)	—	—	1974	Duval	Conti et al. (1984)
Taenia rileyi	NG	NG		NG	NG	NG	Highlands	Layne (1987)
Acanthocephala								
Moniliformis clarki	180	45	(25)	16	1–183	1974	Duval	Conti et al. (1984)
	4	2	(50)	2	1–3	1969	Marion	Parker et al. (1972)
	24	3	(13)	NG[b]	NG	1946	Putnam	Moore (1957)

[a]NG = not given.
[b]Intensities were not given for all 3 squirrels. One had 6 worms; the other 2 had "some."

Table 7-7

Arthropod parasites reported from gray squirrels in Florida

Arthropod	County	Data source
Ticks		
Amblyomma tuberculatum	Putnam	Moore (1957)
Amblyomma americanum	"No. Florida"	Rogers (1953)
	Alachua	Boardman (1929)
Dermacentor variabilis	Duval	Wilson et al. (1991)
Mites		
Eutrombicula alfreddugesi	Alachua, Levy	Rohani & Cromroy (1979), FSCA[a]
	Duval	Wilson et al. (1991)
Eutrombicula splendens	Duval	" " " "
Eutrombicula sp.	Hillsborough	Worth (1950)
Laelaps nuttalli	Hillsborough	" "
Androlaelaps casalis	Duval	Wilson et al. (1991)
	Alachua	FSCA
Androlaelaps fahrenholzi	Duval	Wilson et al. (1991)
Leptotrombidium peromysci	Duval	" " " "
Parasecia g. gurneyi	Duval	" " " "
Fleas		
Hoplopsyllus glacialis affinis	Highlands	Layne (1971), FSCA
Echidnophaga gallinacea	Hillsborough	Layne (1971), Worth (1950), FSCA
Orchopeas howardii	Alachua, Duval, Gilchrist, Highlands, Hillsborough, Indian River, Levy, St. Johns, Sumter	Layne (1971), Worth (1950), FSCA
Pulex simulans	Alachua	FSCA
Sucking lice		
Neohaematopinus sciurinus	Hillsborough	Worth (1950)
	Indian River, Levy	FSCA
Neohaematopinus sciuri	Alachua	Kim et al. (1986)
	Duval	Wilson et al. (1991)
Enderleinellus longiceps	Alachua	FSCA
Hoplopleura sciuricola	Duval	Wilson et al. (1991)
Biting lice		
Penenirmus sp.[b]	Duval	" " " "
Botflies		
Cuterebra emasculator	Alachua	Forrester (1984), Sabrosky (1986)
Phaenicia sp.	Leon	SCWDS records

[a]FSCA = records from the Florida State Collection of Arthropods, Division of Plant Industry, Florida Department of Agriculture, Gainesville, Fla.
[b]One specimen of this biting louse was found on 1 of 180 gray squirrels from Jacksonville. This is normally a parasite of birds and represents an accidental host-parasite association. The squirrel probably acquired the louse while exploring a bird nest.

worm and the acanthocephalan) were higher in urban squirrels (33% and 25%, respectively) than in the nonurban squirrels (6% and 1%). This may be due to differences in host density, home range sizes, stress, habitat diversity, or food quality, availability, and preference. The pathologic significance of these helminths to gray squirrel populations is unknown.

Flyger and Gates (1982) listed 23 species of helminths (9 nematodes, 12 cestodes, and 2 acanthocephalans) from fox squirrels in North America. Little information exists on fox squirrels in Florida. Moore (1957) examined 24 fox squirrels from Putnam County and found infections by *Moniliformis clarki* in four squirrels (17%), with intensities of 1, 1, 10, and 33 per squirrel. He also found the tapeworm *Raillietina bakeri* in two squirrels (one of which had a concurrent infection of *M. clarki*), but gave no values for intensity.

We examined three fox squirrels from Alachua County and two from Glades County from 1975 to 1977. All five had infections of *Strongyloides robustus,* with intensities of 1, 8, and 20 for the Alachua County animals and 1 and 41 for the Glades County animals. Layne (1968) examined one fox squirrel from Alachua County and one from Levy County for infections by *Capillaria hepatica.* Both were negative.

Moore (1957) reported infections of *M. clarki* in 5 of 15 flying squirrels from Putnam County in 1946–1947. Intensities were 1, 1, 1, 7, and 14 worms per squirrel. The pinworm *Syphacia thompsoni* was recorded from a flying squirrel in Highlands County (Layne 1987). Layne (1968) examined two flying squirrels from Alachua County for infections by *Capillaria hepatica.* None was found. No other data are available on helminths of flying squirrels in Florida.

FIGURE 7-2. Gray squirrel from Alachua County with numerous botfly larvae (*Cuterebra emasculator*). Note empty cavity from which larva has emerged (arrow).

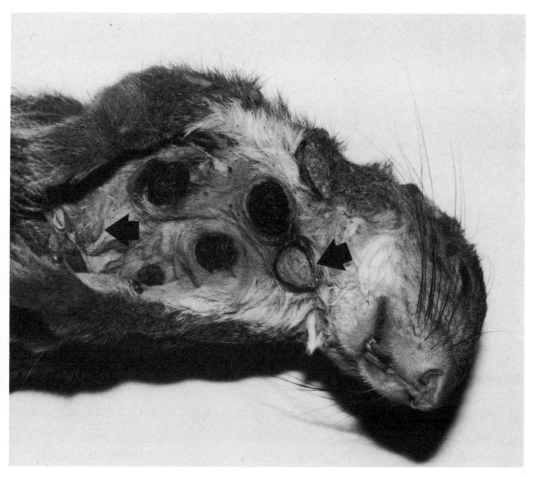

FIGURE 7-3. Close-up of same squirrel shown in Figure 7-2. Note bots *in situ* and empty cavities from which larvae have emerged (arrows).

XII. Arthropods

A checklist of ectoparasites of gray squirrels in North America by Flyger and Gates (1982) included 48 species, of which 25 were ticks and mites, 15 were fleas, 7 were sucking lice, and 1 was a cuterebrid botfly. In Florida 21 species have been reported from gray squirrels, and include 3 ticks, 8 mites, 4 fleas, 4 sucking lice, and 2 bots or warbles (Table 7-7).

The botfly (*Cuterebra emasculator*) is probably the most interesting and commonly noticed ectoparasite of gray squirrels in Flor-

ida, at least in north-central Florida. Its life cycle has not been determined, although it is probably similar to other species known to parasitize rodents and lagomorphs (Harwood and James 1979). In those species eggs are laid in or near the nests or burrows of rodents by the adult fly, which resembles a bumblebee. Larvae hatch from the eggs and enter natural body openings and the skin and grow into grub-like larvae that may reach up to one inch in length (Figure 7-2). The larvae eventually emerge from the animal, pupate on the ground, and develop into an adult fly. The effects of the warbles or bots on gray squirrels are probably minimal and appear more harmful than they actually are. Their occurrence on gray squirrels in north-central Florida is seasonal. We commonly see them in the fall, when we can expect a number of phone calls from people who are alarmed at seeing "tumors" or "bumps" on the backs of squirrels in their backyard. Usually there are one or two bots per squirrel, but we have seen squirrels with more than 10 (Figures 7-2 and 7-3).

Flyger and Gates (1982) listed 24 species of ectoparasites, including 13 ticks and mites, 7 fleas, 3 sucking lice, and 1 botfly from fox squirrels in North America. Fourteen species are known from Florida, largely due to the efforts of Moore (1957), who worked in Putnam County. These include six ticks, three

mites, two fleas, and three sucking lice (Table 7-8).

Seven species of arthropods have been reported from flying squirrels in Florida (Table 7-9), and include four fleas, two sucking lice, and one botfly. Botfly larvae (*Cuterebra* sp.) were found in three young flying squirrels from Alachua County in 1987 (Forrester 1987). This is the first report of this cuterebrid from flying squirrels (Sabrosky 1986).

XIII. Summary and conclusions

Ninety-one different parasites, disease agents, and environmental contaminants have been identified in gray squirrels from Florida. These include 16 pesticides, 4 heavy

Table 7-8
Arthropod parasites reported from fox squirrels in Florida

Arthropod	County	Data source
Ticks		
Ixodes texanus	Taylor	Rogers (1953)
Ixodes scapularis	Putnam	Moore (1957)
Amblyomma americanum	Putnam	" "
Amblyomma maculatum	Putnam	" "
Amblyomma tuberculatum	Putnam	" "
	"Northern Fla."	Rogers (1953)
Dermacentor variabilis	Putnam	Moore (1957)
	"Northern Fla."	Rogers (1953)
Mites		
Eutrombicula alfreddugesi	Putnam	Moore (1957)
Atricholaelaps megaventralis	Putnam	" "
Listrophorus sp.	Putnam	" "
Fleas		
Orchopeas howardii	Alachua, Gilchrist, Highlands, Levy, Putnam, Sumter	Fuller (1943), Layne (1971), Moore (1957)
Hoplopsyllus glacialis affinis	Alachua	FSCA[a]
Sucking lice		
Hoplopleura sciuricola	Putnam	Moore (1957)
Neohaematopinus sciurinus	Putnam	" "
Enderleinellus sp.	Putnam	" "

[a]FSCA = records from the Florida State Collection of Arthropods, Division of Plant Industry, Florida Department of Agriculture, Gainesville, Fla.

Table 7-9
Arthropod parasites reported from flying squirrels in Florida

Arthropod	County	Data source
Fleas		
Orchopeas howardii	Alachua, Clay, Duval, Highlands	Layne (1971)
Opisodasys pseudoarctomys	Dade	Schwartz (1952)
Hoplopsyllus glacialis affinis	Alachua, Clay	FSCA[a]
Polygenis gwyni	NG[b]	Layne (1971)
Sucking lice		
Neohaematopinus sciuropteri	Putnam	Kim et al. (1986)
Hoplopleura trispinosa	Putnam	" " " "
Botflies		
Cuterebra sp.	Alachua	Forrester (1987)

[a]FSCA = records from the Florida State Collection of Arthropods, Division of Plant Industry, Florida Department of Agriculture, Gainesville, Fla.
[b]NG = not given by author.

metals, 1 radionuclide, 5 viruses, 10 bacteria, 19 fungi, 5 protozoa, 9 helminths, and 22 arthropods. Nineteen such disease agents (1 species of bacteria, 1 protozoan, 3 helminths, and 14 arthropods) are known from fox squirrels. Less is known about flying squirrels, for which 12 disease agents (1 virus, 1 rickettsia, 1 protozoan, 2 helminths, and 7 arthropods) have been reported. Nothing is known about the health status of chipmunks and red-bellied squirrels in Florida.

Information on the frequency and distribution of these parasites and diseases is extremely limited. With the exception of rabies virus, ECHO 1/8 complex virus, and some coccidia, no studies have been undertaken to determine the effects of these disease agents on squirrels. It is therefore not possible to draw conclusions at this time concerning the impact of diseases on populations of any of these species of squirrels.

From a public health standpoint the squirrel does not appear to be a serious hazard. Even though there are reports of a number of viruses, bacteria, and fungi that could be transferred from squirrels to man, Bigler and

Hoff (1976) concluded that these are of minor importance. One exception to this might be *Rickettsia prowazekii*, the etiologic agent of epidemic typhus. Bigler and Hoff (1976) concluded that squirrels were sensitive indicators of lead, mercury, and cesium-137, but not pesticides. They further concluded that the gray squirrel could serve as a suitable animal for environmental monitoring in the urban ecosystem.

XIV. Literature cited

Best, R.B. 1977. The eastern gray squirrel (*Sciurus carolinensis*) as a potential reservoir of organisms of public health interest. M.S. thesis, Univ. of Georgia, Athens. 56 pp.

Bigler, W.J., and G.L. Hoff. 1976. Urban wildlife and community health: Gray squirrels as environmental monitors. Proc. Ann. Conf. S.E. Assoc. Game Fish Comm. 30:536–540.

Bigler, W.J., E. Lassing, E. Buff, A.L. Lewis, and G.L. Hoff. 1975. Arbovirus surveillance in Florida: Wild vertebrate studies, 1965–1974. J. Wildl. Dis. 11:348–356.

Boardman, E.T. 1929. Ticks of the Gainesville area. M.S. thesis, Univ. of Florida, Gainesville. 57 pp.

Bond, B.B., and E.C. Bovee. 1957. A redescription of an eimerian coccidian from the flying squirrel *Glaucomys volans,* designating it *Eimeria parasciurorum* nov. sp. J. Protozool. 4:225–229.

Bozeman, F.M., S.A. Masiello, M.S. Williams, and B.L. Elisberg. 1975. Epidemic typhus rickettsiae isolated from flying squirrels. Nature (London) 255:545–547.

Brown, L.N. 1987. A checklist of Florida's mammals. Florida Game and Fresh Water Fish Commission, Tallahassee. 8 pp.

Burridge, M.J., L.A. Sawyer, and W.J. Bigler. 1986. Rabies in Florida. Department of Health and Rehabilitative Services, Tallahassee, Fla. 147 pp.

Burridge, M.J., W.J. Bigler, D.J. Forrester, and J.M. Hennemann. 1979. Serologic survey for *Toxoplasma gondii* in wild animals in Florida. J. Am. Vet. Med. Assoc. 175:964–967.

Chan, M.S., G.L. Hoff, W.J. Bigler, J.A. Tomas, and N.J. Schneider. 1976. Electrophoretic separation of serum proteins from gray squirrels. Am. J. Vet. Res. 37:1237–1239.

Clark, G.M. 1959. Parasites of the gray squirrel. In: Symposium on the gray squirrel. V. Flyger (ed.). Proc. Ann. Conf. S.E. Assoc. Game Fish Comm. 13:356–407.

Conti, J.A., D.J. Forrester, R.K. Frohlich, G.L. Hoff, and W.J. Bigler. 1984. Helminths of urban gray squirrels in Florida. J. Parasitol. 70:143–144.

Davidson, W.R. 1975. Endoparasites of selected populations of gray squirrels, *Sciurus carolinensis* (Gmelin). Ph.D. diss., Univ. of Georgia, Athens. 194 pp.

———. 1976. Endoparasites of selected populations of gray squirrels (*Sciurus carolinensis*) in the southeastern United States. Proc. Helminthol. Soc. Wash. 43:211–217.

Davidson, W.R., and J.P. Calpin. 1976. *Hepatozoon griseisciuri* infection in gray squirrels of the southeastern United States. J. Wildl. Dis. 12:72–76.

Davidson, W.R., and V.F. Nettles. 1988. Field manual of wildlife diseases in the southeastern United States. Southeastern Cooperative Wildlife Disease Study, Univ. of Georgia, Athens. 309 pp.

DeLamater, E.D. 1939. The squirrel as a new host to a ringworm fungus. Mycologia 31:519–526.

Doran, D.J. 1954a. A catalogue of the protozoa and helminths of North American rodents. I. Protozoa and Acanthocephala. Am. Midl. Nat. 52:118–128.

———. 1954b. A catalogue of the protozoa and helminths of North American rodents. II. Cestoda. Am. Midl. Nat. 52:469–480.

———. 1955a. A catalogue of the protozoa and helminths of North American rodents. III. Nematoda. Am. Midl. Nat. 53:162–175.

———. 1955b. A catalogue of the protozoa and helminths of North American rodents. IV. Trematoda. Am. Midl. Nat. 53:446–454.

Flyger, V., and J.E. Gates. 1982. Fox and gray squirrels. In: Wild mammals of North America. J.A. Chapman and G.A. Feldhamer (eds.). Johns Hopkins Univ. Press, Baltimore. pp. 209–229.

Forrester, D.J. 1974. Unpublished data. Univ. of Florida, Gainesville.

———. 1984. Unpublished data. Univ. of Florida, Gainesville.

———. 1987. Unpublished data. Univ. of Florida, Gainesville.

Forrester, D.J., J.D. Shamis, G.L. Hoff, and W.J. Bigler. 1977. Coccidia of urban gray squirrels in northern Florida. J. Parasitol. 63:1045.

Fuller, H.S. 1943. Studies on Siphonaptera of eastern North America. Bull. Brooklyn Entomol. Soc. 38:18–23.

Gainer, J.H. 1961. Studies on the natural and experimental infections of animals in Florida with the encephalomyocarditis virus. Proc. U.S. Livestock San. Assoc. 65:556–572.

———. 1967. Encephalomyocarditis virus infections in Florida, 1960–1966. J. Am. Vet. Med. Assoc. 151:421–425.

Gainer, J.H., and W.J. Bigler. 1967. Encephalomyocarditis (EMC) virus recovered from two cotton rats and a raccoon. J. Wildl. Dis. 3:47–49.

Gates, E.H., J.O. Bond, and A.L. Lewis. 1968. California group arbovirus encephalitis in Florida children. J. Fla. Med. Assoc. 55:37–40.

Harwood, R.F., and M.T. James. 1979. Entomology in human and animal health. 7th ed. Macmillan, New York. 548 pp.

Hoff, G.L., W.J. Bigler, and E.C. Prather. 1975. One-half century of tularemia in Florida. J. Fla. Med. Assoc. 62:35–37.

Hoff, G.L., W.J. Bigler, F.M. Wellings, and A.L. Lewis. 1980. Human enteroviruses and wildlife: Isolation from gray squirrels. J. Wildl. Dis. 16:131–133.

Hoff, G.L., E.B. Lassing, M.S. Chan, W.J. Bigler, and T.J. Doyle. 1976a. Hematologic values for free-ranging urban gray squirrels (*Sciurus c. carolinensis*). Am. J. Vet. Res. 37:99–101.

Hoff, G.L., L.E. McEldowny, W.J. Bigler, L.J. Kuhns, and J.A. Tomas. 1976b. Blood and urinary values in the gray squirrel. J. Wildl. Dis. 12:349–352.

Jenkins, J.H., and T.T. Fendley. 1968. The extent of contamination, detection, and health significance of high accumulations of radioactivity in southeastern game populations. Proc. Ann. Conf. S.E. Assoc. Game Fish Comm. 22:89–95.

Jenkins, J.H., A.H. Davis, W.J. Bigler, and G.J. Hoff. 1980. Mercury and cesium-137 in urban gray squirrels. Bull. Environ. Contam. Toxicol. 25:321–324.

Jennings, W.L., A.L. Lewis, G.E. Staher, W.M. Hammon, and J.O. Bond. 1968. California-encephalitis-group viruses in Florida rabbits: Report of experimental and sentinel studies. Am. J. Trop. Med. Hyg. 17:781–787.

Jennings, W.L., W.G. Winkler, D.D. Stamm, P.H. Coleman, and A.L. Lewis. 1969. Serologic studies of possible avian or mammalian reservoirs of St. Louis encephalitis virus in Florida. In: St. Louis encephalitis in Florida. Fla. State Board Health Monogr. Series, No. 12. Jacksonville. pp. 118–125.

Johnson, W., and C.L. Nayfield. 1970. Elevated

levels of cesium-137 in common mushrooms (Agaricaceae) with possible relationships to high levels of cesium-137 in white-tail deer, 1968–1969. Radiolog. Health Data Rep. 11:527–531.

Joseph, T. 1972. *Eimeria lancasterensis* Joseph, 1969 and *E. confusa* Joseph, 1969 from the grey squirrel (*Sciurus carolinensis*). J. Protozool. 19:143–150.

Karabatsos, N. 1985. International catalogue of arboviruses. 3d ed. Am. Soc. Trop. Med. Hyg., San Antonio, Tex. 1147 pp.

Katz, J.S. 1939. An annotated bibliography of references concerning parasites of squirrels. Ohio Wildl. Res. Sta. Release No. 131. Ohio State Univ., Columbus. 21 pp.

Kilham, L. 1955. Metastasizing viral fibroma of gray squirrels: Pathogenesis and mosquito transmission. Am. J. Hyg. 61:55–63.

Kim, K.C., H.D. Pratt, and C.J. Stojanovich. 1986. The sucking lice of North America. An illustrated manual for identification. Penn. State Press, University Park. 241 pp.

Kissling, R.E., J.M. Vanella, and M. Schaeffer. 1956. Recent isolations of encephalomyocarditis virus. Proc. Soc. Exp. Biol. Med. 91:148–150.

Layne, J.N. 1968. Host and ecological relationships of the parasitic helminth *Capillaria hepatica* in Florida mammals. Zoologica 53:107–122.

———. 1971. Fleas (Siphonaptera) of Florida. Fla. Entomol. 54:35–51.

———. 1987. Unpublished data from the files of Archbold Biological Station, Lake Placid, Fla.

Lewis, E., G.L. Hoff, W.J. Bigler, and M.B. Jefferies. 1975. Public health and the urban gray squirrel: Mycology. J. Wildl. Dis. 11:502–504.

McDade, J.E., 1987. Flying squirrels and their ectoparasites: Disseminators of epidemic typhus. Parasitol. Today 3:85–87.

McKeever, S., G.W. Gorman, and L. Norman. 1958a. Occurrence of a *Trypanosoma cruzi*-like organism in some mammals from southwestern Georgia and northwestern Florida. J. Parasitol. 44:583–587.

McKeever, S., J.H. Schubert, M.S. Moody, G.W. Gorman, and J.F. Chapman. 1958b. Natural occurrence of tularemia in marsupials, carnivores, lagomorphs and large rodents in southeastern Georgia and northwestern Florida. J. Infec. Dis. 103:120–126.

McKeever, S., W. Kaplan, and L. Ajello. 1958c. Ringworm fungi of large wild mammals in southwestern Georgia and northwestern Florida. Am. J. Vet. Res. 19:973–975.

McKeever, S., G.W. Gorman, J.F. Chapman, M.M. Galton, and D.K. Powers. 1958d. Incidence of leptospirosis in wild mammals from southwestern Georgia, with a report of new hosts for six serotypes of leptospires. Am. J. Trop. Med. Hyg. 7:646–655.

McKinnon, J.G., G.L. Hoff, W.J. Bigler, and E.C. Prather. 1976. Heavy metal concentrations in kidneys of urban gray squirrels. J. Wildl. Dis. 12:367–371.

Moore, J.C. 1957. The natural history of the fox squirrel, *Sciurus niger shermani*. Bull. Amer. Mus. Nat. Hist. 113:1–71.

Nally, L., G. Hoff, W. Bigler, and N. Schneider. 1978. Pesticide levels in the omental fat of urban gray squirrels. Bull. Environ. Contam. and Toxicol. 23:42–46.

Parker, J.C. 1971. Protozoan, helminth and arthropod parasites of the gray squirrel in southwestern Virginia. Ph.D. diss., Virginia Polytechnic Inst., Blacksburg. 262 pp.

Parker, J.C., E.J. Riggs, and R.B. Holliman. 1972. Notes on parasites of gray squirrels from Florida. Quart. J. Fla. Acad. Sci. 35:161–162.

Philip, R.N. 1980. Typhus-group rickettsiae. In: CRC handbook series in zoonoses. Section A: Bacterial, rickettsial and mycotic diseases. Vol. 2. J.H. Steele (ed.). CRC Press, Boca Raton, Fla. pp. 317–335.

Prather, E.C., W.J. Bigler, G.L. Hoff, and J.A. Tomas. 1975. Rabies in Florida. History, status, trends. Fla. Div. of Health Monogr. Series, No. 14. Jacksonville. 122 pp.

Rogers, A.J. 1953. A study of the ixodid ticks of northern Florida, including the biology and life history of *Ixodes scapularis* Say (Ixo-

didae: Acarina). Ph.D. diss., Univ. of Maryland, College Park. 191 pp.

Rohani, I.B., and H.L. Cromroy. 1979. Taxonomy and distribution of chiggers (Acarina: Trombiculidae) in northcentral Florida. Fla. Entomol. 62:363–376.

Sabrosky, C.W. 1986. North American species of *Cuterebra*, the rabbit and rodent bot flies (Diptera: Cuterebridae). Entomol. Soc. Am., College Park, Md. 240 pp.

Schwartz, A. 1952. The land mammals of southern Florida and the upper Florida Keys. Ph.D. diss., Univ. of Michigan, Ann Arbor.

Shotts, E.B., C.L. Andrews, and T.W. Harvey. 1975. Leptospirosis in selected wild mammals of the Florida panhandle and southwestern Georgia. J. Am. Vet. Med. Assoc. 167:587–589.

Stockbridge, D.L., and J.H. Jenkins. 1974. Bioaccumulation and seasonal fluctuation of cesium-137 in vegetation from the Waycross State Forest, Georgia. Bull. Ga. Acad. Sci. 32:37–47.

Taylor, D.J., A.L. Lewis, J.D. Edman, and W.L. Jennings. 1971. California group arboviruses in Florida—Host-vector relations. Am. J. Trop. Med. Hyg. 20:139–145.

Venters, H.D., and W.L. Jennings. 1962. Rabies in a flying squirrel. Pub. Health Rep. 77:200.

White, F.H., G.L. Hoff, W.J. Bigler, and E. Buff. 1975. A microbiologic study of the urban gray squirrel. J. Am. Vet. Med. Assoc. 167:603–604.

Williams, K.S., and S.R. Humphrey. 1979. Distribution and status of the endangered Big Cypress fox squirrel (*Sciurus niger avicenna*) in Florida. Fla. Scientist 42:201–205.

Wilson, N.A., S.R. Telford, Jr., and D.J. Forrester. 1991. Ecoparasites of a population of urban gray squirrels in northern Florida. J. Med. Entomol. 28:461–464.

Winkler, W.G. 1972. Rodent rabies in United States. J. Infect. Dis. 126:565–567.

Winkler, W.G., N.J. Schneider, and W.J. Jennings. 1972. Experimental rabies infection in wild rodents. J. Wildl. Dis. 8:99–103.

Wood, D.A. 1990. Official lists of endangered

and potentially endangered fauna and flora in Florida. Florida Game and Fresh Water Fish Commission, Tallahassee. 19 pp.

Worth, C.B. 1950. A preliminary host-ectoparasite register for some small mammals of Florida. J. Parasitol. 36:497–498.

Wright, T.J. 1987. Wildlife harvest and eco-nomic survey. Florida Game and Fresh Water Fish Commission, Tallahassee. P-R Report, W-33.

Yuill, T.M. 1981. Myxomatosis and fibromatosis. In: Infectious diseases of wild mammals. 2d ed. J.W. Davis et al. (eds.). Iowa State Univ. Press, Ames. pp. 154–177.

Pocket Gophers

I. Introduction

The southeastern pocket gopher (*Geomys pinetis* Rafinesque) is abundant in the panhandle and in most of the northern half of peninsular Florida (Stevenson 1976; Brown 1987). Four subspecies are recognized in Florida, one of which (*Geomys pinetis goffi,* Goff's pocket gopher) is listed as endangered by the Florida Game and Fresh Water Fish Commission (Wood 1990). The distribution of Goff's pocket gopher is very limited (Ehrhart 1978). It is found only in Brevard County (Melbourne) and, according to Humphrey (1981) and Humphrey et al. (1987), the subspecies may be extinct.

Pocket gophers are exclusively North American and are among the most highly specialized of all rodents (Lowery 1974). They spend most of their life underground in burrows and are rarely seen. The conspicuous mounds thrown up during construction of their burrows, however, indicate their presence. Local people in Florida often refer to these animals as "salamanders." Several bibliographies and reviews on the parasites of pocket gophers have been prepared (Doran 1954; Doran 1955; Chase et al. 1982; Teipner et al. 1983). The majority of the citations are concerned with arthropods and of those, most deal with biting lice. Very little has been done on the southeastern pocket gopher outside of several reports on parasites.

II. Rabies

One gopher was examined in 1983 and found to be negative for rabies (Burridge et al. 1986). Like other rodents, gophers are most likely of no importance in the epidemiology of rabies in Florida.

III. Helminths

In his study on *Capillaria hepatica,* Layne (1968) examined nine southeastern pocket gophers (one from Alachua County, one from Gilchrist County, two from Highlands County, four from Levy County, and one from St. Johns County). All were negative. A spirurid nematode, *Mastophorus muris* (= *Protospirura ascaroidea*), has been reported from the stomach of southeastern pocket gophers in Alachua and Lake counties (Ross 1976; Hubbell and Goff 1940). Ross (1976) studied seasonal variations in intensities of

infection by this worm and found almost no parasites in gophers during the summer (Figure 8-1). In the fall and winter there was an increase in intensities, with some animals carrying up to 10% of their body weight in stomach worms. He also noted that mortality in the population he studied in Alachua County was greatest during late fall and winter. This mortality was associated with low temperatures and declines in available nutrients and water. *Mastophorus muris* cycles through fleas and cockroaches as intermediate hosts (Miyata 1939) and is common in other rodents in Florida such as cotton rats and rice rats (Kinsella 1974, 1988).

IV. Arthropods

Thirteen species of parasitic arthropods have been reported from the southeastern pocket gopher in Florida and include two ticks, eight

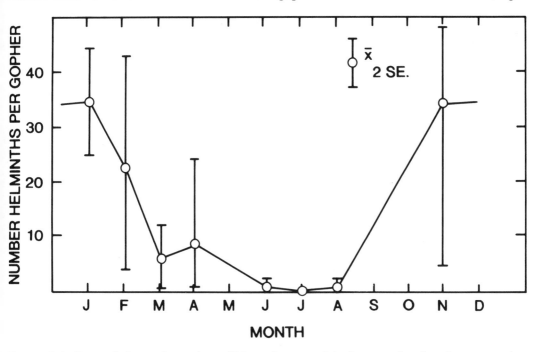

FIGURE 8-1. Seasonal changes in numbers of *Mastophorus muris* in the stomachs of southeastern pocket gophers in Alachua County. (Adapted from Ross 1976.)

mites, two biting lice, and one flea (Table 8-1). One of these records, that of the biting louse, *Geomydoecus scleritus,* from Goff's pocket gopher (Price 1975) is of interest since this subspecies of gopher may now be extinct. The record of the sticktight flea (*Echidnophaga gallinacea*) is curious in that this flea is primarily a parasite of birds or their predators. The presence of this flea on pocket gophers is difficult to explain, although a number of other rodents have been found infested in Florida (Layne 1971).

V. Summary and conclusions

Information on parasites and diseases of the southeastern pocket gopher in Florida is lim-

Table 8-1

Arthropod parasites reported from southeastern pocket gophers in Florida

Arthropod	Location (county)	Data source
Ticks		
Amblyomma americanum	NG[a]	Clifford et al. (1961)
Amblyomma sp.[b]	Alachua	Hubbell & Goff (1940)
Mites		
Geomylichus floridanus	Wakulla, Suwannee, Leon, Hamilton, Alachua	Radford (1949), Fain & Hyland (1974)
Haemolaelaps glasgowi	Alachua	FSCA[c]
Haemolaelaps geomys	NG	Strandtmann (1949)
Haemolaelaps sp.	Alachua[d]	FSCA
	Hillsborough	Worth (1950)
Androlaelaps fahrenholzi	Alachua	FSCA
Laelaptid	Alachua	"
Macrochilid	Alachua[d]	"
Parasitid	Alachua[d]	"
Biting lice		
Geomydoecus scleritus[e]	Lake, Jackson	Hubbell & Goff (1940)[f]
	Highlands	FSCA
	Orange	FSCA, Price (1975)
	Hillsborough	Worth (1950), Price & Timm (1979), Price (1975)
	Pinellas, Putnam, Marion, Duval, Lafayette, Suwannee, Leon, Alachua, Madison, Wakulla, Brevard	Price (1975)
Geomydoecus mobilensis	Walton, Escambia, Washington	" "
Fleas		
Echidnophaga gallinacea	Hillsborough	Worth (1950)

[a]NG = not given by authors.
[b]All specimens were nymphs.
[c]FSCA = records from the Florida State Collection of Arthropods, Division of Plant Industry, Florida Department of Agriculture, Gainesville, Fla.
[d]Specimens collected from burrows of the southeastern pocket gopher.
[e]This species was described by McGregor (1917) from numerous specimens collected from gophers in Florida, but no localities were given.
[f]Hubbell and Goff (1940) reported finding *Geomydoecus geomydis* on pocket gophers from Lake and Jackson counties. These most probably were *G. scleritus.*

ited to a small amount of data on 1 nematode and 13 arthropods. These parasites are believed to have little significance to public health and apparently do not cause adverse effects on populations of pocket gophers (Howard and Childs 1959; Brown 1971; Teipner et al. 1983). Nothing is known about the effects of environmental contaminants, viruses, bacteria, or protozoans on southeastern pocket gophers in Florida.

VI. Literature cited

Brown, L.N. 1971. Breeding biology of the pocket gopher (*Geomys pinetis*) in southern Florida. Am. Midl. Nat. 85:45–53.

———. 1987. A checklist of Florida's mammals. Florida Game and Fresh Water Fish Commission, Tallahassee. 6 pp.

Burridge, M.J., L.A. Sawyer, and W.J. Bigler. 1986. Rabies in Florida. Department of Health and Rehabilitative Services, Tallahassee, Fla. 147 pp.

Chase, J.D., W.E. Howard, and J.T. Roseberry. 1982. Pocket gophers. Geomyidae. In: Wild mammals of North America. J.A. Chapman and G.A. Feldhamer (eds.). Johns Hopkins Univ. Press, Baltimore. pp. 239–255.

Clifford, C.M., G. Anastos, and A. Elbe. 1961. The larval ixodid ticks of the eastern United States (Acarina-Ixodidae). Misc. Publ. Entomol. Soc. Am. 2:213–237.

Doran, D.J. 1954. A catalogue of the protozoa and helminths of North American rodents. II. Cestoda. Am. Midl. Nat. 52:469–480.

———. 1955. A catalogue of the protozoa and helminths of North American rodents. III. Nematoda. Am. Midl. Nat. 53:162–175.

Ehrhart, L.M. 1978. Goff's pocket gopher. In: Rare and endangered biota of Florida. Vol. 1. Mammals. J.N. Layne (ed.). Univ. Presses of Florida, Gainesville. pp. 6–7.

Fain, A., and K. Hyland. 1974. The listrophoroid mites in North America. II. The family Listrophoridae Megnin and Trouessart (Acarina: Sarcoptiformes). Bull. K. Belg. Inst. Nat. Wet. 50:1–69.

Howard, W.E., and H.E. Childs. 1959. Ecology of pocket gophers with emphasis on *Thomomys bottae mewa*. Hilgardia. 29:277–358.

Hubbell, T.H., and C.C. Goff. 1940. Florida pocket gopher burrows and their arthropod inhabitants. Proc. Fla. Acad. Sci. 4:127–166.

Humphrey, S.R. 1981. Goff's pocket gopher (*Geomys pinetis goffi*) is extinct. Fla. Sci. 44:250–252.

Humphrey, S.R., W.H. Kern, Jr., and M.S. Ludlow. 1987. Status survey of seven Florida mammals. Fla. Coop. Fish and Wildl. Res. Unit Tech. Rep. No. 25. 39 pp.

Kinsella, J.M. 1974. Comparison of helminth parasites of the cotton rat, *Sigmodon hispidus*, from several habitats in Florida. Am. Mus. Nov. 2540:1–12.

———. 1988. Comparison of helminths of rice rats, *Oryzomys palustris*, from freshwater and saltwater marshes in Florida. Proc. Helminthol. Soc. Wash. 55:275–280.

Layne, J.N. 1968. Host and ecological relationships of the parasitic helminth *Capillaria hepatica* in Florida mammals. Zoologica. 53:107–122.

———. 1971. Fleas (Siphonaptera) of Florida. Fla. Entomol. 54:35–51.

Lowery, G.W., Jr. 1974. The mammals of Louisiana and its adjacent waters. Louisiana State Univ. Press, Baton Rouge. 565 pp.

McGregor, E.A. 1917. Six new species of Mallophaga from North American mammals. Ann. Ent. Soc. Amer. 10:167–175.

Miyata, I. 1939. Studies on the life history of the nematode *Protospirura muris* (Gmelin) parasitic in the stomach of the rat, especially on the relation of the intermediate hosts, cockroaches, skin moth and rat fleas. Vol. Jub. Yoshida 1:101–136.

Price, R.D. 1975. The *Geomydoecus* (Mallophaga: Trichodectidae) of the southeastern USA pocket gophers (Rodentia: Geomyidae). Proc. Ent. Soc. Wash. 77:61–65.

Price, R.D., and R.M. Timm. 1979. Description of the male of *Geomydoecus scleritus* (Mallophaga: Trichodectidae) from the southeastern pocket gopher. J. Ga. Entomol. Soc. 14:162–165.

Radford, C.D. 1949. New parasitic mites (Acarina: Myialgesidae and Listrophoridae). Proc. Zool. Soc. London 118:933–937.

Ross, J.P. 1976. Seasonal energy budgets of a fossorial rodent *Geomys pinetis*. Ph.D. diss., Univ. of Florida, Gainesville. 153 pp.

Stevenson, H.M. 1976. Vertebrates of Florida. Identification and distribution. Univ. Presses of Florida, Gainesville. 607 pp.

Strandtmann, R.W. 1949. The blood-sucking mites of the genus *Haemolaelaps* (Acarina: Laelaptidae) in the United States. J. Parasitol. 35:325–352.

Teipner, C.L., E.O. Garton, and L. Nelson, Jr. 1983. Pocket gophers in forest ecosystems. USDA Forest Service Gen. Tech. Rep. INT-154. 53 pp.

Wood, D.A. 1990. Official lists of endangered and potentially endangered fauna and flora in Florida. Florida Game and Fresh Water Fish Commission, Tallahassee. 19 pp.

Worth, C.B. 1950. A preliminary host-ectoparasite register for some small mammals of Florida. J. Parasitol. 36:497–498.

Old World Rats and Mice

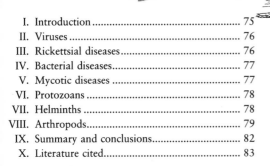

I. Introduction

Three species of Old World or murid rodents occur throughout Florida: the black or roof rat, *Rattus rattus* (L.), the Norway rat, *Rattus norvegicus* (Berkenhout), and the house mouse, *Mus musculus* L. (Brown 1987). All three of these species were introduced into North America by man and his activities. The roof rat and house mouse were introduced first by explorers and colonists. The Norway rat came later (about 1775) and has outcompeted and displaced the roof rat in many areas (Jackson 1982). The Norway rat, however, is much less common and more restricted in distribution than the roof rat. Of the three species of murids, the roof rat is most often encountered in natural habitats, although the house mouse may be common locally in areas distant from development (Layne 1988). These three species are of considerable economic importance. They are responsible for crop damage and the destruction and spoilage of food and stored grain, and harbor a number of zoonotic diseases (Lowery 1974; Jackson 1982). "On a worldwide basis the damage caused by Norway and roof rats alone amounts to billions of dollars, and they are responsible for inestimable human misery" (Lowery 1974, p. 280). Rat-borne diseases such as murine typhus, bubonic plague, leptospirosis, and rat bite fever have caused the loss of more human lives than all the wars and revolutions in recorded history (Lowery 1974). Because of their close association with man and his food and buildings, the murids are often referred to as commensals (Smith et al. 1957; Jackson 1982), which means "sharing the table." On the positive side, the white mutant of the Norway rat has made valuable contributions to the welfare of mankind in that, as a laboratory animal, it has been extremely useful in research laboratories throughout the world. Advancements in many fields of biology and medicine have been possible because of this animal (Lowery 1974).

Brief reviews of the parasites and diseases of murids have been provided by Lowery (1974) and Jackson (1982). Doran (1954a, b, 1955a, b) published a comprehensive catalogue of the protozoans and helminths of rodents in North America. Although these latter lists are now more than 35 years old, they are still of value and provide a good introduction to the older literature.

II. Viruses

Rabies is not common in rodents (Beran 1981; Burridge et al. 1986) and has not been diagnosed in commensal rodents in the United States (Jackson 1982). From 1957 to 1983 over 8,000 rats and mice were examined in Florida for rabies virus (Burridge et al. 1986). All were negative. The species of rats and mice were not given, but it is assumed that many of them were Rattus and Mus. Both house mice and Norway rats are susceptible to rabies as shown by experimental infections (World Health Organization 1973; Winkler et al. 1972), but appear to play no role in the epizootiology of rabies in nature (Beran 1981).

Serum samples from house mice, roof rats, and Norway rats were examined for the presence of antibodies to a number of arboviruses, including all or some of the following: St. Louis encephalitis (SLE) virus, eastern equine encephalomyelitis (EEE) virus, Everglades virus (strains Fe3-7C and TC-83 of the endemic strains of Venezuelan equine encephalomyelitis [VEE] virus), Keystone virus, and Tensaw (TEN) virus (Bigler 1969, 1971; Bigler and McLean 1973; Bigler et al. 1975). These studies took place between 1965 and 1974 and included animals from 38 of Florida's 67 counties. The numbers of rats and mice tested varied from 75 to 108 for each virus. None of the 108 samples from house mice was positive. The only positive samples from Rattus were for roof rats, where 9 of 98 animals were positive for antibodies to Everglades virus (Bigler et al. 1975). The exact locations of these positive animals were not given in the 1975 paper, but in another publication (Bigler 1969) it was stated that 5 of 40 roof rats from Dade County were seropositive for Everglades virus. This virus is probably of little or no significance to murid populations, but along with other species of rodents these Old World rats may be important as reservoirs for this zoonotic virus (Bigler and McLean 1973).

III. Rickettsial diseases

Murine typhus is a rickettsial disease of man caused by Rickettsia typhi (Philip 1980). Commensal rats of the genus Rattus are the primary reservoir host and the oriental rat flea (Xenopsylla cheopis) is the principal vector. Although the disease is seldom fatal (Philip 1980), it is prevalent. In the United States 42,000 cases were reported during 1931–1946 (Harwood and James 1979). Symptoms in man include chills, headache, fever, and rashes. Even though large doses can be lethal for rats and smaller doses cause fever, there is little or no effect on natural populations of rats (Philip 1980).

During the 1940s there was an increase in the number of cases of typhus in the Southeast, including Florida (Philip 1980). This resulted in a flurry of research activity, largely centered around Tampa Bay, which involved serologic studies of wild and commensal rodents and evaluations of their ectoparasites as vectors (Rickard 1951; Rickard and Worth 1951; Worth 1950a–d; Worth and Rickard 1951). In 1948–1949 commensal rats (roof rats and Norway rats) were examined serologically in Hillsborough County and 119 of 729 (16.3%) were positive (Rickard and Worth 1951). Other studies have confirmed that rats of the genus *Rattus* are important reservoirs for murine typhus and that house mice and various species of sylvatic rodents (such as cotton rats and deer mice) are not involved (Traub et al. 1978).

In the 1940s measures undertaken to control murine typhus in the United States were directed at the flea vector and the rat host. Results were spectacularly successful and were due to the use of insecticides, trapping and killing rats, and improving sanitation to prevent build-up of disease potentials (Philip 1980). For additional information on murine typhus, the reader is referred to the thorough review by Traub et al. (1978).

mice in the epizootiology of leptospirosis in Florida is not known.

Hoff et al. (1975) examined 47 house mice, 54 roof rats, and 9 Norway rats for serologic evidence of infection by *Francisella tularensis*, the etiologic agent of tularemia. All were negative.

In 1920, 10 human cases of plague were diagnosed in Pensacola (Escambia County); of these, 7 were fatal (Link 1955). This outbreak stimulated widespread trapping operations and other measures to control roof rats and Norway rats, which serve as reservoir hosts. Over 35,000 rats and mice were examined and fleas from 36 of these were found infected with the plague bacillus (*Yersinia pestis*). The species of fleas involved as vectors were not given by Link (1955), but probably included *Xenopsylla cheopis*, which has been shown to be the most efficient biological vector of plague (Olsen 1981) and is common on roof rats, Norway rats, and house mice in Florida (Tables 9-3 to 9-6). This outbreak of plague was believed to be caused by infected rats being brought into the seaport on ships. The control measures taken were successful in Pensacola, and the disease was eliminated from the area. No further outbreaks of plague have occurred in Florida.

White (1988) cultured the contents of the large intestines of two house mice and two roof rats from Dade County in 1975. No pathogenic bacteria were found.

IV. Bacterial diseases

Shotts et al. (1975) isolated *Leptospira interrogans* serovar *ballum* from a house mouse in the Florida panhandle or in southwestern Georgia. Only one house mouse was examined in that study and the exact locality was not given. Other wild animals are important reservoirs of *ballum* and the role of house

V. Mycotic diseases

We have no information on mycotic diseases of murid rats and mice in Florida. However, two reports from southwestern Georgia are relevant. In one study (Smith et al. 1957) 5 of 84 roof rats and 15 of 350 Norway rats were positive for *Trichophyton mentagrophytes* and 2 of 350 Norway rats were positive for *Microsporum gypseum*. In another study 243 house mice were examined; 1 was positive for *Trichophyton mentagrophytes* and 2 for *Microsporum gypseum* (McKeever et al. 1958). Both species of fungus also infect man.

VI. Protozoans

Only one protozoan has been reported from murids in Florida. Burridge et al. (1979) reported antibodies to *Toxoplasma gondii* in 5 of 38 roof rats, 2 of 8 Norway rats, and none

of 16 house mice. Although these findings are of public health importance, their significance to the rodents concerned is not known.

VII. Helminths

Eight species of helminths have been found in wild murid rodents in Florida (Table 9-1). Layne (1970) found *Capillaria hepatica* in 9 of 109 (8%) roof rats from Highlands County. Most of the infections were "light" in intensity, and the author felt that roof rats do not normally become severely infected.

Table 9-1
Helminths reported from wild murid rodents in Florida

Helminth	No. animals		Intensity		Date	Location (county)	Data source
	Exam.	Inf.	Mean	Range			
Roof rats							
Zonorchis komareki	4	1	15	—	1972	Highlands	Kinsella (1988)
Raillietina sp.	4	1	3	—	1972	Highlands	" "
Taenia taeniaeformis (larvae)	NG[a]	1	NG	NG	NG	Pinellas	Penner (1987)
Capillaria hepatica	109	9	"Light"		1968–69	Highlands	Layne (1970)
	2	0	—	—	1957–64	Alachua	Layne (1968)
	2	0	—	—	1957–64	Duval	" "
	2	0	—	—	1957–64	Monroe	" "
	12	0	—	—	1957–64	Pinellas	" "
Nippostrongylus brasiliensis	4	4	1	—	1972	Highlands	Kinsella (1988)
Physaloptera hispida	4	2	12	10–13	1972	Highlands	" "
	218	88	8	1–67	1974–75	Palm Beach	Forrester & Telford (1990)
Acanthocephala[b]	4	1	1	—	1972	Highlands	Kinsella (1988)
Norway rats							
Capillaria hepatica	1	0	—	—	1957–64	Duval	Layne (1968)
House mice							
Capillaria hepatica	303	0	—	—	1957–64	Alachua	" "
	3	0	—	—	1957–64	Highlands	" "
	19	0	—	—	1957–64	Lee	" "
	3	0	—	—	1957–64	Okaloosa	" "
Syphacia obvelata	1	1	10	—	1972	Highlands	Kinsella (1988)

[a]NG = not given by author.
[b]Unidentified larval stage.

Capillaria hepatica is of public health concern, and a number of cases have been recognized in children, several of which were fatal (Zimmermann 1975). Such infections have been linked to Old World rats (*Rattus* spp.) in areas of low socioeconomic status. The life cycle of *C. hepatica* is discussed in Chapter 10. Infections in children are believed to be due to ingestion of soil containing embryonated eggs (Zimmermann 1975). The importance of this zoonotic problem in Florida is unknown.

No further information is available on the helminths of Florida murids, although studies in various parts of North America have resulted in reports of numerous species of cestodes, trematodes, nematodes, and acanthocephalans (Doran 1954a, b; 1955a, b; Lowery 1974).

VIII. Arthropods

Because of the importance of various ectoparasites as vectors of a number of zoonotic diseases, the arthropod parasites of commensal rodents in Florida have been studied fairly well. Thirty-four species of arthropods have been reported from roof rats, Norway rats, and house mice. These include 3 species of ticks, 16 mites, 8 fleas, 4 sucking lice, and 3 bots (Table 9-2). The roof rat has 28 (Table 9-3), the Norway rat has 18 (Table 9-4), and the house mouse has 8 (Table 9-5) different species of parasitic arthropods.

Two extensive studies on the ectoparasites of commensal rodents have been conducted in Florida. One was in Jacksonville in 1934 (Rumreich and Wynn 1945) and one in Tampa in 1948–1949 (Worth 1950c). Both studies were stimulated by the need to obtain data on these ectoparasites in relation to their role as vectors of murine typhus and bubonic plague.

In the Jacksonville study 89% of 5,245 roof

Table 9-2

Number of species of arthropods reported from commensal rats and mice in Florida

Arthropod group	Roof rats	Norway rats	House mice	All 3 rodents
Ticks	3	0	0	3
Mites	11	8	5	16
Fleas	8	7	3	8
Sucking lice	3	3	0	4
Bots	3	0	0	3
Totals	28	18	8	34

rats and Norway rats had ectoparasites. These consisted of 15 species: 6 were fleas, 6 were mites, and 3 were sucking lice. Fleas were most common and occurred on 83% of the rats. Eight of the species of ectoparasites made up most of the arthropod fauna (Table 9-6).

The Tampa study resulted in the finding of 19 species of arthropods from roof rats and only 8 from Norway rats. Even though fewer species were found in Norway rats, they contained more individual ectoparasites than did roof rats (Table 9-7). Worth (1950c) felt that these observations could be explained by the fact that Norway rats were restricted to a more limited habitat, which led to fewer species being obtained from other rodents. In addition, the burrowing activities of Norway rats may have resulted in higher ectoparasite populations due to the favorable conditions for arthropods in the burrows. Roof rats had a more rural distribution and this resulted in the acquisition of a number of parasites from other wild mammals. A good example was the presence of *Haemaphysalis leporispalustris* on roof rats. This tick is normally a parasite of rabbits.

Several of the ectoparasites of commensal rodents are of importance because they serve as vectors and/or intermediate hosts of other parasites or disease agents that infect man or other animals. *Xenopsylla cheopis,* for exam-

Table 9-3
Arthropods reported from roof rats in Florida

Species of arthropod	Location (county)	Data source
Ticks		
Dermacentor variabilis	Hillsborough	Worth (1950a,b,c)
	Monroe/Dade	Worth (1950a)
Amblyomma maculatum	Hillsborough	Worth (1950a,b,c)
Haemaphysalis leporispalustris	Hillsborough	" "
Mites		
Ornithonyssus bacoti	Hillsborough	Worth (1950c)
	Duval	Rumreich & Wynn (1945)
	Monroe/Dade	Worth (1950a)
Radfordia ensifera	Hillsborough	Worth (1950b,c)
Cheyletus eruditus	Hillsborough	" "
Eutrombicula batatas	Hillsborough	Worth (1950c)
	Monroe/Dade	Worth (1950a,b)
Laelaps nuttalli	Hillsborough	Worth (1950b,c)
Laelaps echidninus	Hillsborough	" "
	Duval	Rumreich & Wynn (1945)
Laelaps hawaiiensis	Duval	" " " "
Cosmolaelaps gurabensis	Monroe	Thurman et al. (1949)
	Hillsborough	Worth (1950b,c)
Gigantolaelaps cricetidarum	Dade	Morlan (1951)
Haemolaelaps glasgowi	Duval	Rumreich & Wynn (1945)
	Hillsborough	Worth (1950b)
Androlaelaps setosus	Duval	Rumreich & Wynn (1945)
	Hillsborough	Worth (1950b)
Fleas		
Echidnophaga gallinacea	Duval	Rumreich & Wynn (1945)
	Hillsborough	Worth (1950b,c)
Ctenocephalides felis	Duval[a]	Rumreich & Wynn (1945)
	Hillsborough	Worth (1950b,c)
Ctenocephalides canis	Santa Rosa[a,b]	Fox & Sullivan (1925)
Xenopsylla cheopis	Duval	Rumreich & Wynn (1945)
	Hillsborough	Worth (1950b,c)
	Leon	Fox (1940)
	Santa Rosa[a]	Fox & Sullivan (1925)
Orchopeas howardii	Leon	Fox (1940)
Polygenis gwyni	Duval[a]	Rumreich & Wynn (1945)
	Hillsborough	Worth (1950a,b,c)
	Highlands	Layne (1971)
Leptopsylla segnis	Duval	Rumreich & Wynn (1945)
	Hillsborough	Worth (1950b,c)
	Leon	Fox (1940)
	Santa Rosa[a]	Fox & Sullivan (1925)
Nosopsyllus fasciatus	Duval	Rumreich & Wynn (1945)
Sucking lice		
Neohaematopinus sciuri	Levy	FSCA[c]
Polyplax spinulosa	Levy, Pinellas	"
	Highlands	"
	Hillsborough	Worth (1950b,c)

(continued)

Table 9-3 (continued)

Species of arthropod	Location (county)	Data source
	Duval	Rumreich & Wynn (1945)
Hoplopleura hirsuta	Duval	" " " "
Bots		
Cuterebra americana	Hillsborough	Worth (1950b,c); Sabrosky (1986)
Cuterebra sp.	Monroe/Dade	Worth (1950a)
Dermatobia-like sp.	Monroe/Dade	Worth (1950a,b)

[a]Authors state that these records are from roof rats and/or Norway rats.
[b]Authors identify these fleas as *Ctenocephalides canis* or *C. felis*.
[c]FSCA = records from the Florida State Collection of Arthropods, Division of Plant Industry, Florida Department of Agriculture, Gainesville, Fla.

Table 9-4
Arthropods reported from Norway rats in Florida

Species of arthropod	Location (county)	Data source
Mites		
Alliea laruei	Hillsborough	Yunker (1960)
Ornithonyssus bacoti	Hillsborough	Worth (1950a,b,c)
	Duval	Rumreich & Wynn (1945)
Hypoaspis murinus	Duval	Strandtmann & Menzies (1948)
Laelaps nuttalli	Hillsborough	Worth (1950b,c)
Laelaps echidninus	Hillsborough	" "
	Duval	Rumreich & Wynn (1945)
Laelaps hawaiiensis	Duval	" " " "
Cosmolaelaps gurabensis	Escambia	Thurman et al. (1949)
Gigantolaelaps cricetidarum	Dade	Morlan (1951)
Fleas		
Echidnophaga gallinacea	Duval	Rumreich & Wynn (1945)
	Hillsborough	Worth (1950b,c)
Ctenocephalides felis	Duval[a]	Rumreich & Wynn (1945)
Ctenocephalides canis	Santa Rosa[a,b]	Fox & Sullivan (1925)
Xenopsylla cheopis	Duval	Fox (1940)
	Hillsborough	Worth (1950b,c)
	Santa Rosa[a]	Fox & Sullivan (1925)
Polygenis gwyni	Duval[a]	Rumreich & Wynn (1945)
	Hillsborough	Worth (1950a,b,c)
Nosopsyllus fasciatus	Duval	Fox (1940), Fox & Sullivan (1925)
	Santa Rosa[a]	Fox & Sullivan (1925)
Leptopsylla segnis	Brevard, Duval	Fox (1940), Fox & Sullivan (1925)
	Santa Rosa[a]	Fox & Sullivan (1925)
Sucking lice		
Polyplax spinulosa	Duval	Rumreich & Wynn (1945)
	Hillsborough	Worth (1950b,c)
Hoplopleura pacifica	Hillsborough	Worth (1950a,b,c)
	Duval	Pritchard (1947)
Hoplopleura hirsuta	Duval	Rumreich & Wynn (1945)

[a]Authors state that these records are from roof rats and/or Norway rats.
[b]Authors identified these fleas as *Ctenocephalides canis* or *C. felis*.

Table 9-5
Arthropods reported from house mice in Florida

Species of arthropod	Location (county)	Data source
Mites		
Ornithonyssus bacoti	Hillsborough	Worth (1950a,d)
Haemolaelaps glasgowi	Hillsborough	Worth (1950a)
Radfordia ensifera	Hillsborough	Worth (1950b)
Eutrombicula sp.	Hillsborough	" "
Listrophorus sp.	Hillsborough	" "
Fleas		
Echidnophaga gallinacea	Duval	Rumreich & Wynn (1945)
	Hillsborough	Worth (1950b)
Xenopsylla cheopis	Duval	Rumreich & Wynn (1945)
Leptopsylla segnis	Duval	" " " "
	Leon	Fox (1940)

Table 9-6
Composition by arthropod group of the most common ectoparasites collected from 5,245 roof rats and Norway rats in Jacksonville, 1934

Arthropod	% composition by arthropod group
Fleas (n = 30,353)	
Xenopsylla cheopis	58.1
Echidnophaga gallinacea	19.7
Leptopsylla segnis	18.9
Nosopsyllus fasciatus	2.0
Ctenocephalides felis	1.3
Mites (n = 3,695)	
Laelaps hawaiiensis	70.2
Echinolaelaps echidninus	17.0
Ornithonyssus bacoti	12.6
Sucking lice (n = 2,441)	
Polyplax spinulosa	63.9
Hoplopleura hirsuta	35.9

Source: Rumreich and Wynn (1945).

Table 9-7
Characteristics of ectoparasites recovered from commensal rodents in Tampa, 1948–49

Characteristic	Roof rats (n = 2,768)	Norway rats (n = 498)
No. species of ectoparasites	19	8
Mean no. fleas[a] per infested rat	4.2	6.4
Prevalence (%) (for fleas[a])	28	43

Source: Worth (1950).
[a]Includes data on all fleas. For roof rats this was for five species; for Norway rats it was for three species.

ple, was very common on all three species of commensal rodents and is a known vector of Yersinia pestis, the bubonic plague bacillus, and Rickettsia typhi, the etiologic agent of murine typhus (Harwood and James 1979). The cat and dog fleas (Ctenocephalides felis and C. canis) are intermediate hosts for the tapeworm Dipylidium caninum, which infects dogs, cats, and man. Several fleas (Xen-opsylla cheopis, Nosopsyllus fasciatus, and Ctenocephalides canis) serve as intermediate hosts of tapeworms of rats and mice, one of which (Hymenolepis nana) frequently infects children (Harwood and James 1979).

No information is available on the effects of arthropod parasites and the diseases they transmit on rodent populations in Florida.

IX. Summary and conclusions

Forty-six different disease agents and parasites have been identified from commensal rats and mice in Florida. These include 1 virus, 1 rickettsia, 1 bacterium, 1 protozoan, 8 helminths, 3 ticks, 16 mites, 8 fleas, 4 sucking lice, and 3 bots. The significance of these agents for populations of roof rats, Norway rats, and house mice is not known. Everglades virus, *Rickettsia typhi, Leptospira ballum, Toxoplasma gondii, Capillaria hepatica,* and a number of the ectoparasites, such as the flea *Xenopsylla cheopis,* are of public health importance. The arthropod parasites have been studied well because of their roles in transmission of zoonotic diseases.

X. Literature cited

Beran, G.W. 1981. Rabies and infections by rabies-related viruses. In: CRC handbook series in zoonoses. J.H. Steele (ed.). CRC Press, Boca Raton, Fla. pp. 57–135.

Bigler, W.J. 1969. Venezuelan encephalitis antibody studies in certain Florida wildlife. Bull. Wildl. Dis. Assoc. 5:267–270.

———. 1971. Serologic evidence of Venezuelan equine encephalitis virus infections in raccoons of south central Florida. J. Wildl. Dis. 7:166–170.

Bigler, W.J., and R.G. McLean. 1973. Wildlife as sentinels for Venezuelan equine encephalomyelitis. J. Am. Vet. Med. Assoc. 163:657–661.

Bigler, W.J., E. Lassing, E. Buff, A.L. Lewis, and G.L. Hoff. 1975. Arbovirus surveillance in Florida: Wild vertebrate studies. J. Wildl. Dis. 11:348–356.

Brown, L.N. 1987. A checklist of Florida's mammals. Florida Game and Fresh Water Fish Commission, Tallahassee. 8 pp.

Burridge, M.J., L.A. Sawyer, and W.J. Bigler. 1986. Rabies in Florida. Department of Health and Rehabilitative Services, Tallahassee, Fla. 147 pp.

Burridge, M.J., W.J. Bigler, D.J. Forrester, and J.M. Hennemann. 1979. Serologic survey for *Toxoplasma gondii* in wild animals in Florida. J. Am. Vet. Med. Assoc. 175:964–967.

Doran, D.J. 1954a. A catalogue of the protozoa and helminths of North American rodents.

I. Protozoa and Acanthocephala. Am. Midl. Nat. 52:118–128.

———. 1954b. A catalogue of the protozoa and helminths of North American rodents. II. Cestoda. Am. Midl. Nat. 52:469–480.

———. 1955a. A catalogue of the protozoa and helminths of North American rodents. III. Nematoda. Am. Midl. Nat. 53:162–175.

———. 1955b. A catalogue of the protozoa and helminths of North American rodents. IV. Trematoda. Am. Midl. Nat. 53:446–454.

Forrester, D.J., and S.R. Telford, Jr. 1990. Unpublished data. Univ. of Florida, Gainesville.

Fox, C., and E.C. Sullivan. 1925. A comparative study of rat-flea data for several seaports of the United States. Pub. Health Rep. 40:1909–1934.

Fox, I. 1940. Fleas of eastern United States. Iowa State Coll. Press, Ames. 191 pp.

Harwood, R.F., and M.T. James. 1979. Entomology in human and animal health. Macmillan, New York. 548 pp.

Hoff, G.L., W.J. Bigler, and E.C. Prather. 1975. One-half century of tularemia in Florida. J. Fla. Med. Assoc. 62:35–37.

Jackson, W.B. 1982. Norway rat and allies. *Rattus norvegicus* and allies. In: Wild mammals of North America. J.A. Chapman and G.A. Feldhamer (eds.). Johns Hopkins Univ. Press, Baltimore. pp. 688–703.

Kinsella, J.M. 1988. Unpublished data. Archbold Biological Station, Lake Placid, Fla.

Layne, J.N. 1968. Host and ecological relationships of the parasitic helminth *Capillaria hepatica* in Florida mammals. Zoologica 53:107–122.

———. 1970. New host records of *Capillaria hepatica* in Florida. Quart. J. Fla. Acad. Sci. 33:18–22.

———. 1971. Fleas (Siphonaptera) of Florida. Fla. Entomol. 54:35–51.

———. 1988. Unpublished data. Archbold Biological Station, Lake Placid, Fla.

Link, V.B. 1955. A history of plague in the United States of America. Pub. Health Monogr. No. 26. 120 pp.

Lowery, G.W., Jr. 1974. The mammals of Louisiana and its adjacent waters. Louisiana State Univ. Press, Baton Rouge. 565 pp.

McKeever, S., R.W. Menges, W. Kaplan, and L. Ajello. 1958. Ringworm fungi of feral rodents in southern Georgia. Am. J. Vet. Res. 19:969–972.

Morlan, H.B. 1951. Notes on the genus *Gigantolaelaps* and description of a new species, *Gigantolaelaps cricetidarum* (Acarina: Laelaptidae). J. Parasitol. 37:273–279.

Olsen, P.F. 1981. Sylvatic plague. In: Infectious diseases of wild mammals. 2d ed. J.W. Davis et al. (eds.). Iowa State Univ. Press, Ames. pp. 232–243.

Penner, L.R. 1987. Unpublished data. Archbold Biological Station, Lake Placid, Fla.

Philip, R.N. 1980. Typhus-group rickettsiae. In: CRC handbook series in zoonoses. Section A: Bacterial, rickettsial and mycotic diseases. Vol. 2. J.H. Steele (ed.). CRC Press, Boca Raton, Fla. pp. 317–335.

Prichard, A.E. 1947. *Hoplopleura oenomydis* Ferris, a louse found on domestic rats in the United States. J. Parasitol. 33:374–375.

Rickard, E.R. 1951. Postinfection murine typhus antibodies in the sera of rodents. Am. J. Hyg. 53:207–216.

Rickard, E.R., and C.B. Worth. 1951. Complement-fixation tests for murine typhus on the sera of wild-caught cotton rats in Florida. Am. J. Hyg. 53:332–336.

Rumreich, A.S., and R.S. Wynn. 1945. A study of the rodent-ectoparasite population of Jacksonville, Fla. Public Health Rep. 60:885–905.

Sabrosky, C.W. 1986. North American species of *Cuterebra*, the rabbit and rodent bot flies (Diptera: Cuterebridae). Entomol. Soc. Am., College Park, Md. 240 pp.

Shotts, E.B., C.L. Andrews, and T.W. Harvey. 1975. Leptospirosis in selected wild mammals of the Florida panhandle and southwestern Georgia. J. Am. Vet. Med. Assoc. 167:587–589.

Smith, W.W., R.W. Menges, and L.K. Georg. 1957. Ecology of ringworm fungi on commensal rats from rural premises in southwestern Georgia. Am. J. Trop. Med. Hyg. 6:81–85.

Strandtmann, R.W., and G.C. Menzies. 1948. A new species of mite, *Hypoaspis murinus*, frequently taken from *Rattus* spp. (Laelaptidae: Hyposaspinae). Ann. Entomol. Soc. Amer. 41:479–482.

Thurman, D.C., J.A. Mulrennan, and N. Branch. 1949. Description of the male of *Cosmolaelaps gurabensis* Fox (Acarina, Laelaptidae). J. Parasitol. 35:496–499.

Traub, R., C.L. Wisseman, Jr., and A. Farhang-Azad. 1978. The ecology of murine typhus—a critical review. Trop. Dis. Bull. 75:237–317.

White, F.H. 1988. Unpublished data. Univ. of Florida, Gainesville.

Winkler, W.G., N.J. Schneider, and W.L. Jennings. 1972. Experimental rabies infection in wild rodents. J. Wildl. Dis. 8:99–103.

World Health Organization. 1973. W.H.O. expert committee on rabies, 6th Rep. WHO, Geneva.

Worth, C.B. 1950a. Observations on ectoparasites of some small mammals in Everglades National Park and Hillsborough County, Florida. J. Parasitol. 36:326–335.

———. 1950b. A preliminary host-ectoparasite register for some small mammals of Florida. J. Parasitol. 36:497–498.

———. 1950c. Field and laboratory observations on roof rats, *Rattus rattus* (Linnaeus), in Florida. J. Mammal. 31:293–304.

———. 1950d. House mice and commensal rats in relation to the dissemination of rat fleas. Am. J. Trop. Med. 30:917–920.

Worth, C.B., and E.R. Rickard. 1951. Evaluation of efficiency of common cotton rat ectoparasites in the transmission of murine typhus. Am. J. Trop. Med. 31:295–298.

Yunker, C.E. 1960. *Alliea laruei*, n. gen., n. sp., (Acarina: Cheyletidae) from *Rattus norvegicus* (Erxleben) in Florida. Proc. Helminthol. Soc. Wash. 27:278–281.

Zimmermann, W.J. 1975. *Capillaria* and *Dioctyophyma* infection. In: Diseases transmitted from animals to man. 6th ed. W.T. Hubbert et al. (eds.). C.C. Thomas, Springfield, Ill. pp. 560–566.

New World Rats and Mice

I. Introduction

Eleven species of New World rats and mice occur in Florida. These include three microtines and eight sigmodontines (= cricetines) (Stevenson 1976; Woods et al. 1982). One of the microtines, the round-tailed muskrat (*Neofiber alleni* True), will be discussed separately in Chapter 11. No parasite/disease data are available on the other two microtines, the pine vole, *Microtus pinetorum* (LeConte), and Duke's saltmarsh vole, *Microtus pennsylvanicus dukecampbelli* Woods, Post, and Kilpatrick. Among the eight species of sigmodontines (Table 10-1), a number of subspecies are recognized, and many of these are listed as endangered, threatened, or species

of special concern, or are under study currently in order to determine their status (Wood 1990; Humphrey et al. 1987; Barbour and Humphrey 1982). Several may be extinct (Humphrey et al. 1987; Humphrey et al. 1988; Humphrey and Barbour 1981; Repenning and Humphrey 1986).

The parasite and disease literature on most of the rodents has been reviewed by Doran (1954a,b; 1955a,b) and Lowery (1974). Whitaker (1968) reviewed the literature on parasites of deer mice and Kinsella (1974a) provided a checklist of the helminths of cotton rats throughout their range. The diseases and parasites of a number of the species of

Table 10-1
Species of New World cricetid rodents that occur in Florida[a]

Common and scientific names	Range in Florida	Status
1. Eastern woodrat *Neotoma floridana* (Ord)	No. 2/3 and Key Largo	Common[b]
2. Hispid cotton rat *Sigmodon hispidus* Say and Ord	Statewide	Abundant[b]
3. Eastern harvest mouse *Reithrodontomys humulus* Audubon and Bachman	No. 2/3	Unknown
4. Marsh rice rat *Oryzomys palustris* (Harlan)	Statewide[c]	Common[b]
5. Florida mouse *Podomys floridanus*	No. 2/3[c]	Common[d]
6. Old-field mouse *Peromyscus polionotus* (Wagner)	No. 2/3	Common[b]
7. Cotton mouse *Peromyscus gossypinus* (LeConte)	Statewide	Abundant[b]
8. Golden mouse *Ochrotomys nuttalli* (Harlan)	No. 2/3	Common

Source: Brown (1987).
[a]Brown (1987) lists an additional species, the Key or silver rice rat (*Oryzomys argentatus*), but according to Humphrey and Setzer (1989), the taxonomic status of this species is questionable. There are no data on its diseases and parasites, and so it will not be discussed further.
[b]Contains one or more subspecies in Florida that are classified as endangered, threatened, species of special concern, or are under review for federal listing.
[c]Absent from the Florida Keys.
[d]Classified as a species of special concern by the Florida Game and Fresh Water Fish Commission (Wood 1990).

New World rats and mice in Florida have been studied and there is considerable information on arboviruses, helminths, and arthropods.

II. Viral diseases

As pointed out previously in Chapter 9 (Old World Rats and Mice), rodents are rarely infected with rabies virus and play an insignificant role in the epidemiology of rabies in Florida (Burridge et al. 1986). The response of cotton rats to infection with rabies virus was studied experimentally by Winkler et al. (1972). They found that 29 of 32 (91%) cotton rats inoculated with virus died of rabies,

but that none of the infected rats had rabies virus in their salivary glands.

In 1966 an outbreak of encephalomyocarditis (EMC) in domestic swine occurred near Winter Haven (Gainer et al. 1968). As a follow-up on that outbreak, two rice rats and six cotton rats were collected and sera were taken for neutralization tests and tissues for virus isolation (Gainer and Bigler 1967). None of the sera was positive, but EMC virus was isolated from two of the cotton rats. Virus was also isolated from one of two raccoons, and the authors speculated that raccoons may acquire EMC virus by ingestion of infected cotton rats (Gainer et al. 1968). There is no evidence that cotton rats are harmed by EMC virus, but they may serve as important reservoirs of the virus (Gaskin et al. 1980).

Twelve other viruses, including six arboviruses, have been reported from New World rats and mice in Florida (Tables 10-2 and 10-3). Four of these (Everglades, Tensaw, SLE, and EEE) are of public health significance in that human infections have been reported

Table 10-2
Prevalence of Everglades virus in New World rodents from Florida

Rodent	No. Exam.	Pos.[a]	Date	Location	Data source
Cotton mice	28	16	1963	Everglades Nat. Park	Chamberlain et al. (1964)
	72	22	1964–65	Everglades Nat. Park	Chamberlain et al. (1969)
	76	0	1961–63	Collier County	" " " "
	35	0	1968	"South Florida"	Bigler (1969)
	33	14	1968	East of Everglades N.P.	" "
	3	1	1969	Indian River County	Bigler (1971)
	6	0	1969–70	Suwannee County	" "
	117	1	1965–69	Big Cypress	Lord et al. (1973)
	208	107	1965–69	Everglades Nat. Park	" " " "
	186	18	1971	Monroe County	Bigler et al. (1974c)
	159	50	1972	Monroe County	" " " "
	248	34	1965–74	NG[b]	Bigler et al. (1975)
Totals	1,171	263 (23%)			
Cotton rats	16	3	1963	Everglades Nat. Park	Chamberlain et al. (1964)
	30	3	1964–65	Everglades Nat. Park	Chamberlain et al. (1969)
	22	0	1961–63	Collier County	" " " "
	306	2	1968	"South Florida"	Bigler (1969)
	61	3	1968	East of Everglades N.P.	" "
	59	3	1969	Indian River County	Bigler (1971)
	26	0	1969–70	Suwannee County	" "
	4	0	1969–70	Hillsborough County	" "
	174	0	1965–69	Big Cypress	Lord et al. (1973)
	130	63[c]	1965–69	Everglades Nat. Park	" " " "
	18	7	1971	Monroe County	Bigler et al. (1974c)
	33	7	1972	Monroe County	" " " "
	578	14	1965–74	NG	Bigler et al. (1975)
Totals	1,457	105 (7%)			
Rice rats	1	0	1964–65	Everglades Nat. Park	Chamberlain et al. (1969)
	45	1	1968	"South Florida"	Bigler (1969)
	54	2	1968	East of Everglades N.P.	" "
	6	0	1965–69	Big Cypress	Lord et al. (1973)
	7	2	1965–69	Everglades Nat. Park	" " " "
	7	0	1971–72	Monroe County	Bigler et al. (1974c)
	172	4	1965–74	NG	Bigler et al. (1975)
Totals	292	9 (3%)			

[a]All prevalence data are from serologic tests.
[b]NG = not given by authors.
[c]Virus was isolated from serum, brain, heart, lung, liver, kidney, spleen, salivary glands, mammary glands, ovary, muscle, and placenta of one of these cotton rats in 1967.

Table 10-3

Prevalence of arboviruses[a] and related viruses in New World rodents from Florida

Virus	Rodent	No. Exam.	No. Pos.[b]	Date	Location	Data source
EEE[c,d]	Cotton rats	578	1	1965–74	NG[f]	Bigler et al. (1975)
	Rice rats	172	0	1965–74	NG	" " " "
	Cotton mice	248	0	1965–74	NG	" " " "
Highlands J[d]	Cotton rats	497	1	1965–74	NG	" " " "
	Rice rats	124	0	1965–74	NG	" " " "
	Cotton mice	179	0	1965–74	NG	" " " "
Tamiami	Cotton rats	294	6 (6)	1975	Everglades Nat. Park	Calisher et al. (1970)
		114	40	1965–74	NG	Bigler et al. (1975)
		1,268[h]	29[h](29)[h]	1963–70	Hillsborough County	Jennings et al. (1970), Wellings et al. (1972)
	Rice rats	149	1 (1)	1963–70	Hillsborough County	Wellings et al. (1972)
		27	4	1965–74	NG	Bigler et al. (1975)
Gumbo Limbo	Cotton rats	22	2 (2)	1963–65	Everglades Nat. Park	Henderson et al. (1969)
		NG	1 (1)	1971	Monroe County	Bigler et al. (1974b)
Keystone[d]	Cotton rats	1,268	3 (3)	1963–70	Hillsborough County	Taylor et al. (1971), Wellings et al. (1972)
		534	1	1964–67	Hillsborough County	Jennings et al. (1968)
		114	3	1965–74	NG	Bigler et al. (1975)
Mahogany Hammock[e]	Cotton rats	22	1 (1)	1963–65	Everglades Nat. Park	Coleman et al. (1969)
Shark River[e]	Cotton rats	22	1 (1)	1963–65	Everglades Nat. Park	Fields et al. (1969)
Tensaw[d]	Cotton rats	356[h]	1[h](1)[h]	1963–70	Hillsborough County	Wellings et al. (1972), Calisher et al. (1986)
	Cotton mice	72	1 (1)	1964–65	Everglades Nat. Park	Chamberlain et al. (1969), Calisher et al. (1986)
Trivittatus[d]	Cotton rats	NG	NG	NG	NG	Karabatsos (1985)
		356[h]	1[h](1)[h]	1963–70	Hillsborough County	Wellings et al. (1972)
Cowbone Ridge[e]	Cotton rats	298	11 (1)	1965	Hendry/Collier County	Calisher et al. (1969), Karabatsos (1985)
	Rice rats	17	0	1965	Hendry/Collier County	Calisher et al. (1969), Karabatsos (1985)
	Cotton mice	210	1	1965	Hendry/Collier County	Calisher et al. (1969), Karabatsos (1985)
SLE[d,g]	Cotton rats	578	7	1965–74	NG	Bigler et al. (1975)
	Rice rats	172	1	1965–74	NG	" " " "
	Cotton mice	248	1	1965–74	NG	" " " "
		NG	1	1968	Dade County	" " " "

[a]Except for Everglades virus (see Table 10-2).
[b]All prevalence data are from serologic tests except virus isolations, which are given in parentheses following the number of animals positive serologically.
[c]EEE = eastern equine encephalomyelitis.
[d]Arboviruses.
[e]May be an arbovirus.
[f]NG = not given by authors.
[g]SLE = St. Louis encephalitis.
[h]356 of these cotton rats were "sentinels" from which one isolant came.

Table 10-4
Mycotic infections reported from New World rodents in southwestern Georgia

Rodent	No. exam.	No. pos. for		
		Trichophyton mentagrophytes	*Microsporum gypseum*	*Microsporum* (red)
Cotton rats	351	1	2	54
Eastern woodrats	7	0	0	2
Eastern harvest mice	24	0	2	1
Golden mice	1	0	0	0
Cotton mice	58	2	2	16
Old-field mice	311	13	6	10

Source: McKeever et al. (1958).

(Karabatsos 1985). With the exception of Everglades virus, the effects of these viruses on populations of native rodents in Florida are unknown. They are probably of little or no significance to native rodents.

The most common and best-studied arbovirus in Florida is Everglades virus, which is an endemic form of Venezuelan equine encephalomyelitis (VEE) virus (McConnell and Spertzel 1981). In contrast to epidemic strains of VEE virus, which do not occur in Florida, Everglades virus is not normally pathogenic for horses (Gibbs 1976). Bigler et al. (1974b) experimentally infected 18 cotton mice with Everglades virus. None of the mice developed clinical signs of involvement of the central nervous system. One animal died between the second and third day postinfection, and Everglades virus was isolated from tissue pools of liver, spleen, and kidney as well as heart and lung. The authors were not sure, however, if the animal died due to Everglades virus infection or if it was killed by its mother. Gibbs (1976) reported that cotton rats were not affected adversely by the virus.

Studies on the epidemiology of Everglades virus began in the early 1960s, when serologic evidence of infections in humans in southern Florida was published (Work 1964). A number of papers appeared during the 1960s and early 1970s (Table 10-2) that showed that Everglades virus was well established in native rodents in southern Florida. Infections were fairly common in cotton mice (23%

Table 10-5
Number of species of helminths reported from New World rats and mice in Florida

Rodent	Trematodes	Cestodes	Nematodes	Acanthocephalans	Total
Cotton rats	7	6	14	0	27
Rice rats	21	4	20	0	45
Florida mice	1	5	13	2	21
Cotton mice	2	4	9	2	17
Old-field mice	1	0	6	1	8
Golden mice	0	1	5	0	6
Woodrats	0	0	2	0	2
Harvest mice	0	0	0	0	0

Table 10-6
Prevalence and intensity of trematodes of cotton rats in Florida, 1970–73

| Trematode | No. rats | | Intensity | | Location |
	Exam.	Inf. (%)	Mean	Range	(county)
Microphallus basodactylophallus	46	0 (—)	—	—	Alachua
	18	5 (28)	8	1–25	St. Johns, Levy
	22	0 (—)	—	—	Highlands
Nudacotyle novicia	46	0 (—)	—	—	Alachua
	18	3 (17)	9	1–20	St. Johns, Levy
	22	0 (—)	—	—	Highlands
Gynaecotyla adunca	46	0 (—)	—	—	Alachua
	18	2 (11)	4	3–5	St. Johns, Levy
	22	0 (—)	—	—	Highlands
Probolocoryphe glandulosa	46	0 (—)	—	—	Alachua
	18	1 (6)	210	—	St. Johns, Levy
	22	0 (—)	—	—	Highlands
Maritrema sp.	46	0 (—)	—	—	Alachua
	18	1 (6)	37	—	St. Johns, Levy
	22	0 (—)	—	—	Highlands
Plagiorchis muris	46	0 (—)	—	—	Alachua
	18	1 (6)	1	—	St. Johns, Levy
	22	0 (—)	—	—	Highlands
Zonorchis komareki	46	0 (—)	—	—	Alachua
	18	0 (—)	—	—	St. Johns, Levy
	22	2 (9)	NG[a]	NG	Highlands

Source: Kinsella (1974a).
[a]NG = not given by author.

prevalence) and less common in cotton rats and rice rats (7% and 3%, respectively). Bigler and coworkers conducted an intensive study of the circulation of Everglades virus in populations of native rodents in Everglades hammocks (Bigler et al. 1974c). Special emphasis was placed on cotton mice, with secondary efforts on cotton rats. They found that the cotton mouse was a good animal for such a study since hemagglutination-inhibition and neutralizing antibodies to Everglades virus persisted for up to 11 months (Bigler et al. 1974a) and the mouse lived for 6 to 12 months and sometimes longer (Bigler et al. 1974c). They also found that there was an annual reintroduction and circulation of the virus in hammocks and that this resulted

in amplification of the virus in the rodents. The virus circulated at low concentrations during spring and early summer, when cotton rats and mice were at their highest population density. Subsequently there was a peak of virus activity (transmission and amplification) during summer and fall (July to October), when rodent populations were declining and were made up mostly of adults (Bigler et al. 1974c).

III. Rickettsial diseases

Murine typhus, as discussed in Chapter 9 (Old World rats and mice), has been reported as a disease of man in Florida. Roof rats and

Table 10-7
Prevalence and intensity of cestodes of cotton rats in Florida

Cestode	No. rats		Intensity			Location	Data Source
	Exam.	Inf. (%)	Mean	Range	Date	(county)	
Monoecocestus sigmodontis	46	30 (66)	6	1–18	1970–73	Alachua	Kinsella (1974a)
	18	6 (34)	5	1–15	1970–73	St. Johns, Levy	" "
	22	1 (5)	3	—	1970–73	Highlands	" "
	NG[a]	1 (—)	"Several"		1929	Dade	McIntosh (1935)
Raillietina bakeri	46	0 (—)	—	—	1970–73	Alachua	Kinsella (1974a)
	18	2 (11)	1	1–2	1970–73	St. Johns, Levy	" "
	22	2 (9)	3	3	1970–73	Highlands	" "
Raillietina sp.	46	0 (—)	—	—	1970–73	Alachua	" "
	18	0 (—)	—	—	1970–73	St. Johns, Levy	" "
	22	19 (86)	24	3–64	1970–73	Highlands	" "
Taenia mustelae (larvae)	142	0 (—)	—	—	1970–73	Alachua	" "
	34	0 (—)	—	—	1970–73	St. Johns, Levy	" "
	22	1 (5)	NG	NG	1970–73	Highlands	" "
Taenia taeniaeformis (larvae)	142	20 (14)	NG	NG	1970–73	Alachua	" "
	34	0 (—)	—	—	1970–73	St. Johns, Levy	" "
	22	0 (—)	NG	NG	1970–73	Highlands	" "
Taenia rileyi (larvae)	142	11 (8)	NG	NG	1970–73	Alachua	" "
	34	0 (—)	—	—	1970–73	St. Johns, Levy	" "
	22	1 (5)	NG	NG	1970–73	Highlands	" "

[a]NG = not given by authors.

Norway rats are involved as reservoir hosts and oriental rat fleas (*Xenopsylla cheopis*) are the most important vectors (Philip 1980). The role of New World rats and mice as reservoirs of this rickettsial disease has been of interest to public health officials for some time. Morlan et al. (1950) conducted a survey of 27 species of mammals (exclusive of *Rattus* spp.) in southwestern Georgia and found 1 of 25 rice rats, 5 of 235 cotton mice, 1 of 217 oldfield mice, and 23 of 841 cotton rats seropositive for murine typhus. A similar survey was undertaken in Florida with emphasis on the Tampa Bay area in 1948–1949. In that study 14.5% of more than 1,000 cotton rats were seropositive (Rickard and Worth 1951). For a number of reasons, however, the authors determined that these titers were nonspecific for *Rickettsia typhi* and concluded that the

cotton rat was not a natural reservoir of murine typhus (Rickard 1951; Rickard and Worth 1951). Because of this and other studies it has been determined that the only reservoir hosts in the southeastern United States are species of *Rattus* and that other findings such as those of Morlan et al. (1950) probably are not of concern (Traub et al. 1978).

IV. Bacterial diseases

Two bacterial diseases have been identified in native rodents in Florida: leptospirosis and tularemia.

Layne (1963) reported that urine samples and kidneys of four Florida mice from sand pine scrub habitat in north-central Florida

Table 10-8

Prevalence and intensity of nematodes of cotton rats in Florida

Nematode	No. rats Exam.	Inf. (%)	Intensity Mean	Range	Date	Location (county)	Data source
Trichostrongylus	46	40 (86)	57	1–625	1970–72	Alachua	Kinsella (1974a)
sigmodontis	NG[a]	NG	NG	NG	1954	Lee	USNM Helm. Coll. (54802)
	18	12 (67)	13	1–88	1970–73	St. Johns, Levy	Kinsella (1974a)
	22	4 (8)	15	1–48	1970–73	Highlands	" "
Hassalstrongylus aduncus[b]	46	37 (81)	55	1–325	1970–73	Alachua	" "
	18	18 (100)	75	6–240	1970–73	St. Johns, Levy	" "
	22	13 (59)	14	1–55	1970–73	Highlands	" "
Trichostrongylus affinis	46	35 (77)	19	1–65	1970–73	Alachua	" "
	18	6 (34)	5	1–11	1970–73	St. Johns, Levy	" "
	22	3 (14)	2	1–3	1970–73	Highlands	" "
Strongyloides sigmodontis	46	29 (64)	42	1–277	1970–73	Alachua	" "
	18	3 (17)	7	3–10	1970–73	St. Johns, Levy	" "
	22	3 (14)	2	1–2	1970–73	Highlands	" "
	6	6[c](100)	NG	NG	NG	Sarasota	Melvin & Chandler (1950)
Litomosoides carinii	46	24 (53)	16	1–69	1970–73	Alachua	Kinsella (1974a)
	18	6 (34)	44	31–50	1970–73	St. Johns, Levy	" "
	22	22 (100)	35	1–135	1970–73	Highlands	" "
	NG	NG (43)	NG	NG	NG	Several[d]	Williams (1948)
	207	72 (35)	10	1–126	1970–71	Alachua	Forrester & Kinsella (1973)
	28	9 (32)	10	1–43	1970–71	Levy	Forrester & Kinsella (1973)
Mastophorus muris	46	13 (28)	2	1–4	1970–73	Alachua	Kinsella (1974a)
	18	7 (39)	5	1–17	1970–73	St. Johns, Levy	" "
	22	11 (50)	12	1–25	1970–73	Highlands	" "
	314	1 (<1)	51	—	1974–75	Palm Beach	Forrester & Telford (1990)
Physaloptera hispida	46	2 (4)	1	1	1970–73	Alachua	Kinsella (1974a)
	18	0 (—)	—	—	1970–73	St. Johns, Levy	" "
	22	11 (50)	10	1–28	1970–73	Highlands	" "
	NG	NG (20)[e]	NG	NG	NG	Sarasota	Schell (1950)
	314	128 (41)	10	1–93	1974–75	Palm Beach	Forrester & Telford (1990)
Physaloptera getula	NG	NG	NG	NG	NG	"Florida"	Morgan (1943)
Physocephalus sexalatus	46	0 (—)	—	—	1970–73	Alachua	Kinsella (1974a)
	18	0 (—)	—	—	1970–73	St. Johns, Levy	" "
	22	1 (5)	4	—	1970–73	Highlands	" "
	NG	1 (NG)	"Several"		NG	Sarasota	Melvin & Chandler (1950)
Gongylonema sp.	46	0 (—)	—	—	1970–73	Alachua	Kinsella (1974a)
	18	0 (—)	—	—	1970–73	St. Johns, Levy	" "
	22	5 (23)	6	1–15	1970–73	Highlands	" "
	NG	1 (NG)	2	—	NG	Sarasota	Melvin & Chandler (1950)

(continued)

Table 10-8 (continued)

Nematode	No. rats Exam.	No. rats Inf. (%)	Intensity Mean	Intensity Range	Date	Location (county)	Data source
Pterygodermatites ondatrae	46	0 (—)	—	—	1970–73	Alachua	Kinsella (1974a)
	18	1 (6)	15	—	1970–73	St. Johns, Levy	" "
	22	0 (—)	—	—	1970–73	Highlands	" "
Syphacia sigmodontis	46	1 (2)	1	—	1970–73	Alachua	" "
	18	4 (22)[f]	84	2–150	1970–73	St. Johns, Levy	" "
	22	0 (—)	—	—	1970–73	Highlands	" "
Monodontus floridanus	NG	1 (NG)	5	—	1929	Dade	McIntosh (1935)
Capillaria hepatica	142	43 (30)	NG	NG	1970–73	Alachua	Kinsella (1974a)
	34	4 (12)	NG	NG	1970–73	St. Johns, Levy	" "
	22	1 (5)	NG	NG	1970–73	Highlands	" "
	427	45 (11)	NG	NG	1957–64	Several[g]	Layne (1968)
	107	4 (4)	NG	NG	1968–69	Highlands	Layne (1970)

[a]NG = not given.
[b]Specimens from cotton rats from Alachua County were used to redescribe this species (see Durette-Desset 1972).
[c]Specimens from these cotton rats were used to describe the species *Strongyloides sigmodontis* (see Melvin and Chandler 1950).
[d]Includes Manatee, Sarasota, DeSoto, Charlotte, Lee, and Collier counties.
[e]Specimens from these cotton rats were used to describe the species *Physaloptera hispida* (see Schell 1950).
[f]Specimens from these cotton rats were used to describe the species *Syphacia sigmodontis* (see Quentin and Kinsella 1972).
[g]Cotton rats came from Alachua, Brevard, Escambia, Highlands, Lee, Levy, Pinellas, St. Johns, and Walton counties. Infected rats were found only in Highlands and Levy counties.

were cultured for leptospires. All were negative. White (1988) cultured the kidneys of 23 rice rats and 21 cotton rats from Alachua County in 1972 and 11 rice rats, 3 cotton rats, and 3 cotton mice from Dade County in 1975. All were negative for leptospires. Shotts et al. (1975), however, cultured *Leptospira interrogans* serovar *ballum* from three of nine cotton rats, and one of nine cotton mice in the Florida panhandle and southwestern Georgia. None of these animals, however, was seropositive for leptospires. Serovar *ballum* has been reported also from feral house mice (Shotts et al. 1975).

In a serological survey Hoff et al. (1975) reported 3 of 359 cotton rats, 2 of 153 cotton mice, and 1 of 3 old-field mice positive for agglutinins to *Francisella tularensis*. None of 85 rice rats and 2 woodrats was positive.

White (1988) cultured the intestines of 23 rice rats and 21 cotton rats from Alachua County (1972) and 11 rice rats, 7 cotton rats, and 3 cotton mice from Dade County (1975). All were negative for such enteric pathogens as *Salmonella* spp. and *Edwardsiella tarda*.

The significance of these findings to native wild rodents is unknown, but they are of importance from a public health standpoint.

Lyme disease is a recently recognized human illness caused by a spirochete (*Borrelia burgdorferi*) that is transmitted by ixodid ticks. In the United States the disease is found mainly in the coastal areas of the Northeast, in the Midwest, and in California, Nevada, and Oregon (Schmid 1984), although several cases have been documented in Florida recently (Conti and Calder 1989). The illness

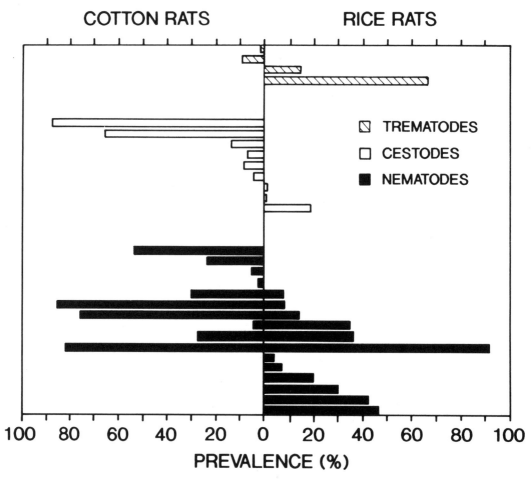

FIGURE 10-1. Comparison of the species of helminths in cotton rats and rice rats in Florida. (Data from Kinsella 1974a, 1988.)

in man is characterized by skin rashes, arthritis, and in some cases neurologic and cardiac abnormalities (Steere et al. 1984). In addition to humans, the disease has been found also in dogs, horses, and cattle (see review in Wright 1987). Rodents have been shown to be important in maintaining the spirochete in endemic areas. In the Northeast, for instance, the white-footed mouse (*Peromyscus leucopus*) is the main reservoir host for the spirochete and the tick *Ixodes dammini* serves as a vector (Donahue et al. 1987; Levine et al. 1985). The ticks and

rodents involved in the epidemiology of this disease in Florida have not been determined. Both cotton rats and *Ixodes scapularis* have been shown experimentally to serve as reservoir hosts and vectors, respectively (Burgdorfer and Gage 1987a, b), and since both are also common and widespread in Florida, they could be important components of the disease cycle in this area. This topic should be further investigated, including studies of other species of Florida rodents and ticks, in order to understand the ecology of this zoonotic disease.

Table 10-9

Prevalence and intensity of trematodes and cestodes of rice rats from freshwater and saltwater marshes in Florida, 1970–72

	Alachua County (freshwater marshes) n = 178				Levy County (saltwater marshes) n = 110[a]			
	Prevalence		Intensity		Prevalence		Intensity	
Helminth	No. inf.	(%)	Mean	Range	No. inf.	(%)	Mean	Range
Trematodes								
Microphallus basodactylophallus	0	0	—	—	103	94	*[b]	*
Microphallus nicolli	0	0	—	—	10	9	*	*
Microphallus sp.	0	0	—	—	11	10	*	*
Maritrema sp. I	0	0	—	—	76	69	*	*
Maritrema sp. II	0	0	—	—	21	19	*	*
Maritrema prosthrometra	0	0	—	—	6	5	*	*
Probolocoryphe glandulosa	0	0	—	—	61	56	*	*
Gynaecotyla adunca	0	0	—	—	17	15	*	*
Levinseniella sp.	0	0	—	—	54	49	*	*
Odhneria odhneri	0	0	—	—	7	6	*	*
Ascocotyle angrense	0	0	—	—	28	25	*	*
Ascocotyle mollenesicola	0	0	—	—	10	9	*	*
Stictodora cursitans	0	0	—	—	57[c]	52	36	(1–100)
Parvatrema sp.	0	0	—	—	29	26	*	*
Lyperosomum intermedium	0	0	—	—	50[d]	45	20	(1–50)
Zonorchis komareki	0	0	—	—	1	1	1	(1)
Echinochasmus schwartzi	0	0	—	—	21	19	4	(1–15)
Catatropis johnstoni	0	0	—	—	33	30	91	(1–500)
Urotrema scabridum	0	0	—	—	25	23	8	(1–25)
Brachylaeme virginianum	27	15	5	(1–23)	0	0	—	—
Fibricola lucida	119	67	143	(1–1975)	12	11	17	(1–65)
Cestodes								
Hymenolepis diminuta	34	19	4	(1–15)	1	1	1	(1)
Taenia rileyi (larvae)[e]	0	0	—	—	1	1	2	(2)
Taenia mustelae (larvae)	1	0.5	NC[f]	NC	0	0	—	—
Cladotaenia circi	1	0.5	NC	NC	1	1	NC	NC

Source: Kinsella (1988).
[a]Prevalence and intensity data for *Catatropis johnstoni* in 91 of these rats are given in Bush and Kinsella (1972).
[b]Asterisk indicates that individual counts of microphallids, heterophyids, and gymnophallids were not made. Total numbers ranged from 40 to 30,000 per rat (mean, 4,050).
[c]Specimens from these rice rats were used to describe the adult form of the species *Stictodora cursitans* (see Kinsella and Heard 1974).
[d]Specimens from these rice rats were used to describe the species *Lyperosomum intermedium* (see Denton and Kinsella 1972).
[e]One larva of *T. rileyi* was also reported from a rice rat from Hillsborough County in 1974 (Rausch 1981).
[f]NC = not counted.

V. Mycotic diseases

There is no published information on mycotic diseases of native rodents in Florida, but McKeever et al. (1958) reported on such diseases in southwestern Georgia. They identified infections of *Trichophyton mentagrophytes, Microsporum gypseum,* and a red

Table 10-10

Prevalence and intensity of nematodes of rice rats in freshwater and saltwater marshes in Florida, 1970–72

Nematode	Alachua County (freshwater marshes) n = 178				Levy County (saltwater marshes) n = 110			
	Prevalence		Intensity		Prevalence		Intensity	
	No. inf.	(%)	Mean	Range	No. inf.	(%)	Mean	Range
Capillaria hepatica[a]	14	8	—	—	7	6	—	—
Capillaria gastrica	7	4	1	1–2	7	6	4	1–10
Capillaria forresteri	82[b]	46	10	1–50	1[b]	1	1	1
Strongyloides sp.	53	30	4	1–30	0	0	—	—
Monodontus sp.	0	0	—	—	1	1	1	1
Hassalstrongylus spp.[c]	164	92	99	1–515	10	9	11	1–75
Trichostrongylus sigmodontis	14	8	4	1–15	3	3	2	1–4
Trichostrongylus affinis	25	14	3	1–14	7	6	7	1–19
Parastrongylus schmidti	12[d]	7	4	1–20	3[d]	3	3	1–8
Syphacia oryzomyos	75[e]	42	34	1–275	0	0	—	—
Physaloptera hispida	62	35	14	1–92	0	0	—	—
Physaloptera sp.	0	0	—	—	4	4	2	1–2
Mastophorus muris	64	36	6	1–70	1	1	1	1
Pterygodermatites spp.[f]	36	20	3	1–9	6	5	3	1–12
Skrjabinoclava thapari	0	0	—	—	31	28	4	1–10
Larval spirurid	0	0	—	—	6	5	2	1–5
Litomosoides scotti	0	0	—	—	63[g]	57	12	1–104

Source: Kinsella (1988).

[a]Layne (1968) examined 32 rice rats from Alachua, Highlands, Lee, and Levy counties. All were negative for *Capillaria hepatica*.

[b]Specimens from these rice rats were used to describe the species *Capillaria forresteri* (see Kinsella and Pence 1987). This species was found also in rice rats from Highlands County (Kinsella and Pence 1987).

[c]A complex of three species (*H. musculi, H. forresteri,* and *H. lichtenfelsi*). The females cannot be distinguished, so data were combined. All three species were described from specimens obtained from a rice rat from Lake Istokpoga (Highlands County).

[d]Specimens from these rice rats were used to describe the species *Angiostrongylus schmidti* (see Kinsella 1971). This species was later referred to the genus *Parastrongylus* (see Ubelaker 1986).

[e]Specimens from these rats were used to describe the species *Syphacia oryzomyos* (see Quentin and Kinsella 1972).

[f]Two species are represented: *P. ondatrae* and *Pterygodermatites* sp. Females of these two species cannot be differentiated, so data were combined.

[g]Specimens from these rice rats were used to describe the species *Litomosoides scotti* (see Forrester and Kinsella 1973).

Microsporum from a number of species of sigmodontine rodents examined between 1954 and 1956 (Table 10-4). In the absence of signs of infection by these fungi, the authors speculated that the rodents were serving as carriers of the spores or fungal elements picked up from the environment. Both *T. mentagrophytes* and *M. gypseum* cause ringworm in man and other animals and therefore are of zoonotic concern.

VI. Protozoans

Several species of protozoans have been found in native rodents in Florida and include coccidia, amoebae, and trichomonads. *Eimeria kinsellai* was reported from a rice rat from Paynes Prairie (Alachua County) by Barnard et al. (1971). Oocysts of two species of *Eimeria* were found in the feces of a Florida mouse from Alachua County (Milstrey and

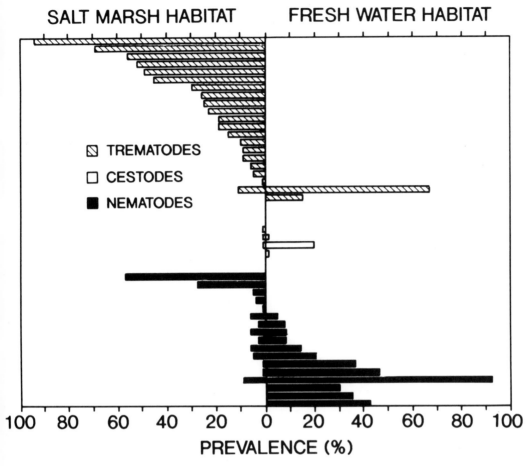

FIGURE 10-2. Comparison of the species of helminths in rice rats from saltmarsh and freshwater habitats in Florida. (Data from Kinsella 1988.)

Greiner 1987), and oocysts of a species of *Eimeria* were reported from feces of 6 of 10 Florida mice from north-central Florida (Layne 1963). Oocysts of a species of *Eimeria* were found in feces from two Eastern woodrats from Putnam County in 1989 and 1990; another woodrat (same locality in 1990) had oocysts of *Isopora* sp. in its feces (Forrester and HaySmith 1989, HaySmith 1991).

In a serosurvey of *Toxoplasma gondii* in wild animals in Florida, Burridge et al. (1979) examined a number of native rodents. Nine of 193 cotton rats, 3 of 62 rice rats, and 1 of

83 cotton mice were seropositive. No antibodies were detected in one woodrat and one old-field mouse. The importance of *Toxoplasma* infections to these rodents is not known, but these findings are significant from a public health standpoint since toxoplasmosis is a serious threat to humans.

Layne (1963) reported infections of *Entamoeba muris*, *Trichomonas muris*, and *Giardia muris* from 2, 17, and 12 of 28 Florida mice examined in north-central Florida. Blood smears from 10 of the above mice were examined for parasites. All were negative.

Table 10-11
Prevalence and intensity of helminths of the Florida mouse

Helminth	No. mice		Intensity		Date	Location (county)	Data source
	Exam.	Inf. (%)	Mean	Range			
Trematodes							
Dicrocoelidae[a]	723	51 (7)	NG[b]	NG	1957–60	Several[c]	Layne (1963)
Cestodes							
Hymenolepis nana	186	9 (5)	3	1–11	1957–60	Several	" "
	102	3 (3)	1	1–2	1972–73	Highlands	Kinsella (1987a)
Raillietina bakeri	102	8 (8)	3	1–7	1972–73	Highlands	" "
Cladotaenia sp. or *Paruterina* sp.[d]	> 700	1 (1)	NG	NG	1957–60	Several	Layne (1963)
Taenia rileyi[d]	> 700	2 (2)	NG	NG	1957–60	Several	" "
Taenia mustelae[d]	102	4 (4)	NG	NG	1972–73	Highlands	Kinsella (1987a)
Nematodes							
Carolinensis peromysci	102	48 (47)	6	1–48	1972–73	Highlands	Kinsella (1987a); Durette-Desset (1974)
Pterygodermatites coloradensis	186	17 (9)	6	2–14	1957–60	Several	Layne (1963)
Pterygodermatites peromysci	NG	NG (—)	NG	NG	1959–60	Levy	Lichtenfels (1970, 1987)
	102	9 (9)	1	1	1972–73	Highlands	Kinsella (1987a)
Trichostrongylus ransomi	186	1 (<1)	1	1	1957–60	Several	Layne, 1963
Trichostrongylus calcaratus	102	2 (2)	1	1	1972–73	Highlands	Kinsella (1987a)
Trichostrongylus affinis	102	2 (2)	1	1	1972–73	Highlands	" "
Capillaria hepatica	723	21 (3)	NG	NG	1956–59	Several	Layne & Griffo (1961)
	1,312[e]	202[e](15)	NG	NG	1957–64	Several	Layne (1968)
	105	66 (63)	NG	NG	1968–69	Highlands	Layne (1970)
	102	61 (60)	NG	NG	1972–73	Highlands	Kinsella (1987a)
Mastophorus numidica	102	1 (1)	3	3	1972–73	Highlands	" "
Physaloptera hispida	102	3 (3)	1	1	1972–73	Highlands	" "
Gongylonema sp.	102	15 (15)	2	1–5	1972–73	Highlands	" "
Syphacia peromysci	102	6 (6)	103	11–250	1972–73	Highlands	" "
Aspicularis americana	102	28 (28)	6	1–15	1972–73	Highlands	" "
Litomosoides carinii	102	4 (4)	3	1–7	1972–73	Highlands	" "
Acanthocephalans							
Moniliformis clarki	102	1 (1)	1	1	1972–73	Highlands	" "
Macracanthorhynchus ingens (larva)	102	1 (1)	1	1	1972–73	Highlands	" "

[a]Identified via eggs in liver tissue.
[b]NG = not given by authors.
[c]Includes Highlands, Levy, and St. Johns counties.
[d]Cysticerci only.
[e]These mice include the ones cited by Layne & Griffo (1961).

Table 10-12
Prevalence and intensity of helminths of cotton mice in Florida

Helminth	No. mice		Intensity		Date	Location (county)	Data source
	Exam.	Inf. (%)	Mean	Range			
Trematodes							
Zonorchis komareki	86	25 (29)	4	1–11	1972–73	Highlands	Kinsella (1974a, 1987a)
Fibricola lucida	86	2 (2)	2	1–3	1972–73	Highlands	Kinsella (1987a)
Cestodes							
Hymenolepis nana	86	5 (6)	2	1–5	1972–73	Highlands	"
Taenia rileyi (larvae)	86	3 (4)	2	1–3	1972–73	Highlands	"
Taenia mustelae (larvae)	NG[a]	NG	NG	NG	NG	Levy	"
Spirometra mansonoides (larvae)	NG	NG	NG	NG	1936	Wakulla	McIntosh (1937)
Nematodes							
Capillaria hepatica	107	3 (3)	NG	NG	1968–69	Highlands	Layne (1970)
	86	6 (7)	NG	NG	1972–73	Highlands	Kinsella (1987a)
Carolinensis peromysci	86	70 (81)	17	1–130	1972–73	Highlands	"
Trichostrongylus affinis	86	1 (1)	1	1	1972–73	Highlands	"
Mastophorus numidica	86	1 (1)	140	140	1972–73	Highland	"
Physaloptera hispida	86	5 (6)	6	1–25	1972–73	Highlands	"
Gongylonema sp.	86	12 (14)	2	1–5	1972–73	Highlands	"
Pterygodermatites peromysci	86	11 (13)	2	1–3	1972–73	Highlands	"
Syphacia peromysci	86	9 (11)	25	1–104	1972–73	Highlands	"
Aspicularis americana	86	2 (2)	1	1	1972–73	Highlands	"
Acanthocephalans							
Moniliformis clarki	86	12 (14)	2	1–6	1972–73	Highlands	"
Macracanthorhynchus ingens (larva)	86	2 (2)	1	1	1972–73	Highlands	"

[a]NG = not given by authors.

VII. Helminths

Information is available on the helminths of seven species of New World rats and mice in Florida. Of those the best-studied are cotton rats, rice rats, and Florida mice (Table 10-5). There is no information on the helminths of harvest mice. The lack of reports on helminths in harvest mice does not mean that they are free of helminths, but rather that they have not been examined.

The helminths of cotton rats have been studied well in Florida and in other parts of the southeastern United States (Kinsella 1974a). A total of 7 trematodes (Table 10-6), 6 cestodes (Table 10-7), and 14 nematodes (Table 10-8) is known from cotton rats in Florida. In the study by Kinsella (1974a) cotton rats from freshwater marshes, saltwater marshes, and upland habitats were sampled. The cotton rat appears to be the primary host of six species of nematodes and two cestodes. Other species of helminths were found also in squirrels, rabbits, deer mice, and rice rats. In Figure 10-1 the species of helminths in cotton rats and rice rats in Florida are compared.

In another study during 1970–72 Kinsella (1988) compared the helminths of rice rats from freshwater and saltwater marshes in Florida. A total of 45 species of helminths was found (Tables 10-9 and 10-10). Rice rats from saltwater marshes had more species (40) than those from freshwater marshes (20) (Figure 10-2). This was due to the large numbers of microphallid and heterophyid trematodes infecting rice rats from saltmarsh habitats. A number of the helminths are specific for rice rats and include *Lyperosomum intermedium*, *Parastrongylus schmidti*, *Syphacia oryzomyos*, *Capillaria forresteri*, and *Litomosoides scotti*. These latter species were described from material obtained from rice rats in Florida and have not been found in other hosts. Other helminths are found in additional hosts such as clapper rails, cotton rats, round-tailed muskrats, cotton mice, marsh rabbits, opossums, and raccoons.

The nature and diversity of the helminth fauna of rice rats are most likely reflections

Table 10-13
Prevalence and intensity of helminths from 41 old-field mice from Highlands County, Florida, 1972–73

Helminth	No. mice		Intensity	
	Inf.	(%)	Mean	Range
Trematodes				
Zonorchis komareki	1	(2)	1	1
Nematodes				
Carolinensis peromysci	11	(27)	6	1–20
Trichostrongylus affinis	2	(5)	1	1–2
Physaloptera hispida	2	(4)	1	1
Gongylonema sp.	4	(10)	2	1–3
Pterygodermatites peromysci	14	(34)	3	1–12
Syphacia peromysci	16	(39)	19	1–127
Acanthocephalans				
Moniliformis clarki	1	(2)	2	2

Source: Kinsella (1987a).

Table 10-14
Prevalence and intensity of helminths in 18 golden mice from
Highlands County, Florida, 1972–73

Helminth	Mice inf.		Intensity[a]	
	No.	(%)	Mean	Range
Cestodes				
Raillietina bakeri	9	(50)	3	1–5
Nematodes				
Carolinensis peromysci	12	(67)	4	1–13
Physaloptera hispida	3	(17)	4	1–8
Gongylonema sp.	2	(11)	4	3, 5
Syphacia peromysci	2	(11)	5	1, 9
Litomosoides carinii	1	(6)	1	1

Source: Kinsella (1987a).
[a]Intensity = number of helminths per infected animal.

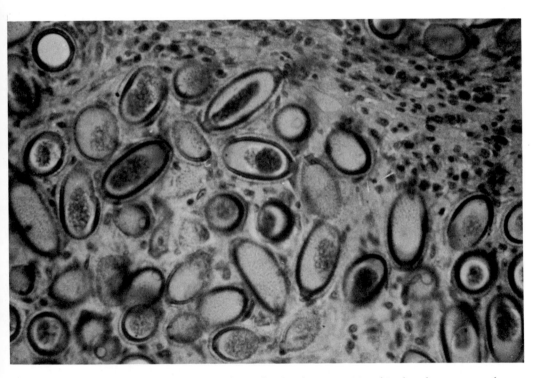

FIGURE 10-3. Eggs of *Capillaria hepatica* in liver of a Florida mouse. Note bipolar plugs on several eggs. (From Layne 1968.)

of the omnivorous food habits of this rodent (Kinsella and Pence 1987). The life cycles of several of the helminths have been studied. The morphology and life cycle of *Stictodora* *cursitans* were investigated by Kinsella and Heard (1974). Intermediate hosts were killifishes (*Fundulus confluentis, F. similis,* and *F. grandis*). *Catatropis johnstoni* also was found

Table 10-15
Number of species of parasitic arthropods reported from New World rats and mice in Florida

Rodent	No. species					
	Ticks	Mites	Sucking lice	Fleas	Botflies	Total
Cotton rat	5	13	2	6	0	26
Rice rat	4	8	1	1	0	14
Florida mouse	5	9	1	5	1	21
Cotton mouse	4	6	0	4	1	15
Old-field mouse	0	0	0	2	0	2
Golden mouse	2	0	0	0	0	2
Woodrat	5	1	0	3	1	10
Harvest mouse	0	0	0	1	0	1

to use the snail *Cerithidea scalariformis* as an intermediate host (Bush and Kinsella 1972). Experimental life cycle studies were conducted on *Parastrongylus schmidti* and *Litomosoides scotti* by Kinsella (1987b) and Forrester and Kinsella (1973), although natural intermediate hosts or vectors were not determined. A number of microphallids were found to use fiddler crabs, blue crabs, and stone crabs as intermediate hosts (Kinsella 1988).

The helminths of Florida mice include 1 trematode, 5 cestodes, 13 nematodes, and 2 acanthocephalans (Table 10-11). Layne (1963) conducted an ecological study of the helminths of Florida mice and examined over 800 animals in 1957–60 from 35 localities, most of which were in the northern half of peninsular Florida. He concluded that factors influencing the patterns of distribution of the parasites of Florida mice were age composition and density of the host population, habitat, and season. He also concluded that parasitism was not a major factor in the regulation of population sizes of Florida mice.

The helminths of cotton mice, old-field mice, and golden mice have received less attention in Florida, but several surveys have been done. These are summarized in Tables

10-12, 10-13, and 10-14. Nothing is known about the effects of these helminths on rodent populations.

One Eastern woodrat from the Ordway Preserve in Putnam County was examined for helminths in 1989. This was an adult male that had infections by two helminths, *Capillaria hepatica* (in the liver) and *Longistriata neotoma* (in the small intestine; 495 specimens) (Forrester and HaySmith 1989; HaySmith 1991). No other information is available on helminths of woodrats in Florida.

Capillaria hepatica is the most extensively studied helminth of rodents in Florida. This is largely due to the efforts of Layne, who has published several papers on the distribution of this nematode (Layne 1968, 1970; Layne and Griffo 1961). This parasite occurs as an adult in the liver of mammals and has a cosmopolitan distribution (Layne 1968). Although rodents are the main hosts, it also occurs in primates (including man; see Chapter 9), lagomorphs, carnivores, and artiodactylids. The adult female of this species lays eggs in the liver (Figure 10-3). These eggs embryonate and infection of the next host occurs when these eggs are ingested. Most investigators believe that the infected liver must be eaten; the eggs then pass out of that

Table 10-16
Arthropod parasites reported from cotton rats in Florida

Species of arthropod	Location (county)	Data source
Ticks		
Dermacentor variabilis	Brevard, Levy, Indian River	FSCA[a]
	"Northern Florida"	Rogers (1953)
	Indian River	Wilson & Kale (1972)
	Orange, Osceola, Collier	Travis (1941)
	NG[b]	Clifford et al. (1961)
	Monroe/Dade	Worth (1950a, 1951)
	Hillsborough	Worth (1950a,b)
Ixodes minor	Levy	FSCA
	Indian River	Wilson & Kale (1972)
Ixodes scapularis	"Northern Florida"	Rogers (1953)
	NG	Williams (1948)
Ixodes sp.	Monroe/Dade	Worth (1950a)
Amblyomma maculatum	Hillsborough	Worth (1950a,b)
Mites		
Haemolaelaps glasgowi	Monroe/Dade	Worth (1950a,b; 1951)
	Alachua	FSCA
Laelaps sp.	Monroe/Dade, Hillsborough	Worth (1950b)
Androlaelaps fahrenholzi	Alachua	FSCA
Atricholaelaps sigmondoni	Monroe/Dade	Williams (1948)
Ornithonyssus bacoti	Monroe/Dade, Hillsborough	Worth (1950a,b)
	Monroe/Dade	Worth (1951)
	NG	Williams (1948)
Eutrombicula splendens	Monroe/Dade, Hillsborough	Worth (1950a,b)
	Hendry	Ewing (1943)
Eutrombicula multisetosa	Monroe/Dade	Worth (1950a,b)
	Lee	Ewing (1943); Rohani & Cromroy (1979)
Eutrombicula sp.	Monroe/Dade	Worth (1951)
Trombiculid	Brevard	FSCA
Tyrophagus sp.	Brevard	"
Parasitid	Alachua	"
Prolistrophorus bakeri	Lee, Leon, Pinellas, Wakulla	Fain & Hyland (1974)
Listrophorid	Monroe/Dade, Hillsborough	Worth (1950a,b); Worth (1951)
Sucking lice		
Hoplopleura hirsuta	Monroe/Dade, Hillsborough	" " " "
	Alachua, Brevard, Levy	FSCA
Polyplax spinulosa	NG	Williams (1948)
Fleas		
Polygenis gwyni	Monroe/Dade, Hillsborough	Worth (1950a,b; 1951)
	Leon	Fox (1940)
	Alachua, Collier, Highlands, Indian R., Lee, Levy, Nassau, Pinellas	Layne (1971)
	Hillsborough, Alachua, Highlands, Indian R.	FSCA
Hoplopsyllus glacialis affinis	Highlands	FSCA, Layne (1971)
Echidnophaga gallinacea	Monroe/Dade, Hillsborough	Worth (1950a,b)
Ctenocephalides canis	Gadsden	" "
Xenopsylla cheopis	Monroe/Dade, Hillsborough	" "
Leptopsylla segnis	Duval	Rumreich & Wynn (1945)

[a]FSCA = records from the Florida State Collection of Arthropods, Division of Plant Industry, Florida Department of Agriculture, Gainesville, Fla.
[b]NG = not given by authors.

Table 10-17
Arthropod parasites reported from rice rats in Florida

Species of arthropod	Location (county)	Data source
Ticks		
Dermacentor variabilis	Monroe/Dade, Hillsborough	Worth (1950a,b)
Ixodes scapularis	Brevard, Levy	FSCA[a]
Ixodes minor	Indian R.	Wilson & Kale (1972)
Ixodes sp.	Monroe/Dade, Indian R.	Worth (1950a,b), FSCA, Wilson & Kale (1972)
Mites		
Ornithonyssus bacoti	Monroe/Dade, Hillsborough	Worth (1950a,b)
Laelaps oryzomydis[b]	Alachua, Hillsborough, Monroe/Dade	Pratt & Lane (1953), Worth (1950a,b)
Haemolaelaps glasgowi	Monroe/Dade, Hillsborough	Worth (1950a,b)
Gigantolaelaps sp.	Monroe/Dade	" "
Eutrombicula splendens	Monroe/Dade, Hillsborough	" "
Eutrombicula multisetosa	Monroe/Dade	" "
Eutrombicula batatas	Monroe/Dade	" "
Listrophorus sp.	Monroe/Dade, Hillsborough	" "
Sucking lice		
Hoplopleura oryzomydis	Monroe/Dade, Hillsborough	Worth (1950a,b), Pratt (1951), Kim et al. (1986)
Fleas		
Polygenis gwyni	Hillsborough	Worth (1950a,b)
	Alachua, Lee, Levy	FSCA
	Broward	Fox (1940)
	Dade, Monroe	Schwartz (1952)
	Alachua, Indian R., Lee	Layne (1971)

[a]FSCA = records from the Florida State Collection of Arthropods, Division of Plant Industry, Florida Department of Agriculture, Gainesville, Fla.
[b]Worth (1950a) reported *Laelaps* sp. from rice rats in Everglades National Park and from Hillsborough County and stated that "This mite will be described and named by Pratt (Personal communication)." It is assumed that *Laelaps oryzomydis* (see Pratt and Lane 1953) was described from material furnished by Worth.

host in its feces onto the ground, where they then embryonate and are infective for another host when ingested (Levine 1980). The study by Layne (1968) involved examination of 2,254 specimens of 27 species of mammals from 22 counties in Florida in nine major habitats. He found infections in only three species of mammals: cotton rats (10.5% prevalence), Florida mice (15.4%), and cotton mice (6.3%). Population levels and prevalence of infection in two populations of Florida mice were inversely related (Layne 1968). Infections were found mainly in rodents in

scrub or related habitats. By contrast Kinsella (1974a) found infections of *C. hepatica* in cotton rats to be more common in freshwater marshes (30% prevalence) than in upland habitats (5% prevalence).

VIII. Arthropods

The arthropod parasites of New World rats and mice have been studied fairly well. This is due in part to their importance as vectors of zoonotic diseases and to interest shown by

Table 10-18
Arthropod parasites reported from Florida mice

Species of arthropod	Location (county)	Data source
Ticks		
Dermacentor variabilis	Several[a]	Layne (1963)
	"Northern Florida"	Rogers (1953)
Ixodes scapularis	Brevard	FSCA[b]
	"Northern Florida"	Rogers (1953)
Ixodes minor	Several	Layne (1963)
Amblyomma maculatum	Several	" "
Amblyomma americanum	Several	" "
Mites		
Euschongastia peromysci	Several	" "
Gahrlepia americana	Several	" "
Trombicula crossleyi	Several	" "
Eulaelaps stabularis	Several	" "
Haemolaelaps glasgowi	Several	" "
Haemolaelaps fahrenholzi	Levy	FSCA
Haemogamasus liponyssoides	Several	Layne (1963)
Ornithonyssus bacoti	Several	" "
Chatia sp.	Levy	FSCA
Fleas		
Polygenis floridanus	Alachua, Levy, Gilchrist, St. Johns,	"
	Highlands	Johnson & Layne (1961),
		Layne (1963), Layne (1971)
Polygenis gwyni	Alachua, Highlands, Levy	Layne (1971)
Ctenophthalmus pseudagyrtes	Alachua	Johnson & Layne (1961),
		Layne (1963), Layne (1971)
Hoplopsyllus glacialis affinis	Highlands	Johnson & Layne (1961),
		Layne (1963), Layne (1971)
Echidnophaga gallinacea	Highlands	Layne (1971)
Sucking lice		
Hoplopleura hirsuta	Several	Layne (1963)
Botflies		
Cuterebra f. fontinella	Several	Layne (1963), Sabrosky (1986)

[a]Includes Alachua, Clay, Gilchrist, Highlands, Levy, Putnam, and St. Johns counties.
[b]FSCA = records from the Florida State Collection of Arthropods, Division of Plant Industry, Florida Department of Agriculture, Gainesville, Fla.

zoologists in these fascinating rodents, which are native to Florida. In Table 10-15 the numbers of species of arthropods from each host are compared. Mites appear to be important components of the arthropod fauna of these rodents.

The most common flea on rodents in Florida is *Polygenis gwyni*. The primary host of this flea is the cotton rat, on which high intensities occur (Layne 1971). In addition, *P. gwyni* also occurs on other rodents such as rice rats, harvest mice, woodrats, Florida mice, cotton mice, old-field mice, roof rats, and Norway rats. On the other hand, *P. floridanus* is unusually host-specific and infests mainly Florida mice (Layne 1971). Layne

Table 10-19
Arthropod parasites reported from cotton mice in Florida

Species of arthropod	Location (county)	Data source
Ticks		
Dermacentor variabilis	Brevard, Indian R., Levy	FSCA[a]
	Monroe/Dade, Hillsborough	Worth (1950a,b)
	Orange, Osceola, Collier	Travis (1941)
	Indian R.	Wilson & Kale (1972)
	"Northern Florida"	Rogers (1953)
Ixodes scapularis	"Northern Florida"	" "
	Indian R.	Wilson & Kale (1972)
Ixodes minor	Indian R.	" " " "
Ixodes sp.	Monroe/Dade, Hillsborough	Worth (1950a,b)
Mites		
Walchia americana	Leon	Rohani & Cromroy (1979)
Clavidromus transvaalensis	Brevard	FSCA
Ornithonyssus bacoti	Monroe/Dade	Worth (1950a,b)
Haemolaelaps glasgowi	Monroe/Dade	" "
Dermatophagoides scheremetewskyi	Monroe/Dade	" "
Listrophorus sp.	Monroe/Dade, Hillsborough	" "
Fleas		
Polygenis gwyni	Hillsborough	" "
	Levy, Lee	FSCA
	Alachua, Highlands, Indian R., Lee, Levy	Layne (1971)
Polygenis floridanus	Highlands	" "
Stenoponia americana	Leon	Fox (1940)
Orchopeas leucopus	Levy, Nassau	Layne (1971)
Botflies		
Cuterebra f. fontinella	NG[b]	Layne (1963), Sabrosky (1986)
Cuterebra sp.[c]	St. Johns	Neuhauser (1978)
	Levy	Pearson (1954)

[a]FSCA = records from the Florida State Collection of Arthropods, Division of Plant Industry, Florida Department of Agriculture, Gainesville, Fla.
[b]NG = not given by authors.
[c]This is probably *C. f. fontinella*. This record is from the Anastasia Island cotton mouse.

(1971) discussed the zoogeographic relationships of fleas in Florida and pointed out that many of the fleas are present only in the northern part of the state and are relatively rare. The range of these fleas farther south in Florida appears to be limited by climatic factors.

HaySmith (1991) recorded botfly larvae in 17 of 54 (31%) Eastern woodrats from the Ordway Preserve in Putnam County during 1988–89. The larvae were located in the neck region, the face, ears, front legs, and back. Two of the larvae were allowed to pupate in the laboratory, and emerging adults were identified as *Cuterebra americana*. There were peaks in prevalence in February, May, and November.

Some of the arthropod parasites of New

Table 10-20
Arthropod parasites reported from Eastern woodrats in Florida

Species of arthropod	Location (county)	Data source
Ticks		
Dermacentor variabilis	Indian R.	FSCA[a]; Wilson & Kale (1972)
	NG[b]	Clifford et al. (1961)
	"Northern Florida"	Rogers (1953)
Ixodes scapularis[c]	Monroe	FSCA
Ixodes minor	Indian R.	Wilson & Kale (1972)
	Putnam	Forrester & HaySmith (1989)
Ornithodoros talaje[c]	Monroe	FSCA
Haemaphysalis leporispalustris	NG	Bishopp & Trembley (1945)
Mites		
Listrophorus neotomae	Leon	Fain & Hyland (1974)
Fleas		
Polygenis gwyni	Monroe	FSCA
	Monroe/Dade, Hillsborough	Worth (1950b)
	Indian R., Monroe	Layne (1971)
Xenopsylla cheopis	Monroe/Dade, Hillsborough	Worth (1950b)
Orchopeas howardii	Monroe	Schwartz (1952)
	Indian R.	Layne (1971)
Botflies		
Cuterebra americana	Hillsborough	Worth (1950a,b), Sabrosky (1986)
	Putnam	HaySmith (1991)
Cuterebra sp.	Alachua	Forrester (1988)

[a]FSCA = records from the Florida State Collection of Arthropods, Division of Plant Industry, Florida Department of Agriculture, Gainesville, Fla.
[b]NG = not given by authors.
[c]These ticks were found in nests of Eastern woodrats.

Table 10-21
Arthropod parasites reported from golden mice, Eastern harvest mice, and old-field mice in Florida

Host and species of arthropod	Location (county)	Data source
Golden mice		
Ticks		
Dermacentor variabilis	Levy	FSCA[a]
	"Northern Florida"	Rogers (1953)
Ixodes scapularis	"Northern Florida"	" "
Harvest mice		
Fleas		
Polygenis gwyni	Alachua	Layne (1971)
Old-field mice		
Fleas		
Polygenis gwyni	Alachua	" "
Ctenophthalmus pseudogyrtes	Jackson	Fuller (1943), Young (1949)

[a]FSCA = records from the Florida State Collection of Arthropods, Division of Plant Industry, Florida Department of Agriculture, Gainesville, Fla.

World rodents are of significance due to their role as vectors and/or intermediate hosts of other parasites or disease agents that infect humans or other animals. The flea *Xenopsylla cheopis,* for example, is a known vector of the agents of plague and typhus and was found on cotton rats and woodrats in several areas of Florida.

Tables 10-16 through 10-21 provide details of records of various arthropods infesting cotton rats, rice rats, Florida mice, cotton mice, woodrats, golden mice, harvest mice, and old-field mice. There is no informa-

tion on the effects of these arthropods on rodent populations in Florida.

IX. Pentastomes

The pentastome *Porocephalus crotali* occurs as an adult in the respiratory passages of crotaline snakes. These adults lay eggs that pass out of the snake and are ingested by rodents or other mammals. In the gut of the mammal the eggs hatch and the larva penetrates the wall of the small intestine, migrates to the

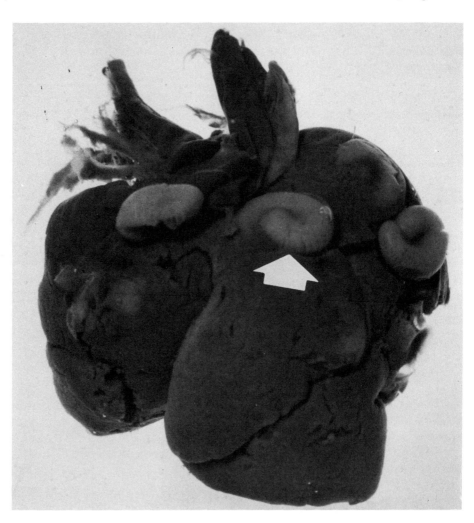

FIGURE 10-4. Nymphs of *Porocephalus crotali* (arrow) on liver of a Florida mouse. (From Layne 1967.)

Table 10-22

Prevalence and intensity of infections of New World rodents in Florida with nymphs of *Porocephalus crotali*

| | No. | | Intensity | | | Locality | |
	Exam.	Pos. (%)	Mean	Range	Date	(county)	Data source
Cotton rats	88	0 (0)	—	—	1970–72	Alachua	Kinsella (1974b)
	35	0 (0)	—	—	1970–72	Levy	" "
	92[a]	1 (1)	"20–25"		NG[b]	Levy	Layne (1967)
Rice rats	105	12 (11)	3	1–12	1970–72	Levy	Kinsella (1974b)
	250	0 (0)	—	—	1970–72	Alachua	" "
	32	0 (0)	—	—	NG	NGS[c]	Layne (1967)
Florida mice	431[d]	8 (2)	NG	1–85	NG	Levy	" "
	114	7 (6)	NG	NG	1957–60	NGS	Layne (1963)
Cotton mice	79[e]	11 (14)	NG	1–15	NG	Levy	Layne (1967)

[a] An additional 335 cotton rats were examined from various localities throughout the state; all were negative.
[b] NG = not given by author.
[c] NGS = locality not given specifically; samples came from 22 counties, most of which were in north-central Florida.
[d] An additional 881 Florida mice were examined from various localities throughout the state; all were negative.
[e] An additional 175 cotton mice were examined from various localities throughout the state; all were negative.

viscera, and develops into a nonmotile nymph (Figure 10-4) that eventually is infective to a snake if ingested (Esslinger 1962). Rodents and other mammals are therefore intermediate hosts for this parasite.

In Florida four species of New World rodents (cotton rats, rice rats, Florida mice, and cotton mice) have been shown to be infected with nymphs of *P. crotali* (Table 10-22). Kinsella (1974b) and Layne (1967) found that infections of rodents in Levy County were more common in the spring and summer months, which is the time of peak activity for many crotaline snakes. Layne (1967) stated that infected rodents did not seem to be adversely affected by the nymphs and felt that these parasites were not significant mortality factors in rodent populations.

X. Summary and conclusions

Seventy different infectious disease agents and parasites have been identified in cotton rats in Florida. These include 13 viruses, 2 bacteria, 1 protozoan, 27 helminths, 26 arthropods, and 1 pentastome. There is information on 65 infectious disease agents and parasites from rice rats; these include 3 viruses, 2 protozoans, 45 helminths, 14 arthropods, and 1 pentastome. For Florida mice there are 49 agents, including 6 protozoans, 21 helminths, 21 arthropods, and 1 pentastome. The list for cotton mice totals 40, and is composed of 4 viruses, 2 bacteria, 1 protozoan, 17 helminths, 15 arthropods, and 1 pentastome. For old-field mice, golden mice, woodrats, and harvest mice the numbers of disease agents are smaller and total 11, 8, 14, and 1, respectively.

The significance of these parasites and disease agents to wild populations of rodents in Florida is largely unknown. Several of the viruses (i.e., Tensaw virus, Everglades virus, EEE virus, and SLE virus), bacteria (i.e., *Leptospira interrogans* and *Francisella tularensis*), and helminths (i.e., *Hymenolepis nana*, *H. diminuta*, and *Capillaria hepatica*) are of public health importance. In addition, some of the mites, ticks, and fleas can serve as vectors of zoonotic disease agents.

XI. Literature cited

Barbour, D.B., and S.R. Humphrey. 1982. Status and habitat of the Key Largo woodrat and cotton mouse (*Neotoma floridana smalli* and *Peromyscus gossypinus allapaticola*). J. Mammal. 63:144–148.

Barnard, W.P., J.V. Ernst, and R.A. Roper. 1971. *Eimeria kinsellai* sp. n. (Protozoa: Eimeriidae) in a marsh rice rat *Oryyomys palustris* from Florida. J. Protozool. 18:546–547.

Bigler, W.J. 1969. Venezuelan encephalitis antibody studies in certain Florida wildlife. Bull. Wildl. Dis. Assoc. 5:267–270.

———. 1971. Serologic evidence of Venezuelan equine encephalitis virus infections in raccoons of south central Florida. J. Wildl. Dis. 7:166–170.

Bigler, W.J., E. Lassing, and A.L. Lewis. 1974a. Persistence of antibody to Venezuelan equine encephalomyelitis virus in cotton mice. J. Am. Vet. Med. Assoc. 165:832–833.

Bigler, W.J., A.L. Lewis, and F.M. Wellings. 1974b. Experimental infection of the cotton mouse (*Peromyscus gossypinus*) with Venezuelan equine encephalomyelitis virus. Am. J. Trop. Med. Hyg. 23:1185–1188.

Bigler, W.J., A.K. Ventura, A.L. Lewis, F.M. Wellings, and N.J. Ehrenkranz. 1974c. Venezuelan equine encephalomyelitis in Florida: Endemic virus circulation in native rodent populations in Everglades hammocks. Am. J. Trop. Med. Hyg. 23:513–521.

Bigler, W.J., E. Lassing, E. Buff, A.L. Lewis, and G.L. Hoff. 1975. Arbovirus surveillance in Florida: Wild vertebrate studies 1965–1974. J. Wildl. Dis. 11:348–356.

Bishopp, F.C., and H.L. Trembley. 1945. Distribution and hosts of certain North American ticks. J. Parasitol. 31:1–54.

Brown, L.N. 1987. A checklist of Florida's mammals. Florida Game and Fresh Water Fish Commission, Tallahassee. 8 pp.

Burgdorfer, W., and K.L. Gage. 1987a. Susceptibility of the hispid cotton rat (*Sigmodon hispidus*) to the Lyme disease spirochete (*Borrelia burgdorferi*). Am. J. Trop. Med. Hyg. 37:624–628.

———. 1987b. Susceptibility of the black-legged tick, *Ixodes scapularis,* to the Lyme disease spirochete, *Borrelia burgdorferi.* Zbl. Bakt. Hyg. A263:15–20.

Burridge, M.J., W.J. Bigler, D.J. Forrester, and J.M. Hennemann. 1979. Serologic survey for *Toxoplasma gondii* in wild animals in Florida. J. Am. Vet. Med. Assoc. 175:964–967.

Burridge, M.J., L.A. Sawyer, and W.J. Bigler. 1986. Rabies in Florida. Department of Health and Rehabilitative Services, Tallahassee, Fla. 147 pp.

Bush, A.O., and J.M. Kinsella. 1972. A natural definitive host for *Catatropis johnstoni* Martin, 1956 (Trematoda: Notocotylidae), with notes on experimental host specificity and intraspecific variation. J. Parasitol. 58:843–845.

Calisher, C.H., J. Daive, P.H. Coleman, R.D. Lord, and T.H. Work. 1969. Cowbone Ridge virus, a new group B arbovirus from south Florida. Am. J. Epidemiol. 89:211–216.

Calisher, C.H., T. Tzianabos, R.D. Lord, and P.H. Coleman. 1970. Tamiami virus, a new member of the Tacaribe group. Am. J. Trop. Med. Hyg. 19:520–526.

Calisher, C.H., D.B. Francy, G.C. Smith, D.J. Muth, J.S. Lazuick, N. Karabatsos, W.L. Jakob, and R.G. McLean. 1986. Distribution of Bunyamwera serogroup viruses in North America, 1956–1984. Am. J. Trop. Med. Hyg. 35:429–443.

Chamberlain, R.W., W.D. Sudia, P.H. Coleman, and T.H. Work. 1964. Venezuelan equine encephalitis virus from south Florida. Science 145:272–274.

Chamberlain, R.W., W.D. Sudia, T.H. Work, P.H. Coleman, V.F. Newhouse, and J.G. Johnston, Jr. 1969. Arbovirus studies in South Florida, with emphasis on Venezuelan encephalomyelitis virus. Am. J. Epidemiol. 89:197–210.

Clifford, C.M., G. Anastos, and A. Elbe. 1961. The larval ixodid ticks of the eastern United States (Acarina-Ixodidae). Misc. Pub. Entomol. Soc. Am. 2:213–237.

Coleman, P.H., S. Ryder, and T.H. Work. 1969. Mahogany Hammock virus, a new Guama group arbovirus from the Florida Everglades. Am. J. Epidemiol. 89:217–221.

Conti, L., and R. Calder. 1989. Lyme disease. Epi-gram. HRS, Tallahassee, Fla. 10:1–2.

Denton, J.F., and J.M. Kinsella. 1972. *Lyperosomum intermedium* sp. n. (Trematoda: Dicrocoelidae) from the rice rat, *Oryzomys palustris,* from southeastern salt marshes. J. Parasitol. 58:226–228.

Donahue, J.G., J. Piesman, and A. Spielman. 1987. Reservoir competence of white-footed mice for Lyme disease spirochetes. Am. J. Trop. Med. Hyg. 36:92–96.

Doran, D.J. 1954a. A catalogue of the protozoa and helminths of North American rodents. I. Protozoa and Acanthocephala. Am. Midl. Nat. 52:118–128.

———. 1954b. A catalogue of the protozoa and helminths of North American rodents. II. Cestoda. Am. Midl. Nat. 52:469–480.

———. 1955a. A catalogue of the protozoa and helminths of North American rodents. III. Nematoda. Am. Midl. Nat. 43:162–175.

———. 1955b. A catalogue of the protozoa and helminths of North Amercian rodents. IV. Trematoda. Am. Midl. Nat. 53:446–454.

Durette-Desset, M.-C. 1972. Compléments morphologiques à l' étude de quelques Nématodes Héligmosomes, parasites de Rongeurs américains. Ann. Parasitol. (Paris) 47:243–249.

———. 1974. Nippostrongylinae (Nematoda: Heligmosomidae) néarctiques. Ann. Parasitol. (Paris) 49:435–450.

Esslinger, J.H. 1962. Hepatic lesions in rats experimentally infected with *Porocephalus crotali* (Pentastomida). J. Parasitol. 48:631–638.

Ewing, H.E. 1943. The American chiggers (larvae of the Trombiculinae) of the genus *Acariscus,* new genus. Proc. Entomol. Soc. Wash. 45:57–66.

Fain, A., and K. Hyland. 1974. The listrophoroid mites in North America. II - The family Listrophoridae Megnin and Trouessart (Acarina: Sarcoptiformes). Bull. K. Belg. Inst. Nat. Wet. 50:1–69.

Fields, B.N., B.E. Henderson, P.H. Coleman, and T.H. Work. 1969. Pahayokee and Shark River, two new arboviruses related to Patois and Zegla from the Florida Everglades. Am. J. Epidemiol. 89:222–226.

Forrester, D.J. 1988. Unpublished data. Univ. of Florida, Gainesville.

———. 1990. Unpublished data. Univ. of Florida, Gainesville.

Forrester, D.J., and L.A. HaySmith. 1989. Unpublished data. Univ. of Florida, Gainesville.

Forrester, D.J., and J.M. Kinsella. 1973. Comparative morphology and ecology of two species of *Litomosoides* (Nematoda: Filarioidea) of rodents in Florida, with a key to the species of *Litomosoides* Chandler, 1931. Int. J. Parasitol. 3:255–263.

Forrester, D.J., and S.R. Telford, Jr. 1990. Unpublished data. Univ. of Florida, Gainesville.

Fox, I. 1940. Fleas of eastern United States. Iowa State Coll. Press, Ames. 191 pp.

Fuller, H.S. 1943. Studies on Siphonaptera of eastern North America. Bull. Brooklyn Entomol. Soc. 38:18–23.

Gainer, J.H., and W.J. Bigler. 1967. Encephalomyocarditis (EMC) virus recovered from two cotton rats and a raccoon. Bull. Wildl. Dis. Assoc. 3:47–49.

Gainer, J.H., J.R. Sandefur, and W.J. Bigler. 1968. High mortality in a Florida swine herd infected with the encephalomyocarditis virus. An accompanying epizootiologic survey. Cornell Vet. 58:31–47.

Gaskin, J.M., M.A. Jorge, C.F. Simpson, A.L. Lewis, J.H. Olson, E.E. Schobert, E.P. Wollenman, C. Marlowe, and M.M. Curtis. 1980. The tragedy of encephalomyocarditis virus infection in zoological parks of Florida. Ann. Proc. Am. Assoc. Zoo Vet. pp. 1–7.

Gibbs, E.P. J. 1976. Equine viral encephalitis. Eq. Vet. J. 8:66–71.

HaySmith, L.A. 1991. Behavioral ecology of the Eastern woodrat *Neotoma floridana floridana* in mesic hardwood forests in north Florida: Population, movements and habitat. M.S. thesis, Univ. of Florida, Gainesville. 118 pp.

Henderson, B.E., C.H. Calisher, P.H. Coleman, B.N. Fields, and T.H. Work. 1969. Gumbo Limbo, a new group C arbovirus from the Florida Everglades. Am. J. Epidemiol. 89:227–231.

Hoff, G.L., W.J. Bigler, and E.C. Prather. 1975. One-half century of tularemia in Florida. J. Fla. Med. Assoc. 62:35–37.

Humphrey, S.R., and D.B. Barbour. 1981. Status and habitat of three subspecies of *Peromyscus polionotus* in Florida. J. Mammal. 60:840–844.

Humphrey, S.R., and H.W. Setzer. 1989. Geographic variation and taxonomic revision of rice rats (*Oryzomys palustris* and *O. argentatus*) of the United States. J. Mammal. 70:557–570.

Humphrey, S.R., W.H. Kern, Jr., and M.E. Ludlow. 1987. Status survey of seven Florida mammals. Fla. Coop. Fish & Wildl. Res. Unit Tech. Rep. No. 25. 39 pp.

Humphrey, S.R., W.H. Kern, Jr., and M.E. Ludlow. 1988. The Anastasia Island cotton mouse (Rodentia: *Peromyscus gossypinus anastasae*) may be extinct. Fla. Sci. 51:150–155.

Jennings, W.L., A.L. Lewis, G.E. Sather, W.M. Hammon, and J.O. Bond. 1968. California-encephalitis-group viruses in Florida rabbits: Report of experimental and sentinel studies. Am. J. Trop. Med. Hyg. 17:781–787.

Jennings, W.L., A.L. Lewis, G.E. Sather, L.V. Pierce, and J.O. Bond. 1970. Tamiami virus in the Tampa Bay area. Am. J. Trop. Med. Hyg. 19:527–536.

Johnson, P.I., and J.N. Layne. 1961. A new species of *Polygenis* Jordan from Florida, with remarks on its host relationships and zoogeographic significance (Siphonaptera: Rhopalopsyllidae). Proc. Entomol. Soc. Wash. 63:115–123.

Karabatsos, N. 1985. International catalogue of arboviruses. 3d ed. Am. Soc. Trop. Med. Hyg., San Antonio, Tex. 1,147 pp.

Kim, K.C., H.D. Pratt, and C.J. Stojanovich. 1986. The sucking lice of North America. An illustrated manual for identification. Penn. State Univ. Press, University Park. 241 pp.

Kinsella, J.M. 1971. *Angiostrongylus schmidti* sp. n. (Nematoda: Metastrongyloidea) from the rice rat, *Oryzomys palustris*, in Florida, with a key to the species of *Angiostrongylus* Kamensky, 1905. J. Parasitol. 57:494–497.

———. 1974a. Comparison of helminth parasites of the cotton rat, *Sigmodon hispidus*, from several habitats in Florida. Am. Mus. Nov. 2540:1–12.

———. 1974b. Seasonal incidence of *Porocephalus crotali* (Pentastomida) in rice rats, *Oryzomys palustris*, from a Florida salt marsh. J. Med. Entomol. 11:116.

———. 1987a. Unpublished data. Archbold Biological Station, Lake Placid, Fla.

———. 1987b. Studies on the life cycle and host specificity of *Parastrongylus schmidti* (Nematoda: Angiostrongylidae). Proc. Helminthol. Soc. Wash. 54:245–248.

———. 1988. Comparison of helminths of rice rats, *Oryzomys palustris*, from freshwater and saltwater marshes in Florida. Proc. Helminthol. Soc. Wash. 55:275–280.

Kinsella, J.M., and R.W. Heard. 1974. Morphology and life cycle of *Stictodora cursitans* n. comb. (Trematoda: Heterophyidae) from mammals in Florida salt marshes. Trans. Am. Micros. Soc. 93:408–412.

Kinsella, J.M., and D.B. Pence. 1987. Description of *Capillaria forresteri* sp. n. (Nematoda: Trichuridae) from the rice rat *Oryzomys palustris* in Florida, with notes on its ecology and seasonal variation. Can. J. Zool. 65:1294–1297.

Layne, J.N. 1963. A study of the parasites of the Florida mouse, *Peromyscus floridanus*, in relation to host and environmental factors. Tulane Stud. Zool. 11:1–27.

———. 1967. Incidence of *Porocephalus crotali* (Pentastomida) in Florida mammals. Bull. Wildl. Dis. Assoc. 3:105–109.

———. 1968. Host and ecological relationships of the parasitic helminth *Capillaria hepatica* in Florida mammals. Zoologica 53:107–122.

———. 1970. New host records of *Capillaria hepatica* in Florida. Quart. J. Fla. Acad. Sci. 33:18–22.

———. 1971. Fleas (Siphonaptera) of Florida. Fla. Entomol. 54:35–51.

Layne, J.N., and J.V. Griffo, Jr. 1961. Incidence of *Capillaria hepatica* in populations of the Florida deer mouse, *Peromyscus floridanus*. J. Parasitol. 47:31–37.

Levine, J.F., M.L. Wilson, and A. Spielman.

1985. Mice as reservoirs of the Lyme disease spirochete. Am. J. Trop. Med. Hyg. 34:355–360.

Levine, N.D. 1980. Nematode parasites of domestic animals and of man. 2d ed. Burgess, Minneapolis. 477 pp.

Lichtenfels, J.R. 1970. Two new species of *Pterygodermatites* (*Paucipectines*) Quentin, 1969 (Nematoda: Rictulariidae) with a key to the species from North American rodents. Proc. Helminthol. Soc. Wash. 37:94–101.

———. 1987. Unpublished data. USDA, Beltsville, Md.

Lord, R.D., C.H. Calisher, W.D. Sudia, and T.H. Work. 1973. Ecological investigations of vertebrate hosts of Venezuelan equine encephalomyelitis virus in south Florida. Am. J. Trop. Med. Hyg. 22:116–123.

Lowery, G.W., Jr. 1974. The mammals of Louisiana and its adjacent waters. Louisiana State Univ. Press, Baton Rouge. 565 pp.

McConnell, S., and R.O. Spertzel. 1981. Venezuelan equine encephalomyelitis (VEE). In: CRC handbook series in zoonoses. Section B: Viral zoonoses. Vol. 1. G.W. Beran (ed.). CRC Press, Boca Raton, Fla. pp. 59–69.

McIntosh, A. 1935. A new hookworm, *Monodontus floridanus* n.sp. from a cotton rat, *Sigmodon hispidus*. Trans. Am. Micr. Soc. 54:28–32.

———. 1937. New host records for *Diphyllobothrium mansonoides* Mueller, 1935. J. Parasitol. 23:313–315.

McKeever, S., R.W. Menges, W. Kaplan, and L. Ajello. 1958. Ringworm fungi of feral rodents in southwestern Georgia. Am. J. Vet. Res. 19:969–972.

Melvin, D.M., and A.C. Chandler. 1950. New helminth records from the cotton rat, *Sigmodon hispidus*. J. Parasitol. 38:346–355.

Milstrey, E.G., and E.C. Greiner. 1987. Unpublished data. Univ. of Florida, Gainesville.

Morgan, B.B. 1943. The *Physaloptera* (Nematoda) of rodents. Wasmann Coll. 5:99–107.

Morlan, H.B., E.L. Hill, and J.H. Schubert. 1950. Serological survey for murine typhus infection in southwest Georgia animals. Pub. Health Rep. 65:57–63.

Neuhauser, H.N. 1978. Anastasia Island cotton mouse. In: Rare and endangered biota of Florida. Vol. 1. Mammals. J.N. Layne (ed.). Univ. Presses of Florida, Gainesville. pp. 45–47.

Pearson, P.G. 1954. Mammals of Gulf Hammock, Levy County, Florida. Am. Midl. Nat. 51:468–480.

Philip, R.N. 1980. Typhus-group rickettsiae. In: CRC handbook series in zoonoses. Section A: Bacterial, rickettsial and mycotic diseases. Vol. 2. J.H. Steele (ed.). CRC Press, Boca Raton, Fla. pp. 317–335.

Pratt, H.D. 1951. *Hoplopleura oryzomydis* new species, with notes on other United States species of *Hoplopleura* (Anoplura: Haematopinidae). J. Parasitol. 37:141–146.

Pratt, H.D., and J.E. Lane. 1953. *Laelaps oryzomydis*, n.sp., with a key to some American species of *Laelaps* (Acarinea: Laelaptidae). J. Wash. Acad. Sci. 43:358–360.

Quentin, J.-C., and J.M. Kinsella. 1972. Etude de trois espèces d'Oxyures *Syphacia* parasites de Rongeurs Cricétidés nord-américains. Hypothèses sur les filiations des espèces américaines. Ann. Parasitol. (Paris) 47:717–733.

Rausch, R.L. 1981. Morphological and biological characteristics of *Taenia rileyi* Loewen, 1929 (Cestoda: Taeniidae). Can. J. Zool. 59:653–666.

Repenning, R.W., and S.H. Humphrey. 1986. The Chadwick Beach cotton mouse (Rodentia: *Peromyscus gossypinus restrictus*) may be extinct. Fla. Sci. 49:259–262.

Rickard, E.R. 1951. Postinfection murine typhus antibodies in the sera of rodents. Am. J. Hyg. 53:207–216.

Rickard, E.R., and C.B. Worth. 1951. Complement-fixation tests for murine typhus on the sera of wild-caught cotton rats in Florida. Am. J. Hyg. 53:332–336.

Rogers, A.J. 1953. A study of the ixodid ticks of northern Florida, including the biology and life history of *Ixodes scapularis* Say (Ixodidae: Acarina). Ph.D. diss., Univ. of Maryland, College Park. 191 pp.

Rohani, I.B., and H.L. Cromroy. 1979. Taxonomy and distribution of chiggers (Acarina: Trombiculidae) in northcentral Florida. Fla. Entomol. 62:363–376.

Rumreich, A.S., and R.S. Wynn. 1945. A study of the rodent-ectoparasite population of Jacksonville, Florida. Pub. Health Rep. 60:885–905.

Sabrosky, C.W. 1986. North American species of *Cuterebra*, the rabbit and rodent bot flies (Diptera: Cuterebridae). Entomol. Soc. Am., College Park, Md. 240 pp.

Schell, S.C. 1950. A new species of *Physaloptera* (Nematoda: Spiruroidea) from the cotton rat. J. Parasitol. 36:423–425.

Schmid, G.P. 1984. The global distribution of Lyme disease. Yale J. Biol. Med. 57:617–618.

Schwartz, A. 1952. The land mammals of southern Florida and the upper Florida Keys. Ph.D. diss., Univ. of Michigan, Ann Arbor.

Shotts, E.B., C.L. Andrews, and T.W. Harvey. 1975. Leptospirosis in selected wild mammals of the Florida panhandle and southwestern Georgia. J. Am. Vet. Med. Assoc. 167:587–589.

Steere, A.C., S.E. Malawista, N.H. Bartenhagen, P.N. Spieler, J.H. Newman, D.W. Rahn, G.J. Hutchinson, J. Green, D.R. Snydman, and E. Taylor. 1984. The clinical spectrum and treatment of Lyme disease. Yale J. Biol. Med. 57:453–461.

Stevenson, H.M. 1976. Vertebrates of Florida. Identification and distribution. Univ. Presses of Florida, Gainesville. 607 pp.

Taylor, D.J., A.L. Lewis, J.D. Edman, and W.L. Jennings. 1971. California group arboviruses in Florida. Host-vector relations. Am. J. Trop. Med. Hyg. 20:139–145.

Traub, R., C.L. Wisseman, Jr., and A. Farhang-Azad. 1978. The ecology of murine typhus—a critical review. Trop. Dis. Bull. 75:237–317.

Travis, B.V. 1941. Examinations of wild animals for the cattle tick *Boophilus annulatus microplus* (Can.) in Florida. J. Parasitol. 27:465–467.

Ubelaker, J.E. 1986. Systematics of species referred to the genus *Angiostrongylus*. J. Parasitol. 72:237–244.

Wellings, F.M., A.L. Lewis, and L.V. Pierce. 1972. Agents encountered during arboviral ecological studies: Tampa Bay area, Florida, 1963 to 1970. Am. J. Trop. Med. Hyg. 21:201–213.

Whitaker, J.O., Jr. 1968. Parasites. In: Biology of *Peromyscus* (Rodentia). J.A. King (ed.). Spec. Pub. No. 2, Am. Soc. Mammalogists. pp. 254–311.

White, F.H. 1988. Unpublished data. Univ. of Florida, Gainesville.

Williams, R.W. 1948. Studies on the life cycle of *Litomosoides carinii*, filariid parasite of the cotton rat, *Sigmodon hispidus litoralis*. J. Parasitol. 34:24–43.

Wilson, N., and H.W. Kale. 1972. Ticks collected from Indian River County, Florida (Acari: Metastigmata: Ixodidae). Fla. Entomol. 55:53–57.

Winkler, W.G., N.J. Schneider, and W.L. Jennings. 1972. Experimental rabies infection in wild rodents. J. Wildl. Dis. 8:99–103.

Wood, D.A. 1990. Official lists of endangered and potentially endangered fauna and flora in Florida. Florida Game and Fresh Water Fish Commission, Tallahassee. 19 pp.

Woods, C.A., W. Post, and C.W. Kilpatrick. 1982. *Microtus pennsylvanicus* (Rodentia: Muridae) in Florida: A Pleistocene relict in a coastal saltmarsh. Bull. Fla. State Mus., Biol. Sci. 28:25–52.

Work, T.H. 1964. Serological evidence of arbovirus infection in the Seminole Indians of southern Florida. Science 145:270–272.

Worth, C.B. 1950a. Observations on ectoparasites of some small mammals in Everglades National Park and Hillsborough County, Florida. J. Parasitol. 36:326–335.

———. 1950b. A preliminary host-ectoparasite register for some small mammals of Florida. J. Parasitol. 36:497–498.

———. 1951. Indirect evidence supporting observations on the range of wild rodents. J. Mammal. 32:76–79.

Wright, S.D. 1987. Experimental infection of the white-footed mouse (*Peromyscus leucopus*) with the Lyme disease spirochete (*Borrelia burgdorferi*). Ph.D. diss., Univ. of Connecticut, Storrs. 106 pp.

Young, F.N. 1949. Insects from burrows of *Peromyscus polionotus*. Fla. Entomol. 32:77.

Round-tailed Muskrats

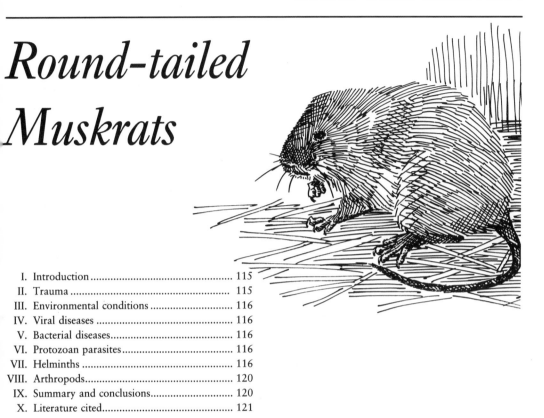

I. Introduction

The round-tailed muskrat (*Neofiber alleni* True) is found in fresh- and saltwater marshes, prairies, and sugarcane fields in Florida and in the Okefenokee Swamp in southern Georgia (Hall 1981; Steffen et al. 1981; Wassmer and Wolfe 1983). It is also known as the Florida water rat (Stevenson 1976), and has been described as "a living link between the muskrat and the field mouse" (True 1884, p. 34). It is currently under review for survival status by the U.S. Fish and Wildlife Service (Wood 1990).

Typical habitats are shallow, emergent marshes with dense stands of maidencane and pickerelweed (Porter 1953; Birkenholz 1963). In areas where sugarcane is cultivated in southern Florida and water levels are maintained at 0.60 to 0.75 m below the soil surface, the round-tailed muskrat builds extensive tunnel systems in the highly organic muck soil. Both in marshes and muck fields, *Neofiber* appears to be colonial (Lefebvre 1982).

II. Trauma

Birkenholz (1963) assessed the impact of predation on round-tailed muskrats on Paynes Prairie in Alachua County. He found that the main predators were marsh hawks, red-tailed hawks, barn owls, barred owls, bobcats, and cottonmouths. Predation was particularly high when high water conditions and poor cover caused displacement of animals. Mortality due to road-kills also increased during these times. Other records of avian predators of round-tailed muskrats include bald eagles (McEwan and Hirth 1980) and great blue herons (Ehrhart 1984). Kinsella (1982) found six adult round-tailed muskrats in the stomach and small intestine of an alligator in Alachua County.

Little evidence was found of intraspecific interactions such as fighting (Birkenholz 1963). Of 326 specimens examined Birkenholz found very few wounds or scars. Seven rats had stub tails of various lengths and seven had torn pinnae. There was no evidence of increased strife among rats at times when population densities were high.

III. Environmental conditions

Birkenholz (1963) concluded that changes in water level had drastic effects on round-tailed muskrat populations. He felt that this was the single most important environmental factor leading to mortality. A population of rats on one pond on Paynes Prairie was reduced by about 85% in a period of two and one-half months after heavy rainfall and a resulting 8-inch rise in water level. This occurred during March, when emergent vegetation had all but disappeared. Juveniles were most severely affected. A year later another high water period occurred and another population was reduced by 50% to 60%.

Birkenholz (1963) also recorded the effects of a severe drought on muskrats on Paynes Paririe. A population of several thousand was reduced to only a few animals in a two-month period during May and June 1961. Rainfall

during that time was almost four inches below normal.

IV. Viral diseases

Almost nothing is known about viral diseases of round-tailed muskrats. An animal found dead in a sugarcane field in Palm Beach County in 1979 was found to have bronchopneumonia probably caused by a virus. Exfoliated epithelial cells in some bronchioles contained dark eosinophilic intranuclear structures that were suggestive of viral inclusion bodies. The pneumonia was judged to be severe enough to have caused the death of the animal. The virus was not isolated or characterized (Forrester 1984).

V. Bacterial diseases

Porter (1953) gave a description of skin abscesses in captive round-tailed muskrats. He attributed these to a bacterial infection, but no bacteriologic studies were conducted. This condition has not been seen in wild muskrats.

VI. Protozoan parasites

The protozoan parasites of round-tailed muskrats have not been studied. The only reference to protozoans is that of Burridge et al. (1979); they tested sera from 12 animals for antibodies to *Toxoplasma gondii*. All samples were negative.

VII. Helminths

The helminths of round-tailed muskrats have been studied by a number of investigators. Fifteen species have been reported, including

Table 11-1
Helminths reported from round-tailed muskrats in Florida

Helminth	No. muskrats Exam.	Inf. (%)	Intensity Mean	Range	Date	Location (county)	Data source
Trematoda							
Quinqueserialis floridensis[a]	2	1 (50)	"Several thousand"		NG[b]	Putnam	Rausch (1952)
	298	39 (13)	NG	—	1958–61	Alachua	Birkenholz (1963)
	10	9 (90)	40[c]	12–135[c]	1970–72	Alachua	Kinsella (1985)
	3	3 (100)	42	22–65	1972	Highlands	" "
Cestoda							
Raillietina sigmodontis	114	6 (5)	4	1–12	1974–75	Palm Beach	Forrester et al. (1987)
Anoplocephaloides neofibrinus	2	1 (50)	NG	—	NG	Putnam	Rausch (1952)
	298	146 (49)	NG	1–20	1958–61	Alachua	Birkenholz (1963)
	10	5 (50)	3	2–3	1970–72	Alachua	Kinsella (1985)
	NG	NG	1	—	1952	Jefferson	Porter (1953)
	3	2 (67)	42	22–65	1972	Highlands	Kinsella (1985)
Pseudocittotaenia praecoquis	2	1 (50)	NG	—	NG	Putnam	Rausch (1952)
	NG	NG	1	—	1952	Jefferson	Porter (1953)
Taenia rileyi (larvae)	2	1 (50)	16	—	NG	Putnam	Rausch (1952, 1981)
Nematoda							
Mastophorus sp.	3	1 (33)	3	—	1972	Highlands	Kinsella (1985)
Physocephalus sexalatus	204	3 (1)	3	1–4	1974–75	Palm Beach	Forrester & Telford (1990)
Physaloptera hispida	3	3 (100)	6	1–13	1972	Highlands	Kinsella (1985)
	204	2 (1)	6	1–11	1974–75	Palm Beach	Forrester & Telford (1990)
Unidentified nematodes[d]	298	20 (7)	NG	—	1958–61	Alachua	Birkenholz (1963)
Carolinensis kinsellai	3	2 (67)	NG	—	1968	Hendry	Durette-Desset (1969)
	114	113 (99)	96	1–537	1974–75	Palm Beach	Forrester et al. (1987)
	10	7 (70)	7	1–25	1970–72	Alachua	Kinsella (1985)
	3	3 (100)	49	15–98	1972	Highlands	" "
	12	6 (50)	NG	?–170	1952	Dade, Hendry	Porter (1953)[e]
Strongyloides sigmodontis	114	77 (68)	69	1–2,056	1974–75	Palm Beach	Forrester et al. (1987)
	3	1 (33)	1	—	1972	Highlands	Kinsella (1985)
Monodontus floridanus	114	83 (73)	7	1–105	1974–75	Palm Beach	Forrester et al. (1987)
Trichostrongylus spp.[f]	114	14 (12)	11	1–62	1974–75	Palm Beach	Forrester et al. (1987)
Capillaria hepatica	114	7 (6)	—	—	1974–75	Palm Beach	Forrester et al. (1987)
	10	4 (40)	—	—	1970–72	Alachua	Kinsella (1985)
Litomosoides sp.	NG	NG	15	—	1952	Brevard	Porter (1953)
	114	8 (7)	1	1–2	1974–75	Palm Beach	Forrester et al. (1987)

[a]Forrester et al. (1987) erroneously stated that Porter (1953) reported this helminth from muskrats in southern Florida. He did not.
[b]NG = not given by authors.
[c]Intensity values based on only 5 of the 10 animals.
[d]Birkenholz (1963) reported unidentified nematodes in the stomachs of 20 of 298 muskrats from Alachua County. These may have been Mastophorus sp. or Physaloptera hispida, but the specimens are not available for examination (Forrester et al. 1987).
[e]Porter (1953) reported Longistriata adunca from the small intestines of 6 of 12 muskrats. It is assumed that these were actually Carolinensis kinsellai, although this cannot be confirmed (Forrester et al. 1987).
[f]A complex of 2 species (T. sigmodontis and T. affinis), considered here as one entity.

1 trematode, 4 cestodes, and 10 nematodes (Table 11-1). Of the species reported, three appear to represent core species: the trematode *Quinqueserialis floridensis,* the cestode *Anoplocephaloides neofibrinus,* and the nematode *Carolinensis kinsellai.* These core species occurred commonly in round-tailed muskrats (four or five of the six localities studied in Florida) and have not been found in other hosts. They are therefore host specialists (Forrester et al. 1987). The other species are less common and are considered satel-

lite species that have been acquired from other hosts. Eleven of these are known to be parasites of cotton rats (Kinsella 1974). These include *S. sigmodontis, T. sigmodontis, T. affinis, M. floridanus, C. hepatica, Litomosoides* sp., *P. hispida, P. sexalatus, Mastophorus* sp., *T. rileyi,* and *R. sigmodontis.* *Trichostrongylus affinis* has been found also in rabbits. *Pseudocittotaenia praecoquis* is a parasite from pocket gophers (Beveridge 1978). These satellite species are found in round-tailed muskrats most likely because of

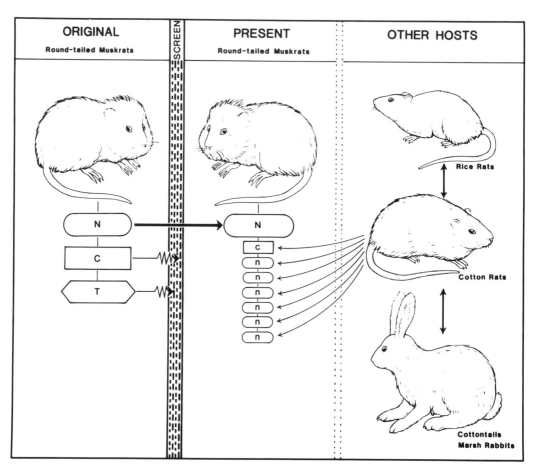

FIGURE 11-1. Diagrammatic representation of the effects of an agricultural "screen" on the helminth fauna of round-tailed muskrats from sugarcane fields in southern Florida. Capital N signifies a core species of nematode; lower case *n* is a satellite species of nematode. Capital C is a core cestode; lower case *c* is a satellite cestode. Capital *T* is a core trematode. (Adapted from data presented by Forrester et al. 1987.)

Table 11-2
Arthropods reported from round-tailed muskrats in Florida

Arthropod	Location (county)	Data source
Mites		
Listrophorus caudatus[a]	Alachua, Highlands	Smith (1986), Fain et al. (1986)
Listrophorus laynei[a]	Alachua, Highlands	" " " " " "
Prolistrophorus birkenholzi[a]	Alachua, Highlands	" " " " " "
Laelaps evansi	Brevard	Tipton (1960)
	Dade, Hendry	Porter (1953)[b]
	Alachua	Birkenholz (1963)
	Highlands	Smith (1986)
Androlaelaps fahrenholzi	Alachua	Birkenholz (1963)
	Highlands	Smith (1986)
Euschongastia splendens	Dade, Hendry	Porter (1953)
	Highlands	Smith (1986)
Radfordia sp.	Highlands	" "
Garmania bulbicola[c]	Dade, Hendry	Porter (1953)
Garmania sp.[c]	Highlands	Smith (1986)
Macrocheles mammifer[c,d]	Dade, Hendry	Porter (1953)
	Highlands	Smith (1986)
Tyrophagus lintneri[c]	Brevard	Porter (1953)
Tyrophagus sp.[c]	Highlands	Smith (1986)
Fleas		
Polygenis gwyni	Highlands	" "

[a]Birkenholz (1963) mentioned the presence of an undescribed species of listrophorid from Alachua County. Smith (1986) examined 2 preserved round-tailed muskrats from Alachua County and found *Listrophorus caudatus*, *L. laynei*, and *Prolistrophorus birkenholzi*.
[b]Porter (1953) reported that he found an undescribed species of *Laelaps* on round-tailed muskrats. These were described later by Tipton (1960) as *L. evansi*.
[c]These are probably not parasites and should be considered as nonparasitic associates.
[d]Smith et al. (1988) referred to this as *Macrocheles* sp., but Krantz and Whitaker (1988) studied these specimens further and determined that they were *M. mammifer*.

the sharing of food and spatial resources with other rodents.

Round-tailed muskrats in sugarcane habitats in Palm Beach County were found to have an unusual helminth fauna (Forrester et al. 1987). Two of the core species (*Q. floridensis* and *A. neofibrinus*) were totally absent. It was postulated that this was due to a "screen" effect caused by a number of agricultural practices such as planting, harvesting, burning, and applying rodenticides, herbicides, and insecticides. These effects probably were mediated through adverse impacts on the intermediate hosts such as snails and insects. This screen effect, therefore, resulted in the removal of two core species and satellite species increased in relative importance (Forrester et al. 1987). These processes are illustrated graphically in Figure 11-1 and provide an example of how habitat changes can have a profound influence on parasites or diseases of wildlife.

Two of the nematodes from round-tailed muskrats (*Monodontus floridanus* and *Strongyloides sigmodontis*) may be of significance as primary pathogens, but this remains to be determined. Closely related species of these two nematodes are known to be pathogenic

(Levine 1980). One of the nematodes (*Capillaria hepatica*) may be of zoonotic concern.

VIII. Arthropods

Twelve species of mites and one flea have been found on round-tailed muskrats in Florida (Table 11-2). Five of these species are considered nonparasitic forms or associates and include *Garmania bulbicola*, *Garmania* sp., *Macrocheles mammifer*, *Tyrophagus lintneri*, and *Tyrophagus* sp. Three of the other eight species were common, with mean numbers of mites per infested host from 200 to over 700 (Table 11-3). One specimen of the flea *Polygenis gwyni* was found on one muskrat. This probably originated from a cotton rat or rice rat and represents an accidental or satellite species. Fleas are rare on aquatic mammals and there are no other reports from *Neofiber*.

Smith et al. (1988) conducted a detailed study of the spatial distribution of the listrophorids of 15 muskrats from Highlands County. They sampled 23 areas of the bodies of the muskrats and determined that the mites were located mainly on the anterior portion of the host (both ventrally and dorsally). The muzzle and the nape of the neck contained the most dense populations of mites.

The pathologic significance of these arthropods to round-tailed muskrat populations is not known. None is of public health concern.

IX. Summary and conclusions

Round-tailed muskrats are known to have 30 parasites and infectious diseases. These include 10 nematodes, 4 cestodes, 1 trematode, 12 mites, 1 flea, 1 virus, and 1 bacterial infection. The role of these disease agents in

Table 11-3
Prevalences and intensities of arthropods from 25 round-tailed muskrats[a] from Florida, 1962–84

Arthropod	No. muskrats Inf.	(%)	Intensity[b]	Tot. no. arthropods collected
Mites				
Listrophorus caudatus	24	(96)	770	18,467
Listrophorus laynei	23	(92)	734	16,890
Prolistrophorus birkenholzi	21	(84)	236	4,950
Laelaps evansi	23	(92)	45	1,043
Androlaelaps fahrenholzi	18	(72)	8	148
Euschongastia splendens	7	(28)	16	109
Garmania sp.	7	(28)	2	12
Radfordia sp.	5	(20)	1	7
Macrocheles mammifer[c]	3	(12)	1	4
Tyrophagus sp.	3	(12)	1	3
Fleas				
Polygenis gwyni	1	(4)	1	1

Source: Smith et al. (1988).
[a]Of these 25 muskrats, 22 came from Highlands County, 2 from Alachua County, and 1 from DeSoto County.
[b]Mean number of arthropods per infested host.
[c]Smith et al. (1988) referred to this as *Macrocheles* sp., but Krantz and Whitaker (1988) studied these specimens further and determined that they were *M. mammifer*.

muskrat populations is uncertain and needs investigation. One of the nematodes (*Capillaria hepatica*) may be of zoonotic concern. Predation, road-kills, and changing water levels appear to be important mortality factors in north-central Florida.

X. Literature cited

Beveridge, I. 1978. A taxonomic revision of the genera *Cittotaenia* Riehm, 1881, *Ctenotaenia* Railliet, 1893, *Mosgovoyia* Spasskii, 1951, and *Pseudocittotaenia* Tenora, 1976 (Cestoda: Anoplocephalidae). Mem. Mus. Nat. Hist. Nat. Ser. A (Paris). 107:1–64.

Birkenholz, D.E. 1963. A study of the life history and ecology of the round-tailed muskrat (*Neofiber alleni* True) in north-central Florida. Ecol. Monogr. 33:187–213.

Burridge, M.J., W.J. Bigler, D.J. Forrester, and J.M. Hennemann. 1979. Serologic survey for *Toxoplasma gondii* in wild animals in Florida. J. Am. Vet. Med. Assoc. 175:964–967.

Durette-Desset, M.-C. 1969. Etude du système des arêtes cuticulaires de trois nématodes héligmosomes: *Longistriata kinsellai* n.sp., *L. seurati* Travassos et Darriba, 1929, *L. hokkaidensis* Chabaud, Rausch et Dessert, 1963, parasites de rongeurs. Ann. Parasit. Hum. Comp. 44:617–624.

Ehrhart, L.M. 1984. Some avian predators of the round-tailed muskrat. Fla. Field Nat. 12:98–99.

Fain, A., M.A. Smith, and J.O. Whitaker. 1986. The fur mites (Acari: Listrophoridae) of the round-tailed muskrat, *Neofiber alleni*. Bull. Ann. Soc. R. Belge Ent. 122:171–181.

Forrester, D.J. 1984. Unpublished data. Univ. of Florida, Gainesville.

Forrester, D.J., and S.R. Telford, Jr. 1990. Unpublished data. Univ. of Florida, Gainesville.

Forrester, D.J., D.B. Pence, A.O. Bush, D.M. Lee, and N.R. Holler. 1987. Ecological analysis of the helminths of round-tailed muskrats (*Neofiber alleni* True) in southern Florida. Can. J. Zool. 65:2976–2979.

Hall, E.R. 1981. The mammals of North America. 2d ed. John Wiley and Sons, New York. 1,175 pp.

Kinsella, J.M. 1974. Comparison of helminth parasites of the cotton rat, *Sigmodon hispidus*, from several habitats in Florida. Am. Mus. Nov. 2540:1–12.

———. 1982. Alligator predation on round-tailed muskrats. Fla. Field Nat. 10:70.

———. 1985. Unpublished data. Archbold Biological Station, Lake Placid, Fla.

Krantz, G.W., and J.O. Whitaker. 1988. Unpublished data. Indiana State University, Terre Haute.

Lefebvre, L.W. 1982. Population dynamics of the round-tailed muskrat (*Neofiber alleni*) in Florida sugarcane. Ph.D. diss., Univ. of Florida, Gainesville. 204 pp.

Levine, N.D. 1980. Nematode parasites of domestic animals and of man. 2d ed. Burgess, Minneapolis. 477 pp.

McEwan, L.L., and D.H. Hirth. 1980. Food habits of the bald eagle in northcentral Florida. Condor 82:229–231.

Porter, R.P. 1953. A contribution to the life history of the water rat, *Neofiber alleni*. M.S. thesis, Univ. of Miami, Coral Gables. 152 pp.

Rausch, R.L. 1952. Helminths from the round-tailed muskrat, *Neofiber alleni nigrescens* Howell, with descriptions of two new species. J. Parasitol. 38:151–156.

———. 1981. Morphological and biological characteristics of *Taenia rileyi* Lowen, 1929. (Cestoda: Taeniidae). Can. J. Zool. 59:653–666.

Smith, M.A. 1986. Ectoparasites of *Neofiber alleni* from Florida with special emphasis on the mites of the family Listrophoridae. M.S. thesis. Indiana State University, Terre Haute. 46 pp.

Smith, M.A., J.O. Whitaker, Jr., and J.N. Layne. 1988. Ectoparasites of the round-tailed muskrat (*Neofiber alleni*) with special emphasis on mites of the family Listrophoridae. Am. Midl. Nat. 120:268–275.

Steffen, D.E., N.R. Holler, L.W. Lefebvre, and P.F. Scanlon. 1981. Factors affecting the occurrence and distribution of Florida water rats in sugarcane fields. Proc. Am. Soc. Sugar Cane Technol. 9:27–32.

Stevenson, H.M. 1976. Vertebrates of Florida. Identification and distribution. Univ. Presses of Florida, Gainesville. 607 pp.

Tipton, V.J. 1960. The genus *Laelaps*, with a review of the Laelaptinae and a new subfamily Alphalaelaptinae (Acarina: Laelaptidae). Univ. Calif. Pub. Entomol. 16:233–356.

True, F.W. 1884. A muskrat with a round tail. Science 4:34.

Wassmer, D.A., and J.L. Wolfe. 1983. New Florida localities for the round-tailed muskrat. Northeast Gulf Sci. 6:197–199.

Wood, D.A. 1990. Official lists of endangered fauna and flora in Florida. Florida Game and Fresh Water Fish Commission, Tallahassee. 19 pp.

Raccoons

I. Introduction

The raccoon (*Procyon lotor* L.) is a common mammal in Florida and is distributed widely throughout the state (Stevenson 1976). Over 45,000 were harvested in 1986–87 by hunters and trappers in Florida (Wright 1987). In many residential areas and state parks this animal has become accustomed to humans and lives in close proximity, at times causing serious problems. Two subspecies of raccoons (the Key Vaca raccoon, *P. l. auspicatus,* and the Key West raccoon, *P. l. incautus*) are currently under review by the U.S. Fish and Wildlife Service in order to determine their survival status (Wood 1990). The literature on parasites and diseases of raccoons in North America was summarized briefly by Kaufman (1982). The literature on helminth parasites was reviewed by Schaffer (1979) and included some information on raccoons in Florida. Bigler et al. (1975a) discussed the diseases and parasites of raccoons that are of public health importance in the southeastern United States.

In recent years considerable concern has been expressed over the translocation of raccoons from Florida to other states in the North because of possible disease introduction (Prather et al. 1975; Nettles and Martin 1978; Nettles et al. 1979; Nettles et al. 1980; Schaffer et al. 1981). A number of serious disease problems have been found associated with these translocated raccoons and will be discussed further in subsequent sections of this chapter.

Baseline values for serum proteins (Doyle et al. 1975) and various determinations on hematology, serum chemistry, and urinalysis (Hoff et al. 1974a) have been published for raccoons in Florida. Data on anesthesia have been presented also (Bigler and Hoff 1974).

II. Environmental contaminants

Residues of 15 different pesticides were reported from omental fat of 24 raccoons collected in Collier County (n = 10), Sarasota County (n = 10), and Duval County (n = 4) (Nalley et al. 1975). These included alpha-BHC, beta-BHC, gamma-BHC, aldrin, dieldrin, octachlor epoxide, heptachlor epoxide, o,p'-DDT, o,p'-DDE, o,p'-DDD, p,p'-DDT, p,p'-DDE, p,p'-DDD, methoxychlor, and trans-nonachlor. Concentrations, for the most part, were less than 1 ppm and of little concern except for methoxychlor, which occurred at 3.1 and 1.8 ppm in each of two raccoons from Collier County (Marco Island) and at 2.7 and 36.8 ppm in each of two raccoons from Sarasota County (Phillipi Creek). The animal with the 36.8 ppm concentration was an adult female; the significance of this is unknown. The authors concluded that raccoons could be used to monitor environmental contamination by certain compounds that are associated with industrial development.

Wheeler et al. (1977) reported residues of the chlorinated hydrocarbon mirex in six raccoons from the Dee Dot Ranch in Duval County. One animal was collected before the area was treated with mirex (for fire ant control), two were collected one month after treatment, one at six months, one at one year,

and one at two years. Concentrations of mirex in brain, fat, liver, muscle, and stomach contents were less than 1 ppm except for the fat samples at one month, which measured 2.24 ppm. The significance of these observations is unknown.

Radionuclide concentrations have been studied in raccoons in several areas of Florida. These were summarized by Bigler et al. (1975a) (Table 12-1). There seemed to be a slight decrease in the concentrations of cesium-137 going from north to south in Florida and the reverse for strontium-90. Bigler et al. (1975a) also learned that raccoons that feed heavily in salt marshes accumulate very small amounts of radioisotopes. This was believed to be due to the dilution of radiocesium because of the availability of potassium and other elements in these marshes and the resultant relative decrease in uptake by these animals. A similar phenomenon has been noted for white-tailed deer that utilize saltmarsh habitats (Jenkins and Fendley 1971).

Hoff et al. (1977) reported on concentrations of lead, zinc, and cadmium in kidneys

Table 12-1
Mean concentrations of cesium-137 (PCI/kg of muscle, wet wt) and strontium-90 (PCI/kg of bone, wet wt) in raccoons from Florida, 1969–73

Location	No. raccoons sampled	Mean	Range
Cesium–137			
North[a]	75	3,255	208–16,805
Central[b]	41	2,759	38–14,070
South[c]	28	2,419	50–11,980
Strontium–90			
Central	5	4,036	2,027–6,524
South	4	4,664	212–11,692

Source: Bigler et al. (1975a).
[a]Various locations north of a line between Citrus and St. Johns counties.
[b]Area between North and South.
[c]Various locations south of a line between Lee and Brevard counties.

Table 12-2
Concentrations (ppm wet wt) of lead, zinc, and cadmium in 14 adult raccoons from Marco Island

Heavy metal	Concentration		Standard deviation
	Mean	Range	
Lead	0.47	0.19–0.73	0.22
Zinc	75.88	45.12–105.00	16.54
Cadmium	2.48	0.85–7.30	1.66

Source: Hoff et al. (1977).

of 14 adult raccoons from an estuarine environment on Marco Island (Collier County). Values are summarized in Table 12-2. Data on concentrations of mercury in raccoons from Florida are given in Table 12-3. Adult raccoons tended to have higher concentrations of mercury than juveniles (Cumbie 1975). The significance of these findings to raccoons is unknown.

Hoff (1973) reported three instances of teeth stained with aluminum in a sample of 17 raccoons trapped in Sarasota County. He postulated that this was due to the animals chewing on aluminum soft drink or beer cans,

and attached no health significance to the observation.

III. Rabies

Undoubtedly the most significant disease of raccoons in Florida is rabies. Currently the raccoon is considered to be the most important reservoir host for rabies virus in Florida (Burridge et al. 1986) and the main source for terrestrial animal rabies in the state (Smith et al. 1990). There is a considerable volume of literature on rabies in Florida, notable of which is the monograph by Prather et al. (1975) that recently has been updated and extensively revised by Burridge et al. (1986). The reader is referred to this latter publication and to the review published by Sikes (1981) for further information on this important disease.

The etiologic agent of rabies is a neurotropic virus in the family Rhabdoviridae (Burridge et al. 1986). Historically it was felt that rabies viruses were similar the world over, but recent research has shown that there are

Table 12-3
Concentrations of mercury in tissues of raccoons from Florida, 1971–74

Tissue	No. raccoons exam.	Concentration (ppm) of mercury		Date	Location
		Mean	Range		
Hair[a]	23	7.50	0.52–35.7	1971–73	No. Fla.[c]
	11	4.35	0.84–10.1	1971–73	So. Fla.[d]
Muscle[b]	3	0.15	NG	1971–73	No. Fla.[c]
	6	0.14	NG	1971–73	So. Fla.[d]
Liver	2	7.05	5.90–8.20	1973–74	Collier Co.
	1	1.20	—	1973	Duval Co.
	1	0.08	—	1974	Alachua Co.

Sources: Data on hair and muscle from Cumbie (1975), Cumbie & Jenkins (1975), and Bigler et al. (1975a); data on liver from Gourlie (1984).
[a]Values are on air-dry weight basis.
[b]Values are on wet-weight basis.
[c]Various locations north of a line between Citrus and St. Johns counties.
[d]Various locations south of a line between Lee and Brevard counties.

a number of distinct antigenic variants (Schneider 1982; Sureau et al. 1983).

Transmission occurs most commonly when saliva containing rabies virus is introduced into an open wound or abrasion of the skin or mucous membranes by the bite of a rabid animal (Burridge et al. 1986). A less common method is via inhalation of airborne virus in caves containing dense populations of infected bats (Constantine 1962).

The first report of a case of rabies in a raccoon occurred in Brevard County in 1947 (Scatterday et al. 1960). The virus appeared to spread northward and southward along major waterways in Florida, and by 1957 it was found throughout peninsular Florida (Bigler et al. 1973). By 1987 rabid raccoons had been reported in all 67 counties in Florida except Escambia (Figure 12-1). There are two annual peaks in prevalence of rabies in raccoons, one in March and one in September (Figure 12-2), possibly due to breeding activities when adult males move extensively and engage in fighting (Bigler et al. 1973; Burridge et al. 1986). The yearly number of cases of rabies in raccoons from 1964 through 1987 is presented in Table 12-4.

Several localized epizootics of raccoon ra-

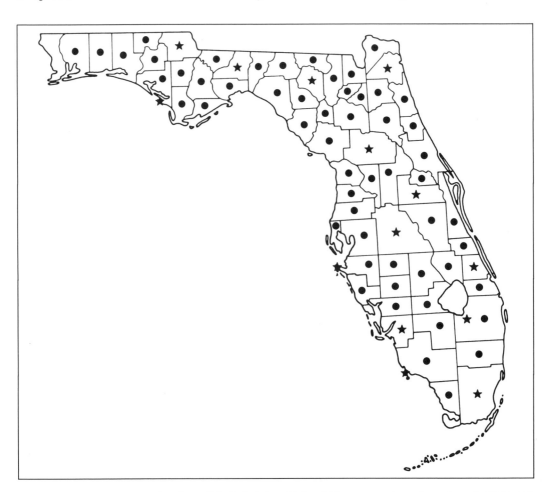

FIGURE 12-1. Counties in Florida (solid circles) in which rabid raccoons have been found, 1947–87. Stars indicate areas where rabies epizootics have occurred. See Table 12-5 for more details. (After Burridge et al. 1986; Bigler 1988.)

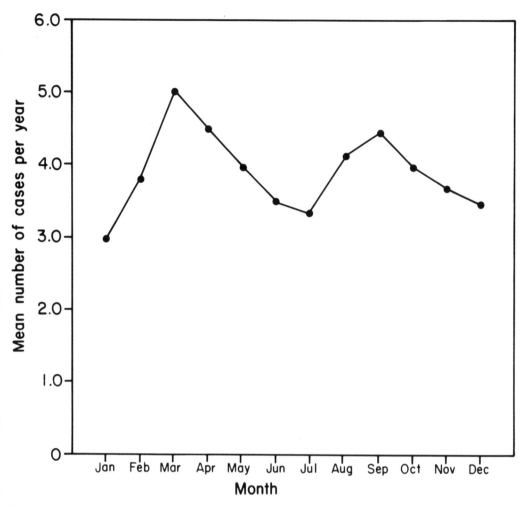

FIGURE 12-2. Monthly distribution of cases of rabies in raccoons in Florida, 1955–83. (From Burridge et al. 1986.)

bies have occurred in Florida. Data on these have been presented and discussed by Kappus et al. (1970), Bigler et al. (1973), and Burridge et al. (1986) and are summarized in Table 12-5. All outbreaks began between October and January. The epizootics on Longboat Key, Marco Island, and Tyndall Air Force Base occurred in urban areas of dense human populations where land development activities had all but eliminated the natural habitat of the raccoons (Bigler et al. 1973). The area with the most dense population of raccoons (Longboat Key) experienced a more rapid

spread of rabies virus than the other two areas with less dense populations (Bigler et al. 1973). Other outbreaks have been more widespread and have lasted for several years. These are also summarized in Table 12-5, although fewer details are available.

The signs of rabies vary considerably from host to host. Those that are suggestive of rabies include behavioral changes, peripheral neuritis, and various types of paralysis (Burridge et al. 1986). The most common signs in raccoons are aggressiveness, wandering into residential areas during the daytime, incoor-

Table 12-4
Number of cases of rabies in raccoons in
Florida, 1964–87

Year	No. cases	Year	No. cases
1964	47	1976	51
1965	32	1977	69
1966	37	1978	33
1967	50	1979	54
1968	82	1980	84
1969	136	1981	79
1970	68	1982	51
1971	48	1983	56
1972	49	1984	92
1973	23	1985	122
1974	39	1986	128
1975	30	1987	71

Sources: Prather et al. (1975); Burridge et al. (1986); Department of Health and Rehabilitative Services (1984); Bigler (1988).

Table 12-5
Summary of epizootics of raccoon rabies in
Florida

Date	Specific area	County	Estimated no. raccoons/ sq. mile
1965–66	South of Lake Okeechobee	Palm Beach	NG[a]
1967–68	Bradenton	Manatee	NG
1969	Longboat Key	Manatee, Sarasota	69
1970–71	Marco Island	Collier	25
1970–71	Tyndall Air Force Base	Bay	32
1974	Matheson Hammock	Dade	NG
1977	NG	Marion	NG
1977	NG	Lee	NG
1980	NG	Duval	NG
1981	NG	Suwannee	NG
1982–85	NG	Leon	NG
1984–87	NG	Polk, Orange	NG
1985–86	NG	Jackson	NG
1987	NG	St. Lucie	NG

Sources: Bigler et al. (1973); Department of Health and Rehabilitative Services (1984); Bigler (1988).
[a]NG = not given by authors.

dination, and inability to walk (McLean 1975).

At the site of inoculation the rabies virus replicates in muscle, connective tissue, or nerves and then progresses into nerves to the spinal cord and eventually the brain. After the virus enters the brain, paralytic signs occur and subsequently this is followed by depression, coma, and death from respiratory arrest (Murphy 1983). There are usually no gross lesions except some cerebral edema. Microscopic lesions include perivascular mononuclear infiltration and in about 80% of the cases the presence of Negri bodies within the cytoplasm of neurons (Burridge et al. 1986).

Rabies is almost always fatal. It has been shown, however, that raccoons can survive the disease and produce antibodies in response to the infection. In several studies, up to 35% of the population has been found to have rabies antibodies, indicating past infection and subsequent survival (McLean 1975; Bigler et al. 1973; Bigler et al. 1983). Recov-

ery, however, in domestic animals and man is very rare (Burridge et al. 1986).

In addition to the harmful effect of rabies on populations of raccoons, the public health implications of this disease must be considered. As previously mentioned, several epizootics along Florida's coastline have occurred in connection with land development activities that have included destruction of habitat via dredging, filling, and clearing operations (Bigler et al. 1973). Outbreaks in other more inland areas such as Orange, Marion, and Leon counties have been associated also with intensive land development (Bigler 1988). This has resulted in the raccoons moving to more urban areas and becoming adapted to close association with man. This situation results in a significant increase in the possibility of transfer of raccoon rabies to humans.

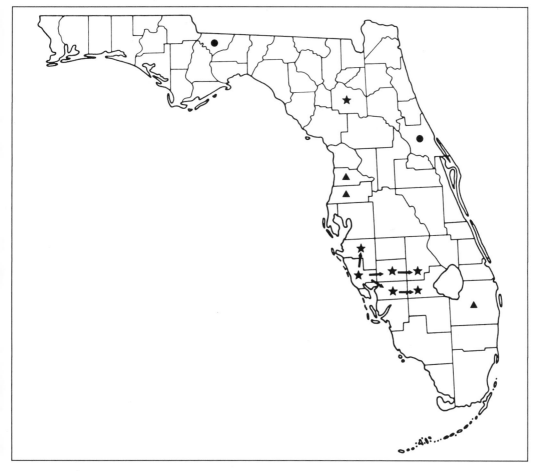

FIGURE 12-3. Counties in Florida in which canine distemper has been diagnosed in raccoons. Stars indicate areas where epizootics of distemper have occurred. Arrows show directions of spread of the 1972–73 epizootic. Triangles indicate counties in which a presumptive diagnosis of canine distemper was made. Solid circle represents a single case reported.

Bigler et al. (1973) stated that raccoons bite or scratch about 350 people per year in Florida. This figure may be much higher now due to the increased human populations, and would result in very significant exposure of people to rabies.

The raccoon is a popular wild animal pet and many are kept as such in Florida. At the present time there is no method available to immunize raccoons against rabies. Because of this, and because of the high prevalence of rabies virus in raccoons, it is recommended

that raccoons not be kept as pets (Burridge et al. 1986).

IV. Canine distemper

Canine distemper (CD) is an acute or sub-acute febrile disease caused by a paramyxovirus known as the virus of Carre. Transmission is by direct contact or aerosol (Budd 1981). Signs include dyspnea, ataxia, clonic convulsions, spasms of hind legs, ascending paralysis, progressive blindness, loss of appetite, emaciation, diarrhea, and coma (Hoff et al. 1974b). There is some evidence that CD virus infection lowers resistance and allows development of latent infections of other diseases such as toxoplasmosis (Moller 1951). In addition to the raccoon the disease also occurs in various wild canids and mustelids (Budd 1981). In Florida, gray foxes are known to have the disease as well as raccoons (Hoff et al. 1974b). Four of the five documented CD epizootics (Figure 12-3) have involved both raccoons and gray foxes.

In 1972–1973 an epizootic of CD occurred in Sarasota County and involved at least 114 raccoons and 8 gray foxes (Hoff et al. 1974b). During this outbreak, which lasted for two years, CD virus was isolated from two clinically ill raccoons on two occasions, seven months apart. The disease appeared first in the fox population and subsequently was introduced into raccoons (Figure 12-4). The source of the virus was not determined. The epizootic spread into the neighboring counties of Manatee, DeSoto, and Charlotte, and by the fall of 1973 it had spread into Glades and Highlands counties (Figure 12-3). During the outbreak there was no observed change in the number of cases of CD reported in domestic dogs in Sarasota County.

In the winter of 1977 an epizootic of CD occurred again in Sarasota County and involved around 100 raccoons and several gray foxes. Two raccoons examined at necropsy had lesions consistent with CD including intracytoplasmic eosinophilic inclusions (Figure 12-5) in the renal pelvis and transitional epithelium of the urinary bladder and focal demyelination of the cerebellar white matter (Woodward 1977).

Canine distemper appears to be enzootic in Sarasota County and neighboring areas with the eruption of periodic epizootics such

as the ones in 1972–1973 and 1977. McLean (1988) conducted serologic studies and found 58 of 145 (40%) raccoons in Manatee County and 48 of 77 (62%) raccoons in Sarasota County to be seropositive. He also found several positive opossums and one positive gray fox. This was in 1968–1969, several years before the 1972–1973 outbreak.

Three other epizootics of CD in Florida have been recognized (Wright and Forrester 1988). These occurred in Alachua County (December 1986–November 1987), Pasco and Hernando counties (February and March 1987), and Palm Beach County (February and March 1988). As in other outbreaks of CD, gray foxes as well as raccoons were affected, except for Alachua County, which involved only raccoons. Large numbers of raccoons were found with signs of CD in the Pasco/Hernando and the Palm Beach outbreaks, but a diagnosis of CD was presumptive, since virus was not isolated and inclusions were not demonstrated histologically. During these die-offs, however, definitive diagnoses were made for gray foxes in these latter two areas and for raccoons in the Alachua County epizootic. The numbers of animals involved in these incidents were not determined, but reports from various observers indicated that they were extensive. Rabies was not a factor, but one raccoon from Alachua County had toxoplasmosis as well as CD.

In 1983 a single case of CD was diagnosed in a raccoon from Gadsden County (SCWDS records), and in 1990 a single case was diagnosed in Volusia County (Forrester 1990).

The impact of these epizootics on raccoon and fox populations is not known, since no studies of the densities of the host species were conducted in connection with the die-offs. Hoff et al. (1974b), however, pointed out that there were considerably fewer "nuisance calls" concerning sick raccoons and

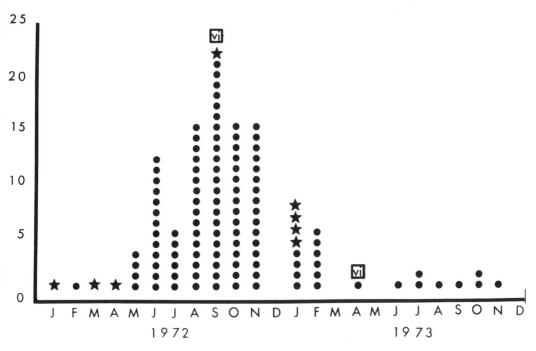

FIGURE 12-4. Epizootic curve for canine distemper outbreak in raccoons (dots) and gray foxes (stars) in Sarasota County, Florida, in 1972–73. Vi = virus isolations. (From Hoff et al. 1974b.)

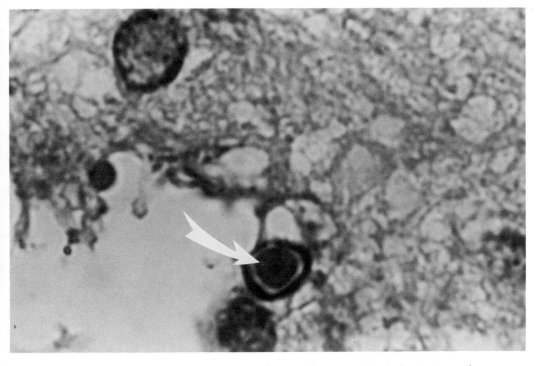

FIGURE 12-5. Intracytoplasmic inclusion (arrow) of canine distemper virus in brain tissue of a raccoon.

foxes received by county animal control officers from the general public after the epizootic of 1972–1973 than before it occurred.

V. Parvovirus infections

Parvovirus infections have been reported in raccoons that were being translocated from Florida, Texas, and Virginia into other parts of the Southeast (Nettles et al. 1980). Many of these animals had severe enteritis. At necropsy the intestinal lesions consisted of edema, hyperemia, and focal mucosal necrosis. This parvovirus has been shown to be different from canine parvovirus (Appel and Parrish 1982).

Five of 30 (17%) raccoons from Collier County were seropositive for parvovirus (Table 12-6). The impact of this virus on raccoon populations is unknown, but because of the severe enteritis caused by it in a number of cases, it may be important.

VI. Arboviruses

Six arboviruses have been reported from raccoons in Florida (Table 12-7). There is no

Table 12-6
Prevalence of serologic reactors to parvovirus in raccoons from Collier County, Florida

Year	No. raccoons exam.	No. raccoons pos.	Reciprocal titers[a]
1967	1	1	10,000
1969	1	0	—
1971	3	0	—
1972	1	1	2,000
1973	2	0	—
1974	8	0	—
1984	1	0	—
1985	13	3	15, 20, 10,000
Total	30	5	—

Source: Roelke (1985).
[a]Serum neutralization titers.

evidence that any of these viruses are harmful to raccoons (Seymour and Yuill 1981). The raccoon, however, may be of some importance as a reservoir host for these viruses; all except Keystone and Sawgrass are of veterinary or public health significance.

VII. Miscellaneous viruses

There are two reports of the isolation of encephalomyocarditis virus from raccoons in Florida. One was from Osceola County in 1961 (Gainer 1961) and one was from a raccoon trapped on a hog farm in Polk County in 1966 (Gainer 1967; Gainer and Bigler 1967; Gainer et al. 1968). This latter observation was made during an investigation of an epizootic of encephalomyocarditis in domestic swine. This cardiovirus is known to cause disease in swine (Gillespie and Timoney 1981) and exotic mammals in zoos in Florida (Gaskin et al. 1980), but its significance to the health of raccoons is unknown. The role of raccoons in dissemination of the virus to domestic and wild swine and other mammals has not been determined.

Laham (1978) isolated a syncytium-forming virus or foamy virus from three of four raccoons from Marco Island, Collier County. The virus, called raccoon syncytium-forming virus (RSFV), was recovered from spleen, greater omentum, kidney, lungs, and peripheral blood leukocytes. Attempts to isolate the virus from two raccoons trapped on Merritt Island (Brevard County) were unsuccessful. Through a serologic survey Laham (1978) found that RSFV was widespread in Florida, discovering 56 positive raccoons in a sample of 120 from 11 counties (Table 12-8). The significance of this virus to raccoons and other species of wildlife is unknown. Syncytium-forming viruses have been isolated from domestic cats and cattle with respiratory diseases and other problems, but experimental

Table 12-7

Arboviruses reported from raccoons in Florida

Virus	No. raccoons Exam.	No. raccoons Pos.	Date	Location	Data source
Everglades	5	0	1966–68	"South Florida"	Bigler (1969)
	10	4	1969	Indian River	Bigler (1971)
	917	39	1965–74	NG[a]	Bigler et al. (1975b)
	107	9	1965–69	"South Florida"[b]	Lord et al. (1973), Berge (1975)
SLE[c]	917	5	1965–74	NG	Bigler et al. (1975b)
	NG	5	1969	Manatee	" " " "
	47[e]	1[e]	1969	Hillsborough	Wellings et al. (1972)
EEE[d]	917	1	1965–74	NG	Bigler et al. (1975b)
	57[e]	2[e]	1963–70	"Tampa Bay Area"	Wellings et al. (1972)
Sawgrass	NG	3	1964	Pinellas, Hillsborough	Sather et al. (1970b)
Tensaw	144	35	1965–74	NG	Bigler et al. (1975b)
Keystone	144	3	1965–74	NG	" " " "
	25	3	1964–67	Hillsborough	Jennings et al. (1968), Taylor et al. (1971)

Note: Unless indicated otherwise, all data are from serosurveys.
[a]NG = not given by authors.
[b]Big Cypress Swamp and the "Everglades."
[c]SLE = St. Louis encephalitis.
[d]EEE = eastern equine encephalomyelitis.
[e]Virus isolations, not serology.

Table 12-8

Prevalence of serologic reactors[a] to raccoon syncytium-forming virus in Florida

County	No. raccoons tested	No. raccoons pos.
Alachua	8	3
Clay	2	1
Collier	68	39
Columbia	4	0
Dade	4	1
Duval	5	1
Levy	3	0
Monroe	3	0
Polk	2	2
Sarasota	16	9
Suwannee	5	3
Totals	120	56

Source: Laham (1978).
[a]Immunodiffusion test.

studies have not shown the virus to be pathogenic (Gillespie and Timoney 1981).

Roelke et al. (1988) examined serologically 18 raccoons from Collier County and 36 from Brevard County for antibodies to pseudorabies virus. The 18 samples from Collier County were negative; three of the samples from Brevard County (Cape Canaveral) were positive. Raccoons are considered to be major reservoir hosts of pseudorabies virus and have been implicated in the spread of the virus to domestic pigs (Thawley and Wright 1982; Wright and Thawley 1980). At one time it was felt that raccoons were dead-end hosts for pseudorabies virus, but studies by Platt et al. (1983) and Goyal et al. (1986) have shown that infections occur naturally in the wild and that the virus can spread from raccoons to other animals. Infected raccoons frequently exhibit depression and localized pruritis (Thawley and Wright 1982; Goyal et al. 1986), but such observations have not been made on raccoons in Florida. The epidemiologic relationship between pseudorabies infections in raccoons and in wild hogs in Florida should be investigated.

Antibodies to infectious canine hepatitis virus were found in 3 of 145 (2%) and 4 of 77 (5%) raccoons from Manatee and Sarasota counties, respectively, in 1968–1969 (McLean 1988). This virus is known to cause encephalitis in foxes (see Chapter 16) and hepatitis in dogs and skunks (Cabasso 1981).

There are, however, reports of seropositive raccoons in other parts of the United States (see review in Cabasso 1981), but nothing is known about the pathogenicity of this virus to raccoons.

VIII. Rickettsiae

Schaffer et al. (1978) found 2 of 20 raccoons from Hillsborough County infected with the rickettsial agent *Haemobartonella procyoni*.

Table 12-9
Summary of findings on bacterial diseases of raccoons in Florida

Disease/agent	Basis of diagnosis	Year	No. raccoons Exam.	Pos.	Location (county)	Data source
Leptospirosis[a]						
Leptospira interrogans	Serology	NG[b]	21[c]	10[d]	Leon[f]	Shotts et al. (1975)
	Necropsy, culture	NG	21[c]	8[e]	Leon[f]	" " " "
	Serology	1968–69	157	80	Manatee	McLean (1988)
	Serology	1968–69	80	7	Sarasota	" "
Brucellosis						
Brucella canis	Serology	1968–69	145	1	Manatee	McLean (1988), Bigler (1973)
	Serology	1968–69	77	3	Sarasota	McLean (1988), Bigler (1973)
	Serology	NG	269	1	NG	Hoff et al. (1974c)
Tularemia						
Francisella tularensis	Serology	1955–57	69	4	Leon	McKeever et al. (1958a)
	Serology	1965–73	801	26	NG	Hoff et al. (1975)
Salmonellosis[g]						
Salmonella spp.	Necropsy, culture	1969–73	168	28	See Table 12–10	Bigler et al. (1974)
		1973–74	42	22		White et al. (1975)
Edwardsiellosis[g]						
Edwardsiella tarda	Necropsy, culture	1973–74	42	7	Collier, Duval	" " " "

[a]McKeever et al. (1958d) cultured 117 raccoons from Decatur and Thomas counties in southern Georgia (near the Florida border) and found 5 positive for *Leptospira*. Two were positive for serovar *grippotyphosa*, 2 for *australis* A, and 1 for *ballum*.
[b]NG = not given by authors.
[c]The same 21 raccoons were examined serologically and at necropsy.
[d]Reacting serovars were *grippotyphosa* (9 raccoons) and *ballum* (1 raccoon).
[e]Reacting serovar was *grippotyphosa* (all 8 raccoons).
[f]Author presented combined data on raccoons from Leon County, Florida, and from South Grady and Thomas counties in southern Georgia without separating out data from each county.
[g]Carrier state, not disease.

Ten other raccoons from Glades County and 3 from Orange County were negative. This rickettsia is believed to be nonpathogenic to raccoons (Schaffer et al. 1978).

IX. Bacterial diseases

A number of bacterial infections have been reported from raccoons in Florida (Table 12-9) and include 19 serovars of *Salmonella* (Table 12-10). The impact of these bacterial infections on populations of raccoons is unknown and their main importance is most likely from a zoonotic standpoint. All of these

Table 12-10
Serovars of *Salmonella* isolated from raccoons in Florida, 1969–74

Serovar	No. isolates	County
S. carrian	7	Collier, Nassau, St. Johns, Volusia
S. meunchen	6	Hillsborough, St. Johns, Suwannee, Bay, Duval
S. anatum	4	Martin, St. Johns, Bay, Collier
S. miami	4	Hillsborough, Bay, Collier, Duval
S. hartford	4	Highlands, Collier, Duval, Indian River
S. java	3	Nassau, Martin, Bay
S. mississippi	3	Bay
S. typhimurium (var.) *copenhagen*	3	Bay
S. bareilly	3	Collier
S. saint-paul	2	Monroe, Collier
S. newport	2	Bay, Collier
S. tallahassee	2	Collier
S. mulado	1	Duval
S. pensacola	1	Collier
S. manhattan	1	Collier
S. oranienburg	1	Collier
S. lichfield	1	Collier
S. javiana	1	Collier
S. infantis	1	Collier

Sources: Bigler et al. (1974); White et al. (1975).

are infective to man and the raccoon may serve as an important reservoir host. Twelve species or serovars of bacteria were isolated from raccoons found clinically ill with canine distemper (Table 12-11). These infections were probably secondary to the primary disease (canine distemper) affecting these raccoons.

X. Mycotic infections

McKeever et al. (1958c) examined 583 raccoons from southeastern Georgia and northwestern Florida for ringworm fungi during 1954 to 1956. A species of *Microsporum* (red variety) was cultured from hair samples from one of these raccoons. This fungus is not believed to be pathogenic and this finding is therefore probably not significant, but represents a case of contamination from soil since this organism is commonly found in such habitats.

XI. Protozoan parasites

The protozoans reported from raccoons in Florida are listed in Table 12-12. The pathologic importance of these eight species has not been determined, but two of them (*Toxoplasma gondii* and *Trypanosoma cruzi*) are zoonotic parasites.

XII. Helminths

Forty-two species of helminths are known from raccoons in Florida. These include 19 species of trematodes, 18 nematodes, 4 cestodes, and 1 acanthocephalan. Data on distribution, prevalence, and intensity are given in Table 12-13 (trematodes), Table 12-14 (nematodes), and Table 12-15 (cestodes and acanthocephalans).

Table 12-11

Bacteria isolated from the blood, brain, and viscera of raccoons clinically ill with canine distemper, Sarasota County, November 1972

Bacterium	No. raccoons pos.[a]						
	Blood	Brain	Liver	Lung	Spleen	Kidney	Intestine
Escherichia coli	0	3	5	3	5	4	4
Proteus mirabilis	2	1	1	1	1	1	3
Clostridium perfringens	2	1	1	0	1	1	0
Staphylococcus, coagulase-positive	0	1	2	0	2	1	0
Staphylococcus, coagulase-negative	3	0	0	0	0	0	0
Streptococcus, beta-hemolytic	0	4	4	3	4	4	0
Streptococcus, beta-hemolytic, Group G	2	0	0	0	0	0	0
Streptococcus faecium	3	0	0	0	0	0	0
Streptococcus faecium var. *durans*	1	0	0	0	0	0	0
Streptococcus faecium var. *liquefaciens*	1	0	0	0	0	0	0
Pseudomonas sp.	0	0	1	0	1	1	0
Bacillus sp.	0	0	0	0	0	1	0

Source: Hoff (1972).
[a]Blood results from 6 raccoons; other results from 5 raccoons.

Little is known about the pathogenicity of many of these parasites. Schaffer (1979) and Schaffer et al. (1981) reviewed the pathogenic effects of various helminths of raccoons in the southeastern United States. One trematode (*Heterobilharzia americana*), one cestode (*Spirometra mansonoides*), and nine nematodes (*Crenosoma goblei, Dracunculus insignis, Filaroides* sp., *Gnathostoma procyonis, Molineus barbatus, Physaloptera rara, Placoconus lotoris, Strongyloides* sp., and *Trichinella spiralis*) were considered by Schaffer (1979) to be pathogenic to raccoons or potentially pathogenic due to their recognized harmful effects in other hosts. Of these 11 species, the most important seem to be: (1) the blood fluke *Heterobilharzia americana*, (2) the lungworms *Crenosoma goblei* and *Filaroides* sp., (3) the stomach worm *Gnathostoma procyonis*, and (4) the hook-worm *Placoconus lotoris*. *Heterobilharzia americana* infections result in livers that are firm, pale, and shrunken. Miscroscopic lesions include severe periportal fibrosis, portal tracts thickened by collagenous fibers, periportal granulomas, and multifocal granulomatous pneumonitis caused by eggs in the lung tissue (Bartsch and Ward 1976; Schaffer 1979). *Crenosoma goblei* and *Filaroides* sp. have been associated with verminous pneumonia (Johnson 1970; Schaffer 1979). Chandler (1942) felt that *Gnathostoma procyonis* was the most pathogenic parasite of raccoons when infections were of high intensity. Migrating larvae cause disruption of the muscle fibers, edema, and hemorrhage (Ash 1962). Adults in the stomach attach to the submucosa or muscularis and provoke the formation of fibroblastic granulomatous nodules (Chandler 1942; Jordan and Hayes 1959;

Table 12-12

Protozoan parasites reported from raccoons in Florida

Protozoan	No. raccoons		Date	County	Basis of diagnosis	Data source
	Exam.	Pos.				
Babesia lotori[a]	170	71	1972–73	Collier	Blood smears	Telford & Forrester (1991)
	14	11	1972–73	Duval	Blood smears	Telford & Forrester (1991)
	10	4	1977	Glades	Blood smears	Schaffer et al. (1978)
	20	7	1976	Hillsborough	Blood smears	" " " "
	3	0	1977	Orange	Blood smears	" " " "
Hepatozoon procyonis	10	1	1977	Glades	Blood smears, HP[b]	" " " "
	20	0	1976	Hillsborough	Blood smears, HP	" " " "
	3	0	1977	Orange	Blood smears, HP	" " " "
	1	1	1983	Gadsden	Blood smears, HP	SCWDS records
Toxoplasma gondii	34	0	1968	Manatee	Serology[d]	McLean (1988)
	16	0	1968	Sarasota	Serology	" "
	4	0	1972	Sarasota	Serology	Hoff (1972)
	530	94	NG[c]	NG	Serology	Burridge et al. (1979)
	1	1	1986	Alachua	Necropsy	Buergelt (1987)
Eimeria nuttalli	34	33	1973–74	Collier	Fecal analysis	Forrester (1985)
	1	1	1973	Indian River	Fecal analysis	" "
	10	7	1985	Monroe	Fecal analysis	" "
Eimeria procyonis	34	19	1973–74	Collier	Fecal analysis	" "
	1	1	1973	Indian River	Fecal analysis	" "
Isospora sp.	34	1	1973–74	Collier	Fecal analysis	" "
	1	0	1973	Indian River	Fecal analysis	" "
Sarcocystis sp.	34	1	1973–74	Collier	Fecal analysis	" "
	1	0	1973	Indian River	Fecal analysis	" "
Trypanosoma cruzi	10	1	1977	Glades	Blood smears, cultures	Schaffer et al. (1978)
	20	3	1976	Hillsborough	Blood smears, cultures	" " " "
	3	0	1977	Orange	Blood smears, cultures	" " " "
	608	9	1954–57	NG[e]	Culture of blood and tissues	McKeever et al. (1958b)
	144	3	1969–71	Alachua, Hillsborough, Levy[f]	Serology[g]	Irons (1971)
	170	1	1972–73	Collier	Blood smears	Telford & Forrester (1991)
	14	1	1972–73	Duval	Blood smears	Telford & Forrester (1991)

[a]Schaffer et al. (1978) referred to this parasite as *Babesia procyonis*, but Anderson et al. (1981) showed that this is invalid and named it *B. lotori*.
[b]HP = histopathology.
[c]NG = not given by authors.
[d]Indirect fluorescent antibody test.
[e]NG = not given by authors; animals were trapped in 9 counties in southwestern Georgia and 1 county (Leon) in Florida.
[f]Raccoons from 17 other counties in Florida were sampled; all were negative.
[g]Ouchterlony gel diffusion method.

Table 12-13
Trematodes reported from raccoons in Florida

Trematode	No. raccoons		Intensity		Date	County	Data source
	Exam.	Inf. (%)	Mean	Range			
Cathaemasiidae							
Ribeiroia ondatrae	20	1(5)	2	2	1976	Hillsborough	Schaffer (1979)
Cyathocotylidae							
Mesostephanus appendiculatoides	NG[a]	NG	NG	NG	NG	Pinellas	Hutton (1964)
Dicrocoelidae							
Lyperosomum sinuosum	31	22(71)	15	1–52	1973–74	Collier	Forrester (1985)
	19	4(21)	5	1–11	1973–74	Duval	" "
	2	1(50)	2	2	1973	Indian River	" "
Diplostomidae							
Fibricola cratera	18	1(1)	11	11	1977	Highlands	Schaffer (1979)
	20	5(25)	347	5–1,907	1976	Hillsborough	Harkema & Miller (1961, 1964)
	19	1(1)	NG	NG	NG	NG	Schaffer (1979)
Parallelorchis diglossus	18	3(17)	45	15–87	1977	Highlands	Schaffer (1979)
Pharyngostomoides adenocephala	19	5(26)	NG	NG	1960	Glades	Harkema & Miller (1961, 1964)
	10	2(20)	184	179–88	1977	Glades	Schaffer (1979)
Pharyngostomoides procyonis	18	15(83)	476	4–1,558	1977	Highlands	" "
	20	5(25)	2,122	15–10,414	1976	Hillsborough	" "
	NG	NG	NG	NG	NG	Jefferson	Loftin (1961)
	10	10(100)	1,163	113–4,607	1977	Glades	Schaffer (1979)
	18	17(94)	885	94–2,539	1977	Highlands	" "
	20	17(85)	1,310	9–7,039	1976	Hillsborough	" "
	3	2(67)	353	13–693	1977	Orange	" "
	19	19(100)	NG	NG	NG	NG	Harkema & Miller (1964)
	NG	NG	NG	NG	NG	Highlands	Kinsella (1987)
Heterophyidae							
Ascocotyle pachycystis	5	4(80)	NG	62–2,000	NG	"South Florida"	Schroeder and Leigh (1965)

Parasite	No. examined	No. infected (%)	No.	Range	Year	County	Reference
Ascocotyle angrense	NG	NG	NG	NG	NG	Pinellas	Sogandares-Bernal & Bridgman (1960), Hutton (1964)
Stictodora cursitans	12	2(17)	20	7–33	1973–74	Collier	Forrester (1985)
	NG	1(—)	NG	NG	1970–71	Levy	Kinsella & Heard (1974)
	NG	1(—)	NG	NG	1966	Monroe	"
Microphallidae							
Microphallus basodactylophallus	12	11(92)	9,950	556–62,570	1973–74	Collier	Forrester (1985)
Carneophallus bilobatus	12	2(17)	2,504	154–4,853	1973–74	Collier	"
C. turgidus	2	2(100)	"Several thousand"		1956	"South Florida"	Leigh (1958)
Gynaecotyla adunca	12	11(92)	534	1–4,140	1973–74	Collier	Forrester (1985)
Levinseniella sp.	12	2(17)	27	12–41	1973–74	Collier	"
Maritrema prosthometra	12	5(42)	2,051	130–6,830	1973–74	Collier	"
Microphallus sp.	12	12(100)	9,950	556–62,970	1973–74	Collier	"
	3	3(100)	NG	NG	1966	Monroe	Heard & Sikora (1969)
Probolocoryphe glandulosa	12	8(67)	20,102	60–151,370	1973–74	Collier	Forrester (1985)
Schistosomatidae							
Heterobilharzia americana	10	5(50)	3	1–6	1977	Glades	Schaffer (1979)
	18	11(61)	11	1–47	1977	Highlands	"
	20	17(85)	12	1–33	1976	Hillsborough	"
	3	3(100)	18	3–46	1977	Orange	"
	19	1(1)	NG	NG	NG	NG	Harkema & Miller (1964)
	18	12(67)	4	1–15	1973–74	Duval	Forrester (1985)

[a]NG = not given by author.

Table 12-14
Nematodes reported from raccoons in Florida

Nematode	No. raccoons		Intensity		Date	County	Data source
	Exam.	Inf. (%)	Mean	Range			
Placoconus lotoris	10	10(100)	69	4–207	1977	Glades	Schaffer (1979)
	18	16(89)	29	1–125	1977	Highlands	" "
	20	19(95)	32	2–98	1976	Hillsborough	" "
	3	1(33)	27	27	1977	Orange	" "
	19	12(63)	35	1–57	1973–74	Collier	Forrester (1985)
	19	19(100)	202	7–540	1973–74	Duval	" "
	1	1(100)	1	1	1973	Indian River	" "
	1	1(100)	6	6	1974	Alachua	" "
	NG[a]	NG	NG	NG	NG	Highlands	Kinsella (1987)
Gnathostoma procyonis	10	8(10)	5	2–10	1977	Glades	Schaffer (1979)
	18	15(83)	9	2–30	1977	Highlands	" "
	20	5(25)	1	1–2	1976	Hillsborough	" "
	19	15(79)	NG	NG	NG	NG	Harkema & Miller (1964)
	NG	NG	NG	NG	NG	"Florida"	Penner (1987)
Gongylonema pulchrum	20	1(5)	1	1	1976	Hillsborough	Schaffer (1979)
Physaloptera rara	18	1(6)	28	28	1977	Highlands	" "
	20	4(20)	2	1–3	1976	Hillsborough	" "
	3	2(67)	18	16–19	1977	Orange	" "
Physaloptera maxillaris	NG	NG	NG	NG	NG	"Florida"	Morgan (1941)
	NG	NG	NG	NG	NG	"Florida"	Penner (1987)
Synhimantus sp.	10	2(20)	21	2–39	1977	Glades	Schaffer (1979)
	18	13(72)	17	1–51	1977	Highlands	" "
	20	2(10)	5	1–8	1976	Hillsborough	" "
Procyonostrongylus muelleri	10	3(30)	3	1–5	1977	Glades	Schaffer (1979), Anderson et al. (1979)
	18	2(11)	4	1–6	1977	Highlands	Schaffer (1979), Anderson et al. (1979)
	20	1(5)	1	1	1976	Hillsborough	Schaffer (1979), Anderson et al. (1979)
Molineus barbatus	10	2(20)	3	1–4	1977	Glades	Schaffer (1979)
	20	15(75)	33	1–80	1976	Hillsborough	" "
	19	3(16)	NG	NG	NG	NG	Harkema & Miller (1964)
	18	13(72)	72	5–290	1973–74	Duval	Forrester (1985)
	18	6(33)	24	1–75	1973–74	Collier	" "
	1	1(100)	51	51	1974	Alachua	" "
Capillaria procyonis	10	4(40)	1	1–2	1977	Glades	Schaffer (1979)
	20	3(15)	2	2–4	1976	Hillsborough	" "
Capillaria putorii	20	2(10)	6	2–9	1976	Hillsborough	" "
Capillaria hepatica	5	0(—)	—	—	NG	Several[b]	Layne (1968)
Capillaria sp.	18	1(6)	1	1	1977	Highlands	Schaffer (1979)
Crenosoma goblei	10	3(30)	1	1	1977	Glades	" "
	18	10(56)	3	1–7	1977	Highlands	" "
	20	16(80)	8	1–26	1976	Hillsborough	" "
	3	1(33)	4	4	1977	Orange	" "
	33	3(9)	4	1–7	1973–74	Collier	Forrester (1985)
	17	3(18)	4	1–7	1973–74	Duval	" "
	1	1(100)	2	2	1974	Alachua	" "

(continued)

Table 12-14 *(continued)*

Nematode	No. raccoons Exam.	No. raccoons Inf. (%)	Intensity Mean	Intensity Range	Date	County	Data source
Filaroides sp.	20	2(10)	22	2–42	1976	Hillsborough	Schaffer (1979)
Dirofilaria tenuis	NG	2(—)	"Several"		1947	Sarasota	McIntosh (1954)
	75	35(47)	NG	NG	1982–83	Indian River	Sauerman & Nayar (1985)
	35	2(6)	NG	NG	NG	Alachua	Isaza & Courtney (1988)
	33	7(21)	NG	NG	NG	Brevard	Isaza & Courtney (1988)
	16	10(63)	NG	NG	1973	Collier	Wong (1973)
	11	5(45)	NG	NG	NG	Collier	Isaza & Courtney (1988)
	170	40(24)	—	—	1972–73	Collier	Telford & Forrester (1991)
Mansonella llewellyni	20	1(5)	1	1	1976	Hillsborough	Schaffer (1979)
	4	2(50)	NG	NG	1973	Duval	Wong (1973)
	14	2(14)	—	—	1972–73	Duval	Telford & Forrester (1991)
Dracunculus insignis	10	4(40)	3	1–8	1977	Glades	Schaffer (1979)
	18	3(17)	3	2–3	1977	Highlands	" "
	20	4(20)	2	1–3	1976	Hillsborough	" "
	19	6(32)	NG	NG	NG	NG	Harkema & Miller (1964)
	1	1(100)	1	1	1955	Alachua	Layne et al. (1960)
	1	1(100)	1	1	1959	Osceola	Layne et al. (1960)
	NG	NG	NG	NG	NG	Osceola	Penner (1987)
Strongyloides sp.	18	2(11)	6	2–9	1977	Highlands	Schaffer (1979)
	20	18(90)	236	2–1,263	1976	Hillsborough	" "
	18	7(39)	12	2–31	1973–74	Duval	Forrester (1985)
	19	1(5)	5	5	1974	Collier	" "
	1	1(100)	735	735	1974	Alachua	" "
Trichinella spiralis	10	1(10)	NG	NG	1977	Glades	Schaffer (1979)
	20	1(5)	NG	NG	1976	Hillsborough	" "
	109	4(4)	NG	NG	1962	Marion	Sholtens & Norman (1971)
	12	0(0)	—	—	1973	Duval	Forrester (1985)

[a]NG = not given by authors.
[b]Alachua, Highlands, Levy, and Monroe.

Table 12-15
Cestodes and acanthocephalans reported from raccoons in Florida

Helminth	No. raccoons		Intensity		Date	County	Data source
	Exam.	Inf. (%)	Mean	Range			
Cestoda							
Atriotaenia procyonis	10	3(30)	16	1–35	1977	Glades	Schaffer (1979)
	20	5(25)	40	1–127	1976	Hillsborough	" "
	19	3(16)	NG[a]	NG	NG	NG	Harkema & Miller (1964)
	NG	NG	NG	NG	NG	Jefferson	Loftin (1961)
Atriotaenia sp.	NG	NG	NG	NG	NG	Jefferson	" "
Mesocestoides variabilis	10	2(20)	215	116–313	1977	Glades	Schaffer (1979)
	18	1(5)	245	245	1977	Highlands	" "
	20	1(5)	13	13	1976	Hillsborough	" "
	19	1(5)	NG	NG	NG	NG	Harkema & Miller (1964)
Spirometra mansonoides	10	6(60)	5	1–11	1977	Glades	Schaffer (1979)
	20	3(15)	2	1–3	1976	Hillsborough	" "
	19	15(79)	NG	NG	NG	NG	Harkema & Miller (1964)
	NG	NG	NG	NG	NG	"Florida"	Penner (1987)
Acanthocephala							
Macracanthorhynchus ingens	10	5(50)	2	1–4	1977	Glades	Schaffer (1979)
	18	5(27)	3	1–5	1977	Highlands	" "
	20	11(55)	3	1–8	1976	Hillsborough	" "
	3	2(67)	13	11–14	1977	Orange	" "
	19	10(53)	NG	NG	NG	NG	Harkema & Miller (1964)
	20	2(10)	2	1–2	1973–74	Collier	Forrester (1985)
	19	4(21)	5	1–12	1973–74	Duval	Forrester (1985)
	NG	NG	NG	NG	NG	Monroe	Penner (1987)

[a]NG = not given by authors.

Ash 1962; Johnson 1970). Hookworm infections by *Placoconus lotoris* cause emaciation, anemia, hair loss, shagginess of the coat, and dark feces (Balasingam 1964a, 1964b). Adult worms attach to the muscosa of the small intestine and cause focal hemorrhage, erosion of the epithelium, atrophy of intestinal glands, and necrosis (Balasingam 1964a). Death has been reported when hookworms occur simultaneously with another nematode, *Molineus barbatus* (Balasingam 1964a). Hookworms are very prevalent

(87% overall) in Florida raccoons (see Table 12-14). Particularly severe infections were noted in animals from Duval County, where the prevalence was 100% and the mean intensity was 202 worms (range, 7–540) per raccoon.

The significance of the microphallid infections is unknown, but the high prevalence and intensities of these trematodes (Table 12-13) are cause for concern. Twelve raccoons from Marco Island (Collier County) contained mixed infections of from one to seven

Table 12-16
Examination of 158 raccoons in Florida for infections of *Baylisascaris procyonis*

County	Date	No. raccoons exam.	Technique	Data source
Alachua	1974	1	Necropsy	Forrester (1985)
	1985	11	Fecal flotation	Matthews (1985)
Brevard	1985	35	Fecal flotation	Forrester (1985)
Collier	1973–74	20	Necropsy	" "
	1985	10	Fecal flotation	Matthews (1985)
Duval	1973–74	19	Necropsy	Forrester (1985)
Glades	1977	10	Necropsy	Schaffer (1979)
Highlands	1976	18	Necropsy	" "
Hillsborough	1976	20	Necropsy	" "
Indian River	1973	1	Necropsy	Forrester (1985)
Monroe	1985	10	Fecal flotation	" "
Orange	1977	3	Necropsy	Schaffer (1979)

Note: All results were negative.

species of microphallids, which averaged 36,723 flukes per animal (range, 23–317,548). One of these species (*Microphallus basodactylophallus*) may be a zoonotic parasite (Heard and Overstreet 1983), but this has not been established. If it is shown to be infective to man, the problem would be associated with ingestion of raw or poorly cooked shrimp and crabs in which the infective stages are found.

Although raccoons are the normal definitive hosts of *Dirofilaria tenuis,* humans are also infected by this subcutaneous filariid (see reviews by Sauerman and Nayar 1985; Isaza and Courtney 1988). Twenty such cases were reported from Florida, 17 of which were from southern Florida (Beaver and Orihel 1965). Isaza and Courtney (1988) found that *D. tenuis* was more prevalent in southern Florida (Collier and Brevard counties) than in northern Florida (Alachua County), and suggested that this may account for the higher prevalence of human infections in southern Florida.

Considerable concern has been expressed recently over the zoonotic status of the raccoon ascaroid nematode *Baylisascaris procy-* *onis.* This nematode lives in the small intestine of raccoons and does little harm to the raccoon. However, infective eggs from raccoon feces can be ingested by other animals and the migrating larvae from these eggs can cause fatal or severe central nervous system disease when they enter the eye, spinal cord, or brain (Kazacos 1983). Fatalities have been reported in mice, squirrels, woodchucks, beaver, nutria, cottontail rabbits, chickens, quail, partridges, pigeons, turkeys, and other birds (Nettles et al. 1975; Kazacos 1983). In addition, there is information on cases in primates and man (Kazacos et al. 1981; Kazacos 1983). Data from 158 raccoons from 10 counties (Table 12-16) indicate that *Baylisascaris procyonis* is not present in Florida, but more animals from other areas should be checked before this is known for certain.

XIII. Arthropods

Ten species of parasitic arthropods are known from raccoons in Florida. These include two species of fleas, five ticks, and three mites (Table 12-17).

Table 12-17
Arthropod parasites reported from raccoons in Florida

Arthropod	Location (county)	Data source
Fleas		
Hoplopsyllus glacialis affinis	Okeechobee	Layne (1971)
Ctenocephalides felis	Hendry	Fox (1940)
Ticks		
Amblyomma americanum	"Northern Florida"	Rogers (1953)
	"Florida"	Bishopp & Trembley (1945)
Dermacentor variabilis	Citrus, Collier, Hendry, Hillsborough, Lee, Marion	Taylor (1951)
	Indian River, Brevard	FSCA[a]
	Indian River	Wilson & Kale (1972)
	Collier	Bigler (1973)
	Alachua	Boardman (1929)
	Hillsborough	Worth (1950)
	"Northern Florida"	Rogers (1953)
	NG[b]	Hoff et al. (1975)
	Palm Beach	Carpenter et al. (1946), SCWDS records
	Collier, Orange, Osceola	Travis (1941)
	Monroe	McLean (1988)
Ixodes texanus	Collier	Bigler (1973)
	Collier, Orange, Osceola	Travis (1941)
	"Northern Florida"	Rogers (1953)
	Liberty	Bigler (1973)
	Citrus, Collier, Hendry, Hillsborough, Lee, Marion	Taylor (1951)
Ixodes cookei	"Northern Florida"	Rogers (1953)
Ixodes scapularis	Collier, Orange, Osceola	Travis (1941)
	Collier	Bigler (1973)
	Indian River	FSCA
	Alachua	Boardman (1929)
	"Northern Florida"	Rogers (1953)
	Palm Beach	SCWDS records
Mites		
Eutrombicula multisetosa	Orange	Ewing (1943), Rohani & Cromroy (1979)
Eutrombicula splendens	Collier	Ewing (1943)
Eutrombicula sp.	Hillsborough	Worth (1950)

[a]FSCA = records from the Florida State Collection of Arthropods, Division of Plant Industry, Florida Department of Agriculture, Gainesville, Fla.
[b]NG = not given by authors.

The flea, *Hoplopsyllus glacialis affinis,* is of interest since it is a western flea normally found on rabbits (Layne 1971). The species may have been introduced into Florida when black-tailed jackrabbits were brought in during the 1930s to be used in training greyhounds. Currently there are wild populations of jackrabbits in Broward, Dade, and Hillsborough counties (Layne 1965, 1988). According to Layne (1971) the flea is well established in the peninsular part of the state and has been reported from cottontails in Dade, Highlands, Polk, and Putnam counties and from marsh rabbits in Lee County. It seems to be more prevalent during the warmer months (Layne 1971).

The American dog tick, *Dermacentor variabilis,* is a vector of the etiologic agent of Rocky Mountain spotted fever and can cause tick paralysis in animals and man (Strickland et al. 1976). Both *D. variabilis* and *Ixodes scapularis* are vectors of *Francisella tularensis,* the causative agent of tularemia.

XIV. Summary and conclusions

One hundred and thirty-two different parasites, disease agents, and environmental contaminants have been identified from raccoons in Florida. These include 16 pesticides, 5 heavy metals, 2 radionuclides, 12 viruses, 1 rickettsia, 35 bacteria, 1 fungus, 8 protozoans, 19 trematodes, 18 nematodes, 4 cestodes, 1 acanthocephalan, and 10 arthropods. Of these, rabies virus and canine distemper virus appear to be of most importance to raccoon populations. Significant epizootics of rabies and distemper have been documented. In addition, stomach worms, blood flukes, lungworms, and hookworms may be of significance.

Twenty of these disease agents are of public health significance and include the agents of rabies, encephalitis, encephalomyocarditis, salmonellosis, edwardsiellosis, tularemia, brucellosis, leptospirosis, toxoplasmosis, Chagas' disease, and filariasis. One microphallid trematode, one flea, three ticks, and one chigger are also potentially harmful to man. People who live in close proximity to raccoons or handle them for various reasons should be aware of these zoonotic diseases and should exercise appropriate precautions.

XV. Literature cited

Anderson, J.F., L.A. Magnarelli, and A.J. Sulzer. 1981. Raccoon babesiosis in Connecticut, USA: *Babesia lotori* sp. n. J. Parasitol. 67:417–425.

Anderson, R.C., A.K. Prestwood, and U.R. Strelive. 1979. *Procyonostrongylus meulleri* gen. et sp. n. (Metastrongyloidea: Angiostrongylidae) from the raccoon (*Procyon l. lotor*). J. Parasitol. 65:811–813.

Appel, M.J.G., and C.R. Parrish. 1982. Raccoons are not susceptible to canine parvovirus. J. Am. Vet. Med. Assoc. 18:1489.

Ash, L.R. 1962. Migration and development of *Gnathostoma procyonis* Chandler, 1942, in mammalian hosts. J. Parasitol. 48:306–313.

Balasingam, E. 1964a. On the pathology of *Placoconus lotoris* infections in raccoons (*Procyon lotor*). Can. J. Zool. 42:903–905.

———. 1964b. Studies on the life cycle and developmental morphology of *Placoconus lotoris* (Schwartz, 1925) Webster, 1956 (Ancylostomidae: Nematoda). Can J. Zool. 42:869–902.

Bartsch, R.C., and B.C. Ward. 1976. Visceral lesions in raccoons naturally infected with *Heterobilharzia americana*. Vet. Pathol. 13:241–249.

Beaver, P.C., and T.C. Orihel. 1965. Human infection with filariae of animals in the United States. Am. J. Trop. Med. Hyg. 14:1010–1029.

Berge, T.O. (ed.). 1975. International catalogue

of arboviruses including certain other viruses of vertebrates. 2d ed. USDHEW Pub. No. (CDC) 75-8301.

Bigler, W.J. 1969. Venezuelan encephalitis antibody studies in certain Florida wildlife. Bull. Wildl. Dis. Assoc. 5:267–270.

———. 1971. Serologic evidence of Venezuelan equine encephalitis virus infections in raccoons of south central Florida. J. Wildl. Dis. 7:166–170.

———. 1973. Unpublished data. HRS, Tallahassee, Fla.

———. 1988. Unpublished data. HRS, Tallahassee, Fla.

Bigler, W.J., and G.L. Hoff. 1974. Anesthesia of raccoons with ketamine hydrochloride. J. Wildl. Manage. 38:364–366.

Bigler, W.J., R.G. McLean, and H.A. Trevino. 1973. Epizootiologic aspects of raccoon rabies in Florida. Am. J. Epidemiol. 98:326–335.

Bigler, W.J., G.L. Hoff, A.M. Jasmin, and F.H. White. 1974. *Salmonella* infections in Florida raccoons, *Procyon lotor*. Arch. Environ. Health. 28:261–262.

Bigler, W.J., J.H. Jenkins, P.M. Cumbie, G.L. Hoff, and E.C. Prather. 1975a. Wildlife and environmental health: Raccoons as indicators of zoonoses and pollutants in southeastern United States. J. Am. Vet. Med. Assoc. 167:592–597.

Bigler, W.J., E. Lassing, E. Buff, A.L. Lewis, and G.L. Hoff. 1975b. Arbovirus surveillance in Florida: Wild vertebrate studies 1965–74. J. Wildl. Dis. 11:348–356.

Bigler, W.J., G.L. Hoff, J.S. Smith, R.G. McLean, H.A. Trevino, and J. Ingwersen. 1983. Persistence of rabies antibody in free-ranging raccoons. J. Infect. Dis. 14:8610.

Bishopp, F.C., and H.L. Trembley. 1945. Distribution and hosts of certain North American ticks. J. Parasitol. 31:1–54.

Boardman, E.T. 1929. Ticks of the Gainesville area. M.S. thesis, Univ. of Florida, Gainesville. 57 pp.

Budd, J. 1981. Distemper. In: Infectious diseases of wild mammals. J.W. Davis et al. (eds.). Iowa State Univ. Press, Ames. pp. 31–44.

Buergelt, C.D. 1987. Unpublished data. (Necropsy Report No. N86-0880, College of Vet. Med., Univ. of Florida, Gainesville).

Burridge, M.J., L.A. Sawyer, and W.J. Bigler. 1986. Rabies in Florida. Department of Health and Rehabilitative Services, Tallahassee, Fla. 147 pp.

Burridge, M.J., W.J. Bigler, D.J. Forrester, and J.M. Hennemann. 1979. Serologic survey for *Toxoplasma gondii* in wild animals in Florida. J. Am. Vet. Med. Assoc. 175:964–967.

Cabasso, V.J. 1981. Infectious canine hepatitis. In: Infectious diseases of wild mammals. J.W. Davis et al. (eds.). Iowa State Univ. Press, Ames. pp. 191–195.

Carpenter, S.J., R.W. Chamberlain, and L. Peoples. 1946. Tick collections at army installations in the Fourth Service Command. Entomol. News. 57:71–76.

Chandler, A.C. 1942. The helminths of raccoons in east Texas. J. Parasitol. 28:255–268.

Constantine, D.G. 1962. Rabies transmission by non-bite route. Public Health Rep. 77:287–289.

Cumbie, P.M. 1975. Mercury in hair of bobcats and raccoons. J. Wildl. Manage. 39:419–425.

Cumbie, P.M., and J.H. Jenkins. 1975. Mercury accumulation in native mammals of the southeast. Proc. Ann. Conf. S.E. Game Fish Comm. 28:639–647.

Department of Health and Rehabilitative Services. 1984. Florida morbidity statistics, 1984. HRS, Tallahassee. 121 pp.

Doyle, T.J., G.L. Hoff, and W.J. Bigler. 1975. Seasonal variations in total serum protein concentration in an estuarine raccoon population. J. Wildl. Dis. 11:58–61.

Ewing, H.E. 1943. The American chiggers (larvae of the Trombiculinae) of the genus *Acariscus*, new genus. Proc. Entomol. Soc. Wash. 45:57–66.

Forrester, D.J. 1985. Unpublished data. Univ. of Florida, Gainesville.

———. 1990. Unpublished data. Univ. of Florida, Gainesville.

Fox, I. 1940. Fleas of eastern United States. Iowa State Coll. Press, Ames. 191 pp.

Gainer, J.H. 1961. Studies on the natural and experimental infections of animals in Florida with the encephalomyocarditis virus. Ann. Proc. U.S. Livestock San. Assoc. 65:556–572.

———. 1967. Encephalomyocarditis virus infections in Florida, 1960–1966. J. Am. Vet. Med. Assoc. 151:421–425.

Gainer, J.H., and W.J. Bigler. 1967. Encephalomyocarditis (EMC) virus recovered from two cotton rats and a raccoon. Bull. Wildl. Dis. Assoc. 3:47–49.

Gainer, J.H., J.R. Sandefur, and W.J. Bigler. 1968. High mortality in a Florida swine herd infected with encephalomyocarditis virus: An accompanying epizootiologic survey. Cornell Vet. 58:31–47.

Gaskin, J.M., M.A. Jorge, C.F. Simpson, A.L. Lewis, J.H. Olson, E.E. Schobert, E.P. Wollenman, C. Marlow, and M.M. Curtis. 1980. The tragedy of encephalomyocarditis virus infection in zoological parks of Florida. Ann. Proc. Am. Assoc. Zoo Vet. pp. 1–7.

Gillespie, J.H., and J.F. Timoney. 1981. Hagan and Bruner's infectious diseases of domestic animals. Cornell Univ. Press, Ithaca. 851 pp.

Gourlie, N. 1984. Unpublished data. DER, Tallahassee, Fla.

Goyal, S.M., R. Drolet, and P. King. 1986. Pseudorabies in free-ranging raccoons. J. Am. Vet. Med. Assoc. 189:1163–1164.

Harkema, R., and G.C. Miller. 1961. *Parallelorchis diglossus* n.g., n. sp., a trematode (Strigeida: Diplostomidae) from the Florida raccoon. J. Parasitol. 47:611–613.

———. 1964. Helminth parasites of the raccoon, *Procyon lotor* in the southeastern United States. J. Parasitol. 50:60–66.

Heard, R.W., and R.M. Overstreet. 1983. Taxonomy and life histories of two North American species of "*Carneophallus*" (= *Microphallus*) (Digenea: Microphallidae) Proc. Helminthol. Soc. Wash. 50:170–174.

Heard, R.W., and W.B. Sikora. 1969. *Probolocoryphe* Otagaki, 1958 (Trematoda: Microphallidae), a senior synonym of *Mecynophallus* Cable, Connor, and Balling, 1960, with notes on the genus. J. Parasitol. 55:674–675.

Hoff, G.L. 1972. Unpublished data. HRS, Tallahassee, Fla.

———. 1973. Raccoon teeth stained with aluminum. J. Wildl. Dis. 9:323.

Hoff, G.L., W.J. Bigler, and J.G. McKinnon. 1977. Heavy metal concentrations in kidneys of estuarine raccoons from Florida. J. Wildl. Dis. 13:101–102.

Hoff, G.L., W.J. Bigler, and E.C. Prather. 1975. One-half century of tularemia in Florida. J. Fla. Med. Assoc. 62:35–37.

Hoff, G.L., W.J. Bigler, L.E. McEldowny, D.W. Peterson, J.P. Trapp, and P.C. Hudgins. 1974a. Blood and urinary values of free-ranging raccoons (*Procyon lotor*) in Florida. Am. J. Vet. Res. 35:861–864.

Hoff, G.L., W.J. Bigler, S.J. Proctor, and L.P. Stallings. 1974b. Epizootic of canine distemper virus infection among urban raccoons and gray foxes. J. Wildl. Dis. 10:423–428.

Hoff, G.L., W.J. Bigler, D.O. Trainer, J.G. Debbie, G.M. Brown, W.G. Winkler, S.H. Richards, and M. Reardon. 1974c. Survey of selected carnivore and opossum serums for agglutinins to *Brucella canis*. J. Am. Vet. Med. Assoc. 165:830–831.

Hutton, R.F. 1964. A second list of parasites from marine and coastal animals of Florida. Trans. Am. Microsc. Soc. 83:439–477.

Irons, E.M. 1971. A survey of the state of Florida for the incidence of American trypanosomiasis in insect vectors and reservoir animals. M.S. thesis, Univ. of Florida, Gainesville. 70 pp.

Isaza, R., and C.H. Courtney. 1988. Possible association between *Dirofilaria tenuis* infections in humans and its prevalence in raccoons in Florida. J. Parasitol. 74:189–190.

Jenkins, J.H., and T.T. Fendley. 1971. Radionuclide biomagnification in coastal plain deer. Proc. 3d Nat. Symp. Radioecol., Oak Ridge, Tenn. 3:116–122.

Jennings, W.L., A.L. Lewis, G.E. Staker, W.M. Hammon, and J.O. Bond. 1968. California-encephalitis-group viruses in Florida rabbits: Report of experimental and sentinel studies. Am. J. Trop. Med. Hyg. 17:781–787.

Johnson, A.S. 1970. Biology of the raccoon (*Procyon lotor varius* Nelsen and Goldman) in Alabama. Auburn Univ. Agric. Exp. Sta. Bull. 402:1–148.

Jordon, H.E., and F.A. Hayes. 1959. Gastrointestinal helminths of raccoons (*Procyon lotor*) from Ossabaw Island, Georgia. J. Parasitol. 45:249–252.

Kappus, K.D., W.J. Bigler, R.G. McLean, and H.A. Trevino. 1970. The raccoon, an emerging rabies host. J. Wildl. Dis. 6:507–509.

Kaufmann, J.H. 1982. Raccoon and allies. In: Wild mammals of North America. J.A. Chapman and G.A. Feldhamer (eds.). Johns Hopkins Univ. Press, Baltimore. pp. 567–585.

Kazacos, K.R. 1983. Raccoon roundworms (*Baylisascaris procyonis*)—a cause of animal and human disease. Purdue Univ. Agr. Exp. Sta. Bull. No. 422. 25 pp.

Kazacos, K.R., W.L. Wirtz, P.P. Burger, and C.S. Christmas. 1981. Raccoon ascarid larvae as a cause of fatal central nervous system disease in subhuman primates. J. Am. Vet. Med. Assoc. 179:1089–1094.

Kinsella, J.M. 1987. Unpublished data. Archbold Biological Station, Gainesville, Fla.

Kinsella, J.M., and R.W. Heard. 1974. Morphology and life cycle of *Stictodora cursitans* n. comb. (Trematoda: Heterophyidae) from mammals in Florida salt marshes. Trans. Am. Micros. Soc. 93:408–412.

Laham, S.N. 1978. Isolation and characterization of a syncytium-forming virus of raccoons. Ph.D. diss., Univ. of Florida, Gainesville. 92 pp.

Layne, J.N. 1965. Occurrence of black-tailed jackrabbits in Florida. J. Mammal. 46:502.

———. 1968. Host and ecological relationships of the parasitic helminth *Capillaria hepatica* in Florida mammals. Zoologica. 53:107–122.

———. 1971. Fleas (Siphonaptera) of Florida. Fla. Entomol. 54:35–51.

———. 1988. Unpublished data. Archbold Biological Station, Lake Placid, Fla.

Layne, J.N., D.E. Birkenholz, and J.V. Griffo, Jr. 1960. Records of *Dracunculus insignis* (Leidy, 1858) from raccoons in Florida. J. Parasitol. 46:685.

Leigh, W.H. 1958. *Carneophallus turgidus* sp.

nov. (Trematoda: Microphallidae) from the raccoon, *Procyon lotor,* in south Florida. J. Parasitol. 44:100–102.

Loftin, H. 1961. An annotated check-list of trematodes and cestodes and their vertebrate hosts from northwest Florida. Quart. J. Fla. Acad. Sci. 23:302–314.

Lord, R.D., C.H. Calisher, W.D. Sudia, and T.H. Work. 1973. Ecological investigations of vertebrate hosts of Venezuelan equine encephalomyelitis virus in south Florida. Am. J. Trop. Med. Hyg. 22:116–123.

McIntosh, A. 1954. A new distribution record of *Dirofilaria tenuis* Chandler, 1949, and the discovery of the male. J. Parasitol. 40 (Suppl.):31.

McKeever, S., J.H. Schubert, M.D. Moody, G.W. Gorman, and J.F. Chapman. 1958a. Natural occurrence of tularemia in marsupials, carnivores, lagomorphs, and large rodents in southwestern Georgia and northwestern Florida. J. Infect. Dis. 103:120–126.

McKeever, S., G.W. Gorman, and L. Norman. 1958b. Occurrence of a *Trypanosoma cruzi*-like organism in some mammals from southwestern Georgia and northwestern Florida. J. Parasitol. 44:583–587.

McKeever, S., W. Kaplan, and L. Ajello. 1958c. Ringworm fungi of large wild mammals in southwestern Georgia and northwestern Florida. Am. J. Vet. Res. 19:973–975.

McKeever, S., G.W. Gorman, J.F. Chapman, M.M. Galton, and D.K. Powers. 1958d. Incidence of leptospirosis in wild mammals from southwestern Georgia, with a report of new hosts for six serotypes of leptospires. Am. J. Trop. Med. Hyg. 7:646–655.

McLean, R.G. 1975. Raccoon rabies. In: The natural history of rabies. Vol. 2. G.M. Baer (ed.). Academic Press, New York. pp. 53–77.

———. 1988. Unpublished data. CDC, Fort Collins, Colo.

Matthews, L. 1985. Unpublished data. Univ. of Florida, Gainesville.

Moller, T. 1951. Et tilfaelde at letalt forlobende toxoplasmose hos en hund. Nord. Vet.-Med. 3:1073–1093.

Morgan, B.B. 1941. A summary of the Physalopterinae (Nematoda) of North America. Proc. Helminthol. Soc. Wash. 8:28–30.

Murphy, F.A. 1983. Pathogenesis of rabies. In: Report on rabies. Veterinary Learning Systems, Princeton Junction, N.J. pp. 7–10.

Nalley, L., G. Hoff, W. Bigler, and W. Hull. 1975. Pesticide levels in the omental fat of Florida raccoons. Bull. Environ. Cont. Toxicol. 13:741–744.

Nettles, V.F., and W.M. Martin. 1978. General physical parameters and health characteristics of translocated raccoons. Proc. Ann. Conf. S.E. Assoc. Fish Wildl. Agencies 32:71–74.

Nettles, V.F., W.R. Davidson, S.K. Fisk, and H.A. Jacobson. 1975. An epizootic of cerebrospinal nematodiasis in cottontail rabbits. J. Am. Vet. Med. Assoc. 167:600–602.

Nettles, V.F., J.E. Pearson, G.A. Gustafson, and J.L. Blue. 1980. Parvovirus infection in translocated raccoons. J. Am. Vet. Med. Assoc. 177:787–789.

Nettles, V.F., J.H. Shaddock, K. Sikes, and C.R. Reyes. 1979. Rabies in translocated raccoons. Am. J. Pub. Health 69:601–602.

Penner, L.R. 1987. Unpublished data. Archbold Biological Station, Lake Placid, Fla.

Platt, K.B., D.L. Graham, and R.A. Faaborg. 1983. Pseudorabies: Experimental studies in raccoons with different virus strains. J. Wildl. Dis. 19:297–301.

Prather, C.E., W.J. Bigler, G.L. Hoff, and J.A. Tomas. 1975. Rabies in Florida. History, status, trends. Fla. Div. of Health Monogr. Series, no. 14. Jacksonville, Fla. 122 pp.

Roelke, M.E. 1985. Unpublished data. Univ. of Florida, Gainesville, and Florida Game and Fresh Water Fish Commission, Gainesville.

Roelke, M.E., E.C. Pirtle, and D.J. Forrester. 1988. Unpublished data. Florida Game and Fresh Water Fish Commission, Gainesville.

Rogers, A.J. 1953. A study of the ixodid ticks of northern Florida, including the biology and life history of *Ixodes scapularis* Say (Ixodidae: Acarina). Ph.D. diss., Univ. of Maryland, College Park. 191 pp.

Rohani, I.B., and H.L. Cromroy. 1979. Taxonomy and distribution of chiggers (Acarina:

Trombiculidae) in northcentral Florida. Fla. Entomol. 62:363–376.

Sather, G.E., A.L. Lewis, W. Jennings, J.O. Bond, and W. McD. Hammon. 1970. Sawgrass virus: A newly described arbovirus in Florida. Am. J. Trop. Med. Hyg. 19:319–326.

Sauerman, D.M., Jr., and J.K. Nayar. 1985. Prevalence of presumed *Dirofilaria tenius* microfilariae in raccoons near Vero Beach, Florida. J. Parasitol. 71:130–132.

Scatterday, J.E., N.J. Schneider, W.L. Jennings, and A.L. Lewis. 1960. Sporadic animal rabies in Florida. Public Health Rep. 75:945–953.

Schaffer, G.D. 1979. Helminth parasites of translocated raccoons (*Procyon lotor*) in the southeastern United States. M.S. thesis. Univ. of Georgia, Athens. 93 pp.

Schaffer, G.D., W.L. Hanson, W.R. Davidson, and V.F. Nettles. 1978. Hematotropic parasites of translocated raccoons in the southeast. J. Am. Vet. Med. Assoc. 173:1148–1151.

Schaffer, G.D., W.R. Davidson, V.F. Nettles, and E.A. Rollor, III. 1981. Helminth parasites of translocated raccoons (*Procyon lotor*) in the southeastern United States. J. Wildl. Dis. 17:217–227.

Schneider, L.G. 1982. Antigenic variants of rabies virus. Comp. Immunol. Microbiol. Inf. Dis. 5:101–107.

Schroeder, R.E., and W.H. Leigh. 1965. The life history of *Ascocotyle pachycystis* sp.n., a trematode (Digenea: Heterophyidae) from the raccoon in south Florida. J. Parasitol. 51:594–599.

SCWDS. 1983. Necropsy records of the Southeastern Cooperative Wildlife Disease Study, Coll. Vet. Med., Univ. of Georgia, Athens.

Seymour, C., and T.M. Yuill. 1981. Arboviruses. In: Infectious diseases of wild mammals. J.W. Davis et al. (eds.). Iowa State Univ. Press, Ames. pp. 54–86.

Sholtens R.G., and L. Norman. 1971. *Trichinella spiralis* in Florida wildlife. J. Parasitol. 57:1103.

Shotts, E.B., Jr., C.L. Andrews, and T.W. Harvey. 1975. Leptospirosis in selected wild mammals of the Florida panhandle and southwestern Georgia. J. Am. Vet. Med. Assoc. 167:587–589.

Sikes, R.K., Jr. 1981. Rabies. In: Infectious diseases of wild mammals. J.W. Davis et al. (eds.). Iowa State Univ. Press, Ames. pp. 3–17.

Smith, J.S., P.A. Yager, W.J. Bigler, and E.C. Hartwig, Jr. 1990. Surveillance and epidemiologic mapping of monoclonal antibody-defined rabies variants in Florida. J. Wildl. Dis. 26:473–485.

Sogandares-Bernal, F., and J.F. Bridgman. 1960. Three *Ascocotyle* complex trematodes (Heterophyidae) encysted in fishes from Louisiana, including the description of a new genus. Tul. Stud. Zool. 8:31–39.

Stevenson, H.M. 1976. Vertebrates of Florida. Identification and distribution. Univ. Presses of Florida, Gainesville. 607 pp.

Strickland, R.K., R.R. Gerrish, J.L. Hourigan, and G.O. Schubert. 1976. Ticks of veterinary importance. APHIS-USDA Agric. Handbook No. 485. U.S. Government Printing Office, Washington, D.C. 122 pp.

Sureau, P., P. Rollin, and T.J. Wiktor. 1983. Epidemiologic analysis of antigenic variations of street rabies virus: Detection by monoclonal antibodies. Am. J. Epidemiol. 117:605–609.

Taylor, D.J. 1951. The distribution of ticks in Florida. M.S. thesis, Univ. of Florida, Gainesville. 124 pp.

Taylor, D.J., A.L. Lewis, J.D. Edman, and W.L. Jennings. 1971. California group arboviruses in Florida: Host-vector relations. Am. J. Trop. Med. Hyg. 20:139–145.

Telford, S.R., Jr., and D.J. Forrester. 1991. Hemoparasites of raccoons (*Procyon lotor*) in Florida. J. Wildl. Dis. 27:486–490.

Thawley, D.G., and J.C. Wright. 1982. Pseudorabies virus infection in raccoons: A review. J. Wildl. Dis. 18:113–116.

Travis, B.V. 1941. Examinations of wild ani-

mals for the cattle tick *Boophilus annulatus microplus* (Can.) in Florida. J. Parasitol. 27:465–467.

Wellings, F.M., A.L. Lewis, and L.V. Pierce. 1972. Agents encountered during arboviral ecological studies: Tampa Bay Area, Florida, 1963–1970. Am. J. Trop. Med. Hyg. 21:201–213.

Wheeler, W.B., D.P. Jouvenaz, D.P. Wojcik, W.A. Banks, C.H. Van Middelem, C.S. Lofgren, S. Nesbitt, L. Williams, and R. Brown. 1977. Mirex residues in nontarget organisms after application of 10-5 bait for fire ant control, northeast Florida, 1972–74. Pest. Monit. J. 11:146–156.

White, F.H., J.J. Watson, G.L. Hoff, and W.J. Bigler. 1975. *Edwardsiella tarda* infections in Florida raccoons, *Procyon lotor*. Arch. Environ. Health 30:602–603.

Wilson, N., and H.W. Kale, III. 1972. Ticks collected from Indian River County, Florida (Acari: Metastigmata: Ixodidae). Fla. Entomol. 55:53–57.

Wong, M.M. 1973. Unpublished data. Univ. of California, Davis.

Wood, D.A. 1990. Official lists of endangered fauna and flora in Florida. Florida Game and Fresh Water Fish Commission, Tallahassee. 19 pp.

Woodward, J.C. 1977. Unpublished data. (Necropsy No. N77-30 and N77-31, College of Vet. Med., Univ. of Florida, Gainesville).

Worth, C.B. 1950. A preliminary host-parasite register for some small mammals of Florida. J. Parasitol. 36:497–498.

Wright, J.C., and D.G. Thawley. 1980. Role of the raccoon in the transmission of pseudorabies: A field and laboratory investigation. Am. J. Vet. Res. 415:581–583.

Wright, S.D., and D.J. Forrester. 1988. Unpublished data. Univ. of Florida, Gainesville.

Wright, T.J. 1987. Wildlife harvest and economic survey. Florida Game and Fresh Water Fish Commission, Tallahassee. P-R Report, W-33.

Mustelids

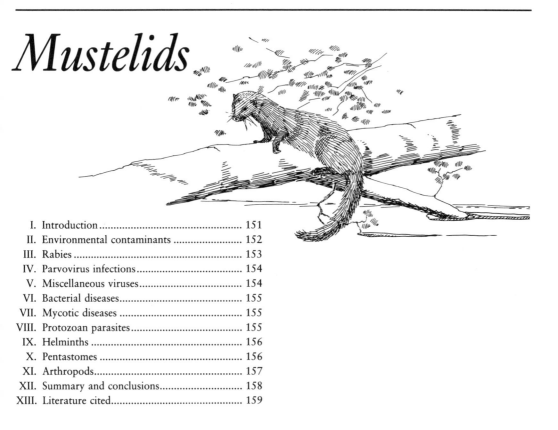

I. Introduction

Five mustelids occur in Florida (Table 13-1). Although river otters appear to be abundant (Robson and Humphrey 1985) and are present in every county (Brady 1977), they are currently listed in Appendix II of the Convention on International Trade in Endangered Species of Wild Fauna and Flora (U.S. Fish and Wildlife Service 1977). This listing means that the U.S. Fish and Wildlife Service must show that harvesting these animals for export is not harmful to the species (Endangered Species Scientific Authority 1978). *Lutra canadensis lataxina* is the subspecies that occurs in Florida (van Zyll de Jong 1972).

Two subspecies of weasels are in Florida:

the southeastern long-tailed weasel (*Mustela frenata olivacea*) and the Florida long-tailed weasel (*M. f. peninsulae*) (Stevenson 1976). The former is found in northern Florida, including the panhandle and the northern third of the peninsula. The latter occurs in the southern two-thirds of the Florida peninsula, but is absent from the Everglades and the Gold Coast area (Brown 1978). According to Layne (1974) these weasels are not common anywhere in Florida and were at one time classified as rare (Brown 1978). Currently the southeastern long-tailed weasel is not listed and the Florida long-tailed weasel is under review for listing (Wood 1990).

Table 13-1
Species of mustelids that occur in Florida

Common and scientific names	Range in Florida	Status
1. River otter *Lutra canadensis* (Schreber)	Statewide[a]	Common
2. Long-tailed weasel *Mustela frenata* Lichtenstein	Statewide[a]	Rare
3. Mink *Mustela vison* Schreber	No. coasts, Everglades	Rare
4. Spotted skunk *Spilogale putorius* (L.)	Statewide[a]	Common
5. Striped skunk *Mephitis mephitis* (Schreber)	Statewide[a]	Common

Source: Brown (1987).
[a]Absent from the Florida Keys

Mink (*Mustela vison*) occur in three disjunct populations in peninsular Florida (Humphrey and Setzer 1989). These include *M. v. mink* (= *M. v. evergladensis*) in freshwater marshes of southern Florida (Everglades, Big Cypress, and Lake Okeechobee); *M. v. lutensis* in the saltwater marshes of the Atlantic Coast from the Georgia border south to Matanzas Inlet; and *M. v. halilimnetes* in the salt marshes of the Gulf Coast. One of these subspecies (*M. v. mink*) is listed as threatened and one (*M. v. lutensis*) is under review for listing (Wood 1990), although Humphrey and Setzer (1989) state that all three subspecies are relatively common in the areas where they occur.

The spotted skunk (*Spilogale putorius ambarvalis*) is distributed throughout most of Florida except for parts of the panhandle, the northwestern corner, and the southwestern tip of the peninsula (Stevenson 1976). Striped skunks (*Mephitis m. elongata*) occur throughout most of mainland Florida (Stevenson 1976). Neither species is extremely

abundant, but the striped skunk is more common than the spotted skunk in southern Florida (Layne 1974).

The literature on parasites and diseases of mustelids has been compiled and reviewed by several authors. Shump et al. (1976) prepared a bibliography on otters and included a number of references on diseases and parasitism; Fleming et al. (1977) and Toweill and Tabor (1982) summarized similar data. Such treatises also have been prepared for weasels (Heidt et al. 1976; Svendsen 1982), mink (Gorham et al 1972; Barber and Lockard 1973; Linscombe et al. 1982), and skunks (Verts 1967; Dyer 1969; Shump et al. 1975; Howard and Marsh 1982; Godin 1982). The checklist of helminth parasites by Erickson (1946) is old but still useful, and contains information on a number of North American mustelids.

II. Environmental contaminants

Very little information is available on environmental contaminants in mustelids in Florida. Limited data are available on mercury concentrations for one long-tailed weasel and four river otters (Table 13-2). Nothing is known about the effects of mercury on weasels. A number of studies, however, in other parts of North America have been conducted on mercury concentrations in river otters (Kucera 1983; O'Connor and Nielson 1981), including two studies in Georgia (Cumbie 1975; Halbrook 1978) and one in Louisiana (Beck 1977). The concentrations of mercury found in the four otters from Florida were similar to those found in otters from Louisiana (1.29 ppm) and in otters from two areas in Georgia (5.11 and 9.16 ppm) (Halbrook 1978; Beck 1977). Based on experimental data presented by O'Connor and Nielsen (1981), these concentrations are below those

Table 13-2

Concentrations of mercury (total Hg in ppm, wet wt) in liver samples from mustelids in Florida

Species of mustelid	Date collected	Age	Sex	Location (county)	Total Hg (mg/kg)
Long-tailed weasel	1974	Immature	F	Alachua	0.86
River otter	1979	Unknown	M	Sumter	1.90
	1979	Unknown	M	Franklin	5.60
	1979	Unknown	M	Broward	9.10
	1979	Unknown	M	Baker	11.00

Sources: Forrester (1987) and Brady (1987).

known to cause clinical signs of mercury intoxication. In the latter study otters fed methylmercury in their food showed anorexia, lethargy, ataxia, and progressive central nervous system deterioration over a 10–14 day period and several died. Residues of mercury in livers ranged from 25 to 39 ppm total mercury. Further studies should be conducted in Florida to assess the significance of mercury in otters.

Data on other types of environmental contaminants are not available for mustelids in Florida. This is unfortunate since they could be important disease factors. Polychlorinated biphenyls, for example, have been shown to cause reproductive failure through resorption of embryos, stillbirths, and neonatal mortality of mink (Platonow and Karstad 1973; Aulerick and Ringer 1977). Contaminant studies such as those conducted in Georgia (Halbrook 1978; Halbrook et al. 1981), Louisiana (Beck 1977), and Maryland (O'Shea et al. 1981) should be undertaken on Florida mustelids, especially otter and mink.

III. Rabies

According to Burridge et al. (1986) rabies is not common in otters. Six cases have been reported in Florida and include one otter each from Collier County (1969), Volusia County (1970), Dade County (1977), Polk County (1984), Brevard County (1986), and Columbia County (1988) (Bigler 1988). The latter is of special interest since it is the only known case of an otter attacking a group of people (Bigler 1988). On July 13, 1988, this otter attacked seven young women who were tubing on the Ichetucknee River in Columbia County. As the tubers floated past the otter, who was sunning himself on the river bank, the animal jumped in the river and climbed onto their inner tubes. He then bit the tubers and inflicted wounds to their heads and extremities. The animal was subsequently killed and the head submitted for testing for rabies virus. It was determined to be positive and as a result 11 people received antirabies prophylaxis. Otters may become infected through encounters with rabid raccoons and, in general, are not considered important in the epidemiology of rabies.

Skunks are only of minor importance in the epidemiology of rabies in Florida (Burridge et al. 1986). Up through 1987, 64 rabid "skunks" (striped and spotted skunks, presumably) were reported from 36 counties throughout the state (Figure 13-1). Skunks require 100 times more virus than foxes to become infected (Sikes 1962). Many rabid

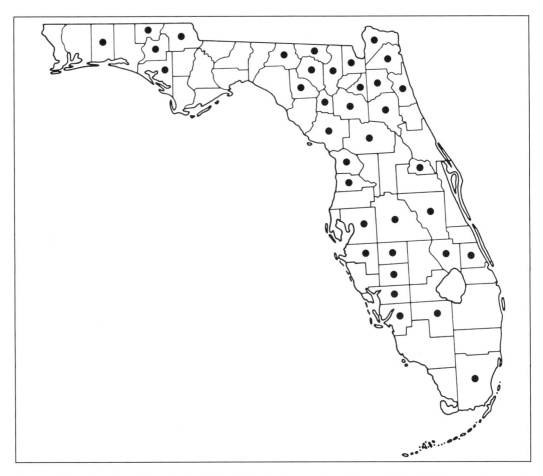

FIGURE 13-1. Counties in Florida in which rabid skunks were found from 1951–87. Data on the species of skunks (spotted versus striped) were not separated. (After Burridge et al. 1986; Department of Health and Rehabilitative Services 1984; Bigler 1988.)

skunks exhibit furious signs and attack and hold on to their victims with tenacity (Burridge et al. 1986).

Between 1975 and 1983, 12 weasels and 6 mink were examined for rabies in Florida (Burridge et al. 1986). All were negative.

IV. Parvovirus infections

Evidence of a parvovirus in otters of Florida has been presented (Roelke et al. 1986). Five of 38 otters from Collier County were sero-

positive. Two mink from Collier County were negative. For additional information on parvoviruses, the reader is referred to Chapter 15 on Florida panthers and bobcats. The significance of this parvovirus to otters is unknown. No such data are available for weasels and skunks in Florida.

V. Miscellaneous viruses

Fifteen striped skunks (mostly from Escambia County) were examined serologically for evidence of infection by various arboviruses (SLE, Everglades, EEE, and Highlands J). One of the 15 was seropositive for EEE (Bigler 1971; Bigler et al. 1975). Two spotted skunks (one from Polk County and one from Hendry County) were negative serologically (Bigler et al. 1975).

In a study of the epidemiology of encephalomyocarditis (EMC) virus at a farm in Polk County, one spotted skunk was tested serologically and an attempt was made to isolate EMC viruses (Gainer and Bigler 1967; Gainer et al. 1968). Results were negative.

Four otters from Collier County were tested serologically for antibodies to pseudorabies virus (Roelke and Pirtle 1988). All were negative.

VI. Bacterial diseases

McKeever et al. (1958c) conducted a survey of wild mammals from southwestern Georgia in order to determine the prevalence of leptospires. Three of the trapping areas were near the Florida border and the results from these localities are of value. Kidneys of 9 of 75 striped skunks were positive, 3 for *Leptospira ballum* and 4 for *L. pomona*. Two isolations were not serotyped. Striped skunks may be secondary hosts for *L. ballum* and accidental hosts for *L. pomona* according to Verts (1967). One otter from southern Thomas County, Georgia, was negative for leptospires (McKeever et al. 1958c).

In two ecological studies on tularemia, 21 striped skunks were seronegative (McKeever et al. 1958d; Hoff et al. 1975).

Hoff et al. (1974) reported that one striped skunk from Florida was seronegative for agglutinins to *Brucella canis*.

White (1987) cultured the contents of the large intestines of eight otters, one from Escambia County (1976), five from Alachua

County (1973–75), one from Polk County (1978), and one from Glades County (1973). The otter from Glades County was positive for *Arizona* sp. and one of the otters from Alachua County (1974) was positive for *Salmonella anatum*. The importance of these enteric bacteria to otters in Florida is unknown. Both may be of zoonotic significance.

VII. Mycotic diseases

McKeever et al. (1958b) reported *Microsporum* (red variety) in the fur of 2 of 239 striped skunks, but in none of 6 spotted skunks and 1 otter from southwestern Georgia and northwestern Florida. This fungal organism was considered to be a new species. There was no evidence that it was pathogenic and the authors concluded that these were instances of the fur being contaminated from the environment rather than the animals being infected.

VIII. Protozoan parasites

Only one protozoan is known from mustelids in Florida. McKeever et al. (1958a) cultured kidneys of 306 striped skunks, 7 spotted skunks, and 1 otter from southwestern Georgia and northwestern Florida. Of these, three striped skunks were infected with a trypanosome that was indistinguishable from *T. cruzi* (Norman et al. 1959). The spotted skunks and the otter were negative. *Trypanosoma cruzi* is the etiologic agent of Chagas' disease in man. No cases of Chagas' disease have been reported in the areas from which the infected skunks came (Norman et al. 1959). This disease is of considerable zoonotic importance in Central and South America.

IX. Helminths

Ten species of helminths occur in river otters in Florida (Table 13-3). These include two trematodes, one cestode, six nematodes, and one acanthocephalan.

There are four records of helminths in skunks in Florida. These include the tapeworm *Oochoristica mephitis* from a striped skunk in Jefferson County (Loftin 1961), *Capillaria hepatica* from a spotted skunk in Highlands County (Layne and Winegarner 1971), *Trichinella spiralis* from a "skunk" (species not given) in Marion County (Scholtens and Norman 1971), and *Physaloptera maxillaria* from a striped skunk (county not given) (Morgan 1941). Layne (1968) examined one striped skunk from Duval County and found it to be negative for *Capillaria hepatica.*

There are no data on the helminths of weasels and mink in Florida. One long-tailed weasel from Alachua County was examined, but was free of helminths (Forrester 1987). The liver of one long-tailed weasel from Duval County was negative for *Capillaria hepatica* (Layne, 1968).

The significance of the helminths that occur in otters and skunks is unknown. Probably the most important pathogen would be *Crenosoma goblei* in otters. Other related species of *Crenosoma,* such as *C. vulpis* in dogs and foxes, are known to cause bronchopneumonia that can be fatal (Anderson 1971). At least three of the helminths are of known zoonotic importance: *Spirometra mansonoides, Capillaria hepatica,* and *Trichinella spiralis.*

X. Pentastomes

Nymphs of *Sebekia mississippiensis* were found in the intestines of one otter from Alachua County (1974), one from Polk County

Table 13-3
Helminths of river otters from Florida

Helminth	Prevalence			Intensity	
	No. exam	No. inf.	(%)	Mean	Range
Trematoda					
Baschkirovitrema incrassatum	61	34	(56)	27	1–248
Enhydridiplostomum alarioides	61	13	(21)	149	1–1,640
Cestoda					
Spirometra mansonoides (sparganum)	10	1	(10)	ND[a]	ND
Nematoda					
Crenosoma goblei	65	40	(62)	13	1–72
Strongyloides lutrae	61	38	(62)	96	1–992
Gnathostoma miyazakii	63	20	(32)	3	2–18
Capillaria plica	57	7	(12)	9	1–49
Dirofilaria lutrae[b]	10	7	(70)	ND	ND
Capillaria hepatica	61	1	(2)	ND	ND
Acanthocephala					
Oncicola sp.	61	4	(7)	2	1–2

Sources: Forrester (1987) and Steers and Forrester (1987).
[a]ND = not determined.
[b]*D. lutrae* was described from material collected from otters in Dade and Collier counties by Orihel (1965).

(1977), and two from Collier County (1976, 1985) (Forrester 1987). Adults of this pentastome occur in the lungs of alligators, and fish serve as intermediate hosts (Boyce et al. 1984). Infections were probably acquired by the otters through eating fish. The pathological significance of this parasite to otters is unknown. The infections in otters may be spurious.

Stiles and Hassall (1894) gave a record of *Porocephalus crotali* from a striped skunk in Florida, but did not give the specific locality or information on the stages found.

XI. Arthropods

Nine species of parasitic arthropods are known from mustelids in Florida. These include three species of ticks (Table 13-4), five fleas (Table 13-5), and one biting louse.

Two of the ticks (*Dermacentor variabilis* and *Amblyomma americanum*) have been found on other mammals in Florida, including deer, hogs, squirrels, opossums, bears,

foxes, bobcats, and panthers. Both species can cause tick paralysis, but no such cases have been seen in mustelids in Florida. Both can also serve as vectors of Rocky Mountain spotted fever and tularemia (Strickland et al. 1976). *Ixodes cookei* is found on carnivores throughout the eastern and central United States and occurs commonly on mustelids in the South (Wilson and Baker 1972; Wilson and Kale 1972). It is not known to be of economic importance since it does not transmit disease agents or seriously affect animals or man (Bishopp and Trembley 1945).

The sticktight flea (*Echidnophaga gallinacea*) is primarily a parasite of domestic fowl and, as Layne (1971) points out, infestations on mammals such as spotted skunks and long-tailed weasels are probably acquired when such mammals associate with poultry houses. Such was the case with the weasel from Highlands County discussed by Layne (1971).

Polygenis gwyni is a very common flea of small mammals in Florida and occurs on rodents such as the cotton rat and also on opossums (Layne 1971). *Hoplopsyllus glacialis af-*

Table 13-4
Ticks from mustelids of Florida

Host Tick	County	Data source
Spotted skunk		
Dermacentor variabilis	Indian R.	Wilson & Kale (1972), FSCA[a]
Ixodes cookei	Indian R., Brevard	" " " " "
Striped skunk		
Dermacentor variabilis	Alachua	Boardman (1929)
Ixodes cookei	NG[b]	Bishopp & Trembley (1945)
Amblyomma americanum	NG	" " " "
	Alachua	Boardman (1929)
Mink		
Amblyomma americanum	NG	Bishopp & Trembley (1945)
River otter		
Ixodes cookei	Glades	Wassef & Hoogstraal (1982)

[a]FSCA = records from the Florida State Collection of Arthropods, Division of Plant Industry, Florida Department of Agriculture, Gainesville, Fla.
[b]NG = not given by authors.

Table 13-5
Fleas of mustelids in Florida

Host Flea	County	Data source
Spotted skunk		
Echidnophaga gallinacea	Indian R.	Hopkins & Rothschild (1953)
	Highlands	Layne (1971)
Ctenocephalides felis	Dade	Schwartz (1952)
Polygenis gwyni	Dade	" "
	Indian R.	Layne (1971)
Hoplopsyllus glacialis affinis	Highlands	FSCA[a]
Striped skunk		
Pulex simulans	Dade	Schwartz (1952)
	Alachua	Layne (1971)
Long-tailed weasel		
Echidnophaga gallinacea	Highlands	" "
Polygenis gwyni	Collier	" "

[a]FSCA = records from the Florida State Collection of Arthropods, Division of Plant Industry, Florida Department of Agriculture, Gainesville, Fla.

finis is primarily a western flea and is believed to have been introduced into Florida on jackrabbits (*Lepus californicus*) in the 1930s. Since then it has become established in Florida and occurs on a number of native rabbits and rodents (Layne 1971).

The one record of a biting louse was obtained from the Florida State Collection of Arthropods. A striped skunk from Alachua County was found infested with *Neotrichodectes mephitidis*. This mallophagan is specific for skunks (Emerson 1972) and its importance to skunks in Florida is unknown.

XII. Summary and conclusions

Seventeen different contaminants, infectious disease agents, and parasites have been identified in river otters in Florida. These include one heavy metal, two viruses, two bacteria, two trematodes, one cestode, six nematodes, one acanthocephalan, one pentastome, and one tick. Mercury contamination may be a serious problem, but we have very little data on this subject in Florida.

Eighteen infectious disease agents and parasites have been documented in skunks in Florida, most in the striped skunk. Among these are two viruses, one fungus, one protozoan, one tapeworm, three nematodes, one pentastome, three ticks, and five fleas.

Almost nothing is known about the diseases and parasites of mink and weasels. We have a little information on heavy metals in one weasel and on fleas and ticks of weasels and mink.

The significance of disease among populations of the five species of mustelids in Florida is unknown. One of the nematodes (*Crenosoma goblei*) may cause verminous pneumonia, but this remains to be studied. Ten of these disease agents are of public health and veterinary significance and include the agents of rabies, eastern equine encephalomyelitis, salmonellosis, arizonosis, Chagas' disease, sparganiasis, capillariasis, and trichinosis. Several of the ticks and fleas can also infest man.

XIII. Literature cited

Anderson, R.C. 1971. Lungworms. In: Parasitic diseases of wild mammals. J.W. Davis and R.C. Anderson (eds.). Iowa State Univ. Press, Ames. pp. 81–126.

Aulerick, R.J., and R.K. Ringer. 1977. Current status of PCB toxicity to mink and ferrets. Arch. Environ. Contam. Toxicol. 9:627–635.

Barber, D.L., and L.L. Lockard. 1973. Some helminths from mink in southwestern Montana, with a checklist of their internal parasites. Great Basin Nat. 33:53–60.

Beck, D.L. 1977. Pesticide and heavy metal residues in Louisiana river otter. M.S. thesis, Texas A. & M. Univ., College Station. 95 pp.

Bigler, W.J. 1971. Serologic evidence of Venezuelan equine encephalitis virus infections in raccoons of south central Florida. J. Wildl. Dis. 7:166–170.

———. 1988. Unpublished data. HRS, Tallahassee, Fla.

Bigler, W.J., E. Lassing, E. Buff, A.L. Lewis, and G.L. Hoff. 1975. Arbovirus surveillance in Florida: Wild vertebrate studies 1965–1974. J. Wildl. Dis. 11:348–356.

Bishopp, F.C., and H.L. Trembley. 1945. Distribution and hosts of certain North American ticks. J. Parasitol. 31:1–54.

Boardman, E.T. 1929. Ticks of the Gainesville area. M.S. thesis, Univ. of Florida, Gainesville. 57 pp.

Boyce, W.M., P. Cardeilhac, T. Lane, C. Buergelt, and M. King. 1984. Sebekiosis in captive alligator hatchlings. J. Am. Vet. Med. Assoc. 185:1419–1420.

Brady, J.R. 1977. Otter Studies XII. Final Job Performance Report. Florida Game and Fresh Water Fish Commission, Tallahassee. 5 pp.

———. 1987. Unpublished data. Florida Game and Fresh Water Fish Commission, Gainesville.

Brown, L.N. 1978. Southeastern weasel and Florida weasel. In: Mammals. Vol. 1. Rare and endangered biota of Florida. J.N. Layne (ed.). Univ. Presses of Florida, Gainesville. pp. 36–39.

———. 1987. A checklist of Florida's mammals. Florida Game and Fresh Water Fish Commission, Tallahassee. 6 pp.

Burridge, M.J., L.A. Sawyer, and W.J. Bigler. 1986. Rabies in Florida. Department of Health and Rehabilitative Services, Tallahassee. 147 pp.

Cumbie, P.M. 1975. Mercury levels in Georgia otter, mink and fresh-water fish. Bull. Environ. Contam. Toxicol. 14:193–196.

Department of Health and Rehabilitative Services. 1984. Florida morbidity statistics. HRS, Tallahassee, Fla. 121 pp.

Dyer, W.G. 1969. Helminths of the striped skunk, Mephitis mephitis, in North America. Am. Midl. Nat. 82:601–604.

Emerson, K.C. 1972. Checklist of the Mallophaga of North America (North of Mexico). Part 1. Suborder Ischnocera. Deseret Test Center, Dugway, Utah. 200 pp.

Endangered Species Scientific Authority. 1978. Export of bobcat, lynx, river otter and ginseng. Fed. Reg. 43:15098–15100.

Erickson, A.B. 1946. Incidence of worm parasites in Minnesota mustelidae and host lists and keys to North American species. Am. Midl. Nat. 36:494–509.

Fleming, W.J., C.F. Dixon, and J.W. Lovett. 1977. Helminth parasites of river otters (Lutra canadensis) from southeastern Alabama. Proc. Helminthol. Soc. Wash. 44:131–135.

Forrester, D.J. 1987. Unpublished data. Univ. of Florida, Gainesville.

Gainer, J.H., and W.J. Bigler. 1967. Encephalomyocarditis (EMC) virus recovered from two cotton rats and a raccoon. Bull. Wildl. Dis. Assoc. 3:47–49.

Gainer, J.H., J.R. Sandefur, and W.J. Bigler. 1968. High mortality in a Florida swine herd infected with the encephalomyocarditis virus. An accompanying epizootiologic survey. Cornell Vet. 58:31–47.

Godin, A.J. 1982. Striped and hooded skunks (Mephitis mephitis and allies). In: Wild mammals of North America. J.A. Chapman and G.A. Feldhamer (eds.). Johns Hopkins Univ. Press, Baltimore. pp. 674–687.

Gorham, J.R., K.W. Hagen, and R.K. Farrell. 1972. Minks: Diseases and parasites. Agr. Handbook No. 175, Washington, D.C. 45 pp.

Halbrook, R.S. 1978. Environmental pollutants in the river otter of Georgia. M.S. thesis, Univ. of Georgia, Athens. 82 pp.

Halbrook, R.S., J.H. Jenkins, P.B. Busch, and N.D. Seabolt. 1981. Selected environmental contaminants in river otters (*Lutra canadensis*) of Georgia and their relationship to the possible decline of otters in North America. In: Worldwide Furbearer Conf. Proc. J.A. Chapman and D. Pursley (eds.). Frostburg, Md. pp. 1752–1762.

Heidt, G.A., A.U. Shump, K.A. Shump, and R.J. Aulerich. 1976. A bibliography of mustelids. Part IV: Weasels. Mich. Agr. Exp. Sta., Michigan State Univ., East Lansing. 47 pp.

Hoff, G.L., W.J. Bigler, and E.C. Prather. 1975. One-half century of tularemia in Florida. J. Fla. Med. Assoc. 62:35–37.

Hoff, G.L., W.J. Bigler, D.O. Trainer, J.G. Debbie, G.M. Brown, W.G. Winkler, S.H. Richards, and M. Reardon. 1974. Survey of selected carnivore and opossum serums for agglutinins to *Brucella canis*. J. Am. Vet. Med. Assoc. 165:830–831.

Hopkins, G.H.E., and M. Rothschild. 1953. An illustrated catalogue of the Rothschild collection of fleas (Siphonaptera) in the British Museum (Natural History). Vol. 1. Tungidae and Pulicidae. British Museum, London. 361 pp.

Howard, W.E., and R.E. Marsh. 1982. Spotted and hog-nosed skunks (*Spilogale putorius* and allies). In: Wild mammals of North America. J.A. Chapman and G.A. Feldhamer (eds.). Johns Hopkins Univ. Press, Baltimore. pp. 664–673.

Humphrey, S.R., and H.W. Setzer. 1989. Geographic variation and taxonomic revision of mink (*Mustela vison*) in Florida. J. Mammal. 70:241–252.

Kucera, E. 1983. Mink and otter as indicators of mercury in Manitoba waters. Can. J. Zool. 61:2250–2256.

Layne, J.N. 1968. Host and ecological relationships of the parasitic helminth *Capillaria hepatica* in Florida mammals. Zoologica 53:107–122.

———. 1971. Fleas (Siphonaptera) of Florida. Fla. Entomol. 54:35–51.

———. 1974. The land mammals of south Florida. In: Environments of south Florida: Present and past. P.J. Gleason (ed.). Miami Geol. Soc. Mem. 2. pp. 386–413.

Layne, J.N., and C.E. Winegarner. 1971. Occurrence of *Capillaria hepatica* (Nematoda: Trichuridae) in the spotted skunk in Florida. J. Wildl. Dis. 7:256–257.

Linscombe, G., N. Kinler, and R.J. Aulerich. 1982. Mink (*Mustela vison*). In: Wild mammals of North America. J.A. Chapman and G.A. Feldhamer (eds.). Johns Hopkins Univ. Press, Baltimore. pp. 629–643.

Loftin, H. 1961. An annotated check-list of trematodes and cestodes and their vertebrate hosts from northwest Florida. Quart. J. Fla. Acad. Sci. 23:302–314.

McKeever, S., G.W. Gorman, and L. Norman. 1958a. Occurrence of a *Trypanosoma cruzi*-like organism in some mammals from southwestern Florida. J. Parasitol. 44:583–587.

McKeever, S., S. Kaplan, and L. Ajello. 1958b. Ringworm fungi of large wild mammals in southwestern Georgia and northwestern Florida. Am. J. Vet. Res. 19:973–975.

McKeever, S., G.W. Gorman, J.F. Chapman, M.M. Galton, and D.K. Powers. 1958c. Incidence of leptospirosis in wild mammals from southwestern Georgia, with a report of new hosts for six serotypes of leptospires. Am. J. Trop. Med. Hyg. 7:646–655.

McKeever, S., J.H. Schubert, M.D. Moody, G.W. Gorman, and J.F. Chapman. 1958d. Natural occurrence of tularemia in marsupials, carnivores, lagomorphs, and large rodents in southwestern Georgia and northwestern Florida. J. Inf. Dis. 103:120–126.

Morgan, B.B. 1941. A summary of the Physalopterinae (Nematoda) of North America. Proc. Helminthol. Soc. Wash. 8:28–30.

Norman, L., M.M. Brooke, D.S. Allain, and G.W. Gorman. 1959. Morphology and virulence of *Trypanosoma cruzi*–like hemoflagellates isolated from wild mammals in Georgia and Florida. J. Parasitol. 45:457–463.

O'Connor, D.J., and S.W. Nielsen. 1981. Environmental survey of methylmercury levels in wild minks (*Mustela vison*) and otter (*Lutra canadensis*) from the northeastern United States and experimental pathology of methylmercurialism in the otter. In: Worldwide Furbearer Conf. Proc. J.A. Chapman and D. Pursley (eds.). Frostburg, Md. pp. 1728–1745.

Orihel, T.C. 1965. *Dirofilaria lutrae* sp. n. (Nematoda: Filarioidea) from otters in the southeast United States. J. Parasitol. 51:409–413.

O'Shea, T.J., T.E. Kaiser, G.R. Askins, and J.A. Chapman. 1981. Polychlorinated biphenyls in a wild mink population. In: Worldwide Furbearer Conf. Proc. J.A. Chapman and D. Pursley (eds.). Frostburg, Md. pp. 1746–1751.

Platonow, N.S., and L.H. Karstad. 1973. Dietary effects of polychlorinated biphenyls on mink. Can. J. Comp. Med. 37:391–400.

Robson, M.S., and S.R. Humphrey. 1985. Inefficacy of scent-stations for monitoring river otter populations. Wildl. Soc. Bull. 13:558–561.

Roelke, M.E., and E.C. Pirtle. 1988. Unpublished data. Florida Game and Fresh Water Fish Commission, Gainesville.

Roelke, M.E., E.R. Jacobson, G.V. Kollias, and D.J. Forrester. 1986. Medical management and biomedical findings on the Florida panther, *Felis concolor coryi*, July 1, 1985 to June 30, 1986. Ann. Rept. Fla. Game and Fresh Water Fish Comm., Gainesville. 65 pp.

Scholtens, R.G., and L. Norman. 1971. *Trichinella spiralis* in Florida wildlife. J. Parasitol. 57:1103.

Schwartz, A. 1952. The land mammals of southern Florida and the upper Florida Keys. Ph.D. diss., Univ. of Michigan, Ann Arbor.

Shump, K.A., A.U. Shump, R.A. Aulerich, and G.A. Heidt. 1976. A bibliography of mustelids. Part V: Otters. Mich. Agr. Exp.

Sta., Michigan State Univ., East Lansing. 32 pp.

Shump, K.A., A.U. Shump, T.W. Nelson, G.A. Heidt, and R.J. Aulerich. 1975. A bibliography of mustelids. Part III: Skunks. Mich. Agr. Exp. Sta., Michigan State Univ., East Lansing. 34 pp.

Sikes, R.K. 1962. Pathogenesis of rabies in wildlife. 1. Comparative effect of varying doses of rabies virus inoculated into foxes and skunks. Am. J. Vet. Res. 23:1041–1047.

Steers, G.C., and D.J. Forrester. 1987. Unpublished data. Univ. of Florida, Gainesville.

Stevenson, H.M. 1976. Vertebrates of Florida. Identification and distribution. Univ. Presses of Florida, Gainesville. 607 pp.

Stiles, C.W., and A. Hassall. 1894. A preliminary catalogue of the parasites contained in the collection of the U.S. Bureau of Animal Industry, U.S. Army Medical Museum, Biological Department of the University of Pennsylvania (Coll. Leidy) and in Coll. Stiles and Coll. Hassall. Vet. Mag. 1:331–354.

Strickland, R.K., R.R. Gerrish, J.L. Hourigan, and G.O. Schubert. 1976. Ticks of veterinary importance. APHIS-USDA Agr. Handbook No. 485. Washington, D.C. 122 pp.

Svendsen, G.E. 1982. Weasels (*Mustela* species). In: Wild mammals of North America. J.A. Chapman and G.A. Feldhamer (eds.). Johns Hopkins Univ. Press, Baltimore. pp. 3–36.

Toweill, D.E., and J.E. Tabor. 1982. River otter (*Lutra canadensis*). In: Wild mammals of North America. J.A. Chapman and G.A. Feldhamer (eds.). Johns Hopkins Univ. Press, Baltimore. pp. 688–703.

U.S. Fish and Wildlife Service. 1977. International trade in endangered species of wild fauna and flora. Fed. Reg. 42:10462–10488.

van Zyll de Long, C.G. 1972. A systematic review of the nearctic and neotropical river otters (genus *Lutra*, Mustelidae, Carnivora). Life Sci. Contrib. R. Ont. Mus. 80:1–104.

Verts, B.J. 1967. The biology of the striped skunk. Univ. of Illinois Press, Urbana. 218 pp.

Wassef, H.Y., and H. Hoogstraal. 1982. Unpublished data. NAMRU, Cairo, Egypt.

White, F.H. 1987. Unpublished data. Univ. of Florida, Gainesville.

Wilson, N., and W.W. Baker. 1972. Ticks of Georgia (Acarina: Metastigmata). Bull. Tall Timbers Res. Sta. 10:1–29.

Wilson, N., and H.W. Kale. 1972. Ticks collected from Indian River County, Florida (Acari: Metastigmata: Ixodidae). Fla. Entomol. 55:53–57.

Wood, D.A. 1990. Official lists of endangered fauna and flora in Florida. Florida Game and Fresh Water Fish Commission, Tallahassee. 19 pp.

CHAPTER FOURTEEN

Black Bears

I. Introduction

The black bear, *Ursus americanus* Pallas, is the largest land mammal in Florida (Brady and Maehr 1985) and, except in Baker and Columbia counties and Apalachicola National Forest, is listed by the Florida Game and Fresh Water Fish Commission as threatened (Wood 1990). The subspecies in Florida is *Ursus americanus floridanus* (Stevenson 1976). The distribution of Florida black bears is widespread, but fragmented and restricted to large undeveloped woodland tracts (Brady and Maehr 1985). A variety of foods (mostly native plants and animals) is utilized, indicating that a diverse habitat is needed by this omnivore (Maehr and Brady 1982b, 1984; Maehr and DeFazio 1985).

A number of reviews of the literature on parasites and diseases of black bears in North America have been published (Hamilton et al. 1974; Rogers and Rogers 1976; Crum 1977; Pelton 1982).

II. Trauma

Wooding and Brady (1987) analyzed the characteristics of black bears killed by vehicles in Florida from 1976–86. During that time period 99 bears were collected from roadsides in 27 of Florida's 67 counties. The largest numbers came from Collier County (n = 23), where most came from the highways that traverse Big Cypress National Preserve. Lake County (n = 15) and Marion County (n = 13) had high numbers also. The other animals came from locations scattered throughout the state. Few animals came from the five counties where hunting is legal. The authors concluded that road-kills represented a major cause of mortality for Florida bears in areas where there is no hunting.

About twice as many males were killed on roads as females. This was attributed to the more extensive movements of males compared to females. There were two peaks in the numbers of bears killed, one in May–July and one in October–December (Figure 14-1). The May–July peak was probably associated with the movements of males in relation to dispersal and breeding, and the October–December peak may have been associated with a search for energy-rich food. There was no concentration of female bears killed at a certain age, but

a higher number of males from one to four years of age was found (Figure 14-2). This was attributed to the breakup of families and the subsequent dispersal of young males outside of their natural home range.

Wooding and Brady (1987) stated that vehicle-related mortality will become more significant as the human population in Florida increases and as black bear populations became more fragmented. They recommended that a number of efforts be instituted in order to reduce this mortality. Such efforts as erection of warning signs in bear crossing areas, fencing along major highways, and building of underpasses may be of help.

III. Environmental contaminants and toxicosis

There is no information available on environmental contaminants in black bears in Flor-

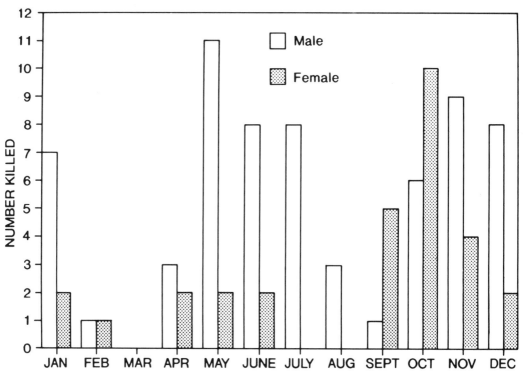

FIGURE 14-1. Numbers of male and female black bears killed each month on highways in Florida during 1976–86. (From Wooding and Brady 1987.)

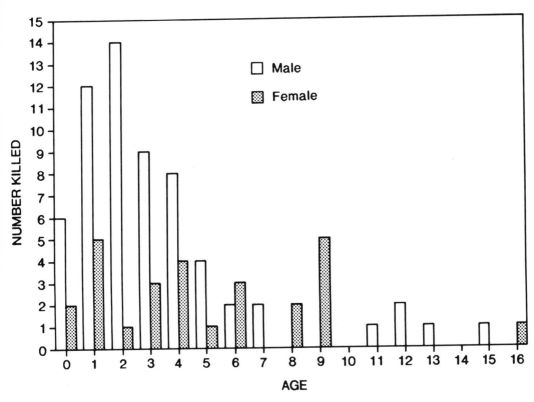

FIGURE 14-2. Age distribution of male and female black bears killed on highways in Florida during 1976–86. (From Wooding and Brady 1987.)

ida. Because of their omnivorous feeding habits, residues of persistent pesticides and herbicides might be expected.

In Florida a number of bears are poisoned by strychnine each year. These unfortunate incidents are believed to be attempts by beekeepers to eliminate problem bears that cause extensive damage to their bee-hives and equipment. Annual losses in Florida are believed to be over $100,000 (Maehr and Brady 1982a). It has been estimated that around a half dozen black bears are killed each year along with other nontarget animals (such as raccoons and opossums) that also eat the poisoned bait, usually strychnine-laced honeycomb (Goodson 1986). The Florida Game and Fresh Water Fish Commission has attempted to decrease these losses by an education campaign and by urging the use of electric fences in problem areas (Maehr and Brady 1982a).

IV. Infectious diseases

Serologic studies on black bears in Idaho (Binninger et al. 1980) and California (Ruppanner et al. 1982) indicate that a variety of viral, rickettsial, fungal, and bacterial diseases, some of public health importance, might be expected in Florida. Such information for Florida bears is limited.

Apparently rabies is not a problem. There are no reports of rabid black bears in Florida (Burridge et al. 1986).

Serologic evidence for the existence of pseudorabies virus in Florida black bears was presented by Pirtle et al. (1986). In that study, 13 animals from Ocala National Forest in 1985 were tested and one (a 10-month-old cub) was seropositive. The cub may have acquired the infection by feeding on the carcass of an infected wild hog. In Florida, wild hogs are commonly infected with pseudorabies virus (Pirtle et al. 1986) and have been found to be utilized as food by black bears (Maehr and Brady 1984).

Sera from 12 black bears in north-central Florida (1985) were tested for antibodies to seven arboviruses and were positive for EEE (3 of 12), SLE (1 of 12), vesicular stomatitis-Indiana (1 of 12), and California group (10 of 11) viruses (McLean and Forrester 1990). The samples were seronegative for Everglades virus, vesicular stomatitis-New Jersey virus, and Tensaw virus.

Serum samples collected from 34 black bears from Columbia/Baker (n = 6), Lake (n = 3), Putnam (n = 13), Marion (n = 8), Orange (n = 1), and Calhoun (n = 3) counties in 1980–87 were tested for antibodies to *Leptospira interrogans*. Only a three-year-old male from Columbia/Baker counties was positive. This animal had a 1:50 titer for serovar *iterohaemorrhagiae*. These same samples

were tested also for *Brucella* antibodies; all were negative (Forrester et al. 1990).

White and Forrester (1988) examined nine bears for enteric bacteria, seven from Osceola National Forest (1976–78), one from Alachua County (1971), and one from Hernando County (1976). The bear from Alachua County, a five-month-old cub, was positive for *Salmonella litchfield*.

The significance of pseudorabies, *Leptospira*, *Salmonella*, and arboviral infections to bear populations is not known. The *Salmonella* and *Leptospira* infections and the arboviruses may be of public health importance.

V. Protozoan parasites

The only protozoan parasite known from black bears in Florida is *Toxoplasma gondii*. Seventeen of 38 (45%) bears were seropositive for *T. gondii* (Table 14-1). Bears from Osceola National Forest (Columbia/Baker counties) had the highest prevalences of infection. Ages of infected bears varied from cubs less than one year to a seven-year-old male. The significance of these findings to bear populations is unknown, although the public

Table 14-1
Results of serologic tests (indirect hemagglutination) for *Toxoplasma gondii* in black bears from Florida

| Locality (county) | No. bears | | | Data source |
	Exam.	Pos.	%	
Calhoun	3	1	33	Forrester et al. (1990)[a]
Columbia/Baker	6	4	67	" " "
Putnam	13	3	23	" " " "
Marion	8	4	50	" " " "
Orange	1	1	100	" " " "
Lake	3	0	0	" " " "
Columbia/Baker	4	4	100	Burridge et al. (1979)[b]
All areas	38	17	45	

[a]1980–1987.
[b]Sampling dates not given by authors.

health considerations are important (Jordan et al. 1975).

Crum (1977) examined four bears in 1973–1974 from Liberty County for *Sarcocystis* infections. None was infected. This parasite has been reported from black bears in North Carolina and West Virginia (Crum 1977; Crum et al. 1978).

Fecal samples from 11 bears in Florida were examined for coccidial oocysts (Forrester 1985). All were negative. Two species of *Eimeria* (*E. albertensis* and *E. borealis*) have been reported from black bears in Canada (Hair and Mahrt 1970).

Blood smears from 19 black bears were examined for parasites and found to be negative (Telford and Forrester 1990). These came from Columbia/Baker counties (n = 16, 1976–80), Osceola County (n = 1, 1979), and Bay County (n = 2, 1990).

VI. Helminths

Twenty species of helminths have been reported from black bears in Florida. These include 17 species of nematodes, 2 trematodes, and 1 acanthocephalan (Table 14-2). Three of these species (*Strongyloides* sp., *Capillaria aerophila*, and *Macracanthorhynchus ingens*) are of concern from a pathological standpoint. All three were very prevalent and, in some cases, intensities were high. Crum et al. (1978) reported that *Capillaria aerophila* in high numbers was associated with catarrhal bronchitis. Several species of *Strongyloides* are known to be pathogenic to young animals (Levine 1980), and it is possible that the species infecting black bears in Florida may cause problems in cubs. The acanthocephalan (*M. ingens*) may also be harmful to young bears due to mechanical damage to the intestines produced by its large and powerful hooks (Petrochenko 1971).

The helminth fauna of black bears in the southeastern United States was studied further by Pence et al. (1983) and compared with data from black bears in other parts of North America. The authors concluded that the helminth fauna of bears in the Southeast (including Florida) was different from that of bears in other regions. They also pointed out that black bears have a number of species of helminths that are found also in raccoons and various canids. These shared species (such as *Placoconus lotoris, Macracanthorhynchus ingens, Ancylostoma caninum,* and *Toxascaris leonina*) make up a large secondary community of parasites. The reader is referred to Pence et al. (1983) for further details on the statistical analyses conducted and their ecological interpretation.

One of the most commonly reported parasites of black bears in other parts of North America is *Trichinella spiralis*, the etiologic agent of trichinosis (Crum 1977). Crum et al. (1978) examined tissues from 50 bears in the Southeast (including four from Liberty County, Florida) and found no *T. spiralis* infections. Conti et al. (1983) tested diaphragm samples from 25 additional bears from various parts of Florida. Most came from Osceola National Forest, where a number of bears are killed and consumed by hunters each year. All were negative for larvae of *T. spiralis*. Thus it appears that Florida bears are not hosts of this zoonotic parasite.

VII. Arthropods

Four species of ticks, one species of mite, and one species of screwworm have been found infesting black bears in Florida (Table 14-3). The primary screwworm (*Cochliomyia hominovorax*) was an important pathogen to Florida wildlife, but was eradicated in the late 1950s and early 1960s (Strickland et al.

Table 14-2
Helminths reported from black bears in Florida

Helminth	No. of bears		Intensity		Date	County	Data source
	Exam.	Infec.(%)	Mean	Range			
Nematoda							
Strongyloides sp.	46	40(87)	412[a]	1–4,767	1976–81	Liberty, Columbia, Baker, Hamilton, Highlands, Marion, Duval, Pasco, Lake, Collier, Alachua	Conti et al. (1983), Forrester & Conti (1985)
Capillaria aerophila	4	3(75)	73	12–104	1973–74	Liberty	Crum (1977)
	41	30(73)	60	4–367	1976–81	Columbia, Baker, Hamilton, Highlands, Marion, Duval, Pasco, Alachua, Collier	Conti et al. (1983), Forrester & Conti (1985)
Molineus barbatus[a]	4	3(75)	32	19–52	1973–74	Liberty	Crum (1977)
	46	21(46)	10	1–79	1976–81	Columbia, Baker, Duval, Alachua	Conti et al. (1983), Forrester & Conti (1985)
Gongylonema pulchrum	4	1(25)	240	240	1973–74	Liberty	Crum (1977)
	34	13(38)	2	1–9	1976–81	Columbia, Baker, Marion, Alachua	Conti et al. (1983), Forrester & Conti (1985)
Placoconus lotoris	4	2(50)	5	1–8	1973–74	Liberty	Crum (1977)
	46	13(28)	4[a]	1–11	1976–81	Columbia, Baker, Hamilton, Liberty	Conti et al. (1983), Forrester & Conti (1985)
Ancylostoma caninum	4	3(75)	1	1–2	1973–74	Liberty	Crum (1977)
Gnathostoma sp. (larvae)	4	2(50)	1	1	1973–74	Liberty	" "
	46	8(17)	2	1–3	1976–81	Columbia, Baker, Liberty	Conti et al. (1983), Forrester & Conti (1985)
Physaloptera sp. (larvae)	46	7(15)	2	1–5	1976–81	Columbia, Baker, Duval, Pasco, Alachua	Conti et al. (1983), Forrester & Conti (1985)
Dirofilaria immitis	4	1(25)	2	2	1973–74	Liberty	Crum (1977)
	40	6(15)	1	1–2	1976–81	Columbia, Baker, Marion, Collier	Conti et al. (1983), Forrester & Conti (1985)

Species					Years	Counties	References
Capillaria putorii	46	4(9)	3	1–5	1976–81	Columbia, Baker	Conti et al. (1983), Forrester & Conti (1985)
Gnathostoma didelphis	4	2(50)	5	1–9	1973–74	Liberty	Crum (1977)
	46	3(7)	1	1–2	1976–81	Columbia, Baker	Conti et al. (1983), Forrester & Conti (1985)
Capillaria plica	20	1(5)	15	15	1976–81	Columbia, Baker	Conti et al. (1983), Forrester & Conti (1985)
Lagochilascaris sprenti	46	2(4)	63	24–103	1976–81	Columbia, Baker, Duval	Conti et al. (1983), Forrester & Conti (1985), Bowman et al. (1983)
Toxascaris leonina	46	2(4)	3	3	1976–81	Columbia, Baker	Conti et al. (1983), Forrester & Conti (1985)
Physaloptera rara	46	2(4)	11	1–20	1976–81	Columbia, Baker	Conti et al. (1983), Forrester & Conti (1985)
Crenosoma vulpis	41	1(2)	1	1	1976–81	Columbia, Baker	Conti et al. (1983), Forrester & Conti (1985)
Crenosoma sp. (larvae)	41	1(2)	1	1	1976–81	Columbia, Baker	Conti et al. (1983), Forrester & Conti (1985)
Trematoda *Pharyngostomoides procyonis*	46	1(2)	1[a]	1	1976–81	Columbia, Baker	Conti et al. (1983), Forrester & Conti (1985)
Heterobilharzia americana	37	1(3)	2	2	1976–81	Collier	Forrester & Conti (1985)
Acanthocephala *Macracanthorhynchus ingens*	46	37(80)	9	1–46	1976–81	Columbia, Baker, Hamilton, Hernando, Highlands, Liberty, Duval, Alachua, Lake	Conti et al. (1983), Forrester & Conti (1985)

[a] = intensity values based on 35 animals.

Table 14-3
Arthropods reported from black bears in Florida

| Species | No. bears | | Counties | Data source |
	Exam.	Inf.(%)		
Ticks				
Dermacentor variabilis	20	15(75)	Baker, Columbia, Collier, Marion, Highlands, Lake, Pasco	Forrester & Brady (1985)
	NG[a]	NG	Collier	Taylor (1951)
Ixodes scapularis	20	8(40)	Baker, Columbia	Forrester & Brady (1985)
	4	NG	"Northern Florida"	Rogers (1953)
Amblyomma maculatum	20	6(30)	Baker, Columbia, Collier, Duval, Lake, Pasco	Forrester & Brady (1985)
Amblyomma americanum	20	5(20)	Baker, Columbia, Marion, Pasco	" " "
Mites				
Demodex sp.	3	3(100)	Bradford, Lake, Marion	Spalding et al. (1990)
Screwworms				
Cochliomyia hominivorax[b]	NG	1(—)	Marion	Strode (1955)

[a]NG = not given by authors.
[b]This parasite has now been eradicated from Florida (Strickland et al. 1976).

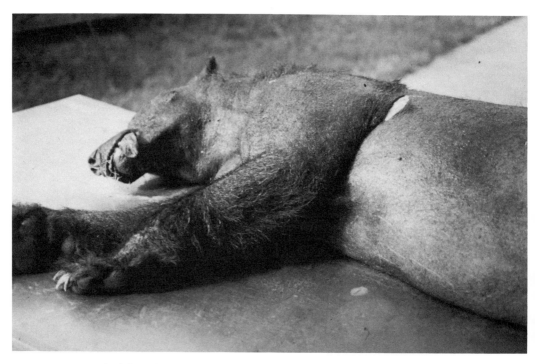

FIGURE 14-3. Black bear from Bradford County, Florida, with severe case of demodectic mange.

1976). *Dermacentor variabilis* is the most common and widely distributed species. Three of the species (*D. variabilis, Amblyomma maculatum,* and *A. americanum*) are known to cause tick paralysis in other hosts (Strickland et al. 1976) and all four have been reported previously from white-tailed deer, wild hogs, and Florida panthers in Florida (Smith 1977; Greiner et al. 1984; Forrester et al. 1985).

A case of demodectic mange was seen in an adult male black bear that had been killed by a vehicle in Bradford County in June 1990 (Spalding et al. 1990). The animal was almost hairless (alopecia) except for sparsely haired areas on the back of the neck and on the ears and limbs (Figure 14-3). Many specimens of *Demodex* sp. were seen in scrapings and histologic sections of the skin. Subsequently two other road-killed bears, one from Marion County and one from Lake County (both in October 1990) were found positive for *Demodex*. Only one, however, had alopecia. This was the bear from Marion County which had hair loss on its face, forearms, and paws but of less severity compared to the bear from Bradford County.

VIII. Summary and conclusions

Little is known about the diseases of black bears in Florida. There is no information on environmental contaminants, neoplasia, or rickettsial and fungal diseases, and only a limited amount of data on five viral and two bacterial infections. Twenty-seven species of parasites have been reported, including 1 protozoan, 17 nematodes, 2 trematodes, 1 acanthocephalan, and 6 arthropods. Of the parasites reported, four may be significant pathologically. These are *Strongyloides* sp., *Capillaria aerophila, Macracanthorhynchus ingens,* and *Demodex* sp. Vehicle-related mortality is a significant factor in Florida black bear populations.

IX. Literature cited

Binninger, C.C., J.J. Beecham, L.A. Thomas, and L.D. Winward. 1980. A serological survey for selected infectious diseases of black bears in Idaho. J. Wildl. Dis. 16:423–430.

Bowman, D.D., J.L. Smith, and M.D. Little. 1983. *Lagochilascaris sprenti* sp. n. (Nematoda: Ascarididae) from the opossum, *Didelphis virginiana* (Marsupialia: Didelphidae). J. Parasitol. 69:754–760.

Brady, J.R., and D.S. Maehr. 1985. Distribution of black bears in Florida. Fla. Field Nat. 13:1–7.

Burridge, M.J., L.A. Sawyer, and W.J. Bigler. 1986. Rabies in Florida. Department of Health and Rehabilitative Services, Tallahassee, Fla. 147 pp.

Burridge, M.J., W.J. Bigler, D.J. Forrester, and J.M. Hennemann. 1979. Serologic survey for *Toxoplasma gondii* in wild animals in Florida. J. Am. Vet. Med. Assoc. 175:964–967.

Conti, J.A., D.J. Forrester, and J.R. Brady. 1983. Helminths of black bears in Florida. Proc. Helminthol. Soc. Wash. 50:252–256.

Crum, J.M. 1977. Some parasites of black bears (*Ursus americanus*) in the southeastern United States. M.S. thesis, Univ. of Georgia, Athens. 76 pp.

Crum, J.M., V.F. Nettles, and W.R. Davidson. 1978. Studies on endoparasites of the black bear (*Ursus americanus*) in the southeastern United States. J. Wildl. Dis. 14:178–186.

Forrester, D.J. 1985. Unpublished data. Univ. of Florida, Gainesville.

Forrester, D.J., and J.R. Brady. 1985. Unpublished data. Univ. of Florida, Gainesville.

Forrester, D.J., and J.A. Conti. 1985. Unpublished data. Univ. of Florida, Gainesville.

Forrester, D.J., J.R. Brady, and J.B. Wooding. 1990. Unpublished data. Univ. of Florida, Gainesville.

Forrester, D.J., J.A. Conti, and R.C. Belden.

1985. Parasites of the Florida panther (*Felis concolor coryi*). Proc. Helminthol. Soc. Wash. 52:95–97.

Goodson, B. 1986. Unpublished data. Florida Game and Fresh Water Fish Commission, Tallahassee.

Greiner, E.C., P.P. Humphrey, R.C. Belden, W.B. Frankenberger, D.H. Austin, and E.P. J. Gibbs. 1984. Ixodid ticks on feral swine in Florida. J. Wildl. Dis. 20:114–119.

Hair, J.D., and J.L. Mahrt. 1970. *Eimeria albertensis* n. sp. and *E. borealis* n. sp. (Sporozoa: Eimeriidae) in black bears, *Ursus americanus*, from Alberta. J. Protozool. 17:663–664.

Hamilton, R.J., F.E. Kellogg, and R.C. Sheard. 1974. Parasites and diseases of the black bear in the Southeast (*Ursus americanus*): A position report. Proc. 2d No. Am. Workshop Black Bear Manage. Res., Gatlinburg, Tenn. 22 pp.

Jordan, G.W., J. Theis, C.M. Fuller, and P.D. Hoeprich. 1975. Bear meat trichinosis with a concomitant serologic response to *Toxoplasma gondii*. Am. J. Med. Sci. 269:251–257.

Levine, N.D. 1980. Nematode parasites of domestic animals and of man. 2d ed. Burgess, Minneapolis. p. 477.

McLean, R.G., and D.J. Forrester, 1990. Unpublished data. CDC, Fort Collins, Colo.

Maehr, D.S., and J.R. Brady. 1982a. Florida black bear–beekeeper conflict: 1981 beekeeper survey. Am. Bee J. 122:372–375.

———. 1982b. Fall food habits of black bears in Baker and Columbia counties, Florida. Proc. S.E. Assoc. Fish Wildl. Agencies 36:565–570.

———. 1984. Food habits of Florida black bears. J. Wildl. Manage. 48:230–235.

Maehr, D.S., and J.T. DeFazio. 1985. Foods of black bears in Florida. Fla. Field Nat. 13:8–12.

Pelton, M.R. 1982. Black bear. In: Wild mammals of North America. J.A. Chapman and G.A. Feldhamer (eds.). Johns Hopkins Univ. Press, Baltimore. pp. 504–514.

Pence, D.B., J.M. Crum, and J.A. Conti. 1983.

Ecological analyses of helminth populations in the black bear, *Ursus americanus*, from North America. J. Parasitol. 69:933–950.

Petrochenko, V.I. 1971. Acanthocephala of domestic and wild animals. Israel Program for Scientific Translation, Ltd., Jerusalem, Israel. 478 pp.

Pirtle, E.C., M.E. Roelke, and J. Brady. 1986. Antibodies against pseudorabies virus in the serum of a Florida black bear cub. J. Am. Vet. Med. Assoc. 189:1164.

Rogers, A.J. 1953. A study of the ixodid ticks of northern Florida, including the biology and life history of *Ixodes scapularis* Say (Ixodidae: Acarina). Ph.D. diss., Univ. of Maryland, College Park. 191 pp.

Rogers, L.L., and S. Rogers. 1976. Parasites of bears: A review. In: Bears—their biology and management. Pelton et al. (eds.). Int. Union Cons. Nature Nat. Res., Morges, Switzerland. New Ser. Publ. No. 40. pp. 411–430.

Ruppanner, R., D.A. Jessup, I. Ohishi, D.E. Behymer, and C.E. Franti. 1982. Serologic survey for certain zoonotic diseases in black bears in California. J. Am. Vet. Med. Assoc. 181:1288–1291.

Smith, J.S. 1977. A survey of ticks infesting white-tailed deer in twelve southeastern states. M.S. thesis, Univ. of Georgia, Athens. 60 pp.

Spalding, M.G., D.J. Forrester and J.B. Wooding. 1990. Unpublished data. Univ. of Florida, Gainesville.

Stevenson, H.M. 1976. Vertebrates of Florida. Identification and distribution. Univ. Presses of Florida, Gainesville. 607 pp.

Strickland, R.K., R.R. Gerrish, J.L. Hourigan, and G.O. Schubert. 1976. Ticks of veterinary importance. APHIS-USDA Agric. Handbook No. 485. U.S. Government Printing Office, Washington, D.C. 122 pp.

Strode, D.D. 1955. The screw-worm problem in the Ocala National Forest deer herd. Proc. Ann. Conf. S.E. Assoc. Game Fish Comm. 8:85–89.

Taylor, D.J. 1951. The distribution of ticks in Florida. M.S. thesis, Univ. of Florida, Gainesville. 124 pp.

Telford, S.R., Jr., and D.J. Forrester. 1990. Unpublished data. Univ. of Florida, Gainesville.

White, F.H., and D.J. Forrester. 1988. Unpublished data. Univ. of Florida, Gainesville.

Wood, D.A. 1990. Official lists of endangered and potentially endangered fauna and flora in Florida. Florida Game and Fresh Water Fish Commission. Tallahassee. 19 pp.

Wooding, J.B., and J.R. Brady. 1987. Black bear roadkills in Florida. Proc. Ann. Conf. S.E. Assoc. Fish Wildl. Agen. 41:438–442.

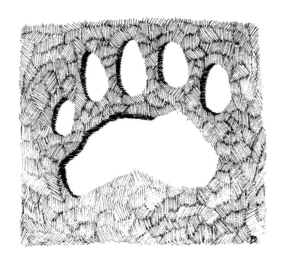

Florida Panthers and Bobcats

I. Introduction

Stevenson (1976) lists three species of wild felids in Florida: the bobcat, *Felis rufus* (Schreber), the Florida panther, *Felis concolor coryi* Bangs, and the jaguarundi, *Felis yagouaroundi* (Berlandier). There is no additional substantiated evidence of the presence of jaguarundis in the state, and therefore they will not be discussed further. The bobcat is distributed widely throughout the state and is found in every county (Brady 1977). The Florida panther consists mainly of a population of 20 to 50 animals in southern Florida (Glades, Hendry, Collier, Broward, Monroe, and Dade counties) (Belden 1986). It was declared an endangered subspecies by the U.S. Department of the Interior in 1967.

McCord and Cardoza (1982) provided a brief review of the parasites and diseases of bobcats and Tumlison et al. (1982) listed 67 references on parasites and diseases in their bibliography of bobcat literature. Anderson (1983) published a critical review of the literature on the puma, and included a section on parasites and diseases. Baseline data on hematology, serum chemistry, and endocrinology have been obtained for the Florida panther by Roelke (1990).

II. Trauma

There are no data on trauma as a cause of death in bobcats from Florida, but it seems reasonable to assume that such mortality may be important. Road-killed bobcats are not an uncommon finding, but no tabulations on the extent of this trauma are available.

Roelke (1988b, 1990) documented the morbidity and mortality of Florida panthers from 1972 to 1990, during which time 43 panthers were injured or known or presumed to have been injured or died (Table 15-1). Of these, 20 were hit by vehicles, 7 were illegal kills, 5 died due to intraspecific aggression by other panthers, 1 died of a heart defect, and 5 others died of disease. One other animal was killed accidentally during a live-capture procedure, and the cause of death of four others was unknown. Roelke et al. (1985) pointed out previously that there was a dramatic increase in mortality from 1979 to 1985 and that this coincided with a considerable increase in the number of people living

Table 15-1
Documented injury/mortality of Florida panthers, 1972–1990

Category	No. panthers Tot. no.	%
Road-killed/injured[a]	20	46.5
Illegally killed	7	16.3
Intraspecific aggression[b]	5	11.6
Capture-related mortality	1	2.3
Congenital heart defect	1	2.3
Disease[c]	5	11.6
Unknown[d]	4	9.3
Total	43	100.0

Sources: Roelke (1988b, 1989, 1990).
[a]This category includes four panthers which were seriously injured, but survived due to medical attention. These would not have survived if left on their own. A fifth panther was struck by a vehicle and escaped; its fate is not known, but it is assumed that it probably died later.
[b]Includes those animals that died of septicemia or toxemia as a result of bite and puncture wounds.
[c]One animal died of each of the following: kidney/liver/thyroid disease, rabies, mercury poisoning, septicemia, and pyothorax.
[d]Only skeletal remains were recovered on these animals; the cause of death was not apparent.

in southern Florida. For example, between 1970 and 1980 the population of Collier County increased by 126%. Concomitantly, there occurred an increase in highway traffic and use of public lands for recreational purposes (camping, fishing, hunting, etc.). The amount of traffic on Alligator Alley increased from 31,977 vehicles per month in 1979–1980 to 55,894 in 1984–1985 (Figure 15-1). Furthermore, when the seasonal pattern of mortality was analyzed (Figure 15-2), it became clear that most of the road-kills or injuries occurred between October and May, when traffic was at its peak. Other causes of death (excluding road-kills) clustered at the same time of year. This could be explained by the fact that during the various hunting seasons, there were more people in areas where panthers occur. Of the panthers killed by vehicles and illegally killed, 60% were between 18 months and 3 years of age. The vulnerability of panthers to vehicle collisions and illegal shooting may be due to dispersal of young and their naïveté concerning the hazards associated with roads and human activities (Roelke et al. 1985). It is obvious from these data that trauma related to the interaction of people and panthers is an important cause of mortality.

III. Environmental contaminants

There is no information on pesticides or radionuclides in bobcats in Florida. Cumbie (1975) and Cumbie and Jenkins (1975), however, gave information on concentrations of mercury in hair, skeletal muscle, and liver samples from bobcats in Florida, Georgia, and South Carolina. Unfortunately, they did not present separate values for animals from Florida. Concentrations varied from 1.1 to 24.0 ppm for hair, 0.02 to 1.9 ppm for muscle, and 0.2 to 4.8 ppm for liver. Jenkins and Fendley (1968) provided data on cesium-137

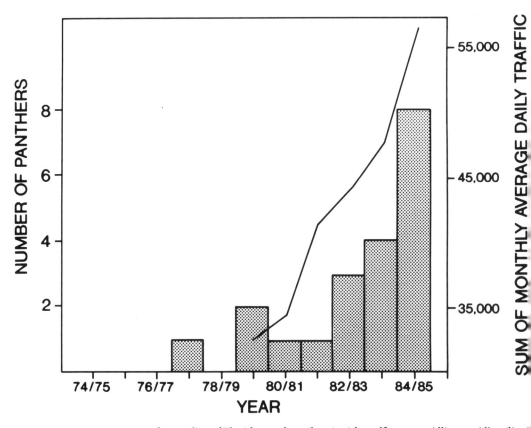

FIGURE 15-1. Comparison of mortality of Florida panthers (bars) with traffic use on Alligator Alley (line) from 1974 to 1985. (From Roelke et al. 1985.)

in bobcats from Georgia and South Carolina, but not Florida.

Tissues from seven Florida panthers have been examined for residues of chlorinated hydrocarbons (Table 15-2). Eight different compounds were identified, including DDE, DDD, DDT, PCB, dieldrin, heptachlor, heptachlor epoxide, and lindane. Concentrations were very low for most compounds. The highest was 32 ppm of DDE in the fat of a panther killed in Glades County. The importance of these findings is unknown, although these low concentrations are most likely of little significance to the health of panthers.

Blood and other tissues from 18 panthers that died of various causes or were "normal animals" sampled during capture operations from 1978 to 1989 were tested for residues of mercury (Technical Subcommittee of the Florida Panther Interagency Committee 1989). Residues were detected in every panther and varied from 0.05 to 130.00 ppm in samples of liver, kidney, and hair (Table 15-3). Residues in muscle samples from eight panthers varied from 0.06 to 4.2 ppm and in blood (collected in EDTA) from 11 panthers varied from 0.07 to 1.83 ppm. One panther (no. 27), a four-year-old female from the northern Shark River Slough (East Everglades) near Everglades National Park, had 110 ppm in its liver and 130 ppm in hair samples and was believed to have died of mercury toxicosis. The source of the mercury for panthers is probably their prey. Concen-

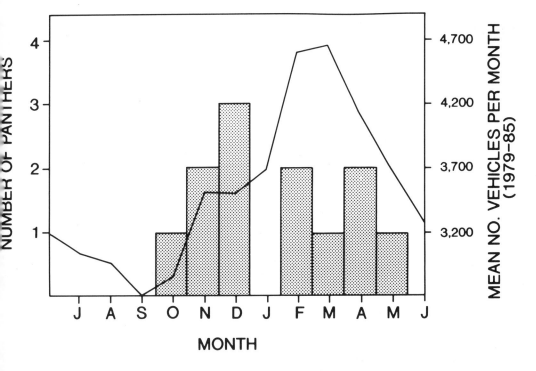

FIGURE 15-2. Comparison of numbers of Florida panthers killed or injured by vehicles (bars) with traffic use on Alligator Alley (line) on a seasonal basis. (From Roelke et al. 1985.)

rations of mercury were considerably higher in panthers from Fakahatchee Strand State Preserve and from East Everglades than in those from other areas (Table 15-3). Panthers in these areas of high mercury concentrations are known to feed primarily on mammals such as raccoons, rabbits, otters, and armadillos, whereas those in other areas utilize deer, hogs, and alligators (Technical Subcommittee of the Florida Panther Interagency Committee 1989). Older panthers had higher concentrations than younger animals. Additional research is needed on the ecological aspects of mercury contamination and its effects on panthers in southern Florida. Mercury contamination could be a very serious factor in panther populations. In addition to causing mortality, mercury poisoning can result in a variety of neurologic problems, teratogenic changes, and abortion (Buck 1989).

Samples of tissues from eight panthers (six from animals examined at necropsy and two from live-captured animals) were tested for residues of lead, selenium, and arsenic. Small amounts of each were found in most samples (Table 15-4). The significance of these findings is unknown, but there may be sublethal effects that are unrecognized at the present time.

IV. Neoplasia

Roelke (1990) reported fribromas or fibropapillomas in the vestibules or vaginas of several Florida panthers. Two animals (11–14 years of age) had advanced cases in which the growths were covered with fingerlike projections 0.5–3.0 mm in length. The growths protruded from the vulvar lips and encircled the

Table 15-2
Residues of chlorinated hydrocarbons in tissues of Florida panthers

Panther no.	78–65	80–4	80–15	81–19	83–1	83–64	83–22
Date	1978	1979	1980	1981	1983	1983	1985
Age	SA	Ad	SA	SA	Ad	Ad	SA
Sex	M	F	M	F	F	M	F
County	Dade	Collier	Collier	Collier	Collier	Collier	Glades
Tissue/Compd				*Residue (ppm)*			
Brain							
DDE	NE[a]	Tr[b]	Tr	Tr	NE	0	NE
DDD	NE	Tr	0	0	NE	0	NE
PCB	NE	0	0	0	NE	0	NE
Others	0	0	Tr[c]	0	NE	0	NE
Muscle							
DDE	Tr	0.1	0	Tr	NE	NE	NE
DDD	0	Tr	0	0	NE	NE	NE
PCB	0.4	0	0	0	NE	NE	NE
Others	Tr[d]	Tr[e]	0	0	NE	NE	NE
Liver							
DDE	0.2	Tr	0	Tr	2.2	0	1.3
DDD	0	Tr	0	0	0	0	0
PCB	0.7	0	0	0	0	0	0
Others	Tr[d]	0	Tr[c,e,f]	0	0	0	0
Fat							
DDE	3.7	2.1	0	0	0	3.1	32.0
DDD	0	0.3	0	0.2	0	0	0
PCB	3.9	0	0	0	0	0	0
Others	Tr[d]	Tr[e]	Tr[e,h]	Tr[g]	0	0	0

Source: Forrester et al. (1985b).
[a]NE = not examined.
[b]Tr = trace (< 0.1 ppm).
[c]Trace amounts of heptachlor epoxide.
[d]Trace amounts of dieldrin.
[e]Trace amounts of heptachlor.
[f]Trace amounts of lindane.
[g]Trace amounts of DDT and Halowax.
[h]0.9 ppm of heptachlor epoxide.

vestibule. Roelke (1990) postulated that these tumors could interfere with conception by hindering successful copulation and movement of spermatoza. Neither of the females reproduced during the 6.5-year period in which they were monitored, even though they were known to associate with males.

V. Anomalies

Five anomalies have been documented in Florida panthers. These include kinked tail tips, mid-dorsal ridges or whorls of hair on the back, cryptorchidism, sperm abnormalities, and congenital heart defects.

Wilkins (1990) reported that 57 of 71 (80%) Florida panthers had a mid-dorsal whorl compared to 2% for other North American cougars and 14% for South American specimens. Kinked tail tips occurred in 44 of 59 (75%) Florida specimens. Prevalences of both whorls and kinks were considerably higher in panthers in southwestern Florida (Big Cypress National Preserve, Fakahatchee Strand State Preserve, etc.) than in

Table 15-3

Concentrations of mercury in tissues of Florida panthers, 1978–89

Area	Panther				ppm (wet wt)		
	No.	Sex	Age[a]	Date	Liver	Hair	Kidney
Northern Fakahatchee[b]	04	M	OA	1985	7.80	NA	11.20
	13	M	A	1987	0.05	NA	0.16
	20	M	A	1988	0.05	NA	0.19
	25	M	YA	1988	2.40	0.2	0.57
Southern Fakahatchee[c]	07	F	OA	1985	2.00	NA	8.50
	08	F	OA	1988	19.00	14.0	1.75
	01	M	OA	1983	3.60	NA	0.70
	PCO-59	F	OA	1986	20.00	0.56	0.52
	G81-19	F	SA	1981	NA	NA	9.10
Eastern Everglades[d]	16	M	SA	1988	NA	82.00	NA
	21	F	YA	1988	NA	14.00	NA
	27	F	A	1989	110.00	130.00	8.70
Long Pine Key[e]	14	F	A	1988	NA	8.50	NA
	15	M	SA	1988	NA	82.00	NA
	22	F	SA	1988	NA	7.10	NA
Corkscrew Swamp[f]	N-89-64	M	YA	1989	1.40	7.00	0.61
Corbett WMA[g]	G84-20	F	Y	1984	12.0	NA	0.24
Raccoon Point[h]	G78-65	M	SA	1978	15.0	NA	NA

Source: Data from Technical Subcommittee of the Florida Panther Interagency Committee (1989).
[a]SA = subadult (1–2 yr), YA = young adult (2–3 yr), A = adult (4–7 yr), and OA = old adult (8+ yr).
[b]Includes the Florida Panther National Wildlife Refuge, Bear Island Unit of the Big Cypress National Preserve, and private land, all in Collier County.
[c]Fakahatchee Strand State Preserve (Collier County).
[d]Area to the north of Long Pine Key (Dade County).
[e]Also known as the Hole-in-the-Donut area (Dade County).
[f]Collier County.
[g]Corbett Wildlife Management Area (Palm Beach County).
[h]Part of the Monument Unit of Big Cypress National Preserve (Collier County).

those in southeastern Florida (Everglades National Park).

Cryptorchidism (one testicle not descending into the scrotum) was present in 12 of 27 (44%) male Florida panthers examined during 1981–1990 (Roelke 1989, 1990). In two animals examined at necropsy, the retained testicles were just outside the abdominal cavity within the inguinal canal and were atrophied and sterile.

Semen from 14 different Florida panthers examined during 1987–1989 contained more than 90% morphologically abnormal sperm (Roelke 1987, 1988b, 1989). Of these defective sperm, 70% were classified as primary

abnormalities that occur during spermatogenesis. The most common (48%) type of defect involved the acrosome (head) of the spermatozoon, which would severely decrease the chances of fertilization occurring (Roelke 1986). These abnormalities are high in prevalence when compared to other cougars in North America (60–75% abnormality) and domestic cats (30%) (Roelke et al. 1986, 1987).

In 1988 the heart of a young adult male panther from Collier County was found to have a congenital defect (Roelke 1989). The problem involved the two atria and resulted in lung changes due to vascular flow prob-

Table 15-4
Concentrations of lead, selenium, and arsenic in tissues of
Florida panthers

Animal no.	Tissue	Lead[a]	Selenium[b]	Arsenic[b]
78–65[c]	Liver	3.0	NE	ND
	Blood	ND[f]	0.45	ND
80–15[c]	Blood	ND	0.38	ND
81–19[c]	Kidney	ND	NE[g]	0.03
83–64[c]	Liver	ND	NE	ND
	Kidney	ND	NE	ND
	Bone	ND	NE	NE
	Blood	ND	0.52	ND
83–22[c]	Blood	ND	0.41	ND
04[d]	Blood	ND	0.28	ND
08[e]	Blood	ND	0.68	ND
27[h]	Liver	ND	22.00	ND

Sources: Roelke (1985, 1990).
[a]Concentrations are in μg/dl for blood and μg/g (= ppm) for liver and kidney samples (wet wt).
[b]Concentrations are in μg/g (= ppm).
[c]See Table 15-2 for collection data.
[d]This panther, a 10+-yr-old male, was captured in the Fakahatchee Strand (Collier County) on January 22, 1984.
[e]This panther, a 7–8-yr-old female, was captured in the Fakahatchee Strand (Collier County) on March 25, 1984.
[f]ND = none detected.
[g]NE = not examined.
[h]This panther, a 4-yr-old female, was found dead in East Everglades (Dade County) on July 26, 1989.

lems. This anomaly was felt to have contributed to the animal's death.

The above anomalies are indicative of inbreeding and subsequent decreased genetic diversity. This could lead to decreased vitality and lowered disease resistance such as seen in the cheetah (O'Brien et al. 1985) and could result in extinction in the wild as occurred recently in the black-footed ferret (Williams et al. 1988). Genetic studies indicate that Florida panthers possess lower amounts of biochemical genetic variation compared to other subspecies of *Felis concolor* (Roelke 1989, 1990). These observations are cause for serious concern for the overall health and survival of Florida panthers due to their restricted population size and poor reproduction potential (Roelke 1989; Seal and Lacy 1989; O'Brien et al. 1990).

VI. Rabies

Rabies is not common in wild felids. According to Burridge et al. (1986), only 21 cases (all bobcats) were diagnosed in the United States during 1978–1982. In Florida 26 rabid bobcats were identified between 1954 and 1987. These included cases from 14 counties (Figure 15-3). Even though rabies is uncommon in bobcats, people handling such animals should use extreme care, especially with those animals that exhibit abnormal behavior or are ill. As an example of what not to do, consider the following episode as presented by Cole et al. (1973). In May 1973, a wild bobcat was trapped near Gainesville and brought to the Santa Fe Community College Zoo. Later that day the animal bit one person and scratched another. Several days

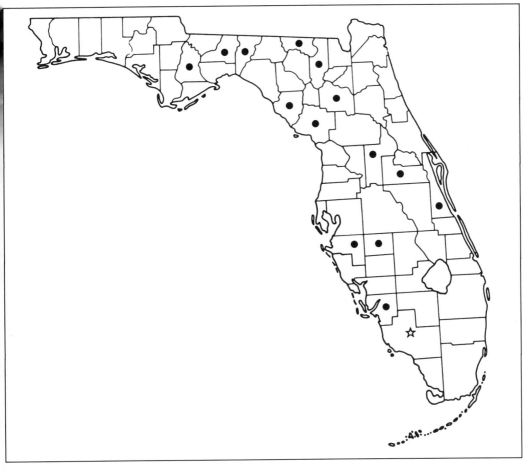

FIGURE 15-3. Counties in Florida in which rabid bobcats (1954–87) and Florida panthers (1989) have been found. Solid circles are localities of rabid bobcats, and the star is the locality of a rabid panther. (Adapted from Burridge et al. 1986; Department of Health and Rehabilitative Services 1984; Bigler 1988; Roelke 1990.)

later the bobcat became ill and a caretaker attempted to tube-feed it. In the process the cat regurgitated the food back through the tube into the caretaker's face and mouth. Later that same day the cat experienced respiratory arrest and one of the caretakers performed mouth-to-mouth resuscitation. Despite these efforts the bobcat died; when the brain was tested it was positive for rabies virus. Fourteen people who had contact with the bobcat were subsequently given postexposure prophylaxis. Sick wild animals should be handled only by professionals who have

the proper skills and knowledge. Keeping wild mammals as pets is not a good idea.

Seven panthers that died of other causes were tested for rabies virus between 1978 and 1983. All were negative (Forrester 1985). In November 1989 a three-year-old free-ranging male Florida panther was found dead in Big Cypress National Preserve (Collier County) (Figure 15-3) and was diagnosed as rabid (Calderwood Mays 1989; Roelke 1990). This is the first report of rabies in Florida panthers, although 11 of 38 nonrabid panthers sampled in southern Florida during

1985–1990 were seropositive (Roelke 1990; Rupprecht and Roelke 1990). Four of the positive animals lived for at least two years after this serologic testing (Roelke 1990). The overall significance of rabies in panther populations in Florida is not known at this time.

VII. Feline panleukopenia

Feline panleukopenia is an acute, highly contagious disease caused by a parvovirus (Bittle 1981). It affects most of the members of the family Felidae and is characterized by an enteritis and a severe decrease in leukocytes in the peripheral circulation (Bittle 1981). It is also known as feline infectious enteritis or feline distemper. The virus is shed in urine, feces, and saliva, and is transmitted by direct contact via inhalation or ingestion (Bittle 1981).

In 1979 an outbreak of panleukopenia was documented in Highlands County during an intense radiotelemetry study being conducted by personnel of Archbold Biological Station (Wassmer et al. 1988). Eight of 17 collared bobcats died; 4 of these were examined and found to have gross and microscopic lesions compatible with feline panleukopenia, and infections with this virus were judged to be the cause of death. No serology or viral isolations were attempted, however, in order to confirm the presence of the virus (Rubin and Layne 1982). This mortality occurred in the winter months (January and February) during the peak of mating activity and frequent social contact, which may have increased the opportunity for transmission to occur (Wassmer 1982; Wassmer et al. 1988). Mortality due to panleukopenia has been reported also in bobcats in southern California during the winter months (Lembeck 1978; Gould 1980). Progulske (1982) reported a die-off of bobcats in Putnam County in 1979 that may have

been due to panleukopenia virus, but carcasses were not available for diagnostic testing.

Serologic data indicate that the panleukopenia virus is widespread in Florida (Figure 15-4). It is present (41% prevalence) in bobcat populations in seven counties, ranging from Wakulla and Baker counties in northern Florida to Dade County in southern Florida (Table 15-5).

Panleukopenia has not been diagnosed as a disease in Florida panthers, but there is serologic evidence that the virus occurs in panther populations in southern Florida (Figure 15-4). Serum neutralization tests were positive for 26 of 40 (65%) panthers examined from 1978 to 1989 (Table 15-6). The significance of these findings to panther populations is unknown. Since this virus is very pathogenic to felids, however, these results are cause for concern.

VIII. Other viruses

Evidence for the presence of feline calicivirus in bobcats and Florida panthers has been obtained by serologic studies. This virus is usually limited to the upper respiratory tract, and causes pneumonia in domestic cats (Gillespie and Timoney 1981). Serum samples from 18 of 41 (44%) panthers and 21 of 73 (29%) bobcats from southern Florida had titers to calicivirus (Roelke et al. 1986; Roelke 1987, 1988, 1989). The significance of this virus to panthers and bobcats is not known.

Feline immunodeficiency virus (FIV) causes an immunodeficiency-like syndrome in domestic cats and is characterized by nonspecific and varied clinical signs and such entities as gingivitis, dermatitis, anemia, and reproductive failure (Barr et al. 1989). Six of 20 Florida panthers and 1 of 11 bobcats from southern Florida (1986–88) were seroposi-

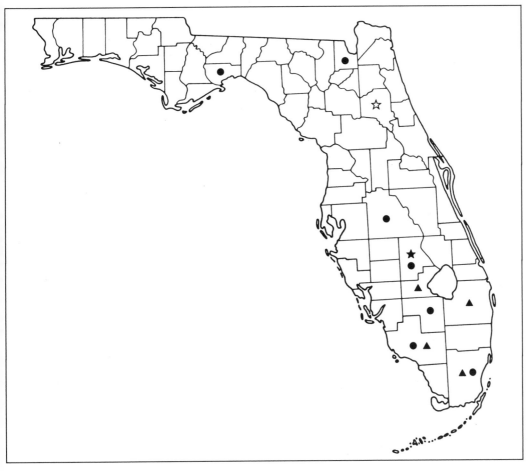

FIGURE 15-4. Distribution of parvovirus in Florida panthers (triangles) and bobcats (circles) in Florida. Solid star indicates location (Highlands County) of a parvovirus epizootic among bobcats in 1979; open star shows location (Putnam County) of a presumptive epizootic among bobcats in 1979. (Data from Wassmer et al. 1988; Roelke 1985, 1987, 1988b; Roelke et al. 1986.)

tive for FIV (Barr et al. 1989). The impact of this virus on panthers and bobcats is unknown. Several of the seropositive panthers either died or experienced reproductive problems. One of these had chronic anemia, weight loss, and reproductive failure, and eventually died of chronic kidney and liver failure; one was in good physical condition, but was reproductively unsuccessful for three years; and one died of fulminating septicemia after being bitten by another panther. Several other seropositive animals, however, were apparently healthy and reproductively successful (Barr et al. 1989; Roelke 1990). Additional research on FIV is needed before its significance to Florida's wild felids can be appreciated.

Hatcher et al. (1990) found 4 of 12 panthers seropositive to feline syncytium-forming virus. The four positive animals were from Collier County. Six panthers from Everglades National Park were negative. Although this virus has been isolated from domestic cats with respiratory disease, exper-

Table 15-5
Prevalence of serologic reactors (serum
neutralization) to feline panleukopenia virus in
bobcats from Florida

		No. bobcats		
County	Year	Tested	Pos.	%
Alachua	1976	1	0	0
	1978	1	0	0
Baker	1979	3	2	67
Collier	1973	1	0	0
	1983–84	15	4	27
	1984–85	55	27	49
	1986–87	8	2	25
	1987–88	3	2	67
Columbia	1978	2	0	0
	1979	1	0	0
Dade	1984–85	3	1	33
	1986–87	4	0	0
Hendry	1987–88	6	5	83
Highlands	1987–88	5	3	60
Levy	1979	3	0	0
Palm Beach	1974	1	0	0
Polk	1979	1	1	100
Wakulla	1979	3	1	33
Totals	1973–88	116	48	41

Sources: Roelke (1985, 1987, 1988); Roelke et al. (1986).

Table 15-6
Prevalence of serologic reactors (serum
neutralization) to feline panleukopenia virus in
Florida panthers

		No. panthers		
County	Year	Tested	Positive	%
Collier	1978	1	1	100
	1980	1	1	100
	1981	1	0	0
	1983	4	4	100
	1984	3	2	67
	1985	1	1	100
	1986	5	5	100
	1987	4	4	100
	1988	3	2	67
	1989	6	1	17
Glades	1983	1	1	100
	1988	1	0	0
Monroe/Dade	1986	2	2	100
	1987	4	0	0
	1988	1	1	100
	1989	1	0	0
Palm Beach	1984	1	1	100
Totals	1978–89	40	26	65

Sources: Roelke (1985, 1987, 1988b, 1989); Roelke et al.
(1986).

imental studies have not shown that it is pathogenic (Gillespie and Timoney 1981). Its effects on panthers are unknown. Hatcher et al. (1990) also tested 15 bobcats from southern Florida, but all were seronegative.

Two of 17 bobcats from the Big Cypress Swamp (Collier County) were positive for antibodies to Everglades virus in 1965 (Lord et al. 1973; Berge 1975). There is no evidence that this arbovirus is harmful to bobcats, but this felid may serve as a reservoir host for this zoonotic pathogen (Seymour and Yuill 1981).

Forty-one panthers and 15 bobcats from southern Florida were tested serologically for feline rhinotracheitis virus and feline leukemia virus. Twenty-five of these panthers and 31 bobcats were tested also for pseudorabies

virus. Results were negative (Roelke 1987, 1988b, 1989).

Serum samples from Florida panthers in southern Florida were tested for antibodies to feline enteric coronavirus/feline infectious peritonitis viruses. Samples from 41 panthers tested by use of the kinetics enzyme-linked assay (KELA) were all negative, but 5 of 27 samples tested by an indirect immunofluorescence assay (IFA) were positive (Roelke 1990). The significance of these findings is unclear. The IFA test results may be indicative of false positives due to cross-reactions with other viruses obtained by the panthers via food ingestion. Further studies are necessary to sort out this problem and to determine if panthers in southern Florida are infected with feline infectious peritonitis virus.

IX. Bacterial diseases

Very little research has been done on the bacterial diseases of bobcats and panthers. Small numbers of animals have been tested serologically for *Leptospira interrogans* and *Francisella tularensis* (Table 15-7). Only one bobcat was positive for *Leptospira interrogans* serovar *grippotyphosa*. In another study in southern Georgia, McKeever et al. (1958c) isolated leptospires from kidney tissues of 3 of 40 bobcats. All positive bobcats were from areas in Decatur and Thomas counties, which are near the northern Florida border. Two cats were positive for serovar *pomona* and one for *ballum*. Forty-one Florida panthers were examined serologically for *Brucella* sp.; one, a three-year-old male from Monroe County, was positive. Four species of enteric pathogens (*Salmonella arizonae*, *Edwardsiella tarda*, *Pleseomonas shigelloides*, and *Campylobacter* sp.) have been isolated from feces of bobcats and Florida panthers (Table 15-7) in southern Florida. White and Forrester (1988) cultured the intestinal contents of six bobcats, five from Alachua County (1976–78) and one from Polk County. All were negative for enteric pathogens. The significance of these findings is unknown.

X. Mycotic diseases

During 1954–1956 McKeever et al. (1958d) cultured the fur and skin of 68 bobcats for mycotic infections in southwestern Georgia and northwestern Florida. None was infected.

XI. Protozoan diseases

Five protozoan parasites have been reported from wild felids in Florida (Table 15-8).

These include *Toxoplasma gondii*, *Cytauxzoon felis*, and *Sarcocystis* sp. from bobcats and panthers, and *Eimeria* sp. and *Isospora* sp. from panthers. The eimerian infection may have been spurious, having been acquired possibly from a prey item.

Toxoplasma gondii is a sporozoan parasite that causes toxoplasmosis, a disease of considerable significance to man, domestic animals, and many species of wildlife. This disease is one of the most widespread zoonotic diseases in North America and probably the world. Numerous species of wild and domestic animals and man serve as intermediate hosts, while the definitive hosts are known only from Felidae (domestic and wild cats). A recent serologic survey of 3,471 wild animals representing 114 species (25 mammals, 82 birds, and 7 reptiles) in Florida showed that infections were present in a number of animals (Burridge et al. 1979). The highest prevalences were in armadillos (19%), raccoons (18%), roof rats (13%), and opossums (11%). The transmission of the parasite occurs when infected tissue or oocysts from the feces of another felid are ingested. Other animals are infected by accidentally ingesting oocysts from cat feces or by consuming tissue from an infected animal (Figure 15-5). Usually the infection in man is not serious, but if a woman is infected during the later stages of pregnancy, the child may be born with abnormalities, including mental retardation, convulsions, spasticity and palsies, severely impaired vision, and hydro- or microcephalus (Dubey and Beattie 1988). Sexual multiplication in the felid usually does not result in serious intestinal damage to the cat, but felids can also get the disease from ingestion of the parenteral stages in infected flesh (Levine and Ivens 1981). The reader is referred to other chapters for additional information on this important parasite of wildlife and man.

An unidentified species of *Sarcocystis* was

Table 15-7
Bacterial diseases of Florida panthers and bobcats

Disease and etiologic agent	Host[a]	Basis of diagnosis	Year	No. animals Exam.	No. animals Pos.	County	Data source
Leptospirosis *Leptospira interrogans*	BC	Serology, necropsy/culture	NG[b]	1	1[c]	Leon[d]	Shotts et al. (1975)
Brucellosis *Brucella canis*	BC	Serology	NG	1	0	NG	Hoff et al. (1974)
Brucella sp.	FP	"	1978–90	41	1	Several[e]	Roelke et al. (1986); Roelke (1988)
	BC	"	1984–89	37	0	Collier, Highlands	Roelke (1990)
Tularemia *Francisella tularensis*	BC	"	1965–73	1	0	NG	Hoff et al. (1975)
	BC	"	1955–57	1	0	Leon	McKeever et al. (1958a)
Salmonellosis *Salmonella* spp.	FP	Culture of feces	1985	8[f]	1[g]	Collier	Roelke (1985)
	FP	"	1978	1	0	Dade	White & Forrester (1988)
	BC	"	1985	4[f]	0	Collier	Roelke (1985)
	BC	"	1976–78	6	0	Alachua, Polk	White & Forrester (1988)
Edwardsiellosis *Edwardsiella tarda*	FP	"	1985	8[f]	3	Collier	Roelke (1985)
	FP	"	1978	1	0	Dade	White & Forrester (1988)
	FP	"	1988	1	1	Dade	Roelke (1988a)
	BC	"	1985	4[f]	0	Collier	Roelke (1985)
	BC	"	1976–78	6	0	Alachua, Polk	White & Forrester (1988)
Plesiomoniasis *Plesiomonas shigelloides*	FP	"	1985	8[f]	2	Collier	Roelke (1985)
	BC	"	"	4[f]	1	"	"
Campylobacterosis *Campylobacter* sp.	FP	"	1988	1	1	Dade	Roelke (1988a)
Septicemia *Escherichia coli*	FP	Culture of organs	1990	1	1	Collier	Roelke (1990)
Streptococcus equismilis	FP	Culture of thoracic exudate	1990	1	1	Monroe	"

[a]BC = bobcat; FP = Florida panther.   [b]NG = not given by authors.   [c]Serovar was *grippotyphosa*.

[d]Author presented combined data on carnivores from Leon County, Florida, and from South Grady and Thomas counties, southern Georgia, without separating data from each county.

[e]Collier, Dade, Glades, Hendry, Highlands, Lee, and Monroe (the positive panther was from Monroe County).

[f]Six of 8 panthers and all 4 bobcats were cultured also for *Shigella*, *Campylobacter*, *Vibrio*, *Yersinia* and *Aeromonas*. Results were negative.

[g]*Salmonella arizonae*.

Table 15-8

Protozoan parasites reported from Florida panthers and bobcats in Florida

Protozoan	Host[a]	No. animals Exam.	Pos.	Date[b]	County	Basis of diagnosis	Data source
Toxoplasma gondii	BC	3	2	NG[b]	NG[c]	Serology	Burridge et al. (1979)
							Roelke (1987, 1990)
	FP	28	2	1986–90	Several[c]	"	Burridge et al. (1979),
	FP	50	5[d]	1978–90	Collier, Glades, Hendry, Highlands, Lee, Monroe	"	Forrester et al. (1985a), Roelke et al. (1985), Roelke (1988, 1989, 1990)
Sarcocystis sp.	BC	60	30	1985–88	Several[e]	Histopathology	Anderson et al. (1990)
	FP	14	11	1983–87	Collier, Palm Beach	"	Greiner et al. (1989)
Eimeria sp.	FP	15	1[f]	1986–87	Collier, Hendry, Monroe	Fecal flotation	Roelke (1987)
Isospora sp.	FP	15	1[f]	1986–87	"	"	"
Cytauxzoon felis	BC	36	1[g]	1984–85	Collier, Baker, Alachua	Blood smear	Roelke & Kocan (1985)
	FP	19	10	1989–90	Several[h]	"	Roelke (1990)
Trypanosoma cruzi–like	BC	63	0	1954–57	NG	Culture	McKeever et al. (1958b)

[a]BC = bobcat; FP = Florida panther.
[b]NG = not given by authors.
[c]Collier and Hendry (n = 11) and Monroe (n = 4) counties.
[d]All 5 positive panthers were from Collier County.
[e]Alachua (0 infected/1 examined), Collier (21/41), Dade (1/2), Duval (1/1), Glades (2/2), Hendry (4/6), Highlands (1/4), Lake (0/1), and Lee (0/2) counties.
[f]The positive panthers were both from Dade County (Everglades National Park).
[g]The 1 positive bobcat was from Alachua County.
[h]Collier, Hendry, Monroe, and Dade counties.

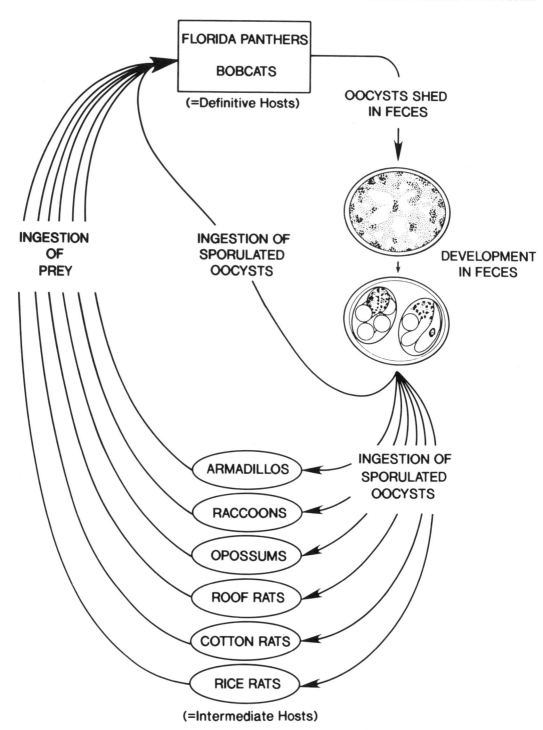

FIGURE 15-5. Transmission of *Toxoplasma gondii* among Florida panthers, bobcats, and other mammals in Florida.

found in 30 of 60 bobcats and 11 of 14 Florida panthers during 1983–1988 (Table 15-8). These sarcocysts (Figure 15-6) were found in the tongue, masseter, heart, diaphragm, intestine, skeletal muscles, and the striated muscles associated with the mammary gland (Greiner et al. 1989; Anderson et al. 1990). The significance of this finding is unknown, but the observations are unusual and unexplained since this stage (the sarcocyst) is usually found in a prey species that serves as an intermediate host for the parasite.

Cytauxzoon felis is a piroplasm that occurs in erythrocytes and reticuloendothelial macrophages of domestic cats and bobcats (Glenn et al. 1982). One of 36 bobcats and 10 of 19 panthers in Florida were infected (Table 15-8). *Cytauxzoon felis* is pathogenic to domestic cats, but apparently is harmless to bobcats (Glenn et al. 1983). Panthers may react to *C. felis* like bobcats do. No clinical signs of cytauxzoonosis were seen in the 10 free-ranging panthers diagnosed with infections (Roelke 1990). In addition, blood from a healthy captive Florida panther (with a *C. felis* parasitemia) was inoculated into a domestic cat that was maintained in isolation facilities. The cat died of cytauxzoonosis within 12 days (Butt et al. 1991), illustrating the susceptibility of the domestic cat to this protozoan disease. The donor panther was infected, but disease-free, that is, an asymptomatic carrier. Blouin et al. (1984) showed that *C. felis* could be transmitted by *Dermacentor variabilis*. This tick has been found on both bobcats and Florida panthers (Rogers 1953; Forrester et al. 1985a), and may be the vector in Florida.

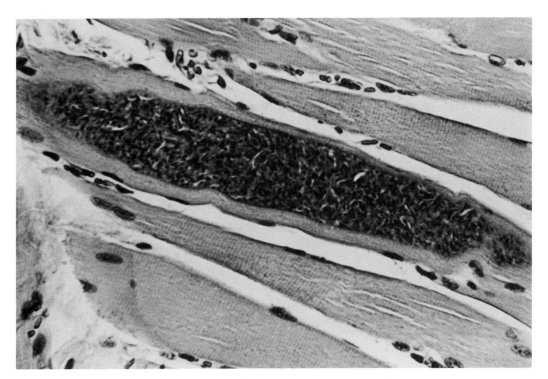

FIGURE 15-6. Photomicrograph of a sarcocyst in tongue of a Florida panther from Collier County. (Photo courtesy of Dr. S.D. Wright.)

Table 15-9
Helminths reported from bobcats in Florida

Helminth	No. bobcats			Intensity		Date	County	Data source
	Exam.	Inf.	%	Mean	Range			
Trematoda								
Alaria marcianae	30	13	44	NG	3–2, 194	1978–79	Several[a]	Bowerman (1980)
Heterobilharzia americana	NG[b]	NG		NG	NG	1907	NG	Price (1943)
Cestoda								
Spirometra mansonoides	30	12	40	NG	1–22	1978–79	Several[a]	Bowerman (1980)
	1	1	100	45	—	1936	Jefferson	McIntosh (1937)
	1	1	100	3	—	1907	Indian River	" "
Taenia pisiformis	NG	NG		NG	NG	NG	Jefferson	Loftin (1961)
Taenia taeniaeformis	NG	NG		NG	NG	NG	Jefferson	" "
Taenia macrocystis	1	1	100	15	—	1936	Jefferson	McIntosh (1937)
Taenia sp.	30	25	83	NG	1–91	1978–79	Several[a]	Bowerman (1980)
Hydatigera lyncis[c]	NG	NG		NG	NG	NG	Jefferson	Loftin (1961)
Nematoda								
Toxocara mystax	30	23	76	NG	1–79	1978–79	Several[a]	Bowerman (1980)
Toxascaris leonina	30	1	5	NG	4	1978–79	Several[a]	" "
Molineus barbatus	30	24	79	NG	1–144	1978–79	Several[a]	" "
Ancylostoma tubaeforme	56	5	9	2	1–3	1979–85	Several[d]	Obstbaum et al. (1987)
Ancylostoma braziliense	56	11	20	3	1–10	1979–85	Several[e]	" "
Ancylostoma pluridentatum	3	2	67	13	10–16	1981	Collier	Forrester et al. (1985a), Forrester (1985)
Ancylostoma caninum	56	12	21	34	1–126	1979–85	Collier	Obstbaum et al. (1987)
	56	10	18	3	1–12	1979–85	Several[f]	" "

Parasite	No. examined	No. infected	%	NG/col	Range	Year	County	Reference
Strongyloides sp.	30	3	10	NG	5–33	1978–79	Several[a]	Bowerman (1980)
Physaloptera sp.	30	7	23	NG	1–3	1978–79	Several[a]	" "
Capillaria aerophila	30	10	33	NG	1–8	1978–79	Several[a]	" "
Capillaria plica	30	5	17	NG	1–7	1978–79	Several[a]	" "
Capillaria sp.	30	3	10	NG	1–13	1978–79	Several[a]	" "
Oslerus rostratus	30	4	14	NG	2–13	1978–79	Several[a]	" "
Dirofilaria immitis	30	1	3	2	2	1979	Wakulla	" "
	29	1	3	2	2	1984–85	Collier	Roelke (1985)
Dirofilaria striata	29[g]	6	21	—	—	1984–85	Collier	" "
	29[g]	16	55[h]	—	—	1984–85	Collier	" "
	3	1	33[h]	—	—	1985	Dade	" "
	7	2	29[h]	—	—	1985	Baker	" "
	1	1	100[h]	—	—	1984	Alachua	" "
	15	0	0	—	—	1960–61	"Central & So. Fla."	Orihel and Ash (1964)
Spirocerca lupi	30	1	5	6	6	1979	Columbia	Bowerman (1980)
Trichinella sp.	25	0	0	—	—	1978–79	Several[a]	" "
(larvae)	11	0	0	—	—	1962	Marion	Scholtens & Norman (1971)
	1	1	100	—	—	1988	Collier	Dame & Wright (1988)
Capillaria hepatica	4	0	0	—	—	1957–64	Several[i]	Layne (1968)

[a]Bowerman (1980) examined 30 bobcats from 7 counties in Florida as follows: Leon (1), Wakulla (5), Columbia (5), Baker (5), Alachua (1), Levy (11), and Polk (2). In her report she did not separate her results by county. In a few instances it was possible to determine the counties involved from original data sheets.

[b]NG = not given by authors.

[c]Probably *Taenia rileyi*.

[d]Alachua, Levy, Lee, and Collier counties.

[e]Wakulla, Baker, Alachua, Levy, Polk, Lee, and Collier counties.

[f]Leon, Wakulla, Alachua, Levy, Polk, Lee, and Collier counties.

[g]Data from the same 29 bobcats. Values are given based on recovery of adult worms at necropsy and on a modified Knott's test for microfilariae.

[h]Data from a modified Knott's test for microfilariae.

[i]Alachua (2 animals), DeSoto, and Taylor counties.

XII. Helminths

Twenty-five species of helminths have been reported from bobcats in Florida (Table 15-9). These include 2 species of trematodes, 6 cestodes, and 17 nematodes. Fifteen species have been found in Florida panthers (Table 15-10), including 2 species of trematodes, 3 cestodes, and 10 nematodes.

The literature on helminths of bobcats of North America has been summarized by McCord and Cardoza (1982). Anderson (1983) and Dixon (1982) discussed the pertinent literature on helminths of *Felis concolor*. None of these publications, however, gave data on bobcats or panthers in Florida. The reader is referred also to articles by Watson et al. (1981), Miller and Harkema (1968), and Stone and Pence (1978) for information on helminths of bobcats in West Virginia, Georgia, North Carolina, South Carolina, and Texas.

The pathologic significance of the helminths of bobcats and Florida panthers is unknown. The trematode *Alaria marcianae* occurs in both animals and is especially prevalent and abundant in panthers. One animal had more than 9,600 adult flukes in its small intestine. Most infections by *Alaria* spp. are considered nonpathogenic (Soulsby 1982), but intense infections can cause catarrhal duodenitis (Erlich 1938). In domestic cats, the life cycle of this trematode includes freshwater snails as the first intermediate host and tadpoles as the second intermediate host (Shoop 1988). The definitive or final host (the cat) becomes infected by ingesting tadpoles that contain infective stages (mesocercariae). Other hosts, such as mice, rats, snakes, alligators, or birds, can also ingest these tadpoles and serve as carrier or paratenic hosts; cats become infected by eating these animals. In the domestic cat the immature flukes go through a complex migration to the lungs and

eventually reach the small intestine (Figure 15-7). In addition, some enter the mammary glands and infection of nursing kittens can occur via the milk. It is not known if *Alaria marcianae* undergoes this type of migration in bobcats or panthers or what damage may occur during the migratory phase, but it could be significant. Of additional concern is the zoonotic potential of *Alaria* spp. There is a report of a man dying of an infection of a species of *Alaria* acquired by eating inadequately cooked frogs' legs (Fernandes et al. 1976). At necropsy the man was found to have several thousand mesocercariae in the peritoneal cavity, brain, heart, kidneys, liver, lungs, lymph nodes, pancreas, spinal cord, spleen, and stomach.

The blood fluke *Heterobilharzia americana* is common in Florida panthers, but in low numbers. Little is known about it in bobcats, except that it occurs in them. In Florida this blood fluke is common also in raccoons (see Chapter 12) and may be of pathologic significance (Bartsch and Ward 1976), but its effect on panthers and bobcats is probably minimal due to its low intensity in these hosts.

Three species of cestodes are known from Florida panthers and four (or perhaps five) from bobcats in Florida (Tables 15-9 and 15-10). These tapeworms are probably of little significance to panthers and bobcats judging from what is known about them in domestic dogs and cats (Soulsby 1982). It is possible that infections with large numbers of worms could cause diarrhea or constipation and result in general unthriftiness. Intestinal obstruction may also occur. Two of these tapeworms (*Mesocestoides* sp. and *Spirometra mansonoides*) have been known to infect man (Soulsby 1982).

According to Levine (1980), hookworms of the genus *Ancylostoma* "are perhaps the most pathogenic parasites of young dogs and cats" (p. 90). The harmful effects of these

Table 15-10

Helminths reported from Florida panthers, 1978–90

Helminth	No. panthers			Intensity		Date	County	Data source
	Exam.	Inf.	%	Mean	Range			
Trematoda								
Alaria marcianae	6	6	100	3,428	238–9,689	1978–83	Collier	Forrester et al. (1985a), Forrester (1985)
Heterobilharzia americana	1	1	100	239	239	1983	Glades	" "
	6	4	67	4	1–7	1978–83	Collier	" "
	1	1	100	3	3	1983	Glades	" "
Cestoda								
Taenia omissa	6	3	50	9	1–15	1978–83	Collier	" "
	1	1	100	1	1	1983	Glades	" "
Spirometra mansonoides	6	4	67	13	4–33	1978–83	Collier	" "
	1	0	0	—	—	1983	Glades	" "
Mesocestoides sp.	6	3	50	280	1–833	1978–83	Collier	" "
	1	1	100	7	7	1983	Glades	" "
Nematoda								
Ancylostoma pluridentatum	6	6	100	254	36–746	1978–83	Collier	" "
	1	0	0	—	—	1983	Glades	" "
Trichinella sp. (larvae)	6	4	67	—[a]	—[a]	1978–83	Collier	" "
	1	0	0	—	—	1983	Glades	" "
Dirofilaria striata	6	3	50	3	1–7	1978–83	Collier	" "
	1	1	100	1	1	1983	Glades	" "
Dracunculus insignis	2	2	100	2	2–3	1989–90	Monroe	Forrester & Roelke (1990), Forrester (1985)
Capillaria aerophila	6	0	0	—	—	1978–83	Collier	" "
	1	0	0	—	—	1983	Glades	Forrester et al. (1985), Forrester (1985)
	6	2	33	2	1–3	1978–83	Collier	" "
Strongyloides sp.	1	0	0	—	—	1983	Glades	" "
	6	2	33	8	1–16	1978–83	Collier	" "
	1	0	0	—	—	1983	Glades	" "
Toxocara mystax	6	0	0	—	—	1978–83	Collier	" "
	1	1	100	2	2	1983	Glades	" "
Toxocara sp. (larvae)	6	1	17	25	25	1978–83	Collier	" "
	1	0	0	—	—	1983	Glades	" "
Molineus barbatus	6	1	17	2	2	1978–83	Collier	" "
	1	0	0	—	—	1983	Glades	" "
Gnathostoma sp.	6	0	0	—	—	1978–83	Collier	" "
	1	0	0	—	—	1983	Glades	" "
	2	1	50	1	1	1989–90	Monroe	Forrester & Roelke (1990)

[a] Intensity was determined for a panther that had 1 larva per gram of diaphragm and psoas muscle.

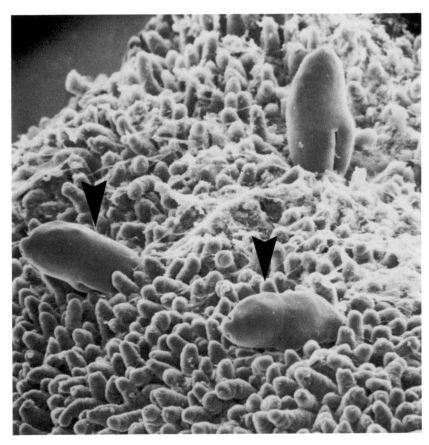

FIGURE 15-7. Electron micrograph of *Alaria marcianae* (arrows) attached to mucosa of the small intestine of a domestic cat. (Photo courtesy of Dr. W.L. Shoop.)

parasites are due mostly to the loss of blood. Signs of infection in domestic cats include anemia, emaciation, edema, weakness, listlessness, and rough hair coat (Levine 1980). Little is known about the actual effects on bobcats or Florida panthers. Roelke et al. (1985) reported on hookworm infections in captive cougars in Florida. Two three-month-old kittens had infections by hookworms (*Ancylostoma* sp.) in which there were 150,000 eggs per gram of feces. These kittens had severe anemia, depressed serum iron, poor weight gain, and in general were unthrifty. If these animals had not been treated with anthelmintics, they probably would have died (Roelke et al. 1985). Combined infections of panleukopenia virus and hookworms may have devastating effects on young bobcats or Florida panthers. This possibility should be studied further.

Ancylostoma pluridentatum has been identified in six of seven panthers (Table 15-10) and 14 of 59 bobcats in southern Florida (Table 15-9). This is the first finding of this species of hookworm in free-ranging cougars and bobcats in North America. Obstbaum et al. (1987) examined bobcats from 10 counties throughout the state and found *A. pluridentatum* only in bobcats from Collier County. Other species of hookworms, however, were found in bobcats in Collier County and in other parts of the state. Preliminary data on the life cycle of this species have been obtained (Rickard et al. 1984). Two samples collected from Collier County and identified as Florida panther feces were cultured in the laboratory. Infective third-stage larvae were obtained and 230 were given by mouth to each of three 12-day-old domestic kittens. Twenty-seven to 30 days later, hookworm eggs were detected in the feces of all three kittens, which clinically were unthrifty and pot-bellied. At necropsy adult hookworms were recovered and identified as *A. pluridentatum*. In other experiments two 10-week-old kittens and two adult cats (previously

Table 15-11
Arthropods reported from bobcats in Florida

Arthropod	Date	County	Data source
Ticks			
Dermacentor variabilis	NG[a]	"North Florida"	Rogers (1953)[b]
	NG	Alachua	Boardman (1929)
	1986	Collier	Forrester & Keirans (1990)
Amblyommna americanum	NG	"North Florida"	Rogers (1953)[c]
	NG	Alachua	Boardman (1929)
	1949–53	Levy	Rogers (1953)[d]
Amblyomma maculatum	1986	Collier	Forrester & Keirans (1990)
Ixodes scapularis	NG	Broward	Taylor (1951)
	NG	"Florida"	Bishopp & Trembley (1945)
	NG	Alachua	Boardman (1929)
	1936–37	Orange, Osceola, Collier	Travis (1941)
	1949–52	"North Florida"	Rogers (1953)[b]
	1984	Lee	FSCA[e]
Ixodes affinis	1948, 1951	Levy	Kohls & Rogers (1953), Rogers (1953)[b]
	1976	Levy	Forrester (1985)
Mites			
Notoedres cati	1979	Highlands	Wassmer (1982)
Lynxacarus morlani[f]	1985	Collier	Milstrey et al. (1985)
Eutrombicula splendens	1985	Collier	" " " "
Fleas			
Cediopsylla simplex	NG	Jefferson	Fox (1940)
	NG	Highlands	Layne (1971)
Echidnophaga gallinacea[g]	NG	Highlands	" "
	1969	Highlands	FSCA
Pulex simulans	NG	Highlands	Layne (1971)
Ctenocephalides felis	NG	Highlands	" "
	1969	Highlands	FSCA

[a]NG = not given by authors.
[b]Nymphs and adults.
[c]Larvae.
[d]Adults.
[e]FSCA = records from the Florida State Collection of Arthropods, Division of Plant Industry, Florida Department of Agriculture, Gainesville, Fla.
[f]Two of 5 bobcats from Collier County were infested.
[g]Layne (1971) reported more than 100 specimens of this flea from a bobcat that also was infested with *Cediopsylla simplex*, *Pulex simulans,* and *Ctenocephalides felis.* The bobcat was trapped near a chicken house.

Table 15-12
Arthropods reported from Florida panthers

Arthropod	No. panthers		Intensity		Date	County	Data source
	Exam.	Pos.	Mean	Range			
Ticks							
Dermacentor variabilis	12	9	8	1–26	1978–83	Collier, Dade, Glades	Forrester et al. (1985a)
Dermacentor nitens	12	1	1	1	1980	Collier	Forrester et al. (1985a), Forrester (1985)
Amblyomma americanum	12	1	8	8	1983	Glades	" "
Amblyomma maculatum	12	1	2	2	1983	Collier	" "
Ixodes scapularis	12	7	49	3–222	1980–83	Collier	" "
Ixodes affinis	12	4	5	1–10	1978–82	Collier, Dade	" "
Mites							
Lynxacarus morlani	1	1[a]	ND[b]	ND	1985	Collier	Milstrey et al. (1985)
Eutrombicula splendens	1	1	ND	ND	1985	Collier	" "
Fleas							
Ctenocephalides felis	12	1	1	1	1983	Collier	Forrester et al. (1985a)
Keds							
Lipoptena mazamae[c]	2	2	1	1–2	1990	Collier	Forrester & Roelke (1990)

[a]Mites found on road-killed animal in October 1985; feces collected 10 months previously from the field were thought to be from the same animal and contained similar mites.
[b]ND = not determined.
[c]These are probably accidental parasites acquired while the panthers fed on white-tailed deer.

exposed to other species of hookworms, but free of infections at the time of the experiment) were found to be resistant to infection by *A. pluridentatum.*

Of interest is the finding of four panthers and one bobcat positive for larvae of *Trichinella* sp. This zoonotic nematode has been found only rarely in mammals in Florida. Scholtens and Norman (1971) reported it from 1 of 17 "foxes" (species not given), 3 of 65 opossums, 4 of 109 raccoons, and 1 of 22 "skunks" (species not given). We found the worm in 1 of 26 wild hogs from Collier County. Hogs and raccoons may be the source of the infection in panthers.

The finding of the dog heartworm (*Dirofilaria immitis*) in two bobcats (one from Collier and one from Wakulla County) is noteworthy since this filarial worm can cause serious morbidity and mortality (Levine 1980). No infections of *D. immitis* were detected in panthers. Another filariid, *Dirofilaria striata*, however, was found in both bobcats and Florida panthers. The adults of this species do not occur in the heart or blood vessels, but in the intermuscular fascia or free in the peritoneal cavity. Nothing is known about its pathogenicity, but the microfilariae could cause damage to the kidneys similar to that described in domestic dogs (Simpson et al. 1974). This aspect should be investigated since chronic kidney disease has been observed in a bobcat from Dade County and in a Florida panther from Collier County (Roelke 1988a, 1988b). This parasite is probably transmitted by a mosquito vector.

XIII. Arthropods

Twelve species of parasitic arthropods have been reported from bobcats in Florida. These include four fleas, five ticks, and three mites (Table 15-11). From the Florida panther 10 species of arthropods are known, and include one flea, six ticks, two mites, and one hippo-

boscid (Table 15-12). Bobcats and Florida panthers share six species of ectoparasites, including one flea (*Ctenocephalides felis*) and five ticks (*Dermacentor variabilis, Amblyomma americanum, Amblyomma maculatum, Ixodes scapularis,* and *Ixodes affinis*).

Of the four species of fleas that occur on bobcats and panthers, two (*Cediopsylla simplex* and *Echidnophaga gallinacea*) are typical of prey animals and two (*Pulex simulans* and *Ctenocephalides felis*) are typical of medium-sized or large mammals (Layne 1971). *Cediopsylla simplex* is most common on rabbits and secondarily on their predators. It is known from Eastern cottontails, marsh rabbits, and gray foxes as well as bobcats in Florida. *Echidnophaga gallinacea,* the sticktight flea, is typical of birds or mammals that prey on birds (particularly domestic fowl). In addition to domestic poultry and bobcats, this flea

FIGURE 15-8. Head of a bobcat from Highlands County showing encrustation and alopecia due to notoedric mange. (Photo courtesy of Dr. J.N. Layne.)

FIGURE 15-9. Close-up of the ear of the same bobcat illustrated in Figure 15-8 showing thick encrustation. (Photo courtesy of Dr. J.N. Layne.)

is known from opossums, red foxes, and gray foxes in Florida (Layne 1971).

Except for *Dermacentor nitens,* which is a parasite of horses in southern Florida (Strickland et al. 1976), the ticks of panthers and bobcats are found also on white-tailed deer and/or wild hogs in Florida (Greiner et al. 1984; Smith 1977).

The pathologic significance of these ectoparasites to bobcats and panthers in Florida is unknown. In other species they cause varying degrees of skin damage, from slight irritation to severe dermatitis and secondary infections (Soulsby 1982). Wassmer et al. (1988) reported a case of notoedric mange in a bobcat in Highlands County. The bobcat, a female, was weak and emaciated when captured and died shortly thereafter. She had been seen periodically over the preceding five weeks and appeared to become progressively thinner and weaker. Her face and ears were heavily encrusted with a dry exudate and there was con-

siderable hair loss (Figures 15-8 and 15-9). Wassmer et al. (1988) trapped and handled several other bobcats in the same general area with apparent mange problems and felt that there was a high prevalence of this disease in Highlands County during 1978–1979. Mortality of bobcats due to mange has been reported also in Texas (Pence et al. 1982). In addition, four of the ticks (*Amblyomma americanum, A. maculatum, Ixodes scapularis,* and *Dermacentor variabilis*) are known to cause tick paralysis in other animals (Gregson 1973; Strickland et al. 1976). The fleas and ticks also may serve as vectors of Rocky Mountain spotted fever or tularemia.

XIV. Summary and conclusions

Forty-eight different parasites and infectious disease agents have been identified in bobcats from Florida. These include 1 heavy metal, 5 viruses, 2 bacteria, 3 protozoans, 2 trematodes, 6 cestodes, 17 nematodes, 4 fleas, 5 ticks, and 3 mites. The most important of these appear to be panleukopenia virus, hookworms (*Ancylostoma* spp.), and notoedric mange, although the evidence for this is largely speculative.

Sixty-one different environmental contaminants, tumors, anomalies, parasites, and infectious disease agents have been documented in Florida panthers. These include 8 chlorinated hydrocarbons, 4 heavy metals, 1 tumor, 5 anomalies, 6 viruses, 7 bacteria, 5 protozoans, 2 trematodes, 3 cestodes, 10 nematodes, 1 flea, 1 hippoboscid, 6 ticks, and 2 mites. Again, the most important agents appear to be panleukopenia virus and hookworms. In addition, trauma (road-kills and illegal kills) ranks as a significant mortality factor. Anomalies, which may be a reflection of inbreeding, are another concern in that lowered disease resistance could be the ultimate result, which would make panthers more prone to serious epizootics.

A number of the disease agents are of public health significance and include the agents of rabies, encephalitis (Everglades virus), leptospirosis, salmonellosis, edwardsiellosis, campylobacterosis, pleseomoniosis, toxoplasmosis, trematodiosis (*Alaria*), cestodiosis (*Mesocestoides* and *Spirometra*), visceral larva migrans (*Toxocara mystax*), cutaneous larva migrans (*Ancylostoma braziliense*), and trichinosis. Many of the fleas, ticks, and mites also can infest man.

XV. Literature cited

Anderson, A.E. 1983. A critical review of literature on puma (*Felis concolor*). Spec. Report No. 54, Colo. Div. Wild., Denver. 91 pp.

Anderson, A.J., E.C. Greiner, M.E. Roelke, and C.T. Atkinson. 1990. Unpublished data. Univ. of Florida, Gainesville.

Barr, M.C., P.P. Calle, M.E. Roelke, and F.W. Scott. 1989. Feline immunodeficiency virus infection in nondomestic felids. J. Zoo Wildl. Med. 20:265–272.

Bartsch, R.C., and B.C. Ward. 1976. Visceral lesions in raccoons naturally infected with *Heterobilharzia americana*. Vet. Pathol. 13:241–249.

Belden, R.C. 1986. Florida panther recovery plan implementation—A 1983 progress report. Proc. 2d Internat. Cat Symp. pp. 159–172.

Berge, T.O. (ed.). 1975. International catalogue of arboviruses including certain other viruses of vetebrates. 2d ed. USDHEW Pub. No. (CDC) 75-8301.

Bishopp, F.C., and H.L. Trembley. 1945. Distribution and hosts of certain North American ticks. J. Parasitol. 31:1–54.

Bittle, J.L. 1981 Feline panleukopenia. In: Infectious diseases of wild mammals. 2d ed. J.W. Davis et al. (eds.). Iowa State Univ. Press, Ames. pp. 97–101.

Blouin, E.F., A.A. Kocan, B.L. Glenn, K.M. Kocan, and J.A. Hair. 1984. Transmission of *Cytauxzoon felis* Kier, 1979 from bobcats, *Felis rufus* (Schreber) to domestic cats by *Dermacentor variabilis* (Say). J. Wildl. Dis. 10:241–42.

Bowerman, B. 1980. A survey of internal parasites of the bobcat in Florida. Unpublished MS, Univ. of Florida, Gainesville. 9 pp.

Brady, J.R. 1977. Unpublished data. Florida Game and Fresh Water Fish Commission, Gainesville.

Buck, W.B. 1989. Effects of mercury on Florida panthers. Report to the Ad Hoc Interagency Working Group of the Florida Panther Interagency Committee, Gainesville, Fla. 6 pp.

Burridge, M.J., L.A. Sawyer, and W.J. Bigler. 1986. Rabies in Florida. Department of Health and Rehabilitative Services, Tallahassee, Fla. 147 pp.

Burridge, M.J., W.J. Bigler, D.J. Forrester, and J.M. Hennemann. 1979. Serologic survey for *Toxoplasma gondii* in wild animals in Florida. J. Am. Vet. Med. Assoc. 175:964–967.

Butt, M.T., D. Bowman, M.C. Barr, and M.E. Roelke. 1991. Iatrogenic transmission of *Cytauxzoon felis* from a Florida panther (*Felis concolor coryi*) to a domestic cat. J. Wildl. Dis. 27: 342–347.

Calderwood-Mays, M.B. 1989. Unpublished data. (Pathology Report No. N89-848, CVM-TH, Univ. of Florida, Gainesville).

Cole, C., J. Nichols, and R.B. Hogan. 1973. Epidemiologic notes and reports. Rabies exposure—Kansas, Florida. CDC Morbid. Mortal. Weekly Rep. 22:209–210.

Cumbie, P.M. 1975. Mercury in hair of bobcats and raccoons. J. Wildl. Manage. 39:419–425.

Cumbie, P.M., and J.H. Jenkins. 1975. Mercury accumulation in native mammals of the southeast. Proc. Ann. Conf. S.E. Game Fish Comm. 28:639–647.

Dame, J.B., and S.D. Wright. 1988. Unpublished data. Univ. of Florida, Gainesville.

Dixon, K.R. 1982. Mountain lion. In: Wild mammals of North America. J.A. Chapman and G.A. Feldhamer (eds.). Johns Hopkins Univ. Press, Baltimore. pp. 711–727.

Dubey, J.P., and C.P. Beattie. 1988. Toxoplasmosis of animals and man. CRC Press, Boca Raton, Fla. 220 pp.

Erlich, R. 1938. Paraziticka fauna pasa s pedrucia grada z agreba. Vet. Arh. 8:531–571.

Fernandes, B.J., J.D. Cooper, J.B. Cullen, R.S. Freeman, A.C. Ritchie, A.A. Scott, and P.F. Stuart. 1976. Systemic infection with *Alaria americana* (Trematoda). Can. Med. Assoc. J. 115:1111–1114.

Forrester, D.J. 1985. Unpublished data. Univ. of Florida, Gainesville.

Forrester, D.J., and J.E. Keirans. 1990. Unpublished data. Univ. of Florida, Gainesville.

Forrester, D.J., and M.E. Roelke. 1990. Unpublished data. Univ. of Florida, Gainesville.

Forrester, D.J., J.A. Conti, and R.C. Belden. 1985a. Parasites of the Florida panther (*Felis concolor coryi*). Proc. Helminthol. Soc. Wash. 52:95–97.

Forrester, D.J., N.P. Thompson, S.F. Sundlof, and W.B. Wheeler. 1985b. Unpublished data. Univ. of Florida, Gainesville.

Fox, I. 1940. Fleas of eastern United States. Iowa State Coll. Press, Ames. 191 pp.

Gillespie, J.H., and J.F. Timoney. 1981. Hagan and Bruner's infectious diseases of domestic animals. Cornell Univ. Press, Ithaca. 851 pp.

Glenn, B.L., A.A. Kocan, and E.F. Bouin. 1983. Cytauxzoonosis in bobcats. J. Am. Vet. Med. Assoc. 183:1155–1158.

Glenn, B.L., R.E. Rolley, and A.A. Kocan. 1982. *Cytauxzoon*-like piroplasms in erythrocytes of wild-trapped bobcats in Oklahoma. J. Am. Vet. Med. Assoc. 181:1251–1253.

Gould, G.I. 1980. Bobcat study, San Diego County, California. P-R report, Calif. Dept. of Fish and Game, Sacramento. 12 pp.

Gregson, J.D. 1973. Tick paralysis. An appraisal of natural and experimental data. Can. Dept. Agr. Monogr. No. 9. 109 pp.

Greiner, E.C., M.E. Roelke, C.T. Atkinson, J.P. Dubey, and S.D. Wright. 1989. *Sarcocystis* sp. in muscles of free-ranging Florida panthers and cougars (*Felis concolor*). J. Wildl. Dis. 25:623–628.

Greiner, E.C., P.P. Humphrey, R.C. Belden, W.B. Frankenberger, D.H. Austin, and E.P.J. Gibbs. 1984. Ixodid ticks on feral swine in Florida. J. Wildl. Dis. 20:114–119.

Hatcher, J.L., J.M. Gaskin, M.E. Roelke, and J.F. Evermann. 1990. Unpublished data. Univ. of Florida, Gainesville.

Hoff, G.L., W.J. Bigler, and E.C. Prather. 1975. One-half century of tularemia in Florida. J. Fla. Med. Assoc. 62:35–37.

Hoff, G.L., W.J. Bigler, D.O. Trainer, J.G. Debbie, G.M. Brown, W.G. Winkler, S.H. Richards, and M. Reardon. 1974. Survey of selected carnivore and opossum serums for agglutinins to *Brucella canis*. J. Am. Vet. Med. Assoc. 165:830–831.

Jenkins, J.H., and T.T. Fendley. 1968. The extent of contamination, detection and health significance of high accumulations of radioactivity in southeastern game populations. Proc. Ann. Conf. S.E. Assoc. Game Fish Comm. 22:89–95.

Kohls, G.M., and A.J. Rogers. 1953. Note on the occurrence of the tick *Ixodes affinis* Neumann in the United States. J. Parasitol. 39:669.

Layne, J.N. 1968. Host and ecological relationships of the parasitic helminth *Capillaria he-*

patica in Florida mammals. Zoologica 53:107–123.

———. 1971. Fleas (Siphonaptera) of Florida. Fla. Entomol. 54:35–51.

Lembeck, M. 1978. Bobcat study, San Diego County, California. P-R report, Calif. Dept. of Fish and Game, Sacramento. 22 pp.

Levine, N.D. 1980. Nematode parasites of domestic animals and of man. 2d ed. Burgess, Minneapolis. 477 pp.

Levine, N.D., and V. Ivens. 1981. The coccidian parasites (Protozoa, Apicomplexa) of carnivores. Ill. Biol. Monogr. #51. Univ. of Illinois Press, Urbana. 248 pp.

Loftin, H. 1961. An annotated check-list of trematodes and cestodes and their vertebrate hosts from Northwest Florida. Quart. J. Fla. Acad. Sci. 23:302–314.

Lord, R.D., C.H. Calisher, W.D. Sudia, and T.H. Work. 1973. Ecological investigations of vertebrate hosts of Venezuelan equine encephalomyelitis virus in south Florida. Am. J. Trop. Med. Hyg. 22:116–123.

McCord, C.M., and J.E. Cardoza. 1982. Bobcat and lynx. In: Wild mammals of North America. J.A. Chapman and G.A. Feldhamer (eds.). Johns Hopkins Univ. Press, Baltimore. pp. 728–766.

McIntosh, A. 1937. New host records for *Diphyllobothrium mansonoides* Mueller, 1935. J. Parasitol. 23:313–315.

McKeever, S., J.H. Schubert, M.D. Moody, G.W. Gorman, and J.F. Chapman. 1958a. Natural occurrence of tularemia in marsupials, carnivores, lagomorphs, and large rodents in southwestern Georgia and northwestern Florida. J. Infect. Dis. 103:120–126.

McKeever, S., G.W. Gorman, and L. Norman. 1958b. Occurrence of a *Typanosoma cruzi*–like organism in some mammals from southwestern Georgia and northwestern Florida. J. Parasitol. 44:583–587.

McKeever, S., G.W. Gorman, J.F. Chapman, M.M. Galton, and D.K. Powers. 1958c. Incidence of leptospirosis in wild mammals from southwestern Georgia with a report of new hosts for six serotypes of leptospires. Am. J. Trop. Med. Hyg. 7:646–655.

McKeever, S., W. Kaplin, and L. Ajello. 1958d. Ringworm fungi of large wild mammals in southwestern Georgia and northwestern Florida. Am J. Vet. Res. 19:973–975.

Miller, G.C., and R. Harkema. 1968. Helminths of some wild mammals in the southeastern United States. Proc. Helminthol. Soc. Wash. 35:118–125.

Milstrey, E.G., A.D. Gettman, and M.E. Roelke. 1985. Unpublished data. Univ. of Florida, Gainesville.

O'Brien, S.J., M.E. Roelke, L. Marker, A. Newman, C.A. Winkler, D. Meltzer, L. Colby, J.F. Evermann, M. Bush, and D.E. Wildt. 1985. Genetic basis for species vulnerability in the cheetah. Science 227:1428–1434.

O'Brien, S.J., M.E. Roelke, N. Yuhki, K.W. Richards, W.E. Johnson, W.L. Franklin, A.E. Anderson, O.L. Bass, Jr., R.C. Belden, and J.S. Martenson. 1990. Genetic introgression within the Florida panther *Felis concolor coryi*. Nat. Geogr. Res. 6:485–494.

Obstbaum, M., D.J. Forrester, M.E. Roelke, and J.R. Brady. 1987. Hookworms of bobcats (*Felis rufus* Schreber) from Florida. Unpublished MS, Univ. of Florida, Gainesville. 12 pp.

Orihel, T.C., and L.R. Ash. 1964. Occurrence of *Dirofilaria striata* in the bobcat (*Lynx rufus*) in Louisiana with observations on its larval development. J. Parasitol. 50:590–591.

Pence, D.B., F.D. Matthews, and L.A. Windberg. 1982. Notoedric mange in the bobcat, *Felis rufus*, from south Texas. J. Wildl. Dis. 18:47–50.

Price, E.W. 1943. A redescription of *Heterobilharzia americana* Price (Trematoda; Schistosomatidae). Proc. Helminthol. Soc. Wash. 10:85–86.

Progulske, D.R., Jr. 1982. Spatial distribution of bobcats and gray foxes in eastern Florida. M.S. thesis, Univ. of Florida, Gainesville. 63 pp.

Rickard, L.G., M.E. Roelke, and D.J. Forrester. 1984. Unpublished data. Univ. of Florida, Gainesville.

Roelke, M.E. 1985. Unpublished data. Florida

Game and Fresh Water Fish Commission, Gainesville.

———. 1987. Florida panther biomedical investigation, July 1, 1986 to June 30, 1987. Ann. Rept. Fla. Game and Fresh Water Fish Comm., Gainesville. 110 pp.

———. 1988a. Unpublished data. Florida Game and Fresh Water Fish Commission, Gainesville.

———. 1988b. Florida panther biomedical investigation, July 1, 1987 to June 30, 1988. Ann. Rept. Fla. Game and Fresh Water Fish Comm., Gainesville. 124 pp.

———. 1989. Florida panther biomedical investigation, July 1, 1988 to June 30, 1989. Ann. Rept. Fla. Game and Fresh Water Fish Comm., Gainesville. 120 pp.

———. 1990. Florida panther biomedical investigation, July 1, 1989 to June 30, 1990. Ann. Rept. Fla. Game and Fresh Water Fish Comm., Gainesville. 175 pp.

Roelke, M.E., and A.A. Kocan. 1985. Unpublished data. Florida Game and Fresh Water Fish Commission, Gainesville.

Roelke, M.E., E.R. Jacobson, G.V. Kollias, and D.J. Forrester. 1985. Medical management and biomedical findings on the Florida panther, *Felis concolor coryi,* July 1, 1983 to June 30, 1985. Ann. Rept. Fla. Game and Fresh Water Fish Comm., Gainesville. 114 pp.

Roelke, M.E., E.R. Jacobson, G.V. Kollias, and D.J. Forrester. 1986. Medical management and biomedical findings on the Florida panther, *Felis concolor coryi,* July 1, 1985 to June 30, 1986. Ann. Rept. Fla. Game and Fresh Water Fish Comm., Gainesville. 65 pp.

Rogers, A.J. 1953. A study of the ixodid ticks of northern Florida, including the biology and life history of *Ixodes scapularis* Say (Ixodidae: Acarina). Ph.D diss., Univ. of Maryland, College Park. 183 pp.

Rubin, H.L., and J.N. Layne. 1982. Unpublished data. Kissimmee Diagnostic Laboratory, Kissimmee, Fla.

Rupprecht, C.E., and M.E. Roelke. 1990. Unpublished data. Wistar Institute, Philadelphia, Pa.

Scholtens, R.G., and L. Norman. 1971. *Trichinella spiralis* in Florida wildlife. J. Parasitol. 57:1103.

Seal, U.S., and R.C. Lacy. 1989. Florida panther (*Felis concolor coryi*) viability analysis and species survival plan. U.S. Fish and Wildlife Service Coop. Agreement #14-16-0004-90-902. 208 pp.

Seymour, C., and T.M. Yuill. 1981. Arboviruses. In: Infectious diseases of wild mammals. J.W. Davis et al. (eds.). Iowa State Univ. Press, Ames. pp. 54–86.

Shoop, W.L. 1988. Trematode transmission patterns. J. Parasitol. 74:46–59.

Shotts, E.B., Jr., C.L. Andrews, and T.W. Harvey. 1975. Leptospirosis in selected wild mammals of the Florida panhandle and southwestern Georgia. J. Am. Vet. Med. Assoc. 167:587–589.

Simpson, C.F., B.M. Gebhardt, R.E. Bradley, and R.E. Jackson. 1974. Glomerulosclerosis in canine heartworm infection. Vet. Pathol. 11:506–514.

Smith, J.S. 1977. A survey of ticks infesting white-tailed deer in 12 southeastern states. M.S. thesis, Univ. of Georgia, Athens. 60 pp.

Soulsby, E.J. L. 1982. Helminths, arthropods and protozoa of domesticated animals. Lea and Febiger, Philadelphia. 809 pp.

Stevenson, H.M. 1976. Vertebrates of Florida. Identification and distribution. Univ. Presses of Florida, Gainesville. 607 pp.

Stone, J.E., and D.B. Pence. 1978. Ecology of helminth parasitism in the bobcat from west Texas. J. Parasitol. 64:295–302.

Strickland, R.K., R.R. Gerrish, J.L. Hourigan, and G.O. Schubert. 1976. Ticks of veterinary importance. APHIS-USDA Agr. Handbook No. 485. Washington, D.C. 122 pp.

Taylor, D.J. 1951. The distribution of ticks in Florida. M.S. thesis, Univ. of Florida, Gainesville. 124 pp.

Technical Subcommittee of the Florida Panther Interagency Committee. 1989. Status report on mercury contamination in the Florida panther. Gainesville, Fla. 19 pp.

Travis, B.V. 1941. Examinations of wild animals for the cattle tick *Boophilus annulatus microplus* (Can.) in Florida. J. Parasitol. 27:465–467.

Tumlison, R., V.R. McDaniel, M.J. Harvey, M.L. Kennedy, and G.A. Heidt. 1982. A bibliography of bobcat literature. Occasional paper. Ecol. Res. Center, Memphis State Univ., Memphis. 30 pp.

Wassmer, D.A. 1982. Demography, movements, activity, habitat utilization and marking behavior of a bobcat (*Lynx rufus*) population in south-central Florida. M.S. thesis, Univ. of South Florida, Tampa. 146 pp.

Wassmer, D.A., D.D. Guenther, and J.N. Layne. 1988. Ecology of the bobcat in south-central Florida. Bull. Fla. State Mus., Biol. Sci. 33:159–228.

Watson, T.G., V.F. Nettles, and W.R. Davidson. 1981. Endoparasites and selected infectious agents in bobcats (*Felis rufus*) from West Virginia and Georgia. J. Wildl. Dis. 17:547–554.

White, F.H., and D.J. Forrester. 1988. Unpublished data. Univ. of Florida, Gainesville.

Wilkins, L. 1990. The Florida panther, *Felis concolor coryi*. A morphological investigation of the subspecies with a comparison to other North American and South American cougars. Unpublished report prepared for the Florida Game and Fresh Water Fish Commission. Florida Museum of Natural History, Univ. of Florida, Gainesville. 70 pp.

Williams, E.S., E.T. Thorne, M.J. G. Appel, and D.W. Belitsy. 1988. Canine distemper in black-footed ferrets (*Mustela nigripes*) from Wyoming. J. Wildl. Dis. 24:385–398.

Foxes and Coyotes

I. Introduction

There are three wild canids in Florida (Stevenson 1976). These include the gray fox, *Urocyon cinereoargenteus* (Schreber), the red fox, *Vulpes vulpes* L., and the coyote, *Canis latrans* Say. The gray fox and the red fox occur throughout Florida, except for the Keys (Brown 1987). Coyotes are distributed throughout most of the panhandle and also along the Central Highland Ridge from Hamilton County south to Polk County. There are no established populations of coyotes in southern Florida (Layne 1974; Brady and Campbell 1983).

The parasites and diseases of foxes in North America have been reviewed by Samuel and Nelson (1982). Extensive reviews have been published on parasites and diseases of coyotes by Custer and Pence (1981) and Pence and Custer (1981).

II. Environmental contaminants

There is no information on the occurrence of heavy metals, pesticides, or radionuclides in foxes and coyotes in Florida. Cumbie and Jenkins (1975), however, gave some data on mercury concentrations in gray and red foxes in Georgia and South Carolina. In another study, concentrations of cesium-137 were reported for gray foxes in Georgia and South Carolina by Jenkins and Fendley (1968).

III. Rabies

The first case of rabies in a fox in Florida occurred in 1913 (Wood 1954). Since that time several epizootics have occurred. These were in 1947–1948 (Jefferson and surrounding counties), 1953–1958 (13 counties in the panhandle), 1966–1967 (Jackson County), and 1969–1970 (Walton and Okaloosa counties) (Wood and Davis 1959; Jennings et al. 1960; Scatterday et al. 1960; Burridge et al. 1986). The most extensive outbreak was the one in 1953–1958, which involved only gray foxes. It began in Holmes, Washington, and Jackson counties in 1953 and subsequently spread to the east along the northern part of the panhandle of Florida and terminated in 1959 in Madison County. Rabid foxes were also found in nearby areas in Alabama and Georgia (Jennings et al. 1960). Although rabid foxes have been found in 49 of 67 counties in Florida between 1951 and 1987 (Figure 16-1), the majority of these have been from the northern part of the state (Jennings et al. 1960; Burridge et al. 1986). Burridge et al. (1986) presented details on fox rabies by county on a year-to-year basis. In spite of the fact that both red and gray foxes are equally susceptible to rabies virus (Schmidt and Sikes 1968), most of the cases of fox rabies in Florida involve gray foxes. The red fox is less common and its distribution more limited, which may account for this phenomenon. No cases of rabies have been reported from coyotes in Florida. It is interesting to note, however, that fox rabies (primarily gray fox rabies) is found mainly in areas where gray foxes, red foxes, and coyotes occur sympatrically (the panhandle and north-central Florida).

Although the occurrence of rabies in foxes is of some concern, it is of lesser importance than rabies in raccoons (see Chapter 12). During 1974 to 1983 only 4% of the rabies cases diagnosed in Florida were foxes (Burridge et al. 1986). Burridge et al. (1986) plotted the cases on a monthly basis from 1955 to 1983 and showed that there was a peak between December and May that coincides with breeding and whelping activities.

The most common behavior among rabid foxes is either aggression or confusion (Jennings et al. 1960). Aggressive behavior is usually in the form of sudden attack on a person or an animal with the delivery of a bite as the result. The other kind of behavior is characterized by a confused or moribund condition during the daytime. The animals will bite dogs, but usually not people. Many are killed by vehicles on highways (Jennings et al. 1960).

IV. Canine distemper

Foxes with canine distemper (CD) exhibit dyspnea, anorexia, emaciation, ascending paralysis, ataxia, convulsions, and coma. Blindness occurs sometimes and animals exhibit a lack of fear of man with tendencies toward wandering and aimless circling, types of behavior exhibited with rabies (Helmboldt and Jungherr 1955; Monson and Stone 1976).

The epizootics of CD described in the chapter on raccoons also involved a small number of gray foxes (see Chapter 12). The die-offs in Sarasota County involved at least eight gray foxes in 1972–1973 (Hoff et al. 1974a) and at least three gray foxes in 1977. In 1972–1973 the disease appeared first in foxes and subsequently spread into the raccoon population (see Figure 12-3). Epizootics also occurred in Pasco and Hernando coun-

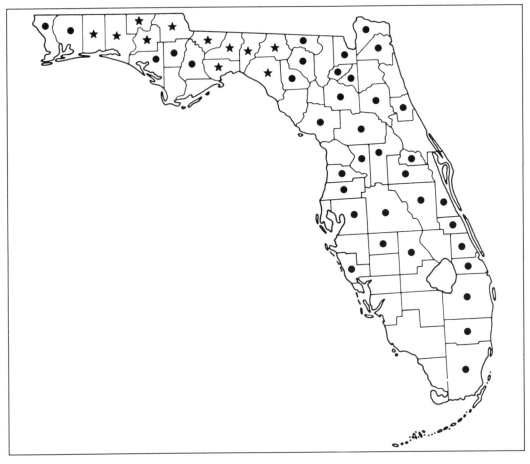

FIGURE 16-1. Distribution of rabid foxes (gray and red foxes combined) in Florida during 1951–87. Solid circles are counties in which rabid foxes have been reported. Stars indicate locations of epizootics. (Adapted from Burridge et al. 1986; Bigler 1988.)

ties in 1987, Palm Beach County in 1988, and Citrus and Volusia counties in 1990 (Figure 16-2) (Wright and Forrester 1988; Forrester and Spalding 1990). One case of CD was reported in a gray fox in Santa Rosa County in 1984 (SCWDS records). In addition, McLean (1988) found one of nine gray foxes in Manatee County to be seropositive.

The full impact of CD on populations of foxes in Florida is not known, but because foxes are quite susceptible to the virus and the prognosis for infected animals is generally poor (Budd 1981), the disease may be impor-

tant. In addition to Florida, over 50 cases of CD have been reported from gray foxes in Georgia, Virginia, West Virginia, Maryland, and Mississippi during the 15-year period 1973–87 (SCWDS records). Six of these foxes also had concurrent infections of toxoplasmosis.

V. Other viruses

Sera from 13 gray foxes were tested for antibodies to St. Louis encephalitis (SLE) virus,

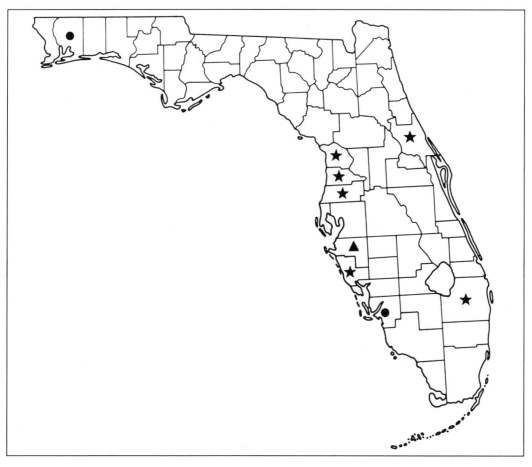

FIGURE 16-2. Distribution of canine distemper in gray foxes in Florida, 1972–90. Solid circle represents county in which a single case of canine distemper has been reported. Solid triangle indicates location of a seropositive animal. Stars indicate locations of epizootics. (Adapted from Hoff et al. 1974a; SCWDS records; McLean 1988; Wright and Forrester 1988; Rubin 1989; Forrester and Spalding 1990.)

Everglades virus, and eastern equine encephalomyelitis (EEE) virus, and one gray fox was tested for antibodies to Highlands J virus (Bigler 1971; Bigler et al. 1975). All were negative except for five foxes that were seropositive for EEE. This virus is not believed to cause significant mortality in populations of wild mammals (Seymour and Yuill 1981), although it is of public health and veterinary importance (Gillespie and Timoney 1981; McLean 1975). According to Bigler et al. (1975) EEE virus has been isolated from mos-

quitoes, horses, humans, and a number of wild birds during every month of the year in Florida. Foxes may play a minor role as a reservoir of the virus.

Tensaw virus was isolated from the brain of a gray fox from Marion County in 1965 (Bigler et al. 1975; Calisher et al. 1986). This fox had been submitted for rabies examination. Tensaw virus is of public health significance, but its importance to fox populations is not known.

In their excellent discourse on fox rabies

in Florida, Jennings et al. (1960) discussed a disease that was identified as "fox encephalitis." A number of gray foxes examined during a rabies epizootic during the 1950s in the panhandle were negative for rabies. Inclusion bodies were seen in brain tissue, however, but were unlike those of rabies virus. The authors (Jennings et al. 1960) reported that similar inclusions were found in dogs with encephalitic diseases of the distemper-hepatitis complex. Helmboldt and Jungherr (1955) reported similar findings in gray foxes. Although this "fox encephalitis" disease was not further identified and the numbers of foxes that died from it were not determined, Jennings et al. (1960) stated that the "violence and magnitude of this die-off were unmatched elsewhere in the period of our observation" (p. 175). Afflicted foxes were seen in large numbers and never were known to attack humans, but often wandered about in a confused and fearless state. The authors further stated that rabies outbreaks were curtailed in areas where "fox encephalitis" occurred (Jennings et al. 1960). This disease was probably infectious canine hepatitis, which is caused by an adenovirus and is known to infect wild and farm-ranched foxes (Gillespie and Timoney 1981). No further information is available on this disease in Florida, except that McLean (1988) found three of nine gray foxes seropositive for infectious canine hepatitis virus in Manatee County in 1968–69.

Wassmer (1984) reported canine parvovirus as the cause of death of a radio-collared gray fox in Highlands County in 1981. In addition, 1 of 12 gray foxes from Collier County was seropositive for parvovirus (Roelke et al. 1986). The significance of these findings to fox populations is unknown.

Roelke et al. (1986) tested one gray fox from Collier County for antibodies to pseudorabies virus. It was negative.

VI. Bacterial diseases

Sera from 10 gray foxes from various areas in Florida and from 9 gray foxes from Manatee County were tested for antibodies to *Brucella canis,* the etiologic agent of brucellosis (Hoff et al. 1974b; McLean 1988). All were negative.

In another study, sera from five gray foxes in Leon County (1955–57) were tested for antibodies to *Francisella tularensis,* the causative agent of tularemia (McKeever et al. 1958a). Two of the foxes were positive. Hoff et al. (1975a) tested 10 gray foxes serologically; all were negative. Foxes probably acquire tularemia from eating infected rodents or rabbits (Jellison 1974). In Florida, there is evidence that tularemia occurs in cottontails, marsh rabbits, cotton rats, cotton mice, and old-field mice (Hoff et al. 1975a, 1975b). These animals may be the source of infection for gray foxes.

Leptospirosis has not been diagnosed in foxes in Florida, but McKeever et al. (1958c) recovered *Leptospira interrogans,* serovar *ballum* from 2 of 52 gray foxes from southwestern Georgia. One of the infected foxes was in southern Seminole County, only a few miles from the Florida border. In another study, however, McLean (1988) found that three of nine gray foxes from Manatee County were positive for leptospire antibodies in 1968–69. The serovar involved was not determined.

Twelve gray and two red foxes from Alachua County were cultured for enteric pathogens in 1970–77. Two of the gray foxes were carriers of *Salmonella;* one was positive for *S. madelia* and one for *S. rubislaw* (White and Forrester 1985).

The significance of these bacterial diseases to fox populations in Florida is unknown. All are of public health importance.

VII. Mycotic infections

McKeever et al. (1958d) examined 95 gray foxes and 20 red foxes for ringworm fungi in southwestern Georgia and northwestern Florida in 1954–56. None was infected.

VIII. Protozoan diseases

Five gray foxes from Florida were examined serologically for antibodies to *Toxoplasma gondii* by Burridge et al. (1979). All were negative. McLean (1988), however, found one of nine gray foxes seropositive in Manatee County in 1968.

McKeever et al. (1958b) cultured 18 red foxes and 118 gray foxes for trypanosomes from 1954 to 1957. Two of the gray foxes were positive for *Trypanosoma cruzi*–like organisms. The authors combined their data from animals trapped in southwestern Georgia and northwestern Florida and therefore it is not possible to determine if the positive foxes were from Florida.

A fecal sample taken from a road-killed gray fox in Alachua County in 1974 contained coccidial oocysts. These measured 15 by 28 microns, but could not be identified further because they would not sporulate. There are no reports of coccidia from gray foxes in North America (Levine and Ivens 1981). It is possible that this finding was a case of spurious parasitism and that the oocysts were from prey animals, as there were the remains of two cotton rats in the stomach of the fox.

IX. Helminths

Twenty-one species of helminths are known from gray foxes in Florida, including 1 trem-atode, 4 cestodes, 4 acanthocephalans, and 12 nematodes (Conti 1984). Twelve species are known from red foxes: 1 cestode and 11 nematodes. Coyotes in Florida have 11 species: 1 trematode, 2 cestodes, 1 acanthocephalan, and 7 nematodes. Data on distribution, prevalence, and intensity of these helminths (except for *Trichinella spiralis*) are given in Tables 16-1 (gray foxes), 16-2 (red foxes), and 16-3 (coyotes). Scholtens and Norman (1971) reported larvae of *Trichinella spiralis* in the diaphragm of 1 of 17 foxes from Marion County in 1962. They stated that they examined both gray and red foxes, but did not say which species was positive.

The pathologic significance of these helminths in populations of foxes and coyotes in Florida is unknown. Most of them, particularly the trematodes, cestodes, and acanthocephalans, occurred in such low prevalences and intensities as to suggest that they would be of little consequence to the host. Among the nematodes, the three most abundant species (*Molineus barbatus*, *Physaloptera rara*, and *Ancylostoma tubaeforme*) may be important, particularly to young animals. The heartworm, *Dirofilaria immitis* (Figure 16-3), may be a morbidity and mortality factor. Pence and Custer (1981) discussed the pathology of *D. immitis* infections in wild canids and concluded that this parasite should be considered as an important pathogen in certain populations. The importance of foxes and coyotes as reservoir hosts of heartworms for domestic dogs is uncertain. In the foxes and coyotes examined in Florida, Conti (1984) reported that only the female worms from the coyote contained microfilariae and hence the infections in foxes would have been "dead end" and of no importance epizootiologically. Several other nematodes (*Capillaria aerophila*, *Ancylostoma* spp., *Strongyloides*

Table 16-1

Helminths reported from 26 gray foxes in Florida, 1972–79

Helminth	Prevalence No. inf. (%)	Intensity Mean	Range	County
Trematoda				
Alaria marcianae	5 (19)	27	1–55	Alachua, Highlands
Cestoda				
Taenia pisiformis	1 (43)	2	3	Alachua
Taenia sp.[a]	2 (8)	2	1–2	Alachua
Mesocestoides sp.[b]	3 (12)	3	1–8	Alachua
Spirometra mansonoides	1 (4)	1	1	Alachua
Acanthocephala				
Centrorhynchus wardae	1 (4)	1	1	Alachua
Pachysentis canicola	1 (4)	1	1	Alachua
Moniliformis moniliformis	1 (4)	8	8	Alachua
Unidentified[c]	1 (4)	1	1	Alachua
Nematoda				
Molinius barbatus	20 (77)	30	1–224	Alachua, Highlands, Levy
Physaloptera rara[d]	18 (69)	11	1–49	Alachua, Highlands, Marion, Levy
Ancylostoma tubaeforme	20 (77)	11	1–48	Alachua, Highlands, Levy
Ancylostoma caninum	1 (4)	6	6	Alachua
Ancylostoma braziliense	1 (4)	4	4	Marion
Trichuris vulpis	6 (23)	9	1–43	Alachua, Highlands, Marion
Spirocerca lupi	3 (12)	1	1	Alachua, Levy
Spirurid larvae	4 (15)	6	1–19	Alachua
Dirofilaria immitis	2 (8)	3	1–5	Alachua
Capillaria aerophila	1 (4)	2	2	Alachua
Strongyloides stercoralis	1 (4)	71	71	Orange

Sources: Conti (1984); Forrester and Conti (1985). Layne (1968) examined the livers of 6 gray foxes from Alachua (n = 3), Flagler (n = 1), Highlands (n = 1), and Putnam (n = 1) counties. All were negative for *Capillaria hepatica.*
[a]Closely resembles *T. macrocystis.*
[b]Unidentified species due to uncertain taxonomic status of members of this genus.
[c]Specimens were immature and probosces were not evaginated. Belong to either the genus *Oncicola* or *Macracanthorhynchus.*
[d]Morgan (1941) reported *Physaloptera rara* from a "Florida gray fox" but gave no details on locality, prevalence, intensity, or the like.

stercoralis, and *Toxocara canis*) are known to cause serious problems in domestic canids (Levine 1968; Pence and Custer 1981) and may do likewise in foxes and coyotes under the proper ecological conditions.

X. Arthropods

Fifteen species of parasitic arthropods are known from foxes in Florida. Thirteen of these occur on gray foxes and three on red foxes (Table 16-4). These include seven species of ticks, one mite, six fleas, and one biting louse.

Three of the fleas—*Cediopsylla simplex, Echidnophaga gallinacea,* and *Orchopeas howardi*—are primarily parasites of rabbits, chickens, and squirrels, respectively, and their presence on foxes is believed to be due to the predation of foxes on these animals (Layne 1971).

Table 16-2
Helminths of 4 red foxes in Florida, 1973–76

Helminth	Prevalence No. inf. (%)	Intensity Mean	Range	County
Cestoda				
Taenia sp.[a]	1 (25)	1	1	Polk
Nematoda				
Molineus barbatus	3 (75)	5	1–9	Alachua, Levy, Polk
Physaloptera rara	2 (50)	27	13–40	Levy, Polk
Ancylostoma tubaeforme	2 (50)	10	5–14	Levy, Polk
Ancylostoma caninum	1 (25)	4	4	Polk
Trichuris vulpis	2 (50)	4	2–6	Alachua, Levy
Spirocerca lupi	1 (25)	2	2	Levy
Spiruid larvae	1 (25)	14	14	Levy
Dirofilaria immitis	1 (25)	1	1	Alachua
Capillaria aerophila	2 (50)	2	1–2	Alachua, Levy
Anafilaroides pararostratus	1 (25)	2	2	Alachua
Toxocara canis	1 (25)	3	3	Levy

Sources: Conti (1984); Forrester and Conti (1985).
[a]No scolices found.

Table 16-3
Helminths of 3 coyotes in Florida, 1979–81

Helminth	Prevalence No. inf. (%)	Intensity Mean	Range	County
Trematoda				
Alaria marcianae	1 (33)	2	2	Lake
Cestoda				
Taenia pisiformis	2 (67)	13	1–24	Escambia, Gadsden
Taenia sp.[a]	1 (33)	8	8	Escambia
Acanthocephala				
Unidentified[b]	1 (33)	1	1	Escambia
Nematoda				
Molineus barbatus	1 (33)	49	49	Gadsden
Physaloptera rara	1 (33)	25	25	Gadsden
Trichuris vulpis	2 (67)	11	9–12	Escambia, Gadsden
Dirofilaria immitis	1 (33)	9	9	Lake
Capillaria aerophila	1 (33)	1	1	Gadsden
Capillaria plica	1 (33)	2	2	Gadsden
Ancylostoma caninum	1 (33)	2	2	Gadsden

Sources: Conti (1984); Forrester and Conti (1985).
[a]Closely resembles *T. macrocystis.*
[b]Specimens were immature and probosces were not evaginated. Belong to either the genus *Oncicola* or *Macracanthorhynchus.*

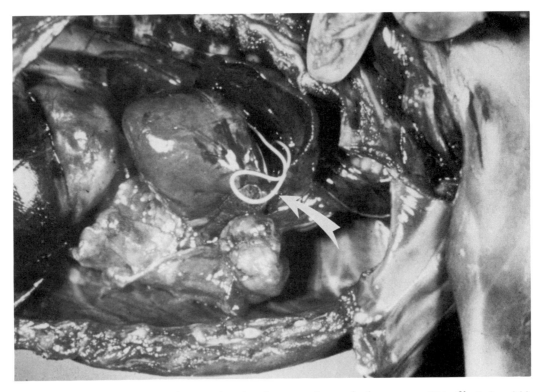

FIGURE 16-3. Thoracic cavity of a gray fox showing a specimen of a heartworm (*Dirofilaria immitis*) (arrow) partially extruding from the heart.

As pointed out in previous chapters, some of the ticks (e.g., *Dermacentor variabilis, Amblyomma maculatum, A. americanum,* and *Ixodes scapularis*) are known to cause tick paralysis (Gregson 1973). Both *Dermacentor variabilis* and *Ixodes scapularis* are vectors of *Francisella tularensis,* the etiologic agent of tularemia (Strickland et al. 1976). *Amblyomma tuberculatum* occurs as an adult only on the gopher tortoise (Rogers 1953). Gray foxes were infected with larvae of this species.

The mange or itch mite, *Sarcoptes scabiei,* infests a number of wild and domestic mammals and is also a zoonotic problem (Harwood and James 1979). Red foxes are affected severely by this mite, whereas gray foxes are relatively poor hosts (Stone et al. 1972), with only an occasional animal showing susceptibility to the disease (Stone et al. 1982). This ectoparasite is felt to be a limiting factor in populations of red foxes in Wisconsin (Trainer and Hale 1969). Sarcoptic mange is also a problem in some populations of coyotes (Pence et al. 1983). The reader is referred to the reviews of this disease by Pence and Custer (1981) and Todd et al. (1981). In April 1976, a red fox in emaciated condition was shot by a farmer near Williston (Levy County). It had a very severe case of sarcoptic mange. The tail was almost completely devoid of hair, and hair was missing over most of the body with extensive crusted areas on the head, legs, back, and tail (Figure 16-4). This disease may be important in red foxes in Florida and other parts of the Southeast. Sarcoptic mange has been reported from a number of red foxes in Georgia and in one red fox from Alabama, and also from coyotes in Louisiana and Georgia (SCWDS records).

Table 16-4
Arthropod parasites reported from foxes in Florida

Arthropod	Host[a]	County	Data source
Ticks			
Dermacentor variablis	G	Bradford	FSCA[b]
	G	Indian River	Wilson & Kale (1972), FSCA
Amblyomma americanum	G	"North Florida"	Rogers (1953)
	G	Alachua	Boardman (1929)
Amblyomma maculatum	G	Indian River	Wilson & Kale (1972)
	G	Alachua	Forrester (1985)
	G	Orange	Boardman (1929)
	G	Orange, Osceola, Collier	Travis (1941)
Amblyomma tuberculatum[c]	G	"North Florida"	Rogers (1953)
	G	Putnam	FSCA
Ixodes scapularis	G	"North Florida"	Rogers (1953)
	G	Orange, Osceola, Collier	Travis (1941)
Ixodes affinis	G	Alachua	Forrester (1985)
Ixodes cookei	G	"Florida"	Clifford et al. (1961)
Mites			
Sarcoptes scabiei	R	Levy	Forrester (1985)
Fleas			
Ctenocephalides canis	G	Leon	Fox (1940)
Ctenocephalides felis	G	Alachua	Layne (1971), FSCA
Cediopsylla simplex	G	Alachua	" " "
Echidnophaga gallinacea	G	Alachua	" " "
Pulex simulans	G	Alachua, Marion	" " "
	R	Alachua	Layne (1971)
Orchopeas howardii	G	NG[d]	Layne (1971)
Biting lice			
Neotrichodectes mephitidis	R	Alachua	FSCA

[a]G = gray fox; R = red fox.
[b]FSCA = records from the Florida State Collection of Arthropods, Division of Plant Industry, Florida Department of Agriculture, Gainesville, Fla.
[c]Larvae only.
[d]NG = not given by author.

XI. Summary and conclusions

Forty-five different parasites and infectious disease agents have been identified in gray foxes in Florida. These include 6 viruses, 2 bacteria, 3 protozoans, 1 trematode, 4 cestodes, 4 acanthocephalans, 12 nematodes, 6 fleas, and 7 ticks. The most important of these appear to be three viral diseases: rabies, canine distemper, and fox encephalitis (= infectious canine hepatitis). Epizootics of all three, sometimes in combination, have been reported. In addition, hookworms, stomach worms, and heartworms may be important.

Fifteen species of parasites have been documented in red foxes in Florida. These include 1 cestode, 11 nematodes, 1 mite, 1 flea, and 1 biting louse. The mite, the causative agent of sarcoptic mange, is of most significance to red fox populations and can cause severe morbidity and mortality.

Coyotes are hosts of at least 11 species of parasites. Among these are 1 trematode, 2 cestodes, 1 acanthocephalan, and 7 nema-

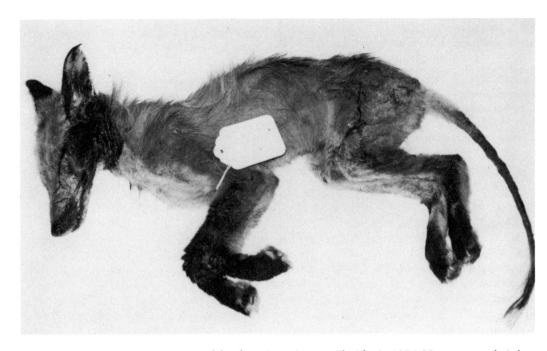

FIGURE 16-4. Sarcoptic mange in a red fox from Levy County, Florida, in 1976. Note extreme hair loss and large areas of crusted skin.

todes. The significance of disease in coyotes in Florida is unknown.

Nine of these disease agents are of public health and veterinary significance and include the agents of rabies, eastern equine encephalomyelitis, tularemia, salmonellosis, Chagas' disease (*Trypanosoma cruzi*), strongyloidosis (*Strongyloides stercoralis*), creeping eruption (*Ancylostoma braziliense*), visceral larva migrans (*Toxocara canis*), and mange (*Sarcoptes scabiei*). Several of the fleas and ticks can also infest man.

XII. Literature cited

Bigler, W.L. 1971. Serologic evidence of Venezuelan equine encephalitis virus infections in raccoons of south central Florida. J. Wildl. Dis. 7:166–170.

———. 1988. Unpublished data. HRS, Tallahassee, Fla.

Bigler, W.J., E. Lassing, E. Buff, A.L. Lewis, and G.L. Hoff. 1975. Arbovirus surveillance in Florida: Wild vertebrate studies 1965–74. J. Wildl. Dis. 11:348–356.

Boardman, E.T. 1929. Ticks of the Gainesville area. M.S. thesis, Univ. of Florida, Gainesville. 57 pp.

Brady, J.R., and H.W. Campbell. 1983. Distribution of coyotes in Florida. Fla. Field Nat. 11:40–41.

Brown, L.N. 1987. A checklist of Florida's mammals. Florida Game and Fresh Water Fish Commission, Tallahassee. 6 pp.

Budd, J. 1981. Distemper. In: Infectious diseases of wild mammals. J.W. Davis et al. (eds.). Iowa State Univ. Press, Ames. pp. 31–44.

Burridge, M.J., L.A. Sawyer, and W.J. Bigler. 1986. Rabies in Florida. Department of Health and Rehabilitative Services, Tallahassee, Fla. 147 pp.

Burridge, M.J., W.J. Bigler, D.J. Forrester, and J.M. Hennemann. 1979. Serologic survey for *Toxoplasma gondii* in wild animals in Florida. J. Am. Vet. Med. Assoc. 175:964–967.

Calisher, C.H., D.B. Francy, G.C. Smith, D.J. Muth, J.S. Lazuick, N. Karabatsos, W.L. Jakob, and R.G. McLean. 1986. Distribution of Bunyamwera serogroup viruses in North America, 1956–1984. Am. J. Trop. Med. Hyg. 35:429–443.

Clifford, C.M., G. Anastos, and A. Elbl. 1961. The larval ixodid ticks of the eastern United States (Acarina—Ixodidae). Misc. Pub. Entomol. Soc. Am. 2:213–237.

Conti, J.A. 1984. Helminths of foxes and coyotes in Florida. Proc. Helminthol. Soc. Wash. 51:365–367.

Cumbie, P.M., and J.H. Jenkins. 1975. Mercury accumulation in native mammals of the southeast. Proc. Ann. Conf. S.E. Assoc. Game Fish Comm. 28:639–648.

Custer, J.W., and D.B. Pence. 1981. Host-parasite relationships in the wild Canidae of North America. I. Ecology of helminth infections in the genus Canis. In: Worldwide Furbearer Conference Proceedings. Chapman and Pursley (eds.). R.R. Donnelley and Sons, Falls Church, Va. pp. 730–759.

Forrester, D.J. 1985. Unpublished data. Univ. of Florida, Gainesville.

Forrester, D.J., and J.A. Conti. 1985. Unpublished data. Univ. of Florida, Gainesville.

Forrester, D.J., and M.G. Spalding. 1990. Unpublished data. Univ. of Florida, Gainesville.

Fox, I. 1940. Fleas of eastern United States. Iowa State Coll. Press, Ames. 191 pp.

Gillespie, J.H., and J.F. Timoney. 1981. Hagan and Bruner's infectious diseases of domestic animals. Cornell Univ. Press, Ithaca. 851 pp.

Gregson, J.D. 1973. Tick paralysis, an appraisal of natural and experimental data. Can. Dept. Agric. Monogr. No. 9. 109 pp.

Harwood, R.F., and M.T. James. 1979. Entomology in human and animal health. 7th ed. Macmillan, New York. 548 pp.

Helmboldt, C.F., and E.L. Jungherr. 1955. Distemper complex in wild carnivores simulating rabies. Am. J. Vet. Res. 16:463–469.

Hoff, G.L., W.J. Bigler, S.J. Proctor, and L.P. Stallings. 1974a. Epizootic of canine distemper virus infection among urban raccoons and gray foxes. J. Wildl. Dis. 10:423–428.

Hoff, G.L., W.J. Bigler, D.O. Trainer, J.G. Debbie, G.M. Brown, W.G. Winkler, S.H. Richards, and M. Reardon. 1974b. Survey of selected carnivore and opossum serums for agglutinins to Brucella canis. J. Am. Vet. Med. Assoc. 165:830–831.

Hoff, G.L., W.J. Bigler, and E.C. Prather. 1975a. One-half century of tularemia in Florida. J. Fla. Med. Assoc. 62: 35–37.

Hoff, G.L., W.J. Bigler, W. Hemonert, and D. Lawrence. 1975b. Tularemia in Florida: Sylvilagus palustris as a source of human infection. J. Wildl. Dis. 11:560–561.

Jellison, W.L. 1974. Tularemia in North America, 1930–1974. Univ. of Montana, Missoula. 276 pp.

Jenkins, J.H., and T.T. Fendley. 1968. The extent of contamination, detection, and health significance of high accumulations of radioactivity in southeastern game populations. Proc. Annu. Conf. S.E. Assoc. Game Fish Comm. 22:89–95.

Jennings, W.L., N.A. Schneider, A.L. Lewis, and J.E. Scatterday. 1960. Fox rabies in Florida. J. Wildl. Manage. 24:171–179.

Layne, J.N. 1968. Host and ecological relationships of the parasitic helminth Capillaria hepatica in Florida mammals. Zoologica 53:107–122.

———. 1971. Fleas (Siphonaptera) of Florida. Fla. Entomol. 54:35–51.

———. 1974. The land mammals of south Florida. In: Environments of south Florida: Present and past. P.J. Gleason (ed.). Miami Geol. Soc. Mem. 2. pp. 386–413.

Levine, N.D. 1968. Nematode parasites of domestic animals and of man. Burgess, Minneapolis. 600 pp.

Levine, N.D., and V. Ivens. 1981. The coccidian parasites (Protozoa, Apicomplexa) of carnivores. Ill. Biol. Monogr. 51, Univ. of Illinois Press, Urbana. 248 pp.

McKeever, S., J.H. Schubert, M.D. Moody, G.W. Gorman, and J.F. Chapman. 1958a. Natural occurrence of tularemia in marsupials, carnivores, lagomorphs, and large rodents in southwestern Georgia and northwestern Florida. J. Infect. Dis. 103:120–126.

McKeever, S., G.W. Gorman, and L. Norman. 1958b. Occurrence of a *Trypanosoma cruzi*–like organism in some mammals from southwestern Georgia and northwestern Florida. J. Parasitol. 44:583–587.

McKeever, S., G.W. Gorman, J.F. Chapman, M.M. Galton, and D.K. Powers. 1958c. Incidence of leptospirosis in wild mammals from southwestern Georgia with a report of new hosts for six serotypes of leptospires. Am. J. Trop. Med. and Hyg. 7:646–655.

McKeever, S., W. Kaplan, and L. Ajello. 1958d. Ringworm fungi of large wild mammals in southwestern Georgia and northwestern Florida. Am. J. Vet. Res. 19:973–975.

McLean, D.M. 1975. Group A mosquito-borne arboviruses, primarily in the western hemisphere. In: Diseases transmitted from animals to man. W.T. Hubbert et al. (eds.). C.C. Thomas, Springfield, Ill. pp. 968–983.

McLean, R.G. 1988. Unpublished data. CDC, Fort Collins, Colo.

Monson, R.A., and W.B. Stone. 1976. Canine distemper in wild carnivores in New York. N.Y. Fish Game J. 23:149.

Morgan, B.B. 1941. A summary of the Physalopterinae (Nematoda) of North America. Proc. Helminthol. Soc. Wash. 8:28–30.

Pence, D.B., and J.W. Custer. 1981. Host-parasite relationships in the wild Canidae of North America. II. Pathology of infectious diseases in the genus *Canis*. In: Worldwide Furbearer Conference Proceedings. Chapman and Pursley (eds.). R.R. Donnelley and Sons, Falls Church, Va. pp. 760–845.

Pence, D.B., L.A. Windberg, B.C. Pence, and R. Sprowls. 1983. The epizootiology and pathology of sarcoptic mange in coyotes, *Canis latrans*, from south Texas. J. Parasitol. 69:1100–1115.

Roelke, M.E., E.R. Jacobson, G.V. Kollias, and D.J. Forrester. 1986. Medical management and biomedical findings on the Florida panther, *Felis concolor coryi*, July 1, 1985 to June 30, 1986. Ann. Rept. Fla. Game and Fresh Water Fish Comm., Gainesville. 65 pp.

Rogers, A.J. 1953. A study of the ixodid ticks of northern Florida, including the biology and life history of *Ixodes scapularis* Say (Ixodidae: Acarina). Ph.D. diss., Univ. of Maryland, College Park. 176 pp.

Rubin, H.L. 1989. Unpublished data. Kissimmee Diagnostic Laboratory, Kissimmee, Fla.

Samuel, D.E., and B.B. Nelson. 1982. Foxes. In: Wild mammals of North America. J.A. Chapman and G.A. Feldhamer (eds.). Johns Hopkins Univ. Press, Baltimore. pp. 475–490.

Scatterday, J.E., N.J. Schneider, W.L. Jennings, and A.L. Lewis. 1960. Sporadic animal rabies in Florida. Pub. Health Rep. 75:945–953.

Schmidt, R.C., and R.K. Sikes. 1968. Immunization of foxes with inactivated-virus rabies vaccine. Am. J. Vet. Res. 29:1843–1847.

Seymour, C., and T.M. Yuill. 1981. Arboviruses. In: Infectious diseases of wild mammals. J.W. Davis et al. (eds.). Iowa State Univ. Press, Ames. pp. 54–86.

Sholtens, R.G., and L. Norman. 1971. *Trichinella spiralis* in Florida wildlife. J. Parasitol. 57:1103.

Stevenson, H.M. 1976. Vertebrates of Florida. Identification and distribution. Univ. Presses of Florida, Gainesville. 607 pp.

Stone, W.B., I.F. Salkin, and A. Martel. 1982. Sarcoptic mange in a gray fox. N.Y. Fish Game J. 29:102–103.

Stone, W.B., Jr., E. Parker, B.L. Weber, and F.J. Parks. 1972. Experimental transfer of sarcoptic mange from red foxes and wild canids to captive wildlife and domestic animals. N.Y. Fish Game J. 19:1–11.

Strickland, R.K., R.R. Gerrish, J.L. Hourigan, and G.O. Schubert. 1976. Ticks of veterinary importance. APHIS-USDA Agric. Handbook No. 485. U.S. Government Printing Office, Washington, D.C. 122 pp.

Todd, A.W., J.R. Gunson, and W.M. Samuel. 1981. Sarcoptic mange: An important disease of coyotes and wolves of Alberta, Canada. Proc. 1st Worldwide Furbearer Conf. Chapman and Pursely (eds.). R.R. Donnelly and Sons, Falls Church, Va. pp. 706–729.

Trainer, D.O., and J.B. Hale. 1969. Sarcoptic mange in red foxes and coyotes of Wisconsin. Bull. Wildl. Dis. Assoc. 5:387–391.

Travis, B.V. 1941. Examinations of wild animals for the cattle tick *Boophilus annulatus microplus* (Can.) in Florida. J. Parasitol. 27:465–467.

Wassmer, D.A. 1984. Movements and activity patterns of a gray fox in south-central Florida. Fla. Sci. 47:76–77.

White, F.H., and D.J. Forrester. 1985. Unpublished data. Univ. of Florida, Gainesville.

Wilson, N., and H.W. Kale II. 1972. Ticks collected from Indian River County, Florida (Acari: Metastigmata: Ixodidae). Fla. Entomol. 55:53–57.

Wood, J.E. 1954. Investigation of fox populations and sylvatic rabies in the southeast. Trans. No. Am. Wildl. Nat. Resour. Conf. 19:131–140.

Wood, J.E., and D.E. Davis. 1959. The prevalence of rabies in populations of foxes in the southern states. J. Am. Vet. Med. Assoc. 135:121–124.

Wright, S.D., and D.J. Forrester. 1988. Unpublished data. Univ. of Florida, Gainesville.

CHAPTER SEVENTEEN

Whales and Dolphins

I. Introduction

Twenty-nine species of cetaceans have been reported from Florida waters and beaches (Moore 1953; Layne 1965, 1978; Schmidly 1981; Caldwell and Caldwell 1983; Mead 1987; Perrin et al. 1987; Bonde and O'Shea 1989). Of these, six are baleen whales and 23 are toothed whales (Table 17-1). Five of these species—namely the sperm whale, sei whale, fin whale, humpback whale, and right whale—are classified by the Florida Game and Fresh Water Fish Commission and the U.S. Fish and Wildlife Service as endangered (Wood 1990). All 29 species are protected by the U.S. Marine Mammal Protection Act of 1972. Information on various aspects of nutrition, respiration, cardiovascular adjust-

ments, oxygen stores, thermoregulation, osmoregulation, reproductive physiology, hematology, and serum chemistry has been reviewed and summarized by a number of authors (Ridgway 1972; Leatherwood and Reeves 1982; Reeves and Brownell 1982; Geraci 1986; Sweeney 1986; Medway and Geraci 1986). The diseases of cetaceans were reviewed by Sweeney and Ridgway (1975), Howard (1983), and Dailey (1985). A checklist of parasites of marine mammals was provided by Dailey and Brownell (1972) and included an extensive section on cetaceans. Delyamure (1968) has published an excellent monograph on the taxonomy and ecology of helminths of marine mammals and Mawdes-

Table 17-1

Cetaceans reported from Florida waters and beaches

Scientific name	Common name
Suborder Mysticeti (Baleen whales)	
1. *Eubalaena glacialis*	Right whale[a]
2. *Balaenoptera borealis*	Sei whale[a]
3. *Balaenoptera physalus*	Fin whale[a]
4. *Balaenoptera edeni*	Bryde's whale
5. *Balaenoptera acutorostrata*	Minke whale
6. *Megaptera novaeangliae*	Humpback whale[a]
Suborder Odontoceti (Toothed whales)	
1. *Physeter catodon*	Sperm whale[a]
2. *Kogia breviceps*	Pygmy sperm whale
3. *Kogia simus*	Dwarf sperm whale
4. *Mesoplodon densirostris*	Dense-beaked whale
5. *Mesoplodon europaeus*	Antillean beaked whale
6. *Mesoplodon mirus*	True's beaked whale
7. *Mesoplodon bidens*	Sowerby's beaked whale
8. *Ziphius cavirostris*	Cuvier's beaked whale
9. *Feresa attenuata*	Pygmy killer whale
10. *Pseudorca crassidens*	False killer whale
11. *Orcinus orca*	Killer whale
12. *Globicephala macrorhynchus*	Short-finned pilot whale
13. *Steno bredanensis*	Rough-toothed dolphin
14. *Lagenodelphis hosei*	Fraser's dolphin
15. *Delphinus delphis*	Common dolphin
16. *Tursiops truncatus*	Bottlenosed dolphin
17. *Grampus griseus*	Risso's dolphin
18. *Stenella frontalis*	Atlantic spotted dolphin
19. *Stenella attenuata*	Pantropical spotted dolphin
20. *Stenella coeruleoalba*	Striped dolphin
21. *Stenella longirostris*	Spinner dolphin
22. *Stenella clymene*	Clymene dolphin
23. *Phocoena phocoena*	Harbor porpoise

Sources: Schmidly (1981); Caldwell and Caldwell (1983); Mead (1987); Perrin et al. (1987); Bonde and O'Shea (1989); Banks et al. (1987).
[a] Classified as endangered by the Florida Game and Fresh Water Fish Commission and the U.S. Fish and Wildlife Service (Wood 1990).

ley-Thomas (1974) published a review of neoplasia in cetaceans.

II. Environmental contaminants

Contamination of the marine environment with various chemicals such as organochlorines has been recognized since the early 1960s (Holden 1981). A number of authors have published data on residues of organochlorines in cetaceans in various parts of the world (Holden and Marsden 1967; Taruski et al. 1975; Alzieu and Duguy 1979; O'Shea et al. 1980; Wagemann and Muir 1984). Since marine mammals lack the enzymes needed to metabolize chlorinated hydrocarbons, they may accumulate residues of such compounds in higher concentrations than other mammals (Tanabe et al. 1988). Infor-

Table 17-2

Concentrations of organochlorines in 19 bottlenosed dolphins from Florida waters

Date collected	Locality	Sex	TL[a]	Sample[b]	Concentration (ppm wet wt)										
					pp'-DDT	pp'-DDE	pp'-DDD	op'-DDT	op'-DDE	Tot. DDT	PCB	Dieldrin	Hept. epox	Hept.	Lindane
1969–70	Off Marco Isl.	F	235	BL	4.1	15.0	3.6	NG[c]	NG	22.7	41.0	0.06	NG	NG	NG
1969–70	Off Marco Isl.	F	205	BL	3.6	6.7	7.8	NG	NG	18.1	29.0	0.05	NG	NG	NG
1969–70	Florida waters	U[d]	U	BL	0.7	1.0	NG	NG	NG	1.7	NG	NG	NG	NG	NG
1969–70	Florida waters	U	U	BL	11.4	16.8	NG	NG	NG	28.2	NG	NG	NG	NG	NG
1984	St. Lucie Co.	M	108	ME	6.6	9.3	ND[e]	ND	3.0	18.8	73.3	4.5	9.8	ND	0.4
1984	Indian R. Co.	M	165	ME	2.2	1.3	ND	ND	0.2	1.6	7.0	1.2	1.5	Tr[f]	Tr
1985	Brevard Co.	M	173	ME	18.2	11.4	12.4	2.6	1.1	44.7	79.6	5.4	9.1	ND	0.2
1986	Brevard Co.	M	176	ME	9.4	14.6	ND	1.9	5.2	21.7	97.1	6.1	14.7	0.5	0.4
1985	Volusia Co.	M	195	ME	9.3	5.5	ND	ND	2.5	17.4	142.5	3.9	8.3	ND	ND
1985	Monroe Co.	M	244	ME	16.3	26.9	ND	7.2	7.2	57.5	101.5	6.6	16.2	2.2	3.4
1983	Brevard Co.	M	255	ME	14.6	9.6	ND	ND	8.9	33.1	113.6	9.6	16.6	1.3	ND
1983	Brevard Co.	M	264	ME	9.7	11.9	ND	ND	10.1	31.7	111.7	10.0	21.7	0.6	ND
1983	Flagler Co.	F	97	ME	0.5	0.2	ND	ND	ND	0.8	1.8	0.4	0.3	Tr	Tr
1985	Brevard Co.	F	109	ME	2.5	2.6	ND	ND	1.3	6.4	33.6	1.2	3.3	ND	ND
1983	Brevard Co.	F	155	ME	2.0	2.1	ND	ND	0.6	4.7	2.2	1.0	3.4	0.4	0.3
1985	Brevard Co.	F	215	ME	0.3	0.2	ND	ND	0.1	0.5	35.3	0.3	0.3	ND	ND
1983	Brevard Co.	F	221	ME	2.6	1.8	ND	ND	0.5	2.3	21.4	1.9	2.5	Tr	0.1
1983	Brevard Co.	F	225	ME	4.0	3.0	1.5	1.3	0.4	10.3	31.9	ND	0.9	ND	0.1
1985	Brevard Co.	F	249	ME	3.0	2.2	ND	ND	0.9	6.1	11.1	1.7	2.4	0.4	0.1

Sources: The 1969–70 data are from Dudok van Heel (1972); the 1983–85 data are from King (1987).

[a]TL = total length in cm.
[b]BL = blubber, ME = melon.
[c]NG = not given by author.
[d]U = unknown.
[e]ND = none detected.
[f]Tr = trace amount (< 0.1 ppm).

mation on organochlorines has been reported for four species of cetaceans from Florida waters, including bottlenosed dolphins (Dudok van Heel 1972; King 1987), pygmy sperm whales (Odell and Asper 1976; King 1987), dwarf sperm whales (Odell and Asper 1976), and pygmy killer whales (Forrester et al. 1980).

The concentrations of DDT and its various metabolites and isomers, PCBs, dieldrin, heptachlor epoxide, heptachlor, lindane, and alpha benzine hexachloride are given for 19 bottlenosed dolphins (Table 17-2), 19 pygmy sperm whales (Table 17-3), and 3 pygmy killer whales (Table 17-4) from Florida waters. It is difficult to compare these findings with published data from other species of odontocetes because of a number of possible variables. King (1987) pointed out this problem and listed such factors as the history of pesticide usage and industrial activity on land masses nearby, differences in food habits, reproductive history, age, sex, distribution, and variations in analytical and reporting methods as being involved. Keeping these limitations in mind, it is still useful to compare data on cetaceans from Florida waters with those reported from animals in other parts of the world. The concentrations of DDT and PCBs in bottlenosed dolphins, pygmy sperm whales, and pygmy killer whales were within the low range of contamination reported from other species throughout the world (King 1987; Forrester et al. 1980). The one exception was that concentrations of PCBs in male bottlenosed dolphins were in the high range (King 1987). Males of all three species examined in Florida had higher concentrations than did females.

King (1987) showed that, in general, the concentrations of organochlorines were higher in bottlenosed dolphins than in pygmy sperm whales. This was attributed to differences in diet (bottlenosed dolphins are mainly

fish-eaters, pygmy sperm whales feed heavily on squid) and distribution (bottlenosed dolphins are mainly inshore animals, pygmy sperm whales are offshore animals). Presumably inshore animals would be more apt to be exposed to contamination than offshore species. It is of interest also to note that the concentrations of DDT reported by Odell and Asper (1976) and by King (1987) for pygmy sperm whales were very similar, indicating almost no change in the amounts of DDT in the ocean during the 10 years that elapsed between studies.

The effect of organochlorines on these cetaceans is unknown (Taruski et al. 1975; O'Shea et al. 1980; King 1987). Critical studies have not been conducted, but since these compounds are known to cause reproductive problems in other mammals and birds (O'Shea et al. 1980), there is reason for concern. Concentrations of DDE and PCBs have been shown to be inversely related to amounts of testosterone in Dall's porpoise (*Phocoenoides dalli*) in the Pacific Ocean, for example (Subramanian et al. 1987).

Dudok van Heel (1972) discussed data on bottlenosed dolphins that were captured in Florida waters and shipped to several locations in Europe where they were maintained for various periods of time in commercial aquaria. Sickness and death of several of these animals were attributed to mercury poisoning. One of the lines of evidence was the above normal concentration of mercury in blood and liver tissues (Tables 17-5 and 17-6) and the higher amounts of mercury in animals in captivity for the shortest length of time (Table 17-5). In addition, the author stated that other causes of morbidity and mortality (bacteria, viruses, etc.) were not established. He further stated that the contamination probably came from fish that the dolphins consumed in Florida waters. It must be noted, however, that he stated in one place in

Table 17-3

Concentrations of organochlorines in melon tissues of 19 pygmy sperm whales from Florida waters

Date collected	Locality	Sex	TL[a]	pp'-DDT	pp'-DDE	pp'-DDD	op'-DDT	op'-DDE	Tot. DDT	PCB	Diel-drin	Hept. epox	Hept.	Lindane
												Concentration (ppm wet wt)		
1985	Monroe Co.	M	161	1.8	2.1	0.8	0.7	0.2	5.6	6.1	0.3	0.5	ND[b]	0.1
1984	West Palm Beach Co.	M	164	1.0	0.5	0.3	0.4	0.1	2.3	1.1	ND	0.3	ND	ND
1983	Brevard Co.	M	278	3.8	2.3	0.7	0.8	0.3	8.0	7.7	ND	0.7	ND	ND
1983	Monroe Co.	M	290	7.6	14.7	1.3	1.3	0.7	25.6	10.3	ND	3.1	ND	ND
1984	Brevard Co.	M	311	6.9	10.8	1.2	0.9	1.4	21.2	2.3	ND	3.2	ND	ND
1985	Brevard Co.	M	320	1.1	0.8	0.4	0.3	0.1	1.6	8.3	ND	0.5	ND	0.1
1985	Brevard Co.	M	327	0.2	0.2	0.5	0.2	0.1	1.2	5.9	0.1	0.3	ND	ND
1983	Brevard Co.	M	335	2.6	2.7	0.5	0.5	0.1	3.7	11.8	ND	0.6	0.1	ND
1985	Volusia Co.	F	132	1.3	4.2	0.3	0.4	0.2	2.1	5.9	ND	0.6	ND	Tr
1984	Indian R. Co.	F	185	Tr[c]	Tr	ND	Tr	Tr	Tr	0.2	ND	Tr	ND	ND
1985	Brevard Co.	F	198	3.3	2.2	0.7	0.6	0.3	7.2	0.2	ND	0.9	ND	ND
1984	Palm Bch. Co.	F	218	1.9	0.7	0.7	0.3	0.1	3.8	1.7	ND	0.4	ND	ND
1983	Martin Co.	F	262	0.7	0.2	0.1	0.2	ND	1.2	1.5	Tr	0.1	ND	ND
1986	Volusia Co.	F	274	0.1	Tr	Tr	Tr	ND	0.2	0.4	ND	ND	ND	ND
1986	Volusia Co.	F	274	0.1	Tr	Tr	Tr	ND	0.2	0.4	ND	ND	ND	ND
1985	Volusia Co.	F	277	0.4	0.3	0.1	Tr	Tr	0.9	0.2	Tr	0.2	ND	ND
1986	St. Lucie Co.	F	292	0.2	0.2	Tr	Tr	Tr	0.3	0.3	ND	0.1	ND	ND
1983	Brevard Co.	F	318	0.6	0.4	Tr	0.1	0.1	1.7	0.4	ND	0.3	ND	ND
1985	Martin Co.	F	323	0.8	0.3	0.3	ND	0.1	1.6	2.3	0.2	0.3	ND	ND

Source: King (1987).
[a] TL = total length in cm.
[b] ND = none detected.
[c] Tr = trace amount (< 0.1 ppm).

Table 17-4

Concentrations of organochlorines in tissues of 3 stranded pygmy killer whales from Florida waters

Date collected	Locality	Sex	TL[a]	Sample[b]	Concentration (ppm wet wt)								
					DDE	DDD	DDT	Tot. DDT	PCB[c]	Dieldrin	Heptachlor	Lindane	αBHC
1975	St. Lucie Co.	M	172	ME	7.3	14.7	5.1	27.1	76.4	ND[d]	ND	ND	ND
				IF	4.7	5.8	12.6	23.1	79.0	Tr[e]	ND	ND	ND
1976	Franklin Co.	F	220	BR	1.7	0.5	1.5	3.7	0.4	ND	ND	ND	ND
				MU	0.8	0.5	1.1	2.4	0.6	ND	ND	ND	ND
				LI	0.2	0.2	Tr	0.4	Tr	ND	ND	ND	ND
				BL	2.0	0.8	2.0	4.8	0.8	ND	ND	ND	ND
1978	Martin Co.	M	221	ME	14.6	3.5	3.0	21.1	29.0	Tr	Tr	ND	ND
				IF	18.9	4.5	3.5	26.9	36.6	ND	Tr	ND	ND
				LI	2.4	0.5	ND	2.9	2.6	ND	Tr	ND	ND
				KI	0.4	0.1	Tr	0.5	1.2	Tr	Tr	Tr	Tr

Source: Forrester et al. (1980).
[a]TL = total length in cm.
[b]ME = melon, IF = intramandibular fat, BR = brain, MU = muscle, LI = liver, BL = blubber, KI = kidney.
[c]Aroclor 1254
[d]ND = none detected.
[e]Tr = trace amount (< 0.1 ppm).

Table 17-5
Concentrations of mercury in blood of 11 bottlenosed dolphins originating in
Florida waters

Dolphin no.	Sex	Date captured	Concentration of mercury (ppm)	
			March 1971	October 1971
1	M	Spring 1965	0.1	0.1
2	M	Spring 1965	NG[a]	0.1
3	F	May 1968	0.1	0.1
4	F	August 1969	0.2	20.2
5	F	September 1969	0.3	0.1
6	F	August 1969	0.3	0.2
7	F	August 1969	0.4	NG
8	F	February 1970	0.1	NG
9	F	February 1970	NG	0.1
10	M	December 1970	0.4	NG
11	F	December 1970	0.8	0.4

Source: Dudok van Heel (1972).
[a]NG = not given by author.

the paper that the food fish being given to the dolphins while they were in captivity were "clean" (i.e., free of toxins), but in another part of the paper he stated that the mackerel and herring that were fed to the dolphins contained mercury. Concentrations of other metals in the livers of five of the dolphins (Table 17-6) were considered to be within normal ranges (Dudok van Heel 1972).

Information on metals in two pygmy sperm whales (Table 17-7) and two dwarf sperm whales (Table 17-8) has been collected (Odell and Asper 1976). The significance of these findings is unknown. The high concentrations of copper and zinc in the liver and lead in the spermaceti organ and brain may be of concern.

Table 17-6
Concentrations (ppm) of heavy metals in liver tissues of 5 bottlenosed
dolphins from Florida waters, 1969–70

Metal	Sex and total length or weight				
	F	F	F	U[a]	U
	235 cm	205 cm	223 cm	130 kg	96 kg
Mercury	58.0	2.2	16.0	136.0	90.0
Selenium	19.0	1.4	6.0	NG[b]	NG
Arsenic	0.3	0.1	0.2	NG	NG
Cadmium	0.3	Tr[c]	0.2	NG	NG
Zinc	43.0	41.0	66.0	NG	NG
Antimony	Tr	Tr	Tr	NG	NG

Source: Dudok van Heel (1972).
[a]U = unknown.
[b]NG = not given by author.
[c]Tr = trace amount (< 0.1 ppm).

Table 17-7

Concentrations of trace metals in tissues from a female pygmy sperm whale and her calf that stranded in Dade County on March 13, 1974

Age	Sex	Length (cm)	Sample	Concentration (ppm)						
				Cr[a]	Cd	Pb	Zn	Cu	Mn	Ag
Adult	F	315	Liver	0.8	7.6	1.1	10.1	2.1	0.8	0.6
			Blubber	5.0	0.5	ND[b]	3.5	0.9	1.0	NS[c]
			Melon	5.2	0.4	ND	4.0	0.3	0.3	NS
			Spermaceti organ	7.0	0.6	ND	4.3	0.5	0.1	NS
			Spermaceti oil	1.5	0.4	ND	1.8	0.2	0.2	NS
Calf	F	156	Liver	4.0	0.2	ND	NS	76.1	NS	0.1
			Blubber	6.2	0.3	ND	2.9	2.3	NS	NS
			Melon	7.7	0.4	ND	4.3	0.9	0.3	NS
			Spermaceti organ	4.9	0.4	42.8	5.9	0.3	0.4	NS
			Intramandibular fat	5.9	0.2	ND	1.5	0.2	0.3	NS

Source: Odell and Asper (1976).
[a]Cr = chromium, Cd = cadmium, Pb = lead, Zn = zinc, Cu = copper, Mn = manganese, Ag = silver.
[b]ND = none detected.
[c]NS = no sample.

Table 17-8

Concentrations of trace metals in tissues from 2 dwarf sperm whales stranded on Florida beaches in 1974

Age	Sex	Length (cm)	Sample	Concentration (ppm)						
				Cr[a]	Cd	Pb	Zn	Cu	Mn	Ag
Adult[b]	M	190	Liver	2.7	1.3	ND[c]	15.0	17.3	2.6	0.1
			Blubber	3.6	0.4	ND	3.3	0.3	0.1	NS[d]
			Melon	1.5	0.2	ND	1.5	0.5	0.5	NS
			Spermaceti organ	3.1	0.2	ND	1.4	0.1	0.1	NS
			Intramandibular fat	5.7	0.3	ND	4.1	0.3	0.1	NS
			Kidney	3.3	3.4	ND	NS	2.1	0.9	NS
			Brain	4.8	0.2	43.9	5.3	3.2	0.7	Tr[e]
			Muscle	4.8	0.2	ND	12.0	1.4	0.8	NS
Calf[f]	M	100	Liver	4.1	0.2	ND	11.4	144.4	4.1	0.2
			Blubber	5.2	0.5	ND	2.9	0.7	0.1	NS
			Melon	25.0	0.2	ND	NS	2.1	NS	NS
			Intramandibular fat	3.6	0.1	ND	2.9	0.5	0.7	NS

Source: Odell and Asper (1976).
[a]Cr = chromium, Cd = cadmium, Pb = lead, Zn = zinc, Cu = copper, Mn = manganese, Ag = silver.
[b]Stranded in Brevard County on July 19, 1974.
[c]ND = none detected.
[d]NS = no sample.
[e]Tr = trace amount (< 0.1 ppm).
[f]Stranded in Brevard County on June 12, 1974.

III. Toxicosis

During the 11-month period from June 1987 to May 1988, large numbers of bottlenosed dolphins died along the Atlantic Coast (Scott et al. 1988). These mortalities began in the coastal area of New Jersey and worked their way southward and eventually reached Florida. In all at least 740 dolphins died, 108 of which died in Florida waters (east coast) from November 1987 to May 1988 (Geraci 1989). It has been estimated that 50% or more of the coastal migratory bottlenosed dolphins located between Florida and New Jersy succumbed during this epizootic (Scott et al. 1988). Necropsy findings in some cases were dramatic. Many animals had skin lesions consisting of blisters, craters, and sloughing of large areas of skin. Some had multiple changes associated with septicemia that led to edema and the accumulation of large amounts of blood-tinged fluids in the body cavities. These and other observations are detailed in the report by Geraci (1989). After extensive studies involving numerous laboratories and individuals over an 18-month period, it was concluded that the proximate cause of the mortality was brevetoxin, a powerful neurotoxin produced by a dinoflagellate, the red tide organism *Ptychodiscus brevis* (Geraci 1989). It was believed that secondary microbial infections (viruses, bacteria, and fungi) and immune suppression were sequels to exposure to brevetoxin and caused the ultimate demise of the dolphins. Concentrations of contaminants such as chlorinated hydrocarbons were extremely high and may have contributed also to the problem by increasing the susceptibility of the dolphins to the brevetoxin or the secondary microbial infections that followed (Geraci 1989).

The details of this extraordinary event are incompletely understood at this time, but dolphins may have been exposed to the brevetoxin via consumption of planktivorous fish (such as menhaden) that had become contaminated by a persistent bloom of the red tide organism. In addition to the coverage in papers by Scott et al. (1988) and Geraci (1989), this massive die-off and its various implications are discussed by Steidinger (1989) and Anderson and White (1989). Gunter et al. (1948) reported "a small number" of bottlenosed dolphins dying during a red tide incident near Fort Myers in 1946–1947, but it is not clear if these deaths were a result of the red tide or merely coincidental with it. Steidinger (1989) concluded that deaths of dolphins due to brevetoxin are "rare events due to unusual timing and environmental conditions" (p. 62). The details of these "conditions" are poorly known and in need of further investigation. The reader is referred to Chapter 19 for a discussion of a die-off of Florida manatees in association with a red tide.

IV. Neoplasia

One case of neoplasia has been reported from a cetacean in Florida waters. In August 1974 an aged bottlenosed dolphin was captured in a weakened condition in the Gulf of Mexico near St. Petersburg Beach (Goldston et al. 1974; Migaki et al. 1978). After four months in captivity the animal was killed because of an actively advancing case of Lobo's disease. At necropsy a solitary renal adenoma was an incidental finding. No evidence of metastases was seen in the regional lymph nodes or in other organs of the dolphin. This tumor was probably of little consequence to the dolphin, but constitutes the first report of a renal adenoma in cetaceans.

V. Cardiomyopathy

Bossart et al. (1985) studied 23 pygmy sperm whales and 6 dwarf sperm whales that had stranded singly or in cow-calf pairs over a four-year period in the southeastern United States, including many from Florida (the exact number not given). They felt that 18 adults and 1 immature whale may have died due to congestive heart failure (Table 17-9). Histopathologic studies indicated that the cardiomyopathy was chronic and progressive rather than acute and terminal. The authors suggested that congestive heart failure and the accompanying hepatic compromise in adult whales would lead to debilitation and subsequently to beaching, depending on ocean currents and weather conditions. Calf strandings would occur along with an adult cow due to maternal bonding (Bossart et al. 1985). Both pygmy sperm whales and dwarf sperm whales strand as singles or as cow-calf pairs rather than in mass strandings as seen in other species (Schmidly 1981). The observations and interpretations of Bossart et al. (1985) may help explain this phenomenon that occurs commonly on Florida beaches. Unfortunately it was not possible for Bossart and coworkers to examine "normal" (non-stranding) adults of *Kogia* spp. to compare the condition of their cardiac tissues with those of stranded animals.

VI. Neuropathology

A four-year study was conducted to assess neurologic disease in stranded and captive cetaceans in Florida (Schimpff and Hall 1979; Hall and Schimpff 1979; Hall et al. 1977). In examinations of more than 75 animals of 7 species, only one case of severe neurologic disease was found. This was a massive intracerebral hemorrhage in a captive bottlenosed dolphin (Hall et al. 1977). The etiology of this hematoma was not established. Three other bottlenosed dolphins (two captive and one stranded) had less severe cases of cerebrovascular disease. One had arterial thrombosis, one a subarachnoid hemorrhage in the cerebral cortex, and one a subarachnoid hemorrhage over the lower brainstem (Schimpff and Hall 1979). Another dolphin (an Atlantic spotted dolphin that died on St. Petersburg Beach) had chronic meningitis.

Table 17-9
Numbers of pygmy and dwarf sperm whales with cardiomyopathy stranded along the coast of the southeastern United States

Species of whale	Age (total length in cm)	Sex	No. whales exam.	No. whales with cardiomyopathy
Pygmy sperm whales	Adult (> 270)	M	8	8
		F	7	7
	Immature (185–270)	M	1	0
		F	2	0
	Calf (< 185)	M	2	0
		F	3	0
Dwarf sperm whales	Adult (> 210)	M	1	1
		F	2	2
	Immature (120–210)	M	3	1
		F	0	—
	Calf (<120)	M	0	—
		F	0	—

Source: Bossart et al. (1985).

One of 23 pygmy sperm whales that stranded had severe, diffuse subdural cerebral hemorrhage along with associated adjacent soft tissue hemorrhage (Bossart et al. 1985). This animal was sexually immature.

In July 1980 a striped dolphin stranded near Pensacola Beach (Escambia County). The animal was kept in a recovery pool and had equilibrium problems (Townsend 1987). Two days later it died. At necropsy the brain was observed to have irregular-shaped areas of brownish discoloration on the surface of the frontal, temporal, and occipital lobes of the right cerebral hemisphere (Figure 17-1). Microscopically these were multifocal areas of liquifactive necrosis within which were trematode eggs (Figure 17-2). In one of the necrotic areas a section of an adult trematode was seen (Figure 17-3). Eggs were also seen in the meninges. These eggs and the adult are probably a species of *Nasitrema* (Buergelt 1980).

In June 1985 a pantropical spotted dolphin was found stranded near Fort Walton Beach (Okaloosa County). In captivity it was observed to be incoordinated and in a few days died with seizures (Townsend 1987). At necropsy the cerebrum had a granulomatous lesion. When sectioned it was found to contain trematode eggs, probably of *Nasitrema* sp. Associated with the eggs were giant cells, macrophages, perivascular cuffing with lymphocytes, neuronal swelling and degeneration, and hemorrhage (Calderwood-Mays 1985).

Townsend (1987) reported two other single strandings in the Fort Walton Beach area. One involved a pantropical spotted dolphin

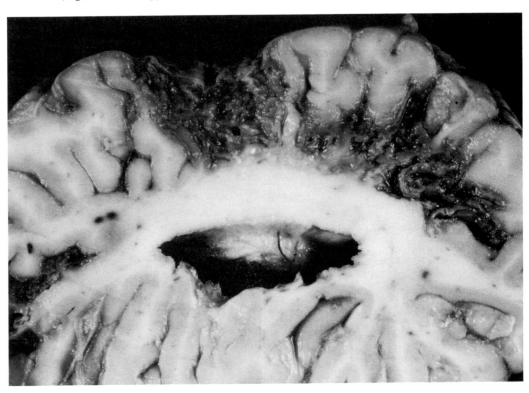

FIGURE 17-1. Cross-section of the cerebrum of a striped dolphin that stranded near Pensacola Beach in 1980. Note the malacic cavitating lesion. (Photograph courtesy of Drs. C.D. Buergelt and F.I. Townsend.)

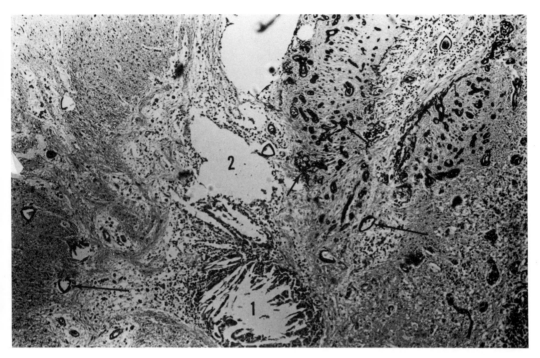

FIGURE 17-2. Photomicrograph of the cerebrum of the striped dolphin referred to in Figure 17-1. Lesion includes cholesterol clefts (1), cavitations (2), mineralized blood vessels (short arrows), and scattered inflammatory cells. Trematode eggs (long arrows) are seen in numerous areas. (Photograph courtesy of Drs. C.D. Buergelt and F.I. Townsend.)

(1984) and the other a rough-toothed dolphin (1985). Trematode eggs resembling those of *Nasitrema* sp. were seen histologically in brain tissue of both of these animals (Calderwood-Mays 1984; Russell 1985).

Neurologic disease may play a role in some single strandings, but significant evidence has not been found in cetaceans involved in mass strandings (i.e., strandings of three or more animals) to implicate brain disease as a primary cause.

VII. Bacterial diseases

Many different bacteria have been isolated from cetaceans in various parts of the world, and are of particular importance in captive animals (Dailey 1985). Very little is known about bacterial infections in cetaceans from Florida waters, however. In 1974 staphylococcal pneumonia was diagnosed in an old male bottlenosed dolphin found in moribund condition near St. Petersburg Beach. The animal was taken into captivity and successfully treated with chloromycetin (Goldston et al. 1974), but four months later was killed because of complications due to Lobo's disease (Migaki et al. 1978).

An outbreak of erysipelas septicemia occurred in four captive bottlenosed dolphins that had been captured six to eight months previously in Florida waters (Geraci et al. 1966). It was not clear if the dolphins became infected while in captivity or if they were carriers of the organism (*Erysipelothrix rusiopathiae*) when captured and the disease was manifested subsequently under influence of

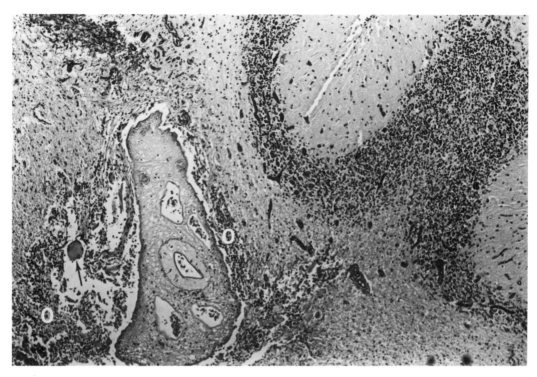

FIGURE 17-3. Photomicrograph of the cerebellum of the striped dolphin referred to in Figure 17-1. Section shows a trematode (probably *Nasitrema* sp.) surrounded by mononuclear (O) and multinuclear (arrow) giant cells. (Photograph courtesy of Drs. C.D. Buergelt and F.I. Townsend.)

unknown predisposing factors as has been shown in domestic swine (Gillespie and Timoney 1981). The authors tested some of the fishes used as food for the dolphins, but were unable to culture *E. rusiopathiae* (Geraci et al. 1966). Seibold et al. (1956) also reported *E. rusiopathiae* from a captive Atlantic spotted dolphin in Florida. This disease has been reported from other cetaceans (Simpson et al. 1958; Ridgway 1972; Sweeney and Ridgway 1975), but its importance to dolphin populations is unknown. This is a zoonotic disease and therefore of public health significance.

Nocardiosis has been diagnosed in the lungs of a pygmy sperm whale (Pier et al. 1970) and from the mouth and snout of a captive bottlenosed dolphin (Jasmin et al. 1972) in Florida. The species from the dolphin was determined to be *Nocardia paraquayensis;* the species from the pygmy sperm whale was not identified. Such reports of nocardial infections in cetaceans are rare and mostly are known from captive animals (Pier et al. 1970). Infection probably occurred from contamination by soil or ocean sediments. This bacterial disease is also of zoonotic concern (Hunter et al. 1976).

Various tissues and organs (including intestines) of several stranded cetaceans were cultured by White and Forrester (1988). These included three short-finned pilot whales (Fort George Inlet, 1978) and one bottlenosed dolphin (Indian River, 1978). No pathogenic bacteria were recovered.

VIII. Mycotic diseases

Five mycotic diseases, all of which are zoonoses, have been reported from captive and free-

Table 17-10
Systemic mycoses reported from captive cetaceans in facilities in
Florida

Mycotic disease	Cetacean	Data source
Candidiosis	Killer whale	Sweeney et al. (1976)
	Bottlenosed dolphin	Bossart & Bossart (1982)
Aspergillosis	Bottlenosed dolphin	Carroll et al. (1968)
Mucormycosis	Bottlenosed dolphin	Sweeney et al. (1976)
Entomophthoromycosis	Bottlenosed dolphin	Migaki & Blumer (1975)

ranging cetaceans in Florida (Tables 17-10 and 17-11). Systemic mycoses, although known from both free-ranging and captive cetaceans (Dailey 1985), appear primarily to be problems of captive animals (Table 17-10). Pulmonary involvement characterizes most of these systemic mycoses. In their review Sweeney et al. (1976) pointed out that soil is the natural source of fungal infections. Cetaceans are infected via contaminated water. Infection of the cetacean occurs when resistance or immunity is depressed by such factors as chronic disease or stress. The high prevalence of systemic mycoses in captive animals, therefore, is most likely related to stress over a prolonged period of time due to conditions of confinement, movement to unfamiliar environments, and poor husbandry techniques (Sweeney et al. 1976).

Lobomycosis (also known as Lobo's disease or keloidal blastomycosis) is a chronic skin infection caused by the fungus *Loboa loboi* and in Florida has been found only in free-ranging bottlenosed dolphins (Table 17-11). Before being reported in dolphins, lobomycosis was known from humans in Central and South America (Migaki et al. 1971). Over 100 cases in humans have been documented (Caldwell et al. 1975). In addition to bottlenosed dolphins the disease has been found in one free-ranging river dolphin (*Sotalia guayanensis*) in Surinam (DeVries and Laarman

Table 17-11
Confirmed cases of lobomycosis reported from free-ranging bottlenosed
dolphins in Florida waters

Date	Sex	Total length (cm)	Location	Data source
March 1970	F	235	Sarasota	Migaki et al. (1971), Migaki & Robinson (1974)
March 1970	F	237	Vero Beach	Woodard (1972), Caldwell et al. (1975)
August 1974	M	NG[a]	St. Petersburg Beach	Goldston et al. (1974), Migaki et al. (1978)
NG	M	246	Fort Lauderdale	Bossart (1984)

Note: As noted in the text, Caldwell et al. (1975) reported a number of other probable cases of lobomycosis in bottlenosed dolphins in addition to the 4 confirmed cases given in this table. Their presumptive diagnoses, based on photographs and descriptions, included animals from off Cedar Key, St. Augustine, Oak Hill, Fort Pierce, and Florida Bay.
[a]NG = not given by authors.

1973). The lesions of this disease occur as white patches, crusts, or raised bumps (Figure 17-4). When examined microscopically they are found to consist of large, discrete, histiocytic granulomas in the dermis that result in severe acanthosis (Migaki et al. 1971). These usually occur on the top of the head, the dorsal fin, the top of the caudal peduncle, and on the tail flukes (Caldwell et al. 1975). The disease can result in loss of mobility and death (Dailey 1985). Woodard (1972) studied the ultrastructure of the lesions. Caldwell et al. (1975) presented an excellent historic and geographic summary of documented cases of lobomycosis in dolphins and provided a number of observations of probable infections in other free-ranging bottlenosed dolphins. The disease dates back at least to 1955 and its distribution includes both coasts of Florida. Caldwell and coworkers (1975) also pointed

out that most of the diseased animals (collected and observed) were from protected waters or were close to land and concluded that infected free-ranging dolphins may live for several years. The full importance of this disease in cetacean populations is not clear.

IX. Protozoans

Several protozoan parasites have been reported from cetaceans in Florida. Woodard et al. (1969) and Caldwell et al. (1971) reported an unidentified holotrich ciliate from the bottlenosed dolphin (24 of 56 were infected), the striped dolphin (1 of 1), and Risso's dolphin (2 of 3). Positive animals were found on both the Atlantic and Gulf coasts of northern Florida. The ciliates were located within the blowhole and in the air passages

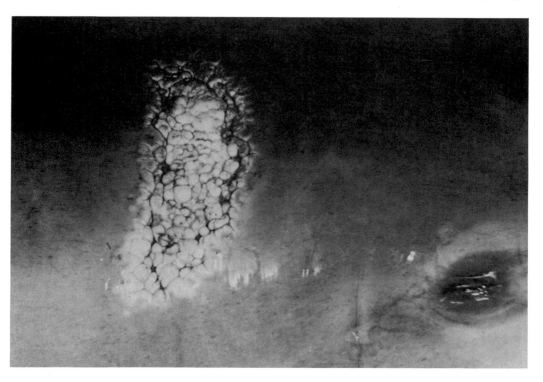

FIGURE 17-4. Skin lesion of lobomycosis in a bottlenosed dolphin from Florida waters. (From Caldwell et al. 1975.)

of the lungs (Caldwell et al. 1971). At necropsy one bottlenosed dolphin had large amounts of yellowish, solidified puriform material in its larynx, trachea, and stem bronchi. There were pneumonic areas in the lungs that contained numerous ciliates (Woodard et al. 1969). Most of the ciliates were in the alveolar spaces. Sometimes ciliates were seen within the lung parenchyma. The full significance of these protozoans to populations of dolphins is not understood.

Unidentified ciliates have been found also in skin lesions of bottlenosed dolphins in Florida (Howard 1983; Inskeep et al. 1990), but are probably opportunistic parasites (Dailey 1985).

Eight bottlenosed dolphins from various locations in Florida waters were examined serologically for antibodies to *Toxoplasma gondii* (Burridge et al. 1979). All were negative. However, *T. gondii* was identified histologically (Figure 17-5) in tissues of a female bottlenosed dolphin and her calf that stranded on Picnic Island in Tampa Bay in 1987 (Goldston 1988; Inskeep et al. 1990). A third case of *T. gondii* infection in a bottlenosed dolphin was reported by Cruickshank et al. (1990) from an immature male found near Ocean Beach, Florida, in 1988. Apparently these are the first reports of *T. gondii* in cetaceans, although it has been found in pinnipeds (Lauckner 1985) and sirenians (Buergelt and Bonde 1983).

X. Helminths

Information is available on helminths of 12 species of odontocete whales and dolphins from Florida waters and beaches (Tables 17-12 through 17-21). Several helminths are significant from a disease standpoint and include species of four genera of nematodes (*Anisakis, Stenurus, Halocercus,* and *Crassi-*

cauda) and four genera of trematodes (*Nasitrema, Campula, Pholeter,* and *Braunina*). The cestodes and the acanthocephalan apparently cause little harm (Dailey 1985).

Species of the genus *Anisakis* are common and have been found in 10 species of odontocetes that have been examined in Florida (Tables 17-12 through 17-20). These nematodes attach to the mucosa of the stomach and may provoke granulomatous nodules (Dailey 1985), although such lesions have not been reported from Florida cetaceans. *Anisakis* spp. are also important because of infections they cause in man (Van Thiel 1962). Fish serve as intermediate hosts (Dailey et al. 1981).

Stenurus species have been found in the cranial sinuses and lungs of pygmy killer whales (Table 17-14) and false killer whales (Table 17-15), and in the cranial sinuses of short-finned pilot whales (Table 17-21) from Florida waters. Some authors have suggested that infections by this nematode in the cranial sinuses, eustachian tubes, and middle ears may cause echolocation problems and result in strandings (e.g., Delyamure 1968), but others disagree (see review by Dailey 1985). An intermediate host may be required in the life cycle of *Stenurus* species, but this has not been determined.

Lung nematodes of the genus *Halocercus* have been reported from bottlenosed dolphins (Table 17-17) and pantropical spotted dolphins (Table 17-19) in Florida. Mucopurulent bronchiolitis and verminous pneumonia were described in several bottlenosed dolphins (captive and wild) infected with *H. lagenorhynchi,* but not all animals infected with the lungworms exhibited clinical signs of disease (Caldwell et al. 1968; Woodard et al. 1969). The importance of infections of *Halocercus* as mortality factors in cetaceans is not fully understood (Dailey 1985). Other factors may interact with lungworm infec-

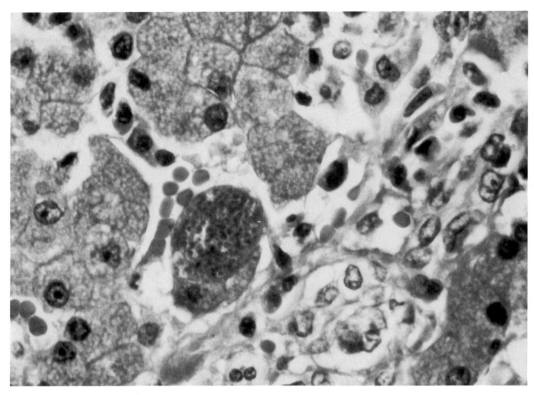

FIGURE 17-5. Cyst of *Toxoplasma gondii* in liver of a bottlenosed dolphin that stranded near St. Petersburg in 1987. (Photograph courtesy of Drs. S.D. Wright and R.T. Goldston.)

tions and result in morbidity and mortality, but these conditions remain unknown. The life cycle of these nematodes has not been determined.

Townsend (1987) recovered a live-stranded and debilitated Cuvier's beaked whale in April 1982 near Panama City Beach (Bay County). After two weeks in captivity the animal died and at necropsy severe chronic verminous nephritis and ureteritis due to an infection by the nematode *Crassicauda* sp. were found (Figure 17-6) (Stetzer 1983). There was massive destruction of entire lobules of the kidney with fibrosis, necrosis, and mixed inflammatory cell infiltrates composed of lymphocytes, plasma cells, macrophages, neutrophils, and eosinophils. Sections of the ureter showed total destruction of the transitional epithelium and underlying

submucosal tissues along with a mixed inflammatory cell infiltrate (Stetzer 1983). In 1986 and 1987 two additional single-stranded Cuvier's beaked whales were found near Panama City Beach. Both had kidney infections of *Crassicauda* sp. that were judged to be moderate to severe (Bonde 1987; Buergelt 1988; Hines 1986). Several species of *Crassicauda* have been found in a number of toothed and baleen whales in various parts of the world (Dailey 1985). The life cycle of these extremely pathogenic nematodes is unknown.

Trematodes of the genus *Nasitrema* are common in odontocetes and in Florida have been found in pygmy killer whales (Table 17-14), bottlenosed dolphins (Table 17-17), pantropical spotted dolphins (Table 17-19), striped dolphins (Table 17-20), and short-

Table 17-12

Helminths reported from pygmy and dwarf sperm whales from waters in northeastern Florida

Helminth	Location in host[a]	No. whales inf.
	Pygmy sperm whales (n = 7)	
Cestoda		
Phyllobothrium delphini (cysticerci)	(1)	3
Nematoda		
Anisakis typica	(2)	5
	Dwarf sperm whales (n = 3)	
Cestoda		
Phyllobothrium delphini (cysticerci)	(1)	3
Nematoda		
Anisakis catodontis	(3)	1
Anisakis typica	(2)	1

Source: Zam et al. (1971).
[a](1) Encysted in blubber, especially on ventral side near anus, (2) forestomach, fundic stomach, pyloric stomach, and the ampulla of the duodenum, (3) forestomach and fundic stomach.

Table 17-13

Helminths reported in a dense-beaked whale from northeastern Florida

Helminth	Location in host
Cestode	
Phyllobothrium delphini (cysticerci)	Blubber layer, primarily on ventral side
Nematoda	
Anisakis simplex	Forestomach
Acanthocephala	
Bolbosoma vasculosum	Intestines

Source: Zam et al. (1971).

finned pilot whales (Table 17-21). The adults of *Nasitrema* are found in the air sinuses of the head and in the eustachian tubes. Sometimes they are found in the lungs as well (Dailey 1985). These trematodes are mobile and often migrate to the brain (Figure 17-3). Dailey and Walker (1978) found adult *Nasitrema* in brains of 18 of 24 (75%) common dolphins that had stranded (single strandings) along the coast of southern California, whereas none of 17 common dolphins that were drowned accidentally in fishing nets off the coast of southern California (i.e., non-stranded controls) had flukes in their brains. Dailey (1985) wrote that these "results clearly indicated that trematodes of the genus *Nasitrema* were the primary cause of single stranding of cetaceans in the area" (p. 817). Four single-stranded dolphins (one striped dolphin in 1980, two pantropical spotted dolphins in 1984 and 1985, and one rough-toothed dolphin in 1985) from the Pensacola/Fort Walton Beach area were found to have trematode eggs in brain tissue (Buergelt 1980; Calderwood-Mays 1984, 1985; Russell 1985). Three of the dolphins were obtained alive and exhibited signs of CNS disease (Townsend 1987). In one of the animals a

Table 17-14
Helminths reported in 7 pygmy killer whales from Florida waters

Helminth	Location in host[a]	No. whales		Intensity	Date	Geographic location	Data source
		Exam.	Inf.				
Cestoda							
Tetrabothrius forsteri	(3)	1	1	"Several"	January 1976	Franklin Co.	Forrester et al. (1980)
		1	1	"Several"	July 1975	St. Lucie Co.	Conti & Frohlich (1984)
Tetrabothrids	(1)	1	1	"Several"	May 1971	Lake Worth	White (1976)
Tetraphyllidean larvae	(5)	1	1	623	January 1976	Franklin Co.	Forrester et al. (1980)
Trigonocotyle sp.	(3)	3	3	6,600, 7,200, 14,500	January 1981	Bay Co.	Conti & Frohlich (1984)
		1	1	2,328	January 1976	Franklin Co.	Forrester et al. (1980) Conti & Frohlich (1984)
Trematoda							
Pholeter gastrophilus	(2, 3)	3	2	1, 3	January 1981	Bay Co.	" " "
Nasitrema lanceolata	(4)	1	1	384[b]	January 1976	Franklin Co.	Forrester et al. (1980)
		1	1	ND[c]	July 1975	St. Lucie Co.	" " " "
		1	1	ND	March 1978	Martin Co.	" " " "
Nematoda							
Stenurus globicephalae	(4)	1	1	ND	July 1975	St. Lucie Co.	Forrester et al. (1980)
	(6)	1	1	5	January 1976	Franklin Co.	" " " "
Pseudalids	(6)	1	1	2	January 1976	Franklin Co.	" " " "
Anisakis typica	(1, 2)	3	3	51, 145, 166	January 1981	Bay Co.	Conti & Frohlich (1984)
Filocapsularia sp.	(1)	1	1	"Several hundred"	May 1971	Lake Worth	White (1976)

[a](1) forestomach, (2) fundic stomach, (3) intestine, (4) cranial sinuses, (5) liver, (6) lungs.
[b]Two immature specimens of *Nasitrema* sp. were found also in the lungs of this animal.
[c]ND = not determined.

Table 17-15
Helminths reported in 8 false killer whales from Florida waters

Helminth	Location in host[a]	No. whales		Intensity	Date	Geographic location	Data source
		Exam.	Inf.				
Trematoda							
Orthosplanchnus elongatus	(1)	2	1	NG[b]	NG	NE Florida	Zam et al. (1971)
Nematoda							
Anisakis simplex	(2)	2	1	NG	NG	Near Fort Pierce[c]	" " " "
	(2)	6	3	NG	July 1976	Near North Captiva Island	Odell et al. (1980)
Anisakis typica	(2)	2	1	NG	NG	Near Daytona Beach[c]	Zam et al. (1971)
Stenurus auditivus	(3)	2	1	NG	NG	Near New Smyrna Beach	" " " "
Stenurus globicephalae	(3)	6	5	"Hundreds"	July 1976	Near North Captiva Island	Odell et al. (1980)
	(4)	6	4	NG	July 1976	" "	" " " "
Acanthocephala							
Bolbosoma capitatum	(5)	6	6	"Hundreds"	July 1976	"	" " " "

[a](1) hepatico-pancreatic duct, (2) stomach, (3) cranial sinuses, (4) lungs, (5) small intestines.
[b]NG = not given by authors.
[c]See Caldwell et al. (1970) for more details on geographic location.

Table 17-16
Helminths of two rough-toothed dolphins from Florida waters,
November 1974

Helminth	Location in host[a]	Adult male dolphin	Adult female dolphin
Cestoda			
Tetrabothrius forsteri	(2)	34	10
Larvae[b]	(3)	0	160
Trematoda			
Campula palliata	(3, 4)	129	218
Pholeter gastrophilus	(1)	11	13
Synthesium tursionis	(2)	0	22
Nematoda			
Anisakis typica[c]	(1, 2)	22	29
Total no. of helminths		196	452

Source: Forrester and Robertson (1975). These two dolphins were found stranded on a sandbar six miles southeast of the mouth of the Suwannee River in the Gulf of Mexico.
[a](1) forestomach, (2) intestine, (3) liver, (4) bile duct.
[b]Probably a larval tetraphyllidean cestode.
[c]Layne (1965) reported roundworms in the stomach of 1 of 11 rough-toothed dolphins that stranded on the coast of Taylor County in May 1961. These may have been anisakid nematodes, but were not specifically identified.

section of an adult fluke was observed histologically (Figure 17-3). From the size and shape of the eggs (Figure 17-2), these were probably a species of *Nasitrema*. This fluke, therefore, may be the cause of some single strandings of odontocetes in Florida as was observed by Dailey and Walker (1978) in California. Morimitsu et al. (1986, 1987) presented evidence that adults of *Nasitrema gondo* may have caused mass strandings of the many-toothed blackfish (*Peponocephala electra*), short-finned pilot whales, and false killer whales in Japan. Numerous flukes were found in the tympanic cavity and were associated also with damage to the octavus nerve, which the authors felt would account for the equilibrium problems and subsequent stranding.

Several species of *Campula* have been found in the ducts of the pancreas and liver of a number of odontocetes in Florida waters (see Tables 17-16 through 17-20). *Campula palliata* was associated with chronic interstitial fibrosis in the pancreas and liver of several bottlenosed dolphins, but the lesions were not judged to be of clinical significance (Woodard et al. 1969).

Pholeter gastrophilus and *Braunina cordiformis* occur commonly in the stomach of cetaceans and a number of infections have been encountered in Florida (see Tables 17-14, and 17-16 through 17-19). The localized lesions caused by these two trematodes have been described (Schryver et al. 1967; Woodard et al. 1969), but probably do not result in serious pathological consequences (Dailey 1985).

XI. Ectoparasites and associates

A variety of organisms are found attached to cetaceans (Dailey 1985). In Florida there are records of copepods, barnacles, and amphipods (whale lice) (Table 17-22). Some of these, such as the barnacles, are probably not parasites but rather are usually associates or epizoites that cause little or no harm. Cald-

Table 17-17

Helminths reported from bottlenosed dolphins in Florida waters

Helminth	Location in host[a]	No. dolphins Exam.	Inf.	Geographic location	Data source
Trematoda					
Campula oblonga	(1)	53	2	NE Florida	Zam et al. (1971)
Campula delphini	(2)	53	2	NE Florida	" " " "
Campula palliata	(2)	53	3	NE Florida	" " " "
Campula sp.	(2)	53	2	NE Florida	" " " "
Nasitrema delphini	(3)	17	2	NE Florida	" " " "
Pholeter gastrophilus	(4)	56	11	NE Florida	" " " "
		2	1	Tampa Bay	Inskeep et al. (1990)
Braunina cordiformis	(5)	64	30	NE Florida, NE and SW Gulf of Mexico	Zam et al. (1971)
		NG[b]	NG	St. Petersburg Beach	Hutton (1964)
		1	1	Titusville	Forrester (1987)
		2	2	"Florida"	McIntosh (1953)
		2	1	Tampa Bay	Inskeep et al. (1990)
Cestoda					
Diphyllobothrium sp.	(6)	6	1	NE Florida	Zam et al. (1971)
Nematoda					
Anisakis typica	(7)	63	3	NE Florida	Zam et al. (1971)
Anisakis tursiopis	(7)	63	1	NE Florida	" " " "
Anisakis marina	(7)	63	1	NE Florida	" " " "
Halocercus lagenorhynchi	(8)	59	46	NE Florida, NE Gulf of Mexico	" " " "
Gnathostoma sp.	(9)	60	1	NE Florida	" " " "

[a](1) pancreatic ducts, (2) ducts of the pancreas and/or liver, (3) cranial sinuses, (4) within cysts in the walls of the fundic and/or pyloric stomachs, (5) fundic stomach, pyloric stomach, or ampulla of the duodenum, (6) intestines, (7) forestomach, (8) air passages of lungs, (9) exact location unknown (found lying on surface of liver during necropsy).
[b]NG = not given by author.

well (1988), however, found one case of a large number of stalked barnacles (*Conchoderma auritum*) associated with severe erosion of the lips of a pilot whale.

The copepod *Harpacticus pulex* was found associated with skin lesions of a captive bottlenosed dolphin (Humes 1964), but it was not clear if the copepods caused the lesions or secondarily invaded lesions caused by something else. This copepod has not been found on free-ranging dolphins; all other known species of *Harpacticus* are free-living (Lauckner 1985).

Whale lice have been found in association with skin lesions of bottlenosed dolphins and

pygmy sperm whales (Caldwell et al. 1971), but these may have been opportunistic associations. These amphipods cause minor skin irritations and are probably of little significance to the health of cetaceans.

XII. Strandings

Most of the 79 species of cetaceans in the world have at one time or another been found stranded on beaches or sandbars (Nowak and Paradiso 1983; Ellis 1987). Many of these are single or cow-calf strandings such as seen commonly in Florida for bottlenosed dol-

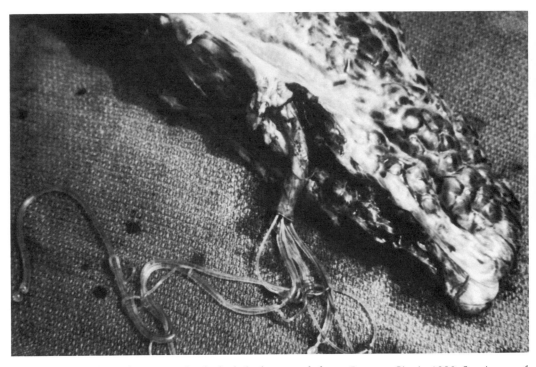

FIGURE 17-6. Kidney of a Cuvier's beaked whale that stranded near Panama City in 1982. Specimens of *Crassicauda* sp. are seen in the ureter. (Photograph courtesy of Dr. F.I. Townsend.)

Table 17-18

Helminths reported from 3 Risso's dolphins from waters in NE Florida

Helminth	Location in host[a]	No. dolphins infected
Trematoda		
Campula palliata	(1)	1
Synthesium tursionis	(2)	1
Pholeter gastrophilus	(3)	1
Cestoda		
Phyllobothrium delphini (cysticerci)	(4)	2
Nematoda		
Anisakis alexandri	(5)	1

Source: Zam et al. (1971).
[a](1) hepatico-pancreatic duct, (2) intestines, (3) wall of abdominal cavity just dorsal to the urogenital region, (4) encysted in mesentery of the right testis and in the blubber, (5) forestomach and intestines.

phins and pygmy sperm whales, respectively. Overall, Florida has more recorded strandings than any other state in the Southeast. This is probably due to a long history of interest in marine mammals in the state and to the fact that Florida has such a long coastline (Schmidly 1981).

The causes of single and cow-calf strandings are poorly understood. Some are believed to be due to diseases such as brain infections by trematodes in striped dolphins, pantropical spotted dolphins, and rough-toothed dolphins, and congestive heart failure in pygmy sperm whales. These conditions have been discussed more completely in earlier sections of this chapter.

Mass strandings involving three or more animals have provoked considerable interest for many years. The phenomenon of large numbers of whales beaching themselves and eventually dying (Figure 17-7) usually re-

Table 17-19

Helminths reported from pantropical spotted dolphins in Florida waters and beaches

Helminth	Location in host[a]	No. dolphins Exam.	Inf.	Geographic location	Data source
Trematoda					
Campula palliata	(1)	17	2	NE Florida	Zam et al. (1971)
Braunina cordiformis	(2)	17	2	NE Florida, NE Gulf of Mexico	" " " "
Nasitrema sp.	(3)	2	2	NE Florida	Forrester (1987)
Pholeter gastrophilus	(4)	17	1	NE Florida	Zam et al. (1971)
Nematoda					
Anisakis alexandri	(5)	17	1	NE Florida	" " " "
Halocercus delphini	(6)	17	3	NE Florida, NE Gulf of Mexico	" " " "

[a](1) hepatico-pancreatic duct, (2) attached in the fundic and pyloric stomachs, (3) cranial sinuses, (4) within cysts in walls of the fundic stomach, (5) forestomach, (6) air passages of the lungs.

ceives a great deal of attention from people in many walks of life. There are records of 69 mass strandings (involving 12 of the 29 species of cetaceans that occur in Florida waters) from 1882 to 1990 (Table 17-23). All of these strandings involved odontocetes; there are no records of baleen whales stranding in large numbers in Florida. The number of strandings in the southeastern United States (including Florida) is greatest during January through April (Schmidly 1981). Additional details of specific mass strandings in Florida have been published, including accounts of short-finned pilot whales (Moore 1953; Layne 1965; Fehring and Wells 1976; Irvine et al 1979), false killer whales (Caldwell et al. 1970; Odell et al. 1980), sperm whales (Caldwell and Caldwell 1980), pygmy killer whales (Caldwell and Caldwell 1975; Conti and Frohlich 1984), rough-toothed dolphins (Layne 1965; Forrester and Robertson 1975), spinner dolphins

Table 17-20

Helminths reported from striped dolphins from Florida waters

Helminth	Location in host[a]	No. dolphins Exam.	Inf.	Geographic location	Data source
Cestoda					
Phyllobothrium delphini (larvae)	(1)	2	1	Indian Rocks Beach	Zam et al. (1971)
Phyllobothrium sp. (larvae)	(2)	1	1	Hutchinson's Island	Odell & Chapman (1976)
Monorygma sp.	(3)	1	1	" "	" " " "
Trematoda					
Nasitrema sp.	(4)	1	1	Pensacola/Fort Walton Beach	Buergelt (1980), Townsend (1987)
Campula rochebruni	(5)	1	1	Hutchinson's Island	Odell & Chapman (1976)
Nematoda					
Anisakis simplex	(6)	2	1	Indian Rocks Beach	Zam et al. (1971)

[a](1) dorsal wall of abdominal cavity, (2) blubber, (3) body cavity, (4) brain, (5) bile ducts, (6) forestomach.

Table 17-21

Helminths from the cranial sinuses of 10 short-finned pilot whales from Florida waters

Helminth	No. whales		Intensity	
	Exam.	Inf.	Mean	Range
Trematoda				
Nasitrema sp.	9[a]	8	77	48–191
Nematoda				
Stenurus	9[a]	7	109	1–524
globicephalae	1[b]	1	2	—

Source: Forrester (1987).

[a]These 9 pilot whales were part of a mass stranding of 138 animals at the mouth of Fort George River (Duval County) in February 1977 (see Irvine et al. 1979 for further details).

[b]This pilot whale was 1 of 8 animals that stranded near Clearwater and Honeymoon Island (Pinellas County) in August 1979.

(Mead et al. 1980), and Fraser's dolphins (Hersh and Odell 1986).

The cause or causes of mass strandings have been the subject of considerable thought and debate for many years. Stranding is not a recent phenomenon. Some 2,300 years ago Aristotle wrote in *Historia Animalium* that it "is not known why they sometimes run aground on the seashore; for it is asserted that this happens rather frequently when the fancy takes them and without any apparent reason." Among the many hypotheses on the cause of mass strandings are: (1) echolocation problems associated with gently sloping beaches, (2) pelagic animals feeding in inshore areas unfamiliar to them, (3) harassment by predators such as sharks, (4) unusual underwater noises such as explosions, (5) pollution, (6) storms, and (7) disease (Geraci

Table 17-22

Ectoparasites and associates reported on cetaceans from Florida waters and beaches

Ectoparasite or associate	Cetacean	Data source
Copepods		
Harpacticus pulex	Bottlenosed dolphin[a]	Humes (1964)
Barnacles		
Xenobalanus globicipitus	Bottlenosed dolphin	Caldwell et al. (1971)
	Pantropical spotted dolphin	" " " "
	Risso's dolphin	" " " "
	False killer whale	" " " "
Xenobalanus sp.	Short-finned pilot whale[b]	Layne (1965)
	Rough-toothed dolphin	Townsend (1987)
Conchoderma auritum	Short-finned pilot whale	Caldwell (1988)
Whale lice (amphipods)		
Cyamidae (several	Bottlenosed dolphin[c]	Caldwell et al. (1971)
unidentified species)	Pantropical spotted dolphin	" " " "
	Pygmy sperm whale	" " " "
	Short-finned pilot whale	Layne (1965)
Syncyamus sp.	Bottlenosed dolphin[d]	Migaki et al. (1978)

[a]Captive animal.

[b]Layne (1965) reported "parasitic copepods" on the flippers of 2 pilot whales; Caldwell et al. (1971) felt that these were *Xenobalanus*, but could not examine specimens to confirm this.

[c]Woodard et al. (1969) mentioned this same finding.

[d]Goldston et al. (1974) discussed this same animal and reported the whale lice as *Cyamus* sp.

FIGURE 17-7. Mass stranding of short-finned pilot whales in northeastern Florida (date unknown). (Photograph courtesy of Marineland of Florida.)

Table 17-23
Summary of mass strandings of odontocete cetaceans on Florida beaches, 1882–1990

Species of cetacean	Mass strandings		No. individuals		
	No.	% of total	Mean	Range	Total
Short-finned pilot whales	29	42	33	3–200+	944
False killer whales	10	14	30	3–150	300
Sperm whales	7	10	8	2–16	55
Pygmy killer whales	5	7	4	3–5	21
Rough-toothed dolphins	5	7	14	6–30	70
Risso's dolphins	3	4	4	3–6	13
Pantropical spotted dolphins	2	3	9	4–15	19
Spinner dolphins	2	3	32	29–36	65
Clymene dolphins	2	3	10	4–17	21
Striped dolphins	2	3	26	3–50	53
Fraser's dolphins	1	1	8	—	8
Pygmy sperm whales	1	1	3	—	3
Totals	69	—	23	3–200+	1,572

Source: Prepared from data provided by Smithsonian Institution, courtesy of Dr. James G. Mead (1991).

1978). Wood (1979) suggested that cetaceans had amphibious ancestors and that when stressed, they regress to fundamental and primitive behaviors mediated by subcortical structures and attempt to return to dry land, that is, strand themselves deliberately. A recent hypothesis, the geomagnetic travel hypothesis, appears to have considerable promise in helping to explain the cause or causes of mass strandings, and deals with geomagnetic fields and migration (Klinowska 1985, 1986; Kirschvink et al. 1986). The explanation is based on the fact that there are highly significant correlations between mass strandings and local magnetic minima. Strandings seem to occur in locations where low anomalies or valleys in the local geomagnetic field intersect coastlines or are blocked by islands. Such stranding events are seen as the result of major orientation mistakes, perhaps caused by illness or other factors (Klinowska 1988). After all is said and done, however, the reasons for cetacean strandings still remain obscure (Geraci 1978).

The role of disease in mass strandings has been considered by numerous investigators (see papers and reviews in Geraci and St. Aubin 1979). Particular interest has been focused on infections by nematodes and trematodes in the brain and in the various air sinuses of the head (Geraci 1978, 1979; Morimitsu et al. 1987). Two mass strandings in Florida resulted in information on these parasitic problems. In July 1976 a recurrent stranding of false killer whales occurred in southwestern Florida (Captiva Island and Loggerhead Key) and involved around 35 animals (Hall and Schimpff 1979; Odell et al. 1980). The middle ear cavities of six of these whales were examined and five contained hundreds of the nematode *Stenurus globicephalae*. There was no evidence of damage to the eighth cranial nerves and brains of these animals. In February 1977 a stranding of 138 short-finned pilot whales occurred at the mouth of Fort George River north of Jacksonville (Figure 17-8) (Irvine et al. 1979). Numerous specimens of *Stenurus globicephalae* and *Nasitrema* sp. (Figure 17-9) were found in the middle ear cavities of seven and nasal sinuses of eight of the nine animals examined (Table 17-21). These infections were associated only with mild inflammation of the sinus linings (Woodard 1987). Brains were grossly and microscopically normal (Hall and Schimpff 1979). Data from these two strandings, therefore, do not implicate these parasitic infections as important causes of the mass strandings. Further studies of stranded and nonstranded cetaceans are needed before the role of disease in mass strandings is understood properly. The "jury is still out" on this topic.

XIII. Summary and conclusions

Information on parasites and diseases is available for 18 of the 29 species of cetaceans that are known from Florida waters. A large number of parasites and disease agents have been identified. These include 7 organochlorines, 11 heavy metals, 1 biological toxin, 2 bacteria, 5 fungi, 2 protozoans, 34 helminths (12 trematodes, 8 cestodes, 12 nematodes, and 2 acanthocephalans), and 8 ectoparasites. In addition, several cases of congestive heart failure, neurologic disease, and neoplasia were recorded. Five mycotic diseases (lobomycosis, candidiasis, aspergillosis, mucormycosis, and entomophthormycosis) and two bacterial diseases (nocardiosis and erysipelas) are zoonoses. The significance of these parasites and disease agents is unclear. Species of the trematode *Nasitrema* may migrate to the brain and cause single strandings of some cetaceans such as striped dolphins, pantropical spotted dolphins, and rough-toothed dol-

FIGURE 17-8. Mass stranding of short-finned pilot whales at Fort George Inlet (Duval County) in 1977.

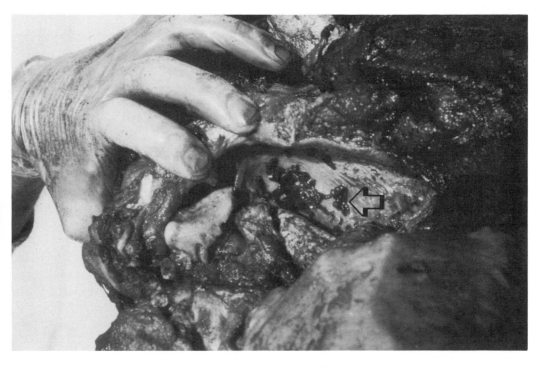

FIGURE 17-9. Opened nasal sinus of a stranded short-finned pilot whale near Fort George Inlet in 1977. Note numerous specimens of *Nasitrema* sp. (arrow) in sinus.

phins. The role of disease in mass strandings, however, is uncertain. Such mass strandings occurred 69 times on Florida beaches between 1882 and 1990 and involved 12 different species, the most common of which were short-finned pilot whales and false killer whales. A massive die-off of bottlenosed dolphins occurred in 1987–88 and was attributed to red tide.

XIV. Literature cited

Alzieu, C., and R. Duguy. 1979. Teneurs en composes organochlores chez les Cetaces et Pinnipèdes frequentant les côtes francaises. Ocean. Acta 2:107–120.

Anderson, D.M., and A.W. White (eds.). 1989. Toxic dinoflagellates and marine mammal mortalities. Woods Hole Oceanogr. Inst. Tech. Rept. WHOI-89-36 (CRC-89-6). 65 pp.

Banks, R.C., R.W. McDiarmid, and A.L. Gardner. 1987. Checklist of vertebrates of the United States, the U.S. territories, and Canada. U.S. Fish Wildl. Serv., Resour. Publ. 166. 79 pp.

Bonde, R.K. 1987. Unpublished data. USFWS, Gainesville, Fla.

Bonde, R.K., and T.J. O'Shea. 1989. Sowerby's beaked whale (*Mesoplodon bidens*) in the Gulf of Mexico. J. Mammal. 70:447–449.

Bossart, G.D. 1984. Suspected acquired immunodeficiency in an Atlantic bottlenosed dolphin with chronic-active hepatitis and lobomycosis. J. Am. Vet. Med. Assoc. 185:1413–1414.

Bossart, G.D., and C. Bossart. 1982. A treatment regimen for candidiasis in an Atlantic bottlenose dolphin. J. Am. Vet. Med. Assoc. 181:1399–1400.

Bossart, G.D., D.K. Odell, and N.H. Altman. 1985. Cardiomyopathy in stranded pygmy and dwarf sperm whales. J. Am. Vet. Med. Assoc. 187:1137–1140.

Buergelt, C.D. 1980. Unpublished data. (Pathology Report No. C80-932, CVM-TH, Univ. of Florida, Gainesville).

———. 1988. Unpublished data. (Pathology Report No. R88-WA, CVM-TH, Univ. of Florida, Gainesville).

Buergelt, C.D., and R.K. Bonde. 1983. Toxoplasmic meningoencephalitis in a West Indian manatee. J. Am. Vet. Med. Assoc. 183:1294–1296.

Burridge, M.J., W.J. Bigler, D.J. Forrester, and J.M. Hennemann. 1979. Serologic survey for *Toxoplasma gondii* in wild animals in Florida. J. Am. Vet. Med. Assoc. 175:964–967.

Calderwood-Mays, M.B. 1984. Unpublished data. (Pathology Report No. C84-1436B, CVM-TH, Univ. of Florida, Gainesville).

———. 1985. Unpublished data. (Pathology Report No. C85-1552, CVM-TH, Univ. of Florida, Gainesville).

Caldwell, D.K. 1988. Unpublished data. Marineland, Fla.

Caldwell, D.K., and M.C. Caldwell. 1975. Pygmy killer whales and short-snouted spinner dolphins in Florida. Cetology 18:1–5.

Caldwell, D.K., and M.C. Caldwell. 1980. An early mass stranding of sperm whales, *Physeter macrocephalus*, in northeastern Florida. Cetology 40:1–3.

Caldwell, D.K., and M.C. Caldwell. 1983. A field guide to marine mammals of the southeastern United States and Caribbean basin. Manuscript report distributed by the U.S. National Marine Fisheries Service at the Western Atlantic Turtle Symposium (WATS), San Jose, Costa Rica, July 17–22. 44 pp.

Caldwell, D.K., M.C. Caldwell, and C.M. Walker, Jr. 1970. Mass and individual strandings of false killer whales, *Pseudorca crassidens*, in Florida. J. Mammal. 51:634–636.

Caldwell, D.K., M.C. Caldwell, and S.G. Zam. 1971. A preliminary report on some ectoparasites and nasal sac parasites from small odontocete cetaceans from Florida and Georgia. In: Marineland Res. Lab., Tech. Rep. #5, ONR Contract NOOC14-70-C-0178. 7 pp.

Caldwell, D.K., M.C. Caldwell, J.C. Woodard, L. Ajello, W. Kaplan, and H.M. McClure. 1975. Lobomycosis as a disease of the Atlantic bottlenosed dolphin (*Tursiops truncatus*

Montagu, 1821). Am. J. Trop. Med. Hyg. 24:105–114.

Caldwell, M.C., D.K. Caldwell, and S.G. Zam. 1968. Occurrence of the lungworm (*Halocercus* sp.) in Atlantic bottlenosed dolphins (*Tursiops truncatus*) as a husbandry problem. Proc. 2d Symp. Dis. Husb. Aquat. Mamm. pp. 11–15.

Carroll, J.M., A.M. Jasmin, and J.N. Baucom. 1968. Pulmonary aspergillosis of the bottlenose dolphin (*Tursiops truncatus*). Vet. Clin. Pathol. 2:139–140.

Conti, J.A., and R.K. Frohlich. 1984. Gastrointestinal parasitism in pygmy killer whales. Proc. Helminthol. Soc. Wash. 51:364–365.

Cruickshank, J.J., D.M. Haines, N.C. Palmer, and D.J. St. Aubin. 1990. Cysts of a *Toxoplasma*-like organism in an Atlantic bottlenose dolphin. Can. Vet. J. 31:213–215.

Dailey, M.D. 1985. Diseases of Mammalia: Cetacea. In: Diseases of marine animals. Vol. 4, pt. 2. Introduction, Reptilia, Aves, Mammalia. O. Kinne (ed.). Biologische Anstalt Helgoland, Hamburg, Germany. pp. 805–847.

Dailey, M.D., and R.L. Brownell, Jr. 1972. A checklist of marine mammal parasites. In: Mammals of the sea. S.H. Ridgway (ed.). C.C. Thomas, Springfield, Ill. pp. 528–589.

Dailey, M.D., and W.A. Walker. 1978. Parasitism as a factor (?) in single strandings of southern California cetaceans. J. Parasitol. 64:593–596.

Dailey, M.D., L.A. Jensen, and B.W. Hill. 1981. Larval anisakine roundworms of marine fishes from southern and central California, with comments on public health significance. Calif. Fish Game 67:240–245.

Delyamure, S.L. 1968. Helminthofauna of marine mammals (ecology and phylogeny). Israel Program for Scientific Translation. Jerusalem. 522 pp.

DeVries, G.A., and J.J. Laarman. 1973. A case of Lobo's disease in the dolphin *Sotalia guianensis*. Aquat. Mammal. 1:26–33.

Dudok van Heel, W.H. 1972. Raised levels of mercury and chlorinated hydrocarbons in newly captured *Tursiops truncatus* from Florida waters. Aquat. Mammal. 1:24–36.

Ellis, R. 1987. Whales. Oceans. pp. 25–29, 63.

Fehring, W.K., and R.S. Wells. 1976. A series of strandings by a single herd of pilot whales on the west coast of Florida. J. Mammal. 57:191–194.

Forrester, D.J. 1987. Unpublished data. Univ. of Florida, Gainesville.

Forrester, D.J., and W.D. Robertson. 1975. Helminths of rough-toothed dolphins, *Steno bredanensis* Lesson 1828, from Florida waters. J. Parasitol. 61:922.

Forrester, D.J., D.K. Odell, N.P. Thompson, and J.R. White. 1980. Morphometrics, parasites, and chlorinated hydrocarbon residues of pygmy killer whales from Florida. J. Mammal. 61:356–360.

Geraci, J.R. 1978. The enigma of marine mammal strandings. Oceanus 21:38–47.

———. 1979. The role of parasites in marine mammal strandings along the New England coast. In: Biology of marine mammals: Insights through strandings. J.R. Geraci and D.J. St. Aubin (eds.). U.S. Dept. of Commerce, Nat. Tech. Inf. Service PB-293 890. pp. 85–91.

———. 1986. Nutrition and nutritional disorders. In: Zoo and wild animal medicine. M.E. Fowler (ed.). W.B. Saunders, Philadelphia. pp. 760–64.

———. 1989. Clinical investigation of the 1987–88 mass mortality of bottlenose dolphins along the U.S. central and south Atlantic Coast. Final Rep. to Nat. Mar. Fish. Serv., U.S. Navy, and Marine Mamm. Comm. Univ. of Guelph, Guelph, Ont. 63 pp.

Geraci, J.R., and D.J. St. Aubin (eds.). 1979. Biology of marine mammals: Insights through strandings. U.S. Dept. of Commerce, Nat. Tech. Inf. Service PB-293 890. 343 pp.

Geraci, J.R., R.M. Sauer, and W. Medway. 1966. Erysipelas in dolphins. Am. J. Vet. Res. 27:597–606.

Gillespie, J.H., and J.F. Timoney. 1981. Hagen and Bruner's infectious diseases of domestic animals. 7th ed. Cornell Univ. Press, Ithaca. 851 pp.

Goldston, R.T. 1988. Unpublished data. St. Petersburg, Fla.

Goldston, R.T., R.A. Whitman, and T.E. Haslett. 1974. Lobo's disease in the Atlantic bottlenosed dolphin (*Tursiops truncatus*). Proc. Am. Assoc. Zoo. Vet. pp. 128–130.

Gunter, G., R.H. Williams, C.C. Davis, and F.G. Smith. 1948. Catastrophic mass mortalities of marine animals and coincident phytoplankton bloom on the west coast of Florida, November 1946 to August 1947. Ecol. Monogr. 18:309–324.

Hall, N.R., and R.D. Schimpff. 1979. Neuropathology in relation to strandings. Mass stranded whales. In: Biology of marine mammals: Insights through strandings. J.R. Geraci and D.J. St. Aubin (eds.). U.S. Dept. of Commerce, Nat. Tech. Inf. Service. PB-293 890. pp. 236–242.

Hall, N.R., R.D. Schimpff, J.C. Woodard, C.C. Carleton, and R.T. Goldston. 1977. Intracerebral hemorrhage in a bottlenosed dolphin (*Tursiops truncatus*). J. Wildl. Dis. 13:341–345.

Hersh, S.L., and D.K. Odell. 1986. Mass stranding of Fraser's dolphin, *Lagenodelphis hosei*, in the western north Atlantic. Mar. Mamm. Sci. 2:73–76.

Hines, S.A. 1986. Unpublished data. (Pathology Report No. N86-0336, CVM-TH, Univ. of Florida, Gainesville).

Holden, A.V. 1981. Organochlorines—an overview. Mar. Poll. Bull. 12:110–115.

Holden, A.V., and K. Marsden. 1967. Organochlorine pesticides in seals and porpoises. Nature 216:1274–1276.

Howard, E.B. (ed.). 1983. Pathobiology of marine mammal diseases. Vols. 1 and 2. CRC Press, Boca Raton, Fla. 477 pp.

Humes, A.G. 1964. *Harpacticus pulex,* a new species of copepod from the skin of a porpoise and a manatee in Florida. Bull. Mar. Sci. Gulf and Caribbean 14:517–528.

Hunter, G.W., J.C. Swartzwelder, and D.F. Clyde. 1976. Tropical medicine. 5th ed. W.B. Saunders, Philadelphia. 900 pp.

Hutton, R.F. 1964. A second list of parasites from marine and coastal animals of Florida. Trans. Am. Micros. Soc. 83: 439–447.

Inskeep, W., II., C.H. Gardiner, R.K. Harris, J.P. Dubey, and R.T. Goldston. 1990. Toxoplasmosis in Atlantic bottle-nosed dolphins. J. Wildl. Dis. 26:377–382.

Irvine, A.B., M.D. Scott, R.S. Wells, and J.G. Mead. 1979. Stranding of the pilot whale, *Globicephala macrorhynchus,* in Florida and South Carolina. Fish. Bull. 77:511–513.

Jasmin, A.M., C.P. Powell, and J.N. Baucom. 1972. Actinomycotic mycetoma in the bottlenose dolphin (*Tursiops truncatus*) due to *Nocardia paraguayensis*. Vet. Med. Sm. Anim. Clin. 67:542–543.

King, C.A. 1987. Organochlorines in bottlenose dolphins (*Tursiops truncatus*) and pygmy sperm whales (*Kogia breviceps*) from southeastern Florida. M.S. thesis, Univ. of Miami, Coral Gables. 92 pp.

Kirschvink, J.L., A.E. Dizon, and J.A. Westphal. 1986. Evidence from strandings for geomagnetic sensitivity in cetaceans. J. Exp. Biol. 120:1–24.

Klinowska, M. 1985. Cetacean live stranding sites relate to geomagnetic topography. Aquat. Mammal. 11:27–32.

———. 1986. The cetacean magnetic sense—evidence from strandings. In: Research on dolphins. M.M. Brydan and R. Harrison (eds.). Clarendon, Oxford. pp. 401–432.

———. 1988. Cetacean "navigation" and the geomagnetic field. J. Navigat. 41:52–71.

Lauckner, G. 1985. Diseases of mammalia: Sirenia. In: Diseases of marine animals. Vol. 4, pt. 2. Introduction, Reptilia, Aves, Mammalia. O. Kinne (ed.). Biologische Anstalt Helgoland, Hamburg, Germany. pp. 795–803.

Layne, J.N. 1965. Observations on marine mammals in Florida waters. Bull. Fla. State Mus. 9:131–181.

———. (ed.). 1978. Rare and endangered biota of Florida. Vol. 1. Mammals. Univ. Presses of Fla., Gainesville. 52 pp.

Leatherwood, S., and R.R. Reeves. 1982. Bottlenose dolphin *Tursiops truncatus* and other toothed cetaceans. In: Wild mammals of North America. J.A. Chapman and G.A. Feldhamer (eds.). Johns Hopkins Univ. Press, Baltimore. pp. 369–414.

McIntosh, A. 1953. New host and distribution records for the Trematoda genus *Braunina* Heider, 1900. J. Parasitol. 39:31.

Mawdesley-Thomas, L.E. 1974. Some aspects of neoplasia in marine animals. Adv. Mar. Biol. 12:151–231.

Mead, J.G. 1991. Unpublished data. Smithsonian Institution, Washington, D.C.

Mead, J.G., D.K. Odell, R.S. Wells, and M.D. Scott. 1980. Observations on a mass stranding of spinner dolphin, *Stenella longirostris*, from the west coast of Florida. Fish. Bull. 78:353–360.

Medway, W., and J.R. Geraci. 1986. Clinical pathology of marine mammals. In: Zoo and wildlife medicine. M.E. Fowler (ed.). W.B. Saunders, Philadelphia. pp. 791–897.

Migaki, G., and P.W. Blumer. 1975. Case for diagnosis. Milit. Med. 140:544, 549.

Migaki, G., and F.R. Robinson. 1974. Case for diagnosis. Milit. Med. 139:201, 210–211.

Migaki, G., J.C. Woodard, and R.T. Goldston. 1978. Renal adenoma in an Atlantic bottle-nosed dolphin (*Tursiops truncatus*). Am. J. Vet. Res. 39:1920–1921.

Migaki, G., M.G. Valerio, B. Irvine, and F.M. Garner. 1971. Lobo's disease in an Atlantic bottle-nosed dolphin. J. Am. Vet. Med. Assoc. 159:578–582.

Moore, J.C. 1953. Distribution of marine mammals to Florida waters. Am. Midl. Nat. 49:117–158.

Morimitsu, T., T. Nagai, M. Ide, A. Ishii, and M. Koono. 1986. Parasitogenic octavus neuropathy as a cause of mass stranding of Odontoceti. J. Parasitol. 72:469–472.

Morimitsu, T., T. Nagai, M. Ide, H. Kawano, A. Naichuu, M. Koono, and A. Ishii. 1987. Mass stranding of Odontoceti caused by parasitogenic eighth cranial neuropathy. J. Wildl. Dis. 23:586–590.

Nowak, R.M., and J.L. Paradiso. 1983. Walker's mammals of the world. 4th ed. Johns Hopkins Univ. Press, Baltimore. 1,362 pp.

Odell, D.K., and E.D. Asper. 1976. Studies on the biology of *Kogia* (Cetacea: Physeteridae) in Florida: Preliminary report to the small whale subcommittee of the International Whaling Commission. Unpublished MS. 12 pp.

Odell, D.K., and C. Chapman. 1976. A striped dolphin, *Stenella coeruleoalba*, from Florida. Cetology 20:1–6.

Odell, D.K., E.D. Asper, J. Baucom, and L.H. Cornell. 1980. A recurrent mass stranding of the false killer whale, *Pseudorca crassidens*, in Florida. Fish. Bull. 78:171–177.

O'Shea, T.J., R.L. Brownell, Jr., D.R. Clark, Jr., W.A. Walker, M.L. Gay, and T.G. Lamont. 1980. Organochlorine pollutants in small cetaceans from the Pacific and South Atlantic oceans, November 1968–June 1976. Pest. Monit. J. 14:35–46.

Pier, A.C., A.K. Tokayama, and A.Y. Miyahara. 1970. Cetacean nocardiosis. J. Wildl. Dis. 6:112–118.

Perrin, W.F., E.D. Mitchell, J.G. Mead, D.K. Caldwell, M.C. Caldwell, P.J. H. van Bree, and W.H. Dawbin. 1987. Revision of the spotted dolphins, *Stenella* spp. Mar. Mamm. Sci. 3:99–170.

Reeves, R.R., and R.L. Brownell, Jr. 1982. Baleen whales *Eubalaena glacialis* and allies. In: Wild mammals of North America. J.A. Chapman and G.A. Feldhamer (eds.). Johns Hopkins Univ. Press, Baltimore. pp. 415–444.

Ridgway, S.H. 1972. Homeostasis in the aquatic environment. In: Mammals of the sea—biology and medicine. S.H. Ridgway (ed.). Charles C. Thomas, Springfield, Ill. pp. 590–747.

Russell, S.W. 1985. Unpublished data. (Pathology Report No. C85-2553, CVM-TH, Univ. of Florida, Gainesville).

Schimpff, R.D., and N.R. Hall. 1979. Neuropathology in relation to strandings. Captive and single stranded cetaceans. In: Biology of marine mammals: Insights through strandings. J.R. Geraci and D.J. St. Aubin (eds.). U.S. Dept. of Commerce, Nat. Tech. Inf. Service PB-293 890. pp. 234–235.

Schmidly, D.J. 1981. Marine mammals of the southeastern United States coast and Gulf of Mexico. U.S. Fish and Wildlife Service,

Office of Biological Services, Washington, D.C. FWS/OBS-90.41. 163 pp.

Schryver, H.F., W. Medway, and J.F. Williams. 1967. The stomach fluke *Braunina cordiformis* in the Atlantic bottle-nosed dolphin. J. Am. Vet. Med. Assoc. 15:884–886.

Scott, G.P., D.M. Burn, and L.J. Hansen. 1988. The dolphin die-off: Longterm effects and recovery of the population. Proc. Oceans '88, Baltimore, Md. pp. 819–823.

Seibold, H.R., and J.E. Neal. 1956. *Erysipelothrix* septicemia in the porpoise. J. Am. Vet. Med. Assoc. 128:537–539.

Simpson, C.F., F.G. Wood, and G. Young. 1958. Cutaneous lesions on a porpoise with erysipelas. J. Am. Vet. Med. Assoc. 133:558–560.

Steidinger, K.A. 1989. Implications of 1986–87 *Ptychodiscus brevis* red tide and 1987–88 mass bottlenose dolphin mortalities. In: Toxic dinoflagellates and marine mammal mortalities. D.M. Anderson and A.W. White (eds.). Woods Hole Oceanog. Inst. Tech. Rept. WHOI-89-36 (CRC-89-6). pp. 56–65.

Stetzer, E.R. 1983. Unpublished data. (Pathology Report No. C83-232, CVM-TH, Univ. of Florida, Gainesville).

Subramanian, A., S. Tanabe, R. Tatsukawa, S. Suito, and N. Miyazaki. 1987. Reduction in the testosterone levels by PCB's and DDE in Dall's porpoises of the northwestern North Pacific. Mar. Pollut. Bull. 18:643–646.

Sweeney, J. 1986. Reproduction. In: Zoo and wildlife medicine. M.E. Fowler (ed.). W.B. Saunders, Philadelphia. pp. 789–790.

Sweeney, J.C., and S.H. Ridgway. 1975. Common diseases of small cetaceans. J. Am. Vet. Med. Assoc. 167:533–540.

Sweeney, J.C., G. Migaki, P.M. Vainik, and R.H. Conklin. 1976. Systemic mycoses in marine mammals. J. Am. Vet. Med. Assoc. 169:946–948.

Tanabe, S., S. Watanabe, H. Kan, and R. Tatsu-

kawa. 1988. Capacity and mode of PCB metabolism in small cetaceans. Mar. Mammal Sci. 4:103–124.

Taruski, A.G., C.E. Olney, and H.E. Winn. 1975. Chlorinated hydrocarbons in cetaceans. J. Fish. Res. Board Can. 32:2205–2209.

Townsend, F.I. 1987. Unpublished data. Fort Walton Beach, Fla.

Van Thiel, P.H. 1962. Anisakiasis. Parasitology 52:16P–17P.

Wagemann, R., and D.C.G. Muir. 1984. Concentrations of heavy metals and organochlorines in marine mammals of northern waters: Overview and evaluation. Can. Tech. Rep. Fish Aquat. Sci. 1279. 97 pp.

White, F.H., and D.J. Forrester. 1988. Unpublished data. Univ. of Florida, Gainesville.

White, J.R. 1976. A pygmy killer whale found on the east coast of Florida. Fla. Sci. 39:31–36.

Wood, D.A. 1990. Official lists of endangered and potentially endangered fauna and flora in Florida. Florida Game and Fresh Water Fish Commission, Tallahassee. 19 pp.

Wood, F.G. 1979. The cetacean stranding phenomenon: An hypothesis. In: Biology of marine mammals: Insights through strandings. J.R. Geraci and D.J. St. Aubin (eds.). U.S. Dept. of Commerce, Nat. Tech. Inf. Service PB-293 890. pp. 129–188.

Woodard, J.C. 1987. Unpublished data. Univ. of Florida, Gainesville.

———. 1972. Electron microscopic study of lobomycosis (*Loboa loboi*). Lab. Invest. 27:606–612.

Woodard, J.C., S.G. Zam, D.K. Caldwell, and M.C. Caldwell. 1969. Some parasitic diseases of dolphins. Pathol. Vet. 6:257–272.

Zam, S.G., D.K. Caldwell, and M.C. Caldwell. 1971. Some endoparasites from small odontocete cetaceans collected in Florida and Georgia. Cetology 2:1–11.

CHAPTER EIGHTEEN

Seals and Sea Lions

I. Introduction

Four species of seals and sea lions have been reported from Florida waters and beaches (Moore 1953; Layne 1965; Stevenson 1976; Schmidly 1981). These include the West Indian or Caribbean monk seal (*Monachus tropicalis*), the hooded or bladdernose seal (*Cystophora cristata*), the harbor seal (*Phoca vitulina*), and the California sea lion (*Zalophus californianus*). The West Indian monk seal, the only pinniped native to the Gulf of Mexico and the Caribbean area (Schmidly 1981), is now extinct (Rice 1977; LeBoeuf et al. 1986). The last specimen was taken near Key West in 1922 (Townsend 1923). Harbor seals and hooded seals occur only as occa-

sional strays (Schmidly 1981). The California sea lion has been introduced into the western North Atlantic and occurs as an exotic animal. Schmidly (1981) listed three captures and eight sightings of California sea lions in Florida waters and beaches. These undoubtedly represented animals that had escaped from display facilities or had been released purposely. They are not known to breed in the Atlantic (Schmidly 1981).

The common diseases of captive and free-ranging pinnipeds have been reviewed by Sweeney (1974), Ridgway et al. (1975), and Lauckner (1985). Information on respiration, oxygen stores, thermoregulation, osmoregulation, reproductive physiology, hematology, serum chemistry, and diseases (including diagnosis and therapy) was summarized by Ridgway (1972). Mortality factors for the various seals and sea lions of North America were discussed in a review by Ronald et al. (1982). The organochlorine and heavy metal residues in seals were examined in a review written by Holden (1978). Dailey and Brownell (1972) provided a checklist of marine mammal parasites that included a section on pinnipeds, and Mawdesley-Thomas (1974) reviewed the status of our knowledge of neoplasia in pinnipeds. The hazards of disease transfer from pinnipeds to land mammals (including man) were discussed by Smith et al. (1978).

II. Viral diseases

The only information available on viruses of pinnipeds in Florida is one case of eastern equine encephalomyelitis (EEE) in a California sea lion (Stetzer et al. 1988). This case was in an eight-year-old male that had been in captivity at Marineland of Florida for about one year. It was on exhibit along with four other sea lions. The animal died following a 24-hour period of progressive lethargy and anorexia.

EEE virus is vectored by mosquitoes (*Culiseta melanura*) and occurs in eastern North America and in the Caribbean region (Seymour and Yuill 1981). California sea lions in their native habitat on the West Coast do not encounter this virus. When introduced into an area like Florida, where the virus is enzootic among populations of mosquitoes and vertebrate hosts, the California sea lion serves as an example of an exotic host coming into contact with a disease agent to which it is susceptible. This viral disease could be an important limiting factor preventing the es-

tablishment of California sea lions introduced into Florida waters.

III. Bacterial diseases

In 1965 a male California sea lion in a zoological park in Florida died and was diagnosed as having bacterial and verminous pneumonia (Wallace et al. 1966). A pure culture of a beta-hemolytic *Streptococcus* was isolated from the lungs and from a bronchial lymph node. *Edwardsiella tarda*, beta-hemolytic streptococci, *Escherichia coli*, and *Bacillus subtilis* were isolated from a mesenteric lymph node. The effect of *E. tarda* on sea lions is unknown. In other hosts it has been associated with hemorrhagic enteritis. It was isolated also from two American alligators in the same zoological park, but both isolants were of different serotypes from the one in the sea lion.

IV. Helminths

During 1970–71 six captive California sea lions from Marineland of Florida were examined at necropsy for filarial worms (Forrester et al. 1973). Results of these examinations are presented in Table 18-1. Heartworms (*Dirofilaria immitis*) were not found in the three young animals, but all three of the older sea lions that had resided in Florida for longer than one year were infected. Gross and histopathologic findings comparable to those of canine heartworm disease were seen in sea lion no. 2. A second filarial worm (*Dipetalonema odendhali*) was found in subcutaneous tissues of all four of the sea lions that were examined for this worm. The evidence indicates the *D. odendhali* is enzootic in California sea lions in their native habitat on the West Coast and that when these pinnipeds

Table 18-1
Data on filarial worms from six captive California sea lions examined at necropsy in Florida

Sea lion no.	Sex	Approx. age (yr)	Time lived in Fla. (mo)	No. *Dirofilaria immitis* adults in heart	*Dipetalonema odendhali* adults present
1	M	3+	18	9	ND[a]
2	M	10	24	6	ND
3	M	8	20	23	yes
4	M	1	1	0	yes
5	F	1	1	0	yes
6	F	1	1	0	yes

Source: Forrester et al. (1973).
[a]ND = not determined.

are introduced into an area such as Florida where *D. immitis* is enzootic, they acquire canine heartworms and subsequent heartworm disease. Thus, another situation exists similar to that described earlier for EEE virus in California sea lions in which a susceptible host is introduced into an area where infection by a pathogenic organism results in morbidity and mortality. Some zoological parks in Florida that wish to maintain sea lions for exhibition purposes have instituted the use of diethylcarbamazine citrate as prophylaxis against canine heartworm infections (Beusse et al. 1977).

In 1975 a hooded seal was examined at necropsy for helminth parasites (Forrester 1987). This animal was found at Jacksonville Beach (Duval County), an apparent victim of a shark attack. It was negative for helminths except for 23 specimens of an unidentified digenetic trematode in its intestines.

No other information is available on helminths of seals and sea lions in Florida.

V. Arthropods

In 1968 Caldwell and Caldwell (1969) found a dead harbor seal near Daytona Beach. It was infested with large numbers of sucking lice (*Echinophthirius horridus*), especially in the dorsolateral region of the head and neck and the ventrolateral region of the posterior belly. This louse has been reported also from a number of other northern species of hair seals (family Phocidae) (Kim et al. 1986).

VI. Summary and conclusions

Seals and sea lions are rare visitors to Florida waters and beaches. California sea lions have been introduced by man, but do not seem to thrive and reproduce in the South Atlantic. Limited observations show that they are susceptible to two diseases that are enzootic to Florida: eastern equine encephalomyelitis and canine heartworm disease. With the exception of intestinal trematodes from a hooded seal and sucking lice from a harbor seal, nothing is known about the parasites and diseases of other pinnipeds in Florida waters.

VII. Literature cited

Beusse, D.O., E.D. Asper, J.N. Baucom, and S.W. Searles. 1977. Diethylcarbamazine citrate for prevention of heartworm (*Dirofilaria immitis*) in the California sea lion (*Zalophus californianus*). Vet. Med./Sm. Anim. Clin. 1977:470–471.

Caldwell, D.K., and M.C. Caldwell. 1969. The harbor seal, *Phoca vitulina concolor,* in Florida. J. Mammal. 50:379–380.

Dailey, M.D., and R.L. Brownell, Jr. 1972. A checklist of marine mammal parasites. In: Mammals of the sea. S.H. Ridgway (ed.). C.C. Thomas, Springfield, Ill. pp. 528–589.

Forrester, D.J. 1987. Unpublished data. Univ. of Florida, Gainesville.

Forrester, D.J., R.F. Jackson, J.F. Miller, and B.C. Townsend. 1973. Heartworms in captive California sea lions. J. Am. Vet. Med. Assoc. 163:568–570.

Holden, A.V. 1978. Pollutants and seals—a review. Mammal. Rev. 8:53–66.

Kim, K.C., H.D. Pratt, and C.J. Stojanovich. 1986. The sucking lice of North America. An illustrated manual for identification. Penn. State Univ. Press, University Park. 241 pp.

Lauckner, G. 1985. Diseases of Mammalia: Pinnipedia. In: Diseases of marine animals. Vol. IV, pt. 2. Introduction, Reptilia, Aves, Mammalia. O. Kinne (ed.). Biologische Anstalt Helgoland, Hamburg, Germany. pp. 683–793.

Layne, J.N. 1965. Observations on marine mammals in Florida waters. Bull. Fla. State Mus. 9:131–181.

LeBoeuf, B.J., K.W. Kenyon, and B. Villa-Ramirez. 1986. The Caribbean monk seal is extinct. Mar. Mamm. Sci. 2:70–72.

Mawdesley-Thomas, L.E. 1974. Some aspects of neoplasia in marine animals. Adv. Mar. Biol. 12:151–231.

Moore, J.C. 1953. Distribution of marine mammals to Florida waters. Am. Midl. Nat. 49:117–158.

Rice, D.W. 1977. A list of the marine mammals of the world. 3d ed. Nat. Oceanic Atmos. Adm., Nat. Mar. Fish. Serv., NOAA Tech. Rep. SSRF-711. 15 pp.

Ridgway, S.H. 1972. Homeostasis in the aquatic environment. In: Mammals of the sea. S.H. Ridgway (ed.). C.C. Thomas, Springfield, Ill. pp. 590–747.

Ridgway, S.H., J.R. Geraci, and W. Medway. 1975. Diseases of pinnipeds. Rapp. P.-v. Reun. Cons. Int. Explor. Mer. 169:327–337.

Ronald, K., J. Selley, and P. Healey. 1982. Seals. In: Wild mammals of North America. J.A. Chapman and G.A. Feldhamer (eds.). Johns Hopkins Univ. Press, Baltimore. pp. 769–827.

Schmidly, D.J. 1981. Marine mammals of the southeastern United States coast and the Gulf of Mexico. U.S. Fish and Wildlife Service, Office of Biological Services. Washington, D.C. 163 pp.

Seymour, C., and T.M. Yuill. 1981. Arboviruses. In: Infectious diseases of wild mammals. 2d ed. J.W. Davis et al. (eds.). Iowa State Univ. Press, Ames. pp. 54–86.

Smith, A.W., N.A. Vedros, T.G. Akers, and W.G. Gilmartin. 1978. Hazards of disease transfer from marine mammals to land mammals: Review and recent findings. J. Am. Vet. Med. Assoc. 173:1131–33.

Stetzer, E.R., R.S. Kingston, and N.M. Young. 1988. Unpublished data. Univ. of Florida, Gainesville.

Stevenson, H.M. 1976. Vertebrates of Florida. Identification and distribution. Univ. Presses of Florida, Gainesville. 607 pp.

Sweeney, J.C. 1974. Common diseases of pinnipeds. J. Am. Vet. Med. Assoc. 165:805–810.

Townsend, C.H. 1923. The West Indian seal. J. Mammal. 4:55.

Wallace, L.J., F.H. White, and H.L. Gore. 1966. Isolation of *Edwardsiella tarda* from a sea lion and two alligators. J. Am. Vet. Med. Assoc. 149:881–883.

Manatees

I. Introduction

The West Indian manatee (*Trichechus manatus* L.) is a member of the order Sirenia and is entirely herbivorous and aquatic. In Florida waters a distinct subspecies occurs, the Florida manatee (*T. m. latirostris*), which is reproductively isolated from the rest of the species (Domning and Hayek 1986). At the present time the species is considered vulnerable or endangered throughout its range and is protected by the Marine Mammal Protection Act of 1972, the Endangered Species Act of 1973, as amended, and the Florida Manatee Sanctuary Act. There are a minimum of 1,200 in Florida (O'Shea 1988; Lefebvre et al. 1989). Florida manatees occur in fresh- and saltwa-

ter systems and during cold winter weather many of them concentrate in warm-water refugia (Bonde 1985). During the summer they disperse along coastal areas, canals, and inland rivers. Lefebvre et al. (1989) have given detailed data on the distribution and status of manatees throughout their range, including Florida.

Baseline values have been published on serum chemistry (White et al. 1976; Irvine et al. 1980; Beusse et al. 1981b; Medway et al. 1982a; O'Shea et al. 1985b), hematology (White et al. 1976; Irvine et al. 1980; Beusse et al. 1981b; Medway et al. 1982c), blood coagulation (Medway et al. 1982b), urine values

(Irvine et al. 1980), metabolic rates (Irvine 1983), milk composition (Bachman and Irvine 1979; Pervaiz and Brew 1986), and respiration (Scholander and Irving 1941).

Several bibliographies and reviews of the literature on manatees and sirenians in general have been published and include references to mortality factors, diseases, parasites, and the like (Whitfield and Farrington 1975; Husar 1977, 1978; Blair 1979; Odell 1982; Caldwell and Caldwell 1985). In addition, two monographs on the manatee were published in the late 1970s (Ronald et al. 1978; Hartman 1979) and contain a wealth of information on the biology of manatees. Bonde et al. (1983) published an excellent manual that describes the procedures for salvage and necropsy of manatees and includes valuable information on anatomy.

II. Trauma

There are a number of publications that discuss mortality of manatees in Florida (Odell and Reynolds 1979; Irvine et al. 1981; Beck et al. 1981; Buergelt et al. 1984; O'Shea et al. 1985a; Bonde and Beck 1990). In an analysis of 406 manatees found dead during 1976–81 in Florida, O'Shea et al. (1985a) attributed the deaths of 142 (35%) animals to trauma due to human causes. These included collisions with boats (Figure 19-1), entrapment by gates of locks and dams, vandalism, poaching, drowning in commercial fishing nets, being caught in large-diameter pipes, or entanglement in fishing lines (Table 19-1). In addition, there are two published reports of intussusceptions as the cause of death of manatees that had ingested fish hooks and/or fishing line (Forrester et al. 1975; Buergelt et al. 1984) and a record of a manatee ingesting a piece of stainless steel wire that punctured the stomach and led to acute peritonitis and death (USFWS records). From these reports

it is clear that human-related activities are very important factors in the mortality of Florida manatees. This situation is cause for considerable concern since the manatee's population dynamics do not indicate that excessive losses of adults can continue without resulting in a population decline (O'Shea et al. 1985a).

Most of the deaths caused by collisions with boats result from vessels with large-horsepower engines, although small boats also kill manatees. Almost 50% of the manatees hit by large boats are killed by impact trauma rather than propeller cuts (Beck et al. 1982). The greatest number of deaths due to boats was found to occur in northeastern Florida, especially Brevard County and the St. Johns River (O'Shea et al. 1985a). In fact, 80% of the animals killed by boats during 1976–81 were in eastern Florida. O'Shea et al. (1985a) pointed out that this mortality correlated with higher levels of human activity and commerce in eastern compared to western Florida. For further details on this aspect, the reader is referred to the thoughtful analysis and discussion provided by O'Shea and associates (1985a). In a recent publication Bonde and Beck (1990) presented data showing a direct correlation between boat-related mortality and the numbers of registered boats in Florida. Mortality increased as the numbers of boats increased from 1976 through 1989 (Figure 19-2).

Since the closely related dugong (*Dugong dugon*) has been found to be prone to capture myopathy (Anderson 1981; Marsh and Anderson 1983), O'Shea et al. (1985b) reviewed the available evidence (published and unpublished) concerning this phenomenon in manatees. They concluded that there were no indications of unusual susceptibility of manatees to capture myopathy based on the capture and handling of 92 animals from 1975 to 1983, and on records of another 150 animals captured during the 1900s.

FIGURE 19-1. Florida manatee that died due to trauma inflicted by propeller blades of a boat. (Photograph courtesy of USFWS.)

III. Cold exposure

Manatees are tropical mammals and in Florida they are at the northern limit of their range. They have low metabolic rates and may become lethargic and anorectic when water temperatures reach 16°C for prolonged periods (Campbell and Irvine 1981; Irvine 1983).

There are a number of documented deaths of manatees in association with cold winter weather in Florida. The earliest report was on the death of two manatees in 1886 following a freeze (Bangs 1895). Other such reports have been given by Cahn (1940), Hamilton (1941), Moore (1956), Layne (1965), Campbell and Irvine (1981), Buergelt et al. (1984), and O'Shea et al. (1985a). In recent years these occurrences have been studied and documented carefully. Cold-related deaths numbered 38 in 1977, 30 in 1981, 34 in 1984, and 47 in 1990 following severe cold spells

(Campbell and Irvine 1981; Buergelt et al. 1984; Wright 1990). During normal winters only seven or eight cold-related deaths would be documented (Buergelt et al. 1984).

In a detailed study of mortality during 1976–81 it was found that the majority of manatees dying during cold snaps were juvenile/subadult animals (O'Shea et al. 1985a). In a study of the carcasses of several of these manatees, it was noted that there was serous atrophy of fat, emaciation, and absence of food in the gastrointestinal tract. It was felt that during these times of cold weather, manatees became lethargic and anorectic and died of hypothermia through metabolic drains to the environment. Young animals seem to be especially susceptible due to their surface-to-volume relationships (Buergelt et al. 1984). Although it has been suggested that the crowding of animals together at warm-water outlets (such as power-plant effluents) may predispose manatees to viral or bacterial

Table 19-1
Causes of death for 406 manatees in Florida,
1976–81

Cause of death	No. cases	% of total
Collisions with boats	87	21
Entrapment by gates of locks and dams	35	9
Shot by vandals	5	1
Poaching	4	< 1
Drowning in commercial fishing nets	4	< 1
Caught in large-diameter pipes	3	< 1
Infections due to entanglement of flippers in fishing lines or crab-trap lines	4	< 1
Perinatal/early juvenile death (stillbirths, neonate mortality, orphans)	58	14
Aborted fetus	1	< 1
Hemorrhagic enteritis	3	< 1
Respiratory tract infections	5	1
Pustular dermatitis	4	< 1
Septicemia	1	< 1
Ruptured uterus	1	< 1
Cachectic condition associated with cold winter weather	4	< 1
Undetermined	187[a]	46
TOTAL	406	100

Source: O'Shea et al. (1985a).
[a]Many of these deaths actually may have been due to severe cold weather such as was experienced in 1977 and 1981 (O'Shea 1986).

pneumonia (Gallivan et al. 1983), this does not seem to be the case. Although pneumonia was diagnosed in a manatee that died in the 1977 cold snap (Campbell and Irvine 1981), this is an uncommon finding as a primary cause of death.

IV. Environmental contaminants

Organochlorine contamination does not appear to be a significant factor in manatees. O'Shea et al. (1984) tested blubber samples from 26 animals and found residues of metabolites of DDT in five and dieldrin in four. Concentrations were less than 1 ppm. Forrester et al. (1975) found similar concentrations of DDE and PCBs in samples of liver, muscle, blubber, and brain from a manatee. Dieldrin (< 1 ppm) was found only in liver and brain. O'Shea found PCBs in 13 of 26 manatees at concentrations ranging from 0.5 to 4.6 ppm (mean, 1.4 ppm). All manatees with residues of PCB were from the urban areas of northeastern Florida. Analyses for residues of other organochlorines were conducted on 26 manatees at the 0.1 ppm level of sensitivity. These included endrin, HCB, mirex, heptachlor epoxide, and metabolites and components of chlordane and toxaphene. None was detected (O'Shea et al. 1984).

O'Shea et al. (1984) also examined a series of manatee tissues for mercury, lead, cadmium, copper, iron, and selenium. They found that concentrations of all but copper were not excessive (Table 19-2). Copper concentrations, however, were significantly elevated in manatees from areas such as Crystal River, where copper herbicides were used for weed control. These values were higher than those reported previously for any wild mammal and were at concentrations that are known to cause toxic effects in several domestic animals (O'Shea et al. 1984).

Hartman (1979) cited J.A. Powell as reporting arsenic in the tissues of a dead calf from Crystal River in 1976, but further details were not given, nor was it stated that the arsenic was the cause of death.

V. Toxicosis

Deaths of manatees have been linked circumstantially to outbreaks of red tide caused by blooms of the toxic dinoflagellate *Ptychodiscus brevis*. Layne (1965) reported seven dead

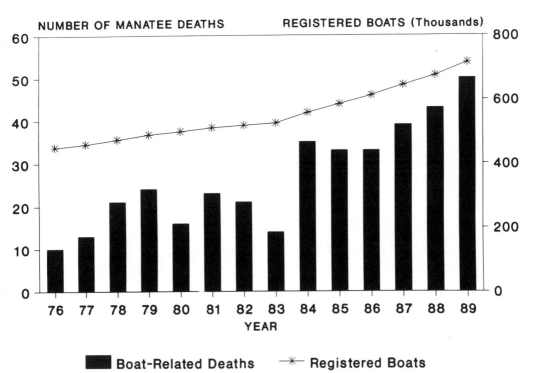

FIGURE 19-2. Mortality of manatees due to boat-related incidents compared to numbers of registered boats in Florida, 1976–89. (From Bonde and Beck 1990.)

Table 19-2
Concentrations of metals in tissues of manatees in Florida,
1977–81

	No. manatees		Concentration (ppm dry wt)	
Tissue and metal	Exam.	Pos.	Mean	Range
Kidney				
Cadmium	38	36	25.7	0–190
Lead	20	20	5.2	3.3–7.1
Liver				
Copper	54	54	175	4.4–1,200
Iron	35	35	1,920	460–8,200
Lead	19	19	2.7	1.8–4.4
Mercury	19	1	0.2	0.2
Selenium	19	11	0.42	0–1.1
Muscle				
Mercury	27	0	—	—

Source: O'Shea et al. (1984).

manatees near Fort Myers (Lee County) during March and April 1963. At the same time there was a red tide outbreak in the Englewood area nearby, and there were reports of mortality of cormorants, gulls, and raccoons as well. During February to April 1982, another die-off involving 41 manatees occurred in the same general area in Lee County in the lower Caloosahatchee River (O'Shea and Rathbun 1982; Buergelt et al. 1984). This die-off was linked also to an outbreak of red tide, but this relationship was not established conclusively. In a 39-page report supplemented with a 650-page appendix of supporting documents, O'Shea and Rathbun (1982) discussed the evidence (largely circumstantial) that led them to suspect that red tide was a cause of the die-off. This included (1) a red tide concurrent with the manatee mortality, (2) mortality of other animals (i.e., catfish, mullet, and cormorants) that are known to be susceptible to red tide toxins, (3) neurologic signs typical of red tide poisoning, (4) record of a similar event in the same general area in 1963, (5) many of the dead manatees containing ascidians (= tunicates) in their gastrointestinal tracts (means of exposure to red tide toxins), and (6) mortality of manatees terminating shortly after the red tide ended. O'Shea and Rathbun (1982) concluded tentatively that "this event occurred as a result of the cooccurrence of several normally unrelated events: a seasonal dispersal of manatees from winter aggregations at the power plant; an unusual drought and compensatory water management practices which produced high salinities, poor flushing of the lower Caloosahatchee and a decline of freshwater vegetation; a red tide outbreak; and an apparently unusual occurrence of relatively dense patches of ascidians." Ascidians are filter feeders and could thereby concentrate red tide toxin; they were probably ingested accidentally by manatees as they fed on sea grasses. This epizootic is discussed further by O'Shea et al. (1991).

VI. Anomalies and morphological variations

There are several reports on congenital malformations in manatees. Watson and Bonde (1986) gave data on three cases of congenital ectrodactyly of the flipper, including one case of bilaterally symmetrical cleft hand. The authors state that the observed frequency of this anomaly (three cases out of 784 carcasses examined in Florida over a 10-year period) is high in manatees compared to similar conditions in humans. The significance of this observation to manatee populations is not known.

Valvular endocardiosis or valvular fibrosis was seen in 8 of 26 neonatal and subadult manatees (Buergelt et al. 1990). This morphological/physiological variation involved the atrioventricular valves and seemed to regress as manatees aged. These are not felt to be of pathologic significance.

Bonde (1987) observed one manatee that had the descending mesocolon attached to the lateral margin of the right kidney. Normally it attaches to the left kidney. This anomaly did not appear to incapacitate the animal.

VII. Viral diseases

No viruses or viral diseases are known from Florida manatees. Irvine et al. (1981) reported that pneumonia virus was isolated from one specimen during the 1977 cold-related die-off. A check of the original pathologist's report revealed that bacterial pneumonia, not viral pneumonia, was diagnosed (Popp 1977).

VIII. Bacterial diseases

Forty-eight species of bacteria have been isolated from captive and free-ranging manatees in Florida (Table 19-3). Some of these may not be of pathologic significance; others have been isolated from lesions and/or diseased animals. Apart from secondary infection of wounds and septicemia (which are common sequelae to trauma from boats, etc.), five bacterial diseases have been identified in manatees in Florida. These include pustular dermatitis, pneumonia, meningoencephalitis, typhlitis/colitis, and omphalitis/peritonitis.

Five cases of severe pustular dermatitis have been found in free-ranging manatees (O'Shea et al. 1985a; Beck 1986). A number of bacteria have been cultured from these lesions, including *Aeromonas hydrophila*, *Bacillus* sp., *Corynebacterium* sp., *Escherichia coli*, *Klebsiella pneumoniae*, *Pseudomonas aeruginosa*, *P. florescens*, *P. putrefaciens*, and *Streptococcus epidermidis*. Fungi also were involved and will be discussed in the following section. The pathogenesis of this condition and the role of these bacteria are unknown. Dermatitis is common in captive manatees (Irvine et al. 1980; Cardeilhac et al. 1981; Jenkins 1981; Bartmann 1974). Irvine et al. (1980) and Jenkins (1981) discussed the occurrence of dermatitis in four captive manatees. A female and its calf developed multiple furuncles associated with hair follicles on the dorsal and lateral surfaces within three weeks after the animals were handled and fresh water was added to the tank. These lesions were noted to regress gradually after the tank water was changed to saltwater, but they never healed completely. Similar bacteria as cultured from the wild-caught manatees were isolated from the lesions of these captive animals. Irvine et al. (1980) felt that the dermatitis was initiated by trauma to the skin during handling and subsequent secondary bacterial infections. Similar situations have been reported by Murie (1872) and Bartmann (1974). Boever et al. (1976) reported numerous pustules covering the entire body of a captive Amazonian manatee (*Trichechus inunguis*) from which *Mycobacterium chelonei* was cultured.

Several cases of pneumonia have been reported (Buergelt and Bonde 1983; Buergelt et al. 1984; Beck 1986; Campbell and Irvine 1981; Cardeilhac et al. 1981; Beusse et al. 1981a), but these may be problems secondary to trauma or cold exposure. *Aeromonas hydrophila* and *Proteus* sp. have been cultured from lungs of manatees with pneumonia (UF-CVM/USFWS records), but may have been contaminants (Buergelt 1986). Much of the lay literature on manatees discusses pneumonia, but these actually may have been cases of cold exposure/cachexia as discussed previously. Pyogranulomatous pneumonia due to infection with *Mycobacterium marinum* was diagnosed in a captive Amazonian manatee maintained in an aquarium with various species of fish and turtles for 17 years (Morales et al. 1985).

One case of meningoencephalitis due to gram-positive coccoid bacteria was reported by Buergelt et al. (1984). This was a subadult male found in the Orange River (Lee County) in May 1981. The animal was cachectic; the bacterial infection was believed to have led to secondary malnutrition.

A two-month-old calf from Rattlesnake Key (Levy County) was found in moribund condition and subsequently died in November 1984. At necropsy it was found to have acute, severe necrotizing colitis and typhlitis (Figure 19-3) due to *Aeromonas hydrophila*. There was also an interstitial pneumonia and a severe pustular dermatitis, all of which contributed to the death of this animal (Russell and Cooley 1985).

Walsh et al. (1987) described omphalitis

Table 19-3

Bacteria isolated from captive and free-ranging manatees in Florida

Species	Site of isolation	Data source
Aeromonas hydrophila	Lung, bronchus, nares, skin, small and large intestines, lymph node, abscess, uterus	UF-CVM/USFWS records,[a] Irvine et al. (1980), Jenkins (1981)
Aeromonas sp.	Lung	UF-CVM/USFWS records
Bacillus sp.	Skin	" " "
Bacteroides fragilis	Stomach, duodenal ampulla	Cerniglia & Odell (1987)
Bacteroides sp.	Duodenal ampulla	" " "
Citrobacter sp.	Skin (wounds)	Beusse et al. (1981a, 1981b)
Clostridium bifermentans	Cecum	Cerniglia & Odell (1987)
Clostridium butyricum	Duodenal ampulla	" " " "
Clostridium clostridiiforme	Duodenal ampulla	" " " "
Clostridium paraputrificum	Cecum	" " " "
Clostridium sp.	Muscle	UF-CVM/USFWS records
Corynebacterium sp.	Skin	" " "
Edwardsiella tarda	Small and large intestines, lymph nodes	UF-CVM/USFWS records, Forrester et al. (1975), O'Shea & Rathbun (1982)
Edwardsiella sp.	Liver, lung, spleen	Beusse et al. (1981a)
Enterobacter agglomerans	Lung, stomach	UF-CVM/USFWS records
Enterobacter cloacae	Stomach contents	O'Shea & Rathbun (1982)
Enterobacter sp.	Pleura	UF-CVM/USFWS records
Escherichia coli	Small and large intestines, bronchus, uterus, liver, skin, abdominal fluid	UF-CVM/USFWS records, Irvine et al. (1980), Walsh et al. (1987)
Eubacterium lentum	Cecum	Cerniglia & Odell (1987)
Eubacterium sp.	Duodenal ampulla, upper large intestine	" " " "
Fusobacterium varium	Stomach	" " " "
Klebsiella pneumoniae	Skin, stomach contents, feces	UF-CVM/USFWS records, O'Shea & Rathbun (1982)
Lactobacillus sp.	Upper large intestine	Cerniglia & Odell (1987)
Pasteurella hemolytica	Bronchus, stomach, small intestine	UF-CVM/USFWS records
Pasteurella multocida	Bronchus, brain	" " "
Pasteurella sp.	Urine	" " "
Plesiomonas shigelloides	Abdominal fluid	Walsh et al. (1987)
Proteus mirabilis	Lung	UF-CVM/USFWS records
Proteus morganii	Lung, nares	" " "
Proteus vulgaris	Lung, uterus	" " "
Proteus sp.	Brain, skin (wound), lungs, liver, urine	UF-CVM/USFWS records, Buergelt and Bonde (1983)
Pseudomonas aeruginosa	Urine, pleura, skin	UF-CVM/USFWS records, Irvine et al. (1980), Jenkins (1981)
Pseudomonas florescens	Skin	Irvine et al. (1980), Jenkins (1981)
Pseudomonas mallophilia	Lung	UF-CVM/USFWS records
Pseudomonas putrefaciens	Lung, stomach, skin	UF-CVM/USFWS records, Irvine et al. (1980), Jenkins (1981)
	Abdominal fluids	Walsh et al. (1987)
Pseudomonas sp.	Skin (wound), bronchus	UF-CVM/USFWS records
Salmonella heidelberg	Intestinal contents	Cardeilhac et al. (1981)
Serratia liquifaciens	Pleura	UF-CVM/USFWS records
Serratia marcescens	Pleura	" " "

(continued)

Table 19-3 (*continued*)

Species	Site of isolation	Data source
Staphylococcus aureus	Pleura, abscess	UF-CVM/USFWS records, O'Shea & Rathbun (1982)
Staphylococcus epidermidis	Bronchus	UF-CVM/USFWS records
Staphylococcus sp.	Pleura, skin (wounds)	UF-CVM/USFWS records, Beusse et al. (1981b)
Streptococcus epidermidis	Skin	UF-CVM/USFWS records
Streptococcus faecium	Abdominal fluids	Walsh et al. (1987)
Streptococcus mutans	Stomach contents	O'Shea & Rathbun (1982)
Streptococcus sp.	Bronchus, nares, skin (wound), cecum, upper large intestine	UF-CVM/USFWS records, Cerniglia & Odell (1987)
Vibrio cholerae[b]	Feces	O'Shea & Rathbun (1982)
Vibrio alginolyticus	Feces	" " " "

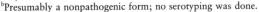

[a]UF-CVM/USFWS indicates records on file in the University of Florida, College of Veterinary Medicine, and in the Sirenia Project Office of the U.S. Fish and Wildlife Service in Gainesville, Fla.
[b]Presumably a nonpathogenic form; no serotyping was done.

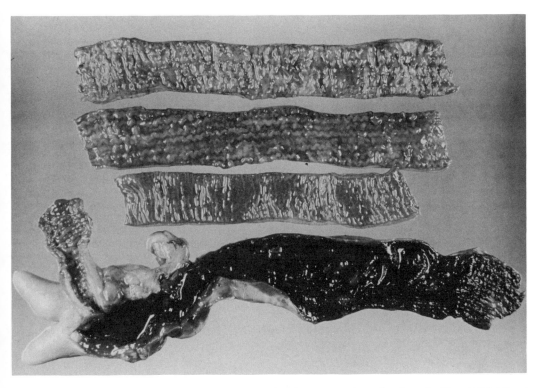

FIGURE 19-3. Necrotizing colitis and typhlitis in a Florida manatee from Rattlesnake Key, 1984. The 3 upper segments are small intestine and illustrate hyperemia; the lower section shows necrosis and hemorrhage in the cecum and colon. (Photograph courtesy of Dr. J. Cooley.)

and peritonitis in a young manatee from the west coast of Florida in September 1985. *Streptococcus faecium, Plesiomonas shigelloides, Pseudomonas putrefaciens,* and *Escherichia coli* were cultured from the animal. The manatee died as a result of terminal septicemia. The events leading to the development of omphalitis were not determined. Some of the bacteria may have been involved in the pathogenesis of this disease process.

IX. Mycotic diseases

Two manatees with pustular dermatitis (Figure 19-4) were found to have mycotic infections (UF-CVM/USFWS records). In one of these the fungus involved was not identified, but in the other, *Fusarium* sp. and *Blasto-*

myces dermatitidis were identified tentatively along with an array of bacteria as discussed in the previous section. The role of these fungi in the dermatitis problems of manatees is unknown. Four captive West Indian manatees in an aquarium in Japan developed dermatitis that was believed to be related to fungi of the genera *Cephalosporium* and *Mucor* (Tabuchi et al. 1974). Mok and Best (1979) colonized a hyphomycete from skin lesions of a captive Amazonian manatee and tentatively identified it as a species of *Cercospora*.

X. Protozoan parasites

Three protozoans have been found in the Florida manatee: *Toxoplasma gondii, Eimeria manatus,* and *Eimeria nodulosa.* Buer-

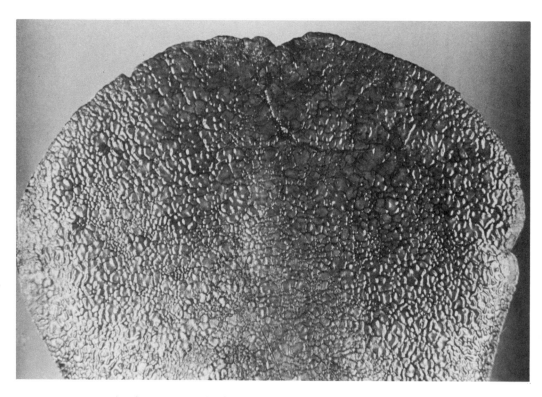

FIGURE 19-4. Pustular dermatitis on the fluke of a Florida manatee from Rattlesnake Key, 1984. Note the generalized cracks and fissures. Histologically dense mats of fungal hyphae were seen invading the epidermis. (Photograph courtesy of Dr. J. Cooley.)

gelt and Bonde (1983) described a case of toxoplasmic meningoencephalitis (Figure 19-5) in a young female (less than one year of age) from Indian River (St. Lucie County). The animal also had bacterial pneumonia and multiple skin abscesses. The authors speculated that this manatee was infected by ingestion of oocyst-contaminated water. Manatees have been seen drinking from sewer effluents (Shane 1981), and this may have been the source of infection.

Two species of *Eimeria* have been described from captive and free-living Florida manatees (Upton et al. 1989). Prevalences were 31% and 44%, respectively, for *E. nodulosa* and *E. manatus* in 16 animals examined during 1987 and 1988. Captive animals were from several marine mammal facilities in central and southern Florida. Free-living manatees were from Indian River (n = 3), St. Johns River (n = 2), and New Smyrna Beach

(n = 1). The life cycles and effects of these coccidia on manatees are unknown.

XI. Helminths

The helminths of manatees in Florida have been well studied. Bonde (1985) and Beck and Forrester (1988) reviewed the literature (Table 19-4) and presented data on helminths collected at necropsy for 215 animals during 1974–1982.

Six species of helminths were found, including 4 species of trematodes, 1 nematode, and 1 cestode. The prevalence and intensity of each of these species are given in Table 19-5. None of the manatees was infected with either 5 or 6 species; 5 manatees had 4 species, 37 had 3, 53 had 2, and 61 had 1 species. Fifty-nine were helminth-free, 30 of which were calves.

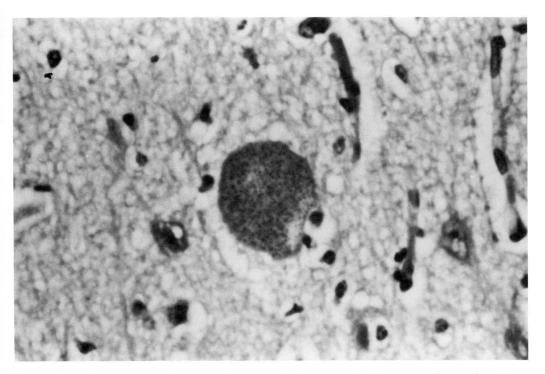

FIGURE 19-5. *Toxoplasma* cyst in the cerebral neuropil of a young Florida manatee from Indian River, St. Lucie County. (Photograph courtesy of Dr. C.D. Buergelt.)

Table 19-4

Helminths reported from Florida manatees

Helminth	Site	Data source
Trematoda		
Chiorchis fabaceus	Lumen of cecum and colon	Buergelt et al. (1984), Bonde (1985), Forrester et al. (1975), Forrester et al. (1980), Hutton (1964), Radhakrishnan & Bradley (1970), Beck & Forrester (1988)
Cochleotrema cochleotrema	Nares, lungs	Buergelt et al. (1984), Blair (1981), Bonde (1985), Forrester et al. (1980), Beck & Forrester (1988)
Moniligerum blairi	Mucosa and submucosa of small intestine	Bonde (1985), Reynolds (1980), Dailey et al. (1988), Beck & Forrester (1988)
Nudacotyle undicola	Lumen of small intestine	Bonde (1985), Forrester et al. (1980), Dailey et al. (1988), Beck & Forrester (1988)
Nematoda		
Heterocheilus tunicatus	Lumen and mucosa of stomach and small intestine	Buergelt et al. (1984), Bonde (1985), Forrester et al. (1980), Radhakrishnan & Bradley (1970), Sprent (1980), Beck & Forrester (1988)
Rhabditoid sp.	Skin	UF-CVM/USFWS records,[a] Greiner (1986)
Cestoda		
Anoplocephala sp.	Lumen of small intestine	Bonde (1985), Beck & Forrester (1988)

[a]UF-CVM/USFWS indicates records on file in the University of Florida, College of Veterinary Medicine, and in the Sirenia Project Office of the U.S. Fish and Wildlife Service in Gainesville, Fla.

Helminth data were studied in relation to sex, age class, season and location of recovery, and cause of death of the host. There were no statistically significant associations of any of these factors with the intensity of the helminths. Similarly, there were no associations of prevalence of helminths with sex, season of recovery, or cause-of-death category. There were, however, significant associations of the prevalence of *Chiorchis fabaceus*, *Cochleotrema cochleotrema*, and *Heterocheilus tunicatus* with age of the host. The prevalences of all three species were higher in juveniles and adults than in calves. There were higher prevalences of *H. tunicatus*

in western and southern Florida and a higher prevalence of *C. cochleotrema* in eastern Florida. The low prevalence of these parasites in calves was thought to be due to the limited intake of vegetation (with larvae or intermediate hosts). The regional differences may be due to the distribution of the intermediate hosts of these parasites (Bonde 1985; Beck and Forrester 1988).

The pathologic significance of parasitism to manatees is poorly understood. Two manatees were affected severely by infections of the nasal fluke *Cochleotrema* (Bonde 1985) (Figure 19-6). One of these was an animal that died of verminous pneumonia (Buergelt

Table 19-5
Prevalence and intensity of helminths from salvaged manatees in Florida,
1974–82

Helminth	Prevalence		Intensity[a]		
	No. exam.	% inf.	No. exam.	Mean	Range
Trematoda					
Chiorchis fabaceus	203	66	29	2,731	15–24,976
Cochleotrema cochleotrema	146	38	19	54	2–250
Nudacotyle undicola	31	90	4	44,223	169–132,110
Moniligerum blairi	39	18	ND[b]	ND	ND
Nematoda					
Heterocheilus tunicatus	185	39	19	228	2–1,693
Cestoda					
Anoplocephala sp.	205	0.5	205	1	1

Sources: Bonde (1985); Beck and Forrester (1988).
[a] No. helminths per infected manatee.
[b] ND = not determined.

FIGURE 19-6. Nasal flukes (*Cochleotrema cochleotrema*) in the nasal passages of a Florida manatee.

et al. 1984). The lungs of that manatee had 490 specimens of the nasal fluke, many of which were blocking the larger bronchioles. The nares of this animal were not examined and the count may have actually been higher. Another manatee was infected with 250 nasal flukes and had severe rhinitis and pulmonary edema, possibly due to the fluke infection (Bonde 1985). A third manatee died of hemorrhagic enteritis and over 1,125,000 specimens of *Nudacotyle undicola* were present in its intestines (Bonde 1985). The paramphistome fluke (*Chiorchis fabaceus*) (Figure 19-7) has not been associated with pathologic changes other than localized irritation of the intestinal mucosa, even though it occurs in high numbers in some cases. *Moniligerum blairi* was found in pairs in small cysts in the mucosa and submucosa of the small intestine (Figure 19-8), but since it is rare in occurrence

it may be of little pathologic importance. The ascarid nematode (*H. tunicatus*) has been found occasionally to be partly embedded in the gastric mucosa (Figure 19-9), but this may occur after the death of the animal. No perforation of the gastrointestinal tract has been observed (Bonde 1985).

One specimen of a sexually immature tapeworm (*Anoplocephala* sp.) was found in the small intestine of a manatee. This was thought to be an accidental infection, possibly of an equine tapeworm that was acquired by a manatee feeding on vegetation along a shore near a horse pasture (Bonde 1985).

Rhabditoid nematodes were observed in skin sections of one manatee with a severe case of pustular dermatitis (UF-CVM/USFWS records; Greiner 1986). These nematodes were present in the superficial surface of the skin and may represent contamination or a

FIGURE 19-7. Paramphistome flukes (*Chiorchis fabaceus*) in the large intestine of a Florida manatee.

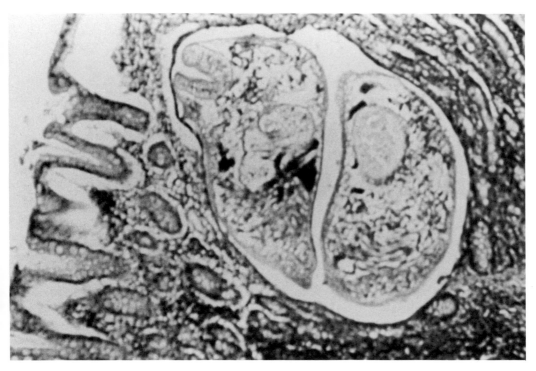

FIGURE 19-8. Section of the small intestine of a Florida manatee showing a pair of opisthotrematid flukes (*Moniligerum blairi*) in a cyst in the mucosa and submucosa.

spurious infection by a free-living nematode. Hartman (1979) also mentioned finding nematodes in epidermal scrapings of wild manatees.

XII. Ectoparasites and associates

Skin sections of the same manatee mentioned above (with the rhabditoid nematodes) also contained mites (UF-CVM/USFWS records). These were not further identified (Greiner 1986) and their significance is unknown.

A variety of organisms have been found associated with the skin of manatees (Husar 1977; Hartman 1979). These include copepods (*Harpacticus pulex*), barnacles (*Chelonibia manati*), remoras (*Echeneis naucrates*), blue-green algae (*Lyngbya martensiana*), red algae (*Compsopogen coeruleus*), diatoms (*Zygnema* and *Navicula*), and various protozoans, ostracods, amphipods, isopods, dipteran larvae, gastropods, and small leeches (Husar 1977; Humes 1964; Hartman 1979; Pilsbry 1916; Bonde 1985). Most if not all of these are probably commensals and live on manatees temporarily. Some—such as diatoms, barnacles, and remoras—are acquired in saltwater and die or drop off when manatees enter freshwater. They are probably of little significance to the overall health of manatees, with the exception of the copepod, *Harpacticus pulex*. Two cases of infection by this copepod were described by Zeiller (1981). Apparently these are the same cases discussed by Humes (1964). Both cases were on captive manatees at the Miami Seaquarium. The copepods were found associated with skin lesions, but it was not determined if the copepods were responsible for the le-

FIGURE 19-9. Ascaroid nematodes (*Heterocheilus tunicatus*) embedded in the gastric mucosa of a Florida manatee found dead in the Withlacoochee River in 1975.

sions or secondarily invaded lesions caused by something else. Control was achieved by changing the water of the tank to freshwater and by adding copper sulfate to the pool.

XIII. Summary and conclusions

Mortality of Florida manatees is largely due to human-related causes (i.e., trauma due to boat accidents, entrapment by gates of locks and dams or fishing nets and lines, ingestion of foreign objects, vandalism, or poaching) or to undiagnosed factors especially during the winter months. Juvenile and subadult manatees are susceptible to cold exposure during winters of unusually low temperatures. One epizootic of manatees involving 41 animals occurred during the winter of 1982 and was linked circumstantially to red tide intoxication. Anomalies and morphological variations found included congenital ectrodactyly and valvular endocardiosis.

Eighty-four different commensals, parasites, disease agents, and environmental contaminants have been identified from Florida manatees. These include 3 organochlorines, 6 metals, 48 species of bacteria, 2 fungi, 3 protozoans, 4 trematodes, 2 nematodes, 1 cestode, and 15 external associates (including remoras, barnacles, mites, dipteran larvae, copepods, ostracods, amphipods, isopods, gastropods, leeches, protozoans, algae, and diatoms). Some of these have been associated with morbidity or mortality of individual manatees and include several species of bacteria and/or fungi (pneumonia, pustular dermatitis, meningoencephalitis, typhlitis/

colitis, and omphalitis/peritonitis), *Toxoplasma gondii* (meningoencephalitis), *Cochleotrema cochleotrema* (verminous pneumonia), and *Nudacotyle undicola* (hemorrhagic enteritis). None of these disease agents is known to cause epizootics and their overall importance from a pathologic standpoint is probably minor.

Toxoplasma gondii and two of the species of bacteria (*Salmonella heidelberg* and *Edwardsiella tarda*) are of zoonotic importance, but their prevalences among manatee populations are fairly low and therefore they are of limited significance to public health.

XIV. Literature cited

Anderson, P.K. 1981. The behavior of the dugong (*Dugong dugon*) in relation to conservation and management. Bull. Mar. Sci. 31:640–647.

Bachman, K.C., and A.B. Irvine. 1979. Composition of milk from the Florida manatee (*Trichechus manatus latirostris*). Comp. Biochem. Physiol. 62A:873–878.

Bangs, O. 1895. The present standing of the Florida manatee, *Trichechus latirostris* (Harlan) in the Indian River waters. Am. Nat. 29:783–787.

Bartmann, W. 1974. Management of sea cows (*Trichechus manatus*) in the Duisburg Zoo. Aquat. Mammal. 2:13–15.

Beck, C.A. 1986. Unpublished data. USFWS, Gainesville, Fla.

Beck, C.A., and D.J. Forrester. 1988. Helminths of the Florida manatee, *Trichechus manatus latirostris,* with a discussion and summary of the parasites of sirenians. J. Parasitol. 74:628–637.

Beck, C.A., R.K. Bonde, and D.K. Odell. 1981. Manatee mortality in Florida during 1978. In: The West Indian manatee in Florida. R.L. Brownell, Jr., and K. Ralls (eds.). Fla. Dept. Nat. Res., Tallahassee, Fla. pp. 76–85.

Beck, C.A., R.K. Bonde, and G.B. Rathbun.

1982. Analyses of propeller wounds on manatees in Florida. J. Wildl. Manage. 46:531–535.

Beusse, D.O., Jr., E.D. Asper, and S.W. Searles. 1981a. Some causes of manatee mortality. In: The West Indian manatee in Florida. R.L. Brownell, Jr., and K. Ralls (eds.). Fla. Dept. Nat. Res., Tallahassee, Fla. pp. 98–101.

Beusse, D.O., Jr., E.D. Asper, and S.W. Searles. 1981b. Diagnosis and treatment of manatees at Sea World of Florida. In: The West Indian manatee in Florida. R.L. Brownell, Jr., and K. Ralls (eds.). Fla. Dept. Nat. Res., Tallahassee, Fla. pp. 111–120.

Blair, D. 1979. An annotated bibliography of the helminth parasites of the Sirenia. Dugong Workshop, James Cook Univ. 24 pp.

———. 1981. The monostome flukes (Digenea: Families Opisthotrematidae Poche and Rhabdiopoeidae Poche) parasitic in sirenians (Mammalia: Sirenia). Aust. J. Zool. Suppl. Ser. 81. 54 pp.

Boever, W.J., C.O. Thoen, and J.D. Wallach. 1976. *Mycobacterium chelonei* infection in a Natterer manatee. J. Am. Vet. Med. Assoc. 169:927–929.

Bonde, C.B. 1985. Helminth parasites of the West Indian manatee, *Trichechus manatus* L., in Florida. M.S. thesis, Univ. of Florida, Gainesville. 89 pp.

Bonde, R.K. 1987. Unpublished data. USFWS, Gainesville, Fla.

Bonde, R.K., and C.A. Beck. 1990. How the Florida manatees fare today. Whalewatcher. 24:8–9.

Bonde, R.K., T.J. O'Shea, and C.A. Beck. 1983. Manual of procedures for the salvage and necropsy of carcasses of the West Indian manatee (*Trichechus manatus*). NTIS PB83-255273. 175 pp.

Buergelt, C.D. 1986. Unpublished data. Univ. of Florida, Gainesville.

Buergelt, C.D., and R.K. Bonde. 1983. Toxoplasmic meningoencephalitis in a West Indian manatee. J. Am. Vet. Med. Assoc. 183:1294–1296.

Buergelt, C.D., R.K. Bonde, C.A. Beck, and T.J. O'Shea. 1984. Pathologic findings in manatees in Florida. J. Am. Vet. Med. Assoc. 185:1331–1334.

Buergelt, C.D., R.K. Bonde, C.A. Beck, and T.J. O'Shea. 1990. Myxomatous transformation of heart valves in Florida manatees. J. Zoo. Wildl. Med. 21:220–227.

Cahn, A.R. 1940. Manatees and the Florida freeze. J. Mammal. 21:222–23.

Caldwell, D.K., and M.C. Caldwell. 1985. Manatees. *Trichechus manatus* Linnaeus, 1758; *Trichechus senegalensis* Link, 1795 and *Trichechus inunguis* (Natterer, 1883). In: Handbook of marine mammals. Vol. 3. The sirenians and baleen whales. S.H. Ridgway (ed.). Academic, New York. pp. 33–66.

Campbell, H.W., and A.B. Irvine. 1981. Manatee mortality during the unusually cold winter of 1976–1977. In: The West Indian manatee in Florida. R.L. Brownell, Jr., and K. Ralls (eds.). Fla. Dept. Nat. Res., Tallahassee, Fla. pp. 86–91.

Cardeilhac, P.T., C.M. Walker, R.L. Jenkins, J.A. Popp, D.J. Forrester, F.H. White, and R.T. Smith. 1981. Complications in the formula-rearing of infant manatees associated with bacterial infections. In: The West Indian manatee in Florida. R.L. Brownell, Jr., and K. Ralls (eds.). Fla. Dept. Nat. Res., Tallahassee, Fla. pp. 141–146.

Cerniglia, C.E., and D.K. Odell. 1987. Unpublished data. Univ. of Miami, Miami.

Dailey, M.D., W. Vogelbein, and D.J. Forrester. 1988. *Moniligerum blairi* n.g., n.sp. and *Nudacotyle undicola* n.sp. (Trematoda: Digenea) from the West Indian manatee, *Trichechus manatus* L. System. Parasitol. 11:159–163.

Domning, D.P., and L.C. Hayek. 1986. Interspecific and intraspecific morphological variation in manatees (Sirenia: *Trichechus*). Mar. Mamm. Sci. 2:87–144.

Forrester, D.J., F.H. White, J.C. Woodard, and N.P. Thompson. 1975. Intussusception in a Florida manatee. J. Wildl. Dis. 11:566–568.

Forrester, D.J., D.J. Black, D.K. Odell, J.E. Reynolds, C.A. Beck, and R.K. Bonde. 1980. Parasites of manatees (*Trichechus manatus*) in Florida. Abstract in: Conf. Proc. Aq. An.

Med.: A State of the Art. Fla. Sea Grant Rep. No. 32. pp. 103–104.

Gallivan, G.J., R.C. Best, and J.W. Kanwisher. 1983. Temperature regulation in the Amazonian manatee, *Trichechus inunguis*. Physiol. Zool. 56:255–262.

Greiner, E.C. 1986. Unpublished data. Univ. of Florida, Gainesville.

Hamilton, W.J., Jr. 1941. Notes on some mammals of Lee County, Florida. Am. Midl. Nat. 25:686–691.

Hartman, D.S. 1979. Ecology and behavior of the manatee (*Trichechus manatus*) in Florida. Spec. Pub. No. 5 Am. Soc. Mammal. 153 pp.

Humes, A.G. 1964. *Harpacticus pulex,* a new species of copepod from the skin of a porpoise and a manatee in Florida. Bull. Mar. Sci. Gulf Carib. 14:517–27.

Husar, S.L. 1977. The West Indian manatee (*Trichechus manatus*). U.S. Dept. Int., Fish and Wildl. Serv., Wildl. Res. Rep. 7. 22 pp.

———. *Trichechus manatus*. Mammalian Species No. 93:1–5.

Hutton, R.F. 1964. A second list of parasites from marine and coastal animals of Florida. Trans. Am. Micro. Soc. 83:439–447.

Irvine, A.B. 1983. Manatee metabolism and its influence on distribution in Florida. Biol. Conserv. 25:315–34.

Irvine, A.B., D.K. Odell, and H.W. Campbell. 1981. Manatee mortality in the southeastern United States from 1974 through 1977. In: The West Indian manatee in Florida. R.L. Brownell, Jr., and K. Ralls (eds.). Fla. Dept. Nat. Res., Tallahassee, Fla. pp. 67–75.

Irvine, A.B., F.C. Neal, P.T. Cardeilhac, J.A. Popp, F.H. White, and R.L. Jenkins. 1980. Clinical observations on captive and free-ranging West Indian manatees, *Trichechus manatus,* in Florida. Aquat. Mammal. 8:2–10.

Jenkins, R.L. 1981. Captive husbandry of the manatees at Marineland of Florida. In: The West Indian Manatee in Florida. R.L. Brownell, Jr., and K. Ralls (eds.). Fla. Dept. Nat. Res., Tallahassee, Fla. pp. 128–130.

Layne, J.N. 1965. Observations on marine

mammals in Florida waters. Bull. Fla. State Mus. 9:131–181.

Lefebvre, L.W., T.J. O'Shea, G.B. Rathbun, and R.C. Best. 1989. Distribution, status, and biogeography of the West Indian manatee. In: Biogeography of the West Indies. C.A. Woods (ed.). Sandhill Crane, Gainesville. pp. 567–610.

Marsh, H., and P.K. Anderson. 1983. Probable susceptibility of dugongs to capture stress. Biol. Conserv. 25:1–3.

Medway, W., M.L. Bruss, J.L. Bengtson, and D.J. Black. 1982a. Blood chemistry of the West Indian manatee (*Trichechus manatus*). J. Wildl. Dis. 18:229–234.

Medway, W., W.J. Dodds, A.C. Moynihan, and R.K. Bonde. 1982b. Blood coagulation of the West Indian manatee (*Trichechus manatus*). Cornell Vet. 72:120–127.

Medway, W., G.B. Rathbun, and D.J. Black. 1982c. Hematology of the West Indian manatee (*Trichechus manatus*). Vet. Clin. Pathol. 11:11–15.

Mok, W.Y., and R.C. Best. 1979. Saprophytic colonization of a hyphomycete in the Amazonian manatee *Trichechus inunguis* (Mammalia: Sirenia). Aquat. Mammal. 7:79–82.

Moore, J.C. 1956. Observations of manatees in aggregations. Am. Mus. Novit. 1811:1–24.

Morales, P., S.H. Madin, and A. Hunter. 1985. Systemic *Mycobacterium marinum* infection in an Amazon manatee. J. Am. Vet. Med. Assoc. 187:1230–1231.

Murie, J. 1872. On the form and structure of the manatee (*Manatus americanus*). Trans. Zool. Soc. Lond. 8:127–202.

Odell, D.K. 1982. West Indian manatee. In: Wild mammals of North America. J.A. Chapman and G.A. Feldhamer (eds.). Johns Hopkins Univ. Press, Baltimore. pp. 828–837.

Odell, D.K., and J.E. Reynolds. 1979. Observations on manatee mortality in south Florida. J. Wildl. Manage. 43:572–577.

O'Shea, T.J. 1986. Unpublished data. USFWS, Gainesville, Fla.

———. 1988. The past, present, and future of manatees in the southeastern United States: Realities, misunderstandings, and enigmas. In: Proc. 3d S.E. Nongame and Endangered Wildlife Symp. R.R. Odom et al. (eds.). Ga. Dept. Nat. Res., Social Circle, Ga. pp. 184–204.

O'Shea, T.J., and G.B. Rathbun. 1982. Summary report on a die-off of the West Indian manatee (*Trichechus manatus*) in Lee County, Florida, Spring 1982. Unpublished report, Denver Wildlife Research Center, Gainesville, Fla. 689 pp.

O'Shea, T.J., J.F. Moore, and H.I. Kochman. 1984. Contaminant concentrations in manatees in Florida. J. Wildl. Manage. 48:741–748.

O'Shea, T.J., C.A. Beck, R.K. Bonde, H.I. Kochman, and D.K. Odell. 1985a. An analysis of manatee mortality patterns in Florida, 1976–81. J. Wildl. Manage. 49:1–11.

O'Shea, T.J., G.B. Rathbun, E.D. Asper, and S.W. Searles. 1985b. Tolerance of West Indian manatees to capture and handling. Biol. Conserv. 33:335–349.

O'Shea, T.J., G.B. Rathbun, R.K. Bonde, C.D. Buergelt, and D.K. Odell. 1991. An epizootic of Florida manatees associated with a dinoflagellate bloom. Mar. Mammal Sci. 7:118–146.

Pervaiz, S., and K. Brew. 1986. Purification and characterization of the major whey proteins from the milk of the bottlenose dolphin (*Tursiops truncatus*), the Florida manatee (*Trichechus manatus latirostris*) and the beagle (*Canis familiaris*). Arch. Biochem. Biophys. 246:846–854.

Pilsbry, H.A. 1916. The sessile barnacles (Cirripedia) contained in the collections of the U.S. National Museum including a monograph of the American species. USNM Bull. 93:261–267, 284–287, 354–357.

Popp, J.A. 1977. Unpublished data. (Pathology Report No. N77-25, Coll. of Vet. Med., Univ. of Florida, Gainesville).

Radhakrishnan, C.V., and R.E. Bradley. 1970. Some helminths from animals at Busch Gardens Zoological Park. Assoc. Southeast. Biol. Bull. 17:58–59.

Reynolds, J.E., III. 1980. Aspects of the structural and functional anatomy of the gastrointestinal tract of the West Indian manatee, *Trichechus manatus*. Ph.D. diss., Univ. of Miami, Coral Gables. 110 pp.

Ronald, K., L.J. Shelley, and E.C. Amoroso. 1978. Biological synopsis of the manatee. Internat. Dev. Res. Centre, Ottawa, Canada. 112 pp.

Russell, S.W., and J. Cooley. 1985. Unpublished data. (Pathology Report No. N84-1004, Coll. of Vet. Med., Univ. of Florida, Gainesville).

Scholander, P.F., and L. Irving. 1941. Experimental investigations on the respiration and diving of the Florida manatee. J. Cell. Comp. Physiol. 17:169–191.

Shane, S.H. 1981. Abundance, distribution, and use of power plant effluents by manatees (*Trichechus manatus*) in Brevard County, Florida. U.S. Fish and Wildlife Service, National Fish and Wildlife Laboratory Contract Report No. 61552-86540 to Florida Power and Light Company. NTIS Pub. No. PB 81-147019. 244 pp.

Sprent, J.F. A. 1980. Ascaridoid nematodes of sirenians—the Heterocheilinae redefined. J. Helminthol. 45:309–27.

Tabuchi, K., T. Muku, T. Satomichi, M. Hara, N. Imai, and Y. Iwamoto. 1974. A dermatosis in manatee (*Trichechus manatus*): Mycological report of a case. Bull. Azabu. Vet. Coll. 28:127–134.

Upton, S.J., D.K. Odell, G.D. Bossart, and M.T. Walsh. 1989. Description of the oocysts of two new species of *Eimeria* (Apicomplexa: Eimeriidae) from the Florida manatee, *Trichechus manatus* (Sirenia: Trichechidae). J. Protozool. 36:87–90.

Walsh, M.T., G.D. Bossart, W.G. Young, Jr., and P.M. Rose. 1987. Omphalitis and peritonitis in a young West Indian manatee (*Trichechus manatus*). J. Wildl. Dis. 23:702–704.

Watson, A.G., and R.K. Bonde. 1986. Congenital malformations of the flipper in three West Indian manatees, *Trichechus manatus,* and a proposed mechanism for development of ectrodactyly and cleft hand in mammals. Clin. Orthoped. 202:294–301.

White, J.R., D.R. Harkness, R.E. Isaacks, and D.A. Duffield. 1976. Some studies on blood of the Florida manatee, *Trichechus manatus latirostris*. Comp. Biochem. Physiol. 55A: 413–417.

Whitfield, W.K., and S.L. Farrington. 1975. An annotated bibliography of Sirenia. Fla. Dept. Nat. Resour. Mar. Res. Publ. 7. 44 pp.

Wright, S.D. 1990. Unpublished data. DNR, St. Petersburg, Fla.

Zeiller, W. 1981. The management of West Indian manatees (*Trichechus manatus*) at the Miami Seaquarium. In: The West Indian manatee in Florida. R.L. Brownell, Jr., and K. Ralls (eds.). Fla. Dept. Nat. Res., Tallahassee, Fla. pp. 103–110.

White-tailed Deer

I. Introduction

Two species of deer occur in Florida, the white-tailed deer, *Odocoileus virginianus* (Zimmermann), which is native to the state, and the sambar deer, *Cervus unicolor* (Cuvier), which was introduced (Brown 1987). Whitetails are abundant and widespread throughout the state. They are an important game species; in the 1986–87 season close to 90,000 were killed by hunters (Wright 1987). Two subspecies occur on the Florida mainland: *O. v. osceolus* and *O. v. seminolus* (Stevenson 1976). A third subspecies, the Key deer (*O. v. clavium*), is found only in the Florida Keys and, because of its unique and endangered status, will be discussed separately in the following chapter. The sambar deer is found only on St. Vincent Island and also will be dealt with elsewhere (Chapter 22).

There is no doubt that white-tailed deer have received more attention from the parasite/disease standpoint than any other species of wildlife in Florida. This is obvious from the published literature and from numerous unpublished reports and documents. The great bulk of our knowledge stems from the efforts of the personnel of the Southeastern Cooperative Wildlife Disease Study (SCWDS) at the University of Georgia (Athens). In the 25-year period 1963–1987, for example, SCWDS personnel obtained data from over 450 deer from 24 counties in Florida (SCWDS records). Much of their work has been summarized in numerous journal articles and reports and in a book edited by Davidson et al. (1981) entitled *Diseases and Parasites of White-Tailed Deer*. This excellent book contains a wealth of detailed information on deer in Florida and in other parts of its range.

II. Trauma

Wobeser (1981) analyzed the literature on injuries to white-tailed deer and reported that trauma was responsible for 72% to 98% of all deer mortality, not counting that induced by hunters. He stated that long-term or chronic morbidity due to trauma was insignificant and cited a study done in the Southeast by Nettles et al. (1976).

Injuries may be classified into three major categories: (1) intraspecific conflicts; (2) interspecific conflicts; and (3) inanimate factors. Intraspecific conflicts occur mainly between bucks during the rut. There is not much evidence that injury due to fighting is very common in the Southeast (Nettles et al. 1976), but such conflict can result in skull fractures and secondary bacterial infections of the brain (Davidson et al. 1990). Four such cases were seen in Florida deer (Table 20-11), all during the month of October.

Interspecific conflicts are a result of encounters with man or his machinery and structures and also with predators. Encounters between deer and motor vehicles are usually fatal (Nettles et al. 1976). The number of deer killed on highways is considerable. In a study published in 1964 it was estimated that 800 deer were killed on Florida highways that year (Thompson 1964). At the present time this figure is certainly much higher considering the growth of population and the expanded road systems in the state. In addition to road-kills, deer are known to die from encounters with fences and other structures. Strode (1954) reported four such instances where deer were found entangled with barbed wire fences. In 1977 a yearling buck was found in a weakened condition next to a chain-link fence in Alachua County. The animal did not respond to treatment and died two days later. At necropsy it was found to have a fractured neck that may have been associated with the deer becoming entangled in the fence (Forrester 1984). A similar incident was recorded in Marion County in 1980. Such happenings may be more common than is realized.

Capture myopathy (or exertional rhabdomyolysis) is sometimes seen in restrained deer. A concise summary of this degenerative disease of skeletal muscles has been given by Wobeser (1981). He states that the problem may be more common than suspected. Signs include depression, incoordination, muscle stiffness, and sometimes paralysis, coma, and death. At necropsy such animals may have pale or streaked muscles and hemorrhage. Kidneys often are pale and swollen, and the urinary bladder may contain dark, wine-colored urine (Wobeser 1981). This condition was seen in a doe that had been live-trapped in 1979 at Cape Canaveral (Brevard County). The day following capture and tagging, it was found moribund. At necropsy the classic signs of capture myopathy were evident. This particular condition should be kept in mind during capture-release operations with deer and may be a cause of losses that appear to occur for no obvious reason.

The overall significance of trauma due to predators such as Florida panthers, bobcats, coyotes, black bears, and domestic dogs is poorly known. Two of six stomachs and 28 of 61 scats from Florida panthers in southern Florida contained remains of white-tailed deer (Belden 1986), indicating that this predator relies fairly heavily on deer as a food item. Maehr et al. (1990) examined 270 scats from panthers in southwestern Florida and found that white-tailed deer were the second most common prey (28% frequency of occurrence) next to wild hogs (42%). Deer were more frequently taken (41%) in the southern areas (Fakahatchee Strand State Preserve and Big Cypress National Preserve) studied by Maehr et al. (1990) than in the northern areas (Florida Panther National Wildlife Refuge and other areas in northern Collier County) (36%). Of almost 400 stomachs from bobcats obtained throughout the state of Florida, less than 2% (by volume) contained deer remains (Maehr 1984). Land (1990) studied white-tailed deer in the Bear Island Unit of the Big Cypress National Preserve from 1986 to 1990 and found that of 20 radio-tagged deer found dead, 9 deaths were from predation, 5 by bobcats and 4 by Florida panthers. Personnel of the SCWDS examined 2 deer in 1982 from Broward County that they felt had been attacked by predators. One was diagnosed as having died of trauma and suffocation due to attack by a bobcat. The other had signs of trauma and subsequent secondary bacterial infection and toxemia. Stomachs from several coyotes in Florida contained no deer material (Maehr 1984). The black bear is known to consume deer occasionally (Maehr and Brady 1984), but this may be carrion-feeding rather than predation. In 1979 an adult buck from DeSoto County was found in debilitated condition. Upon examination it was found to have an old granulated wound on its right hindquarter with secondary bacterial infection of the leg and scrotum. The wound may have been inflicted initially by a predator. This type of situation has not been found very often. Nettles et al. (1976) examined over 1,000 deer in the Southeast (including a number from Florida) for evidence of chronic debilitation. These were deer that were collected for scien-

tific purposes other than studies of trauma. Only 7.6% of these deer showed evidence of previous injury. Thirty percent of these injuries were related to gunshot or arrow wounds, but the remainder were not identified as to the cause. Some of those might have been caused by predators.

III. Inclement weather

Inclement weather can result in some mortality of deer. Storms, cold weather, and flooding are likely causes in Florida. The Everglades deer herd in southern Florida appears to be prone to mortality due to extended high water conditions. Loveless (1959, p. 43), for instance, reported that during "the critical winter high water period of 1957–58 it was estimated that the Everglades herd was reduced by approximately 30 percent as a result of starvation and associated disease." During that same winter, along with the high water were unusually low temperatures and chilling winds that, according to Loveless (1959), were related to an increased prevalence of pneumonia. He also stated that during times of prolonged high water the deer become crowded on elevated "islands," experience a decline in general health, and are more susceptible to parasitism and other diseases in concert with malnutrition. Similar die-offs have occurred at other times in the Everglades deer herd such as in 1968–69, 1979, and 1982 (Prestwood et al. 1973; Florida Game and Fresh Water Fish Commission 1983).

IV. Toxicosis and environmental contaminants

According to Murphy (1981), who reviewed the literature on white-tailed deer, toxicosis is not an important factor. He pointed out that there are occasional deaths of deer from poisoning (poisonous plants, inorganic and organic chemicals, etc.), but that "large scale die-offs are rare" (p. 43). Hayes and Jenkins (1959), however, in a discussion of poisonous plants and their impact on deer in the southeastern United States, pointed out that because published records on this topic are rare, it may be a mistake to assume that there is little cause for concern. They stated that there are approximately 100 species of poisonous plants in the Southeast and virtually every deer habitat has one or more such plants. The reader is referred to their paper on this subject for further details and to the review by Fowler (1983) for a discussion of poisonous plants and their effects on wildlife.

Several studies have been conducted on radionuclide concentrations in white-tailed deer of Florida. Most of Florida lies within an area of high fallout bioaccumulation (Jenkins and Fendley 1971). A variety of plants, animals, and animal products from several southeastern states (including Florida) were analyzed for radionuclide concentrations by Jenkins and Fendley (1968). Cesium-137 was the most important isotope and high concentrations that were over 300 times those of domestic livestock were found in muscles of white-tailed deer (Table 20-1). Concentra-

tions in deer from other states (North Carolina, Alabama, Virginia, South Carolina, and Georgia) were considerably lower (Cummings et al. 1971; Jenkins and Fendley 1968). The apparent source of the cesium-137 is plants that obtain it from the atmosphere or via uptake from soil. These plants are then eaten by deer in which the cesium-137 accumulates (Roessler et al. 1969). Johnson and Nayfield (1970) found that the common gill mushroom in Duval, Clay, and Dixie counties showed concentrations of cesium-137 that were an order of magnitude higher than other vegetation consumed by deer. Jenkins and Fendley (1968) concluded that the long-term effects of these radionuclide concentrations on deer were unknown. In addition, the effects on human consumption were considered minimal since the concentrations in deer muscle were found to vary seasonally and the high concentrations occurred after the hunting season was over. Nevertheless, it is good news that concentrations of radionuclides in Florida's environment decreased considerably in the 1980s (Roessler 1984).

Cumbie and Jenkins (1975) found residues of mercury in the hair of five deer from Eglin Air Force Base (Walton County) in 1973–1974. Concentrations varied from 0.13 to

Table 20-1
Concentrations of cesium-137 in samples of muscle from white-tailed deer in Florida

Location	No. deer sampled	Date	Picocuries of cesium-137		
			Mean	Range	S.E.
Eglin Air Force Base					
(Walton Co.)	5	May 1967	5,577	879–15,815	2,665
	5	August 1967	7,913	2,486–13,218	1,675
	5	November 1967	24,018	12,416–29,513	2,683
		February 1968	120,861	80,713–	12,442
	5			152,940	
	8	March 1968	41,111	2,660–77,060	8,042
	5	May 1968	4,968	2,387–7,543	733
Big Cypress Swamp					
(Collier Co.)	5	January 1968	3,050	2,321–4,710	387

Source: Jenkins and Fendley (1968).

0.40 ppm that, according to the authors, were below lethal concentrations. In other studies in Collier, Monroe, and Dade counties, concentrations of mercury in liver and kidney samples varied between 0.06 and 0.80 ppm (Table 20-2). These data are comparable to those obtained from white-tailed deer in Oklahoma (Kocan et al. 1980) and probably should be considered to be normal values.

Concentrations of cadmium in deer from Collier, Monroe, and Dade counties varied

from 0.03 to 3.34 ppm in liver and kidney samples (Table 20-2). These amounts are low and should be considered normal background concentrations (Eisler 1985). In Collier, Monroe, and Dade counties, low concentrations of lead (0.05–0.23 ppm) and arsenic (0.02–0.13 ppm) were found (Wright et al. 1988; Sundlof and Forrester 1990). Chromium concentrations in these same deer were low (Table 20-2), although one deer (three years of age) from Stairsteps had residues

Table 20-2
Concentrations (ppm wet wt) of heavy metals in livers and kidneys of white-tailed deer from southern Florida, 1984–88

Metal	Date	Locality (county)	Liver No. deer Exam.	Liver No. deer Pos.	Liver Mean[a]	Liver Range[a]	Kidney No. deer Exam.	Kidney No. deer Pos.	Kidney Mean[a]	Kidney Range[a]	Data source
Mercury[b]	1984	Collier	10	10	0.25	0.14–0.41	10	10	0.23	0.06–0.80	Wright et al. (1988)
	1985	Collier	9	9	0.30	0.21–0.40	9	9	0.39	0.17–0.62	" "
	1986	Collier	9	9	0.26	0.12–0.45	9	9	0.50	0.37–0.62	" "
	1988	Monroe/ Dade	10	5	0.12	0.09–0.16	10	6	0.12	0.09–0.16	Sundlof & Forrester (1990)
Cadmium[c]	1984	Collier	10	10	0.21	0.08–0.55	10	10	0.99	0.23–2.36	Wright et al. (1988)
	1985	Collier	9	9	0.31	0.05–0.57	9	9	1.36	0.16–2.14	" "
	1986	Collier	9	9	0.18	0.09–0.42	9	9	0.64	0.20–1.60	" "
	1988	Monroe/ Dade	10	10	0.08	0.03–0.28	10	10	1.79	0.28–3.34	Sundlof & Forrester (1990)
Chromium[d]	1984	Collier	10	10	0.06	0.03–0.08	10	10	0.05	0.03–0.09	Wright et al. (1988)
	1985	Collier	9	9	0.04	0.03–0.07	9	9	0.10	0.03–0.44	" "
	1986	Collier	9	9	0.06	0.03–0.11	9	9	0.11	0.03–0.25	" "
	1988	Monroe/ Dade	10	10	0.52	0.10–1.62	10	10	0.56	0.03–3.38	Sundlof & Forrester (1990)
Lead[e]	1984	Collier	10	2	0.14	0.12–0.15	10	2	0.16	0.12–0.20	Wright et al. (1988)
	1985	Collier	9	0	—	—	9	0	—	—	" "
	1986	Collier	9	1	0.17	—	9	0	—	—	" "
	1988	Monroe/ Dade	10	8	0.12	0.06–0.23	10	10	0.09	0.05–0.20	Sundlof & Forrester (1990)

Note: Most of the deer were 1- to 3-year-old females.
[a]Values are for samples that were positive for the metal; negative samples are not included in these calculations.
[b]Lowest level of detection for mercury = 0.05 ppm.
[c]Lowest level of detection for cadmium = 0.005 ppm.
[d]Lowest level of detection for chromium = 0.02 ppm.
[e]Lowest level of detection for lead = 0.05 ppm.

above 3 ppm, which may be presumptive evidence of chromium contamination (Eisler 1986).

The sublethal effects of these heavy metals on white-tailed deer are unknown. This neglected topic should be investigated.

Studies have been conducted on pesticide residues in white-tailed deer in South Carolina (Barrier et al. 1970) and Mississippi (Cotton and Herring 1970), but not in Florida. Such studies should be done since pesticides are known to increase postpartum mortality, slow down development of immature deer, and impair initial conception by young does (Murphy and Korschgen 1970). Other environmental pollutants such as polychlorinated biphenyls, certain fungicides, and gaseous pollutants are known to damage the immune system (Caren 1981) and such deleterious effects could occur in white-tailed deer. At the present time, however, we have no indication that this is occurring in Florida.

V. Neoplasia

A number of tumors have been reported from white-tailed deer. Cosgrove et al. (1981) listed 13 benign and 16 malignant tumors and emphasized that the most frequent were skin tumors and lymphomas. Neoplasia of the central nervous system was also common. Only one internal neoplasm was found in over 1,000 deer from throughout the Southeast that were examined at necropsy (Cosgrove et al. 1981). Three visceral tumors have been reported from deer in Florida and include single cases of lymphosarcoma, nasal squamous cell carcinoma, and hepatocellular carcinoma (Table 20-3). These tumors are not of overall significance to deer populations in Florida.

By far the most common neoplasms are infectious cutaneous fibromas. Seven such

cases have been reported from Florida (Table 20-3). The lesions on the deer from Marion County are illustrated in Figures 20-1 through 20-4. They varied in size from very tiny nodules (Figure 20-1) to massive confluent areas (Figure 20-2). Some were pedunculated or pendulous (Figures 20-3 and 20-4). Sometimes the tumors are damaged, which results in bleeding and secondary bacterial infections. They are usually pigmented and warty in appearance and when incised are found to have a white fibrotic core (Cosgrove and Fay 1981).

There have been several studies that give the prevalence of this tumor as 1.4% of 3,000 deer in New York, 1.7% of almost 3,000 deer in Connecticut, and 1.3% of 1,065 deer in the Southeast (including one from Florida) (Friend 1967; Cosgrove et al. 1981; Sundberg and Neilsen 1982). The study by Sundberg and Neilsen (1982) indicated that the prevalence may be much higher in deer populations since small tumors may be easily overlooked. They found prevalences of 10.3% of 146 deer in New York and 6.6% of 136 deer in southern Vermont when all tumors (even the smallest) were considered, but when they recalculated their data based only on the most prominent tumors, they obtained prevalences of 6.6% and 1.5%, respectively—values that are similar to many of those published from other studies.

Cutaneous fibromas are caused by viruses (papovaviruses) that are transmitted from deer to deer by direct contact, insect vectors (such as mosquitoes), and mechanical injury (Cosgrove and Fay 1981). Young males are infected more commonly and this has been attributed to wounds produced during fighting and antler rubbing (Friend 1967; Cosgrove et al. 1981). All seven of the cases in Florida were seen in October, November, or February, which is after the peak mosquito season.

Table 20-3
Cases of neoplasia reported from white-tailed deer in Florida

Tumor	Age (yr)	Sex	Year	County	Data source
Cutaneous fibroma	NG[a]	NG	1962	NG	Harlow & Jones (1965)
	NG	F	1966	Jackson	SCWDS records
	4.5	M	1968	Okaloosa	" "
	2.5	F	1973	Flagler	Forrester (1988a)
	Ad	F	1976	Marion	" "
	3	M	1981	Gadsden	" "
	1.5	F	1988	Collier	Wright (1988a)
Lymphosarcoma	15[b]	F	1984	Columbia	Calderwood-Mays (1984)
Nasal squamous cell carcinoma	5.5	F	1984	Leon	SCWDS records
Hepatocellular carcinoma	6.5	F	1987	Gadsden	" "

[a]NG = not given by authors.
[b]This deer was semitame and was from Oleno State Park.

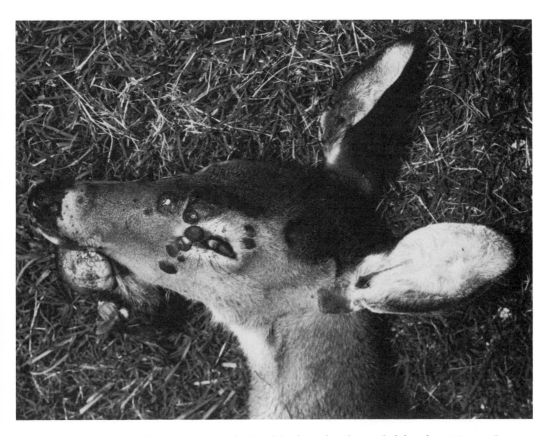

FIGURE 20-1. Cutaneous fibromas on the left side of the face of a white-tailed deer from Marion County, Florida.

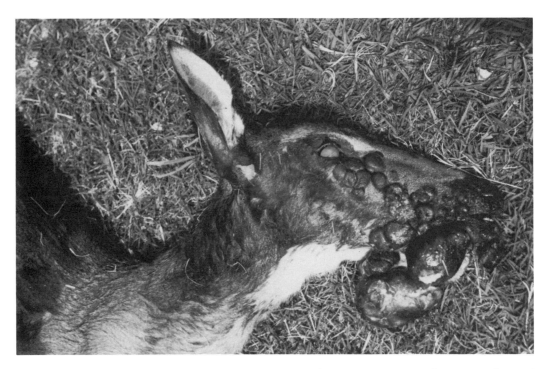

FIGURE 20-2. Right side of face of same deer as in Fig. 20-1 showing numerous small tumors and several large tumors on the lower jaws. Several are confluent. Some are damaged and have secondary infections.

FIGURE 20-3. Large tumor near base of tail of deer shown in Fig. 20-1.

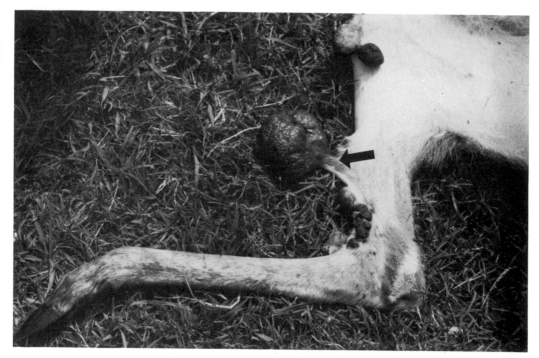

FIGURES 20-4. Baseball-size tumor on left rear leg of same deer as in Fig. 20-1. Note pedunculated attachment (arrow).

The consensus of various reports on cutaneous fibromas is that they are self-limiting and of little consequence to deer populations. Occasionally a severe infection may result in massive lesions that interfere with vision, respiration, feeding, and other activities of an individual deer. SCWDS records give two cases of impaired vision by these tumors. Of the cases we have seen, only one was judged to be of serious consequence to the deer.

For further details on this topic, the reader is referred to the reviews by Fay (1970), Cosgrove and Fay (1981), and Cosgrove et al. (1981).

VI. Hemorrhagic disease

The term *hemorrhagic disease* (HD) refers to a syndrome caused by bluetongue virus (BTV), epizootic hemorrhagic disease virus (EHDV), or dual infections of both viruses (Prestwood et al. 1974a). This disease is probably the most important infectious disease of white-tailed deer in the Southeast and in Florida. Two excellent reviews on HD have been published (Hoff and Trainer 1981; Thomas 1981).

Both viruses are orbiviruses and are antigenically distinct. For some time they were thought to be the same virus because they are identical morphologically and cause the same signs and lesions in deer (Thomas 1981). For all practical purposes it is useful to consider them together. There are five serotypes of BTV and probably one or two serotypes of EHDV that occur in North America (Greiner et al. 1985; Thomas 1981).

Both BTV and EHDV are transmitted by biting midges of the genus *Culicoides*. In most of North America where white-tailed deer occur, the only proven vector is *Culi-*

coides variipennis. In the southern half of the Florida peninsula, however, *C. variipennis* does not occur and instead the neotropical species *C. insignis* is believed to be the vector (Kramer et al. 1985a; Greiner et al. 1985). Hemorrhagic disease is usually seen in late summer and early fall in the acute form (Couvillion et al. 1981), and this occurrence of the disease correlates with the peak populations of *Culicoides* in Florida (Kramer et al. 1985b). The chronic form of the disease is known to occur in fall and winter (Couvillion et al. 1981).

Hemorrhagic disease viruses are widespread in deer throughout the Southeast (Couvillion et al. 1981, Stallknecht et al. 1991). Serologic tests on 504 deer from 17 counties in Florida from 1965 to 1990 have been conducted, and the results indicated that 37% were positive for antibodies to BTV and 39% for antibodies to EHDV (Table 20-4). Some deer were positive for both. In recent years there have been a number of outbreaks of HD in the Southeast. The most severe of these occurred in 1949, 1954, 1955, 1971, and 1980 (Prestwood et al. 1974a; Couvillion et al. 1981). It is not clear if Florida deer were involved in 1949, 1954, and 1955, but they were in the 1971 and 1980 outbreaks. In both 1971 and 1980 the disease was confirmed in northern Florida. In 1971, 25 of 400 deer in an enclosure in Liberty County died during September–December and many more were moribund (Prestwood et al. 1974a). In 1980 other outbreaks occurred in Leon and Union counties. Chronic HD was diagnosed by SCWDS in a single deer in 1973 (Gadsden County) and 1981 (Leon County). In 1982 we examined a 1 1/2-year-old deer from Liberty County that had the chronic form of hemorrhagic disease. It was a hunter-killed buck that was killed on November 29. It appears that HD viruses are enzootic throughout Florida, particularly in the north-

ern half of the state, but that outbreaks of the disease occur only in the panhandle (Figure 20-5). The reasons for this pattern are unclear at this time, but could be related to densities of deer and vectors, or the virulence of the virus strains in that area, or combinations of these factors. It is also possible that the observations are an artifact of reporting and that the disease is occurring but is not being recognized and reported as readily in some areas as in others.

Prevalences of both viruses appear to be similar among age classes greater than one year as was shown in a study conducted in the Big Cypress National Preserve during 1984–1986 (Tables 20-5 and 20-6). Local variations in prevalence can also occur as illustrated by the Big Cypress study in which antibodies to BTV and EHDV were 81% and 77% in deer from Bear Island and only 21% and 14% in deer from Raccoon Point. These differences are probably due to a number of ecological factors that may lead to variations in vector abundance and also may be related to the presence of range cattle on the Bear Island area and their absence from Raccoon Point. Both EHDV and BTV are common in cattle in Florida and both viruses have been isolated from *Culicoides* feeding on cattle (Kramer et al. 1985a; Greiner et al. 1985). The relationship of cattle and deer as reservoirs of the virus for each other is unknown.

Many domestic and wild ruminants become infected with BTV and EHDV, but the white-tailed deer appears to be the most susceptible to HD as a result of these infections. The viruses replicate in many different tissues of the deer's body, especially in association with the vascular endothelial cells and some of the cells in the hemopoietic system (Thomas 1981). The signs and lesions associated with the disease are related to the cytopathology of these cells. The review by Thomas (1981) has an excellent description of the dis-

Table 20-4

Distribution and numbers of white-tailed deer seropositive for bluetongue and epizootic hemorrhagic disease (EHD) viruses, 1965–90

County	Year	No. deer tested	Bluetongue virus		EHD virus		Data source
			No. deer pos.	%	No. deer pos.	%	
Broward	1982	37	16	43	11	30	SCWDS records
Clay	1968	5	0	0	0	0	Thomas & Prestwood (1976)
Collier	1968	12	0	0	0	0	" " " "
	1984–86	110	55	50	49	45	Forrester & Roelke (1986)
	1986	22	15	68	12	55	Wright & Forrester (1987)
	1987	33	25	76	25	76	Forrester (1989a)
	1988	54	29	54	30	56	" "
	1989	33	12	36	7	19	" "
	1990	39	20	51	17	44	Forrester (1990)
Dade	1987	14	0	0	0	0	Wright & Smith (1988)
Duval	1965	10	0	0	0	0	Thomas & Prestwood (1976)
	1971	5	0	0	0	0	" " " "
Franklin	1984	6	1	17	2	33	SCWDS records
Indian R.	1987	1	1	100	1	100	Forrester (1988a)
Leon	1970	6	0	0	2	33	Thomas & Prestwood (1976)
Levy	1984	4	0	0	3	75	SCWDS records
	1986	5	1	20	0	0	" "
Liberty	1971	1	0	0	0	0	Thomas & Prestwood (1976)
Marion	1980	10	0	0	1	10	SCWDS records
Monroe/Dade	1988	15	1	7	1	7	Forrester (1989b)
	1989	13	1	8	1	8	" "
Nassau	1970	7	0	0	3	43	Thomas & Prestwood (1976)
Osceola	1987	5	4	80	4	80	SCWDS records
	1987	1	1	100	1	100	Forrester (1988a)
St. Lucie	1986	1	0	0	0	0	" "
Wakulla	1981	10	0	0	5	50	SCWDS records
	1983	5	0	0	4	80	" "
	1985	5	1	20	4	80	" "
	1986	5	1	20	1	20	" "
	1987	5	1	20	2	40	" "
Walton	1967	15	1	7	8	53	Thomas & Prestwood (1976)
	1968	8	0	0	5	63	" " " "
	1969	2	0	0	0	0	" " " "
Totals	1965–90	504	186	37	199	39	

ease as it is manifested in deer and is accompanied by a series of color plates. Additional details are given by Howerth (1986). Prestwood et al. (1974a) described three forms of the disease as observed in the 1971 outbreak: peracute, acute, and chronic. The peracute form is accompanied by few gross lesions except for massive pulmonary edema that causes death. Acute HD was characterized by hemorrhages throughout the body of the deer, particularly the digestive tract. Erosions of the dental pad (Figure 20-6), hard

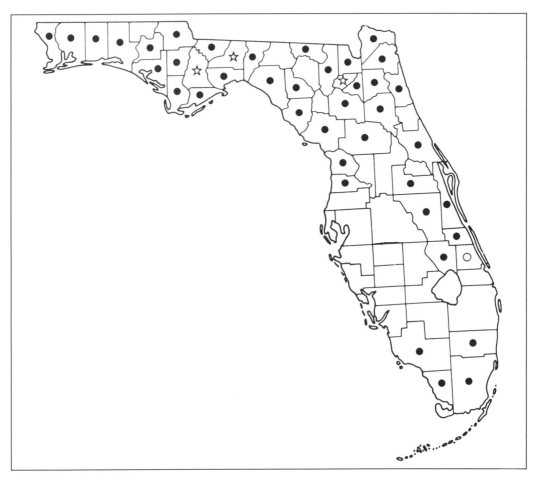

FIGURE 20-5. Distribution of hemorrhagic disease viruses in white-tailed deer in Florida. Stars indicate locations of epizootics. Closed circles indicate counties where serologic or pathologic evidence indicates virus activity. Open circles represent areas where tests on deer were negative. (From Couvillion et al. 1981; Forrester 1988a; Forrester and Roelke 1986; Prestwood et al. 1974a; SCWDS records; Thomas and Prestwood 1976; Wright 1988a.)

palate, and tongue were common. Some cases of coronitis also were seen (Figure 20-7). The chronic disease was associated with a variety of conditions, the most common of which were lesions of the digestive tract and feet. These included ulcers of the dental pad, hard palate, and tongue; ulceration and sloughing of the lining of the forestomachs; gastritis; enteritis; and various foot lesions (coronitis and laminitis) including complete sloughing of the hooves and secondary infec-

tions and abscesses of the feet. Surviving deer often become lame and move about on their carpal joints and sternum, which results in abrasions (Figure 20-8). These deer often have scars and atrophied villi in their rumens (Figure 20-9).

Most deer infected with BTV or EHDV die or else recover completely. The mortality rate is high among acutely ill deer, but the morbidity rate is quite variable (Thomas 1981). Secondary bacterial or mycotic infections may

Table 20-5

Prevalence of antibodies to bluetongue virus in various age classes of white-tailed deer from the Bear Island and Raccoon Point areas of the Big Cypress National Preserve, 1984–86

Age class (yr)	Bear Island		Raccoon Point		Both areas	
	N	Prevalence (%)	N	Prevalence (%)	N	Prevalence (%)
Fawns (< 1)	7	14	11	9	18	6
1	12	92	12	17	24	54
2	16	88	14	29	30	60
3	9	89	9	33	18	61
4	5	100	5	20	10	60
5	2	100	6	33	8	50
6	2	100	0	—	2	100
All ages	53	81	57	21	110	50

Source: Forrester and Roelke (1986).

Table 20-6

Prevalence of antibodies to EHD virus in various age classes of white-tailed deer from the Bear Island and Raccoon Point areas of the Big Cypress National Preserve, 1984–86

Age class (yr)	Bear Island		Raccoon Point		Both areas	
	N	Prevalence (%)	N	Prevalence (%)	N	Prevalence (%)
Fawns (< 1)	7	0	11	0	18	0
1	12	83	12	17	24	50
2	16	88	14	14	30	53
3	9	89	9	11	18	50
4	5	100	5	20	10	60
5	2	100	6	33	8	50
6	2	100	0	—	2	100
All ages	53	77	57	14	110	45

Source: Forrester and Roelke (1986).

have serious effects on deer as well. Additional losses may occur *in utero* since BTV has been shown to cause early absorption or abortion of the fetus in experimentally infected white-tailed deer (Thomas and Trainer 1970). As mentioned earlier in this chapter, this disease is probably the most important infectious disease of white-tailed deer in Florida and can be the cause of extensive morbidity and mortality.

VII. Arboviruses

In addition to bluetongue virus and EHD virus, nine other arboviruses have been reported from deer in Florida (Table 20-7). With the exception of vesicular stomatitis (VS) virus, none of these is of pathologic significance to deer. Some, however, are of zoonotic importance, being associated with encephalitis or febrile diseases in humans

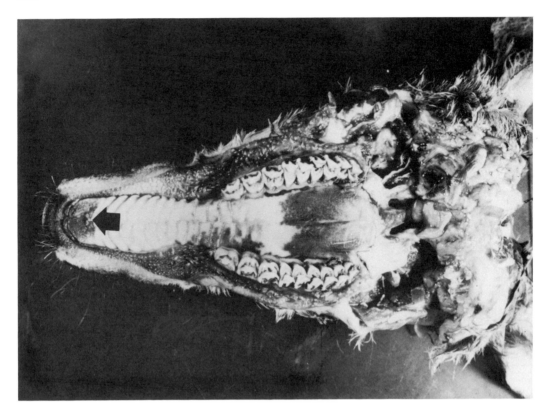

FIGURE 20-6. Erosions of dental pad (arrow) in acute form of hemorrhagic disease in white-tailed deer. (Photo courtesy of SCWDS.)

(Richards 1981). Mosquitoes are the vectors for these viruses and a large number of wild mammals (other than deer), domestic mammals, and birds are involved in their epidemiology and distribution (Richards 1981). The reader is referred to the review by Seymour and Yuill (1981) for further details on arboviruses in wildlife.

Vesicular stomatitis virus causes a disease characterized by the development of vesicles (blisters) on the skin of the mouth or feet (Karstad 1981). The virus is indigenous to North America and in the southeastern United States infections occur almost on an annual basis in some areas. In addition to white-tailed deer, antibodies have been found in humans, swine, cattle, horses, bobcats, and raccoons (Hanson 1968). Transmission is via direct contact or by biting insects, although the latter method is apparently rare in Florida and the only area where viral activity in deer has been demonstrated is in southern Florida (i.e., Collier and Monroe counties), where serological evidence of its presence has been obtained (Table 20-7). No clinical cases of VS have been reported in Florida deer. The overall importance of VS to white-tailed deer in Florida is probably very minor. Deer with vesicular lesions in their mouths or on their feet should be reported to the proper authorities, however, because of the possibility of such a disease being foot-and-mouth disease, the clinical signs of which are very similar to VS (Karstad 1981).

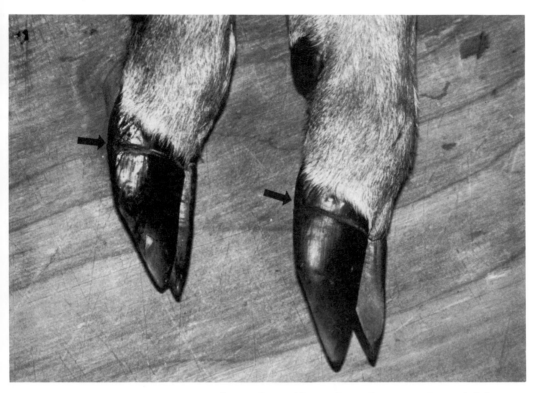

FIGURES 20-7. Laminitis (arrows) in chronic form of hemorrhagic disease in white-tailed deer.

VIII. Other viral diseases

There is evidence for the occurrence of three other viruses in white-tailed deer in Florida, all of which are primarily viruses of cattle. These include infectious bovine rhinotracheitis (IBR) virus, bovine virus diarrhea (BVD) virus, and parainfluenza-3 virus (PI-3) virus (Table 20-8).

Antibodies to IBR were found in only one deer from Collier County (Forrester and Roelke 1986). This herpesvirus causes respiratory disease in cattle and is probably of little consequence to white-tailed deer (Richards 1981).

On the other hand, BVD virus, a togovirus, is of more importance since it is pathogenic to white-tailed deer (Richards 1981). In Florida, antibodies to BVD virus were found in three deer from Broward County and one deer from Collier County (Table 20-8). These findings probably indicate contact with infected cattle from which the deer acquired the virus. Clinical cases of BVD have not been recognized in Florida deer, however.

Parainfluenza-3 virus is a paramyxovirus that is part of a pneumonia syndrome in calves called shipping fever. Typically the disease requires stress, the PI-3 virus, and secondary bacterial invasion (Richards 1981). Twelve of 282 deer from Collier County were seropositive for this virus. The overall importance of this virus to deer in Florida is unknown.

Whitetails are susceptible to a number of other viral diseases, including foot-and-mouth disease, malignant catarrhal fever, rabies, and pseudorabies (Karstad 1981; Richards 1981). There is no evidence, however, that any of these latter viruses occur in white-tailed deer in Florida.

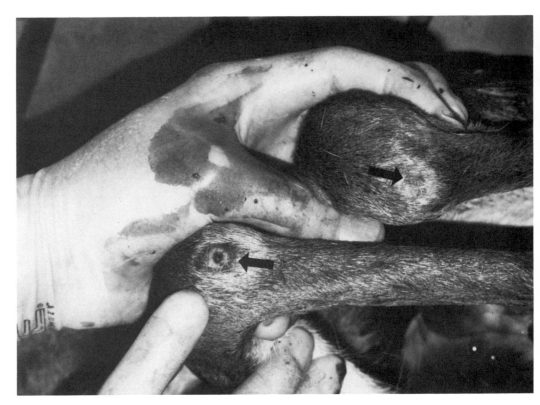

FIGURES 20-8. Abrasions on carpal joints (arrows) in chronic form of hemorrhagic disease in white-tailed deer.

IX. Anaplasmosis

Anaplasmosis is a disease of ruminants that is caused by a rickettsia, *Anaplasma marginale*. This is primarily a disease of cattle in which severe debilitation and death can occur. Transmission is believed to occur by the bite of ticks, horseflies, or mosquitoes (Kuttler 1981). Florida is considered an endemic area for this disease in cattle and surveys have shown that the prevalence is above 10% (McCallon 1973). Even though white-tailed deer are susceptible to experimental infection of the disease (Roberts and Lancaster 1963), there is only one report that it occurs in deer in Florida. Harlow and Jones (1965) reported that 2 of 20 deer from Eglin Air Force Base were positive in 1958. A detailed subinoculation study was conducted by Bedell and Miller (1966) in which 270 white-tailed deer in the southeastern United States (including 51 deer from Florida) were found to be free of the rickettsia. It has been concluded, therefore, that even though under experimental conditions whitetails are susceptible, exhibit minimal clinical signs of infection, and retain latent infections for long periods of time, they do not serve as carriers or reservoirs in the wild (Kuttler 1984). For further information, the reader is referred to the reviews on anaplasmosis by Kuttler (1981, 1984).

X. Bacterial diseases

A number of bacterial pathogens are known from white-tailed deer in Florida. These include the etiologic agents of leptospirosis, bru-

FIGURES 20-9. Atrophied rumen villi in chronic form of hemorrhagic disease in white-tailed deer. Normal villi (large arrow) shown in contrast to atrophied villi (small arrow).

cellosis, anthrax, salmonellosis, dermato-philosis, tularemia, pneumonia, and abscesses (Tables 20-9, 20-10, and 20-11). None of these except perhaps anthrax is of serious concern in relation to large-scale epizootics.

Leptospirosis is caused by the spirochete *Leptospira interrogans,* of which there are 12 serovars known from whitetails (Shotts 1981a). These bacteria are infectious to man and various domestic mammals as well (Shotts 1981b) and herein lies the reason for considerable interest in the role of wildlife in the maintenance and spread of the disease. The current body of knowledge indicates that deer are not important reservoirs of the bacteria and the serologic evidence of infections in deer probably is a reflection of the deer being exposed to the bacteria via other animals. Mammals such as striped skunks, raccoons, opossums, foxes, and mice serve as reservoirs of infection (Shotts 1981a). Sur-

veys of white-tailed deer in Florida for antibodies to *Leptospira interrogans* are summarized in Table 20-9. Seventeen percent of 452 deer examined from 1958–89 were positive. Nine serovars were identified: *canicola* (40 positive deer), *grippotyphosa* (12 deer), *ballum* (9 deer), *pomona* (6 deer), *hardjo* (4 deer), *autumnalis* (3 deer), *bratislava* (2 deer), *pyrogenes* (1 deer), and *icterohaemorrhagiae* (1 deer). The identification of such a high number of deer positive for *canicola* in southern Florida was unusual. In 1987 and 1988 Wright and Miller (1988) cultured kidneys of a number of deer from Collier, Monroe, and Dade counties and identified serogroup *canicola,* serovar Portland-Vere from two deer—one from Bear Island and one from Faka-hatchee Strand State Preserve. The significance of these findings is unknown. Although these results show that a number of deer are exposed to leptospiral organisms, there are

Table 20-7
Arboviruses (other than hemorrhagic disease viruses) reported from white-tailed deer in Florida

Virus	No. deer Exam.	No. deer Pos.	Date	Location (county)	Data source
SLE[a]	143	0	1965–74	NG[b]	Bigler et al. (1975)
	212	12	1984–88	Collier	McLean et al. (1990)
	11	0	1988	Monroe/Dade	" " " "
EEE[c]	143	1	1965–74	NG	Bigler et al. (1975)
	212	11	1984–88	Collier	McLean et al. (1990)
	11	0	1988	Monroe/Dade	" " " "
Highlands J	126	0	1965–74	NG	Bigler et al. (1975)
	182	2	1984–88	Collier	McLean et al. (1990)
Everglades	143	5	1965–74	NG	Bigler et al. (1975)
	3	1	1965–69	Collier	Lord et al. (1973)
	5	2	1967–68	"	Bigler (1969)
	212	33	1984–88	"	McLean et al. (1990)
	11	9	1988	Monroe/Dade	" " " "
Tensaw	211	201	1984–88	Collier	" " " "
	11	5	1988	Monroe/Dade	
Keystone	185	131	1984–88	Collier	" " " "
	11	5	1988	Monroe/Dade	" " " "
Vesicular stomatitis[d]	10	0	1981	Citrus	Stallknecht & Erickson (1986)
	5	0	1968	Clay	Jenney et al. (1970)
	10	0	1966	Collier	" " " "
	6	0	1984	"	Stallknecht & Erickson (1986)
	212	24[e]	1984–88	"	McLean et al. (1990)
		6[f]	1984–88	"	" " " "
	11	3[e]	1988	Monroe/Dade	" " " "
		1[f]	1988	" "	" " " "
	20	0	1965	Duval	Jenney et al. (1970)
	6	0	1984	Franklin	Stallknecht & Erickson (1986)
	7	0	1968	Hernando	Jenney et al. (1970)
	5	0	1983	Leon	Stallknecht & Erickson (1986)
	9	0	1981	Orange	" " " "
	10	0	1981	Wakulla	" " " "
	20	0	1958–59	Walton	Harlow & Jones (1965)
	35	0	1967–69	"	Jenney et al. (1970)
Trivittatus	210	95	1984–88	Collier	McLean et al. (1990)
	11	5	1988	Monroe/Dade	" " " "
Jamestown	211	76	1984–88	Collier	" " " "
Canyon	11	9	1988	Monroe/Dade	" " " "

Note: All data are from serosurveys.
[a]SLE = St. Louis encephalitis.
[b]NG = not given by authors.
[c]EEE = eastern equine encephalomyelitis.
[d]VS virus is considered here to be an arbovirus, although it is recognized that there is some question about this characterization (Karstad 1981).
[e]Vesicular stomatitis—New Jersey virus.
[f]Vesicular stomatitis—Indiana virus.

Table 20-8

Miscellaneous viruses reported from white-tailed deer in Florida

Virus	No. deer Exam.	No. deer Pos.	Date	Location (county)	Data source
IBR[a]	37	0	1982	Broward	SCWDS records
	282	1	1984–90	Collier	Forrester & Roelke (1986), Wright & Forrester (1987), Wright (1988b), Forrester (1991)
	41	0	1988–89	Monroe/ Dade	Forrester (1991)
	11	0	1984, '86	Franklin	SCWDS records
	10	0	1984, '86	Levy	" "
	10	0	1980	Marion	" "
	5	0	1987	Osceola	" "
	30	0	1981–87	Wakulla	" "
BVD[b]	37	3	1982	Broward	SCWDS records
	282	1	1984–90	Collier	Forrester & Roelke (1986), Wright & Forrester (1987), Wright (1988b), Forrester (1991)
	41	0	1988–89	Monroe/ Dade	Forrester (1991)
	11	0	1984, '86	Franklin	SCWDS records
	10	0	1984, '86	Levy	" "
	10	0	1980	Marion	" "
	5	0	1987	Osceola	" "
	30	0	1981–87	Wakulla	" "
PI–3[c]	37	0	1982	Broward	SCWDS records
	282	12	1984–90	Collier	Forrester & Roelke (1986), Wright & Forrester (1987), Wright (1988b), Forrester (1991)
	41	0	1988–89	Monroe/ Dade	Forrester (1991)
	11	0	1984, '86	Franklin	SCWDS records
	10	0	1984, '86	Levy	" "
	10	0	1980	Marion	" "
	5	0	1987	Osceola	" "
	30	0	1981–87	Wakulla	" "
BRSV[d]	172	0	1986–90	Collier	Wright & Forrester (1987), Wright (1988b), Forrester (1991)
	41	0	1988–89	Monroe/ Dade	Forrester (1991)

Note: All data are from serosurveys.

[a] IBR = infectious rhinotracheitis virus.

[b] BVD = bovine virus diarrhea virus.

[c] PI–3 = parainfluenza-3 virus.

[d] BRSV = bovine respiratory syncytial virus.

Table 20-9

Results of serologic surveys for antibodies to *Leptospira interrogans* in white-tailed deer in Florida

| County | Year | No. deer | | Data source |
		Exam.	Pos.	
NG[a]	1958–59	69	8	Shotts & Hayes (1970)
Broward	1982	37	0	SCWDS records
Collier	1984–86	110	12[b]	Forrester & Roelke (1986)
	1986	22	13[c]	Wright & Forrester (1987)
	1987	33	9[d]	Wright (1988b)
	1988	32	15[e]	Forrester & Wright (1989a)
	1989	33	10[f]	Forrester & Telford (1990)
Franklin	1984, '86	11	0	SCWDS records
Leon[g]	NG	6	0	Shotts et al. (1975)
Levy	1984, '86	10	0	" " " "
Marion	1980	10	0	" " " "
Monroe/Dade	1988	11	5[h]	Forrester & Wright (1989b)
	1989	13	2[i]	Forrester & Telford (1990)
Osceola	1987	5	1[j]	SCWDS records
Wakulla	1981–87	30	4[k]	" "
Walton	1958–59	20	0	Harlow and Jones (1965)
Totals	1958–89	452	79 (17%)	

[a]NG = not given by authors.
[b]10 were serovar *canicola*, 1 was *pomona*, and 1 was *grippotyphosa*.
[c]9 were serovar *canicola*, and 4 were *grippotyphosa*.
[d]7 were serovar *canicola*, and 2 were *pomona*.
[e]6 were serovar *canicola*, 4 were *grippotyphosa*, 4 were *hardjo*, and 1 was *pomona*.
[f]5 were serovar *canicola*, 8 were *ballum*, 2 were *autumnalis*, 2 were *bratislava*, and 1 was *pyrogenes* (5 deer were positive for more than 1 serovar).
[g]Data on deer from Leon County, Florida, and South Grady/Thomas counties, Georgia, were not presented separately by the authors.
[h]3 were serovar *canicola*, and 1 was *pomona*.
[i]1 was serovar *autumnalis*, and 1 was *ballum*.
[j]Serovar *pomona*.
[k]3 were serovar *grippotyphosa*, and 1 was *icterohaemorrhagiae*.

no recognized cases of leptospirosis in deer in Florida. This information may be important from a zoonotic standpoint, however, although no human cases have been linked to contact with deer (Shotts 1981a).

Brucellosis occurs in many species of wildlife as well as in man and domestic animals (Witter 1981). Fay (1961) pointed out that an analysis of published information on 12,706 white-tailed deer in the United States (prior to 1961) revealed that only 20 deer (less than 1%) had antibody titers for *Brucella*. In 1981 he updated this claim and stated that things had not changed (Rinehart and Fay 1981). The situation in Florida is similar (Table 20-

10). Of 910 deer examined, only 3 were seropositive for *Brucella abortus*. There are no known clinical cases of brucellosis in deer in Florida or any other part of its range in North America (Rinehart and Fay 1981). Deer are not important from a reservoir viewpoint and this bacterial disease is not of significance to deer populations in Florida.

Anthrax is often a fatal disease of mammals and is caused by *Bacillus anthracis*, a large spore-forming bacterium (Van Ness 1981). It is most common in herbivores and is characterized by a rapid and fatal course, dark and bloody fluid exuding from body openings, a dark and enlarged spleen, and

Table 20-10
Results of serologic surveys for antibodies to *Brucella abortus* in white-tailed deer in Florida

County	Year	No. deer Exam.	Pos.	Data source
NG[a]	1958–60	494	3	Hayes et al. (1960)
Broward	1982	37	0	SCWDS records
Collier	1984–86	110	0	Forrester & Roelke (1986)
	1986	22	0	Wright & Forrester (1987)
	1987	33	0	Wright (1988b)
	1988	32	0	Forrester & Wright (1989a)
	1989	33	0	Forrester & Telford (1990)
	1990	39	0	Forrester (1991)
Franklin	1984, 86	11	0	SCWDS records
Levy	1984, 86	10	0	" "
Marion	1980	10	0	" "
Monroe/Dade	1988	11	0	Forrester & Wright (1989b)
	1989	13	0	Forrester & Telford (1990)
Osceola	1987	5	0	SCWDS records
Wakulla	1981–87	30	0	" "
Walton	1958–59	20	0	Harlow & Jones (1965)
Totals	1958–90	910	3 (0.3%)	

[a]NG = not given by authors.

subcutaneous edema (Choquette and Broughton 1981). It is a zoonotic disease affecting man and domestic animals. It has been reported in every state and province in the United States and Canada, but there are certain areas where the disease is enzootic. In these areas the occurrence of the disease is correlated with "alkaline or neutral soils rich in organic matter which are subject to periodic flooding and drought" (Van Ness 1981, p. 162). The limestone regions of Florida apparently fit this description. Stein and Stoner (1952) reported an outbreak of anthrax in southern Florida where 13 deer were found dead in an area where there was an ongoing epizootic of anthrax in cattle. This is the only report of anthrax in Florida deer. The overall importance of this disease to deer populations in Florida is probably minor.

Salmonellosis is a bacterial disease caused by a number of different serotypes of *Salmonella* (Robinson 1981). The disease has been recognized as important in Texas (Robinson et al. 1970), where fawn mortality was considerable due to gastroenteritis. In Florida *Salmonella anatum* was isolated from two fawns suffering from diarrhea in a captive herd (Forrester et al. 1974a). These same two fawns were also afflicted with strongyloidosis. White (1984) cultured *Salmonella* from the intestines of one of five wild whitetails in Florida. The positive deer was a two-year-old buck from Columbia County that died of haemonchosis. This latter finding is of interest since Robinson (1981) stated that adult "carrier" deer have not been identified in Texas, where the disease is believed to be enzootic.

Single cases of pneumonia, endocarditis, and dermatophilosis were seen in deer from Bay, Columbia, and Leon counties (Table 20-11). Five cases of cerebral abscesses were seen in deer from Alachua, Clay, Columbia, Liberty, and Leon counties. Four of the five were bucks and, as indicated in the section on trauma, these were probably secondary infections resulting from skull fractures due to

Table 20-11
Summary of findings on miscellaneous bacterial diseases of white-tailed deer in Florida

Disease	Bacterium	Basis of diagnosis	Year	No. deer inf.	Age	County	Data source
Anthrax	Bacillus anthracis	Necropsy	1951	13	NG[a]	Southern Florida[b]	Stein & Stoner (1952)
Salmonellosis[c]	Salmonella anatum	Necropsy, isolation	1969	2/12[d]	Fawns	Alachua	Forrester et al. (1974a)
	Salmonella sp.	Necropsy, isolation	1974	1	2 yrs.	Columbia	White (1984)
Tularemia	Francisella tularensis	Serology	1965–73	2/56	NG	NG	Hoff et al. (1975)
Pneumonia	Staphylococcus aureus and Corynebacterium sp.	Necropsy, isolation	1979	1	Fawn	Bay	Forrester (1984)
Pneumonia and endocarditis	Undetermined	Necropsy	1983	1	1.5 yrs.	Columbia	" "
Cerebral abscesses	Actinomyces pyogenes	Necropsy	1982	1	3+ yrs.	Alachua	" "
		Necropsy	1985	1	2 yrs.	Clay	Forrester (1985)
		Necropsy	1986	1	1.5 yrs.	Leon	Davidson et al. (1990)[f]
		Necropsy	1989	1	1.5 yrs.	Columbia	Forrester (1989)
Foot abscesses	Various[e]	Necropsy	1982	12/37	0.5 to 3.5 yrs.	Broward	SCWDS records
Dermatophilosis	Dermatophilus congolensis	Necropsy	1984	1	2 wks.	Leon	" "

[a]NG = not given by author.
[b]Counties not given in the paper, but from the map on p. 317 it would appear to be either Palm Beach, Broward, or Dade County. Harlow and Jones (1965) described an anthrax outbreak in cattle in Broward County in 1951 that may have been related to these infections in deer reported by Stein and Stoner (1952).
[c]"Carrier state," not disease.
[d]Captive animals.
[e]Beta-hemotytic Streptococcus, alpha-hemolytic Streptococcus, Pseudomonas aeruginosa, Enterobacter cloacae, Klebsiella oxytoca, Acinetobacter calcoaceticus, and Moraxella spp.
[f]Davidson et al. (1990) reported also a cerebral abscess in a 3½-year-old female from Liberty County in 1971. The abscess was not cultured.

fighting. These are believed to be isolated incidents and of little overall significance to deer populations.

White-tailed deer have been implicated in the epidemiology of Lyme disease, an important zoonotic disease (Magnarelli et al. 1984), although the competence of deer as reservoirs of the etiologic agent (the spirochete *Borrelia burgdorferi*) has been disputed (Telford et al. 1988). The importance of deer may be in their maintenance of the tick vectors, particularly adult ticks. Nevertheless, white-tailed deer were examined serologically for evidence of infection by the spirochete (Nettles 1985). Serum samples from 144 deer from 13 southeastern states (including 14 samples from Florida) were negative. The Florida samples came from Broward County (n = 5), Escambia County (n = 5), and Orange County (n = 4). See Chapter 10 for more information on Lyme disease.

XI. Protozoan parasites

Twelve species of parasitic protozoans have been reported from white-tailed deer (Kingston 1981). Ten of these species have been found in Florida whitetails (Table 20-12)—nine sporozoans and one flagellate. It is interesting that a checklist of the parasites of deer published in 1970 (Walker and Becklund 1970) contained no reports of protozoa from deer in Florida. During the past 20 years there has been a flurry of research activity on deer parasites and the result has been considerable expansion of our knowledge of protozoan infections and diseases. An excellent review of protozoan parasites of deer has been published (Kingston 1981).

Sarcosporidiasis in white-tailed deer in Florida is caused by at least two sporozoans of the genus *Sarcocystis* (Figures 20-10 and 20-11), although the species involved have not been determined. *Sarcocystis odocoileocanis* was described by Crum et al. (1981), and was found in 51% of 390 whitetails from the southeastern United States (Crum and Prestwood 1982); it may be present in Florida, although this has not been determined. Infections are widespread in deer in Florida, with prevalences up to 100% in some areas (Table 20-12). Deer are the intermediate hosts of these parasites. Infections take the form of microscopic cysts (sarcocysts) in various locations such as skeletal muscles, tongue, heart, esophagus, and diaphragm. The definitive or final hosts are unknown, but probably are carnivores such as bobcats and Florida panthers in whose intestines the sexual phase of the life cycle would occur. Carnivores would be infected by ingesting venison containing the sarcocysts and deer would be infected by ingesting oocysts from carnivore feces.

A study of white-tailed deer in the Southeast showed that 24% of 360 deer had serologic evidence of infection with *Toxoplasma gondii* (Oertley 1981). Of these deer, nine of 50 from Florida were positive (Table 20-12). Experimental studies have shown that infections of *T. gondii* in white-tailed deer result

in mild transient clinical problems, including diarrhea, lethargy, and weakness (Oertley 1981). From this we can assume that toxoplasmosis is probably not very significant to the overall health of deer in Florida, although it may at times result in severe disease in young or debilitated animals. There are only two reports of toxoplasmosis in deer. One was in a whitetail fawn from Mississippi that was subjected to stress due to flooding, starvation, and severe parasitism (SCWDS records). The other dealt with two mule deer that were translocated from New Mexico to Wisconsin (Trainer 1962). The lack of reports of toxoplasmosis in an animal such as white-tailed deer that has been studied extensively for diseases and parasites is probably a good indication of the rarity of the disease, although the infection is fairly common (Oertley 1981). Kingston (1981) stated that there has never been a proven case of infection of man by ingestion of deer meat, but Sacks et al. (1983) presented evidence that three deer hunters (one from Alabama and two from South Carolina) acquired toxoplasmosis from consuming raw or nearly raw venison. Eating inadequately cooked deer meat should be discouraged to avoid the possibility of *Toxoplasma* infection.

The third type of sporozoan that infects white-tailed deer is intestinal coccidia of the genus *Eimeria*. Four species are reported to infect whitetails (Kingston 1981): *Eimeria mccordocki, E. virginianus, E. odocoilei,* and *E. madisonensis*. All of these develop in the mucosal lining of the intestinal tract, where they produce oocysts that leave the deer via their feces. The infection is passed on to the next host by accidental ingestion of the oocysts after they develop (sporulate) to the infective stage. The life cycle, therefore, is direct, no intermediate host being required. The deer is the definitive and only host in this case. These parasites are highly host-specific and

Table 20-12
Protozoan parasites reported from white-tailed deer in Florida

Protozoan	No. deer			Date	County	Basis of diagnosis	Data source
	Exam.	Inf.	%				
Sarcocystis sp.[a]	18	11	61	1988	Baker, Columbia	HP(T)[d]	Forrester (1989b)
	5	4	80	1988	Bay	"	" "
	40	NG[b]	NG	1969–80	Brevard, Duval, Escambia, Gadsden, Lake	HP[c]	Crum & Prestwood (1982)
	5	5	100	1988	Calhoun	HP(T)	Forrester (1989b)
	254	97	38	1984–90	Collier	HP	Wright (1988a), Forrester & Wright (1989a), Forrester & Telford (1990)
	4	1	25	1973	Duval	"	Oertley (1981)
	5	5	100	1977	Escambia	"	" "
	10	8	80	1988	"	HP(T)	Forrester (1989b)
	5	1	20	1973	Gadsden	HP	Oertley (1981)
	7	7	100	1988	"	HP(T)	Forrester (1989b)
	5	5	100	1988	Gulf	"	" "
	10	1	10	1980	Lake	HP	SCWDS records
	5	0	0	1986	Levy	"	" "
	10	6	60	1980	Marion	"	" "
	26	20	77	1988	"	HP(T)	Forrester (1989b)
	26	1	4	1988–89	Monroe/Dade	"	Forrester & Wright (1989b), Forrester (1989b)
	5	0	0	1978	Orange	HP	SCWDS records
	5	0	0	1987	Osceola	"	" "
	20	12	60	1988	Palm Beach	HP(T)	Forrester (1989b)
	25	0	0	1981–87	Wakulla	HP	SCWDS records
Toxoplasma gondii	5	0	0	1968	Clay	Serology[e]	Oertley (1981)
	5	0	0	1973	Duval	"	" "
	5	1	20	1977	Escambia	"	" "
	5	4	80	1973	Gadsden	"	" "
	5	0	0	1980	Lake	"	" "
	5	1	20	1972	Liberty	"	" "
	5	0	0	1970	Nassau	"	" "
	5	1	20	1978	Orange	"	" "
	5	2	40	1977	Osceola/Brevard	"	" "
	5	0	0	1969	Walton	"	" "
Eimeria mccordocki	261	14	5	1984–89	Collier	Fecal analysis	Forrester (1988a, 1988b, 1990)
	12	0	0	1988–89	Dade	" "	Forrester & Wright (1989b), Forrester & Telford (1990)
	25	0	0	1988–89	Monroe	" "	Forrester & Wright (1989b), Forrester & Telford (1990)
Eimeria odocoilei	261	8	3	1984–89	Collier	" "	Forrester (1988a, 1988b, 1990)
	12	0	0	1988–89	Dade	" "	Forrester & Wright (1989b), Forrester & Telford (1990)
	25	0	0	1988–89	Monroe	" "	Forrester & Wright (1989b), Forrester & Telford (1990)
Eimeria madisonensis	261	2	1	1984–89	Collier	" "	Forrester (1988a, 1988b, 1990)
	12	0	0	1988–89	Dade	" "	Forrester & Wright (1989b), Forrester & Telford (1990)
	25	0	0	1988–89	Monroe	" "	Forrester & Wright (1988b), Forrester & Telford (1990)

(continued)

Table 20-12 *(continued)*

Protozoan	No. deer Exam.	Inf.	%	Date	County	Basis of diagnosis	Data source
Eimeria virginianus	261	3	1	1984–87	Collier	Fecal analysis	Forrester (1988b, 1990)
	12	0	0	1988–89	Dade	" "	Forrester & Wright (1989b), Forrester & Telford (1990)
	25	0	0	1988–89	Monroe	" "	Forrester & Wright (1989b), Forrester & Telford (1990)
Theileria cervi	55	29	53	1976–81	Citrus, Escambia, Lake, Marion, Wakulla	Blood smears	Davidson et al. (1983)
	37	0	0	1982	Broward	" "	SCWDS records
	11	4	36	1984, '86	Franklin	" "	SCWDS records, Davidson et al. (1987)
	10	8	80	1980	Lake	" "	SCWDS records
	5	5	100	1986	Levy	" "	" "
	10	8	80	1980	Marion	" "	" "
	5	0	0	1978	Orange	" "	" "
	5	0	0	1987	Osceola	" "	" "
	25	14	56	1981–87	Wakulla	" "	" "
	16	16	100	1978–79	Duval	" "	Telford & Forrester (1991)
	2	2	100	1976–77	Alachua	" "	" " " "
Babesia odocoilei	1	1	100	1990	Citrus	" "	" " " "
Trypanosoma cervi	NG[f]	NG[f]	NG[f]	1968–69	Clay, Walton	Culture of blood	Kistner & Hanson (1969)
	55	23	42	1976–81	Citrus, Lake, Marion, Orange, Wakulla	Blood smears	Davidson et al. (1983)
	37	13	35	1982	Broward	" "	SCWDS records
	152	150	98	1984–86	Collier	Culture of blood	Forrester & Roelke (1986)
	30	25	83	1988	"	" "	Forrester & Wright (1989a)
	34	33	97	1989	"	" "	Forrester & Telford (1990)
	40	39	98	1990	"	" "	" " " "
	11	3	27	1984, '86	Franklin	" "	SCWDS records, Davidson et al. (1987)
	10	1	10	1980	Lake	" "	SCWDS records
	5	1	20	1986	Levy	" "	" "
	10	6	60	1980	Marion	" "	" "
	10	9	90	1988	Monroe/Dade	Culture of blood	Forrester & Wright (1989b)
	14	5	36	1989	Monroe/Dade	" "	Forrester & Telford (1990)
	5	4	80	1978	Orange	Blood smears	SCWDS records
	5	0	0	1987	Osceola	" "	" "
	25	6	24	1981–87	Wakulla	" "	" "
	20	0	0	1958–59	Walton	NG	Harlow & Jones (1965)

[a]May represent 2 or more species.

[b]NG = not given by authors.

[c]HP = histopathologic study of tongue and heart and in some cases diaphragm, esophagus, and skeletal muscles.

[d]HP(T) = histopathologic study of tongue only.

[e]Indirect fluorescent antibody test.

[f]NG = not given by authors, but 14 of 18 deer from Clay County and Walton County, Florida, Liberty County, Georgia, and Assumption Parrish, Louisiana, were positive for trypanosomes. Some of the infected deer were from Florida, but the authors did not say how many.

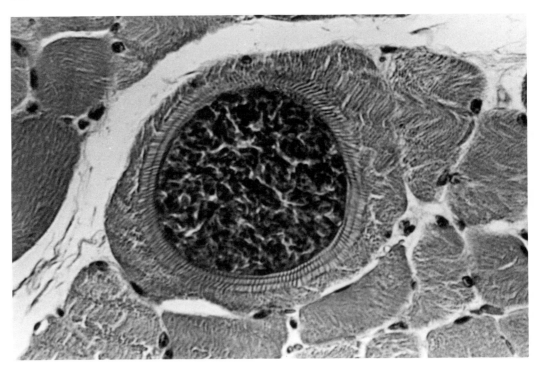

FIGURE 20-10. Thick-walled sarcocyst in tongue of a white-tailed deer in Collier County. (Photo courtesy of Dr. Scott D. Wright.)

deer are their only known hosts. They do not infect man. In 1984–1989 oocysts of all four species were found in feces from deer in southern Florida (Table 20-12). In an earlier study, oocysts of *Eimeria* spp. were found in 29 of 584 (5%) whitetails examined in 13 southeastern states (SCWDS records). *Eimeria mccordocki* is the only species that has been studied experimentally to determine its pathogenicity to white-tailed deer. Conlogue and Foreyt (1984) infected seven 8-month-old fawns with oocysts of *E. mccordocki* and saw no indication of the clinical signs of coccidiosis that are seen so often in domestic livestock (i.e., diarrhea, rough hair coat, weakness, dehydration, prolapse, emaciation, or death). In another experimental study with mule deer, Abbas and Post (1980) found that young debilitated deer were more susceptible to the harmful effects of this species of coccidia. The deer used by Conlogue and

Foreyt (1984) were older and in much better physical condition at the initiation of the trial in comparison to those of Abbas and Post (1980). These studies, therefore, indicate that this species of *Eimeria* may be of limited importance to well-nourished and healthy whitetails, but that if some other factor or factors such as inclement weather, diminished food supply, or other diseases and parasites interact with coccidial infections, the result might be the manifestation of disease.

There are three blood protozoans that infect Florida white-tailed deer: *Theileria cervi* and *Babesia odocoilei*, which are piroplasms, and *Trypanosoma cervi*, which is an extracellular blood flagellate (Table 20-12). *Theileria cervi* is transmitted by ticks (principally *Amblyomma americanum*, the lone star tick) (Kingston 1981; Kuttler et al. 1967), and the distribution of the parasite in deer is correlated closely with the distribution of the tick vector

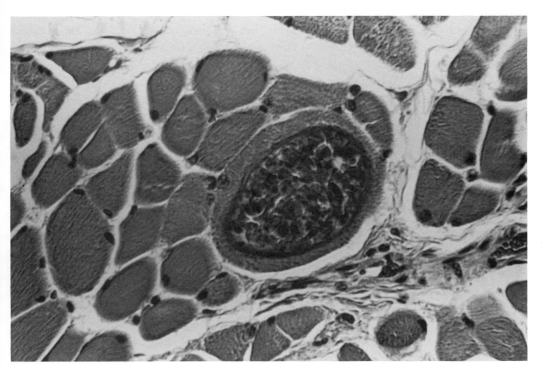

FIGURE 20-11. Thin-walled sarcocyst in tongue of a white-tailed deer in Collier County. (Photo courtesy of Dr. Scott D. Wright.)

in the Southeast (Davidson et al. 1983). Infections in deer usually are of low intensity and are of very little significance (Kingston 1981). When this parasite occurs along with other complicating factors such as high population densities of deer, malnutrition, and other diseases, however, it may contribute to die-offs (Robinson et al. 1967). Such a syndrome has not been recognized in Florida, but since the parasite is fairly prevalent in northern Florida, such an event is quite possible.

Babesia odocoilei was found in only one deer from Citrus County and apparently is not common in Florida. This piroplasm has been reported from Texas (Emerson and Wright 1968; Emerson 1970) and Virginia (Perry et al. 1985), but was not seen in a survey of 240 white-tailed deer from 10 southeastern states (including 55 deer from Florida, some of which were from Citrus County) (Davidson et al. 1983). The patho-

logic significance of this parasite to Florida deer is not known.

Trypanosoma cervi is probably transmitted from deer to deer by horseflies, but this has not been determined (Kingston 1981). They are not known to be pathogenic to deer and even though they are very common in Florida deer, they are of no known significance. The reader is referred to the paper by Telford et al. (1991) for further details on the prevalence and distribution of *T. cervi* in white-tailed deer in southern Florida.

XII. Trematodes

White-tailed deer are known to be parasitized by six species of flukes (Foreyt 1981). These include *Fascioloides magna*, *Fasciola hepatica*, *Paramphistomum liorchis*, *Dicrocoelium dendriticum*, *Heterobilharzia americana*, and *Zygocotyle lunata*. Two of these, the giant liver fluke (*Fascioloides magna*) and the rumen fluke (*Paramphistomum liorchis*), are common. The others are rare and of little consequence. The giant liver fluke and the rumen fluke are the only two flukes known to occur in white-tailed deer in Florida.

Fascioloides magna is a remarkable parasite because of its size (Figure 20-12). Its name (*magna*) is very fitting. The life cycle of this fluke involves lymnaeid snails as intermediate hosts (Foreyt 1981). At least 13 species have been determined to be suitable intermediate hosts, but these have been studied only in the western and midwestern United States and Canada, and in Texas (Foreyt et al. 1977). No studies have been conducted in the southeastern United States to determine which snails are the intermediate hosts. The eggs of the fluke leave the deer via its feces; once outside the host they develop and then hatch. A free-swimming miracidium leaves the egg and lo-

cates and penetrates a snail. Inside the snail it develops through several stages and multiplies until eventually hundreds of free-swimming cercariae emerge from the snail. These cercariae eventually attach to vegetation and form a protective covering over themselves that is very resistant to environmental extremes. These are metacercariae and are the infective stages. The length of time for the above events to occur varies with temperature and the amount of moisture available. Once ingested by a deer as it browses on vegetation, the metacercaria excysts and migrates to the parenchyma of the liver, where it becomes an adult fluke and eventually produces eggs. Once in the liver it takes about seven months for the fluke to become mature.

Fascioloides magna is distributed widely in white-tailed deer in North America, but it appears to be most common in the southeastern United States (from North Carolina to

FIGURE 20-12. Giant liver flukes (*Fascioloides magna*) removed from the sliced-open liver of a white-tailed deer. Note size of fluke in comparison to man's fingers.

Texas), around the Great Lakes, and in New York (Foreyt 1981). Pursglove et al. (1977) examined over 4,000 white-tailed deer in 13 southeastern states and found the giant liver fluke in 13%. The prevalence is higher in Florida (30%), where there are three main endemic areas: one in the southeastern panhandle, one in east-central Florida, and one in southern Florida (Figure 20-13; Table 20-13). Most of the sites where the infections are enzootic are moist lowlands or swamps in association with major drainage systems (Pursglove et al. 1977). This is related to the

need for water in order for the life cycle to be completed. The number of flukes per infected deer (intensity) is usually 30 or less. Infections of as many as 100 or more occur, but this is exceptional (Foreyt 1981). The mean number of flukes in a sample of 352 infected deer in Florida was 9, with a range of 1 to 117 flukes per animal (Table 20-13).

For the most part deer tolerate infections with the giant liver fluke without much difficulty. In the study by Pursglove et al. (1977), for example, only one of over 4,000 deer was considered to be adversely affected by the

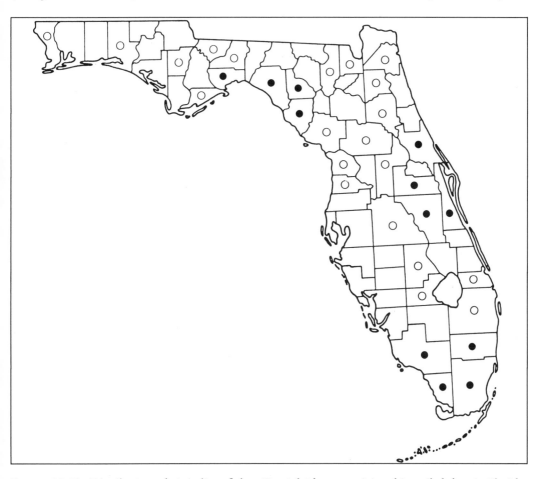

FIGURE 20-13. Distribution of giant liver flukes (*Fascioloides magna*) in white-tailed deer in Florida. Closed circles indicate counties where infected deer have been reported; open circles are counties in which deer have been examined and found free of liver flukes. (From Dinaburg 1939; Forrester 1984; Harlow and Jones 1965; Pursglove et al. 1977; SCWDS records; Forrester and Wright 1989b.)

Table 20-13
Characteristics of infections of the giant liver fluke (*Fascioloides magna*) in white-tailed deer in Florida

County	Year	No. deer Exam.	No. deer Pos.	%	Intensity Mean	Intensity Range	Data source
Baker/Columbia	1957–63	8	0	0	—	—	Harlow & Jones (1965)
Brevard	1977	5	5	100	12	1–30	SCWDS records
Broward/Dade/ Palm Beach	1957–63	22	0	0	—	—	Harlow & Jones (1965)
Broward	1982	31	19	61	39	3–117	SCWDS records
Citrus/Hernando	1957–63	27	0	0	—	—	Harlow & Jones (1965)
	1962, '66	21	0	0	—	—	SCWDS records
Clay	1957–63	22	0	0	—	—	Harlow & Jones (1965)
	1968	5	0	0	—	—	SCWDS records
Collier	1957–63	5	4	80	NG[a]	1–23	Harlow & Jones (1965)
	1957–76	16	9	56	NG	NG	Pursglove et al. (1977)
	1966, '68	20	5	25	6	2–18	SCWDS records
	1984–86	110	69	62	8	1–47	Forrester & Roelke (1986)
	1986	20	12	60	4	1–8	Wright & Forrester (1987)
	1987	44	36	82	9	1–35	Wright (1988b)
	1988	47	36	77	8	2–21	Forrester & Wright (1989a)
	1989	38	26	68	9	2–35	Forrester & Telford (1990)
	1990	40	24	60	7	1–21	" " " "
Dixie/Lafayette	1957–63	6	1	17	NG	3	Harlow & Jones (1965), Pursglove et al. (1977)
Duval	1971, '73	10	0	0	—	—	SCWDS records
	1978–79	18	0	0	—	—	Forrester (1984)
Escambia	1977	5	0	0	—	—	SCWDS records
Franklin	1984, '86	11	0	0	—	—	" "
Gadsden	1973	10	0	0	—	—	" "
Glades	1938–39	8	0	0	—	—	Dinaburg (1939)
Highlands/Polk	1957–63	25	0	0	—	—	Harlow & Jones (1965)
Highlands	1938–39	72	0	0	—	—	Dinaburg (1939)
Lake/Marion/ Putnam	1957–63	34	0	0	—	—	Harlow & Jones (1965)
Lake	1980	17	0	0	—	—	SCWDS records
Leon/Wakulla	1957–63	3	0	0	—	—	Harlow & Jones (1965)
Levy	1986	5	0	0	—	—	SCWDS records
Liberty	1972	5	0	0	—	—	" "
Martin/Palm Bch	1957–63	5	0	0	—	—	Harlow & Jones (1965)
Marion	1980	10	0	0	—	—	SCWDS records
Monroe/Dade	1988	15	2	13	2	2–3	Forrester & Wright (1989b)
	1989	23	7	30	6	1–18	Forrester & Telford (1990)
Orange	1938–39	175	22	13	NG	NG	Dinaburg (1939)
	1978	5	4	80	6	3–7	SCWDS records
Osceola	1938–39	53	37	70	NG	NG	Dinaburg (1939)
	1957–63	17	11	65	NG	1–40	Harlow & Jones (1965), Pursglove et al. (1977)
	1987	5	4	80	2	1–3	SCWDS records
Volusia/Brevard	1957–63	69	17	25	NG	1–16	Harlow & Jones (1965), Pursglove et al. (1977)
Wakulla	1981–87	25	2	8	8	5–11	SCWDS records
Walton	1957–63	27	0	0	—	—	Harlow & Jones (1965)
	1967–69	40	0	0	—	—	SCWDS records
Totals	1938–90	1,179	352	30	9	1–117	

Note: In addition to the data given in this table, Holland (1959) stated that the giant liver fluke infects deer in "restricted areas" in Florida, but he gave no specific localities.
[a]NG = not given by authors.

infection to the point that it was contributory to the death of the deer. However, Cheatum (1951) reported that winter-killed deer in New York had more flukes (and also lungworms) than did healthy deer. It is possible that severe fluke infections may pose a serious threat to deer when other stress factors such as inclement weather or malnutrition come into play. Migrating immature flukes cause hemorrhage in the liver (Whitlock 1939). The liver reacts to the mature flukes by enclosing them in fibrous cysts. Associated with the cysts, mesenteric tissues, and lymph nodes is a black pigmentation caused by the breakdown of red blood cells and the excreta of the flukes (Foreyt 1981).

As emphasized by Pursglove et al. (1977) there are important implications of giant liver fluke infections for domestic livestock. Deer serve as significant reservoir hosts of the fluke for infections in cattle, sheep, and swine. In cattle a thick-walled cyst forms around the flukes and the liver undergoes fibrosis and changes in pigmentation, which result in the condemnation of the liver for human consumption. In sheep the flukes are not usually found in cysts but migrate extensively through the liver causing considerable damage that is commonly lethal (Foreyt 1981).

The life cycle of the rumen fluke, *Paramphistomum liorchis*, is similar in some ways to that of *F. magna*. A number of genera of snails including *Lymnaea* are involved (Foreyt 1981), although nothing is known about the snails serving as intermediate hosts in Florida. Deer become infected by ingesting metacercariae on vegetation. Prestwood et al. (1970) reported an overall prevalence of 7% in 788 deer from 13 southeastern states. Prevalences from location to location varied from 8% to 100%, with intensities from less than 100 up to 3,000 flukes per deer. In Florida prevalences varied from 10 to 100% (average 43%) in 951 deer examined (Table 20-14). Infected deer

have been recorded from 19 counties with a wide distribution throughout the state (Figure 20-14). The adult flukes in large numbers cause inflammation and thickening of the rumen lining (Prestwood et al. 1970), but in general they are considered relatively harmless to deer (Foreyt 1981). Migrating stages sometimes cause inflammation and edema in the upper small intestine (Prestwood et al. 1970).

XIII. Cestodes

Six species of tapeworms have been reported from white-tailed deer (Foreyt 1981; Stubblefield et al. 1987). These include *Moniezia benedeni*, *M. expansa*, and *Thysanosoma actinoides*, which occur as adults in the small intestines or bile ducts of deer, and *Taenia hydatigena*, *T. omissa*, and *Echinococcus granulosus*, which occur as larval forms (cysticerci and hydatid cysts) in various parts of the deer's body.

Three of the above tapeworms have been reported from deer in Florida: *Taenia hydatigena* (cysticerci), *Taenia omissa* (cysticerci), and *Moniezia* sp. (adults) (Harlow and Jones 1965; Walker and Becklund 1970; Prestwood 1971; Forrester and Rausch 1990). All three species occurred in low numbers and in only a few animals (Table 20-15). They are considered to be nonpathogenic to deer and of little consequence (Foreyt 1981). *Taenia hydatigena* and *Moniezia* sp. are common in domestic animals and probably their infection of deer is accidental. The third species (*Taenia omissa*) occurred in 9 of 124 deer examined in Collier County during 1984–86 (Table 20-15). These larval tapeworms were located in the thoracic cavity, often near the sternum. Adults of *T. omissa* are found in Florida panthers (Forrester et al. 1985); adults of *T. hydatigena* occur in domestic and wild canids (Foreyt 1981).

Table 20-14
Characteristics of infections of the rumen fluke (*Paramphistomum liorchis*) in white-tailed deer in Florida

County	Year	No. deer Exam.	Pos.	%	Intensity Mean	Range	Data source
Alachua	1976–81	3	0	0	—	—	Forrester (1984)
Baker	1961–69	1	0	0	—	—	Prestwood et al. (1970)
Brevard	1977	5	3	60	278	1–731	SCWDS records
	1980	1	0	0	—	—	Forrester (1984)
Broward	1961–69	10	10	100	593	ND[a]	Prestwood et al. (1970)
	1982	37	24	65	ND	ND	SCWDS records
Citrus	1962, '66	21	0	0	—	—	" "
Clay	1968	5	0	0	—	—	" "
	1976	2	0	0	—	—	Forrester (1984)
Collier	1966	10	9	90	293	1–1,000	SCWDS records
	1968	10	8	80	330	27–900	" "
	1984–86	110	91	83	ND	ND	Forrester & Roelke (1986)
	1986	19	15	79	ND	ND	Wright & Forrester (1987)
	1987	44	33	75	ND	ND	Wright (1988b)
	1988	47	30	64	ND	ND	Forrester & Wright (1989a)
	1989	37	28	76	ND	ND	Forrester & Telford (1990)
	1990	40	27	68	ND	ND	" " " "
Columbia	1961–69	1	0	0	—	—	Prestwood et al. (1970)
	1974–82	1	1	100	ND	ND	Forrester (1984)
DeSoto	1979	1	1	100	ND	ND	" "
Duval	1971	5	3	60	53	4–89	SCWDS records
	1973	5	5	100	570	1–1,314	" "
	1978–79	18	5	28	ND	ND	Forrester (1984)
Escambia	1977	5	1	20	80	80	SCWDS records
Franklin	1984	6	6	100	32	3–50	SCWDS records, Davidson et al. (1987)
	1986	5	0	0	—	—	SCWDS records
Gadsden	1973	10	0	0	—	—	" "
Glades	1938–39	8	6	75	ND	ND	Dinaburg (1939)
	1976	1	1	100	ND	ND	Forrester (1984)
Highlands	1938–39	72	14	19	ND	ND	Dinaburg (1939)
Lake	1980	5	4	80	47	1–115	SCWDS records
Levy	1974–82	1	1	100	ND	ND	Forrester (1984)
	1986	5	0	0	—	—	SCWDS records
Liberty	1950	NG[b]	NG	—	NG	NG	USDA Par. Coll. 47328[c]
	1973	5	2	40	9	5–14	SCWDS records
Marion	1963	20	2	10	ND	ND	Harlow & Jones (1965)
	1980	10	0	0	—	—	SCWDS records
Monroe/Dade	1988	15	12	80	ND	ND	Forrester & Wright (1989a)
	1989	22	14	64	ND	ND	Forrester & Telford (1990)
Orange	1938–39	175	40	23	ND	ND	Dinaburg (1939)
	1978	5	4	80	2,060	467–4,835	SCWDS records
Osceola	1938–39	53	8	15	ND	ND	Dinaburg (1939)
	1987	5	2	40	300	200–400	SCWDS records
Wakulla	1981	10	0	0	—	—	" "
Walton	1961–69	40	0	0	—	—	Prestwood et al. (1970)
	1967–69	40	0	0	—	—	SCWDS records
Totals	1938–90	951	410	43	387	1–4,835	

Note: In addition to the references given in the table, Price and McIntosh (1944) recorded rumen flukes from deer in Florida but gave no specific localities.
[a]ND = not determined.   [b]NG = not given.   [c]U.S. National Parasite Collection, Beltsville, Md.

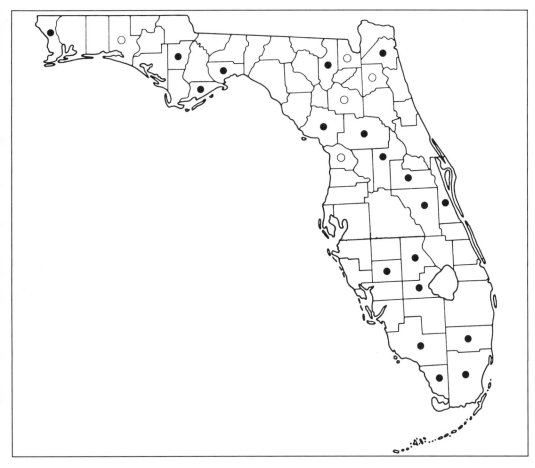

FIGURE 20-14. Distribution of rumen flukes (*Paramphistomum liorchis*) in white-tailed deer in Florida. Closed circles indicate counties where infected deer have been reported; open circles are counties in which deer have been examined and found free of rumen flukes. (From Dinaburg 1939; Forrester 1984; Harlow and Jones 1965; Prestwood et al. 1970; SCWDS records; Forrester and Wright 1989b.)

XIV. Lungworms

Six species of lung nematodes are known to infect white-tailed deer in North America (Anderson and Prestwood 1981). These include *Dictyocaulus viviparus, D. filaria, Parelaphostrongylus tenuis, P. andersoni, Protostrongylus coburni,* and *Vareostrongylus alpenae.* Only three of these species occur in whitetails in Florida: *Dictyocaulus viviparus, Parelaphostrongylus andersoni,* and *P. tenuis.* The latter is known from only one deer and hence does not appear to be of significance to deer in Florida (Prestwood and Smith 1969; Prestwood et at. 1971; Prestwood et al. 1974b).

Dictyocaulosis is caused by *Dictyocaulus viviparus,* a trichostrongyloid nematode. The life cycle of *D. viviparus* has not been studied in white-tailed deer, but is probably similar to that in cattle or sheep (Anderson and Prestwood 1981). Adults are found in the large air passages of the lungs (Figures 20-15 and 20-16). Eggs and larvae are coughed up, swallowed, and hatch on the way out of the body. Outside of the deer the larvae develop

Table 20-15
Characteristics of tapeworm infections in white-tailed deer in Florida

Tapeworm	County	Date	No. deer		Intensity		Data source
			Exam.	Pos.	Mean	Range	
Moniezia sp.[a]	Citrus/Hernando	1962	10	1	1	1	SCWDS records
	Marion	1934	NG[b]	NG	NG	NG	USDA Par. Coll. 41319[c]
Taenia hydatigena[d]	Walton	1967–69	40	1	1	1	SCWDS records
	Collier	1984–86	124	1	1	1	Forrester & Rausch (1990)
	Leon	1984	NG	NG	NG	NG	SCWDS records
Taenia omissa[d]	Collier	1984–86	124	9	5	1–15	Forrester & Rausch (1990)

[a]Adults from small intestine.
[b]NG = not given by author.
[c]National Parasite Collection, Beltsville, Md.
[d]Larval forms in peritoneal cavity.

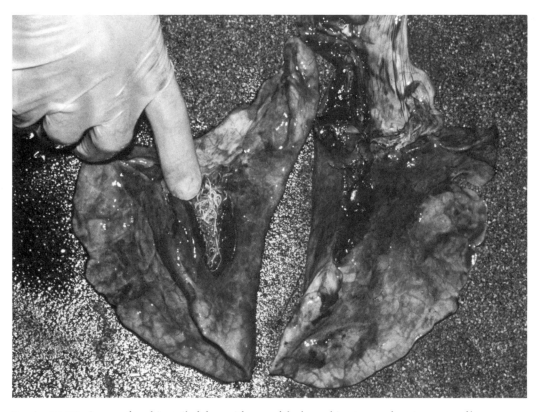

FIGURE 20-15. Lungs of a white-tailed deer with one of the bronchi cut open showing mass of lungworms (*Dictyocaulus viviparus*).

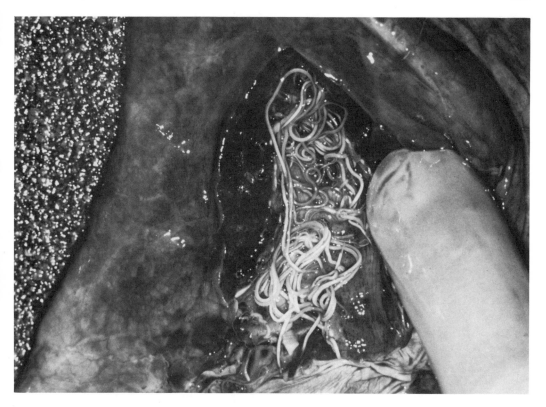

FIGURE 20-16. Close-up of lungworms in air passages of a white-tailed deer.

and molt from first stage to third stage or infective larvae. The infective larvae have two sheaths that provide protection from desiccation. Infective larvae are ingested as a deer feeds and pass to the intestine where they penetrate the wall, enter lymph nodes, and eventually reach the lungs.

Dictyocaulus viviparus is distributed widely in North America (Anderson and Prestwood 1981) and was found in 30% of 806 deer from 13 southeastern states (Prestwood et al. 1971). Infected deer from Baker, Clay, Columbia, Escambia, Walton, Collier, and Broward counties were reported in that paper, although prevalences and intensities were not given on a county basis. Lower intensities of lungworms are evident in deer collected during the winter months than at other times of the year. Mean intensities var-

ied from 13.6 in fall to 6.5 in winter (Anderson and Prestwood 1981). In Florida 46% of 597 deer from 21 counties were infected with *D. viviparus,* with a mean of 21 worms per infected deer (range, 1–420) (Table 20-16). The nematode is distributed throughout the state (Figure 20-17).

There have been no experimental studies done to describe the signs and lesions of dictyocaulosis in deer (Anderson and Prestwood 1981). Nearly all infections of *D. viviparus* were accompanied by other parasitic infections (Prestwood et al. 1971). Localized mild bronchitis and peribronchitis were seen in a few deer with low numbers of lungworms, and verminous pneumonia was common. In some cases air passages can be obstructed and result in suffocation and death (Anderson and Prestwood 1981). A young doe from Levy

Table 20-16

Characteristics of lungworm (*Dictyocaulus viviparus*) infections in white-tailed deer in Florida

County	Year	No. deer Exam.	Pos.	%	Intensity Mean	Range	Data source
Brevard	1977	5	2	40	2	1–3	SCWDS records
Broward, Dade,	1957	5	1	20	ND[a]	ND	Harlow & Jones (1965)
Palm Beach	1958	5	2[b]	40	"Slight"		Hayes et al. (1958)
Broward	1982	37	17	46	5	1–25	SCWDS records
Citrus	1962	10	0	0	—	—	" "
	1966	11	0	0	—	—	" "
Clay	1968	5	2	40	4	2–5	" "
Collier	1966	10	5	50	9	1–13	" "
	1968	10	4	40	5	1–13	" "
	1984–86	127	50	39	11	1–185	Forrester & Roelke (1986)
	1986	21	12	57	4	1–7	Wright & Forrester (1987)
	1987	44	25	57	3	1–10	Wright (1988b)
	1988	47	35	74	7	1–62	Forrester & Wright (1989a)
	1989	37	1	3	2	2	Forrester & Telford (1990)
	1990	40	25	63	5	1–13	" " " "
Duval	1971	5	3	60	15	2–22	SCWDS records
	1973	5	5	100	5	3–7	" "
	1978–79	18	17	94	7	1–45	Forrester (1984)
Escambia	1977	5	4	80	8	4–15	SCWDS records
Franklin	1984	6	5	83	2	1–3	SCWDS records, Davidson et al. (1987)
	1986	5	1	20	4	4	SCWDS records
Gadsden	1973	10	8	80	6	1–12	" "
Lake	1980	5	5	100	9	4–21	" "
Levy	1982	1	1	100	420	420	Forrester (1984)
	1986	5	4	80	10	1–25	SCWDS records
Liberty	1973	5	5	100	3	1–7	" "
Marion	1980	10	0	0	—	—	" "
Monroe/Dade	1988	14	6	43	3	1–9	Forrester & Wright (1989a)
	1989	19	0	0	—	—	Forrester & Telford (1990)
Orange	1978	5	3	60	2	1–3	SCWDS records
Osceola	1987	5	5	100	7	1–16	" "
Wakulla	1981	10	7	70	15	1–33	" "
	1985–87	15	12	80	9	1–46	" "
Walton	1967–69	40	2	5	1	1	" "
Totals	1957–90	597	272	46	21[c]	1–420	

[a]ND = not determined.
[b]Hayes et al. (1958) listed these lungworms as *Dictyocaulus* sp.
[c]The mean intensity is 6 if the 1 deer from Levy County with 420 worms is omitted from the list. This was an abnormally high infection.

County that died of haemonchosis and verminous pneumonia in 1982 had 420 lungworms present in its air passages. This is an extremely high intensity for a white-tailed deer. Infections are usually less than 10 worms per deer (Table 20-16).

Adult deer seem to be able to tolerate mild infections, but young animals less than six

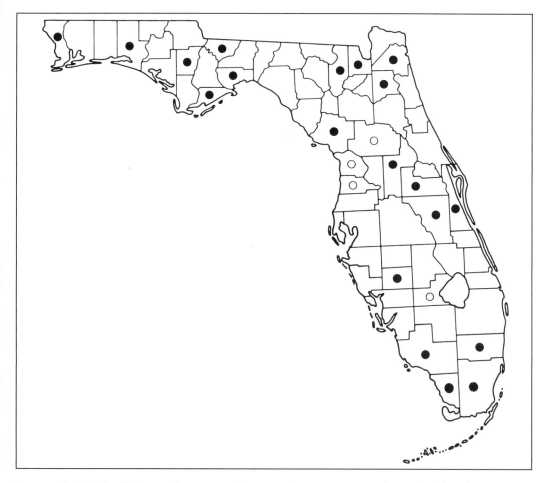

FIGURE 20-17. Distribution of lungworms (*Dictyocaulus viviparus*) in white-tailed deer from Florida. Closed circles indicate counties where infected deer have been reported; open circles are counties in which deer have been examined and found free of lungworms. (From Forrester 1984; Forrester and Roelke 1986; Harlow and Jones 1965; Prestwood et al. 1971; SCWDS records; Wright 1988b; Wright and Forrester 1987; Forrester and Wright, 1989b.)

months of age have been diagnosed with fatal dictyocaulosis in association with malnutrition and concomitant gastrointestinal nematode infections (Anderson and Prestwood 1981; Davidson et al. 1980). Cross-infection of *D. viviparus* between deer and domestic livestock may occur, but the relationship is incompletely understood at this time.

Two species are associated with parelaphostrongylosis, the meningeal worm (*P. tenuis*) and the muscleworm (*P. andersoni*). The adults of the former are located in the meninges of the cranial vault or cranium, and adults of the latter in musculature of the hindbody (Anderson and Prestwood 1981). In both species eggs are carried to the lungs via the blood, where they lodge in capillaries and hatch. First-stage larvae are then coughed up, swallowed, and exit via the feces of the deer. Land snails are required as intermediate hosts, although the species of such have not been determined for Florida. Meningeal worms are usually harmless to white-tailed deer, but when they infect other domestic animals (such as sheep and goats) and wild ungulates (such as moose, caribou, elk, or mule deer) they cause serious neurologic disease. The meningeal worm has been found only once in Florida; this was in a deer from Collier County. The origin of this infection may be a result of the translocation of deer from northern states years ago. The deer currently in Collier County, for instance, are believed to be descendents of whitetails introduced from Wisconsin in 1948 after the native Florida deer had been eradicated to control tropical cattle fever ticks (Prestwood and Smith 1969). Muscleworms are more prevalent than meningeal worms in Florida. Infections have been found in Brevard, Collier, Dade, Duval, and Monroe counties (Table 20-17). In Collier County infections were lowest in August and October (Table 20-18) and in fawns less than one year of age (Table 20-19). The adult worms of *P. andersoni* cause little damage to the musculature where they reside, but massive numbers of larvae can cause pulmonary damage to deer that may be serious when they are stressed by predators or other factors (Nettles 1976).

The reader is referred to the review by Anderson and Prestwood (1981) for more details on these two parasites, which are more prevalent and very important in other parts of eastern North America. Comer et al. (1991) recently published an update on the distribution of meningeal worms in the Southeast.

XV. Gastrointestinal nematodes

There are at least 32 species of nematodes that parasitize the gastrointestinal tract of white-tailed deer in North America (Prestwood and Pursglove 1981). Many of these have been reported rarely, however, and undoubtedly represent accidental infections. Twenty-one of these species are known to occur in deer in Florida (Table 20-20). The distribution, prevalence, and intensity of each of the species are given in Tables 20-21 through 20-34. The two species of *Gongylonema* require coprophagous beetles as intermediate hosts to complete the life cycle. Deer become infected by ingesting beetles containing infective larvae. The other 19 species have direct life cycles and do not require inter-

Table 20-17
Prevalence of muscleworms (*Parelaphostrongylus andersoni*) in white-tailed deer in Florida

Location	No. deer Exam.	Inf.	%	Date	Data Source
Brevard	5	2	40	1977	SCWDS records
Collier	110	43[a]	39	1984–86	Forrester & Roelke (1986)
	25	13[a]	52	1986	Wright (1988a)
	44	28[a]	64	1987	Wright (1988b)
	47	28[a]	60	1988	Forrester & Wright (1989a)
	37	21[a]	57	1989	Forrester & Telford (1990)
	40	18[a]	45	1990	" " " "
Duval	5	1	20	1973	SCWDS records, Prestwood et al. (1974b)
Monroe/Dade	14	9	64	1988	Forrester & Wright (1989b)
	9	6	67	1989	Forrester & Telford (1990)

[a]Diagnosis was by establishing the presence of parelaphostrongylid larvae in lungs and feces and the absence of adult *Parelaphostrongylus tenuis* as determined by necropsy.

Table 20-18

Prevalence of muscleworms (*Parelaphostrongylus andersoni*) in various seasons in white-tailed deer from the Bear Island and Raccoon Point areas of the Big Cypress National Preserve, 1984–86

	Bear Island		Raccoon Point		Both areas	
Date	N	Prevalence (%)	N	Prevalence (%)	N	Prevalence (%)
August–September 1984	6	33	6	50	12	42
October 1984	5	20	6	17	11	18
March 1985	5	40	7	71	12	58
June 1985	6	67	6	83	12	75
August 1985	7	14	6	17	13	15
October 1985	8	13	7	14	15	7
March 1986	10	60	11	36	21	48
June 1986	6	50	8	38	14	43
Total	53	38	57	40	110	39

Note: Data from Forrester and Roelke (1986). Diagnosis was by establishing the presence of parelaphostrongylid larvae in lungs and feces and the absence of adult *Parelaphostrongylus tenuis* as determined by necropsy.

Table 20-19

Prevalence of muscleworms (*Parelaphostrongylus andersoni*) in various age classes of white-tailed deer from the Bear Island and Raccoon Point areas of the Big Cypress National Preserve, 1984–86

	Bear Island		Raccoon Point		Both areas	
Age class (yr)	N	Prevalence (%)	N	Prevalence (%)	N	Prevalence (%)
Fawns (< 1)	7	29	11	0	18	11
1	12	42	12	42	24	42
2	16	31	14	57	30	43
3	9	56	9	56	18	56
4	5	40	5	40	10	40
5	2	50	6	50	8	50
6	2	0	0	—	2	0
All ages	53	38	57	40	110	39

Note: Data from Forrester and Roelke (1986). Diagnosis was by establishing the presence of parelaphostrongylid larvae in lungs and feces and the absence of adult *Parelaphostrongylus tenuis* as determined by necropsy.

mediate hosts (Levine 1980). Prestwood and Pursglove (1981) reviewed the literature on these parasites and concluded that most "species of gastrointestinal nematodes are non-pathogenic or only mildly pathogenic in the numbers usually encountered in free-ranging white-tailed deer" (p. 318). Except for *Haemonchus contortus* and *Strongyloides papillosus,* which are known to be patho-

genic, these parasites will not be individually discussed further. For additional information, the reader may consult Prestwood and Pursglove (1981) and Levine (1980). Abomasal nematodes as a group will be discussed later in reference to their relationship to deer population densities and the implications of this for management practices.

Haemonchosis is caused by a trichostron-

Table 20-20
Prevalence, intensity, and abundance of gastrointestinal nematodes reported from white-tailed deer in Florida, 1938–87

Site	Nematode species	No. deer Exam.	Prevalence (%)	Intensity Mean	Range	Abundance
Esophagus	*Gongylonema pulchrum*	800	23	18	1–257	4
Rumen	*Gongylonema verrucosum*	800	15	43	1–392	6
Abomasum	*Mazamastrongylus odocoilei*	958	69	574	7–5,016	396
	Haemonchus spp.[a]	958	66	822	6–15,574	543
	Trichostrongylus askivali	958	8	124	3–1,938	10
	Trichostrongylus dosteri	958	6	159	17–2,345	10
	Ostertagia mossi	958	6	106	13–1,076	6
	Mazamastrongylus pursglovei	958	5	757	61–3,656	38
	Trichostrongylus axei	958	5	359	15–10,710	18
	Ostertagia dikmansi	958	1	90	31–359	1
	Ostertagia ostertagi	958	1	106	13–274	1
Small intestine	*Capillaria bovis*	614	4	13	1–220	< 1
	Monodontus louisianensis	614	2	5	1–13	< 1
	Strongyloides papillosus	622	1	127	2–947	1
	Cooperia punctata	614	< 1	11	7–15	< 1
	Nematodirus odocoilei	614	< 1	45	2–164	< 1
Large intestine	*Eucyathostomum webbi*	609	4	6	1–26	< 1
	Oesophagostomum venulosum	609	1	4	1–9	< 1
Cecum	*Trichuris odocoileus*	609	1	9	1–36	< 1

Sources: Davidson et al. (1980); Dikmans and Lucker (1935); Dinaburg (1939); Florida Game and Fresh Water Fish Commission (1983); Forrester (1984); Forrester and Roelke (1986); Forrester et al. (1974b); Harlow and Jones (1965); Prestwood et al. (1970); Prestwood et al. (1973); SCWDS records; Wright and Forrester (1987); Wright (1988b).
[a]Includes *Haemonchus contortus*, *H. similis*, and *H. placei*. See text for more details on the distribution, prevalence, and intensity of these three species.

glylid nematode, *Haemonchus contortus,* which is also called the barberpole worm (live specimens of females are red-and-white striped due to their blood-engorged intestines showing up against their white, egg-filled uteri) or the large stomach worm. This species is very common in domestic and wild ruminants throughout the world. Adults are found in the abomasum (Figure 20-18) (Prestwood and Pursglove 1981). In addition to *H. contortus,* two other species of *Haemonchus* also occur in white-tailed deer in Florida: *H. similis* and *H. placei.* Ross and Forrester (1991) examined 1,904 specimens of *Haemonchus* taken from 242 different deer from Collier, Dade, and Monroe counties during 1984–

1988 and found *Haemonchus* species in the following prevalences: *H. contortus* (84%), *H. placei* (8%), intermediate forms between *H. contortus* and *H. placei* (4%), and *H. similis* (3%). The composition of species of *Haemonchus* in other areas of the state has not been determined. *Haemonchus similis,* however, has been reported from 6 of 175 deer from Orange County, 1 of 53 deer in Osceola County, 1 of 72 deer from Highlands County, and 1 of 8 deer from Glades County (Dinaburg 1939). Other than the data from Ross and Forrester (1991), there are no other reports of *H. placei* in Florida deer. Both *H. similis* and *H. placei* have been reported from cattle in Florida (Dikmans 1934; Porter

Table 20-21

Characteristics of infections of the gullet worm (*Gongylonema pulchrum*) in white-tailed deer from Florida

County	Year	No. deer Exam.	Pos.	%	Intensity Mean	Range	Data source
Alachua	1976–81	4	3	75	ND[a]	ND	Forrester (1984)
Baker	1961–69	1	1	100	24	NG	Prestwood et al. (1970)
Broward	1961–69	10	0	0	—	—	" " " "
Brevard/Osceola	1977	5	5	100	9	1–17	SCWDS records
	1987	5	1	20	1	1	" "
Citrus/Hernando	1962	10	10	100	NG[b]	NG	Harlow & Jones (1965), SCWDS records
	1966	10	10	100	27	5–125	SCWDS records, Prestwood et al. (1970)
Clay	1968	5	3	60	6	5–7	SCWDS records, Prestwood et al. (1970)
	1961–69	11	0	0	—	—	Prestwood et al. (1970)
Collier	1984–90	281	0	0	—	—	Forrester & Roelke (1986), Wright & Forrester (1987), Wright (1988a), Forrester & Wright (1989a), Forrester & Telford(1990)
Columbia	1961–69	1	1	100	NG	NG	Prestwood et al. (1970)
	1974	1	1	100	ND	ND	Forrester (1984)
Duval	1971	5	4	80	16	3–34	SCWDS records
	1973	5	5	100	29	25–34	" "
	1978–79	17	16	94	ND	ND	Forrester (1984)
Escambia	1977	5	4	80	9	1–14	SCWDS records
Franklin	1984	6	6	100	23	12–40	SCWDS records, Davidson et al. (1987)
	1986	5	5	100	19	2–60	SCWDS records
Gadsden	1973	10	10	100	26	3–100	" "
Levy	1986	5	3	60	3	1–5	" "
Liberty	1972	5	5	100	25	14–35	" "
Marion	1963	20	17	85	NG	NG	Harlow & Jones (1965)
	1980	5	5	100	14	6–32	SCWDS records
Monroe/Dade	1988–89	33	0	0	—	—	Forrester & Wright (1989b), Forrester & Telford (1990)
Orange	1978	5	4	80	4	2–5	SCWDS records
Wakulla	1981	10	6	60	NG	NG	" "
	1983	5	0	0	—	—	" "
	1985–87	15	12	80	17	1–39	" "
Walton	1963	10	10	100	NG	NG	Harlow & Jones (1965)
	1967–69	40	39	98	51	4–257	SCWDS records, Prestwood et al. (1970)

[a]ND = not determined.
[b]NG = not given by authors.

Table 20-22
Characteristics of infections of the rumen nematode *Gongylonema verrucosum* in white-tailed deer
from Florida

County	Year	No. deer			Intensity		Data source
		Exam.	Pos.	%	Mean	Range	
Baker	1961–69	1	1	100	1	1	Prestwood et al. (1970)
Brevard	1977	5	1	20	1	1	SCWDS records
Broward	1961–69	10	0	0	—	—	Prestwood et al. (1970)
Citrus/Hernando	1962	10	8	80	—	—	SCWDS records
	1961–69	10	9	90	52	12–200	Prestwood et al. (1970), SCWDS records
Clay	1961–69	5	2	40	12	2–21	Prestwood et al. (1970), SCWDS records
Collier	1961–69	11	0	0	—	—	Prestwood et al. (1970)
	1984–90	281	0	0	—	—	Forrester & Roelke (1986), Wright & Forrester (1987), Wright (1988a), Forrester & Wright (1989a), Forrester & Telford (1990)
Columbia	1961–69	1	1	100	NG[a]	NG	Prestwood et al. (1970)
Duval	1971	5	4	80	35	4–61	SCWDS records
	1973	5	5	100	227	9–392	" "
	1978	18	2	11	ND[b]	ND	Forrester (1984)
Escambia	1977	5	5	100	60	1–148	SCWDS records
Franklin	1984	6	5	83	41	15–75	SCWDS records, Davidson et al. (1987)
Gadsden	1973	10	7	70	35	3–100	" " " "
Glades	1938–39	8	0	0	—	—	Dinaburg (1939)
Highlands	1938–39	72	0	0	—	—	" "
Lake	1980	5	4	80	13	2–23	SCWDS records
Liberty	1972	5	3	60	7	4–10	" "
Marion	1934	NG	NG	—	NG	NG	Dikmans & Lucker (1935), USDA Par. Coll. 40468[c]
	1963	20	14	70	NG	NG	Harlow & Jones (1965)
	1980	5	5	100	29	5–85	SCWDS records
Monroe/Dade	1988–89	37	0	0	—	—	Forrester & Wright (1989b), Forrester & Telford (1990)
Orange	1938–39	175	4	2	NG	NG	Dinaburg (1939)
	1978	5	4	80	39	6–79	SCWDS records
Osceola	1938–39	53	0	0	—	—	Dinaburg (1939)
Wakulla	1981–87	30	7	23	42	12–100	SCWDS records
Walton	1963	10	10	100	NG	NG	Harlow & Jones (1965)
	1967–69	40	19	48	48	4–120	SCWDS records, Prestwood et al. (1970)

[a]NG = not given by authors.
[b]ND = not determined.
[c]U.S. National Parasite Collection, Beltsville, Md.

Table 20-23

Characteristics of infections of the abomasal nematode *Mazamastrongylus odocoilei* in white-tailed deer from Florida

County	Year	No. deer Exam.	No. deer Pos.	No. deer %	Intensity Mean	Intensity Range	Data source
Baker	1974	7	7	100	979	291–1,844	SCWDS records
Brevard/Osceola	1977	54	48	89	325	19–1,720	" "
	1987	5	5	100	542	200–1,120	" "
Broward	1982	37	37	100	1,093	66–4,238	" "
Citrus/Hernando	1962	10	6	60	NG[a]	NG	Harlow & Jones (1965)
	1966	10	10	100	419	50–841	SCWDS records
Clay	1968	5	5	100	191	120–230	" "
	1974	21	21	100	655	20–2,167	" "
	1979–80	19	19	100	764	50–2,484	" "
Collier	1966	10	8	80	294	40–762	" "
	1968	10	10	100	722	182–1,766	" "
	1984–86	136	135	99	599	10–3,050	Forrester & Roelke (1986)
	1986	20	20	100	673	153–2,150	Wright & Forrester (1987)
	1987	44	44	100	1,073	50–3,086	Wright (1988b)
	1988	45	45	100	986	10–3,260	Forrester & Wright (1989a)
	1989	36	32	89	511	20–1,540	Forrester & Telford (1990)
	1990	40	40	100	661	50–2,700	" " " "
Duval	1971	5	5	100	629	200–1,260	SCWDS records
	1973	5	5	100	497	80–1,160	" "
	1978	8	7	88	116	20–256	" "
Franklin	1974	11	1	9	33	33	" "
	1984	6	1	17	178	178	SCWDS records, Davidson et al. (1987)
	1986	10	2	20	102	50–154	SCWDS records
Gadsden	1973	10	5	50	988	162–3,833	" "
Glades	1938–39	8	3	38	NG	NG	Dinaburg (1939)
Highlands	1938–39	72	9	13	NG	NG	" "
Lake	1980	8	8	100	391	120–831	SCWDS records
Levy	1984–86	10	9	90	698	207–1,273	" "
Liberty	1972	5	5	100	647	160–1,260	" "
Marion	1980	17	15	88	331	50–1,228	" "
Monroe/Dade	1988	15	13	87	327	20–1,520	Forrester & Wright (1989b)
	1989	24	24	100	624	20–2,660	Forrester & Telford (1990)
Orange	1938–39	175	71	41	NG	NG	Dinaburg (1939)
	1978–81	44	44	100	858	40–3,565	SCWDS records
Osceola	1938–39	53	24	45	NG	NG	Dinaburg (1939)
Palm Beach	1978	10	10	100	1066	200–5,016	SCWDS records
Wakulla	1981–87	30	22	73	686	39–4,263	" "
Walton	1967–69	40	40	100	509	7–1,500	" "

Note: Much of the information cited in this table as SCWDS records was used in a recent publication by Strohlein et al. (1988) to construct distribution maps of *Mazamastrongylus pursglovei* and *M. odocoilei* in the southeastern United States.

[a]NG = not given by authors.

Table 20-24

Characteristics of infections of abomasal nematodes (*Haemonchus* spp.) in white-tailed deer from Florida

County	Year	No. deer Exam.	Pos.	%	Intensity Mean	Range	Data source
Alachua	1976–81	3	2	67	ND[a]	ND	Forrester (1984)
Baker	1974	7	6	86	536	223–1,080	SCWDS records
Brevard/Osceola	1977–78	58	44	76	1,804	19–13,526	SCWDS records, Davidson et al. (1980)
	1987	5	5	100	1,448	20–4,540	SCWDS records
Broward/Palm Beach	1957	5	2	40	NG[b]	NG	Harlow & Jones (1965)
	1958	5	2	40	"Moderate"		Hayes et al. (1958)
	1961–72	10	10	100	464	60–1,436	Prestwood et al. (1973)
	1982	32	29	91	1,364	48–12,568	SCWDS records, Fla. Game Comm. (1983)
Citrus/Hernando	1962	10	10	100	119	7–666	SCWDS records, Harlow & Jones (1965), Prestwood et al. (1973)
	1966	10	9	90	107	19–362	SCWDS records, Prestwood et al. (1973)
Clay	1968	5	4	80	218	67–362	SCWDS records, Prestwood et al. (1973)
	1974	21	21	100	758	20–5,014	SCWDS records
	1979–80	19	13	68	710	20–3,805	SCWDS records, Davidson et al. (1980)
	1985	1	1	100	206	206	Forrester (1988a)
Collier	1966	10	10	100	428	33–1,298	SCWDS records
	1968	10	10	100	611	6–4,326	SCWDS records, Prestwood et al. (1973)
	1984–86	136	123	90	310	7–5,394	Forrester & Roelke (1986)
	1986	20	20	100	533	20–2,840	Wright & Forrester (1987)
	1987	44	39	89	479	7–2,960	Wright (1988b)
	1988	45	39	87	466	7–6,652	Forrester & Wright (1989a)
	1989	36	34	94	486	20–3,260	Forrester & Telford (1990)
	1990	40	29	73	530	20–3,020	" " " "
Duval	1971	5	4	80	596	116–1,312	SCWDS records, Prestwood et al. (1973)
	1973	5	3	60	236	20–649	SCWDS records
	1978	8	5	63	686	64–1,741	SCWDS records, Davidson et al. (1980)
Escambia	1977	5	3	60	87	68–103	SCWDS records
Franklin	1974–86	27	0	0	—	—	" "
Gadsden	1973	10	5	50	55	13–120	" "
Glades	1938–39	8	1	13	NG	NG	Dinaburg (1939)
Highlands	1938–39	72	6	8	NG	NG	" "
Lake	1980	8	8	100	1,674	27–8,509	SCWDS records
Levy	1984–86	10	6	60	790	96–2,893	" "
Liberty	1972	5	1	20	34	34	" "
Marion	1980	22	20	91	405	20–1,132	" "
Monroe/Dade	1988	15	5	33	135	7–350	Forrester & Wright (1989b)
	1989	24	20	83	187	20–1,000	Forrester & Telford (1990)
Orange	1938–39	175	77	44	NG	NG	Dinaburg (1939)
	1978–81	44	33	75	681	20–3,740	SCWDS records, Davidson et al. (1980)
Osceola	1938–39	53	32	60	NG	NG	Dinaburg (1939)
Palm Beach	1978	10	7	70	8127	50–15,574	SCWDS records, Davidson et al. (1980)
Wakulla	1981–87	30	17	57	111	20–525	SCWDS records
Walton	1958	20	17	85	NG	NG	Harlow & Jones (1965)
	1967–69	40	31	78	146	7–1,601	SCWDS records, Prestwood et al. (1973)

[a]ND = not determined.   [b]NG = not given by authors.

Table 20-25

Characteristics of infections of the abomasal nematode *Trichostrongylus askivali* in white-tailed deer from Florida

County	Year	No. deer			Intensity	
		Exam.	Pos.	%	Mean	Range
Brevard	1977–78	35	11	31	113	40–413
Broward	1982	10	3	30	61	38–160
Duval	1971–73	10	6	60	99	20–158
	1978	8	1	12	140	140
Franklin	1974	11	5	45	34	3–62
	1984[a]	6	6	100	200	45–446
	1986	5	2	40	90	70–109
Orange	1978–81	44	29	66	310	39–672
Palm Beach	1978	10	1	10	50	50
Wakulla	1983–87	35	10	29	74	49–192

Source: SCWDS records.
[a]These data are also found in Davidson et al. (1987).

Table 20-26

Characteristics of infections of the abomasal nematode *Ostertagia mossi* in white-tailed deer from Florida

County	Year	No. deer			Intensity	
		Exam.	Pos.	%	Mean	Range
Brevard	1978	5	1	20	13	13
	1987	5	2	40	46	40–51
Broward	1982	15	5	33	60	33–124
Clay	1974	21	5	24	125	41–271
	1979–80	19	10	53	131	35–249
Escambia	1977	5	4	80	489	170–1,076
Gadsden	1973	10	6	60	91	18–291
Levy	1984	5	2	40	58	42–73
Liberty	1972	5	1	20	34	34
Palm Beach	1978	10	8	80	280	100–1,029
Wakulla	1981–87	30	13	43	66	13–149

Source: SCWDS records.

1942; Das and Whitlock 1960; Becklund 1961; Lichtenfels et al. 1986) and this may be the source of the infections for deer since range cattle are common in the counties from which the infected deer came. From the above information it appears that *H. contortus* is the species of most significance to white-tailed deer in Florida, although additional studies such as the one done on deer in Collier County should be undertaken.

Haemonchus contortus is distributed widely throughout the range of the white-tailed deer (Prestwood and Pursglove 1981). In a survey of 939 whitetails in the Southeast, *Haemonchus contortus* was found in 26% of the animals, with a mean of 84 and a high of

Table 20-27

Characteristics of infections of the abomasal nematode
Trichostrongylus dosteri in white-tailed deer from Florida

County	Year	No. deer Exam.	Pos.	%	Intensity Mean	Range
Brevard	1977–78	49	20	42	87	17–707
	1987	5	4	80	170	40–120
Broward	1982	5	1	20	38	38
Franklin	1986	5	2	40	100	60–140
Orange	1978–81	44	33	75	408	28–2,345

Source: SCWDS records.

Table 20-28

Characteristics of infections of the abomasal nematode
Mazamastrongylus pursglovei in white-tailed deer from Florida

County	Year	No. deer Exam.	Pos.	%	Intensity Mean	Range
Escambia	1977	5	5	100	1,240	408
Franklin	1974	11	11	100	647	61–3,656
	1984[a]	6	6	100	1,894	635–2,846
	1986	10	10	100	622	80–1,386
Gadsden	1973	10	5	50	633	180–1,096
Levy	1986	5	1	20	340	340
Wakulla	1981–87	30	10	33	395	176–1,279

Note: Data from SCWDS records. Much of the information cited in this table was used in a recent publication by Strohlein et al. (1988) to construct distribution maps of *Mazamastrongylus pursglovei* and *M. odocoilei* in the southeastern United States.
[a]These data are also found in Davidson et al. (1987).

Table 20-29

Characteristics of infections of the abomasal nematode *Trichostrongylus axei* in white-tailed deer from Florida

County	Year	No. deer Exam.	Pos.	%	Intensity Mean	Range	Data source
Baker	1974	7	2	29	48	39–57	SCWDS records
Brevard	1977–78	49	23	47	359	25–1,332	" "
	1987	5	1	20	40	40	" "
Citrus/Hernando	1966	10	1	10	29	29	" "
Collier	1986	20	1	5	9	9	Forrester (1988a)
Duval	1971–73	10	5	50	1,476	20–10,710	SCWDS records
Franklin	1986	5	2	40	171	70–271	" "
Lake	1980	5	1	20	68	68	" "
Orange	1978–81	44	7	16	264	46–1,010	" "
Wakulla	1981–87	30	3	10	99	15–160	" "

Table 20-30
Characteristics of infections of the abomasal nematodes
Ostertagia dikmansi and *O. ostertagi* in white-tailed deer from
Florida

| County | Year | No. deer | | | Intensity | |
		Exam.	Pos.	%	Mean	Range
Ostertagia dikmansi						
Escambia	1977	5	5	100	146	34–359
Gadsden	1973	10	3	30	67	37–116
Wakulla	1981–87	30	3	10	58	31–99
Ostertagia ostertagi						
Brevard	1978	29	4	14	109	41–274
Lake	1980	5	2	40	147	13–80
Orange	1978–81	34	4	12	81	45–220

Source: SCWDS records.

Table 20-31
Characteristics of infections of the intestinal nematode *Capillaria bovis* in white-tailed deer from
Florida

| County | Year | No. deer | | | Intensity | | Data source |
		Exam.	Pos.	%	Mean	Range	
Brevard	1977	5	2	40	14	3–24	SCWDS records
Citrus/Hernando	1966	10	1	10	1	1	" "
Collier	1968	5	2	40	3	1–5	" "
Duval	1971–73	10	3	30	7	2–10	" "
Lake	1980	5	4	80	5	3–7	" "
Liberty	1972	5	4	80	73	7–220	" "
Orange	1938–39	175	3	2	NG[a]	NG	Dinaburg (1939)
	1978	5	3	60	8	6–9	SCWDS records
Osceola	1938–39	53	3	6	NG	NG	Dinaburg (1939)
Walton	1967–69	40	1	3	1	1	SCWDS records

[a]NG = not given by author.

4,326 worms per deer (Prestwood et al. 1973). Data on distribution, prevalence, and intensity in Florida deer are summarized in Table 20-24. Deer with the highest numbers of worms were from Brevard, Osceola, Broward, Lake, and Palm Beach counties. Overall 66% of 958 deer examined were infected with a mean of 822 worms per infected deer and a high of over 15,000. When these data were grouped according to geographic areas (Figure 20-19), it was found that there was a gradient of infection with the smallest prevalences and numbers of worms per deer in the north and the greatest prevalences and numbers in the southern part of the state (Table 20-35).

The life cycle of *H. contortus* is direct, that is, no intermediate host is used. Adults in the abomasum of deer produce eggs that pass out in the feces. Once in the external environment

Table 20-32

Characteristics of infections of the intestinal nematodes *Monodontus louisianensis*, *Strongyloides papillosus*, *Cooperia punctata*, and *Nematodirus odocoilei* in white-tailed deer from Florida

County	Year	No. deer Exam.	Pos.	%	Intensity Mean	Range	Data source
Monodontus louisianensis							
Duval	1971–73	10	3	30	9	7–13	SCWDS records
Lake	1980	5	4	80	5	1–8	" "
Levy	1976	1	1	100	3	3	Forrester (1988a)
Marion	1980	5	1	20	1	1	SCWDS records
Orange	1978	5	2	40	2	1–2	" "
Strongyloides papillosus							
Collier	1966	10	4	40	251	3–947	" "
Dixie	1973	2	1	50	ND[a]	ND	Forrester (1984)
Hamilton	1973	1	1	100	ND	ND	Forrester et al. (1974b)
Levy	1973	2	1	50	ND	ND	" " " "
	1976	1	1	100	ND	ND	Forrester (1988a)
Nassau	1973	1	1	100	ND	ND	Forrester et al. (1974b)
Union	1973	2	1	50	ND	ND	" " " "
Cooperia punctata							
Collier	1984–85	9	1	11	7	7	Forrester & Roelke (1986)
Duval	1973	5	1	20	15	15	SCWDS records
Nematodirus odocoilei							
Duval	1971	5	3	60	5	2–7	" "
Escambia	1977	5	2	40	84	4–164	" "

[a]ND = not determined.

the egg develops and hatches. A first-stage larva emerges and develops into a second- and then an infective third-stage larva under proper conditions of oxygen, temperature, and moisture. This infective larva migrates up on vegetation, where it is eaten by a deer. Once inside a deer it passes to the abomasum, where it molts to the fourth stage and then to the adult stage. Both fourth-stage larvae and adults are blood-feeders. It takes about two to three weeks from the time infective larvae are ingested and eggs are produced by the adults resulting from that infection (Levine 1980).

Haemonchus contortus is one of the most pathogenic nematodes of deer and by itself is a primary pathogen (Davidson et al. 1980;

McGhee et al. 1981; Prestwood and Pursglove 1981). The signs are related to blood loss: weakness, emaciation, and anemia (Foreyt and Trainer 1970; Davidson et al. 1980). Deer often are stunted and the mucous membranes and pinnae of the ears are blanched. Sometimes the lymph nodes are swollen and fluid accumulates under the jaws ("bottle jaw") and in the body cavities. Tissues and organs are pale and the abomasum contains many worms and is eroded, ulcerated, and reddened (Prestwood and Pursglove 1981). Davidson et al. (1980) described experimental and natural cases of haemonchosis in the Southeast. They reviewed 15 cases of naturally occurring haemonchosis in deer; 3 were in adult deer and 12 in fawns (9

Table 20-33

Characteristics of infections of the intestinal nematodes *Eucyathostomum webbi* and
Oesophagostomum venulosum in white-tailed deer from Florida

County	Year	No. deer Exam.	Pos.	%	Intensity Mean	Range	Data source
Eucyathostomum webbi[a]							
Collier	1968	10	8	80	5	1–11	SCWDS records
Duval	1971–73	10	7	70	8	1–26	" "
Orange	1938–39	175	6	34	NG[b]	NG	Dinaburg (1939)
Osceola	1938–39	53	6	11	NG	NG	" "
Oesophagostomum venulosum							
Brevard	1977	5	2	40	2	1–3	SCWDS records
Collier	1984–85	11	3	27	6	1–9	Forrester & Roelke (1986), Forrester (1988a)
Duval	1971	5	3	60	2	1–3	SCWDS records
Orange	1978	5	1	20	4	4	" "

[a]Pursglove (1976) examined specimens of *Eucyathostomum* sp. from the U.S. National Parasite Collection (USNM Helm. Coll. No. 43678) and identified them as *E. webbi*. The deer came from Florida, but the specific locality and the date of collection are unknown.
[b]NG = not given by author.

Table 20-34

Characteristics of infections of the whipworm *Trichuris odocoileus*[a] from white-tailed deer in Florida

County	Year	No. deer Exam.	Pos.	%	Intensity Mean	Range	Data source
Brevard	1977	5	1	20	11	11	SCWDS records
Citrus/Hernando	1966	10	1	10	1	1	" "
Collier	1966	10	1	10	1	1	" "
Duval	1973	5	1	20	36	36	" "
Franklin	1984	6	1	17	1	1	SCWDS records, Davidson et al. (1987)
Marion	1980	5	1	20	1	1	" " " " "
Orange	1938–39	175	1	< 1	NG[b]	NG	Dinaburg (1939)

[a]*Trichurus odocoileus* was described by Knight (1983) in part from specimens obtained from white-tailed deer in Florida.
[b]NG = not given by the author.

months of age or less). Fawns were the most severely affected and in these animals haemonchosis was usually concomitant with malnutrition and other parasitic infections, especially lungworms. Surveys of 73 fawns and 111 adults from nine counties in Florida showed that average numbers of worms were almost four times higher in fawns than in adults (Table 20-36). In Brevard County the numbers in fawns were almost 26 times

greater than in adults. Davidson et al. (1980) concluded that an intensity of infection near 1,000 worms was "the level at which pathogenic effects become detectable" (p. 506). They also suggested that numbers of worms should be evaluated on a basis of the numbers per kg of body weight. Infections of 75 or more worms per kg were considered harmful. During 1968–90 intensities of *Haemonchus* spp. above 75 per kg were observed in

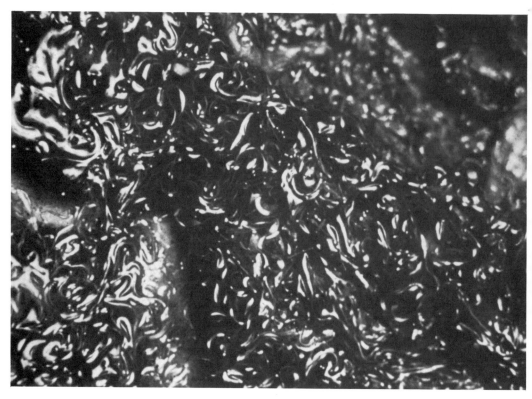

FIGURE 20-18. View of opened-up abomasum of a white-tailed deer showing numerous specimens of *Haemonchus* spp.

45 deer from 10 counties in Florida (Table 20-37). Four of these were adult deer, whereas 6 were yearlings and 35 were fawns. During 1968–87, 108 fawns were examined and 29% had intensities of *Haemonchus* greater than 75 per kg of body weight (mean, 283; range, 90–1,011). The highest intensities were found in Palm Beach County (Table 20-37). Often other factors such as high numbers of ticks and concomitant lungworm infections play an important role in this haemonchosis/malnutrition syndrome.

Davidson et al. (1980) suggested that this syndrome may occur but go unrecognized and unreported since this type of mortality is of a covert nature rather than being recognized as a die-off. However, there have been a number of die-offs in southern Florida (Col-

lier and Broward counties) that may have been caused by haemonchosis. These occurred in 1957–58, 1968–69, and 1979–80 (Loveless 1959; Prestwood et al. 1973; Eve and Kellogg 1977; Florida Game and Fresh Water Fish Commission 1983). During each of these years extensive flooding in the Everglades resulted in concentrations of deer for several months on small areas of land, loss of health and condition in the deer, and subsequent mortality. *Haemonchus* infections were prevalent and large numbers of worms per deer were common. Many questions remain unanswered in connection with these die-offs, and an intensive study of the situation in southern Florida is needed before the impact of haemonchosis on the deer population can be fully understood. Southern Florida is so different from the

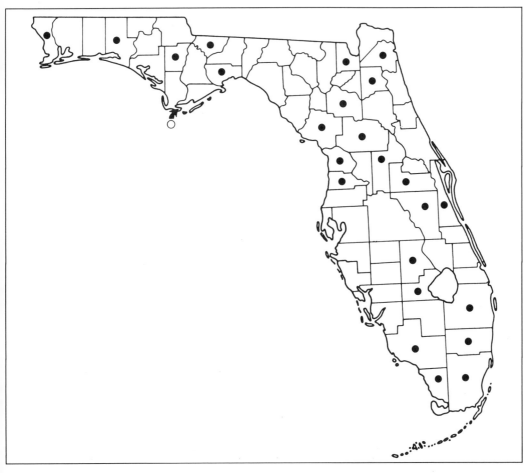

FIGURE 20-19. Distribution of *Haemonchus* spp. in white-tailed deer from Florida. Closed circles indicate counties where infected deer have been reported; open circle is the county where deer have been examined and found free of *Haemonchus* spp. (From Davidson et al. 1980; Dinaburg 1939; Forrester 1984; Forrester and Roelke 1986; Harlow and Jones 1965; Prestwood et al. 1973; SCWDS records; Wright 1988b; Wright and Forrester 1987; Forrester and Wright 1989b.)

Table 20-35

Comparison of numbers of abomasal nematodes (*Haemonchus* spp.) in adult white-tailed deer from various regions of Florida during June–September in various years, 1966–87

Region	County	No. deer exam.	Prevalence (%)	Mean intensity
Panhandle	Walton, Liberty, Wakulla	44	59	194
North-central	Duval, Marion, Levy, Orange, Osceola, Brevard	51	73	540
Southern	Broward, Collier	82	85	637
Statewide	All the above	177	75	523

Sources: SCWDS records; Forrester and Roelke (1986).

Table 20-36

Comparisons of prevalence and intensity of abomasal nematodes (*Haemonchus* spp.) in young and adult white-tailed deer from various counties in Florida

County	Date	Fawns			Adults		
		No. exam.	Prevalence (%)	Mean intensity	No. exam.	Prevalence (%)	Mean intensity
Brevard	January 1978[a]	5	80	2,546	5	20	98
	December 1978[a]	9	100	3,310	10	60	272
Broward	July 1982[a]	9	100	225	12	92	1,587
Citrus/Hernando	February 1962[a]	4	100	244	6	100	36
Clay	November/December 1974[a]	5	100	1,780	16	100	541
	January 1979[a]	4	50	45	5	60	62
Collier	August 1966[a]	4	100	283	6	100	525
	October 1985[b]	5	100	1,505	6	83	138
	March 1986[b]	4	100	782	13	77	243
	October/November 1986[c]	5	100	1,046	10	100	379
	October/November 1987[d]	5	100	2,006	8	100	183
Duval	December 1978[a]	4	100	842	4	20	64
Orange	February 1979[a]	5	100	732	5	60	140
Palm Beach	November 1978[a]	5	100	10,545	5	40	2,083
Totals	1962–87	73	96	1,959	111	79	504

[a]From SCWDS records.
[b]From Forrester and Roelke (1986).
[c]From Wright and Forrester (1987).
[d]From Wright (1988b).

habitat of white-tailed deer in other parts of its range that transfer of information obtained from other areas should be done with great caution, if at all.

The numbers of abomasal parasites (including *H. contortus*) per deer have been used to assess deer populations in relation to carrying capacity (Eve and Kellogg 1977; Eve 1981; Couvillion 1981; Davidson et al. 1982). This technique is based on the assumption that abomasal nematodes are density-dependent, that is, their numbers will be high when deer populations are high or above carrying capacity and low when deer populations are low. The entire nematode fauna of the abomasum is considered (which involves 11 species in Florida), all of which have direct life cycles. The species composition of this fauna varies from locality to locality, but the group as a whole is regarded as ubiquitous

(Eve 1981). Eve and Kellogg (1977) found a significant correlation between the average numbers of adult abomasal nematodes (designated the abomasal parasite count or APC) in a sample of 5 to 10 adult deer from a herd and the density of the herd in relation to carrying capacity. This technique was developed using data collected from mid-summer to early fall from 939 deer from 69 herds in 13 southeastern states (including Florida). The details of the APC procedure are given by Eve and Kellogg (1977) and Prestwood and Pursglove (1981). APCs of 0–500 were judged to be indicative of suboptimal population density (i.e., below carrying capacity), 500–1,500 of optimal density (i.e., near carrying capacity), and over 1,500 to signify overpopulation. Davidson et al. (1982) conducted further studies and concluded that the intensity of abomasal parasitism was inversely related to physical condition on an individual animal and a herd basis. The technique has been further studied in relation to season of collection of the deer. Many wildlife agencies are interested in using hunter-killed animals in the fall rather than having to collect deer in the summer for the APCs. Couvillion et al. (1982) reported that there was a decline in APCs from summer to fall throughout the Southeast, but the timing and magnitude varied according to the physiographic province. The decline in the APCs begins in November in the coastal plain province (which would include Florida). Therefore, it would be possible to use APCs from deer collected in November or later in Florida, but the values should be expected to be lower and should therefore be interpreted appropriately (Couvillion et al. 1982). This latter study was done with data from a number of areas in the Southeast, including five areas in northern Florida. The APC technique is being used fairly extensively in the southeastern states, including Florida (Couvillion 1981), where it has shown some value in gaining public support for deer management practices (Jeter 1979). As pointed out by Eve and Kellogg (1977) and Davidson et al. (1980), the APC technique is also useful in that high APCs provide an "early warning system" for the detection of impending infectious and parasitic diseases in the deer population. The haemonchosis/malnutrition syndrome, for example, could be monitored readily via the use of the APC technique.

The relationship of *Haemonchus contortus* infections in deer to those in livestock is of some concern. Prestwood et al. (1973) stated that *H. contortus* from deer are able to infect cattle and vice versa and that perhaps cattle are the source of the worm for deer. Cattle may also be the source of infections by *H. similis* and *H. placei* in deer in Florida. Our knowledge of this particular topic is based on very little scientific data. Until experimental cross-transmission studies such as those conducted by McGhee et al. (1981) are performed using strains of all three species of *Haemonchus* from deer and cattle in Florida, it will not be possible to draw any firm conclusions on this aspect.

Strongyloidosis is caused by the rhabditoid nematode, *Strongyloides papillosus*. It is known as the threadworm because of its small size. The life cycle of *S. papillosus* is very unusual (Levine 1980). The only parasitic form is a parthenogenic female that is found in the upper small intestine. Embryonated eggs are laid, pass out with the feces, hatch, and produce larvae that eventually become free-living adult males and females. These adults mate and produce eggs from which infective larvae eventually develop. These infective larvae infect deer via any of four ways: (1) ingestion with food or water, (2) penetration of the skin, (3) via the colostrum or milk, or (4) prenatal invasion of the fetal fawn (Prestwood and Pursglove 1981).

Strongyloides is known from whitetails in three areas: Florida (Forrester et al. 1974a, 1974b), North Carolina (Pursglove et al. 1976), and Texas (Glazener and Knowlton 1967). In Florida a captive herd of whitetailed deer at the University of Florida experienced 39% mortality due to strongyloidosis among 251 fawns born from 1963 to 1972 (Forrester et al. 1974a). At necropsy one fawn had 50,000 females of *Strongyloides papillosus* in its small intestine. Six of 14 wild-caught fawns were positive for *Strongyloides* (Forrester et al. 1974b). Infected fawns were between 1 and 19 days of age and all were from northern Florida (Union, Dixie, Levy, Hamilton, and Nassau counties). Pursglove et al. (1976) reported one fawn in Collier County with nearly 950 worms. This parasite is probably more widely distributed and prevalent than these reports indicate, but as

Table 20-37

White-tailed deer in Florida with intensities of *Haemonchus* spp. greater than 75 per kg. of body weight (1968–90)

Age	Weight (kg)	Date mo/yr	No. Haemonchus		PCV[a] (vol. %)	Tot. plasma proteins[b] (g/dl)	Additional factors	County	Data source
			Total	per kg					
Adults									
3.5 yr.	34	9/82	5,140	151	20	ND[c]	Lungworms (10)	Broward	SCWDS records
2.5 yr.	30	9/74	7,500	205	19	"	Emaciation, ticks	Columbia	Forrester (1984)
2.5 yr.	45	1/81	3,740	83	ND	"	Unknown	Orange	SCWDS records
2.5 yr.	34	10/88	6,652	196	77	7.0	None	Collier	Forrester & Wright (1989a)
Yearlings									
12 mo.	30	5/77	3,959	132	"	"	"	Brevard	" "
18 mo.	33	7/82	12,568	380	16	"	"	Broward	" "
15 mo.	22	6/85	1,927	88	70	5.4	Lungworms (27)	Collier	Forrester & Roelke (1986)
12 mo.	18	3/86	2,993	166	22	3.8	Emaciated	"	" "
18 mo.	34	10/89	3,260	96	39	8.4	Nasal bots (21)	"	Forrester & Telford (1990)
18 mo.	23	11/78	4,115	181	ND	ND	Unknown	Palm Beach	SCWDS records
Fawns									
3 mo.	21	10/77	2,256	107	"	"	"	Brevard	" "
2.5 mo.	15	"	1,500	100	"	"	"	"	" "
3 mo.	24	"	4,197	175	"	"	"	"	" "
5 mo.	24	"	4,128	172	"	"	"	"	" "
4.5 mo.	22	11/77	4,951	101	"	"	"	"	" "
2.5 mo.	17	"	2,200	129	"	"	"	"	" "
3 mo.	17	11/77	6,296	370	"	"	"	"	" "
10 mo.	25	1/78	2,589	102	"	"	"	"	" "
5 mo.	15	"	5,912	394	"	"	"	"	" "
7 mo.	21	2/78	13,526	644	"	"	"	"	" "
6 mo.	17	"	2,148	126	"	"	"	"	" "
7 mo.	18	"	3,305	184	"	"	"	"	" "
6 mo.	22	1/87	4,540	208	37	"	"	"	" "
6 mo.	22	"	2,540	117	51	"	"	"	" "
5 mo.	18	9/82	11,380	632	23	"	"	Broward	" "
6 mo.	26	10/68	4,326	164	ND	"	"	Collier	" "
7 mo.	16	10/85	5,394	337	19	2.6	Emaciated	"	Forrester & Roelke (1986)
8 mo.	24	10/86	2,840	118	43	5.6	None	"	Wright & Forrester (1987)
7 mo.	16	10/87	2,600	164	41	7.8	"	"	Wright (1988a, 1988b)
9 mo.	23	"	2,770	122	ND	7.0	"	"	" "
8 mo.	20	"	2,960	147	"	7.6	"	"	" "

(continued)

Table 20-37 (*continued*)

Age	Weight (kg)	Date mo/yr	No. Haemonchus Total	per kg	PCV[a] (vol. %)	Tot. plasma proteins[b] (g/dl)	Additional factors	County	Data source
7 mo.	25	10/88	2,500	100	36	7.6	None	Collier	Forrester & Wright (1989a)
7 mo.	26	10/89	2,300	90	27	8.4	"	"	Forrester & Telford (1990)
7 mo.	20	10/90	3,020	155	36	6.7	Nasal bots (12)	"	" " "
8 mo.	17	"	2,340	139	15	6.0	None	"	" " "
6 mo.	20	11/74	5,014	250	ND	ND	"	Clay	SCWDS records
6 mo.	16	10/80	2,908	182	"	"	"	"	" " "
6 mo.	19	12/78	1,741	94	"	"	"	Duval	" " "
7 mo.	21	2/80	1,920	90	"	"	"	Lake	" " "
9 mo.	20	"	8,509	417	"	"	"	"	" " "
6 mo.	14	12/82	5,460	393	"	"	Lungworms (420), ticks	Levy	Forrester (1984)
8 mo.	20	11/78	4,854	243	"	"	Unknown	Palm Beach	SCWDS records
8 mo.	30	"	14,822	502	"	"	"	"	" " "
8 mo.	16	"	14,959	965	"	"	"	"	" " "
8 mo.	15	"	15,574	1,011	"	"	"	"	" " "

[a]Normal values = 39–58%.
[b]Normal values = 5.0–7.8 g/dl.
[c]ND = not determined.

pointed out by Forrester et al. (1974a) it has not been found because most surveys of deer do not include data on young fawns a few weeks of age. *Strongyloides papillosus* is more common in young animals and quite rare in older ones due to the development of immunity (Levine 1980).

Fawns with strongyloidosis become listless, usually experience diarrhea, and die within 12 to 36 hours (Forrester et al. 1974a). At necropsy the fawns have acute hemorrhagic enteritis. In many cases this is accompanied by bronchopneumonia in association with migrating *Strongyloides* larvae.

The significance of strongyloidosis to whitetail populations in Florida is unknown. There is, however, the potential for this disease to assume an important role under the proper ecological circumstances. Such a situation might include the high water levels seen periodically in southern Florida as described by Loveless (1959) and others. Animals crowded onto small areas of dry land would be subject to infections by *Strongyloides* with devastating effects on fawns. The mortality described by Loveless (1959) and attributed to pneumonia and malnutrition may also have involved strongyloidosis or concomitant infections with *Haemonchus*.

Since *Strongyloides papillosus* is a common parasite of cattle (Levine 1980), there is a possible relationship between deer and livestock from the standpoint of cross-transmission. At the present time we have no data relating to this possibility, but it should be investigated.

XVI. Filarial worms

White-tailed deer are hosts for three species of filarial nematodes (Hibler and Prestwood 1981): the arterial worm (*Elaeophora schneideri*), the abdominal worm (*Setaria yehi*), and the foot worm (*Onchocerca cervipedis*). Only the arterial worm and the abdominal worm have been found in Florida deer and of these, only the arterial worm is of pathologic significance.

Elaeophorosis is caused by the filarial worm *Elaeophora schneideri,* which as an adult is found in the common carotid or internal maxillary arteries and sometimes other parts of the arterial system or in the heart. Microfilariae are found in the skin of the deer's forehead and face (Hibler and Prestwood 1981).

The life cycle involves tabanid horseflies as intermediate hosts. The species of fly involved has not been determined for Florida, but on the coast of South Carolina (Couvillion et al. 1984, 1986b) the main intermediate host appears to be *Tabanus lineola hinellus.* Horseflies feed on the forehead and facial region of infected deer and acquire microfilariae, which develop to the third or infective stage in the fly in about two weeks. As an infected horsefly feeds, these infective larvae are transferred to another deer, where they reach the circulatory system and eventually arrive in the leptomeningeal arteries and then move to the cerebral arteries. Later they move back to the common carotid arteries, mature, mate, and produce microfilariae. The microfilariae are carried to the capillaries that supply the skin of the face and forehead of the deer (Hibler and Prestwood 1981).

Elaeophora schneideri is common in mule deer in the western United States and this host is considered the normal host. Infections in whitetails are rather uncommon and are known only from a few localities in Arizona, Arkansas, Texas, Oklahoma, Georgia, South Carolina, and Florida (Couvillion et al. 1985; Hibler and Prestwood 1981; Prestwood and Ridgeway 1972; Hibler and Adcock 1971). In Florida there appear to be three enzootic areas: one in Duval County, one in Franklin County, and one in Walton County (Table 20-38). In 1963 one infected deer was found in Marion County, but subsequent studies have failed to reveal infections. Prestwood and Ridgeway (1972) suggested that the discontinuous distribution of *E. schneideri* indicates that it was introduced into deer of those regions. It is curious why the parasite is not more widespread since horseflies are prevalent where deer occur.

Most of the natural infections of *E. schneideri* in whitetails do not seem to cause serious damage to the host. However, there are several reported cases, including one from Walton County, Florida (Prestwood and Ridgeway 1972), of infections in aged deer associated with enlargement beneath the rami of the lower jaw, debilitation, and incoordination. These deer seemed unafraid of man and the sublingual area contained masses of chewed food and debris (Prestwood and Ridgeway 1972; Hibler and Prestwood 1981). Experimentally infected fawns died or exhibited transitory signs of dyspnea, ataxia, and incoordination (Titche et al. 1979). *Elaeophora schneideri* may cause partial paralysis because of blockage of blood flow to the muscles forming the floor of the mouth, but the exact cause of the sublingual impaction is unclear (Hibler and Prestwood 1981; Couvillion et al. 1986a). Blockage of the coronary artery by immature *E. schneideri* was known to cause the death of an experimentally infected fawn four weeks after infection (Titche et al. 1979).

The impact of elaeophorosis on whitetailed deer in Florida is probably minor since the infections appear to be confined to three or possibly four localities. The parasite seems to be poorly adapted to whitetails, however,

Table 20-38
Characteristics of infections of the arterial worm (*Elaeophora schneideri*) in white-tailed deer from Florida

County	Year	No. deer Exam.	Pos.	%	Intensity Mean	Range	Data source
Duval	1971	5	1	20	6[a]	6	SCWDS records, Prestwood & Ridgeway (1972)
	1973	5	1	20	1	1	SCWDS records
	1978–79	17	5	29	3	1–6	Forrester (1984)
Franklin	1984	6	1	17	5	5	SCWDS records, Davidson et al. (1987)
Leon	1962	NG[b]	NG	—	NG	NG	USNM Helm. Coll. 59909[c]
Marion	1963	20	1	5	NG	NG	Harlow & Jones (1965)
	1980	10	0	0	—	—	SCWDS records
Walton	1962	1	1	100	14	14	Prestwood & Ridgeway (1972)
	1962–63	77	7	9	NG	1–15	" " " "
	1963	10	3	30	NG	NG	Harlow & Jones (1965)
	1967–69	40	1	3	1	1	SCWDS records

[a]Prestwood and Ridgeway (1972) reported the number of worms from this animal as 7, whereas the original SCWDS records give it as 6.
[b]NG = not given.
[c]U.S. National Parasite Collection, Beltsville, Md.

and the evidence indicates that the disease can be expected occasionally in the enzootic areas. Harmful effects of this parasite are known for domestic sheep and Sika deer (facial dermatitis) and other species of big game such as elk ("clear-eyed blindness" and ischemic necrosis of the tips of the ears and muzzle) (Hibler and Prestwood 1981). Therefore, it would not be wise to introduce these animals into the enzootic areas in Florida.

Setaria yehi as an adult is a large filarial worm that is found free in the thoracic and abdominal cavities of white-tailed deer (Figure 20-20). Occasionally degenerating adult worms are found encysted on the surface of the liver or other organs, but are of little or no pathologic significance. The worm is believed to be transmitted by mosquitoes and is more prevalent in fawns than in older deer. Infections are widespread throughout the range of white-tailed deer. Prestwood and Pursglove (1977) reported it in 27% of 1,045 deer in the Southeast. Infected deer have been found throughout Florida (Table 20-39).

Numbers of worms per deer are usually small. Prestwood and Pursglove (1977) reported that the average infection was 2.6 worms per deer. More than 50 worms per deer was unusual. A mild to moderate fibrinous peritonitis is a common finding in infected deer, but it is not thought to be of much pathological significance (Prestwood and Pursglove 1977). Hunters should be advised that, even though these worms are obvious and objectionable from an aesthetic point of view, they in no way should result in a deer carcass being condemned for human consumption. Other than one report from a sambar deer on St. Vincent Island (Davidson et al. 1987), this worm has not been reported in other wild and domestic animals in Florida.

XVII. Arthropods

White-tailed deer have a number of different species of ectoparasites. These include ticks, mites, screwworms, blowflies, bots, keds,

FIGURE 20-20. View of peritoneal cavity of a white-tailed deer showing several specimens of the abdominal worm (*Setaria yehi*).

sucking lice, biting lice, and fleas. Some of these parasitize only deer, whereas others are not host-specific and feed on a large number of wild and domestic animal species (Strickland et al. 1981). The reader is referred to the reviews and checklists by Anderson (1962), Walker and Becklund (1970), and Strickland et al. (1981) for further information on this topic. Twenty-nine species of parasitic arthropods are known from Florida deer (Tables 20-40 and 20-41). These include 11 species of ticks, 4 mites, 2 screwworms, 4 blowflies, 1 bot, 1 ked, 3 sucking lice, 2 biting lice, and 1 flea. Several of the more important ectoparasites will be discussed in more detail.

Ticks are by far the most important ectoparasite of whitetails (Strickland et al. 1981). The harmful effects of ticks include local irri-

tation, blood loss, skin wounds with resultant secondary infections, disease transmission, and tick paralysis. The full significance of these factors on whitetails in Florida is not known, but it is clear that ticks have an important role in the health and well-being of deer. Of the 11 species of ticks that infest deer in Florida, the most common are *Ixodes scapularis*, *Amblyomma maculatum*, and *Amblyomma americanum*, which occurred on 54%, 32%, and 26%, respectively, of 429 deer from 21 counties in Florida examined in 1974–75 (Smith 1977) (Table 20-42). *Ixodes scapularis* is especially widespread and has been found on deer in 43 counties (Figure 20-21). The composition of the tick fauna of deer from area to area can vary considerably. As an example a study done in Big Cypress Na-

Table 20-39
Characteristics of infections of the abdominal worm (*Setaria yehi*) in white-tailed deer from Florida

County	Year	No. deer Exam.	Pos.	%	Intensity Mean	Range	Data source
Broward	1982	37	6	16	1	1	SCWDS records
Clay	1968	5	1	20	1	1	" "
	1982	2	1	50	ND[a]	ND	Forrester (1984)
	1985	1	1	100	2	2	Forrester (1985)
Collier	1966	10	0	0	—	—	SCWDS records
	1968	10	0	0	—	—	" "
	1984–86	136	3	2	1	1–2	Forrester & Roelke (1986)
	1986	20	0	0	—	—	Wright & Forrester (1987)
	1987	44	0	0	—	—	Wright (1988b)
	1988	49	1[b]	2	1	1	Wright (1988a)
Duval	1971	5	3	60	9	2–18	SCWDS records
	1973	5	1	20	5	5	" "
	1977–79	14	5	36	ND	ND	Forrester (1984)
Escambia	1977	5	4	80	2	1–4	SCWDS records
Franklin	1984	6	6	100	10	1–35	SCWDS records, Davidson et al. (1987)
	1986	5	2	40	58	1–114	SCWDS records
Gadsden	1973	10	2	20	2	1–3	" "
Lake	1980	10	9	90	21	2–64	" "
Levy	1976	2	1	50	ND	ND	Forrester (1984)
	1986	5	3	60	1	1–3	SCWDS records
Liberty	1973	5	1	20	6	6	" "
Marion	1979–80	2	2	100	ND	ND	Forrester (1984)
	1980	10	6	60	2	1–3	SCWDS records
Monroe	1988	6	3	50	1	1	Wright (1988a)
Orange	1978	5	1	20	1	1	SCWDS records
Osceola	1985	ND	3[c]	—	ND	ND	Forrester & McCraken (1985)
	1987	5	2	40	1	1–2	SCWDS records
Wakulla	1981	10	5	50	ND	ND	" "
	1985–87	15	3	20	7	1–14	" "
Walton	1967–69	40	11	28	2	1–8	" "

[a]ND = not determined.
[b]Worm was encysted on the serosa of the uterus.
[c]Degenerating adults were found encysted on the surfaces of the livers of these 3 deer.

tional Preserve can be cited. Over a two-year period (1984–1986) 110 deer were collected from two areas located about 30 miles apart. Fifty-three deer came from Bear Island and 57 from Raccoon Point. *Ixodes scapularis* was more than three times as prevalent on deer from Bear Island than on deer from Raccoon Point (Table 20-43). In addition, an-

other species of *Ixodes* (*I. affinis*) was not even represented at Raccoon Point. Numerous factors such as differences in habitat, local weather conditions, and other mammalian and avian hosts present could account for such observations.

Four of the species of ticks found in Florida whitetails (*Amblyomma americanum, A.*

Table 20-40
Ticks reported from white-tailed deer in Florida

Species of tick	Location (county)	Data source
Amblyomma americanum (TP)[a]	Clay, Levy, Marion, Taylor, Wakulla	Smith (1977)
	Citrus, Duval, Levy, Pasco/ Hernando, Union, Volusia, Walton	Harlow & Jones (1965)
	Leon, Wakulla, Lake, St. Johns, Gadsden, Liberty, Columbia, Walton, Okaloosa	SCWDS records
	"Statewide"	Boardman (1929)
	Hernando	USDA Par. Coll. 34117[b]
	"Northern Florida"	Rogers (1953)
	Franklin	Davidson et al. (1987)
Amblyomma maculatum (TP)	Citrus, Clay, Duval, Highlands, Jackson, Levy, Martin/Palm Beach, Union, Volusia/Brevard, Walton	Harlow & Jones (1965)
	Franklin	Davidson et al. (1987)
	Broward, Charlotte, Clay, Flagler, Glades, Highlands, Jackson, Levy, Marion, Nassau, Osceola, Palm Beach, Volusia, Wakulla	Smith (1977)
	Liberty, Columbia, Baker, Polk	SCWDS records
	Orange	Travis (1941)
	Collier[c]	Forrester & Telford (1990)
	Collier	USDA Par. Coll. 44853[b]
	Lee	Taylor (1951)
	Polk	USDA Par. Coll. 34090[b]
	St. Lucie	USDA Par. Coll. 34174[b]
	Osceola	USDA Par. Coll. 32472[b]
	Osceola/Orange	USDA Par. Coll. 34250, 42219[b]
Amblyomma tuberculatum	Citrus, Clay, Marion, Osceola	Smith (1977)
Boophilus microplus (E)[d]	Orange[e]	Travis (1941)
	Orange, Osceola	Knapp (1940)
	Orange, Osceola[f]	Marshall et al. (1963)
	Collier	FSCA[g], USDA Par. Coll. 44854[b]
	Central & southern Florida[h]	McIntosh (1934)
	Polk	USDA Par. Coll. 34090[b]
Boophilus annulatus (E)	Brevard	USDA Par. Coll. 33831[b]
	Collier	USDA Par. Coll. 42221[b]
	Lee	USDA Par. Coll. 33858[b]
	Orange	USDA Par. Coll. 30296, 31511, 34257[b]
	Orange/Osceola	USDA Par. Coll. 32474, 42218[b]
	St. Lucie	USDA Par. Coll. 33832, 33833[b]
	"East Florida"	Say (1821)
Dermacentor nigrolineatus	Marion	Smith (1977), USDA Par. Coll. 56080[b]
	Clay, Citrus, Marion, Martin/ Palm Beach, Volusia/Brevard	Harlow & Jones (1965)
	Lake	SCWDS records

(Continued)

Table 20-40 *(continued)*

Species of tick	Location (county)	Data source
Dermacentor variabilis (TP)	Citrus, Marion, Martin/Palm Beach, Pasco/Hernando, Volusia/Brevard	Harlow & Jones (1965)
	Franklin, Clay, Broward, Dade	SCWDS records
	Collier[i]	USDA Par. Coll. 44852[b], Forrester & Telford (1990)
Dermacentor nitens	Southern Florida	Strickland & Gerrish (1964)
Ixodes scapularis (TP)	Bay, Broward, Citrus, Clay, Flagler, Glades, Highlands, Jackson, Jefferson, Lafayette, Levy, Marion, Nassau, Osceola, Palm Beach, Polk, Sumter, Taylor, Volusia, Wakulla	Smith (1977)
	Bay, Citrus, Clay, Columbia Duval, Highlands, Jackson, Leon, Levy, Liberty, Marion, Martin/Palm Beach, Osceola, Pasco/Hernando, Sumter, Union, Volusia/Brevard, Walton	Harlow & Jones (1965)
	Orange	Travis (1941)
	Orange/Osceola	USDA Par. Coll. 42220[b]
	"Northern Florida"	Rogers (1953)
	Alachua	Wassef & Hoogstraal (1982)
	Putnam	Moore (1957)
	Collier[j]	Forrester & Telford (1990)
	Franklin	Davidson et al. (1987)
	St. Lucie	USDA Par. Coll. 33834[b]
	Escambia, Dixie, Okaloosa, Baker, Gadsden, Dade, Lake	SCWDS records
	Highlands, Orange, Collier	USDA Par. Coll. 42222[b]
	Monroe/Dade[k]	Forrester & Telford (1990)
Ixodes affinis	Clay, Levy, Marion, Taylor	Smith (1977)
	Alachua, Glades	Wassef & Hoogstraal (1982)
	Collier[l]	Forrester & Telford (1990)
Ixodes sp.	Dade	Taylor (1951)
	St. Lucie	USDA Par. Coll. 33834[b]
Rhipicephalus sanguineus (TP)	Levy, Osceola	Harlow & Jones (1965)
	Collier	USDA Par. Coll. 44111[b]
	Highlands	USDA Par. Coll. 42965[b]

[a](TP) = species known to cause tick paralysis (Strickland et al. 1976; Gregson 1973).

[b]U.S. National Parasite Collection, Beltsville, Md.

[c]16 of 237 (7%) deer were infested (1984–89).

[d](E) = eradicated from Florida (Strickland et al. 1976).

[e]4 of 22 (18%) were infested; mean intensity was 69 (range, 3–182)(1936–37).

[f]22 of 715 (17%) were infested (1937–39).

[g]FSCA = records from the Florida State Collection of Arthropods, Division of Plant Industry, Florida Department of Agriculture, Gainesville, Fla.

[h]McIntosh (1934) reported this tick from cattle, horses, deer, goats, and dogs from 23 counties in central and southern Florida, but did not state the localities for deer separate from the other hosts.

[i]1 of 237 (< 1%) were infested (1984–89).

[j]41 of 237 (17%) were infested (1984–89).

[k]6 of 26 (23%) were infested (1988–89).

[l]16 of 237 (7%) were infested (1984–89).

Table 20-41
Arthropod parasites (other than ticks) reported from white-tailed deer in Florida

Species of arthropod	Location (county)	Data source
Mites		
Eutrombicula splendens	Orange	Ewing (1943)
	Collier[a]	Forrester & Telford (1990)
	Franklin	Davidson et al. (1987)
	Wakulla	SCWDS records
Eutrombicula sp.	Collier	Kellogg et al. (1971)
Demodex odocoilei	Gadsden, Levy, Bay	Forrester (1988a)
	Escambia, Gadsden, Washington	SCWDS records
Psoroptes cuniculi	Wakulla	" "
Sucking lice		
Haematopinus suis	NG[b]	Kellogg et al. (1971)
	Walton	SCWDS records
Solenopotes binipilosus	NG	Kellogg et al. (1971)
	Leon	Kim et al. (1986)
	Collier[c]	Forrester & Telford (1990)
	Gadsden, Walton	SCWDS records
Solenopotes ferrisi	Orange	FSCA[d]
	Lake	SCWDS records
Solenopotes sp.	Franklin	" "
Biting lice		
Tricholipeurus lipeuroides	NG	Kellogg et al. (1971)
	Citrus	Harlow & Jones (1965)
	Franklin	Davidson et al. (1987)
	Lake, Escambia, Gadsden, Citrus, Hernando, Okaloosa, Walton, Collier, Brevard, Wakulla	SCWDS records
	Collier[e]	Forrester & Telford (1990)
Tricholipeurus parallelus	Franklin	Davidson et al. (1987)
	Lake, Marion, Gadsden, Duval, Liberty, Walton	SCWDS records
Bots		
Cephenemyia sp.	Citrus, Collier	Nettles & Doster (1975)
	Collier[f]	Forrester (1989)
	Levy, Marion	Forrester (1988a)
	Broward	SCWDS records
	Monroe/Dade[g]	Forrester (1989)
	Bay, Nassau, Columbia, Sumter, Bradford, Clay, Putnam, Alachua, Dixie, Levy, Marion, Citrus, Hernando, Pasco, Polk, Osceola, Okeechobee, Martin, Palm Beach, Broward, Dade, Monroe, Collier, Gulf	Cogley & Forrester (1991)
Keds		
Lipoptena mazamae	NG	Kellogg et al. (1971)
	Volusia	Harlow & Jones (1965)
	Collier	USDA Par. Coll. 44855[h]
	Collier	Bequaert (1942)
	Collier[i]	Forrester & Telford (1990)
	Monroe/Dade[j]	" " " "
	Levy, Marion	Forrester (1988a)
	Wakulla, Orange, Lake, Palm Beach, Broward, Osceola, Brevard	SCWDS records
	Citrus, Clay, Columbia	Forrester & Wilson (1990)

(continued)

Table 20-41 (*continued*)

Species of arthropod	Location (county)	Data source
Screwworms		
Cochliomyia hominivorax (E)[k]	Charlotte, Glades, Highlands, Marion, Martin/ Palm Beach	Harlow & Jones (1965)
	"Statewide"	Allen (1951)
	Marion[l]	Strode (1955)
	Walton	Allen (n.d.)
Cochliomyia macellaria	Northern Florida[m]	Anonymous (1933)
Blowfly larvae		
Sarcophaga sp.	Marion	SCWDS records
Calliphora sp.	Marion	" "
Phormia regina	Marion	" "
Phaenicia sp.	Taylor	" "
Fleas		
Ctenocephalides felis	Levy	Forrester (1984)
	Liberty	SCWDS records

[a]7 of 237 (3%) were infested (1984–89).
[b]NG = not given by authors.
[c]3 of 237 (1%) were infested (1984–89).
[d]FSCA = records from the Florida State Collection of Arthropods, Division of Plant Industry, Florida Department of Agriculture, Gainesville, Fla.
[e]18 of 237 (8%) were infested (1984–89).
[f]102 of 227 (45%) were infected; intensity ranged from 1–37 (mean = 5) per infected deer (1984–89).
[g]25 of 35 (71%) were infected; intensity ranged from 1–50 (mean = 8) per infected deer (1988–89).
[h]U.S. National Parasite Collection, Beltsville, Md.
[i]200 of 237 (84%) were infested (1984–89).
[j]8 of 26 (31%) were infested (1988–89).
[k](E) = eradicated from Florida (Strickland et al. 1976).
[l]Strode (1955) reported finding 10, 13, and 18 deer infested with screwworms in 1952, 1953, and 1954, respectively.
[m]Infestations were reported in 12 counties in northern Florida. The names of the counties were not given.

maculatum, Dermacentor variabilis, and *Ixodes scapularis*) are known to cause tick paralysis (Gregson 1973), although this condition has not been documented in deer from Florida. Tick paralysis is an acute flaccid ascending paralysis that occurs as a result of the attachment of certain ticks to the head and neck region of animals and man. It can and often does lead to death. *Amblyomma americanum* has been shown by Kuttler et al. (1967) to be the vector of *Theileria cervi,* and also has been found to cause severe losses in young fawns in Oklahoma (Bolte et al. 1970). In that study almost 20% of wild fawns examined had tick bite damage around the eyes, and many fawns were blind. Experimental work showed that infestation of 100 ticks caused anemia and death in young deer

(Barker et al. 1973). We have seen several deer in Florida that exhibited severe allergic reactions to tick bites. One of these deer, a four-year-old doe from Duval County (1974), had a very heavy infestation of *Amblyomma americanum* (several thousand) and some *Ixodes scapularis*. There was severe alopecia (hair loss) on the face and around the eyes, and the ears were thickened and crusty and had undergone some necrosis at the tips of the pinnae (Figure 20-22).

The two species of *Boophilus* listed in Table 20-40 have been eradicated from the state of Florida (Strickland et al. 1976). These species are known as cattle fever ticks and are vectors of *Babesia bigemina,* a protozoan that is highly pathogenic to cattle and causes Texas cattle fever or piroplasmosis. In the

Table 20-42

Number of infested deer examined and species of ticks encountered in 21 counties in Florida during the 1974–75 hunting season

County	No. deer infested	Amblyomma americanum	Amblyomma maculatum	Amblyomma tuberculatum	Dermacentor nigrolineatus	Dermacentor variabilis	Ixodes affinis	Ixodes scapularis
Bay	4	—	—	—	—	—	—	+
Broward	2	—	+	—	—	—	—	+
Charlotte	2	—	+	—	—	—	—	—
Citrus	38	—	—	+	—	—	—	+
Clay	36	+	+	+	—	—	+	+
Flagler	4	—	+	—	—	—	—	+
Glades	3	—	+	—	—	+	—	+
Highlands	19	—	+	—	—	—	—	+
Jackson	2	—	+	—	—	—	—	+
Jefferson	12	—	—	—	—	—	—	+
Lafayette	5	—	—	—	—	—	—	+
Levy	11	+	+	—	—	—	+	+
Marion	95	+	+	+	+	—	+	+
Nassau	2	—	+	—	—	—	—	+
Osceola	46	—	+	+	—	—	—	+
Palm Beach	42	—	+	—	—	—	—	+
Polk	26	—	—	—	—	—	—	+
Sumter	12	—	—	—	—	—	—	+
Taylor	4	+	—	—	—	—	+	+
Volusia	5	—	+	—	—	—	—	+
Wakulla	59	+	+	—	—	—	—	+
Total	429	26%[a]	32%	11%	4%	0.5%	2%	54%

Source: Smith (1977).
[a] % of deer positive for each species of tick.

early 1900s an attempt was made to eradicate the cattle fever ticks in Florida to alleviate the tremendous losses being suffered by the cattle industry. Because deer were found to be secondary hosts of the ticks, thousands were slaughtered between 1937 and 1939 amid much controversy. An estimated 10,000 to 20,000 deer were killed (Harlow and Jones 1965; Kistner 1969). The slaughter program was initiated in Orange and Osceola counties and then undertaken in Highlands, Glades, Polk, Okeechobee, Charlotte, Hernando, Collier, Hendry, and other counties. Opponents of the deer slaughter pointed out that in other parts of the United States it had been found possible to eradicate the tick by exten-

sive chemical dipping of cattle and that this resulted in subsequent reduction in ticks on deer as well. In any case the slaughter continued and the last Boophilus-infested deer was seen in March 1939. A detailed summary of the eradication program and the controversy it caused was presented by Marshall et al. (1963). Deer have been shown to serve as hosts for Boophilus ticks (Park et al. 1966; Kistner and Hayes 1970), but only for short periods of time (Davey 1990). In addition, attempts to transmit Texas cattle fever to deer via Boophilus spp. have been unsuccessful (Kuttler et al. 1972). The issue is now closed, but, should the ticks be reintroduced into Florida from the Caribbean area or Mexico

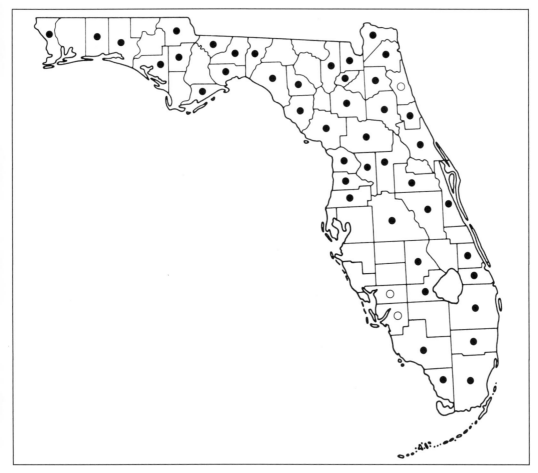

FIGURE 20-21. Distribution of the black-legged tick (*Ixodes scapularis*) on white-tailed deer in Florida. Solid circles indicate counties where infestations have been found on deer; open circles are counties in which deer have been examined, but found negative. (From Smith 1977; Harlow and Jones 1965; Travis 1941; Wassef and Hoogstraal 1982; Davidson et al. 1987; Moore 1957; USDA Par. Coll. 33834 and 42220; SCWDS records; Forrester and Telford 1990.)

Table 20-43
Prevalence of ticks on white-tailed deer from Big Cypress
National Preserve, Collier County, Florida, 1984–86

		Prevalence (%)		
Area	No. deer examined	*Ixodes scapularis*	*Amblyomma maculatum*	*Ixodes affinis*
Bear Island	53	23	4	4
Raccoon Point	57	7	5	0
Totals	110	15	5	4

Note: Data from Forrester and Roelke (1986). Deer were collected from both areas at various seasons of the year over the 2-year period.

FIGURE 20-22. White-tailed deer from Duval County, Florida, with alopecia of facial region and cropped ears due to tick-bite dermatitis.

where they still occur, the initiation of localized deer depopulation may again be suggested as a control measure (Strickland et al. 1981).

Mange in white-tailed deer caused by the follicular mite *Demodex odocoilei* has been found in a number of states, including Oklahoma, Virginia, North Carolina, South Carolina, Georgia, and Florida (Desch and Nutting 1974; Forrester 1984). Six deer from Florida (two from Gadsden County, one from Washington County, one from Escambia County, one from Bay County, and one from Levy County) were found with this condition (Table 20-44). In the deer from Levy County

(a yearling buck) there was extensive involvement, including severe alopecia and secondary skin infections particularly in the abdominal areas and on all legs (Figure 20-23). Thousands of follicular mites were seen when scrapings of the skin lesions were examined microscopically. The overall significance of this mange condition is unknown, but since it occurs at such a low frequency it may not be significant. The mite may be more common than is realized, however, and the mange condition may be manifested when deer become compromised immunologically by factors such as other diseases or malnutrition.

Hunters occasionally encounter the nasal

Table 20-44
Cases of demodectic mange reported from white-tailed deer in Florida

Case no.	Age (yr)	Sex	Year	County	Data source
1.	Adult	M	1977	Levy	Forrester (1988a)
2.	Adult	M	1979	Bay	" "
3.	10.5	F	1981	Gadsden	" "
4.	2.5	M	1982	Gadsden	SCWDS records
5.	6.5	M	1983	Escambia	" "
6.	5.5	F	1984	Washington	" "

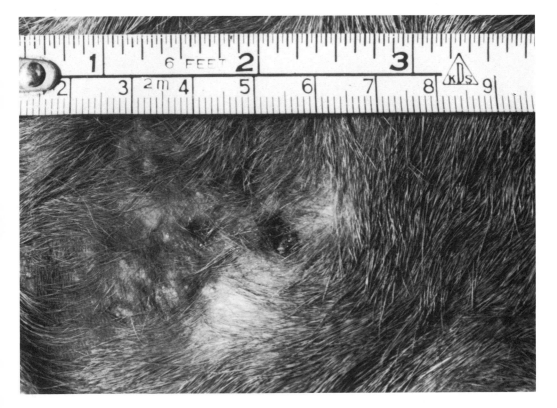

FIGURE 20-23. Close-up of skin of a white-tailed deer from Levy County showing area of hair loss and swelling due to demodectic mange.

or pharyngeal bot (*Cephenemyia* sp.) in the retropharyngeal pouch of whitetails (Figure 20-24). The species concerned has not been determined (Nettles and Doster 1975, Cogley and Forrester, 1991), but may be a subspecies of *C. phobifer* or a new species (Cogley 1989). They can also be found in the nasal passages, trachea, and bronchi. Deer are in-fected when adult flies deposit larvae in the nostrils of the host. These larvae crawl to the retropharyngeal pouch and develop to the third instar. They escape via the sneezing of the deer and the larvae then pupate in the soil and eventually develop into adult flies (Strickland et al. 1981). In a survey of 2,423 deer in the Southeast, Nettles and Doster

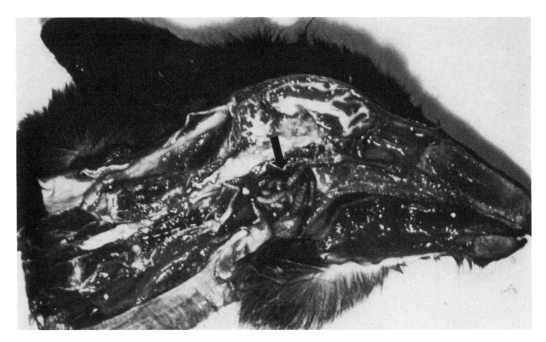

FIGURE 20-24. Sagittal view of the head of a white-tailed deer showing bots (*Cephenemyia* sp.) in retropharyngeal pouch (arrow). (Photo courtesy of SCWDS.)

(1975) found bots in 107 deer (4%) from 10 states, including Florida. The mean intensity was 9 larvae per infected deer and only 5 animals had more than 30 larvae. In Florida nasal bots have been found in deer from 24 widely distributed counties from Columbia in the north to Monroe in the south (Table 20-41). Quantitative data are not available for deer in north-central Florida, but in Collier, Dade, and Monroe counties annual prevalences varied from 32% to 78% (mean, 49%) in 1984–89 and intensities per infested deer from 1 to 50 (mean, 3) (Forrester 1988a; Wright 1988a; Forrester and Telford 1990). Nettles and Doster (1975) felt that bots were not a serious disease problem in deer in the Southeast, but Hair et al. (1969) considered heavy infestations to be a serious health threat to whitetails in Oklahoma. From a practical standpoint these bots are of concern to hunters who find them and wonder about their effect on the edibility of their deer. Infec-

tions by these bots do not cause a deer carcass to be unfit for human consumption (Nettles and Doster 1975).

The primary screwworm (*Cochliomyia hominivorax*) is an obligatory myiasis-producing parasite. The female fly deposits larvae in an open wound on a deer or any number of other species of wild and domestic animals. These larvae feed on the tissues around the wound, causing direct damage and secondary infection. Often tick bite wounds and the unhealed umbilical cord of fawns are sites of infections. Larvae eventually drop off the deer, pupate on the ground, and eventually develop into an adult (Strickland et al. 1981).

Before this parasite was eradicated from Florida it was the most important arthropod parasite of white-tailed deer. In 1958 a program was initiated in the Southeast to eliminate screwworms by the release of male flies that had been sterilized by radiation exposure. These sterile males would mate with female flies, but no offspring would be produced. Since female screwworm flies only mate once in their lifetime, this procedure resulted in drastic reduction in screwworm populations (Diamant 1963). In two years' time the screwworms were gone and deer populations began increasing in southern Florida (Harlow and Jones 1965). A dramatic increase occurred, for instance, in the deer herd of Fisheating Creek in Glades County. In 1950–1951 the herd was estimated at 60 to 70 head; by 1963–1964 it had increased to 750 animals. Similar increases were noted in other herds in southern Florida (Harlow and Jones 1965). Screwworms could return to the state of Florida and continued vigilance is necessary to detect such an occurrence and take appropriate action.

XVIII. Summary and conclusions

White-tailed deer in Florida are known to have 120 different parasites, infections, and disease conditions, not counting various types of trauma. Of these, 70 are parasites (10 protozoans, 2 trematodes, 3 cestodes, 26 nematodes, and 29 arthropods), 25 are bacteria, 1 is a rickettsia, 14 are viruses, 4 are tumors, and 6 are environmental contaminants. Some of these are primary pathogens while others are secondary pathogens or relatively nonpathogenic organisms or conditions. It must be remembered, however, that many "nonpathogenic" agents can cause considerable harm under the proper ecological situation. An example of this might be *Strongyloides papillosus,* which is present in low intensities in fawns in Florida. Under conditions of crowding such as seen in captive herds, an increase in the numbers of nematodes can reach dangerous levels. If at the same time the fawns are undergoing nutri-

tional stress or some other factor weakens their resistance, an outbreak of strongyloidosis may result. Another example might be the haemonchosis/malnutrition syndrome, which can be exacerbated by conditions of heavy rainfall and subsequent flooding.

Although every deer in Florida is not plagued with all 120 disease agents and conditions at one time, it must be remembered that the "average deer" in Florida will be host to a number of parasites and infectious agents simultaneously. These concomitant infections can have interactive effects on the host that may be considerably more serious than the effects of each of them separately. For example, deer on a lowered plane of nutrition and with infestations of large numbers of ticks may be prime candidates for disease due to these factors plus haemonchosis and lungworm infections.

The great bulk of our knowledge of the diseases and parasites of deer in Florida has been obtained during the past 40 years. The beginning of this upsurge of information can be traced back to 1949, when a widespread die-off of deer (now believed to have been due to hemorrhagic disease) caught the attention of many wildlife biologists in the Southeast. Certainly the subsequent formation of the Southeastern Cooperative Wildlife Disease Study in Athens, Georgia, was a milestone in stimulating the accumulation of information on deer diseases and determining something of what it all means. We in Florida owe them a huge debt of gratitude for the pioneering work they did and the contributions they made. Much of what has gone before was of a descriptive and survey nature, which was both necessary and proper in order to discover what was there. However, the pathogenesis and epizootiology of many deer diseases are understood only partially. The significance of these diseases to populations needs further investigation and study. At the same time diagnostic and descriptive work must continue so that we remain alert to "what's out there" and "what it's doing."

The most important deer diseases in Florida appear to be haemonchosis (including the haemonchosis/malnutrition syndrome in fawns), lungworm pneumonia (and perhaps a combination of the latter two), and hemorrhagic disease. The epizootiological facets of these diseases should be studied on a long-term basis to gain a better understanding of the dynamic ecological relationships of these diseases, their hosts, and the environment.

Several of the diseases and parasites of white-tailed deer in Florida are of public health concern and include five of the arboviruses (SLE virus, EEE virus, Everglades virus, Tensaw virus, and VS virus), and the etiologic agents of leptospirosis, anthrax, salmonellosis, tularemia, dermatophilosis, toxoplasmosis, and trichostrongylosis. Many of the ticks will also infest man.

XIX. Literature cited

Abbas, B., and G. Post. 1980. Experimental coccidiosis in mule deer fawns. J. Wildl. Dis. 16:565–570.

Allen, G.W. 1951. Effects of screw-worm on deer in the southeast. Trans. No. Am. Wildl. Conf. 16:135–145.

Allen, R.H. n.d. The screwworm and its effect on the deer herd in the southeast. Alabama Department of Conservation. Unpublished MS. 8 pp.

Anderson, R.C. 1962. The helminth and arthropod parasites of the white-tailed deer (*Odocoileus virginianus*). Trans. R. Can. Inst. 34:57–92.

Anderson, R.C., and A.K. Prestwood. 1981. Lungworms. In: Diseases and parasites of white-tailed deer. W.R. Davidson et al. (eds.). Misc. Pub. No. 7, Tall Timbers Research Station, Tallahassee, Fla. pp. 226–317.

Anonymous. 1933. Screw worm. Insect Pest. Surv. Bull. 13:339.

Barker, R.W., A.L. Hock, R.G. Buckner, and J.A. Hair. 1973. Hematological changes in white-tailed deer fawns, *Odocoileus virginianus*, infested with *Theileria*-infected lone star ticks. J. Parasitol. 59:1091–1098.

Barrier, M.J., J.K. Reed, and L.G. Webb. 1970. Pesticide residues in selected tissues of the white-tailed deer, *Odocoileus virginianus*, in Calhoun County, South Carolina. Proc. S.E. Assoc. Game Fish Comm. 24:31–45.

Becklund, W.W. 1961. Helminth infections of healthy Florida cattle, with a note on *Cooperia spatula*. Proc. Helminthol. Soc. Wash. 28:183–184.

Bedell, D.M., and J.G. Miller. 1966. A report of the examination of 270 white-tailed deer (*Odocoileus virginianus*) from anaplasmosis enzootic areas of southeastern United States for evidence of anaplasmosis. Univ. of Georgia, Tifton. 158 pp.

Belden, R.C. 1986. Florida panther recovery plan implementation. A 1983 progress report. Proc. 2d Internat. Cat Symp. pp. 159–172.

Bequaert, J.C. 1942. A monograph of the Melophaginae, or ked-flies, of sheep, goats, deer and antelopes (Diptera, Hippoboscidae). Ent. Am. 22:1–210.

Bigler, W.J. 1969. Venezuelan encephalitis antibody studies in certain Florida wildlife. Bull. Wildl. Dis. Assoc. 5:267–270.

Bigler, W.J., E. Lassing, E. Buff, A.L. Lewis, and G.L. Hoff. 1975. Arbovirus surveillance in Florida: Wild vertebrate studies 1965–1974. J. Wildl. Dis. 11:348–356.

Boardman, E.T. 1929. Ticks of the Gainesville area. M.S. thesis, Univ. of Florida, Gainesville. 57 pp.

Bolte, J.R., J.A. Hair, and J. Fletcher. 1970. White-tailed deer mortality following tissue destruction induced by lone star ticks. J. Wildl. Manage. 34:546–552.

Brown, L.N. 1987. A checklist of Florida's mammals. Florida Game and Fresh Water Fish Commission, Tallahassee. 6 pp.

Calderwood-Mays, M.B. 1984. Unpublished

data. (Pathology Report No. N84-298, CVM-TH, Univ. of Florida, Gainesville).

Caren, L.D. 1981. Environmental pollutants: Effects on the immune system and resistance to infectious disease. Bioscience 31:582–586.

Cheatum, E.L. 1951. Disease in relation to winter mortality of deer in New York. J. Wildl. Manage. 15:216–220.

Choquette, L.P. E., and E. Broughton. 1981. Anthrax. In: Infectious diseases of wild mammals. J.W. Davis et al. (eds.). Iowa State Univ. Press, Ames. pp. 288–296.

Cogley, T.P. 1989. First account of an adult deer bot (Diptera: Oestridae) from Florida. Fla. Entomol. 72:553–554.

Cogley, T.P., and D.J. Forrester. 1991. Distribution of bot larvae, Cephenemyia spp. (Diptera: Oestridae) from white-tailed deer (Odocoileus virginianus) in Florida. Fla. Entomol. (in press).

Comer, J.A., W.R. Davidson, A.K. Prestwood, and V.F. Nettles. 1991. An update on the distribution of Parelaphostrongylus tenuis in the southeastern United States. J. Wildl. Dis. 27:348–354.

Conlogue, G.C., and W.J. Foreyt. 1984. Experimental infections of Eimeria mccordocki (Protozoa, Eimeriidae) in white-tailed deer. J. Wildl. Dis. 20:31–33.

Cosgrove, G.E., and L.D. Fay. 1981. Viral tumors. In: Infectious diseases of wild mammals. J.W. Davis et al. (eds.). Iowa State Univ. Press, Ames. pp. 424–428.

Cosgrove, G.E., L.C. Satterfield, and V.F. Nettles. 1981. Neoplasia. In: Diseases and parasites of white-tailed deer. W.R. Davidson et al. (eds.). Misc. Pub. No. 7, Tall Timbers Research Station, Tallahassee, Fla. pp. 62–71.

Cotton, D., and J. Herring. 1970. A preliminary survey of pesticide residues in white-tailed deer (Odocoileus virginianus). Proc. S.E. Assoc. Game Fish Comm. 24:23–30.

Couvillion, C.E. 1981. A comparison of summer and fall abomasal parasite counts (APC) of southeastern white-tailed deer. M.S. thesis, Univ. of Georgia, Athens. 58 pp.

Couvillion, C.E., C.B. Crow, and W.R. Davidson. 1982. An evaluation of hunter-killed white-tailed deer for abomasal parasite count (APC) studies. Proc. Ann. Conf. S.E. Fish Wildl. Agencies 36:427–435.

Couvillion, C.E., W.R. Davidson, and V.F. Nettles. 1985. Distribution of Elaeophora schneideri in white-tailed deer in the southeastern United States, 1962–1983. J. Wildl. Dis. 21:451–453.

Couvillion, C.E., V.F. Nettles, W.R. Davidson, and J.E. Pearson. 1981. Hemorrhagic disease among white-tailed deer in the southeast from 1971 through 1980. Proc. 85th Ann. Meet. U.S. Am. Health Assoc. pp. 522–537.

Couvillion, C.E., V.F. Nettles, C.A. Rawlings, and R.L. Joyner. 1986a. Elaeophorosis in white-tailed deer: Pathology of the natural disease and its relation to oral food impactions. J. Wildl. Dis. 22:214–223.

Couvillion, C.E., D.C. Sheppard, V.F. Nettles, and O.M. Bannaga. 1984. Intermediate hosts of Elaeophora schneideri Wehr and Dikmans, 1935 on South Island, South Carolina. J. Wildl. Dis. 20:59–61.

Couvillion, C.E., V.F. Nettles, D.C. Sheppard, R.L. Joyner, and O.M. Bannaga. 1986b. Temporal occurrence of third-stage larvae of Elaeophora schneideri in Tabanus lineola hinellus on South Island, South Carolina. J. Wildl. Dis. 22:196–200.

Crum, J.M. 1981. Studies on the epizootiology of Sarcocystis spp. in white-tailed deer of the southeastern United States. Ph.D. diss., Univ. of Georgia, Athens. 121 pp.

Crum, J.M., and A.K. Prestwood. 1982. Prevalence and distribution of Sarcocystis spp. among white-tailed deer of the southeastern United States. J. Wildl. Dis. 18:195–203.

Crum, J.M., R. Fayer, and A.K. Prestwood. 1981. Sarcocystis spp. in white-tailed deer. I. Definitive and intermediate host spectrum with a description of Sarcocystis odocoileocanis n. sp. J. Wildl. Dis. 17:567–579.

Cumbie, P.M., and J.H. Jenkins. 1975. Mercury accumulation in native mammals of the southeast. Proc. Ann. Conf. S.E. Game Fish Comm. 28:639–647.

Cummings, S.L., J.H. Jenkins, T.T. Fendley, L. Bankert, P.H. Bedrosian, and C.R. Porter. 1971. Cesium-137 in white-tailed deer as related to vegetation and soils of the southeastern United States. In: Radionuclides in Ecosystems. Proc. 3d Nat. Symp. on Radioecol. D.J. Nelson (ed.). USAEC Symp. Series Conf.-71051-Pl. pp. 123–128.

Das, K.M., and J.H. Whitlock. 1960. Subspeciation in *Haemonchus contortus* (Rudolphi, 1803) Nematoda, Trichostrongyloidea. Cornell Vet. 50:182–197.

Davey, R.B., 1990. Failure of white-tailed deer, *Odocoileus virginianus* L., to sustain a population of cattle ticks, *Boophilus annulatus* (Say), through successive generations. J. Parasitol. 76:356–359.

Davidson, W.R., J.S. Osborne, and F.A. Hayes. 1982. Abomasal parasitism and physical condition in southeastern white-tailed deer. Proc. Ann. Conf. S.E. Assoc. Fish Wildl. Agencies 36:436–444.

Davidson, W.R., C.B. Crow, J.M. Crum, and R.R. Gerrish. 1983. Observations on *Theileria cervi* and *Trypanosoma cervi* in white-tailed deer (*Odocoileus virginianus*) from the southeastern United States. Proc. Helminthol. Soc. Wash. 50:165–169.

Davidson, W.R., F.A. Hayes, V.F. Nettles, and F.E. Kellogg (eds.). 1981. Diseases and parasites of white-tailed deer. Misc. Pub. No. 7, Tall Timbers Research Station, Tallahassee, Fla. 458 pp.

Davidson, W.R., M.B. McGhee, V.F. Nettles, and L.C. Chappell. 1980. Haemonchosis in white-tailed deer in the southeastern United States. J. Wildl. Dis. 16:499–508.

Davidson, W.R., V.F. Nettles, L.E. Hayes, E.W. Howerth, and C.E. Couvillion. 1990. Epidemiologic features of an intracranial abscessation/suppurative meningoencephalitis complex in white-tailed deer. J. Wildl. Dis. 26:460–467.

Davidson, W.R., J.L. Blue, L.B. Flynn, S.M. Shea, R.L. Marchinton, and J.A. Lewis. 1987. Parasites, diseases and health status of sympatric populations of sambar deer and white-tailed deer in Florida. J. Wildl. Dis. 23:267–272.

Desch, C.E., and W.B. Nutting. 1974. *Demodex odocoilei* sp. nov. from the white-tailed deer, *Odocoileus virginianus*. Can. J. Zool. 52: 785–789.

Diamant, G. 1963. Screwworm eradication in southeastern United States. Am. J. Pub. Health Assoc. 53:22–26.

Dikmans, G. 1934. New records of helminth parasites. Proc. Helminthol. Soc. Wash. 1:63–64.

Dikmans, G., and J.T. Lucker. 1935. New records of nematode parasites from deer in the United States. Proc. Helminthol. Soc. Wash. 2:83.

Dinaburg, A.G. 1939. Helminth parasites collected from deer, *Odocoileus virginianus*, in Florida. Proc. Helminthol. Soc. Wash. 6: 102–104.

Eisler, R. 1985. Cadmium hazards to fish, wildlife, and invertebrates: A synoptic review. U.S. Fish Wildl. Serv. Biol. Rep. 85(1.2). 46 pp.

———. 1986. Chromium hazards to fish, wildlife, and invertebrates: A synoptic review. U.S. Fish Wildl. Serv. Biol. Rep. 85(1.6). 60 pp.

Emerson, H.R. 1970. Correction. Re: The isolation of a *Babesia* in white-tailed deer. Bull. Wildl. Dis. Assoc. 6:519.

Emerson, H.R., and W.T. Wright. 1968. The isolation of a *Babesia* in white-tailed deer. Bull. Wildl. Dis. Assoc. 4:142–143.

Eve, J.H. 1981. Management implications of disease. In: Diseases and parasites of white-tailed deer. W.R. Davidson et al. (eds.). Misc. Pub. No. 7, Tall Timbers Research Station, Tallahassee, Fla. pp. 413–423.

Eve, J.H., and F.E. Kellogg. 1977. Management implications of abomasal parasites in southeastern white-tailed deer. J. Wildl. Manage. 41:169–177.

Ewing, H.E. 1943. The American chiggers (larvae of the Trombiculinae) of the genus *Acariscus*, new genus. Proc. Entomol. Soc. Wash. 45:57–66.

Fay, L.D. 1961. The current status of brucellosis in white-tailed and mule deer in the United States. Trans. No. Am. Wildl. Resource Conf. 26:203–211.

———. 1970. Skin tumors of the Cervidae. In: Infectious diseases of wild mammals. J.W. Davis et al. (eds.). Iowa State Univ. Press, Ames. pp. 385–392.

Florida Game and Fresh Water Fish Commission. 1983. Everglades emergency deer hunt controversy. Tallahassee, Fla. 29 pp.

Foreyt, W.J. 1981. Trematodes and cestodes. In: Diseases and parasites of white-tailed deer. W.R. Davidson et al. (eds.). Misc. Pub. No. 7, Tall Timbers Research Station, Tallahassee, Fla. pp. 237–265.

Foreyt, W., and D.O. Trainer. 1970. Experimental haemonchosis in white-tailed deer. J. Wildl. Dis. 6:35–42.

Foreyt, W.J., W.M. Samuel, and A.C. Todd. 1977. *Fascioloides magna* in white-tailed deer (*Odocoileus virginianus*): Observations on the pairing tendency. J. Parasitol. 63:1050–1052.

Forrester, D.J. 1984. Unpublished data. Univ. of Florida, Gainesville.

———. 1985. Unpublished data. Univ. of Florida, Gainesville.

———. 1988a. Unpublished data. Univ. of Florida, Gainesville.

———. 1988b. Intestinal coccidia of white-tailed deer in southern Florida. J. Wildl. Dis. 24:369–370.

———. 1989a. Unpublished data. Univ. of Florida, Gainesville.

———. 1989b. Wildlife disease and parasite research. P-R report. Florida Game and Fresh Water Fish Commission, Gainesville. 10 pp.

———. 1990. Unpublished data. Univ. of Florida, Gainesville.

Forrester, D.J., and R. McCraken. 1985. Unpublished data. Univ. of Florida, Gainesville.

Forrester, D.J., and R.L. Rausch. 1990. Cysticerci (Cestoda: Taeniidae) from white-tailed deer, *Odocoileus virginianus*, in southern Florida. J. Parasitol. 76:583–585.

Forrester, D.J., and M.E. Roelke. 1986. Health/disease study of white-tailed deer in the Big Cypress (July 1, 1984–June 30, 1986). P-R report. Florida Game and Fresh Water Fish Commission, Gainesville. 60 pp.

Forrester, D.J., and S.R. Telford, Jr. 1990. Unpublished data. Univ. of Florida, Gainesville.

Forrester, D.J., and S.R. Telford, Jr. 1991. Unpublished data. Univ. of Florida, Gainesville.

Forrester, D.J., and S.D. Wright. 1989a. Health/disease study of white-tailed deer in southern Florida. P-R report. Florida Game and Fresh Water Fish Commission, Gainesville. 39 pp.

Forrester, D.J., and S.D. Wright. 1989b. Studies on the health and diseases of white-tailed deer in Everglades National Park and Big Cypress National Preserve. Ann. Rep. on Subagreement No. 6 to Coop. Agreement CA-5000-7-8007. Gainesville. 32 pp.

Forrester, D.J., J.A. Conti, and R.C. Belden. 1985. Parasites of the Florida panther (*Felis concolor coryi*). Proc. Helminthol. Soc. Wash. 52:95–97.

Forrester, D.J., W.J. Taylor, and K.P. C. Nair. 1974a. Strongyloidosis in captive white-tailed deer. J. Wildl. Dis. 10:11–17.

Forrester, D.J., W.J. Taylor, and P.P. Humphrey. 1974b. Strongyloidiasis in white-tailed deer fawns in Florida. J. Wildl. Dis. 10:146–148.

Fowler, M.E. 1983. Plant poisoning in free-living wild animals: A review. J. Wildl. Dis. 19:34–43.

Friend, M. 1967. Skin tumors in New York deer. Bull. Wildl. Dis. Assoc. 3:102–104.

Glazener, W.C., and F.F. Knowlton. 1967. Some endoparasites found in Welder Refuge deer. J. Wildl. Manage. 31:595–597.

Gregson, J.D. 1973. Tick paralysis. An appraisal of natural and experimental data. Monogr. No. 9, Canada Dept. of Agriculture, Ottawa, Ont. 109 pp.

Greiner, E.C., T.L. Barber, J.E. Pearson, W.L. Kramer, and E.P. J. Gibbs. 1985. Orbiviruses from *Culicoides* in Florida. Proc. Internat. Symp. on Bluetongue and Related Orbiviruses. Alan R. Liss, Monterey, Calif. pp. 195–200.

Hair, J.A., D.E. Howell, C.E. Rogers, and J. Fletcher. 1969. Occurrence of the pharyngeal bot *Cephenemyia jellisoni* in Oklahoma white-tailed deer, *Odocoileus virginianus*. Ann. Entomol. Soc. Am. 62:1208–1210.

Hanson, R.P. 1968. Discussion of the natural

history of vesicular stomatitis. Am. J. Epidemiol. 87:264–266.

Harlow, R.F., and F.K. Jones. 1965. The white-tailed deer in Florida. Fla. Game and Fresh Water Fish Comm. Tech. Bull. No. 9. 240 pp.

Hayes, F.A., and J.H. Jenkins. 1959. Some theoretical implications of poisonous plants and southeastern deer diseases. Proc. Ann. Conf. S.E. Assoc. Fish. Wildl. Agencies 13:173–177.

Hayes, F.A., W.E. Greer, and E.B. Shotts. 1958. A progress report from the Southeastern Cooperative Deer Disease Study. Trans. No. Am. Wildl. Conf. 23:133–136.

Hayes, F.A., W.T. Gerard, E.B. Shotts, and G.J. Dills. 1960. Further serologic studies of brucellosis in white-tailed deer of the southeastern United States. J. Am. Vet. Med. Assoc. 137:190–191.

Hibler, C.P., and J.L. Adcock. 1971. Elaeophorosis. In: Parasitic diseases of wild mammals. J.W. Davis and R.C. Anderson (eds.). Iowa State Univ. Press, Ames. pp. 263–278.

Hibler, C.P., and A.K. Prestwood. 1981. Filarial nematodes of white-tailed deer. In: Diseases and parasites of white-tailed deer. W.R. Davidson et al. (eds.). Misc. Pub. No. 7, Tall Timbers Research Station, Tallahassee, Fla. pp. 413–423.

Hoff, G.L., and D.O. Trainer. 1981. Hemorrhagic diseases of wild ruminants. In: Infectious diseases of wild mammals. J.W. Davis et al. (eds.). Iowa State Univ. Press, Ames. pp. 45–53.

Hoff, G.L., W.J. Bigler, and E.C. Prather. 1975. One-half century of tularemia in Florida. J. Fla. Med. Assoc. 62:35–37.

Holland, J.B., Jr. 1959. Liver flukes in the southeastern white-tailed deer. Proc. Ann. Conf. S.E. Assoc. Game Fish Comm. 12:224–227.

Howerth, E.W. 1986. Studies on the pathogenesis of bluetongue virus infection in white-tailed deer (*Odocoileus virginianus*). Ph.D. diss., Univ. of Georgia, Athens. 115 pp.

Jenkins, J.H., and T.T. Fendley. 1968. The extent of contamination, detection, and health significance of high accumulations of radio-activity in southeastern game populations. Proc. Ann. Conf. S.E. Assoc. Game Fish Comm. 22:89–95.

Jenkins, J.H., and T.T. Fendley. 1971. Radionuclide biomagnification in coastal-plain deer. In: Radionuclides in Ecosystems. Proc. 3d Nat. Symp. in Radioecol. D.J. Nelson (ed.). USAEC Symp. Series Conf.-710501-P1. pp. 116–122.

Jenny, E.W., F.A. Hayes, and C.L. Brown. 1970. Survey for vesicular stomatitis virus neutralizing antibodies in serums of white-tailed deer *Odocoileus virginianus* of the southeastern United States. J. Wildl. Dis. 6:488–493.

Jeter, L.K. 1979. The value of abomasal parasite counts and deer management in Florida. Proc. 2d Ann. Meet. Southeast Deer Study Group. Mississippi State Univ. (abstract).

Johnson, W., and C.L. Nayfield. 1970. Elevated levels of cesium-137 in common mushrooms (Agaricaceae) with possible relationship to high levels of cesium-137 in whitetail deer, 1968–1969. Radiol. Health Data Rep. 11:527–531.

Karstad, L. 1981. Vesicular diseases. In: Diseases and parasites of white-tailed deer. W.R. Davidson et al. (eds.). Misc. Pub. No. 7, Tall Timber Research Station, Tallahassee, Fla. pp. 97–107.

Kellogg, F.E., T.P. Kistner, R.K. Strickland, and R.R. Gerrish. 1971. Arthropod parasites collected from white-tailed deer. J. Med. Entomol. 8:495–498.

Kim, K.C., H.D. Pratt, and C.J. Stojanovich. 1986. The sucking lice of North America. An illustrated manual for identification. Penn. State Univ. Press, University Park. 241 pp.

Kingston, N. 1981. Protozoan parasites. In: Diseases and parasites of white-tailed deer. W.R. Davidson et al. (eds.). Misc. Pub. No. 7, Tall Timbers Research Station, Tallahassee, Fla. pp. 193–236.

Kistner, T.P. 1969. A study to determine the role of white-tailed deer as reservoir hosts of cattle fever ticks. M.S. thesis, Univ. of Georgia, Athens. 73 pp.

Kistner, T.P., and W.L. Hanson. 1969. Trypanosomiasis in white-tailed deer. Bull. Wildl. Dis. Assoc. 5:398–99.

Kistner, T.P., and F.A. Hayes. 1970. White-tailed deer as hosts of cattle fever-ticks. J. Wildl. Dis. 6:437–40.

Knapp, J.V. 1940. Existence of tropical variety of cattle-fever tick (= *Boophilus annulatus* var. *australis*) complicates tick eradication in Florida. J. Am. Vet. Med. Assoc. 96:607–608.

Knight, R.A. 1983. *Trichuris odocoileus* sp. n. (Nematoda: Trichuridae) from white-tailed deer, *Odocoileus virginianus*, in southeastern U.S., and a key to trichurids in North American ruminants. J. Parasitol. 69:1156–1159.

Kocan, A.A., M.G. Shaw, W.C. Edwards, and J.H. Eve. 1980. Heavy metal concentrations in the kidneys of white-tailed deer in Oklahoma. J. Wildl. Dis. 16:593–596.

Kramer, W.L., E.C. Greiner, and E.P.J. Gibbs. 1985a. A survey of *Culicoides* midges (Diptera: Ceratopogonidae) associated with cattle operations in Florida, USA. J. Med. Entomol. 22:153–162.

Kramer, W.L., E.C. Greiner, and E.P.J. Gibbs. 1985b. Seasonal variations in population size, fecundity, and parity rates of *Culicoides insignis* (Diptera: Ceratopogonidae) in Florida, USA. J. Med. Entomol. 22:163–169.

Kuttler, K.L. 1981. Anaplasmosis. In: Diseases and parasites of white-tailed deer. W.R. Davidson et al. (eds.). Misc. Pub. No. 7, Tall Timbers Research Station, Tallahassee, Fla. pp. 126–137.

———. 1984. *Anaplasma* infections in wild and domestic ruminants: A review. J. Wildl. Dis. 20:12–20.

Kuttler, K.L., R.M. Robinson, and R.R. Bell. 1967. Tick transmission of theileriasis in a white-tailed deer. Bull. Wildl. Dis. Assoc. 3:182–183.

Kuttler, K.L., O.H. Graham, S.R. Johnson, and J.L. Trevino. 1972. Unsuccessful attempts to establish cattle *Babesia* infections in white-tailed deer. J. Wildl. Dis. 8:63–66.

Land, E.D. 1990. Big Cypress deer/panther relationships: Deer mortality, July 1, 1989 to June 30, 1990. Ann. Rept. Fla. Game and Fresh Water Fish Comm., Naples, Fla. 22 pp.

Levine, N.D. 1980. Nematode parasites of domestic animals and of man. 2d ed. Burgess, Minneapolis. 477 pp.

Lichtenfels, J.R., P.A. Pilitt, and L.F. LeJambre. 1986. Cuticular ridge patterns of *Haemonchus contortus* and *Haemonchus placei* (Nematoda: Trichostrongyloidea). Proc. Helminthol. Soc. Wash. 53:94–101.

Lord, R.D., C.H. Calisher, W.D. Sudia, and T.H. Work. 1973. Ecological investigations of vertebrate hosts of Venezuelan equine encephalomyelitis virus in south Florida. Am. J. Trop. Med. Hyg. 22:116–123.

Loveless, C.M. 1959. The Everglades deer herd, life history and management. Fla. Game and Fresh Water Fish Comm. Tech. Bull. No. 6. 104 pp.

McCallon, B.R. 1973. Prevalence and economic aspects of anaplasmosis. Proc. 6th Nat. Anaplasmosis Conf., Las Vegas, Nev. pp. 1–3.

McGhee, M.B., V.F. Nettles, E.A. Roller, III, A.K. Prestwood, and W.R. Davidson, 1981. Studies on cross-transmission and pathogenicity of *Haemonchus contortus* in white-tailed deer, domestic cattle and sheep. J. Wildl. Dis. 17:353–364.

McIntosh, A. 1934. Distribution of *Boophilus annulatus australis* (Fuller) in the United States. Proc. Helminthol. Soc. Wash. 1:22.

McLean, R.G., S.D. Wright, D.J. Forrester, and S.R. Ubico. 1990. Unpublished data. CDC, Fort Collins, Colo.

Maehr, D.S. 1984. Unpublished data. Florida Game and Fresh Water Fish Commission, Gainesville.

Maehr, D.S., and J.R. Brady. 1984. Food habits of Florida black bears. J. Wildl. Manage. 48:230–235.

Maehr, D.S., R.C. Belden, E.D. Land, and L. Wilkins. 1990. Food habits of panthers in southwest Florida. J. Wildl. Manage. 54:420–423.

Magnarelli, L.A., J.F. Anderson, and W.A. Chappell. 1984. Antibodies to spirochetes in white-tailed deer and prevalence of infected ticks from foci of Lyme disease in Connecticut. J. Wildl. Dis. 20:21–26.

Marshall, C.M., G.A. Seaman, and F.A. Hayes. 1963. A critique on the tropical cattle fever tick controversy and its relationship to white-tailed deer. Trans. No. Am. Wildl. Nat. Resour. Conf. 28:225–232.

Moore, J.C. 1957. The natural history of the fox squirrel, *Sciurus niger shermani*. Bull. Am. Mus. Nat. Hist. 113:1–71.

Murphy, D.A. 1981. Toxicosis. In: Diseases and parasites of white-tailed deer. W.R. Davidson et al. (eds.). Misc. Pub. No. 7, Tall Timbers Research Station, Tallahassee, Fla. pp. 43–51.

Murphy, D.A., and L.J. Korschgen. 1970. Reproduction, growth, and tissue residues of deer fed dieldrin. J. Wildl. Manage. 34:887–903.

Nettles, V.F. 1976. Pathology of *Parelaphostrongylus andersoni* in white-tailed deer. Ph.D. diss., Univ. of Georgia, Athens. 81 pp.

——. 1985. Unpublished data. SCWDS, Univ. of Georgia, Athens.

Nettles, V.F., and G.L. Doster. 1975. Nasal bots of white-tailed deer in the southeastern United States. Proc. Ann. Conf. S.E. Assoc. Fish Wildl. Agencies. 29:651–655.

Nettles, V.F., F.A. Hayes, and W.M. Martin. 1976. Observations on injuries in white-tailed deer. Proc. Ann. Conf. S.E. Assoc. Game Fish Comm. 30:474–480.

Oertley, K.D. 1981. Studies on toxoplasmosis in white-tailed deer (*Odocoileus virginianus*). M.S. thesis, Univ. of Georgia, Athens. 124 pp.

Park, R.L., O. Skov, G.A. Seaman, and R.M. Bond. 1966. Deer and cattle fever ticks. J. Wildl. Manage. 30:202–203.

Perry, B.D., D.K. Nichols, and E.S. Cullom. 1985. *Babesia odocoilei* Emerson and Wright, 1970 in white-tailed deer, *Odocoileus virginianus* (Zimmemann), in Virginia. J. Wildl. Dis. 21:149–152.

Porter, D.A. 1942. Incidence of gastrointestinal nematodes of cattle in the southeastern United States. Am. J. Vet. Res. 3:304–307.

Prestwood, A.K. 1971. Cestodes of white-tailed deer (*Odocoileus virginianus*) in the southeastern United States. J. Parasitol. 57:1292.

Prestwood, A.K., and S.R. Pursglove. 1977. Prevalence and distribution of *Setaria yehi* in southeastern white-tailed deer. J. Am. Vet. Med. Assoc. 171:933–935.

Prestwood, A.K., and S.R. Pursglove. 1981. Gastrointestinal nematodes. In: Diseases and parasites of white-tailed deer. W.R. Davidson et al. (eds.). Misc. Pub. No. 7, Tall Timbers Research Station, Tallahassee, Fla. pp. 318–350.

Prestwood, A.K., and T.R. Ridgeway. 1972. Elaeophorosis in white-tailed deer of the southeastern U.S.A.: Case report and distribution. J. Wildl. Dis. 8:233–236.

Prestwood, A.K., and J.F. Smith. 1969. Distribution of meningeal worm (*Pneumostrongylus tenuis*) in deer in the southeastern United States. J. Parasitol. 55:720–725.

Prestwood, A.K., J.F. Smith, and J. Brown. 1971. Lungworms in white-tailed deer of the southeastern United States. J. Wildl. Dis. 7:149–154.

Prestwood, A.K., J.F. Smith, and W.E. Mahan. 1970. Geographic distribution of *Gongylonema pulchrum*, *Gongylonema verrucosum*, and *Paramphistomum liorchis* in white-tailed deer of the southeastern United States. J. Parasitol. 56:123–127.

Prestwood, A.K., F.A. Hayes, J.H. Eve, and J.F. Smith. 1973. Abomasal helminths of white-tailed deer in southeastern United States, Texas, and the Virgin Islands. J. Am. Vet. Med. Assoc. 163:556–561.

Prestwood, A.K., T.P. Kistner, F.E. Kellogg, and F.A. Hayes. 1974a. The 1971 outbreak of hemorrhagic disease among white-tailed deer of the southeastern United States. J. Wildl. Dis. 10:217–224.

Prestwood, A.K., V.F. Nettles, and F.E. Kellogg. 1974b. Distribution of muscleworm, *Parelaphostrongylus andersoni*, among white-tailed deer of the southeastern United States. J. Wildl. Dis. 10:404–409.

Price, E.W., and A. McIntosh. 1944. Paramphistomes of North American domestic ruminants. J. Parasitol. 30 (Suppl.):9.

Pursglove, S.R. 1976. *Eucyathostomum webbi* sp. n. (Strongyloidea: Cloacinidae) from white-tailed deer (*Odocoileus virginianus*). J. Parasitol. 62:574–578.

Pursglove, S.R., A.K. Prestwood, V.F. Nettles, and F.A. Hayes. 1976. Intestinal nematodes of white-tailed deer in southeastern United States. J. Am. Vet. Med. Assoc. 169:896–900.

Pursglove, S.R., A.K. Prestwood, T.R. Ridgeway, and F.A. Hayes. 1977. *Fascioloides magna* infection in white-tailed deer of southeastern United States. J. Am. Vet. Med. Assoc. 171:936–938.

Richards, S.H. 1981. Miscellaneous viral diseases. In: Diseases and parasites of white-tailed deer. W.R. Davidson et al. (eds.). Misc. Pub. No. 7, Tall Timbers Research Station, Tallahassee, Fla. pp. 108–125.

Rinehart, J.E., and L.D. Fay. 1981. Brucellosis. In: Diseases and parasites of white-tailed deer. W.R. Davidson et al. (eds.). Misc. Pub. No. 7, Tall Timbers Research Station, Tallahassee, Fla. pp. 148–154.

Roberts, H.H., and J.L. Lancaster. 1963. Determining susceptibility of white-tailed deer to anaplasmosis. Ark. Farm Res., Ark. Agric. Exp. Sta. Bull. 12:12.

Robinson, R.M. 1981. Salmonellosis. In: Diseases and parasites of white-tailed deer. W.R. Davidson et al. (eds.). Misc. Pub. No. 7, Tall Timbers Research Station, Tallahassee, Fla. pp. 155–160.

Robinson, R.M., K.L. Kuttler, J.W. Thomas, and R.G. Marburger. 1967. Theileriasis in Texas white-tailed deer. J. Wildl. Manage. 31:455–459.

Robinson, R.M., R.J. Hidalgo, W.S. Daniel, D.W. Rideout, and R.G. Marburger. 1970. Salmonellosis in white-tailed deer fawns. J. Wildl. Dis. 6:389–396.

Roessler, C.E. 1984. Unpublished data. Univ. of Florida, Gainesville.

Roessler, C.E., G.S. Roessler, and B.G. Dunavant. 1969. Unusual behavior of cesium in the Florida biosphere. Quart. J. Fla. Acad. Sci. 32:1–11.

Rogers, A.J. 1953. A study of the ixodid ticks of northern Florida, including the biology and life history of *Ixodes scapularis* Say (Ixodidae: Acarina). Ph.D. diss., Univ. of Maryland, College Park. 191 pp.

Ross, S.E., and D.J. Forrester. 1991. Unpublished data. Univ. of Florida, Gainesville.

Sacks, J.J., D.G. Delgado, H.O. Lobel, and R.L. Parker. 1983. Toxoplasmosis infection associated with eating undercooked venison. Am. J. Epidemiol. 118:832–38.

Say, T. 1821. An account of the arachnides of the United States. J. Acad. Nat. Sci. Phila. 2:59–82.

Seymour, C., and T.M. Yuill. 1981. Arboviruses. In: Infectious diseases of wild mammals. 2d ed. J.W. Davis et al. (eds.). Iowa State Univ. Press, Ames. pp. 54–86.

Shotts, E.B. 1981a. Leptospirosis. In: Diseases and parasites of white-tailed deer. W.R. Davidson et al. (eds.). Misc. Pub. No. 7, Tall Timbers Research Station, Tallahassee, Fla. pp. 138–147.

———. 1981b. Leptospirosis. In: Infectious diseases of wild mammals. J.W. Davis et al. (eds.). Iowa State Univ. Press, Ames. pp. 323–331.

Shotts, E.B., and F.A. Hayes. 1970. Leptospiral antibodies in white-tailed deer of the southeastern United States. J. Wildl. Dis. 6:295–298.

Shotts, E.B., C.L. Andrews, and T.W. Harvey. 1975. Leptospirosis in selected wild mammals of the Florida panhandle and southwestern Georgia. J. Am. Vet. Med. Assoc. 167:587–589.

Smith, J.S. 1977. A survey of ticks infesting white-tailed deer in 12 southeastern states. M.S. thesis, Univ. of Georgia, Athens. 60 pp.

Stallknecht, D.E., and G.A. Erickson. 1986. Antibodies to vesicular stomatitis New Jersey type virus in a population of white-tailed deer. J. Wildl. Dis. 22:250–254.

Stallknecht, D.E., J.L. Blue, E.A. Roller III, V.F. Nettles, W.R. Davidson, and J.E. Pearson. 1991. Precipitating antibodies to epizootic hemorrhagic disease and bluetongue viruses in white-tailed deer in the southeastern United States. J. Wildl. Dis. 27:238–247.

Stein, C.D., and M.G. Stoner. 1952. Anthrax in livestock during 1951 and comparative data on the disease from 1945 through 1951. Vet. Med. 47:315–320.

Stevenson, H.N. 1976. Vertebrates of Florida. Identification and distribution. Univ. Presses of Florida, Gainesville. 607 pp.

Strickland, R.K., and R.R. Gerrish. 1964. Distribution of the tropical horse tick in the United States, with notes on associated cases of equine piroplasmosis. J. Am. Vet. Med. Assoc. 144:875–878.

Strickland, R.K., R.R. Gerrish, and J.S. Smith. 1981. Arthropods. In: Diseases and parasites of white-tailed deer. W.R. Davidson et al. (eds.). Misc. Pub. No. 7, Tall Timbers Research Station, Tallahassee, Fla. pp. 363–389.

Strickland, R.K., R.R. Gerrish, J.L. Hourrigan, and G.O. Schubert. 1976. Ticks of veterinary importance. Agr. Handbook No. 485, APHIS, USDA, Washington, D.C. 122 pp.

Strode, D.D. 1954. The Ocala deer herd. Fla. Game and Fresh Comm. Game Pub. No. 1. 42 pp.

———. 1955. The screw-worm problem in the Ocala National Forest Deer Herd. Proc. Ann. Conf. S.E. Assoc. Game Fish Comm. 8:85–89.

Strohlein, D.A., C.B. Crow, and W.R. Davidson. 1988. Distribution of Spiculopteragia pursglovei and S. odocoilei (Nematoda: Trichostrongyloidea) from white-tailed deer (Odocoileus virginianus) in the southeastern United States. J. Parasitol. 74:347–349.

Stubblefield, S.S., D.B. Pence, and R.J. Warren. 1987. Visceral helminth communities of sympatric mule and white-tailed deer from the Davis Mountains of Texas. J. Wildl. Dis. 23:113–120.

Sundberg, J.P., and S.W. Nielsen. 1982. Prevalence of cutaneous fibromas in white-tailed deer (Odocoileus virginianus) in New York and Vermont. J. Wildl. Dis. 18:359–360.

Sundlof, S.F., and D.J. Forrester. 1990. Unpublished data. Univ. of Florida, Gainesville.

Taylor, D.J. 1951. The distribution of ticks in Florida. M.S. thesis, Univ. of Florida, Gainesville. 124 pp.

Telford, S.R., Jr., and D.J. Forrester. 1991. Piroplasms of white-tailed deer (Odocoileus virginianus) in Florida. Fla. Field Nat. 19:49–51.

Telford, S.R., Jr., D.J. Forrester, S.D. Wright, M.E. Roelke, S.A. Ferenc, and J.W. McCown. 1991. The identity and prevalence of trypanosomes in white-tailed deer (Odocoileus virginianus) from southern Florida. J. Helminthol. Soc. Wash. 58:19–23.

Telford, S.R., III, T.N. Mahter, S.I. Moore, M.L. Wilson, and A.S. Spielman. 1988. Incompetence of deer as reservoirs of the Lyme disease spirochete. Am. J. Trop. Med. Hyg. 39:105–109.

Thomas, F.C. 1981. Hemorrhagic disease. In: Diseases and parasites of white-tailed deer. W.R. Davidson et al. (eds.). Misc. Pub. No. 7, Tall Timbers Research Station, Tallahassee, Fla. pp. 87–96.

Thomas, F.C., and A.K. Prestwood. 1976. Plague neutralization test reactors to bluetongue and EHD viruses in the southeastern U.S.A. In: Wildlife diseases. L.A. Page (ed.). Plenum, New York. pp. 401–411.

Thomas, F.C., and D.O. Trainer. 1970. Bluetongue virus: (1) in pregnant white-tailed deer (2) a plague reduction neutralization test. J. Wildl. Dis. 6:384–388.

Thompson, F.A. 1964. Deer on highways. New Mexico Dept. Game and Fish. 14 pp.

Titche, A.R., A.K. Prestwood, and C.P. Hibler. 1979. Experimental infection of white-tailed deer with Elaeophora schneideri. J. Wildl. Dis. 15:273–280.

Trainer, D.O. 1962. Protozoan diseases of white-tailed deer. Proc. 1st Nat. White-tailed Deer Symp. Univ. of Georgia, Athens. pp. 155–161.

Travis, B.V. 1941. Examinations of wild animals for the cattle tick Boophilus annulatus microplus (Can.) in Florida. J. Parasitol. 27:465–467.

Van Ness, G.B. 1981. Anthrax. In: Diseases and parasites of white-tailed deer. W.R. Davidson et al. (eds.). Misc. Pub. No. 7, Tall Timbers Research Station, Tallahassee, Fla. pp. 161–167.

Walker, M.L., and W.W. Becklund. 1970. Checklist of the internal and external parasites of deer, *Odocoileus hemionus* and *O. virginianus*, in the United States and Canada. Spec. Pub. No. 1, Index Cat. Med. Vet. Zool. U.S. Government Printing Office, Washington, D.C. 45 pp.

Wassef, H.Y., and H. Hoogstraal. 1982. Unpublished data. NAMRU, Cairo, Egypt.

White, F.H. 1984. Unpublished data. Univ. of Florida, Gainesville.

Whitlock, S.C. 1939. The prevalence of disease and parasites of white-tail deer. Trans. No. Am. Wildl. Conf. 4:244–49.

Witter, J.F. 1981. Brucellosis. In: Infectious diseases of wild mammals. J.W. Davis et al. (eds.). Iowa State Univ. Press, Ames. pp. 280–287.

Wobeser, G.A. 1981. Trauma. In: Diseases and parasites of white-tailed deer. W.R. Davidson et al. (eds.). Misc. Pub. No. 7, Tall Timbers Research Station, Tallahassee, Fla. pp. 35–42.

Wright, S.D. 1988a. Unpublished data. Univ. of Florida, Gainesville.

———. 1988b. Health/disease study of white-tailed deer in southern Florida (July 1, 1987–June 30, 1988). P-R report. Florida Game and Fresh Water Fish Commission, Gainesville. 27 pp.

Wright, S.D., and D.J. Forrester. 1987. Health/disease study of white-tailed deer in southern Florida (July 1, 1986–June 30, 1987). P-R report. Florida Game and Fresh Water Fish Commission, Gainesville. 27 pp.

Wright, S.D., and D.A. Miller. 1988. Unpublished data. Univ. of Florida, Gainesville.

Wright, S.D., and T.R. Smith. 1988. Unpublished data. Univ. of Florida, Gainesville.

Wright, S.D., J.U. Bell, and D.J. Forrester. 1988. Unpublished data. Univ. of Florida, Gainesville.

Wright, T.J. 1987. Wildlife harvest and economic survey. Florida Game and Fresh Water Fish Commission, Tallahassee. P-R Report, W-33.

CHAPTER TWENTY-ONE

Key Deer

I. Introduction

The Key deer (*Odocoileus virginianus clavium* Barbour and Allen) was described as a distinct geographic race or subspecies of *O. virginianus* in 1922 (Barbour and Allen 1922). It is the smallest of the various races of North American deer; males and females average 80 and 63 lbs., respectively (Klimstra et al. 1978). This unique animal is found only on several islands in the lower Florida Keys in the vicinity of Big Pine Key, where the largest concentration occurs (U.S. Fish and Wildlife Service 1985; Klimstra et al. 1978). Populations of Key deer were abundant when the early explorers arrived (Layne 1974), but were reduced by hunting pressure to a low

of about 26 in 1945 (U.S. Fish and Wildlife Service 1985). In 1939 the state of Florida banned hunting of Key deer and in 1957 the National Key Deer Refuge was established (Humphrey and Bell 1986). The Key deer was declared an endangered species in 1967 and is protected by the Endangered Species Act of 1973. The combination of elimination of hunting and some habitat preservation resulted in an increase in the population to 350 to 400 deer by 1974 (Silvy 1975), but by 1982 there was another reduction to 250 to 300 animals that was judged to be due to habitat loss and to mortality associated with land development in critical areas (U.S. Fish and Wildlife Service 1985). Humphrey and Bell (1986) evaluated the current population status and by analysis of transect counts confirmed that there was an alarming downward trend in the numbers of Key deer. The reader is referred to Chapter 20 for details of many of the parasites and diseases discussed herein.

II. Trauma

Klimstra et al. (1974) reported that seven adult male Key deer were found dead with severe injuries to the skull and other parts of the body and felt that these were due to intraspecific conflicts between bucks. These represented 2% of 304 deaths that the authors catalogued between 1968 and 1973.

The largest proportion of the mortality documented by Klimstra et al. (1974) was due to highway accidents. Over a six-year period road-kills comprised 76% of the known mortality. Although this mortality occurred throughout the year, there were peaks in November and April/May corresponding to breeding activities and fawning, respectively. More males than females were killed, which was attributed to behavioral factors. Humphrey and Bell (1986) pointed out that road-kills during 1969–1984 were 10–20% of the estimated population. In Table 21-1 data are

presented for 1973–1984 and indicate that 83% of the mortality was due to road-kills.

Dog-related deaths are a significant problem, particularly on Big Pine Key (U.S. Fish and Wildlife Service 1985). Between 1973 and 1984, 25 deer were known to have been killed by dogs and it was felt that the actual number was probably higher since such mortality is difficult to document and often occurs in remote areas.

In addition to encounters with vehicles, Key deer are injured or die due to entanglement with fences or other structures. Klimstra et al. (1974) reported injuries to three Key deer that were attributed to fences. Drainage ditches constructed for mosquito control became the cause of death by drowning for 11 fawns during 1968–1973 (Klimstra et al. 1974). There are approximately 163 kilometers of mosquito ditches in Big Pine Key and these pose a threat to fawns, which are unable to pull themselves up over the vertical walls if they fall into the ditches (U.S. Fish and Wildlife Service 1985).

III. Neoplasia

Infectious cutaneous fibromas are the only tumors reported from Key deer. Klimstra et al. (1974) found fibromas the size of golf balls

Table 21-1
Documented causes of mortality in Key deer, 1973–84

Mortality	Year												
	1973	1974	1975	1976	1977	1978	1979	1980	1981	1982	1983	1984	Total
Road-kill	46	40	45	43	47	59	60	50	48	45	42	29	554
Unknown/natural	6	1	2	4	3	6	18	7	4	3	4	4	62
Dog-related	0	0	0	1	2	1	5	2	4	1	5	4	25
Poaching	0	2	1	0	0	3	5	2	3	2	0	0	18
Drowning	4	0	0	0	1	1	0	0	0	1	2	1	10
Totals	56	43	48	48	53	70	88	61	59	52	53	38	669

Source: U.S. Fish and Wildlife Service (1985).

on the neck and shoulders of an adult male Key deer. This deer was recaptured several months later and the tumors were gone. As pointed out in Chapter 20, these fibromas are benign and self-limiting and usually are of little consequence unless they interfere with vision or feeding.

IV. Viral diseases

Blood samples from 51 Key deer collected during 1986–90 were tested for antibodies to the etiologic agents of infectious bovine rhinotracheitis, bovine virus diarrhea, parainfluenza-3, epizootic hemorrhagic disease, and bluetongue (SCWDS records). Results of all tests were negative except for two deer in 1986, both of which were seropositive for epizootic hemorrhagic disease virus and bluetongue virus and one deer in 1989 that was seropositive for bluetongue virus. The significance of these two viruses to Key deer populations is not known.

V. Bacterial diseases

From 1986 to 1990 sera from 51 Key deer were tested for antibodies to the etiologic agents of leptospirosis (five serovars: *pomona*, *hardjo*, *grippotyphosa*, *icterohemorrhagiae*, and *canicola*) and brucellosis (SCWDS records). All were negative except for four deer in 1988 that were seropositive for *Leptospira interrogans* serovar *hardjo*. The significance of this is unknown. Six deer were tested in 1990 for antibodies to *Borrelia burgdorferi*, the etiologic agent of Lyme disease (SCWDS records). All were negative.

VI. Protozoan parasites

Of 88 fecal samples from Key deer on Big Pine Key, 59 (67%) contained oocysts of *Eimeria*

spp. (Schulte et al. 1976). The species involved were not determined. Four species of *Eimeria* have been found in white-tailed deer in southern Florida (Forrester 1988a, 1988b). The pathologic significance of these coccidia to Key deer has not been determined.

Two of five Key deer from Big Pine Key were positive for *Sarcocystis* sp. in their musculature in 1986 (SCWDS records). The species involved is not known, nor are the effects of this protozoan on Key deer. Klimstra et al. (1974) examined blood smears from 12 deer from Big Pine Key in 1968–73. All were negative for blood protozoans.

VII. Trematodes

Liver flukes (*Fascioloides magna*) and rumen flukes (*Paramphistomum liorchis*) were not found in the five deer from Big Pine Key examined in 1986 (SCWDS records). As mentioned in Chapter 20, these two flukes are common in deer from other parts of southern Florida.

One of 88 fecal samples from Key deer on Big Pine Key was positive for eggs of a dicrocoelid trematode (Schulte et al. 1976). Although *Dicrocoelium dendriticum* has been found in white-tailed deer in New York (Mapes and Baker 1950), this species has not been recorded from whitetails in Florida.

VIII. Nematodes

Seven species of nematodes have been found in Key deer (Table 21-2). None of these occurred in intensities high enough to be of pathologic significance. *Haemonchus contortus* and *Dictyocaulus viviparus*, however, are pathogenic to other races of white-tailed deer and could potentially be harmful to Key deer as well. The small intestines of six fawns obtained by Klimstra during his 1968–1973

Table 21-2
Nematodes reported from Key deer in Florida

Site	Nematode	Year	No. deer Exam.	Pos.	%	Intensity Mean	Range	Data source
Esophagus/rumen	*Gongylonema* sp.	NG[a]	88	1	1	NG	NG	Schulte et al. (1976)
Abomasum	*Haemonchus*	1986	13	11	85	97	20–200	SCWDS records
	contortus	1987	21	17	81	224	20–1,140	" "
		1988	4	4	100	110	60–220	" "
		1989	15	13	87	143	20–400	" "
		1990	7	7	100	80	20–160	" "
	Mazamastrongylus sp.	1986	13	1	8	20	20	" "
		1987–90	47	0	0	—	—	" "
Small intestine	*Neoascaris* sp.[b]	NG[a]	88	2	2	NG	NG	Schulte et al. (1976)
Large intestine	*Oesophagostomum* sp.	NG[a]	88	4	5	NG	NG	" " " "
Cecum	*Trichuris* sp.	1986	5	1	20	1	1	SCWDS records
Lungs	*Dictyocaulus* *viviparus*	1986	5	1	20	4	4	" "

[a]NG = not given by authors. This date probably included the years 1968–73, since the same authors published other papers on Key deer dealing with data collected during that time-span (Klimstra et al. 1974).
[b]This record is doubtful. It was based on finding eggs in feces and since species of *Neoascaris* have never been found in white-tailed deer (Walker and Becklund 1970; Prestwood and Pursglove 1981), this may represent spurious parasitism or erroneous identification.

study on Big Pine Key were examined for infections by *Strongyloides papillosus*. These fawns ranged in age from one day to six weeks. All were negative (Forrester 1988a).

IX. Arthropods

Ixodes scapularis was reported from the ears of several Key deer in 1968–1973 by Klimstra et al. (1974) and from one deer (site not given) in 1989 (SCWDS records). One of five deer examined from Big Pine Key in 1986 was infested with ticks and two were infested with lice (species not given) (SCWDS records). These infestations were of low intensities and were most likely of little significance. In 1990, six biting lice were collected from a Key deer and may represent an undescribed species or contamination from some other host (SCWDS records).

Mosquitoes and deer flies (species not given) were reported as serious pests of Key deer (Klimstra et al. 1974). After heavy rains

in 1968–1969 and 1969–1970 deer were noticeably bothered by mosquitoes. They moved onto roadways and open areas so as to bed down in a breeze and avoid the mosquitoes, which were numerous in thicker cover. Deer were seen with their heads and legs covered with mosquitoes. Blood spots were present around their eyes and on their faces (Klimstra et al. 1974). The authors felt that at times mosquitoes could cause extensive blood loss in young fawns, which might result in debilitation or even death.

X. Summary and conclusions

Information on the parasites and diseases of Key deer is limited. Eighteen different parasites, diseases, and disease agents are recorded, and include one tumor, two viruses, one bacterium, two protozoans, one trematode, seven nematodes, and four arthropods. The significance of these is essentially unknown.

Road-kills are the most significant mortality factor affecting Key deer and during 1973–1984 accounted for 83% of the recorded mortality. Harassment by dogs and sometimes mosquitoes also may be important. None of the parasites or other disease agents is of public health concern with the possible exception of *Leptospira interrogans* and the tick *Ixodes scapularis*.

XI. Literature cited

Barbour, T., and G.M. Allen. 1922. The white-tailed deer of eastern United States. J. Mammal. 3:65–78.

Forrester, D.J. 1988a. Unpublished data. Univ. of Florida, Gainesville.

———. 1988b. Intestinal coccidia of white-tailed deer in southern Florida. J. Wildl. Dis. 24:369–370.

Humphrey, S.R., and B. Bell. 1986. The Key deer population is declining. Wildl. Soc. Bull. 14:261–265.

Klimstra, W.D., J.W. Hardin, and N.J. Silvy. 1978. Population ecology of Key deer. Nat. Geogr. Soc. Res. Rept., 1969. pp. 313–321.

Klimstra, W.D., J.W. Hardin, N.J. Silvy, B.N. Jacobson, and V.A. Terpening. 1974. Key deer investigations final report. Period of study: December 1967–June 1973. Southern Illinois Univ., Carbondale. 184 pp.

Layne, J.N. 1974. The land mammals of south Florida. In: Environments of South Florida: Present and past. P.J. Gleason (ed.). Miami Geol. Soc., Mem. 2. pp. 386–413.

Mapes, C.R., and D.W. Baker. 1950. The white-tailed deer, a new host of *Dicrocoelium dendriticum* (Rudolphi, 1819) Looss, 1899 (Trematoda: Dicrocoelidae). Cornell Vet. 40:211–212.

Prestwood, A.K., and S.R. Pursglove. 1981. Gastrointestinal nematodes. In: Diseases and parasites of white-tailed deer. W.R. Davidson et al. (eds.). Misc. Pub. No. 7, Tall Timbers Research Station, Tallahassee, Fla. pp. 318–350.

Schulte, J.W., W.D. Klimstra, and W.G. Dyer. 1976. Protozoan and helminth parasites of Key deer. J. Wildl. Manage. 40:579–581.

Silvy, N.J. 1975. Population density, movements, and habitat utilization of Key deer (*Odocoileus virginianus clavium*). Ph.D. diss., Southern Illinois Univ., Carbondale. 152 pp.

U.S. Fish and Wildlife Service. 1985. Florida Key deer recovery plan. U.S. Fish and Wildlife Service, Atlanta, Ga. 46 pp.

Walker, M.L., and W.W. Beckland. 1970. Checklist of the internal and external parasites of deer, *Odocoileus hemionus* and *O. virginianus*, in the United States and Canada. Spec. Pub. No. 1, Index Cat. Med. Vet. Zool. U.S. Government Printing Office, Washington, D.C. 45 pp.

Sambar Deer

I. Introduction

The sambar deer, *Cervus unicolor* (Cuvier), is native to the Indian subcontinent and southeastern Asia. It has been introduced and established in Australia, New Zealand, and several areas in the United States—California, Texas, and Florida (Slee and Presidente 1981a; Flynn 1986). The Indian sambar (*C. u. niger*) was established in Florida on St. Vincent Island (Franklin County) in 1908, when four animals were introduced (Newman 1948). By 1940 the herd had grown to several hundred animals, but after World War II it declined to less than 50 due to excessive hunting. In 1983–1986 the herd numbered between 167 and 209 (Flynn 1986).

The sambar is a very large deer; mature females weigh 300 to 500 lbs. and males weigh 500 to 700 lbs. (Flynn 1986). Presidente (1984) provided a review of the parasites and diseases of sambar deer in its native range and in Australia and New Zealand. Studies on hematology, serum chemistry, infectious diseases, and parasites have been conducted in Victoria, Australia (Slee and Presidente 1981a, b). Flynn (1986) reviewed the literature on arthropods (mainly ticks) and helminths reported from sambar in India and southeast Asia and reported on examinations of 10 sambar from St. Vincent Island. The latter information also formed the basis of the one publication on parasites and diseases of this introduced species in Florida (Davidson et al. 1987).

II. Infectious diseases

Serum samples from 10 sambar deer collected in 1984 were tested for antibodies to the etiologic agents of bovine virus diarrhea, infectious bovine rhinotracheitis, parainfluenza-3, vesicular stomatitis (Indiana and New Jersey serotypes), bluetongue, epizootic hemorrhagic disease, brucellosis, and leptospirosis (*pomona, hardjo, grippotyphosa, icterohemorrhagiae,* and *canicola* serovars). All were negative (Davidson et al. 1987).

III. Protozoans

Blood films from 10 sambar deer collected in 1984 were negative for blood protozoans. Fecal samples were negative for coccidial oocysts (Davidson et al. 1987).

IV. Helminths

Eight species of helminths (seven nematodes and one trematode) were found in a sample of 10 sambar deer examined in 1983–1984 on St. Vincent Island (Davidson et al. 1987) (Table 22-1). With the exception of one of the nematodes (*Capillaria bovis*), the same helminths occurred in white-tailed deer from St. Vincent Island collected and examined at the same time. In comparison to the white-tailed deer, sambar deer had low intensities of parasites. No lesions were found in the sambar deer that were attributed to the helminth infections and overall, parasitism did not appear to be a significant health factor.

V. Arthropods

Five species of arthropods (four ticks and one mite) were found on sambar deer from St. Vincent Island in 1983–1984 (Davidson et al. 1987) (Table 22-2). Mild focal cutaneous and subcutaneous inflammation was associated with some of the tick bites. These same species of arthropods were found in white-tailed deer and/or feral hogs on the island.

VI. Summary and conclusions

Only a limited amount of information is available on the parasites and diseases of sam-

Table 22-1
Helminths of 10 sambar deer from St. Vincent Island, 1983–84

Site	Helminth[a]	No. deer		Intensity	
		Pos.	%	Mean	Max.
Arteries	*Elaeophora schneideri*(N)	1	10	2	2
Body cavity	*Setaria yehi*(N)	1	10	2	2
Esophagus	*Gongylonema pulchrum*(N)	9	90	17	58
Rumen	*Gongylonema verrucosum*(N)	3	30	10	15
	Paramphistomum liorchis(T)	7	70	582	2,000
Abomasum	*Trichostrongylus askivali*(N)	3	30	19	26
Small intestine	*Capillaria bovis*(N)	2	20	1	1
Large intesine/cecum	*Trichuris* sp.(N)	2	20	2	2

Source: Davidson et al. (1987).
[a](N) = nematode; (T) = trematode.

Table 22-2
Arthropods from 10 sambar deer from
St. Vincent Island, 1983–84

	No. deer	
Arthropod	Pos.	%
Ticks		
Amblyomma americanum	9	90
Amblyomma maculatum	3	30
Dermacentor variabilis	1	10
Ixodes scapularis	4	40
Chiggers		
Eutrombicula splendens	2	20

Source: Davidson et al. (1987).

bar deer in Florida. Ten deer from St. Vincent Island had 13 species of parasites, including 7 nematodes, 1 trematode, 4 ticks, and 1 mite. These were most likely derived from sympatric populations of white-tailed deer and wild hogs. Intensities of these parasitic infections were low and consequently parasitism was considered to be of minor consequence. No evidence of viral, bacterial, or protozoan diseases was obtained. Sambar deer on St. Vincent Island were in better overall physical condition than were white-tailed deer. This may have been due to their ability to use many forage sources not eaten by whitetails (Shea 1986), which gave them a competitive advantage (Davidson et al. 1987).

VII. Literature cited

Davidson, W.R., J.L. Blue, L.B. Flynn, S.M. Shea, R.L. Marchinton, and J.A. Lewis. 1987. Parasites, diseases and health status of sympatric populations of sambar deer and white-tailed deer in Florida. J. Wildl. Dis. 23:267–272.

Flynn, L.B. 1986. Sambar deer on St. Vincent NWR: Population statistics, health, and habitat use. M.S. thesis, Univ. of Georgia, Athens. 90 pp.

Newman, C. 1948. Florida's big game. Fla. Wildl. 1:4–5, 8.

Presidente, P.J.A. 1984. Ectoparasites, endoparasites and some diseases reported from sambar deer throughout its native range and in Australia and New Zealand. Proc. Refresh. Course for Vet., Univ. of Sydney, Sydney, Australia. 72:543–557.

Shea, S.M. 1986. The ecology of sambar deer: Social behavior, movement ecology, and food habits. M.S. thesis, Univ. of Georgia, Athens. 117 pp.

Slee, K.J., and P.J. A. Presidente. 1981a. Biological and pathological features of sambar in Victoria. Part I. Haematology, biochemistry and serology. Aust. Deer. 6:7–14

Slee, K.J., and P.J.A. Presidente. 1981b. Biological and pathological features of sambar in Victoria. Part II. Parasitological and pathological findings. Aust. Deer. 6:5–11.

CHAPTER TWENTY-THREE

Wild Hogs

I. Introduction

Wild hogs (*Sus scrofa* L.) were introduced into Florida by Spanish explorers more than 400 years ago (Lewis 1907). The populations now are estimated to total more than 500,000 (Degner et al. 1983) and occur in 66 of Florida's 67 counties (Frankenberger and Belden 1976). In parts of Florida they are considered game animals and from 1972 to 1987 between 30,000 and 80,000 were taken by hunters each year (Wright 1972–87). In other areas in Florida the wild hog is considered a nuisance species and is actively trapped and removed (Belden and Frankenberger 1977). Wild hogs intermingle with domestic stock in many areas and some are live-trapped and sold in livestock auctions and to hunting preserves in other states. Overall, this animal has a commercial value to hunters, trappers, taxidermists, and landowners of more than $8 million per year in Florida (Degner et al. 1983).

II. Trauma

Many wild hogs are injured or killed on Florida's highways, but there is no information on the exact number. It may be considerable in certain areas of the state where hog populations are dense.

The significance of trauma due to predation is also poorly understood. There are some records of Florida panthers preying on hogs. Hamilton (1941) reported a sow and a pig killed by a panther, and Belden (1986) found that 15% of 61 panther scats contained remains of wild hogs. Maehr et al. (1990) examined 270 scats from panthers in southwestern Florida and found that wild hogs were the most common prey (42% frequency of occurrence). Alligators and bobcats may take some young pigs (Hanson and Karstad 1959). Analyses of bobcats' stomachs in Florida showed evidence that 6 of 379 bobcats had eaten wild hogs (Brady 1984).

III. Pseudorabies

Pseudorabies or Aujesky's disease is caused by a herpesvirus and is an acute disease especially in young animals (Gillespie and Timoney 1981). The virus is transmitted directly via inhalation of nasal discharges, contact during coitus, or ingestion of milk (Trainer 1981). Domestic swine are believed to be the principal reservoir of this disease, but the virus has been recovered also from a large variety of domestic and wild mammals, including cattle, goats, sheep, dogs, cats, rodents, opossums, raccoons, and striped skunks (Gillespie and Timoney 1981; Trainer 1981). Several cases in man are recorded from Europe, but these accounts are sketchy and their validity has been questioned (Trainer 1981). A serologic survey of 423 wild hogs in the Southeast revealed that 22% were positive (Nettles and Erickson 1984). In Florida 28% of 1,037 hogs examined between 1979 and 1987 were seropositive (Table 23-1). Positive animals were found in the panhandle and in central and southern Florida (Figure 23-1). Pseudorabies virus was isolated from 1 of 158 of these hogs. The raccoon has been studied extensively as a host for pseudorabies virus (Thawley and Wright 1982), and recent data show that it is naturally infected in the wild. Infections can be passed on from raccoons to

other animals (Platt et al. 1983). Previously it was thought that the virus was at a "dead end" in raccoons and other species. The role of raccoons in Florida as far as pseudorabies is concerned is uncertain, but since this animal is common throughout the state in areas where wild hogs occur, this would be an important topic to investigate. Roelke et al. (1988), as mentioned in Chapter 12, found three seropositive raccoons from Cape Canaveral (Brevard County).

Up until the 1960s pseudorabies in swine resulted in a mild disease with low mortality. In 1962, however, virulent strains appeared, mortality increased, and the disease has taken on an important status in the domestic swine industry (Trainer 1981). In most adults the disease is mild and may result in fever, depression, and some vomiting, with recovery occurring in four to eight days. Some sows show respiratory signs and go off feed; about 50% of the pregnant ones will abort. Severe losses may occur in young pigs, with mortality as high as 100% (Gillespie and Timoney 1981). The situation in wild hogs is uncertain. Nothing is known about the effects on wild hog populations in Florida. A recent study in Italy showed that experimentally infected wild hogs (16 weeks of age) exhibited no signs of disease, but the virus was demonstrated to be passed on to other noninfected animals (Tozzini et al. 1982). Results may have been different if more virulent strains or younger animals had been used. Further research on this disease is needed in order to properly assess its importance to wild hogs in Florida. The role of raccoons and other wildlife in the epizootiology of pseudorabies should be determined also.

IV. Other viral and rickettsial diseases

Wild hogs are susceptible to a number of other viral diseases such as encephalomyeli-

Table 23-1
Summary of findings on pseudorabies virus in wild hogs from Florida

County	Year	No. wild hogs			Basis of diagnosis	Data source
		Exam.	Inf.	%		
Brevard	1981	10	0	0	Serology	Nettles (1984)
		10	0	0	Virus isolation[a]	" "
	1986–87	71	18	25	Serology	Becker et al. (1988)
Collier	1986–87	20	6	30	Serology	" " " "
Franklin	1981	10	2	20	Serology	Nettles (1984)
		10	0	0	Virus isolation[a]	" "
Glades	1979–80	637	140	22	Serology	Gibbs (1984)
		81	0	0	Virus isolation[a]	" "
	1986–87	51	26	51	Serology	Becker et al. (1988)
Hendry	1981	10	6	60	Serology	Nettles (1984)
Lake	1980	1	1	100	Serology	" "
Orange	1980	10	6	60	Serology	" "
		10	1[b]	10	Virus isolation[a]	" "
	1981	6	2	33	Serology	" "
		5	0	0	Virus isolation[a]	" "
Osceola	1980	20	9	45	Serology	" "
		20	0	0	Virus isolation[a]	" "
Pasco	1986–87	21	1	5	Serology	Becker et al. (1988)
Sarasota	1979	24	3	13	Serology	Nettles (1984)
		10	0	0	Virus isolation[a]	" "
	1986–87	134	73	54	Serology	Becker et al. (1988)
Wakulla	1981	12	2	17	Serology	Nettles (1984)
		12	0	0	Virus isolation[a]	" "

[a]Hogs used for virus isolation attempts were from the group of animals shown in the line above examined via serological techniques.
[b]This hog had a purulent metritis, ulcerative dermatitis, and a concurrent infection of *Brucella suis* (Nettles and Erickson 1984).

tis, vesicular stomatitis, hog cholera, swine pox, and swine influenza (Hanson and Karstad 1959). Serologic evidence of vesicular stomatitis virus has been found in wild hogs from Wakulla County, and reovirus was isolated from hogs in Osceola and Orange counties (Table 23-2). Both were in low prevalences and the significance to hog populations is probably negligible. Hog cholera occurred in wild hogs from Dixie County in the 1960s (Campbell 1983), but since then has been eradicated. Recent serologic studies and attempts at isolation of hog cholera virus from wild hogs were all negative (Table 23-2). Similar negative results were found for swine in-

fluenza virus, adenovirus, encephalomyocarditis virus, porcine parvovirus, porcine enterovirus, hemagglutinating encephalomyelitis virus, rotavirus, and transmissible gastroenteritis virus (Nettles 1984; Woods et al. 1990).

The rickettsial organism *Eperythrozoon suis* is widespread in domestic swine in the United States (Gillespie and Timoney 1981) and has been reported from a wild hog in Louisiana (Smith et al. 1982). In the latter study 180 wild hogs from 11 southeastern states (including 40 from Florida) were examined. None of the Florida hogs was positive (Table 23-2). Serologic examinations of 95

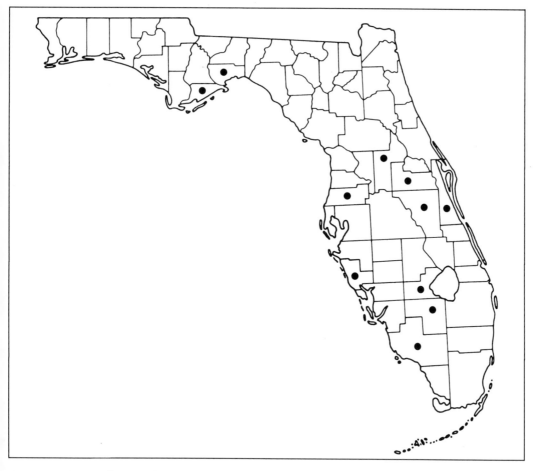

FIGURE 23-1. Distribution of pseudorabies virus in wild hogs from Florida. Solid circles indicate counties where seropositive hogs were found.

sera from wild hogs in Glades County were also negative (Becker 1984). A review of eperythrozoonosis in wildlife has been published (Howe 1981).

V. The African swine fever threat

African swine fever (ASF) is a disease of considerable concern. Currently it is one of the most economically severe and lethal viral diseases of domestic swine in the world (Plowright 1981). It is believed to have originated in Africa, where it is maintained in wart hogs and bush pigs and is transmitted there by soft ticks (*Ornithodoros moubata porcinus*) that act as biological vectors (Butler and Gibbs 1984). In 1978 the disease became established in the Dominican Republic and then spread to Haiti and Cuba (Gibbs and Butler 1984). There is no evidence that ASF occurs in Florida. Becker (1984) examined 95 wild hogs from Glades County in 1977–1978 and Nettles (1984) examined 48 from the following counties: Hendry (n = 10), Wakulla (n = 12), Franklin (n = 10), Orange (n = 6), and Brevard (n = 10). All were seronegative. There has been considerable concern ex-

Table 23-2
Summary of findings on viruses (other than pseudorabies virus) and rickettsia of wild hogs in Florida

Disease agent	Basis of diagnosis	Year	No. hogs			County	Data source
			Exam.	Inf.	%		
Eperythrozoon suis	Serology	1977–78	95	0	0	Glades	Becker (1984)
	Serology, blood smear	1979–80	40	0	0	Orange (10), Osceola (20), Sarasota (10)	Smith (1981)
Vesicular stomatitis virus	Serology	1977–78	95	0	0	Glades	Becker (1984)
	"	1979	24	0	0	Sarasota	Stallknecht et al. (1986)
	Virus isolation[a]	1979	10	0	0	"	Nettles (1984)
	Serology	1980	1	0	0	Lake	Stallknecht et al. (1986)
	"	1980–81	16	0	0	Orange	" " " "
	Virus isolation	1980–81	15	0	0	"	Nettles (1984)
	Serology	1980	20	0	0	Osceola	Stallknecht et al. (1986)
	Virus isolation[a]	1980	20	0	0	"	Nettles (1984)
	Serology	1981	10	0	0	Brevard	Stallknecht et al. (1986)
	Virus isolation[a]	1981	10	0	0	"	Nettles (1984)
	Serology	1981	10	0	0	Franklin	Stallknecht et al. (1986)
	Virus isolation[a]	1981	10	0	0	"	Nettles (1984)
	Serology	1981	10	0	0	Hendry	Stallknecht et al. (1986)
	"	1981	12	4[b]	33	Wakulla[c]	" " " "
	Virus isolation[a]	1981	12	0	0	"	Nettles (1984)
Hog cholera virus[d]	Serology	1980	24	0	0	Sarasota	"
	"	1980	20	0	0	Osceola	"
	Virus isolation[a]	1980	10	0	0	"	"
	Serology	1980–81	16	0	0	Orange	"
	Virus isolation[a]	1980–81	15	0	0	"	"
	Serology	1981	10	0	0	Hendry	"
	"	1981	12	0	0	Wakulla	"
	"	1981	10	0	0	Franklin	"
	"	1981	10	0	0	Brevard	"
Swine influenza virus	Serology	1977–78	95	0	0	Glades	Becker (1984)
	Virus isolation[a]	1980	20	0	0	Osceola	Nettles (1984)

Virus	Method	Year	No. tested	No. positive	County	Reference
Adenovirus, encephalomyocarditis virus, and porcine parvovirus	"	1980	15	0	Orange	"
	"	1981	12	0	Wakulla	"
	"	1981	10	0	Franklin	"
	"	1981	10	0	Brevard	"
	"	1980	24	0	Sarasota	"
	"	1980	20	0	Osceola	"
	"	1980	15	0	Orange	"
	"	1981	12	0	Wakulla	"
	"	1981	10	0	Franklin	"
	"	1981	10	0	Brevard	"
Porcine enterovirus and hemagglutinating encephalomyelitis virus	"	1980	20	0	Osceola	"
	"	1980	15	0	Orange	"
	"	1981	12	0	Wakulla	"
	"	1981	10	0	Franklin	"
	"	1981	10	0	Brevard	"
Reovirus	"	1980	20	5	Osceola	"
	"	1980	15	7	Orange	"
	"	1981	12	0	Wakulla	"
	"	1981	10	0	Franklin	"
	"	1981	10	0	Brevard	"
Rotavirus	"	1980	10	0	Osceola	"
	"	1980	10	0	Orange	"
Transmissible gastroenteritis virus	"	1980	10	0	Osceola	"
	"	1980	10	0	Orange	"
	Serology	NG[e]	262	0	NG[f]	Woods et al. (1990)

[a] Hogs used for virus isolation attempts were from the group in the line above examined via serological techniques.

[b] All were positive for New Jersey serotype.

[c] These hogs came from St. Marks National Wildlife Refuge.

[d] Some of the data given here on hog cholera virus appeared also in Nettles et al. (1989).

[e] NG = not given by authors.

[f] Specific locations not given, but authors stated that samples came "from three locations in Florida."

pressed over the possibility of ASF spreading to Florida and becoming established in the wild hog populations. Such an introduction of the ASF virus can be visualized when one realizes that there is extensive legal and illegal traffic of people and pork products between Florida and the Caribbean countries (Gibbs and Butler 1984). Wild hogs in Florida have been shown to be susceptible to ASF (McVicar et al. 1981) and two species of soft ticks (*Ornithodoros turicata* and *O. talaje*) occur in areas in Florida where wild hogs exist (Butler and Gibbs 1984). The most important tick is *O. turicata,* which is widespread in Florida and is found commonly in the burrows of gopher tortoises (Gibbs and Butler 1984). *Ornithodoros turicata* is capable of serving as a biological vector of ASF virus to pigs (Butler and Gibbs 1984; Hess et al. 1987), so the stage appears to be set. Florida has large susceptible populations of wild hogs and tick vectors in association with each other; the missing link is the ASF virus, which could be introduced at any time. Fortunately this likelihood has been diminished somewhat by the fact that the depopulation phase of the control program in the Caribbean was completed in June 1983 in the Dominican Republic and Haiti and no cases of ASF have been detected in either country since (Gibbs and Butler 1984). However, the introduction of the virus in infected pork or porcine products from other areas of the world where ASF is endemic could still occur. If such an event does occur, the impact on wild and domestic hog populations due to the devastating effects of this disease and the resultant depopulation measures used as a means of control could be severe. For reviews on ASF, the reader is referred to Plowright (1981) and Gibbs and Butler (1984).

VI. Brucellosis

Brucellosis is probably the most important bacterial disease of wild hogs and has serious

Table 23-3
Prevalences of *Brucella* infections in wild hogs as determined by serologic studies in several states

State	No. hogs tested	% pos.	Data source
Florida	1,367	37	See Table 23-4
South Carolina	255	18	Wood et al. (1976)
California	136	15	Clark et al. (1983)
Hawaii	268	8	Zygmont (1981)
Texas	124	3	Corn et al. (1986)

veterinary and public health implications as well. In the United States considerable effort has been made to control brucellosis in domestic swine. Between 1973 and 1979, for instance, almost 14.6 million swine were tested for the disease (Johnson 1979).

In wild hogs, brucellosis is usually caused by *Brucella suis* biotype 1 (Wood et al. 1976; Becker et al. 1978; Zygmont et al. 1982), although studies in California resulted in the identification of *B. suis* biotype 3 (Clark et al. 1983). These are small, gram-negative, nonmotile, non-spore-forming rods (Witter 1981).

Infections are usually transmitted by oral exposure as well as by contamination of the eyes, wounds, and the genital tract (Witter 1981). Becker et al. (1978) cultured *Brucella suis* from seminal vesicles and uterine tissues of several wild hogs, indicating that transmission of brucellosis via sexual activity may be important. Currently there is no evidence in the United States that other wild animal reservoirs might be involved in the transmission of *Brucella* to wild hogs such as is known for wild boar and hares in Germany and Denmark (Zygmont 1981).

Evidence of *Brucella* infections has been reported from wild hogs in Arkansas, California, Florida, Georgia, Hawaii, Louisiana, South Carolina, and Texas (Wood et al. 1976; Becker et al. 1978; Zygmont et al. 1982; Clark et al. 1983; Corn et al. 1986).

Prevalences of infection varied from 3% in Texas to 37% in Florida (Table 23-3). Infections in Florida have been demonstrated in hogs from 16 counties distributed throughout the state (Fig. 23-2), with highest prevalences occurring in hogs from Glades County (Table 23-4). Necropsy and culture studies have resulted in the isolation of *Brucella suis* biotype 1 from hogs in four counties (Table 23-4). Becker et al. (1978) found no differences between prevalences of *Brucella* infections in males versus females, but found that prevalences were significantly lower in hogs less than six months of age (11%) compared to older animals (53–70%).

Clinical signs of brucellosis in domestic hogs vary and depend on the age of the animal, previous exposure to the bacteria, and the organs infected. The disease is more common in adult animals than in young pigs and can result in abortion, metritis, spondylitis, lameness, and paralysis (Gillespie and Timoney 1981). Similar effects are probably produced in wild hogs, but this has not been studied.

Brucellosis undoubtedly causes significant losses in wild hogs in Florida, but there are few data to support this statement. The fact that over 50% of the hogs in some populations (such as at Fisheating Creek in Glades

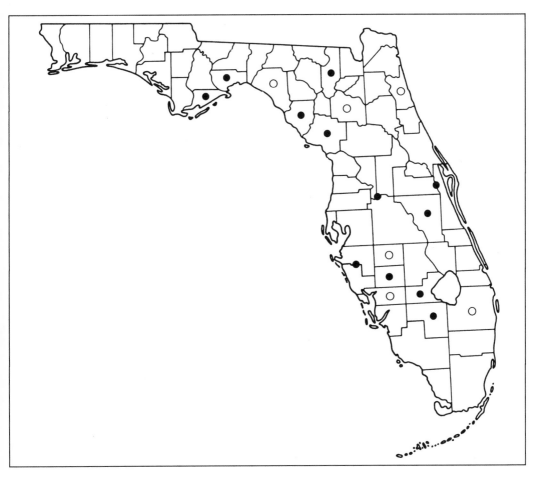

FIGURE 23-2. Map of Florida showing locations where wild hogs were examined for *Brucella* either by necropsy and culture or serologically. Solid black circles = positive; open circles = negative.

Table 23-4
Prevalence of *Brucella* infections in wild hogs of Florida

Organism	Basis of diagnosis	Year	No. hogs Exam.	Inf.	%	County	Data source
Brucella suis biotype 1	Necropsy, culture	1977–78	9	9	100	Glades	Becker et al. (1978)
		1979	10	0	0	Manatee, Sarasota	Zygmont (1981)
		1980	10	1	10	Orange, Brevard	" "
		1980	20	1	5	Osceola	" "
Brucella sp.	Serology	1979	7	0	0	Alachua	Becker & Nicoletti (1988)
		1981	10	0	0	Brevard	Nettles (1984)
		1988	52	0	0	Charlotte	Van der Leek et al. (1990)
		1977, '79	14	2	14	Columbia	Becker & Nicoletti (1988)
		1978	167	21	13	DeSoto	" " " "
		1978	9	1	11	Dixie	" " " "
		1974, '76, '78	15	1	7	Franklin	" " " "
		1981	10	0	0	"	Nettles (1984)
		1977–78	95	50	53	Glades	Becker et al. (1978)
		1979–80	766	393	51	"	Becker & Nicoletti (1988)
		1977	2	0	0	Hardee	" " " "
		1981	10	2	20	Hendry	Nettles (1984)
		1977–79	10	5	50	Levy	Becker & Nicoletti (1988)
		1979	27	2	7	Manatee, Sarasota	" " " "
		1980–81	15	5	33	Orange	Nettles (1984)
		1979–88	29	7	24	"	Becker & Nicoletti (1988)
		1980	20	10	50	Osceola	Nettles (1984)
		1988	23	0	0	"	Van der Leek et al. (1990)
		1988	9	3	33	Polk, Sumter, Lake	" " " " " "
		1988	18	0	0	Palm Beach	" " " " " "
		1979	24	1	4	Sarasota	Nettles (1984)
		1988	4	0	0	St. Johns	Van der Leek et al. (1990)
		1988	19	0	0	Taylor	" " " " " "
		1981	12	1	8	Wakulla	Nettles (1984)
Totals (serology)		1974–88	1,367	504	37	—	—

County) are infected indicates a need for more research on this subject. The relationships of *Brucella* infections in wild hogs and cattle (especially range cattle) should be studied, since *B. suis* biotype 1 was isolated from 16 cattle in Florida during 1983–88 (Payeur 1989). Cattle infections with *B. suis* could have originated either from domestic or wild hogs, but since Florida has such a widespread (66 of 67 counties; Frankenberger and Belden 1976) and large population of wild hogs (estimated at 500,000 by Degner et al. 1983), the sylvatic origin of at least some of these cattle infections should be suspected. Another im-

WILD·HOG·HUNTERS
BE·AWARE!

FLORIDA·WILD·HOGS·MAY·INFECT·YOU·WITH
SWINE · BRUCELLOSIS

Hunting wild hogs is a long-standing tradition with Florida hunters. These popular game animals are found in almost every county of the state, and during the 1980-81 hunting season, more than 20,000 hunters killed more than 100,000 of them.

Until recent scientific studies were made of Florida's wild hog population, it was not known that perhaps half of them could have brucellosis, and that hunters might become infected when these game animals are dressed.

If you have dressed wild hogs, and have symptoms of illness that may be similar to flu symptoms (headaches, fever, muscle soreness, nausea or breathing difficulties), see your physician. A simple blood test can diagnose swine brucellosis in humans.

PRECAUTIONS
WHICH MAY REDUCE RISK:

1. Always wear disposable plastic or rubber gloves when dressing and cleaning wild hogs. Keep several pair in your field hunting supply kit. Avoid direct contact with blood whenever possible.
2. As soon as possible, wash with soap and hot water after dressing wild hogs.
3. Gloves and remains from dressing wild hogs should be buried or burned.
4. Meat from wild hogs should always be thoroughly cooked before consumption.

**FLORIDA GAME AND
FRESH WATER FISH
COMMISSION**

FIGURE 23-3. Warning to wild hog hunters in Florida concerning the dangers of brucellosis. (From inside cover of *Florida Wildlife*, 38 [May–June 1984]).

plication of these data relates to the public health aspect of this infection. Brucellosis is a zoonotic disease, and in Florida there are a number of confirmed reports of infections contracted by hunters (Bigler et al. 1977). Education concerning the risks involved in handling and processing wild hogs should be a high priority. Warnings such as the one printed on the inside front cover of the May–June (1984) issue of *Florida Wildlife* (Figure 23-3) are helpful and will inform hunters of the potential problems.

VII. Other bacterial diseases

Wild hogs are susceptible to a number of other bacterial diseases, such as leptospirosis, tuberculosis, yersiniosis, atrophic rhinitis, salmonellosis, and pneumonia (Clark et al. 1983; Zygmont 1981; Essey et al. 1981). Of these, however, only leptospirosis, salmonellosis, and pneumonia are known to occur in Florida hogs.

Seven serovars of *Leptospira interrogans* have been identified in wild hogs in Florida (Table 23-5). Of 79 hogs examined from six counties, 15% were infected. Transmission is by contact with infected urine. Many such infections in domestic swine are subclinical and mild. Acute infections result in fever, anorexia, icterus, hemoglobinuria, and death (Gillespie and Timoney 1981). Infertility, abortions, and stillbirths are associated commonly with leptospirosis in domestic swine, but nothing is known about the effects on wild hogs. They probably are similar, but this needs to be studied. A review of leptospirosis

in wildlife has been published by Shotts (1981).

Salmonella anatum was isolated from one of 20 hogs from Osceola County (Table 23-6). Zygmont (1981) examined 165 other wild hogs from 11 southeastern states and found only one other *Salmonella* infection. She concluded that *Salmonella* infections in wild hogs are probably not important.

Bacterial pneumonia caused by *Corynebacterium* sp. and several other unidentified species of bacteria was seen in a hunter-killed wild hog from St. John's County in 1980. Such infections may cause occasional morbidity and mortality.

Forty wild hogs from several counties in Florida were cultured for *Bordetella bronchiseptica* and *Yersinia enterocolitica* and found to be negative (Table 23-6).

Both leptospirosis and salmonellosis are zoonotic diseases and precautions such as mentioned for brucellosis would apply to these diseases as well.

VIII. Protozoan diseases

Twelve species of parasitic protozoans are known to infect wild hogs in Florida (Table 23-7). One of these is a ciliate and the other

Table 23-5

Prevalence of *Leptospira interrogans* in wild hogs in Florida

County	No. hogs exam.	No. hogs inf. (%)	Basis of diagnosis	Year	Data source
Glades	39	9(23)[a]	Serology	1979	White (1984)
Manatee, Sarasota	10	1(10)[b]	Necropsy, isolation	1979	Zygmont (1981)
Orange, Brevard	10	2(20)[c]	" "	1980	" "
Osceola	20	0(0)	" "	1980	" "
Totals	79	12(15)	—	1979–80	—

[a]Includes 2 hogs seropositive for 4 serovars (i.e., *ballum, canicola, icterohemorrhagiae,* and *pyrogenes*), 1 hog positive for 2 serovars (*autumnalis* and *pomona*), and 6 hogs positive for 1 serovar each (1 for *autumnalis,* 4 for *canicola,* and 1 for *grippotyphosa*).
[b]Identified as *Leptospira interrogans, grippotyphosa,* Andaman (Moskva V).
[c]One isolate was identified as *L. interrogans, pomona,* Mozdok, 5621, and one as *L. interrogans, canicola,* canicola.

Table 23-6

Summary of findings on atrophic rhinitis, yersiniosis, and salmonellosis based on necropsy and culture of various organs of wild hogs in Florida, 1979–80

| Disease | Bacterium | No. of hogs | | | Counties |
		Exam.	Inf.	%	
Atrophic rhinitis	Bordetella bronchiseptica	40	0	0	Orange, Brevard, Manatee, Sarasota, Osceola
Yersiniosis	Yersinia enterocolitica	40	0	0	Orange, Brevard, Manatee, Sarasota, Osceola
Salmonellosis	Salmonella anatum	20	1	5	Osceola
		20	0	0	Orange, Brevard, Manatee, Sarasota

Source: Zygmont (1981).

11 are coccidia. Of interest is the lack of infection by *Sarcocystis suicanis*, which was found in 32% of 192 wild hogs from Alabama, Arkansas, Georgia, Louisiana, Mississippi, North Carolina, South Carolina, Tennessee, Virginia, and West Virginia (Barrows et al. 1981). The reason or reasons for the absence of this parasite from Florida hogs is unknown.

Balantidium coli is a very common parasite of swine and the statement has been made that "it is likely that it will be found in any pig if an adequate examination is made" (Soulsby 1968, p. 758). This ciliate is usually regarded as a commensal and resides in the lumen of the large intestine, but sometimes it invades the mucosa and can cause ulceration and enteritis that may lead to hemorrhagic dysentery. Infections in man are possible with similar results (Soulsby 1968). Its presence in wild hogs in Florida (Table 23-7) adds another disease to the already crowded list of zoonotic problems associated with wild hogs.

Toxoplasma gondii was found in 3% of 457 wild hogs from five counties in Florida (Table 23-7). This parasite has been reported also from wild hogs in California at a much

higher prevalence (13%) (Clark et al. 1983). The zoonotic importance of toxoplasmosis has been discussed in Chapter 15, and the reader is referred to the appropriate section in that chapter for further information.

Nine eimerian and one isosporan species of coccidia were reported by Greiner et al. (1982) from wild hogs in Florida (Table 23-7). Several of these—*Eimeria debliecki*, *E. polita*, *E. scabra*, *E. spinosa*, and *Isospora suis*—are thought to be pathogens of domestic swine (see review in Greiner et al. 1982), but, with the exception of *I. suis*, nothing is known about their effects on wild hogs. Lindsay et al. (1985) showed experimentally that neonatal feral piglets were susceptible to coccidiosis caused by *I. suis*. Signs included mild lethargy and diarrhea; no mortality occurred. At necropsy mild villous atrophy was observed in the intestines. More than 80% of the hogs examined by Greiner et al. (1982) had two or more species of coccidia. They also found that the hogs became infected with coccidia at an early age and remained infected throughout their life (Figure 23-4). There were no seasonal variations in prevalence except for *E. polita* and *I. suis*, which were

Table 23-7

Protozoan parasites reported from wild hogs in Florida

Protozoan	No. hogs			Date	County	Basis of diagnosis	Data source
	Exam.	Inf.	%				
Ciliates							
Balantidium coli	40	0	0	1979–80	None[a]	Fecal analysis	Smith et al. (1982)
	20	0	0	1988	None[b]	"	Greiner & Clarkson (1990)
	27	3	11	1977	Glades	"	Forrester (1984)
	34	2	29	1988	Charlotte	"	Greiner & Clarkson (1990)
	13	2	15	1988	Osceola	"	" " " "
	7	1	14	1988	Polk	"	" " " "
	10	1	10	1988	Taylor	"	" " " "
Coccidia							
Sarcocystis suicanis	57	0	0	1979–80	None[c]	Tissue digestion	Barrows et al. (1981)
Toxoplasma gondii	457	12	3	1977–79	Levy, Columbia, Franklin, DeSoto, Glades	Serology	Burridge et al. (1979)
Eimeria porci	251	113	45	1979–80	Levy, Glades	Fecal analysis	Greiner et al. (1982)
Eimeria debliecki	251	103	41	1979–80	Levy, Columbia, Glades	"	" " " "
Eimeria neodebliecki	251	82	33	1979–80	Levy, Columbia, Alachua, Glades	"	" " " "
Eimeria scabra	251	67	27	1979–80	Levy, Columbia, Glades	"	" " " "
Eimeria suis	251	60	24	1979–80	Levy, Glades	"	" " " "
Eimeria cerdonis	251	29	12	1979–80	Levy, Glades	"	" " " "
Eimeria polita	251	24	10	1979–80	Levy, Alachua, Glades	"	" " " "
Eimeria perminuta	251	23	9	1979–80	Glades	"	" " " "
Eimeria spinosa	251	2	1	1979–80	Levy, Glades	"	" " " "
Isospora suis	251	6	2	1979–80	Alachua, Glades	"	" " " "

[a]Hogs were examined from Orange, Brevard, Osceola, Sarasota, and Manatee counties.
[b]Hogs were examined from Collier (n = 3), Orange (n = 7), Palm Beach (n = 6), and St. Johns (n = 4) counties.
[c]Hogs were examined from Orange, Osceola, Sarasota, and Wakulla counties.

more common in summer and fall months, respectively.

IX. Lungworms

Wild hogs in Florida are infected commonly with lungworms (Table 23-8). Three species are involved (*Metastrongylus apri, M. salmi,* and *M. pudendotectus*), all of which utilize earthworms as intermediate hosts. In a study of the lungworms in wild hogs at Fisheating Creek (Glades County) the prevalences of *M. apri, M. salmi,* and *M. pudendotectus* were 94%, 76%, and 64%, respectively (Forrester et al. 1982). The mean number of lungworms per infected hog was 155, with numbers varying from 1 to 1,980. *Metastrongylus apri* was

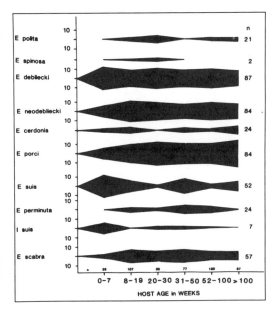

FIGURE 23-4. Kite diagram showing the relative frequencies of various species of coccidia in wild hogs at Fisheating Creek (Glades County). Sample sizes (right side) are the total number of infections for each species. (From Greiner et al. 1982.)

found by itself or concurrently with one or both of the other species. Infections of only *M. salmi* or *M. pudendotectus* or concurrent infections with both species were not encountered. Juvenile hogs (up to seven weeks of age) were infected with *M. apri* only, but older animals were infected with all three species. There were higher numbers of lungworms of all three species in hogs collected during October, November, and December than in hogs collected at other times of the year. This may have been caused by the above-average rainfall that the Fisheating Creek area received for several months prior to October. This would favor survival of lungworm eggs and their transmission to earthworms or perhaps the concentration of earthworms in sites more accessible to hogs.

These lungworms may cause significant morbidity and mortality in wild hog populations in Florida. The lungworms themselves

are pathogenic and are known to obstruct bronchioles (Figures 23-5 and 23-6) and cause lung consolidation and emphysema (Smith et al. 1982; Levine 1980). In addition, they are known to transmit viral diseases such as hog cholera and swine influenza and to exacerbate mycoplasmal pneumonia and swine influenza (Forrester et al. 1982). Fortunately, there is no evidence that these latter diseases are present in wild hog populations in Florida. Smith et al. (1982) stated that verminous pneumonia along with poor nutrition and severe environmental factors could have detrimental effects on wild hogs.

X. Kidney worms

The kidney worm (*Stephanurus dentatus*) is another common nematode of wild hogs in Florida, where an overall prevalence of 68% has been found (Table 23-9). Adults of this worm are found in cysts that connect with the ureters (Figure 23-7). Eggs pass out of the hog's body in the urine and once outside they develop to the infective stage. This larval stage then can infect a new host in any of several ways: by penetration of the skin, by direct ingestion, or by being ingested in transport hosts such as earthworms. Once inside the hog the migrating larvae cause inflammation, abscesses, cirrhosis, and adhesions. Many of them migrate through the liver and cause extensive damage. Larvae may enter the spinal cord and cause posterior paralysis (Levine 1980). In 1977 we saw a case of this condition in a young boar from Levy County that had spinal cord abscesses caused by migrating kidney worm larvae. Prestwood et al. (1975) presented similar data on wild swine on Ossabaw Island, Georgia. Migrating larvae can also penetrate the placenta and cause prenatal infections. Infected animals are ema-

Table 23-8

Characteristics of infections of lungworms (*Metastrongylus* spp.) in wild hogs in Florida

Lungworm	No. hogs			Intensity		Date	County	Data source
	Exam.	Inf.	%	Mean	Range			
Metastrongylus apri	5	3	60	172	68–248	1980	Orange, Brevard	Smith (1981)
	10	7	70	381	38–1,300	1980	Osceola	" "
	5	3	60	113	35–267	1979	Sarasota, Manatee	" "
	90	85	94	114	1–1,099	1978–79	Glades	Forrester et al. (1982)
	2	1	50	37	—	1977	Levy	Forrester (1984)
Metastrongylus salmi	90	68	76	20	1–198	1978–79	Glades	Forrester et al. (1982)
	2	1	50	19	—	1977	Levy	Forrester (1984)
Metastrongylus pudendotectus	5	1	20	124	—	1980	Orange, Brevard	Smith (1981)
	90	58	64	39	1–683	1978–79	Glades	Forrester et al. (1982)
	2	1	50	20	—	1977	Levy	Forrester (1984)
Metastrongylus spp.	10	4	40	28	4–55	1980	Osceola	Smith (1981)
	5	1	20	3	—	1979	Sarasota, Manatee	" "
	2	1	50	62	—	1977	Levy	Forrester (1984)

ciated and often have secondary bacterial infections (Levine 1980).

The full impact of kidney worms on populations of wild hogs in Florida is not known. They undoubtedly are responsible for considerable morbidity and some mortality, but this has not been measured.

XI. Trichinosis

The trichina worm (*Trichinella spiralis*) infects a large number of mammalian hosts (including man) throughout the world except in Australia and certain islands (Levine 1980). Adult worms occur in the small intestine and larvae are found in striated muscle (Figure 23-8). Transmission occurs when meat containing larvae is ingested by a new host. *Trichinella* has been found in wild hogs in Hawaii (Griffin 1978), but none of 185 wild hogs from 11 southeastern states was infected (Smith et al. 1982). This latter survey included 20 hogs from Florida. In another study, samples of diaphragm and/or tongue from 26 wild hogs in Collier County were examined, and one was positive for larvae of *Trichinella* sp. (Forrester et al. 1985). These hogs came from areas where four of seven Florida panthers examined at necropsy were found infected with trichinosis. The parasite may be acquired by panthers from wild hogs since they utilize hogs as a food source in

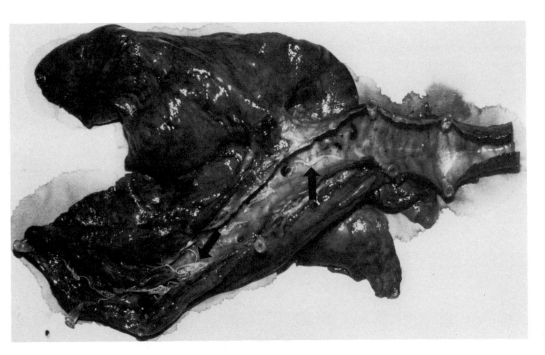

FIGURE 23-5. Trachea and bronchi have been opened, revealing numerous adult lungworms (*Metastrongylus*) (arrows) in a wild hog from Fisheating Creek (Glades County).

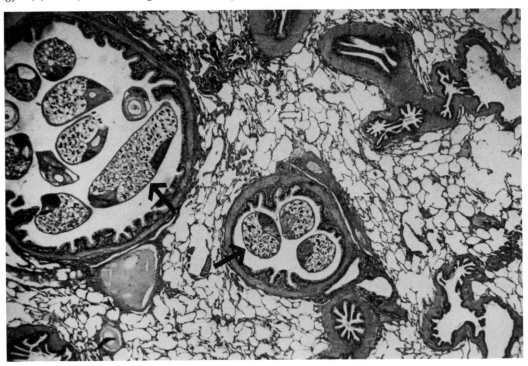

FIGURE 23-6. Section of lung showing cross-sections of lungworms (arrows) in air passages of a wild hog from Fisheating Creek (Glades County).

Table 23-9

Characteristics of infections of kidney worms (*Stephanurus dentatus*) in wild hogs in Florida

County	Date	No. hogs Exam.	No. hogs Inf.	No. hogs %	Intensity[a] Mean	Intensity[a] Range	Data source
Orange, Brevard	1980	5	5	100	38	15–77	Smith (1981)
Osceola	1980	10	10	100	53	4–154	" "
Sarasota, Manatee	1979	5	5	100	29	9–64	" "
Glades	1978–79	79	45	57	8	1–42	Forrester (1984)
DeSoto	NG[b]	26	20	77[c]	43[d]	NG	Becker & Bradley (1981)
Taylor	1988	10	2	20[e]	1[e]	1–2	Greiner & Clarkson (1990)
Osceola	1988	11	2	18[e]	1[e]	1	" " " "
Totals	1978–80	125	85	68	34	1–154	

[a]Number of kidney worms per infected hog.
[b]NG = not given by authors.
[c]This prevalence value was based on examination of urine samples for kidney worm eggs.
[d]This intensity value was based on necropsies of 10 of the 20 infected hogs selected at random.
[e]These values were based on examination of livers only. Another 55 hogs were examined also from Charlotte (n = 28), Collier (n = 3), Orange (n = 7), Palm Beach (n = 6), Polk (n = 7), and St. Johns (n = 4) counties; all were negative.

FIGURE 23-7. Kidney worms (large arrow) in perirenal fat of wild hog. Kidney (small arrow) is seen on the right of the photograph.

FIGURE 23-8. Trichina worm larvae (*Trichinella* sp.) in muscle of hog (arrows).

southern Florida (Belden 1986). In a recent serologic study by Van der Leek and Dame (1990), 5 of 179 (2.8%) wild hogs were positive (Table 23-10). Infected animals came from Osceola/Orange (n = 3), Palm Beach (n = 1), and Taylor (n = 1) counties. The significance of *Trichinella* to wild hog populations is probably minor, but the public

health consequences are of concern since this is a zoonotic parasite.

XII. Gastrointestinal helminths

Thirteen species of gastrointestinal helminths (including 1 acanthocephalan and 12 nematodes) have been reported from wild hogs in Florida (Table 23-11). Several of these (i.e., *Gongylonema pulchrum, Ascarops strongylina, Physocephalus sexalatus,* and *Macracanthorhynchus hirudinaceus*) require arthropods (usually beetles) as intermediate hosts. The others have direct life cycles.

The pathogenic effects of these helminths vary, among other factors, according to the species of worm. The acanthocephalan *M. hirudinaceus* is known to perforate the intestines of domestic swine and cause peritonitis, but this condition has not been encountered in wild hogs in the Southeast (Smith et al. 1982). The stomach nematodes, however, are known to cause gastritis (hyperemia and mucosal erosions) in wild hogs when several

Table 23-10
Seroprevalence[a] of *Trichinella* in wild hogs in Florida, 1988–89

Locality (county)	No. wild hogs		
	Exam.	Pos.	%
Charlotte	58	0	0
Manatee/Sarasota	44	0	0
Osceola/Orange	27	3	11.1
Palm Beach	18	1	5.5
Polk	9	0	0
St. Johns	4	0	0
Taylor	19	1	5.3
Totals	179	5	2.8

Source: Van der Leek and Dame (1990).
[a]Seroprevalence determined by ELISA and Western Blot tests.

Table 23-11

Gastrointestinal helminths of wild hogs in Florida

Site	Species	No. hogs			Intensity		Date	County	Data source
		Exam.	Inf.	%	Mean	Range			
Tongue and esophagus	*Gongylonema pulchrum*	20	5	25	4	1–8	1980	Orange, Brevard, Osceola	Smith (1981)
Stomach	*Ascarops strongylina*	20	1	5	25	—	1980	Orange, Brevard	"
		44	9	20	5	1–21	1978–79	Glades	Forrester (1984)
	Physocephalus sexalatus	20	20	100	327	19–1,436	1979–80	Orange, Brevard, Osceola, Sarasota, Manatee	Smith (1981)
		44	30	68	17	1–149	1978–79	Glades	Forrester (1984)
		2	1	50	172	—	1977	Levy	"
	Hyostrongylus rubidus	20	15	75	961	21–6,175	1980	Orange, Brevard, Osceola	Smith (1981)
Small intestine	*Trichostrongylus axei*	44	1	2	3	—	1979–80	Glades	Forrester (1984)
	Macracanthorhynchus hirudinaceus	20	7	35	3	1–6	1980	Orange, Brevard, Osceola	Smith (1981)
	Ascaris suum[a]	20	12	60	6	1–24	1980	Orange, Brevard, Osceola	"
		3	2	67	3	2–4	1979	Glades	Forrester (1984)
		155	35	23[b]	—	—	1977–78	Glades, Columbia, Levy	"
		34	10	29[b]	—	—	1988	Charlotte	Greiner & Clarkson (1990)
		7	2	29[b]	—	—	1988	Orange	"
		13	2	15[b]	—	—	1988	Osceola	"
		6	1	17[b]	—	—	1988	Palm Beach	"
		4	2	50[b]	—	—	1988	St. Johns	"
	Globocephalus urosubulatus	20	13	65	93	3–442	1979–80	Orange, Brevard, Osceola, Sarasota, Manatee	Smith (1981)
	Strongyloides ransomi[c]	2	2	100	23	12–33	1977	Levy	Forrester (1984)
		155	60	39[b]	—	—	1977–78	Glades, Levy	"
		2	1	50[d]	111	—	1977	Levy	"

Location	Species							Counties	Reference
		1	1	100[e]	551	—	1974	Alachua	" "
		3	1	33[f]	347	—	1979	Glades	" "
		34	6	18[b]	—	—	1988	Charlotte	Greiner & Clarkson (1990)
Large intestine	*Oesophagostomum brevicaudum*	13	7	54[b]	—	—	1988	Osceola	" "
		6	1	17[b]	—	—	1988	Palm Beach	" "
		7	4	57[b]	—	—	1988	Polk	" "
		4	1	25[b]	—	—	1988	St. Johns	" "
		10	3	30[b]	—	—	1988	Taylor	" "
		20	16	80	167	3–1,538	1979–80	Orange, Brevard, Osceola, Sarasota, Manatee	Smith (1981)
	Oesophagostomum dentatum	20	15	75	175	5–641	1980	Orange, Brevard, Osceola	" "
	Oesophagostomum quadrispinulatum	20	20	100	285	4–1,667	1979–80	Orange, Brevard, Osceola, Sarasota, Manatee	" "
	Oesophagostomum spp.	2	1	50	11	—	1977	Levy	Forrester (1984)
		155	89	57[b]	—	—	1977–78	Glades, Columbia, Levy	" "
Cecum	*Trichuris suis*[g]	3	2	67	448	387–509	1979	Glades	" "
		20	2	10	3	1–4	1979–80	Osceola, Sarasota, Manatee	Smith (1981)
		3	1	33	1	—	1979	Glades	Forrester (1984)
		155	31	20[b]	—	—	1977–78	Glades, Columbia, Levy	" "
		34	3	9[b]	—	—	1988	Charlotte	Greiner & Clarkson (1990)
		6	2	33[b]	—	—	1988	Palm Beach	" "
		10	1	10[b]	—	—	1988	Taylor	" "

[a] Greiner & Clarkson (1990) also examined wild hogs from Collier (n = 3), Polk (n = 7), and Taylor (n = 10) counties; all were negative for *Ascaris suum* eggs.

[b] These prevalence values were based on fecal analyses.

[c] Greiner & Clarkson (1990) also examined wild hogs from Collier (n = 3) and Orange (n = 7) counties; all were negative for *Strongyloides ransomi* eggs.

[d] This young pig weighed 52 lbs.

[e] This young pig weighed 17 lbs.

[f] This young pig weighed 47 lbs.

[g] Greiner & Clarkson (1990) also examined wild hogs from Collier (n = 3), Orange (n = 7), Osceola (n = 13), Polk (n = 7), and St. Johns (n = 4) counties; all were negative for *Trichuris suis* eggs.

species are present in large numbers (Smith et al. 1982). *Ascaris suum* has been labeled as "the most pathogenic and important parasite of swine" (Levine 1980, p. 268). In domestic swine it is responsible for tremendous losses. Migrating larvae cause liver damage and verminous pneumonia. Stray larvae sometimes migrate into the brain, resulting in posterior paralysis. Adult worms cause emaciation and retarded growth when present in large numbers. In addition, ascarids may carry or exacerbate several viral diseases such as hog cholera and mycoplasmal pneumonia in a fashion similar to that reported for lungworms (Levine 1980). Currently there is no information on these types of effects in wild hogs.

Strongyloides ransomi is found typically in young domestic swine and causes enteritis, anorexia, vomiting, and diarrhea, which can lead to death (Levine 1980). Older animals are less severely affected. Nothing is known about the effects on wild hogs, but damage similar to that reported in domestic swine may occur under certain ecological conditions.

Other gastrointestinal helminths such as *Gongylonema pulchrum*, *Trichuris suis*, and the three species of *Oesophagostomum* are not believed to be harmful to wild hogs normally (Smith et al. 1982).

XIII. Arthropods

Wild hogs in Florida are known to serve as hosts for seven species of parasitic arthropods (Table 23-12). An eighth species, the screwworm (*Cochliomyia hominivorax*), was known to parasitize wild hogs in the past (Hanson and Karstad 1959), but is no longer a problem since this pest has been eradicated from Florida. For more information on

screwworms, the reader is referred to Chapter 20 on white-tailed deer.

The sucking louse, *Haematopinus suis*, is a common ectoparasite of wild hogs. Smith et al. (1982) found it to be the most frequently encountered arthropod, especially in the coastal plain region. This louse is quite large (up to 6 mm in length) and has been called "the very large louse of pigs" by some authors (Soulsby 1968, p. 370) and is found wherever swine occur (Harwood and James 1979). It can cause irritation of the skin that leads to extensive scratching and hence reduced food consumption and growth in domestic hogs (Dobson 1986). There is no information on its effects on wild hogs.

The ticks that are found on wild hogs in Florida have been studied by Greiner et al. (1984) and Smith (1981). Four species are known (Table 23-12), two of which (*Dermacentor variabilis* and *Amblyomma maculatum*) are very common and numerous. *Dermacentor variabilis*, for instance, was found on 99.6% of 645 wild hogs examined in southern Florida (Greiner et al. 1984). *Amblyomma maculatum* was common also and occurred on 85.9% of the hogs. Both of these are three-host ticks that use three different hosts for the completion of their life cycles. The adults infest wild hogs and other large mammals while the immature stages are found on birds and small mammals (Strickland et al. 1976). Pigs are infested by 7 to 22 days of age; by the time they reach 6 weeks of age, 95% of them are carrying ticks (Greiner et al. 1984). Figure 23-9 illustrates the distribution of the four species of ticks on wild hogs in southern Florida by site on the host and by season. *Dermacentor variabilis* was found on hogs throughout the year and localized mainly on the venter of the hogs, whereas *Amblyomma maculatum* was absent from the hogs in the spring and was found during other times of the year attached to the

Table 23-12

Arthropod parasites collected from wild hogs in Florida

Arthropod	No. hogs			Date	County	Data source
	Exam.	Inf.	%			
Sucking lice						
Haematopinus suis	40	37	93	1979–80	Orange, Brevard, Osceola, Sarasota, Manatee	Smith (1981)
	29	17	59	1977–78	Glades	Forrester (1984)
Ticks						
Dermacentor variabilis	40	13	33	1979–80	Osceola, Sarasota, Manatee	Smith (1981)
	NG	NG	—	1963	Broward, Dade, Palm Beach	SCWDS records
	645	639	99	1979–81	Glades	Greiner et al. (1984)
	10	7	70	1981	Franklin	Davidson et al. (1987), SCWDS records
Amblyomma maculatum	40	1	3	1979–80	Osceola	Smith (1981)
	645	577	86	1979–81	Glades	Greiner et al. (1984)
	NG	NG	—	1969	Palm Beach	SCWDS records
Amblyomma americanum	40	0	0	1979–80	None	Smith (1981)
	645	3	1	1979–81	Glades	Greiner et al. (1984)
Ixodes scapularis	40	9	23	1979–80	Sarasota, Manatee	Smith (1981)
	645	6	1	1979–81	Glades	Greiner et al. (1984)
	NG	NG	—	1963	Broward, Dade, Palm Beach	SCWDS records
Mites						
Demodex phylloides	40	14	35	1979–80	Orange, Brevard, Osceola, Sarasota, Manatee	Smith (1981)
Sarcoptes scabiei	40	2	5	1979–80	Orange, Brevard	" "

ears. Neither *Dermacentor variabilis* nor *A. maculatum* are known to serve as vectors of parasites or disease agents of hogs, but both are known to cause tick paralysis (Strickland et al. 1976); it is not known if this occurs in wild hogs. Local irritation, blood loss, and secondary infections of skin wounds most likely occur in Florida wild hog populations as a result of tick infestations.

The impact of infestations by the two mites (*Demodex phylloides* and *Sarcoptes scabiei*) has not been determined. From what is known about the effects of these parasites on domestic swine, both have the potential of causing severe skin disease. *Demodex phylloides* (the hog follicle mite) can cause nodular lesions (Harwood and James 1979) that can become secondarily invaded by bacteria (Soulsby 1968). *Sarcoptes scabiei* causes sarcoptic mange, which can result in intense itching and scratching, hair loss, and ultimately emaciation and death (Smith et al. 1982;

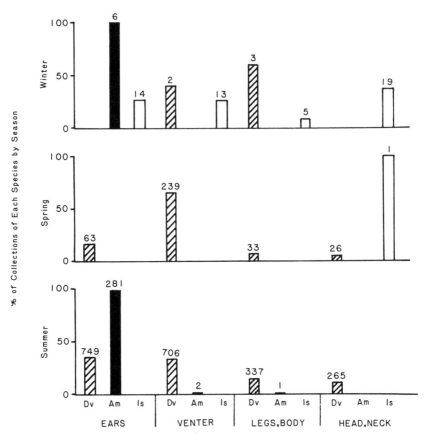

FIGURE 23-9. Distribution of ticks on wild hogs during different seasons (Fisheating Creek). The numbers above the bars are the numbers of each tick recovered from hogs during that season. Dv = *Dermacentor variabilis*, Am = *Amblyomma maculatum*, Is = *Ixodes scapularis*. (From Greiner et al. 1984.)

Soulsby 1968). This mite can infest man and therefore this represents a zoonotic disease.

XIV. Summary and conclusions

Wild hogs in Florida are known to have 47 different parasitic and infectious diseases. Etiologic agents include 37 parasites (12 protozoans, 17 nematodes, 1 acanthocephalan, 1 sucking louse, 4 ticks, and 2 mites), 7 bacteria, and 3 viruses. In addition, a number of other parasites and diseases are probably present (but currently undetected) since they occur in hogs in neighboring states.

Much of what is known about the significance of the diseases of wild hogs has been extrapolated from information on domestic swine and should be interpreted carefully. There is undoubtedly a more than casual relationship between domestic and wild hogs in Florida and other parts of the Southeast. Because of the close association of domestic and wild hogs in many areas of the state there is an opportunity for exchange of a number of parasites and diseases.

Among the most important diseases among wild hogs in Florida appear to be brucellosis, leptospirosis, coccidiosis, verminous pneumonia, kidney worm infections, ascariasis, tick infestations, and mange. Individually or in various combinations, these parasites and diseases may seriously affect hog populations. At the present time very little is known about this aspect. Our information on the distribution of these diseases is spotty and incomplete, but does provide a basis from which to plan further research. The list of zoonotic diseases in wild hogs in Florida is impressive. Eight parasitic and infectious diseases of wild hogs can infect man. These include brucellosis, leptospirosis, salmonellosis, toxoplasmosis, balantidiasis, trichinosis, trichostrongylosis, and sarcoptic mange. In addition, all four species of ticks will feed on man if the opportunity is presented. These potential public health threats should be kept in mind by those who hunt, study, or manage the wild hog in Florida.

XV. Literature cited

Barrows, P.L., H.M. Smith, Jr., A.K. Prestwood, and J. Brown. 1981. Prevalence and distribution of *Sarcocystis* sp. among wild swine of southeastern United States. J. Am. Vet. Med. Assoc. 179:1117–1118.

Becker, H.N. 1984. Unpublished data. Univ. of Florida, Gainesville.

Becker, H.N., and R.E. Bradley. 1981. Fenbendazole as a therapy for naturally acquired *Stephanurus dentatus* and gastrointestinal nematodes in feral swine. Vet. Parasitol. 9:111–115.

Becker, H.N., and P.L. Nicoletti. 1988. Unpublished data. Univ. of Florida, Gainesville.

Becker, H.N., R.C. Belden, T. Breault, M.J. Burridge, W.B. Frankenberger, and P. Nicoletti. 1978. Brucellosis in feral swine in Florida. J. Am. Vet. Med. Assoc. 173:1181–1182.

Becker, H.N., E.C. Pirtle, R.C. Belden, W.R. Frankenberger, B.P. All, H.L. Ruben, and E.P. Gibbs. 1988. Preliminary observations on the presence of pseudorabies antibodies in domestic and feral swine in Florida. Unpublished MS. 8 pp.

Belden, R.C. 1986. Florida panther recovery plan implementation: A 1983 progress report. Proc. 2d Internat. Cat Symp. pp. 159–172.

Belden, R.C., and W.B. Frankenberger. 1977. Management of feral hogs in Florida—past, present, and future. In: Research and management of wild hog populations: Proceedings of a symposium. G.W. Wood (ed.). Georgetown, S.C. pp. 5–10.

Bigler, W.J., G.L. Hoff, W.H. Hemmert, J.A. Thomas, and H.T. Janowski. 1977. Trends of brucellosis in Florida. An epidemiologic review. Am J. Epidemiol. 105:245–251.

Brady, J.R. 1984. Unpublished data. Florida Game and Fresh Water Fish Commission, Gainesville.

Burridge, M.J., W.J. Bigler, D.J. Forrester, and J.M. Hennemann. 1979. Serologic survey for *Toxoplasma gondii* in wild animals in Florida. J. Am. Vet. Med. Assoc. 175:964–967.

Butler, J.F., and E.P.J. Gibbs. 1984. Distribution of potential soft tick vectors of African swine fever in the Caribbean region (Acari: Argasidae). Prev. Vet. Med. 2:63–70.

Campbell, C.L. 1983. Unpublished data. State veterinarian's office, Tallahassee, Fla.

Clark, R.K., D.A. Jessup, D.W. Hird, R. Ruppanner, and M.E. Meyer. 1983. Serologic survey of California wild hogs for antibodies against selected zoonotic disease agents. J. Am. Vet. Med. Assoc. 183:1248–1251.

Corn, J.L., P.K. Swiderek, B.O. Blackburn, G.A. Erickson, A.B. Thiermann, and V.F. Nettles. 1986. Survey of selected diseases in wild swine in Texas. J. Am. Vet. Med. Assoc. 189:1029–1032.

Davidson, W.R., J.L. Blue, L.B. Flynn, S.M. Shea, R.L. Marchinton, and J.A. Lewis. 1987. Parasites, diseases and health status of sympatric populations of sambar deer and white-tailed deer in Florida. J. Wildl. Dis. 23:267–272.

Degner, R.L., L.W. Rodan, W.K. Mathis, and E.P.J. Gibbs. 1983. The recreational and commercial importance of feral swine in Florida. Prev. Vet. Med. 1:371–381.

Dobson, K.J. 1986. External parasites. In: Diseases of swine. 6th ed. Leman et al. (eds.). Iowa State Univ. Press, Ames. pp. 664–675.

Essey, M.A., R.L. Payne, E.M. Himes, and D. Luchsinger. 1981. Bovine tuberculosis surveys of axis deer and feral swine on the Hawaiian island of Molokai. Proc. Ann. Meet. U.S. Anim. Health Assoc. 85:538–549.

Forrester, D.J. 1984. Unpublished data. Univ. of Florida, Gainesville.

Forrester, D.J., J.A. Conti, and R.C. Belden. 1985. Parasites of the Florida panther (*Felis concolor coryi* Bangs). Proc. Helminthol. Soc. Wash. 52:95–97.

Forrester, D.J., J.H. Porter, R.C. Belden, and W.B. Frankenberger. 1982. Lungworms of feral swine in Florida. J. Am. Vet. Med. Assoc. 181:1278–1280.

Frankenberger, W.B., and R.C. Belden. 1976. Distribution, relative abundance and management needs of feral hogs in Florida. Proc. Ann. Conf. S.E. Assoc. Game Fish Comm. 30:641–644.

Gibbs, E.P.J. 1984. Unpublished data. Univ. of Florida, Gainesville.

Gibbs, E.P.J., and J.F. Butler. 1984. African swine fever—an assessment of risk for Florida. J. Am. Vet. Med. Assoc. 184:644–647.

Gillespie, J.H., and J.F. Timoney. 1981. Hagan and Bruner's infectious diseases of domestic animals. Cornell Univ. Press, Ithaca. 851 pp.

Greiner, E.C., and T.C. Clarkson. 1990. Unpublished data. Univ. of Florida, Gainesville.

Greiner, E.C., C. Taylor, III, W.B. Frankenberger, and R.C. Belden. 1982. Coccidia of feral swine from Florida. J. Am. Vet. Med. Assoc. 181:1275–1277.

Greiner, E.C., P.P. Humphrey, R.C. Belden, W.B. Frankenberger, D.H. Austin, and E.P.J. Gibbs. 1984. Ixodid ticks on feral swine in Florida. J. Wildl. Dis. 20:114–119.

Griffin, J. 1978. Ecology of the feral pig on the island of Hawaii. Final Report, P-R. Project W-15-3, Study No. II. Honolulu, Hawaii Department of Land and Natural Resources, Division of Fish and Game.

Hamilton, W.J., Jr. 1941. Notes on some mammals of Lee County, Florida. Am. Midl. Nat. 25:686–691.

Hanson, R.P., and L. Karstad. 1959. Feral swine in the southeastern United States. J. Wildl. Manage. 23:64–74.

Harwood, R.F., and M.T. James. 1979. Entomology in human and animal health. 7th ed. Macmillan, New York. 548 pp.

Hess, W.R., R.G. Endris, T.M. Haslett, M.J. Monahan, and J.P. McCoy. 1987. Potential arthropod vectors of African swine fever virus in North America and the Caribbean Basin. Vet. Parasitol. 26:145–155.

Howe, D.L. 1981. Eperythrozoonosis. In: Infectious diseases of wild mammals. 2d ed. J.W. Davis et al. (eds.). Iowa State Univ. Press, Ames. pp. 415–417.

Johnson, B.G. 1979. Status of the cooperative state-federal brucellosis eradication program. Proc. Ann. Meet. U.S. Anim. Health Assoc. 83:105–117.

Karstad, L.H., and R.P. Hanson. 1958. Infections in wildlife with the viruses of vesicular stomatitis and eastern equine encephalomyelitis. Trans. No. Am. Wildl. Conf. 23:175–186.

Levine, N.D. 1980. Nematode parasites of domestic animals and of man. 2d ed. Burgess, Minneapolis. 477 pp.

Lewis, T.H. 1907. Spanish explorers in the southern United States 1528–1543. Charles Scribner's Sons, New York. 411 pp.

Lindsay, D.S., B.L. Blagburn, J.V. Ernst, and W.L. Current. 1985. Experimental coccidiosis (*Isospora suis*) in a litter of feral piglets. J. Wildl. Dis. 21:309–310.

McVicar, J.W., C.A. Mebus, H.N. Becker, R.C. Belden, and E.P.J. Gibbs. 1981. Induced African swine fever in feral pigs. J. Am. Vet. Med. Assoc. 179:441–446.

Maehr, D.S., R.C. Belden, E.D. Land, and L. Wilkins. 1990. Food habits of panthers in southwest Florida. J. Wildl. Manage. 54:420–423.

Nettles, V.F. 1984. Unpublished data. SCWDS, Univ. of Georgia, Athens.

Nettles, V.F., and G.A. Erickson. 1984. Pseudorabies in wild swine. Proc. Ann. Mtg. U.S. Anim. Health Assoc. 88:505–506.

Nettles, V.F., J.L. Corn, G.A. Erickson, and

D.A. Jessup. 1989. A survey of wild swine in the United States for evidence of hog cholera. J. Wildl. Dis. 25:61–65.

Payeur, J.B. 1989. Feral swine: A potential threat to domestic cattle and swine. Proc. Feral Pig Sym. Livestock Conservation Institute, Madison, Wis. pp. 19–33.

Platt, K.B., D.L. Graham, and R.A. Faaborg. 1983. Pseudorabies: Experimental studies in raccoons with different virus strains. J. Wildl. Dis. 19:297–301.

Plowright, W. 1981. African swine fever. In: Infectious diseases of wild mammals. 2d ed. J.W. Davis et al. (eds.). Iowa State Univ. Press, Ames. pp. 178–190.

Prestwood, A.K., F.E. Kellogg, S.R. Pursglove, and F.A. Hayes. 1975. Helminth parasitism among intermingling insular populations of white-tailed deer, feral cattle and feral swine. J. Am. Vet. Med. Assoc. 166:787–789.

Roelke, M.E., E.C. Pirtle, and D.J. Forrester. 1988. Unpublished data. Florida Game and Fresh Water Fish Commission, Gainesville.

Shotts, E.B., Jr. 1981. Leptospirosis. In: Infectious diseases of wild mammals. J.W. Davis et al. (eds.). Iowa State Univ. Press, Ames. pp. 323–331.

Smith, H.M., Jr. 1981. Parasites of wild swine (*Sus scrofa*) in the southeastern United States. M.S. thesis, Univ. of Georgia, Athens, 126 pp.

Smith, H.M., Jr., W.R. Davidson, V.F. Nettles, and R.R. Gerrish. 1982. Parasitisms among wild swine in southeastern United States. J. Am. Vet. Med. Assoc. 181:1281–1284.

Soulsby, E.J.L. 1968. Helminths, arthropods and protozoa of domesticated animals. Williams and Wilkins, Baltimore. 824 pp.

Stallknecht, D.E., V.F. Nettles, G.A. Erickson, and D.A. Jessup. 1986. Antibodies to vesicular stomatitis virus in populations of feral swine in the United States. J. Wildl. Dis. 22:320–325.

Strickland, R.K., R.R. Gerrish, J.L. Hourigan, and G.O. Schubert. 1976. Ticks of veterinary importance. APHIS-USDA Agric. Handbook No. 485. U.S. Government Printing Office, Washington, D.C. 122 pp.

Thawley, D.G., and J.C. Wright. 1982. Pseudorabies virus infection in raccoons: A review. J. Wildl. Dis. 18:113–116.

Tozzini, F., A. Poli, and G.D. Croce. 1982. Experimental infection of European wild swine (*Sus scrofa* L.) with pseudorabies virus. J. Wildl. Dis. 18:425–428.

Trainer, D.O. 1981. Pseudorabies. In: Infectious diseases of wild mammals. 2d ed. J.W. Davis et al. (eds.). Iowa State Univ. Press, Ames. pp. 102–107.

Van der Leek, M.L., and J.B. Dame. 1990. Unpublished data. Univ. of Florida, Gainesville.

Van der Leek, M.L., C.L. Adams, and P.L. Nicoletti. 1990. Unpublished data. Univ. of Florida, Gainesville.

White, F.H. 1984. Unpublished data. Univ. of Florida, Gainesville.

Witter, J.F. 1981. Brucellosis. In: Infectious diseases of wild mammals. 2d ed. J.W. Davis et al. (eds.). Iowa State Univ. Press, Ames. pp. 280–287.

Wood, G.W., and R.H. Barrett. 1979. Status of wild pigs in the United States. Wildl. Soc. Bull. 7:237–246.

Wood, G.W., J.B. Hendricks, and D.E. Goodman. 1976. Brucellosis in feral swine. J. Wildl. Dis. 12:579–582.

Woods, R.D., E.C. Pirtle, J.M. Sacks, and E.P.J. Gibbs. 1990. Serologic survey for transmissible gastroenteritis virus neutralizing antibodies in selected feral and domestic swine sera in the southern United States. J. Wildl. Dis. 26:420–422.

Wright, T.J. 1972–87. Wildlife harvest and economic surveys. Florida Game and Fresh Water Fish Commission, Tallahassee. P-R Report, W-33.

Zygmont, S.M. 1981. A study of selected bacteria in wild swine in the southeastern United States and Hawaii. M.S. thesis, Univ. of Georgia, Athens. 51 pp.

Zygmont, S.M., V.F. Nettles, E.B. Shotts, Jr., W.A. Carmen, and B.O. Blackburn. 1982. Brucellosis in wild swine: A serologic and bacteriologic survey in the southeastern United States and Hawaii. J. Am. Vet. Med. Assoc. 181:1285–1287.

CHAPTER TWENTY-FOUR

Summary and Conclusions

It is evident from the preceding chapters that a large number and variety of diseases, parasites, and other morbidity/mortality factors have been recognized in wild mammals in Florida. It is also obvious that the story is incomplete. Even though some parasite/disease information is known for 69 of the 96 species of mammals found in Florida, the coverage for each mammal is quite variable. Very little is known about some mammals, and nothing is known for 27 species. Most of these 27 species are bats, rodents, or marine mammals and are rare statewide or common only in restricted areas (Table 24-1). Some are listed as endangered or threatened species. The low relative abundance and lack of study of these animals may account for the absence of information on them. Other species such as white-tailed deer and wild hogs have been well studied, probably because of their abundance and economic importance, while animals such as raccoons and murid rodents have attracted attention due to their role in the transmission of diseases of public health significance.

The importance of the diseases of wild mammals in Florida can be assessed in three ways: (1) the effects of these diseases on wild mammal populations; (2) the relationships of these diseases to domesticated animals; and (3) their public health significance.

Table 24-1

Species of mammals in Florida for which there are no data on parasites and diseases

Mammal		Relative abundance[a]
Family Soricidae (shrews)		
Southeastern shrew	*Sorex longirostris*	Rare
Family Vespertilionidae (vespertilionid bats)		
Little brown bat	*Myotis lucifugus*	Rare
Keen's bat	*Myotis keenii*	Rare
Indiana bat	*Myotis sodalis*	Rare
Silver-haired bat	*Lasionycteris noctivagans*	Rare
Rafinesque's big-eared bat	*Plecotus rafinesquii*	Unknown
Big brown bat	*Eptesicus fuscus*	Rare
Family Molossidae (free-tailed bats)		
Wagner's mastiff bat	*Eumops glaucinus*	Rare
Family Leporidae (rabbits & jackrabbits)		
Black-tailed jackrabbit	*Lepus californicus*[b]	Rare
Family Sciuridae (squirrels)		
Eastern chipmunk	*Tamias striatus*	Rare
Mexican red-bellied squirrel	*Sciurus aureogaster*[b]	Common (on Elliot Key only)
Family Castoridae (beavers)		
Beaver	*Castor canadensis*	Common
Family Cricetidae (New-World rats, mice & voles)		
Key rice rat	*Oryzomys argentatus*	Rare
Pine vole	*Microtus pinetorum*	Common
Meadow vole	*Microtus pennsylvanicus*	Rare
Family Myocastoriidae (nutrias)		
Nutria	*Myocastor coypus*	Common
Family Delphinidae (dolphins & porpoises)		
Common dolphin	*Delphinus delphis*	Common
Family Phocoenidae (porpoises)		
Harbor porpoise	*Phocoena phocoena*	Rare
Family Ziphiidae (beaked whales)		
Antillean beaked whale	*Mesoplodon europaeus*	Rare
True's beaked whale	*Mesoplodon mirus*	Rare
Sowerby's beaked whale	*Mesoplodon bidens*	Rare
Family Balaenopteridae (fin-backed whales)		
Fin whale	*Balaenoptera physalus*	Rare
Minke whale	*Balaenoptera acutorostrata*	Rare
Sei whale	*Balaenoptera borealis*	Rare
Bryde's whale	*Balaenoptera edeni*	Rare
Humpback whale	*Megaptera novaeangliae*	Rare
Family Balaenidae (right whales)		
Right whale	*Balaena glacialis*	Rare

[a]Adapted from Brown (1987); Bonde and O'Shea (1989).
[b]Non-native species.

Table 24-2

Summary of the major diseases and morbidity/mortality factors of Florida wild mammals

Mammal	No. disease agents and morbidity/ mortality factors[a]	Major problems/diseases, etc. in Florida		Comments[b]
		Significant	Potentially significant	
Opossums	49	Unknown	Unknown	Not well studied
Moles & shrews	11	"	"	Poorly studied
Bats	25	Rabies Histoplasmosis	Environmental contaminants	Poorly studied, except for rabies and histoplasmosis
Armadillos	27	Unknown	Unknown	Poorly studied
Cottontails	26	"	Tularemia	" "
Marsh rabbits	15	"	"	" "
Gray squirrels	91	Probably none	Hepatozoonosis	Fairly well studied
Fox squirrels	19	Unknown	Unknown	Poorly studied
Flying squirrels	12	"	"	" "
Pocket gophers	14	"	"	" "
Old-World rats and mice	46	"	"	Viruses and ectoparasites well studied because of their zoonotic importance
Cotton rats	70	Probably none	Probably none	Fairly well studied
Rice rats	65	"	"	" " "
Florida mice	49	"	"	" " "
Cotton mice	40	Probably none	Probably none	Fairly well studied
Old-field mice	11	Unknown	Unknown	Poorly studied
Golden mice	8	"	"	" "
Woodrats	14	"	"	" "
Harvest mice	1	"	"	" "
Round-tailed muskrats	33	Probably none	Inclement weather	Helminths and ectoparasites well studied
Raccoons	132	Rabies Canine distemper	Stomach worms Blood flukes Lungworms Hookworms	Well studied, especially rabies
Otters	17	Unknown	Mercury toxicosis Parvovirus	Parasites studied; other aspects neglected
Skunks	18	"	Unknown	Poorly studied
Mink	1	"	PCBs	" "
Weasels	3	"	Unknown	" "
Black bears	36	Trauma	Nematode infections	Parasites studied; other aspects neglected
Panthers	61	Trauma	Parvovirus Hookworms	Fairly well studied
Bobcats	48	Parvovirus	Notoedric mange Hookworms	Not well studied
Gray foxes	45	Rabies Canine distemper	Hookworms Heartworms Stomach worms Infectious canine hepatitis	Infectious and parasitic diseases fairly well studied

(Continued)

Table 24-2 *(continued)*

Mammal	No. disease agents and morbidity/ mortality factors[a]	Major problems/diseases, etc. in Florida		Comments[b]
		Significant	Potentially significant	
Red foxes	15	Sarcoptic mange	Hookworms Heartworms	Poorly studied
Coyotes	11	Unknown	Hookworms Heartworms	" "
Whales & dolphins	72	Strandings	Helminth infections Red tide	" "
Seals & sea lions	9	Unknown	EEE Heartworms	" "
Manatees	91	Trauma Cold weather	Red tide	Well studied
White-tailed deer	120	Haemonchosis	Hemorrhagic disease Lungworms	Well studied
Key deer	19	Trauma	Hemorrhagic disease Haemonchosis	Poorly studied
Sambar deer	13	Unknown	Unknown	" "
Wild hogs	47	Brucellosis	Coccidiosis Leptospirosis Kidney worms Lungworms	Fairly well studied

[a]These include infectious and parasitic diseases, environmental contaminants, trauma, inclement weather, neoplasia, anomalies, and the like identified from Florida mammals. Although the numbers in this column may be large for some mammals, these may only represent recognition of the presence of the agents or conditions and not necessarily reflect a knowledge of their epidemiology or significance to natural populations.
[b]In this column subjective assessments are given for each mammal or group of mammals in Florida in relation to the status of information on the significance of their parasites and diseases.

In Table 24-2 the major diseases and morbidity/mortality factors of Florida wild mammals are summarized. These are judged as significant or as potentially significant based on their prevalence and their known effects on mammals in Florida and elsewhere. Also indicated in Table 24-2 is an assessment of how well studied the diseases of each mammal or group of mammals are as of 1991. An examination of this table will reveal numerous areas where research is needed. Even though the list of parasites, diseases, and other factors is fairly extensive for some species, our understanding of their significance is rather sketchy. There is a need for innovative and long-term studies to be conducted so that the effects of these diseases on populations of mammals can be defined.

At least 119 parasites and diseases are interchangeable between wild and domestic mammals in Florida (Tables 24-3 through 24-13). These include viruses (13), bacteria (7), fungi (5), protozoans (13), trematodes (4), acanthocephalans (1), cestodes (5), nema-

Table 24-3
Viral diseases of wild mammals in Florida that can infect domestic mammals

Viral disease	Wild mammal hosts in Florida[a]		Susceptible domestic mammals
	Primary	Secondary	
Rabies	Raccoons	Opossums Otters Bobcats Skunks Bats Foxes	All mammals
Canine distemper	Raccoons Foxes	Opossums	Dogs
Feline panleukopenia	Bobcats Panthers	Raccoons (?) Otters (?) Foxes (?)	Cats
Feline calicivirus	Bobcats Panthers	None known	Cats
Infectious canine hepatitis	Foxes	Raccoons	Dogs
Pseudorabies	Wild hogs	Raccoons	Swine, cattle, goats, dogs, cats
Bluetongue	White-tailed deer	None known	Cattle, sheep, goats
EHD[b]	White-tailed deer	None known	Cattle, sheep
Vesicular stomatitis	White-tailed deer	Wild hogs	Horses, cattle, swine
IBR[c]	White-tailed deer	None known	Cattle, goats, swine
BVD[d]	White-tailed deer	None known	Cattle
PI–3[e]	White-tailed deer	None known	Cattle
EEE[f]	None known	Opossums Cotton rats Raccoons Skunks Foxes Black bears White-tailed deer	Horses

[a]Primary hosts are those in which the disease is moderately common or common; secondary hosts are those in which the disease is uncommon or rare.
[b]EHD = epizootic hemorrhagic disease.
[c]IBR = infectious bovine rhinotracheitis.
[d]BVD = bovine virus diarrhea.
[e]PI–3 = parainfluenza-3.
[f]EEE = eastern equine encephalomyelitis.

todes (45), ticks (10), mites (6), fleas (5), fly larvae (4), and sucking lice (1). These figures are perhaps inflated by the inclusion of wild hogs and domestic swine in the calculations. Since these are the same species, it is not surprising that a number of parasites and diseases are shared by these two populations. The list, in fact, would be reduced by 28 species if hogs were excluded. As was pointed out by Pastoret et al. (1988), the number of infec-

tions or infestations shared by wild and domestic animals is actually small. Most diseases and parasites are not shared, but are very specific, being limited to a single host species or to species that are closely related. When considering the list of diseases and parasites common to wild and domestic mammals in Florida, it is important to remember that the "flow" of these diseases is not always in one direction. Some of the shared diseases

Table 24-4
Bacterial diseases of wild mammals in Florida that can infect domestic mammals

Bacterial disease (agent)	Wild mammal hosts in Florida[a]		Susceptible domestic mammals
	Primary	Secondary	
Anthrax (*Bacillus anthracis*)	None known	White-tailed deer	Cattle, horses, sheep, goats
Brucellosis (*Brucella canis*)	None known	Raccoons	Dogs
Brucellosis (*Brucella suis*)	Wild hogs	None known	Swine, cattle
Leptospirosis (numerous serovars of *Leptospira interrogans*)	Opossums Armadillos Raccoons White-tailed deer Wild hogs Cotton rats Foxes	Shrews Rabbits Squirrels House mice Cotton mice Bobcats Bears	Cattle, swine, dogs
Nocardiosis (*Nocardia* sp.)	None known	Armadillos Cetaceans	Cattle, horses, swine, dogs, cats
Salmonellosis (numerous serovars of *Salmonella*)	Opossums Armadillos Raccoons	Otters Black bears Panthers Gray foxes White-tailed deer Wild hogs	Cattle, horses, swine
Tularemia (*Francisella tularensis*)	Cottontails Marsh rabbits	Opossums Armadillos Cotton rats Cotton mice Old-field mice Raccoons Gray foxes White-tailed deer	Sheep, horses, dogs, cats

[a]Primary hosts are those in which the disease is moderately common or common; secondary hosts are those in which the disease is uncommon or rare.

are primarily diseases of wild animals and secondarily infect domestic mammals and vice versa. The full picture of this aspect of the diseases listed in Tables 24-3 through 24-13 is not available. For some diseases, such as rabies, wild mammals (i.e., raccoons) serve as the primary reservoirs of the virus, whereas for others such as heartworm disease, domestic mammals (i.e., dogs) are the main hosts. In some cases when diseases are controlled in domestic animals, there is a subsequent decrease in infections in wildlife. An example of this was the reduction in cattle fever ticks on deer as a result of an extensive program of chemical dipping of cattle (Marshall et al. 1963). Much is yet to be learned about the complex relationships of diseases shared by wild and domestic mammals in Florida. Additional studies such as those conducted by Prestwood et al. (1975, 1976) should be initiated. In those studies the relationships of parasites of white-tailed deer, sheep, cattle, and

Table 24-5

Mycotic diseases of wild mammals in Florida that can infect domestic mammals

Fungal disease (agent)	Wild mammal hosts in Florida	Susceptible domestic mammals
Candidiosis (*Candida albicans*)	Gray squirrels	Cattle, sheep, dogs, cats
Histoplasmosis (*Histoplasma capsulatum*)	Bats	Dogs, cats, cattle, horses, swine
Mucormycosis (*Mucor* sp.)	Gray squirrels	Cattle, horses
Ringworm (*Microsporum gypseum*)	Gray squirrels	Dogs, cats, horses
Ringworm (*Trichophyton mentagrophytes*)	Opossums, gray squirrels	Cattle, sheep, horses, dogs, cats

Table 24-6

Protozoan diseases of wild mammals in Florida that can infect domestic mammals

Protozoan disease (agent)	Wild mammal hosts in Florida[a]		Susceptible domestic mammals
	Primary	Secondary	
Balantidiosis (*Balantidium coli*)	Wild hogs	None known	Swine
Chagas' disease (*Trypanosoma cruzi*)	Opossums	Raccoons Striped skunks Gray foxes	Dogs, cats
Coccidiosis (9 species of *Eimeria* and 1 species of *Isospora*)	Wild hogs	None known	Swine
Toxoplasmosis (*Toxoplasma gondii*)	Bobcats Panthers Armadillos Raccoons Bears	Opossums Rabbits Rodents Foxes White-tailed deer Wild hogs	All mammals

[a]Primary hosts are those in which the disease is moderately common or common; secondary hosts are those in which the disease is uncommon or rare.

feral swine were investigated. The authors found that the parasites of each species were distinct, for the most part, with little exchange occurring among hosts. The information that we now have available as presented in this chapter and throughout the book should be interpreted with caution. Much of it is indirect data (i.e., serologic) and experimental studies are needed to verify the susceptibility of various wild mammals to the pathogens of domestic mammals. Pastoret et al. (1988) recommended that four important questions be answered in order to determine the potential role of wildlife in the persistence and dissemination of diseases shared with domestic animals:

Table 24-7

Trematodes and acanthocephalans of wild mammals in Florida that can infect domestic mammals

Helminth	Wild mammal hosts in Florida	Susceptible domestic mammals
Trematodes (flukes)		
Alaria marcianae (intestinal fluke)	Panthers Bobcats Gray foxes Coyotes	Cats
Fascioloides magna (giant liver fluke)	White-tailed deer	Cattle, sheep
Heterobilharzia americana (blood fluke)	Raccoons Panthers Bobcats Black bears	Dogs, cats
Paramphistomum liorchis (rumen fluke)	White-tailed deer	Cattle
Acanthocephalans (thorny-headed worms)		
Macracanthorhynchus hirudinaceus (thorny-headed worm)	Wild hogs	Swine, cattle

Table 24-8

Cestodes of wild mammals in Florida that can infect domestic mammals

| Cestode (tapeworm) | Wild mammal hosts in Florida[a] | | Susceptible domestic mammals |
	Definitive	Intermediate	
Moniezia sp.	White-tailed deer	None[a]	Cattle, sheep
Spirometra mansonoides	Bobcats Panthers Gray foxes	Cotton mice Otters	Dogs, cats
Taenia hydatigena	Unknown	White-tailed deer	Dogs
Taenia pisiformis	Coyotes Gray foxes Bobcats	Cottontails	Dogs
Taenia taeniaeformis	Bobcats	Roof rats, cotton rats	Dogs, cats

[a]Orbatid mites serve as intermediate hosts.

1. Which species are susceptible to infection?
2. Do these species develop clinical disease and do they excrete the causal agent accordingly?
3. Which species become asymptomatic carriers after infection?

4. Are the wildlife carriers capable of transmitting the disease to other animals, particularly domestic species?

Such criteria need to be determined and evaluated for wild mammals in Florida before the relationships among the various diseases and

Table 24-9
Nematodes of wild mammals in Florida that can infect domestic mammals

Nematode	Wild mammal hosts in Florida	Susceptible domestic mammals
Dirofilaria immitis (heartworm)	Coyotes Gray foxes Red foxes Black bears Bobcats California sea lions	Dogs mainly, but also cats
Dirofilaria striata (subcutaneous worm)	Bobcats Panthers	Dogs, cats
Dracunculus insignis (guinea worm)	Raccoons Panthers	Dogs
Capillaria aerophila (lungworm)	Black bears Bobcats Panthers Gray foxes Red foxes Coyotes	Dogs, cats
Crenosoma vulpis (lungworm)	Black bears	Dogs
Capillaria plica (bladder worm)	Black bears Bobcats Coyotes Otters	"
Spirocerca lupi (esophageal worm)	Bobcats Gray foxes Red foxes	"
Ancylostoma caninum (hookworm)	Black bears Bobcats Gray foxes Red foxes Coyotes	Dogs, cats
Ancylostoma tubaeforme (hookworm)	Bobcats Gray foxes Red foxes	Cats
Ancylostoma braziliense (hookworm)	Bobcats Gray foxes	"
Ancylostoma pluridentatum (hookworm)	Bobcats Panthers	"
Toxocara canis (roundworm)	Red foxes	Dogs, cats
Toxocara mystax (roundworm)	Bobcats Panthers	Cats
Toxascaris leonina (roundworm)	Bobcats	"
Strongyloides stercoralis (threadworm)	Gray foxes	Dogs, cats
Physaloptera rara (stomach worm)	Raccoons Gray foxes Red foxes Coyotes Black bears	Dogs, cats
Trichuris vulpis (whipworm)	Gray foxes Red foxes Coyotes	Dogs

(Continued)

Table 24-9 *(continued)*

Nematode	Wild mammal hosts in Florida	Susceptible domestic mammals
Elaeophora schneideri (arterial worm)	White-tailed deer	Sheep, goats
Dictyocaulus viviparus (lungworm)	" " "	Cattle
Gongylonema pulchrum (gullet worm)	Black bears White-tailed deer Wild hogs	Cattle, sheep, goats, horses, swine
Gongylonema verrucosum (rumen nematode)	White-tailed deer	Cattle, sheep, goats
Haemonchus contortus (stomach worm)	" " "	Cattle, sheep, goats
Haemonchus placei (stomach worm)	" " "	Cattle
Haemonchus similis (stomach worm)	" " "	"
Trichostrongylus axei (stomach worm)	" " " Wild hogs	Cattle, sheep, goats, horses, swine
Ostertagia ostertagi (stomach worm)	White-tailed deer	Cattle
Capillaria bovis (intestinal worm)	" " "	"
Cooperia punctata (intestinal worm)	" " "	"
Oesophagostomum venulosum (nodular worm)	" " "	Sheep, goats
Strongyloides papillosus (threadworm)	" " "	Sheep, cattle
Trichinella spiralis (trichina worm)	Wild hogs Panthers Foxes Opossums Raccoons Skunks	Swine
Stephanurus dentatus (kidney worm)	Wild hogs	Swine, cattle
Metastrongylus apri (lungworm)	" "	Swine
Metastrongylus salmi (lungworm)	" "	"
Metastrongylus pudendotectus (lungworm)	" "	"
Ascarops strongylina (stomach worm)	" "	"
Physocephalus sexalatus (stomach worm)	" "	"
Hyostrongylus rubidus (stomach worm)	" "	"
Ascaris suum (intestinal worm)	" "	"
Globocephalus urosubulatus (hookworm)	" "	"
Strongyloides ransomi (threadworm)	" "	"
Oesophagostomum brevicaudum (nodular worm)	" "	"
Oesophagostomum dentatum (nodular worm)	" "	"
Oesophagostomum quadrispinulatum (nodular worm)	" "	"
Trichuris suis (whipworm)	" "	"

Table 24-10

Ticks of wild mammals in Florida that can infest domestic mammals

Tick	Wild mammal hosts in Florida	Susceptible domestic mammals
Amblyomma americanum (lone star tick)	Opossums, cottontails, gray squirrels, fox squirrels, pocket gophers, Florida mice, raccoons, striped skunks, mink, panthers, bobcats, gray foxes, black bears, white-tailed deer, wild hogs	Dogs, cats, cattle, sheep, goats, horses, swine
Amblyomma maculatum (Gulf Coast tick)	Fox squirrels, roof rats, cotton rats, Florida mice, panthers, gray foxes, black bears, white-tailed deer, wild hogs, bobcats	Dogs, cats, cattle, sheep, goats, horses, swine
Dermacentor nitens (tropical horse tick)	Panthers, white-tailed deer	Mainly horses, but also cattle, sheep, goats, swine
Dermacentor variabilis (American dog tick)	Opossums, cottontails, marsh rabbits, gray squirrels, fox squirrels, roof rats, woodrats, cotton rats, rice rats, Florida mice, cotton mice, spotted skunks, striped skunks, panthers, bobcats, gray foxes, black bears, white-tailed deer, wild hogs, raccoons	Dogs, cats, cattle, sheep, goats, horses, swine
Haemaphysalis leporispalustris (rabbit tick)	Cottontails, marsh rabbits, roof rats, woodrats	Dogs, cats, cattle, sheep, goats
Ixodes cookei (no common name)	Raccoons, spotted skunks, striped skunks, otters, gray foxes	Dogs, cats, cattle, horses, swine
Ixodes scapularis (black-legged tick)	Opossums, least shrews, cottontails, marsh rabbits, fox squirrels, woodrats, cotton rats, rice rats, Florida mice, cotton mice, golden mice, raccoons, panthers, bobcats, gray foxes, black bears, white-tailed deer, wild hogs	Dogs, cats, cattle, sheep, goats, horses, swine
Ixodes texanus (no common name)	Fox squirrels, raccoons	Dogs, cats
Ornithodoros talaje (no common name)	Woodrats	Dogs, cats
Rhipicephalus sanguineus (brown dog tick)	White-tailed deer	Dogs, cats, cattle, sheep, goats

Table 24-11

Mites of wild mammals in Florida that can infest domestic mammals

Mite	Wild mammal hosts in Florida	Susceptible domestic mammals
Demodex phylloides (follicle mite)	Wild hogs	Swine
Eutrombicula alfreddugesi (chigger)	Gray squirrels, fox squirrels	Dogs, cats, sheep, goats, horses
Eutrombicula batatas (chigger)	Roof rats, rice rats	Dogs, cats
Notoedres cati (no common name)	Bobcats	Cats
Ornithonyssus bacoti (tropical rat mite)	Opossums, marsh rabbits, roof rats, Norway rats, house mice, cotton rats, rice rats, Florida mice, cotton mice	Dogs, cats
Sarcoptes scabiei (sarcoptic scab mite)	Red foxes, wild hogs	Dogs, cats, cattle, sheep, goats, horses, swine

Table 24-12

Fleas of wild mammals in Florida that can infest domestic mammals

Flea	Wild mammal hosts in Florida	Susceptible domestic mammals
Cediopsylla simplex (rabbit flea)	Cottontails, marsh rabbits, gray foxes, bobcats	Dogs, cats, rabbits
Ctenocephalides canis (dog flea)	Roof rats, Norway rats, cotton rats, gray foxes	Dogs, cats
Ctenocephalides felis (cat flea)	Opossums, least shrews, cottontails, roof rats, raccoons, spotted skunks, bobcats, panthers, gray foxes, white-tailed deer, Norway rats	Dogs, cats
Echidnophaga gallinacea (sticktight flea)	Opossums, cottontails, gray squirrels, pocket gophers, roof rats, Norway rats, cotton rats, Florida mice, spotted skunks, long-tailed weasels, bobcats, gray foxes	Sheep, goats, horses, swine, dogs, cats
Pulex simulans (no common name)	Opossums, cottontails, gray squirrels, Norway rats, striped skunks, bobcats, gray foxes, red foxes	Swine, dogs, cats

parasites shared by wild and domestic mammals can be understood. It will then be possible to consider the diseases in the categories suggested by Pastoret et al. (1988):

1. Diseases and parasites having a known wildlife reservoir (i.e., rabies, tularemia, and giant liver fluke infections)

Table 24-13
Fly larvae and sucking lice of wild mammals in Florida that can infest domestic mammals

Arthropod	Wild mammal hosts in Florida	Susceptible domestic mammals
Fly larvae		
Cochliomyia macellaria (secondary screwworm)	White-tailed deer	Cattle, sheep, goats, horses, dogs, cats
Cuterebra buccata (rabbit bot)	Cottontails	Cattle
Cuterebra spp. (rodent bot)	Rodents	Dogs, cats
Phormia regina (blowfly)	White-tailed deer	Cattle, sheep, goats
Sucking lice		
Haematopinus suis (common hog louse)	Wild hogs, white-tailed deer	Swine

Table 24-14
Viral and rickettsial diseases of wild mammals in Florida that can also infect man

Type of agent	Disease	Transmission[a]	Wild mammal hosts in Florida	Comments
Viruses	EEE[b]	(1)	Opossums, cotton rats, raccoons, striped skunks, gray foxes, black bears, white-tailed deer	Most prevalent in gray foxes (38%).
	Everglades encephalitis	(1)	Opossums, cotton mice, roof rats, cotton rats, rice rats, bobcats, raccoons, white-tailed deer	Common in southern Florida, especially in rodents. Prevalence in cotton mice = 23%.
	Rabies	(2)	Raccoons, bats, skunks, foxes, opossums, otters, bobcats, panthers	Most important hosts are raccoons.
	SLE[c]	(1)	Opossums, gray squirrels, cotton mice, raccoons, white-tailed deer	Prevalence in white-tailed deer in Collier County = 6%.
	Tensaw encephalitis	(1)	Marsh rabbits, cotton rats, cotton mice, raccoons, gray foxes, white-tailed deer	Common in white-tailed deer (95%) and raccoons (24%).
	Vesicular stomatitis	(3)	White-tailed deer, wild hogs, black bears	11% prevalence in deer from Collier County, 33% in hogs from St. Marks NWR.
Rickettsia	Epidemic typhus (*Rickettsia prowazekii*)	(4)	Flying squirrels	High prevalence (48%) in flying squirrels in northern and central Florida. No human cases known from Florida, however.
	Murine typhus (*Rickettsia typhi*)	(5)	Roof rats, Norway rats	Common during the 1940s, but controlled since then.

[a](1) = mosquitoes, (2) = bite wounds, (3) = direct contact or arthropod bites, (4) = aerosol, (5) = fleas.
[b]EEE = eastern equine encephalomyelitis.
[c]SLE = St. Louis encephalitis.

2. Diseases and parasites affecting many wild and domestic mammals, but without a known wildlife reservoir (i.e., salmonellosis, sticktight flea infestations, and black-legged tick infestations)

3. Diseases and parasites distributed equally among wild and domestic mammals (i.e., bluetongue, toxoplasmosis, and hookworm disease)

At least 60 parasites and diseases of wild mammals in Florida can also infect man and are therefore zoonotic (Tables 24-14 through 24-22). These include viruses (6), rickettsia (2), bacteria (12), fungi (7), protozoans (3), trematodes (1), cestodes (4), nematodes (7), ticks (6), mites (3), and fleas (9). Of these, only 11 are of significance, and include rabies, EEE, SLE, leptospirosis, salmonellosis, tula-

Table 24-15
Bacterial diseases of wild mammals in Florida that can also infect man

Disease	Etiologic agent	Transmission[a]	Wild mammal hosts in Florida	Comments
Leptospirosis	*Leptospira interrogans*	(1)	Opossums, armadillos, raccoons, white-tailed deer, wild hogs, cotton rats, cotton mice, house mice, foxes, shrews, rabbits, squirrels, bobcats, bears	Numerous serovars of *L. interrogans* have been identified. Highest prevalences were in raccoons (38%), foxes (33%), and cotton rats (33%).
Plesiomoniasis	*Plesiomonas shigelloides*	(2)	Panthers, bobcats, manatees	Uncommon.
Salmonellosis	*Salmonella* sp.	(2)	Opossums, raccoons, otters, panthers, gray foxes, black bears, manatees, white-tailed deer, wild hogs	Numerous serovars isolated. High prevalences in raccoons (24%), from which 19 serovars were identified.
Edwardsiellosis	*Edwardsiella tarda*	(2)	Raccoons, panthers, California sea lions, manatees, armadillos	Highest prevalence in raccoons (17%).
Tularemia	*Francisella tularensis*	(3)	Opossums, armadillos, cottontails, marsh rabbits, cotton rats, cotton mice, old-field mice, gray foxes, white-tailed deer, raccoons	Human cases found throughout the state in low numbers. Most contracted from wild rabbits.
Plague	*Yersinia pestis*	(4)	Roof rats, Norway rats	Only 1 outbreak has occurred in Florida (1920).
Anthrax	*Bacillus anthracis*	(5)	White-tailed deer	Only 1 outbreak reported in Florida deer (1951).
Brucellosis	*Brucella suis*	(6)	Wild hogs	Infections are prevalent in wild hogs (37%) and distributed throughout Florida.
Brucellosis	*Brucella canis*	(6)	Raccoons	Uncommon.
Nocardiosis	*Nocardia* spp.	(6)	Armadillos, cetaceans	Uncommon.
Dermatophilosis	*Dermatophilus congolensis*	(7)	White-tailed deer	Only 1 case reported in Florida deer (1984).
Erysipelothrix infection	*Erysipelothrix rhusiopathiae*	(6)	Cetaceans	Reported several times from Florida marine mammals.

[a](1) = contact with infected urine, (2) = fecal-oral, (3) = tick bites or wound infection, (4) = flea bites or wound infection, (5) = airborne, biting arthropods, or ingestion, (6) = direct contact, (7) = wound infection or biting arthropods.

Table 24-16
Fungal diseases of wild mammals in Florida that can also infect man

Disease	Etiologic agent	Transmission[a]	Wild mammal hosts in Florida	Comments
Aspergillosis	Aspergillus fumigatus	(1)	Gray squirrels, cetaceans	Uncommon.
Candidiosis	Candida albicans	(2)	Gray squirrels, cetaceans	Uncommon in squirrels. Reported from captive cetaceans.
Entomophthoro-mycosis	Entomophthora coronata	(3)	Cetaceans	Captive mammals only.
Histoplasmosis	Histoplasma capsulatum	(1)	Bats	Common in Florida bats, especially southeastern brown bats.
Lobomycosis	Loboa loboi	(2)	Bottlenosed dolphins	Reported several times from free-ranging animals.
Mucormycosis	Mucor sp.	(4)	Cetaceans, gray squirrels	Captive cetaceans.
Ringworm	Trichophyton mentagrophytes	(2)	Opossums, gray squirrels	Common in gray squirrels.
Ringworm	Microsporum gypseum	(2)	Opossums, gray squirrels	Common in gray squirrels.

[a](1) = direct contact and airborne, (2) = direct contact, (3) = inhalation, (4) = inhalation or ingestion.

Table 24-17
Protozoan diseases of wild mammals in Florida that can also infect man

Disease	Etiologic agent	Transmission[a]	Wild mammal hosts in Florida	Comments
Balantidiosis	Balantidium coli	(1)	Wild hogs	Poorly studied. May be quite common.
Chagas' disease	Trypanosoma cruzi	(2)	Opossums, raccoons, striped skunks, gray foxes	No human cases yet reported in Florida.
Toxoplasmosis	Toxoplasma gondii	(1)	Bobcats, panthers, opossums, rabbits, rodents, raccoons, foxes, white-tailed deer, wild hogs, armadillos, bears	Very common and widespread.

[a](1) = ingestion, (2) = fecal material of triatomid bug.

remia, brucellosis, histoplasmosis, toxoplasmosis, cutaneous larva migrans, and visceral larva migrans. The other diseases and infections occur at low prevalences and result in only occasional exposure to humans. Nevertheless, it is important that people working closely with wild mammals be aware of the fact that there are disease problems associated with such activities. Rabies is probably the most important and dangerous zoonotic disease in Florida wild mammals. Any wild mammal, especially a raccoon, bat, or skunk, that behaves abnormally should be suspected as being rabid and should be treated accord-

Table 24-18

Trematodes and cestodes of wild mammals in Florida that can also infect man

Disease	Etiologic agent	Transmission[a]	Wild mammal hosts in Florida	Comments
Trematodes				
Swimmer's itch	*Heterobilharzia americana*	(1)	Raccoons, black bears, bobcats, panthers	Very common in raccoons (56%).
Cestodes				
Cestodiosis	*Mesocestoides* sp.	(2)	Panthers, raccoons	Uncommon.
Dwarf tapeworm infection	*Hymenolepis nana*	(3)	Florida mice, cotton mice	Uncommon.
Rat tapeworm infection	*Hymenolepis diminuta*	(3)	Rice rats	Uncommon.
Sparganosis	*Spirometra mansonoides*	(4)	Otters, panthers, bobcats, gray foxes	Common in bobcats and panthers.

[a](1) = penetration of skin by cercariae in water, (2) = ingestion of infected mice or snakes, (3) = ingestion of eggs in food, fleas, or mealworms, (4) = ingestion of larvae in copepods or in tissues of an amphibian, reptile, bird, or mammal or penetration of skin or mucous membranes by larvae.

Table 24-19

Nematodes of wild mammals in Florida that can also infect man

Disease	Etiologic agent	Transmission[a]	Wild mammal hosts in Florida	Comments
Anisakiasis	*Anisakis* sp.	(1)	Cetaceans	Uncommon.
Capillariasis	*Capillaria hepatica*	(2)	Rabbits, rodents, skunks, otters	Very common in Florida mice.
Cutaneous larva migrans	*Ancylostoma braziliense*	(3)	Bobcats, gray foxes	Common.
Filariasis	*Dirofilaria tenuis*	(4)	Raccoons	20 human cases reported in Florida.
Trichinosis	*Trichinella spiralis*	(5)	Opossums, raccoons, skunks, panthers, foxes, wild hogs	High prevalence (57%) in panthers.
Trichostrongylosis	*Trichostrongylus axei*	(2)	White-tailed deer, wild hogs	Uncommon.
Visceral larva migrans	*Toxocara canis* *Toxocara mystax*	(2) (2)	Red foxes, bobcats, panthers	Common.

[a](1) = ingestion of infected fish, (2) = ingestion of eggs, (3) = penetration of skin by larvae, (4) = mosquitoes, (5) = ingestion of larvae in tissues.

ingly and reported to the proper authorities. Most of the zoonotic diseases can be prevented, however, by observing careful practices of sanitation and cleanliness. Certainly it must be remembered that not all mammals in Florida are diseased and not all have zoonotic infections or diseases. A balanced and informed viewpoint is necessary in order to keep these aspects in proper prospective.

The impact and importance of environ-

Table 24-20
Ticks of wild mammals in Florida that can also infest man

Tick	Wild mammal hosts in Florida	Diseases caused or transmitted
Amblyomma americanum	Opossums, rabbits, squirrels, rodents, raccoons, skunks, mink, panthers, bobcats, foxes, bears, deer, hogs	Tick paralysis, Rocky Mountain spotted fever, tularemia, Q fever
Amblyomma maculatum	Squirrels, rodents, panthers, foxes, bears, deer, hogs, bobcats	Tick paralysis
Dermacentor variabilis	Opossums, rabbits, squirrels, rodents, skunks, panthers, bobcats, foxes, bears, deer, hogs, raccoons	Tick paralysis, Rocky Mountain spotted fever, tularemia
Ixodes scapularis	Opossums, shrews, rabbits, squirrels, rodents, panthers, bobcats, foxes, bears, deer, hogs, raccoons	Tick paralysis, tularemia, Lyme disease[a]
Ornithodoros talaje	Woodrats	Relapsing fever
Rhipicephalus sanguineus	White-tailed deer	Tick paralysis, Rocky Mountain spotted fever, Q fever, tularemia

[a] Presumptive.

Table 24-21
Mites of wild mammals in Florida that can also infest man

Mite	Wild mammal hosts in Florida	Diseases caused or transmitted
Eutrombicula alfreddugesi	Squirrels	Chigger dermatitis
Ornithonyssus bacoti	Opossums, rabbits, rodents	Skin irritation
Sarcoptes scabiei	Red foxes, wild hogs	Scabies or "seven-year itch"

mental contamination (radionuclides, pesticides, heavy metals, etc.) on wild mammals in Florida are poorly understood. A few species such as bats, gray squirrels, raccoons, Florida panthers, manatees, bottlenosed dolphins, and white-tailed deer have been studied to some degree, but more needs to be done. As Florida's human population grows, environmental contamination will become more and more of a serious problem. Wild mammals have been recognized as being important indicators or monitors of the status of environmental health. Urban gray squirrels (Bigler and Hoff 1976) and raccoons (Bigler et al. 1975) have been studied in Florida as models of this type of approach. The gray squirrel was determined to be a sensitive indicator of lead in water, cesium-137, and mercury, but not pesticides. Similarly the raccoon was recognized as a useful sentinel for encephalitis viruses, leptospirosis, tularemia, some enteric bacteria and viruses, certain pesticide residues, and for heavy metals such as mercury. Other mammals may prove useful for such purposes as well.

In any case it is very important that surveillance of diseases, parasites, and environmental contaminants be conducted as an ongoing activity. This is necessary in order to recognize modifications in environmental health and also in the health of wild mammal populations. Health and disease in natural popula-

Table 24-22
Fleas of wild mammals in Florida that can also infest man

Flea	Wild mammal hosts in Florida	Diseases caused or transmitted
Cediopsylla simplex	Rabbits, bobcats, foxes	Skin irritation
Ctenocephalides canis	Roof rats, Norway rats, cotton rats, foxes	Tapeworm infections (*Dipylidium caninum* and *Hymenolepis nana*)
Ctenocephalides felis	Opossums, shrews, rabbits, roof rats, Norway rats, raccoons, skunks, panthers, bobcats, foxes, deer, roof rats	Tapeworm infections (*Dipylidium caninum*)
Echidnophaga gallinacea	Opossums, rabbits, squirrels, gophers, rodents, skunks, weasels, bobcats, foxes	Skin irritation
Hoplopsyllus glacialis affinis	Rabbits, squirrels, cotton rats, Florida mice, raccoons, skunks	Skin irritation
Nosopsyllus fasciatus	Roof rats, Norway rats	Tapeworm infections (*Hymenolepis diminuta*), murine typhus, plague
Orchopeas howardii	Opossums, squirrels, roof rats, woodrats, foxes	Skin irritation
Pulex simulans	Opossums, rabbits, squirrels, skunks, bobcats, foxes	Tapeworm infections (*H. nana* and *D. caninum*)
Xenopsylla cheopis	Opossums, shrews, rodents	Plague, murine typhus, tapeworm infection (*H. diminuta* and *H. nana*)

tions of wildlife are dynamic and changes are the rule rather than the exception. Continuous monitoring will not only allow recognition of new problems, but will also ensure that useful information will be available for the improved management and conservation of Florida's unique and valuable wild mammal resource.

Literature cited

Bigler, W.J., and G.L. Hoff. 1976. Urban wildlife and community health: Gray squirrels as environmental monitors. Proc. Ann. Conf. S.E. Assoc. Game Fish Comm. 30:536–540.

Bigler, W.J., J.H. Jenkins, P.M. Cumbie, G.L. Hoff, and E.C. Prather. 1975. Wildlife and environmental health: Raccoons as indicators of zoonoses and pollutants in southeastern United States. J. Am. Vet. Med. Assoc. 167:592–597.

Bonde, R.K., and T.J. O'Shea. 1989. Sowerby's beaked whale (*Mesoplodon bidens*) in the Gulf of Mexico. J. Mammal. 70:447–449.

Brown, L.N. 1987. A checklist of Florida's mammals. Florida Game and Fresh Water Fish Commission, Tallahassee. 6 pp.

Marshall, C.M., G.A. Seaman, and F.A. Hayes. 1963. A critique on the tropical cattle fever tick controversy and its relationship to white-tailed deer. Trans. No. Am. Wildl. Nat. Resour. Conf. 28:225–232.

Pastoret, P.-P., E. Thiry, B. Brochier, A. Schwers, I. Thomas, and J. Dubuisson. 1988. Diseases of wild animals transmissible to domestic animals. Rev. Sci. Tech. Off. Int. Epiz. 7:705–736.

Prestwood, A.K., S.R. Pursglove, and F.A. Hayes. 1976. Parasitism among white-tailed deer and domestic sheep on common range. J. Wildl. Dis. 12:380–385.

Prestwood, A.K., F.E. Kellogg, S.R. Pursglove, and F.A. Hayes. 1975. Helminth parasitisms among intermingling insular populations of white-tailed deer, feral cattle, and feral swine. J. Am. Vet. Med. Assoc. 166:787–789.

Glossary

Acanthocephalan a nonsegmented intestinal helminth (worm) that has an attachment organ or proboscis with spines and no digestive tract; also called a thorny-headed worm.

Acanthosis a thickening of the skin.

Acute happening quickly or coming to a crisis speedily.

Adenopathy a disease or disorder of the glands, especially the lymph glands.

Adhesion a fibrous connection by which organs or tissues are joined abnormally.

Agglutinin an antibody that aggregates an antigen.

Alopecia deficiency or lack of hair where it is present normally.

Amplification the process whereby a microorganism such as a virus multiplies considerably in a host and that increases its chance of being transferred to the next host; usually used in reference to a reservoir host that serves a significant role in the spread of a virus through the amplification process.

Anomaly a marked change from normal.

Anorexia a lack or loss of normal appetite for food.

Antibody a modified serum protein (globulin) synthesized in response to an antigenic stimulus and specific for that particular antigen.

Antigen a high molecular weight substance (usually protein) that stimulates the production of specific antibodies; antigens can be toxins or various disease agents like bacteria and viruses.

Arbovirus an RNA virus transmitted by a blood-feeding arthropod; some infect man as well as other animals and cause encephalitis.

Ataxia an irregularity or lack of muscle coordination.

Atrophy a wasting away or shrinking of the size of a cell, tissue, organ, or body part.

Benign Tumor a localized mass of new tissue that grows independently, but does not spread to other parts of the body.

Biotype a group of organisms that possess the same genotype.

Blood Chemistry same as serum chemistry.

Bronchiolitis inflammation of the bronchioles.

Cachectic characterized by being in overall poor health and in a state of malnutrition.

Capture Myopathy a disease of muscles that is caused by excessive struggling of a wild animal when captured and restrained and is characterized by damage to and subsequent breakdown of muscle.

Carcinoma a malignant new growth of tissue made up of epithelial cells.

Cardiomyopathy disease or disorder of the heart muscle.

Carrier State a condition in which an animal harbors disease agents without being harmed by them; this results in the distribution of the infection or disease to other animals.

Catarrhal Bronchitis inflammation of the bronchi that results in a discharge of mucus.

Catarrhal Duodenitis inflammation of the upper small intestine that results in a discharge of mucus into the lumen.

Cestode a segmented intestinal helminth; also known as a flatworm or tapeworm.

Chlorinated Hydrocarbon a synthetic organic compound with low acute toxicity, but which is persistent in the environment; many are insecticides or pesticides.

Chronic occurring over a long period of time.

Cirrhosis a liver change in which there is destruction of liver cells and an increase in connective tissue.

Colitis inflammation of the colon.

Commensal an organism that lives in or on another organism and causes no harm to that organism.

Congenital Ectrodactyly a malformation that develops before birth and is characterized by missing digits or bones of digits.

Core Species a species of parasite that is common and abundant (high in prevalence and intensity) and occurs exclusively or almost exclusively in a given species of host.

Coronitis inflammation of the coronary band of the hoof of an animal.

Creeping Eruption same as cutaneous larva migrans.

Cutaneous Larva Migrans a disease condition caused by larvae of nematodes (especially hookworms) migrating under the skin and resulting in dermatitis; the host involved is an abnormal host for the particular species of nematode involved; also called creeping eruption.

Cyst a normal or abnormal sac that contains liquid or other substances; in parasitology a cyst is a structure or stage in the cycle of a parasite that is resistant to environmental extremes and usually contains the infective stage or stages.

Cysticercus a larval tapeworm or cestode that consists of a fluid-filled, bladder-like structure containing an immature scolex (attachment organ).

Definitive Host the host in which sexual reproduction of a parasite occurs; also called the final host.

Dermatitis inflammation of the skin.

Dyspnea difficulty or distress in breathing.

Ectoparasite a parasite, frequently an arthropod, which attaches to or lives on the outside of the host's body.

Edema an accumulation of large amounts of fluid in cells, tissues, or cavities.

Emphysema the abnormal accumulation of air in the alveoli or in the tissues connecting the alveoli of the lungs.

Encephalitis inflammation of the brain.

Encephalomyelitis acute inflammation of the brain and spinal cord.

Encephalomyocarditis inflammation of the brain, spinal cord, and heart.

Endemic the continuing presence of a disease agent or parasite in a population of humans in the absence of an epizootic; often used to describe the same process in animals as well as man.

Endocarditis inflammation of the internal membrane lining the heart.

Endoparasite a parasite that lives inside the body of the host animal.

Enteric pertaining to the intestine.

Enteritis inflammation of the intestine.

Environmental Contaminant a man-made chemical such as a pesticide or some other substance that can contaminate the environment and be taken up by animals and may be passed along and accumulated in the food chain.

Enzootic the continuing presence of a disease agent or parasite in a population of animals in the absence of an epizootic; same as endemic.

Epidemiology the study of diseases in populations of people; usually includes distribution and causes of epidemics; this term is often used to refer to the study of diseases in animal as well as human populations and is equivalent to epizootiology.

Epizoite an organism that lives on the surface of an animal and causes little or no harm; sometimes called an associate.

Epizootic an outbreak of disease in a large number of animals simultaneously; same as epidemic.

Epizootiology the study of diseases in populations of animals; usually includes distribution and causes of epizootics; the term is equivalent to epidemiology.

Etiologic Agent an agent, living or otherwise, which causes a disease.

Etiology the study of the causes of disease.

Fibroma a harmless or benign tumor that is derived from fibrous connective tissue.

Fibrosis the formation of fibrous tissue as a healing process after an injury.

Gastritis inflammation of the stomach.

Granuloma a tumor or nodule made up of granulation tissue; often seen as small, rounded, fleshy projections of connective tissue on the surface of a wound.

Helminth an endoparasitic worm such as a nematode (roundworm), cestode (tapeworm), trematode (fluke), or acanthocephalan (thorny-headed worm).

Hematology the study of blood and blood-forming tissues.

Hematoma a tumor or swelling that contains blood (outside of the vascular system).

Hemoglobinuria the presence of hemoglobin in urine.

Hemolysin a substance that causes destruction of red blood cells.

Hepatitis inflammation of the liver.

Histopathology the study of pathologic changes in the microscopic structures of tissues and organs.

Hyperemia an excessive amount of blood in any part of an animal's body within its vascular system.

Hypothermia a condition in which an animal has an abnormally low body temperature.

Icterus a yellow staining of tissues due to bile pigments; also called jaundice.

Inclusion Body structure of uncertain nature in the nucleus or cytoplasm of animals with certain viral infections; often is visible at the light-microscope level; also referred to as an inclusion.

Infection invasion of an animal by a disease agent such as a bacterium, virus, or protozoan.

Infestation external parasitism of an animal by arthropods such as ticks, mites, or flies.

Infiltration the accumulation of cells or other substances in a tissue where they normally do not occur.

Inflammation the fundamental process of cellular and tissue reactions that occur in blood vessels and adjacent tissues when an animal is injured or harmed by a physical, chemical, or biologic agent.

Intensity the number of parasites or disease agents in an infected animal; sometimes incorrectly referred to as a load or burden.

Intermediate Host the biotic environment in which asexual maturity and reproduction of a parasite occurs.

Intussusception the infolding or telescoping of part of the intestine within itself.

Ischemia the lack of blood supply to a local area usually due to mechanical obstruction within the vascular system.

Laminitis inflammation of the lamina portion of the hoof of an animal.

Latent Infection usually used for certain viral or protozoan infections and refers to an infection that is present, but is not obvious and is difficult to detect.

Lesion an injury or wound; a pathologic change in tissue that is usually defined or circumscribed.

Lymphoma a neoplastic disease of lymphoid tissues.

Lymphosarcoma a malignant neoplastic disease of lymphoid tissue.

Malignant Tumor a growth of new tissue that is uncontrolled and spreads to other parts of the body (metastasis) and is life-threatening.

Mange a skin infection caused by mites that is often associated with hair loss.

Mass Stranding the phenomenon whereby a group of three or more marine mammals of the same species intentionally beach themselves.

Meninges the membranes surrounding the brain and spinal cord.

Meningitis inflammation of the meninges.

Meningoencephalitis inflammation of the meninges and the brain.

Metastasis the transfer of malignant cells or tissues from one part of the body to another.

Metritis inflammation of the uterus.

Microfilaria the embryonic form of a filarial worm such as the heartworm (*Dirofilaria immitis*), which is produced by adult worms, carried in the bloodstream, and eventually ingested by the arthropod vector.

Morbidity the rate of disease in a population, that is, the number of sick or diseased animals in the population per unit of time.

Moribund at the brink of death.

Mortality the rate of death in a population, that is, the number of animals dying in a population per unit of time.

Mucopurulent an exudate that contains pus and mucous material.

Mycotic Disease a disease caused by a fungus.

Myiasis an infection caused by the invasion of the body of an animal by dipteran (fly) larvae.

Myopathy a disease or disorder of muscles.

Necropsy the examination of an animal after it has died; sometimes referred to as autopsy or postmortem examination.

Necrosis the death of a cell, a group of cells, or a portion of a tissue or organ, resulting from irreversible damage prior to the death of the animal.

Negri Body an inclusion body in a nerve cell of an animal infected with rabies virus; its presence is considered diagnostic of rabies.

Neoplasia the process of the formation of a neoplasm or tumor.

Neoplasm a new and abnormal growth of tissue that grows independently of its surrounding tissue.

Nephritis inflammation of the kidney.

Neuritis inflammation of a nerve or nerves.

Neurotropic an affinity for nervous tissue, especially the central nervous system.

Omphalitis inflammation of the umbilicus.

Oocyst the cyst stage of coccidian and malarial parasites that contains a zygote.

Organochlorine same as chlorinated hydrocarbon.

Pathogen any microorganism that can cause disease.

Pathogenesis the progressive development of a disease or disease process; usually includes the various factors and conditions that influence such development.

Pathogenic causing damage or disease.

PCB polychlorinated biphenyl; a group of man-made chemicals that are persistent in the environment and are toxic to some animals.

Pentastome a worm-like parasite closely related to arthropods.

Peracute extremely acute.

Peritonitis inflammation of the peritoneum or lining of the abdomen.

Per Os by mouth.

Pneumonia inflammation of the lungs.

Pneumonitis localized and acute inflammation of the lung.

Polychlorinated Biphenyl same as PCB.

Prevalence the number of animals infected with a parasite or disease in relation to the number of animals examined; usually is expressed as a percentage.

Prophylaxis treatment given to prevent a disease or infection.

Pruritis intense itching of the skin.

Pustular Dermatitis inflammation of the skin involving the formation of elevations of the epithelium filled with pus.

Radioisotope a chemical element with an unstable nucleus that is decaying and emitting radiation.

Radionuclide an atom that is disintegrating and emitting radiation; fallout from the explosion of nuclear devices is an important source of radionuclides.

Red Tide an abnormal bloom or growth of marine dinoflagellates; these flagellates in turn produce toxins that cause morbidity and mortality in animals.

Reservoir Host   an animal commonly infected with a parasite or other disease agent, but which is not harmed by the agent; it is responsible for the maintenance of that agent in a particular geographic location or ecosystem.

Residue   any chemical, element, or compound or its analog or metabolite that is not a normal constituent of an animal.

Rhinitis   inflammation of the mucous membranes lining the nasal passage.

Rickettsia   small pleomorphic bacteria-like parasitic microorganisms transmitted usually by blood-sucking arthropods; many are important disease agents.

Saprophyte   an organism that lives on dead or decaying organic matter; saprophytes are usually plants such as bacteria or fungi.

Satellite Species   species of parasites that are not common or abundant, that is, have low prevalence and intensity, and occur more commonly in other host species than in the one under consideration.

Septicemia   systemic disease due to microorganisms (such as bacteria and the toxins they produce) circulating in the bloodstream.

Serology   the study of antibodies in the serum.

Seronegative   absence of specific antibodies in a serum sample.

Seropositive   presence of specific antibodies in a serum sample.

Serotype   a specific subpopulation of microorganisms (such as bacteria or viruses) that is identified as having similar antigenic characteristics; also called serovar.

Serous Atrophy   a degenerative change in which fat cells are absorbed and replaced by serous fluid.

Serovar   same as serotype; often used in describing strains or types of leptospires.

Serum Chemistry   a study of the various chemical constituents (proteins, enzymes, etc.) of the serum component of blood; sometimes referred to as blood chemistry.

Signs   any observed evidence of a disease or infection in an animal.

Spondylitis   inflammation of the vertebrae.

Spurious Infection   an accidental infection whereby an animal becomes infected abnormally; usually an infection in a predator due to ingestion of prey that has parasites not normally infective for the predator.

Stranding   the phenomenon whereby marine mammals intentionally beach themselves.

Syndrome   a number of signs that occur together and characterize a particular disease.

Systemic   a term applied to a disease or infection that is spread throughout an organ system or the body of an animal.

Thrombosis   the formation of a clot (thrombus) from the elements of blood within the vascular system.

Tick Paralysis   an ascending paralysis of man and animals caused by the secretion of certain chemicals by an attached tick.

Toxicosis   any disease condition caused by poisoning.

Trauma   a wound or injury caused by some physical agent; usually is associated with sudden phenomena.

Trematode   a fluke; a parasitic flatworm.

Tumor   a neoplasm; an abnormal mass of new tissue that grows independently of its surrounding tissue.

Typhlitis   inflammation of the cecum.

Ureteritis   inflammation of the ureter.

Valvular Endocardiosis a disease of the lining of the valves of the heart.

Vector an organism that actively deposits a parasite or disease agent in or on the surface of a host animal; vectors can be mechanical (no development or multiplication of the disease agent occurs within the vector) or biological (essential development or multiplication occurs within the vector).

Verminous Pneumonia inflammation of the lungs caused by a helminth infection (usually nematodes).

Virulence the degree of pathogenicity of a microorganism as judged by the harm it causes.

Visceral Larva Migrans a disease or condition caused by larvae of nematodes (especially ascarids) migrating through internal organs (liver, lungs, brain, eyes, etc.) of a host that is abnormal for that particular species of nematode.

Zoonosis a disease of animals (wild or domestic) that can infect man.

Zoonotic Disease a zoonosis.

Index

Boldface numbers refer to pages on which general information such as etiology, transmission, pathology, etc. concerning a specific disease or condition is given. For example, rabies is discussed in many chapters throughout the book, but details such as mentioned above are given only in the raccoon chapter (Chapter 12) and the pages of this section are given in the Index as **125–129**.

In cases where negative data are given these are indicated in the Index as (neg). If a disease or condition is discussed in the text, but specific information is unknown for Florida mammals, this is indexed and is followed by (nd).

About the Author

Donald J. Forrester is professor of parasitology in the Department of Infectious Diseases, College of Veterinary Medicine, and affiliate professor of wildlife ecology, School of Forest Resources and Conversation, both at the University of Florida, Gainesville. He holds an undergraduate degree in wildlife from the University of Massachusetts, a master's degree in wildlife from the University of Montana, and a doctorate in zoology from the University of California at Davis. He taught at Clemson University before joining the University of Florida faculty in 1969.

Dr. Forrester was president of the Wildlife Disease Association in 1977–79 and received its distinguished service award in 1986. From 1981 to 1986 he was editor of the *Journal of Wildlife Diseases*. He also served as coeditor of two volumes of proceedings on wildlife diseases and has authored or coauthored more than 135 papers in national and international journals.